MW01198866

eːnVision® Integrated
MATHEMATICS II

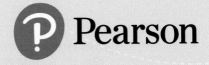 Pearson

Boston, Massachusetts   Chandler, Arizona
Glenview, Illinois   New York, New York

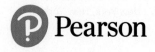

ISBN-13: 978-1418-28377-3
ISBN-10:   1418-28377-0

7 19

Contents in Brief

enVision Integrated MATHEMATICS II

Reviewers & Consultants

Mathematicians

David Bressoud, Ph.D.
Professor Emeritus of Mathematics
Macalester College
St. Paul, MN

Karen Edwards, Ph.D.
Mathematics Lecturer
Harvard University
Cambridge, MA

Teacher Reviewers

Jennifer Barkey
K-12 Math Supervisor
Gateway School District
Monroeville, PA

Miesha Beck
Math Teacher/Department Chair
Blackfoot School District
Blackfoot, ID

Joseph Brandell, Ph.D.
West Bloomfield High School
West Bloomfield Public Schools
West Bloomfield, MI

Andrea Coles
Mathematics Teacher
Mountain View Middle School
Blackfoot, ID

Julie Johnson
Mathematics/CS teacher (9 - 12)
Williamsville Central Schools
Williamsville, NY

Tamar McPherson
Plum Sr HS/Math Teacher
Plum School District
Pittsburgh, PA

Melisa Rice
Math Department Chairperson
Shawnee Public Schools
Shawnee, OK

Ben Wilson
Camille Casteel HS Teacher
Chandler Unified School District
Chandler, AZ

Erin Zitka
6-12 Math Coordinator
Forsyth County
Cumming, GA

Jeff Ziegler
Teacher
Pittsburgh City Schools
Pittsburgh, PA

Authors

Dan Kennedy, Ph.D

- Classroom teacher and the Lupton Distinguished Professor of Mathematics at the Baylor School in Chattanooga, TN
- Co-author of textbooks Precalculus: Graphical, Numerical, Algebraic and Calculus: Graphical, Numerical, Algebraic, AP Edition
- Past chair of the College Board's AP Calculus Development Committee.
- Previous Tandy Technology Scholar and Presidential Award winner

Eric Milou, Ed.D

- Professor of Mathematics, Rowan University, Glassboro, NJ
- Member of the author team for Pearson's **enVision**math**2.0** 6-8
- Member of National Council of Teachers of Mathematics (NCTM) feedback/advisory team for the Common Core State Standards
- Author of *Teaching Mathematics to Middle School Students*

Christine D. Thomas, Ph.D

- Professor of Mathematics Education at Georgia State University, Atlanta, GA
- Past-President of the Association of Mathematics Teacher Educators (AMTE)
- Past NCTM Board of Directors Member
- Past member of the editorial panel of the NCTM journal *Mathematics Teacher*
- Past co-chair of the steering committee of the North American chapter of the International Group of the Psychology of Mathematics Education

Rose Mary Zbiek, Ph.D

- Professor of Mathematics Education, Pennsylvania State University, College Park, PA
- Series editor for the NCTM *Essential Understanding* project

Contributing Author

Al Cuoco, Ph.D

- Lead author of CME Project, a National Science Foundation (NSF)-funded high school curriculum
- Team member to revise the Conference Board of the Mathematical Sciences (CBMS) recommendations for teacher preparation and professional development
- Co-author of several books published by the Mathematical Association of America and the American Mathematical Society
- Consultant to the writers of the Common Core State Standards for Mathematics and the PARCC Content Frameworks for high school mathematics

About enVision Integrated
MATHEMATICS II

enVision® Integrated Mathematics II offers a carefully constructed lesson design to help you succeed in math.

Step 1 At the start of each lesson, you and your classmates will work together to come up with a solution strategy for the problem or task posed. After a class discussion, you'll be asked to reflect back on the processes and strategies you used in solving the problem.

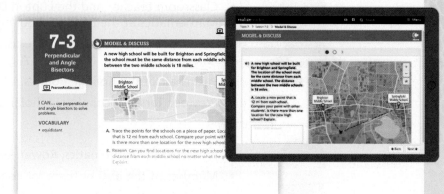

Step 2 Next, your teacher will guide you through new concepts and skills for the lesson.

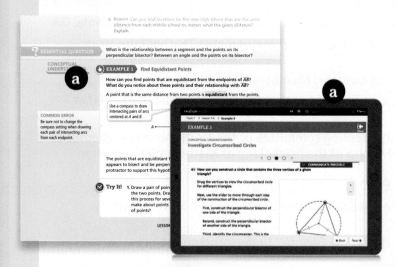

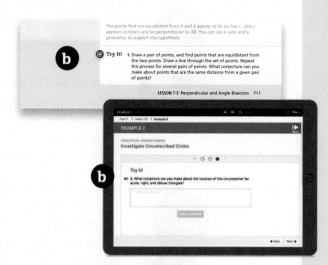

After each example **a**, you work out a problem called the **Try It!** **b** to solidify your understanding of these concepts.

In addition, you will periodically answer **Habits of Mind** **c** questions to refine your thinking and problem-solving skills.

Step 2 cont. This part of the lesson concludes with a Lesson Check that helps you to know how well you are understanding the new content presented in the lesson. With the exercises in the **Do You Understand?** and **Do You Know How?**, you can gauge your understanding of the lesson concepts.

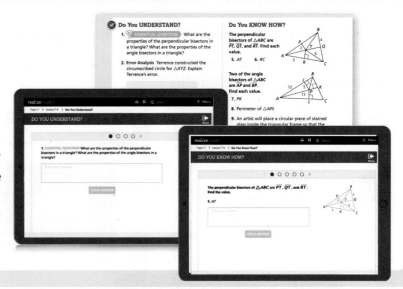

Step 3 In Step 3, you will find a balanced exercise set with **Understand** exercises that focus on conceptual understanding, **Practice** exercises that target procedural fluency, and **Apply** exercises for which you apply concept and skills to real-world situations **d**.

The **Assessment and Practice e** exercises offer practice for high stakes assessments. Your teacher may have you complete the assignment in your Student Edition, Student Companion, or online at PearsonRealize.com.

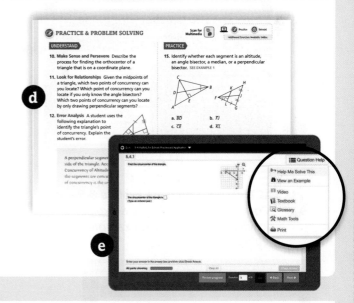

Step 4 Your teacher may have you take the Lesson Quiz after each lesson. You can take the quiz online or in print. To do your best on the quiz, review the lesson problems in that lesson.

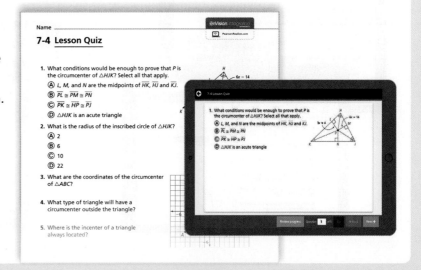

Digital Resources

Everything you need for math, anytime, anywhere.

PearsonRealize.com is your gateway to all of the digital resources for
enVision® Integrated Mathematics II.

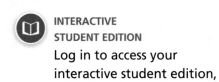

INTERACTIVE STUDENT EDITION
Log in to access your interactive student edition, called Realize Reader.

ACTIVITIES Complete *Explore & Reason*, *Model & Discuss*, *Critique & Explain* activities. Interact with *Examples* and *Try Its*.

ANIMATION View and interact with real-world applications.

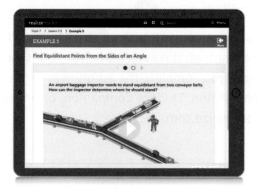

PRACTICE Practice what you've learned.

VIDEOS Watch clips to support Mathematical Modeling in 3 Acts Lessons and **enVision**® STEM Projects.

CONCEPT SUMMARY Review key lesson content through multiple representations.

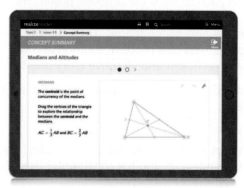

ASSESSMENT Show what you've learned.

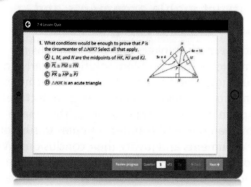

GLOSSARY Read and listen to English and Spanish definitions.

TUTORIALS Get help from Virtual Nerd, right when you need it.

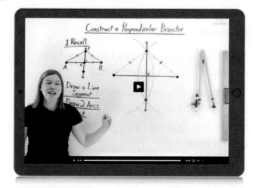

MATH TOOLS Explore math with digital tools and manipulatives.

Mathematical Practices and Processes

Problem Solving

Make sense of problems and persevere in solving them.

Proficient math thinkers are able to read through a problem situation and can put together a workable solution path to solve the problem posed. They analyze the information provided and identify constraints and dependencies. They identify multiple entries to a problem solution and will choose an efficient and effective entry point.

Consider these questions to help you make sense of problems.

- What am I asked to find?
- What are the quantities and variables? The dependencies and the constraints? How do they relate?
- What are some possible strategies to solve the problem?

Attend to precision.

Proficient math thinkers communicate clearly and precisely the approach they are using. They identify the meaning of symbols that they use and always remember to specify units of measure and to label accurately graphical models. They use mathematical terms precisely and express their answers with the appropriate degree of accuracy.

Consider these questions to help you attend to precision.

- Have I stated the meaning of the variables and symbols I am using?
- Have I specified the units of measure I am using?
- Have I calculated accurately?

Reasoning and Communicating

Reason abstractly and quantitatively.

Proficient math thinkers make sense of quantities in problem situations. They represent a problem situation using symbols or equations and explain what the symbols or equation represent in relationship to a problem situation. As they model a situation symbolically or mathematically, they explain the meaning of the quantities.

Consider these questions to help you reason abstractly and quantitatively.

- How can I represent the problem using equations or formulas?
- What do the numbers, variables, and symbols in the equation or formula represent?

Construct viable arguments and critique the reasoning of others.

Proficient math thinkers and problem solvers communicate their problem solutions clearly and convincingly. They construct sound mathematical arguments and develop and defend conjectures to explain mathematical situations. They make use of examples and counterexamples to support their arguments and justify their conclusions. When asked, they respond clearly and logically to the positions and conclusions of others, and compare two arguments, identifying any flaws in logic or reasoning that the arguments may contain. They ask questions to clarify or improve the position of a classmate.

Consider these questions to help you construct mathematical arguments.

- What assumptions can I make when constructing an argument?
- What conjectures can I make about the solution to the problem?
- What arguments can I present to defend my conjectures?

Representing and Connecting

Model with mathematics.

Proficient math thinkers use mathematics to represent a problem situation and make connections between a real-world problem situation and mathematics. They see the applicability of mathematics to solve every-day problems and explain how geometry can be used to solve a carpentry problem or algebra to solve a proportional relationship problem. They define and map relationships among quantities in a problem, using appropriate tools. They analyze the relationships and draw conclusions about the solutions.

Consider these questions to help you model with mathematics.

- What representations can I use to show the relationship among quantities or variables?
- What assumptions can I make about the problem situation to simplify the problem?

Use appropriate tools strategically.

Proficient math thinkers strategize about which tools are more helpful to solve a problem situation. They consider all tools, from paper and pencil to protractors and rulers, to calculators and software applications. They articulate the appropriateness of different tools and recognize which would best serve the needs for a given problem. They are especially insightful about technological tools and use them in ways that deepen or extend their understanding of concepts. They also make use of mental tools, such as estimation, to determine the appropriateness of a solution.

Consider these questions to help you use appropriate tools.

- What tool can I use to help me solve the problem?
- How can technology help me solve the problem?

Seeing Patterns and Generalizing

Look for and make use of structure.

Proficient math thinkers see mathematical patterns in the problems they are solving and generalize mathematics principles from these patterns. They see complicated expressions or equations as single objects composed of many parts.

Consider these questions to help you see structure.

- Can I see a pattern in the problem or solution strategy?
- How can I use the pattern I see to help me solve the problem?

Look for generalizations.

Proficient math thinkers notice when calculations are repeated and can uncover both general methods and shortcuts for solving similar problems.

Consider these questions to help you look for regularity in repeated reasoning.

- Do I notice any repeated calculations or steps?
- Are there general methods that I can use to solve the problem?
- What can I generalize from one problem to another?
- How reasonable are the results that I am getting?

MATHEMATICAL PRACTICES AND PROCESSES

Go Online | PearsonRealize.com

Proficiency with key concepts and skills of Integrated Mathematics II is often cited as a requisite for college- and career readiness.

These foundational concepts of algebraic and geometric thinking provide the gateway to advanced mathematics.

Listed below are the key concepts that you will be studying in **enVision Integrated Mathematics II**.

Functions

- The average rate of change of a function can be estimated from a graph or calculated algebraically.
- The average rate of change of a function over a given interval reveals information about the relationship between the two quantities that the model represents.
- The domain of a function can be determined from its graph.
- Standard functions can be combined using arithmetic operations.
- The graph of a function reveals the type of the function. For example, the graph of these functions is easily recognizable: square root, cube root, and piecewise-defined functions, which include step functions and absolute value functions.
- Changing parameters of a function leads to transformations in the graph of the function.
- The graphs of functions can be transformed in similar and predictable ways.
- A function can have an inverse function.

Exponential Functions and Equations

- An exponential function grows by equal factors over equal intervals.
- An exponential function represents a situation in which a quantity grows or decays by a constant rate per unit interval relative to another.
- A geometric sequence is a type of exponential function. It can be defined recursively or explicitly. It can be used to model a real-world situation.
- The domain of a geometric sequence is a subset of the integers.
- The graph of an exponential function shows x- and y-intercepts, when appropriate, and end behavior.
- A quantity that increases exponentially eventually exceeds a quantity increasing linearly or quadratically.
- The parameters of an exponential function reveal important information about the context that the function represents.
- The properties of exponents can be used to interpret expressions for exponential functions.
- The properties of exponents can be used to transform expressions for exponential functions.

Go Online | **PearsonRealize.com**

Quadratic Functions and Equations

- A quadratic function or equation can be solved by taking square roots, by completing the square, by using the quadratic formula, or by factoring.
- Factoring a quadratic expression reveals the zeros of the function it defines.
- Completing the square in a quadratic expression reveals the maximum or minimum value and the symmetry of the function it defines.
- The parameters of a quadratic function, a, b, and c, in the quadratic function $f(x) = ax^2 + bx + c$ reveal important information about the graph of the function.
- The graph of a quadratic function shows the x-intercepts (when they exist), the y-intercept, the vertex, intervals where the function increases and decreases and the maximum or minimum.

Triangle Relationships

- The circumcenter of a triangle is the point that is equidistant from the vertices. This is where the perpendicular bisectors intersect.
- The incenter of a triangle is the point where the angle bisectors intersect. It is equidistant from the sides.
- Inscribed and circumscribed circles of a triangle are constructed to find the incenter and circumcenter of a triangle.

Similarity

- Two triangles are similar if all corresponding pairs of angles are congruent and all corresponding pairs of sides are proportional.
- The properties of similarity transformations can be used to establish the Angle-Angle criterion for two triangles to be similar.
- Similarity criteria for triangles can be used to solve problems and to prove relationships in geometric figures.
- By similarity, side ratios in right triangles are properties of the angles in the triangle, leading to definitions of trigonometric ratios for acute angles.

Geometric Figures and Measurements

- Volume formulas for cylinders, pyramids, cones, and spheres can help solve real-world and mathematical problems.
- The cross-sections of three-dimensional objects are two-dimensional figures.
- The properties and measures of geometric figures can be used to describe real-world objects.
- Concepts of density based on area and volume can be used to model real-world situations.
- Geometric methods can help solve design problems.

Probability

- Probability events are subsets of a sample space. The outcomes can be categorized as unions, intersections, or complements of other events ("or," "and," "not").
- Two events A and B are independent if the probability of A and B occurring together is the product of their probabilities.
- The probability that event A occurs given event B is called a conditional probability. It is expressed $\frac{P(A \text{ and } B)}{P(B)}$.
- When two events, A and B are mutually exclusive, the probability of A OR B occurring is the sum of the probability of each event, also known as the Addition Rule, that is $P(A \text{ or } B) = P(A) + P(B)$.
- When two events, A and B are not mutually exclusive, the probability of A OR B occurring is found using the Addition Rule, that is $P(A \text{ or } B) = P(A) + P(B) - P(A \text{ and } B)$.
- If A and B are dependent events, the probability of A AND B occurring is $P(A \text{ and } B) = P(A)P(B|A)$ or $P(B)P(A|B)$.
- Permutations and combinations are used to compute probabilities of compound events. A combination shows the probability of compound events when order does not matter while a permutation shows the probability of compound events when order does matter.
- An expected value is a predicted value of a random variable. It is a probability-weighted averages of all possible values.

Circles

- All circles are similar.
- The length of the arc of a circle intercepted by an angle is proportional to the radius of the circle.
- The radian measure of an angle is the ratio of the arc length of a circle and the radius of the circle. It is a constant of proportionality between arc length and radius.
- The equation of a circle of given center and radius can be derived using the Pythagorean Theorem.
- Tangent lines only intersect the circle at one point. They are perpendicular to the radius that intersects the circle at that point.
- When two segments are tangent to a circle and have a common endpoint outside of the circle, the segments are congruent.
- When a tangent intersects the endpoint of a chord, the measure of the angle formed is half the measure of its intercepted arc.
- The measure of an angle inscribed in a circle is half the measure of the arc it intercepts.
- Two inscribed angles that intercept the same arc are congruent.
- If the chords in a circle are congruent, their central angles are congruent.
- If chords are the same distance from the center of a circle, they are congruent.
- If the diameter intersects the chord at $90°$, then it bisects the chord.
- If arcs of a circle are congruent, their chords are also congruent.

Exponents and Roots

TOPIC 3

Quadratic Functions

TOPIC 5

Quadratic Equations and Complex Numbers

TOPIC 6

Working With Functions

Quadrilaterals and Other Polygons

Go Online | PearsonRealize.com

TOPIC 9

Similarity and Right Triangles

Probability

Go Online | PearsonRealize.com

TOPIC 11

Coordinate Geometry

TOPIC
12

Circles

TOPIC

13

Two- and Three-Dimensional Models

Exponents and Roots

? TOPIC ESSENTIAL QUESTION

How do you use exponential, square root, and cube root functions to model situations and solve problems?

Topic Overview

enVision® STEM Project:
   Program a Square Root Algorithm

1-1 Operations on Real Numbers

1-2 Rational Exponents and Properties of Exponents

1-3 Exponential Models

Mathematical Modeling in 3 Acts:
   Edgy Tiles

1-4 The Square Root Function

1-5 The Cube Root Function

Topic Vocabulary

- asymptote
- constant ratio
- cube root function
- element of a set
- exponential function
- rational exponent
- set
- square root function
- subset

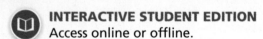

Digital Experience

INTERACTIVE STUDENT EDITION
Access online or offline.

ACTIVITIES Complete *Explore & Reason, Model & Discuss*, and *Critique & Explain* activities. Interact with Examples and Try Its.

ANIMATION View and interact with real-world applications.

PRACTICE Practice what you've learned.

Go online | **PearsonRealize.com**

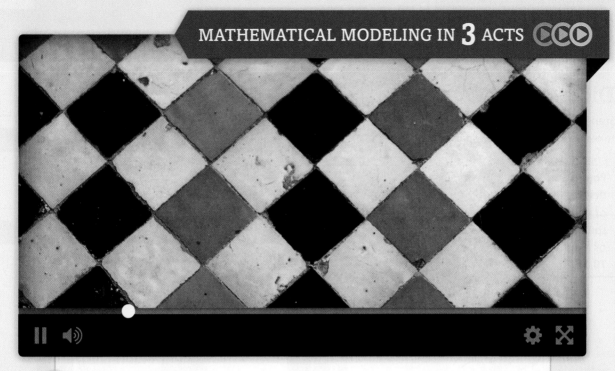

▶ Edgy Tiles

For more than 3,000 years, people have glazed ceramics and other materials to make decorative tile patterns. Tiles used to be used only in important buildings or by the very rich, but now you can find tiles in almost any house.

Before you start tiling a wall, floor, or other surface, it's important to plan out how your design will look. Think about this during the Mathematical Modeling in 3 Acts lesson.

VIDEOS Watch clips to support *Mathematical Modeling in 3 Acts Lessons* and **enVision®** *STEM Projects*.

CONCEPT SUMMARY Review key lesson content through multiple representations.

ASSESSMENT Show what you've learned.

GLOSSARY Read and listen to English and Spanish definitions.

TUTORIALS Get help from *Virtual Nerd*, right when you need it.

MATH TOOLS Explore math with digital tools and manipulatives.

enVision® STEM

Did You Know?

Standing up, the average **person** takes up **2 square feet** of space.

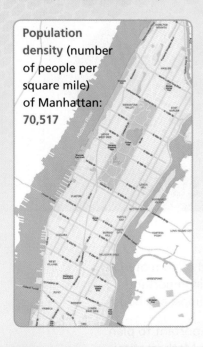

Population density (number of people per square mile) of Manhattan: 70,517

Land Area

Earth: 196.9 million mi^2

United States: 3.535 million mi^2

Population

Earth: 7.648 billion people

United States: 325 million people

San Francisco

Chicago

New York

The cities of San Francisco, Chicago, and New York all have population density greater than 10,000.

For the Chicago Cubs World Series parade and rally on November 4, 2016, an estimated **5 million people** lined the streets of Chicago, Illinois.

Your Task: Program a Square Root Algorithm

Sports arenas and open spaces are designed to hold great numbers of people. You and your classmates will design a square building to hold a given number of people.

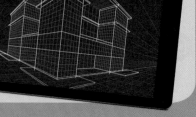

1-1

Operations on Real Numbers

PearsonRealize.com

I CAN... reason about operations on real numbers.

VOCABULARY
• element of a set
• set
• subset

🖑 **CRITIQUE & EXPLAIN**

Cindy and Victor are playing a math game. The winner must get three in a row of the same type of real number and justify how the numbers are alike. Cindy said she won because she was able to get three rational numbers on a diagonal. Victor said he won with three positive numbers in a column.

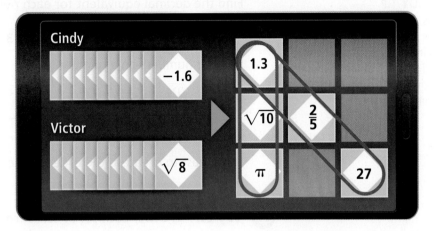

A. Can both players say they won for different reasons? Explain.

B. **Reason** Can you make other groups using the numbers shown that are all the same kind of real number? In how many ways can you do this?

❓ **ESSENTIAL QUESTION** How can you classify the results of operations on real numbers?

🖑 **EXAMPLE 1** Understand Sets and Subsets

In the set of numbers from 1 to 10, which elements are in both the subset of even numbers, and the subset of multiples of 5?

A **set** is a collection of objects such as numbers. An **element of a set** is an object that is in the set. Write a set by listing the elements, enclosed in curly braces ("{" and "}").

Name of the set → $A = \{$ 1, 2, 3, 4, 5, 6, 7, 8, 9, 10 $\}$
                               └─ Elements of the set

Set B is a **subset** of set A if each element of B is also an element of A.

$B = \{2, 4, 6, 8, 10\}$ ← Elements of A that are even

$C = \{5, 10\}$ ← Elements of A that are multiples of 5

MAKE SENSE AND PERSEVERE
Write out each subset. Then see which elements are common to both.

The number 10 is the only number that is an element of both subsets.

☑ **Try It!** 1. Which numbers in set A are elements in both the subset of odd numbers and the subset of multiples of 3?

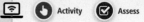

APPLICATION **EXAMPLE 2** **Compare and Order Real Numbers**

Jim is playing a math game where he needs to put a set of three cards in numerical order. His cards show $\frac{40}{11}$, $\sqrt{\frac{324}{36}}$, and $\sqrt{10}$. Order the cards from least to greatest.

STUDY TIP
It is easier to compare and order real numbers when they are all in the same form. Rewrite real numbers to the equivalent decimal form so you can compare them easily.

Find the decimal equivalent for each number.

$$\frac{40}{11} = 3.\overline{63} \qquad \sqrt{\frac{324}{36}} = \frac{18}{6} = 3 \qquad \sqrt{10} \approx 3.2$$

Plot the numbers on a number line.

From least to greatest, the order of the cards is $\sqrt{\frac{324}{36}}$, $\sqrt{10}$, and $\frac{40}{11}$.

✅ **Try It!** **2.** Order each set of cards from least to greatest.

a. 0.25, $\sqrt{\frac{1}{9}}$, $\frac{6}{25}$
b. $\sqrt{\frac{121}{25}}$, 2.25, $\sqrt{5}$

CONCEPTUAL UNDERSTANDING **EXAMPLE 3** **Operations With Rational Numbers**

A. Is the sum of two rational numbers always a rational number?

You can try several different cases of adding two rational numbers.

$$\frac{1}{2} + \frac{1}{3} = \frac{5}{6} \qquad \frac{7}{8} + \frac{3}{4} = \frac{13}{8} \qquad \frac{11}{5} + \frac{1}{6} = \frac{71}{30}$$

In each case, the sum is also rational. But you cannot try *every* pair of rational numbers since there are infinitely many of them. How can you know whether it is true for *all* rational numbers?

Use variables to represent any rational number.

> a, b, c, and d are integers with $b \neq 0$, and $d \neq 0$.

$$\frac{a}{b} + \frac{c}{d} = \frac{ad}{bd} + \frac{bc}{bd}$$

> Since $b \neq 0$ and $d \neq 0$, $bd \neq 0$ also.

$$= \frac{ad + bc}{bd}$$

Since $ad + bc$ and bd are integers, and $bd \neq 0$, the sum is rational.

B. Is the product of two rational numbers always a rational number?

Use the same strategy as in part A, using variables to represent any rational number.

> a, b, c, and d are integers with $b \neq 0$, and $d \neq 0$.

$$\frac{a}{b} \cdot \frac{c}{d} = \frac{ac}{bd}$$

> Since $b \neq 0$ and $d \neq 0$, $bd \neq 0$ also.

Since ac and bd are integers, and $bd \neq 0$, the product is rational.

✅ **Try It!** **3.** Is the quotient of two rational numbers always a rational number? Explain.

👆 **EXAMPLE 4**   **Operations With Rational and Irrational Numbers**

A. **Is the sum of a rational number and an irrational number rational or irrational?**

If you could write the sum of an irrational and a rational number as a rational number, you could write the following equation.

irrational

rational $\dfrac{a}{b} + c = \dfrac{p}{q}$ rational

$$c = \dfrac{pb - aq}{bq}$$

In the rational numbers above, a, b, p, and q are integers, with $b \neq 0$ and $q \neq 0$. This means that

- $pb - aq$ is an integer and
- bq is an integer not equal to 0.

Therefore $\dfrac{pb - aq}{bq}$ is a rational number. But this is equal to c, an irrational number. Can a number be both rational and irrational? No, it cannot.

So what went wrong? The mistake was to assume that you could write the sum $\dfrac{a}{b} + c$ in the form $\dfrac{p}{q}$.

The sum of a rational number and an irrational number is always an irrational number.

B. **Is the product of a rational number and an irrational number rational or irrational?**

Write the product as a rational number.

irrational

rational $\dfrac{a}{b} \cdot c = \dfrac{p}{q}$ rational

$$c = \dfrac{bp}{aq}$$

As in part A, c is both rational and irrational. So the assumption that you can write $\dfrac{a}{b} \cdot c$ as $\dfrac{p}{q}$ at all is wrong.

Also notice that in order to divide by a when calculating c, you have to assume that $a \neq 0$. What happens in the original equation if $a = 0$?

Then $\dfrac{a}{b} = 0$, and $\dfrac{a}{b} \cdot c = 0$ for *any* number c.

So the product of a rational number and an irrational number is always irrational, unless the rational number in the product is 0.

COMMON ERROR
If you do not address the case where $a = 0$, you might conclude that the product of any rational number and any irrational number is irrational. But that is not true.

☑ **Try It!**   4. Is the difference of a rational number and an irrational number always irrational? Explain.

WORDS	The sum of two rational numbers is always rational.	The sum of a rational number and an irrational number is always irrational.
	The product of two rational numbers is always rational.	The product of a nonzero rational number and an irrational number is always irrational.

NUMBERS	Sums: $\frac{2}{9} + \frac{4}{6} = \frac{32}{36}$	Sums: $\sqrt{3} + \frac{1}{3} = \frac{3\sqrt{3} + 1}{3}$
	Products: $\frac{2}{9} \cdot \frac{4}{6} = \frac{8}{54}$	Products: $\sqrt{3} \cdot \frac{1}{3} = \frac{\sqrt{3}}{3}$

ALGEBRA	Sums: $\frac{a}{b} + \frac{c}{d} = \frac{ad + cb}{bd}$	Sums: $\frac{a}{b} + c \neq \frac{p}{q}$, when c is irrational
	Products: $\frac{a}{b} \cdot \frac{c}{d} = \frac{ac}{bd}$	Products: $\frac{a}{b} \cdot c \neq \frac{p}{q}$, when c is irrational

Do You UNDERSTAND?

1. **ESSENTIAL QUESTION** How can you classify the results of operations on real numbers?

2. **Communicate Precisely** Explain why the sum of a rational number and an irrational number is always irrational.

3. **Vocabulary** Are the rational numbers a *subset* of the *set* of all real numbers? Are the rational numbers a *subset* of the irrational numbers? Explain?

4. **Error Analysis** Jacinta says that the product of a rational number and an irrational number is always irrational. Explain her error.

5. **Reason** Let $D = \{-2, -1, 0, 1, 2\}$. Is D a subset of itself? Explain.

Do You KNOW HOW?

Determine whether set B is a subset of set A.

6. $A = \{0, 1, 2, 3, 4\}$
   $B = \{1, 2\}$

7. $A = \{2, 3, 5, 7, 11\}$
   $B = \{3, 5, 7, 9, 11\}$

Order each set of numbers from least to greatest.

8. $\sqrt{200}$, 14, $\frac{41}{3}$

9. $\frac{2}{3}$, $\sqrt{\frac{9}{16}}$, 0.6

10. The park shown is in the shape of a square. Is the perimeter rational or irrational?

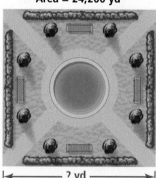

Area = 24,200 yd²

|← ? yd →|

UNDERSTAND

11. **Reason** Identify each solution as rational or irrational.

   a. $\frac{4}{7} + \frac{-1}{3}$ b. $\sqrt{4} \cdot \frac{2}{5}$

12. **Higher Order Thinking** Is the product of two irrational numbers always an irrational number? Explain.

13. **Error Analysis** Describe and correct the error a student made when ordering numbers from least to greatest.

$$\sqrt{144}, \frac{234}{3}, 68.12$$

$$\sqrt{144} = 72$$

$$\frac{234}{3} = 78$$

$$68.12, \sqrt{144}, \frac{234}{3} \quad \times$$

14. **Mathematical Connections** The bulletin board is in the shape of a square. Find two rational numbers that are within $\frac{1}{8}$ in. of the actual side length.

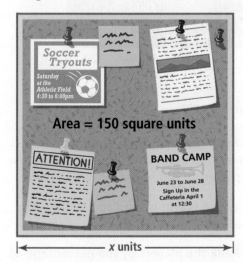

Area = 150 square units

|← x units →|

15. **Construct Arguments** Tell whether each statement is *always true, sometimes true,* or *never true*. Explain.

   a. An integer is a whole number.

   b. A natural number is a rational number.

   c. An irrational number is an integer.

PRACTICE

List all subsets of the real numbers from the list below that each number belongs to. **SEE EXAMPLE 1**

- real numbers
- irrational numbers
- rational numbers
- integers
- whole numbers

16. 10.5

17. $\frac{4}{7}$

18. 6

19. 0

20. $\sqrt{2}$

21. −29

Order the numbers shown from least to greatest. **SEE EXAMPLE 2**

22. $3.5, \frac{10}{3}, \sqrt{14}$

23. $\frac{1}{3}, 0.1\overline{6}, \sqrt{\frac{1}{4}}$

Match each number to the letter that represents its position on the number line. **SEE EXAMPLE 2**

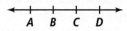

$A \quad B \quad C \quad D$

24. $-\sqrt{120}$

25. $-\sqrt{\frac{400}{4}}$

26. $-\frac{23}{2}$

27. −11.75

Determine whether each sum, difference, product, or quotient represents a rational number or an irrational number. Explain how you know without simplifying. **SEE EXAMPLES 3 AND 4**

28. $\frac{6}{23} - \frac{\sqrt{2}}{2}$

29. $\frac{6}{23} - \frac{15}{127}$

30. $\frac{6}{23} \div \frac{15}{127}$

31. $\frac{6}{23} \div \frac{\sqrt{2}}{2}$

32. Is the difference of two rational numbers always a rational number? Explain. **SEE EXAMPLE 3**

33. Is the quotient of a rational number and an irrational number always irrational? Explain. **SEE EXAMPLE 4**

APPLY

34. **Make Sense and Persevere** Adam wraps the top edge of the gift box shown with gold ribbon.

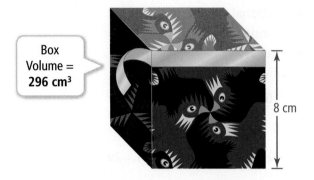

Box Volume = 296 cm³

8 cm

The top and bottom edges of the box are square. If Adam has $24\frac{1}{4}$ in. of gold ribbon, does he have enough to decorate the top of the box?

35. **Reason** In statistics, *continuous data* can have values equal to any real number, such as the average temperature for an area or the number of inches of rainfall. Other sets of data are *discrete*. Examples of discrete data are the number of students in a school district, the number of home runs hit by a baseball team in a season, and the number of letters handled by the post office each month. Which subset of the real numbers is the best one to use to describe discrete data?

36. **Make Sense and Persevere** Helena builds a shed in her backyard. There is a larger section for large tools, like her lawn mower, and a smaller section for small tools. Each section has a square floor. What is the length of the entire shed? What type of number is the length? List as many types of numbers for the length as you can.

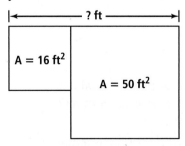

? ft

A = 16 ft²

A = 50 ft²

ASSESSMENT PRACTICE

37. Is 0.62473 a member of the set? For each set of real numbers, select *Yes* or *No*.

	Yes	No
natural numbers	☐	☐
whole numbers	☐	☐
integers	☐	☐
rational numbers	☐	☐
irrational numbers	☐	☐
real numbers	☐	☐

38. **SAT/ACT** What is the square root of $\sqrt{\frac{144}{256}}$?

Ⓐ $\frac{2}{3}$ Ⓑ $\frac{3}{4}$ Ⓒ $\frac{3}{16}$ Ⓓ $\frac{9}{4}$ Ⓔ $\frac{9}{16}$

39. **Performance Task** A basketball coach is considering three players for Most Valuable Player (MVP). The table shows the proportion of shots each player made of the shots they attempted.

Player	Free Throws	Field Goals (2 pts)	3-Point Shots
Martin	71%	49.5%	32%
Corey	$\frac{4}{5}$	$\frac{9}{20}$	$\frac{1}{3}$
Kimberly	0.857	0.448	0.338

Part A For a technical foul, the team can pick any player they want to shoot the free throw. Which player should the team pick? Explain.

Part B Which player is most successful with their field goal shots? Explain.

Part C Rank the players by the percentage of the 3-point shots each made.

Part D If all the players attempted the same number of shots, which player would you choose as the MVP? Justify your answer.

1-2

Rational Exponents and Properties of Exponents

 PearsonRealize.com

I CAN... use properties of exponents to solve equations with rational exponents.

VOCABULARY
• rational exponent

☝ **CRITIQUE & EXPLAIN**

Students are asked to write an equivalent expression for 3^{-3}.

Casey and Jacinta each write an expression on the board.

A. Who is correct, Casey or Jacinta? Explain.

B. Reason What is the most likely error that was made?

> **Casey**
>
> $3^{-3} = -27$

> **Jacinta**
>
> $3^{-3} = \frac{1}{27}$

❓ **ESSENTIAL QUESTION**   What are the properties of rational exponents and how are they used to solve problems?

CONCEPTUAL UNDERSTANDING

☝ **EXAMPLE 1**   **Write Radicals Using Rational Exponents**

What does $3^{\frac{1}{2}}$ equal?

You can think of exponentiation as repeated multiplication.

$3^2 = 3 \cdot 3$ ············· Multiply 3 by itself 2 times.

$3^3 = 3 \cdot 3 \cdot 3$ ············· Multiply 3 by itself 3 times.

$3^4 = 3 \cdot 3 \cdot 3 \cdot 3$ ············· Multiply 3 by itself 4 times.

etc.

GENERALIZE
The Power of a Power Property says that $(a^m)^n = a^{mn}$ for all integers m and n.

But what does $3^{\frac{1}{2}}$ mean? You cannot multiply 3 by itself $\frac{1}{2}$ times. Since interpreting exponents as repeated multiplication does not work in this case, you have to *define* a new meaning for expressions like $3^{\frac{1}{2}}$.

Whatever the new definition is, you want it to obey the same rules of exponents that you know for integers, such as the Power of a Power Property.

$$\left(3^{\frac{1}{2}}\right)^2 = 3^{\frac{1}{2} \cdot 2} = 3^1 = 3$$

> When you square $3^{\frac{1}{2}}$ ...

> ... the result is 3.

You know that a number whose square is 3 is $\sqrt{3}$. So in order to define raising a number to the $\frac{1}{2}$ power in a way that makes sense, define $3^{\frac{1}{2}}$ to be $\sqrt{3}$.

You can define the meaning of other rational exponents in a similar way. If the nth root of a is a real number and m is an integer, then $a^{\frac{1}{n}} = \sqrt[n]{a}$, and $a^{\frac{m}{n}} = \sqrt[n]{a^m} = (\sqrt[n]{a})^m$.

 Try It!   **1.** What does $2^{\frac{1}{3}}$ equal? Explain.

 EXAMPLE 2 | **Use the Product of Powers Property to Solve Equations With Rational Exponents**

What is the solution of $\left(3^{\frac{x}{2}}\right)\left(3^{\frac{x}{3}}\right) = 3^9$?

Rewrite the left side of the equation with one exponent.

$$\left(3^{\frac{x}{2}}\right)\left(3^{\frac{x}{3}}\right) = 3^9$$

$$3^{\frac{x}{2} + \frac{x}{3}} = 3^9 \quad \cdots\cdots\cdots \text{ Product of Powers Property}$$

$$3^{\frac{3x}{6} + \frac{2x}{6}} = 3^9 \quad \cdots\cdots\cdots \text{ Write the exponents with a common denominator.}$$

$$3^{\frac{5x}{6}} = 3^9$$

$$\frac{5x}{6} = 9 \quad \cdots\cdots\cdots \text{ The bases are the same, so set the exponents equal.}$$

$$\frac{6}{5}\left(\frac{5x}{6}\right) = \frac{6}{5}(9) \quad \cdots\cdots\cdots \text{ Multiply both sides by } \frac{6}{5}.$$

$$x = \frac{54}{5}$$

The solution is $\frac{54}{5}$.

> **STUDY TIP**
> To multiply two powers with a common base, keep the common base and add the exponents.

☑ **Try It!** 2. What is the solution of $\left(2^{\frac{x}{4}}\right)\left(2^{\frac{x}{6}}\right) = 2^3$?

👆 **EXAMPLE 3** | **Use the Power of a Power Property to Solve Equations With Rational Exponents**

A. What is the solution of $27^{x-4} = 3^{2x-6}$?

$$27^{x-4} = 3^{2x-6}$$

$$(3^3)^{x-4} = 3^{2x-6} \quad \cdots\cdots\cdots \text{ Rewrite 27 with a base of 3.}$$

$$3^{3x-12} = 3^{2x-6} \quad \cdots\cdots\cdots \text{ Power of a Power Property}$$

$$3x - 12 = 2x - 6 \quad \cdots\cdots\cdots \text{ Write the exponents as an equation.}$$

$$3x - 12 - 3x = 2x - 6 - 3x$$

$$-12 = -x - 6$$

$$-12 + 6 = -x - 6 + 6$$

$$-6 = -x$$

$$6 = x$$

> **STUDY TIP**
> To find the power of a power, keep the base and multiply the exponents.

The solution is 6.

B. What is the solution of $\left(\frac{1}{125}\right)^{-\frac{x}{2}} = \left(\frac{1}{25}\right)^{-\frac{x}{3} - 2}$?

Step 1 Rewrite the equation so both sides have the same base.

$$\left(\frac{1}{125}\right)^{-\frac{x}{2}} = \left(\frac{1}{25}\right)^{-\frac{x}{3} - 2}$$

$$(5^{-3})^{-\frac{x}{2}} = (5^{-2})^{-\frac{x}{3} - 2} \quad \text{ Rewrite } \frac{1}{125} \text{ and } \frac{1}{25} \text{ as powers of 5.}$$

$$5^{\frac{3x}{2}} = 5^{\frac{2x}{3} + 4} \quad \cdots\cdots\cdots \text{ Power of a Power Property}$$

CONTINUED ON THE NEXT PAGE

EXAMPLE 3 CONTINUED

Step 2 Write the exponents as an equation and solve.

$$\frac{3x}{2} = \frac{2x}{3} + 4$$

$$6\left(\frac{3x}{2}\right) = 6\left(\frac{2x}{3} + 4\right)$$

$$9x = 4x + 24$$

$$9x - 4x = 4x + 24 - 4x$$

$$5x = 24$$

$$\frac{5x}{5} = \frac{24}{5}$$

$$x = 4.8$$

The solution is $x = 4.8$.

 Try It! **3.** What is the solution of each equation?

a. $256^{x+2} = 4^{3x+9}$ **b.** $\left(\frac{1}{8}\right)^{\frac{x}{2}-1} = \left(\frac{1}{4}\right)^{\frac{x}{3}}$

APPLICATION   **EXAMPLE 4**   **Use the Power of a Product Property to Solve Equations With Rational Exponents**

Adam is setting up for an outdoor concert. He places three square blankets near the band as shown in the picture. What is the area of Blanket C?

Formulate ◀

Area	=	length	•	width
12	=	$8^{\frac{1}{2}}$	•	$x^{\frac{1}{2}}$

Area of the grass rectangle   Side length of Blanket B   Side length of Blanket C

Compute ◀   Solve for x, the area of Blanket C.

$$12 = \left(8^{\frac{1}{2}}\right)\left(x^{\frac{1}{2}}\right)$$

$$12 = (8x)^{\frac{1}{2}}$$ Multiply the bases and keep the exponent.

$$12^2 = \left[(8x)^{\frac{1}{2}}\right]^2$$

$$144 = 8x$$ Square both sides.

$$\frac{144}{8} = \frac{8x}{8}$$

$$18 = x$$

Blanket A

Blanket B
8 yd²

Blanket C
x yd²

12 yd²

Interpret ◀   The area of Blanket C is 18 yd².

Check Compare the product of $\sqrt{18}$ and $\sqrt{8}$ to the rectangular area of 12.

$$(\sqrt{8})(\sqrt{18}) = \left(8^{\frac{1}{2}}\right)\left(18^{\frac{1}{2}}\right)$$

$$= (8 \cdot 18)^{\frac{1}{2}} = 144^{\frac{1}{2}}$$

$$= 12$$

 Try It! **4.** When the side length of Blanket A is multiplied by $2^{\frac{1}{2}}$ the result is 6 yards. Find the area of Blanket A.

APPLICATION 👆 **EXAMPLE 5** **Use the Quotient of Powers Property to Solve Equations With Rational Exponents**

Terrarium A and Terrarium B are cubes. The side length of Terrarium A is twice the side length of Terrarium B. What is the value of x?

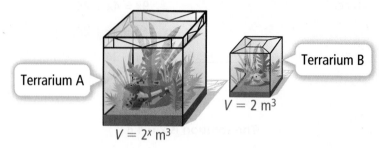

Terrarium A

Terrarium B

$V = 2$ m³

$V = 2^x$ m³

Step 1 Write a proportion using the side lengths.

$$\frac{(2^x)^{\frac{1}{3}}}{2^{\frac{1}{3}}} = 2 \qquad \text{The ratio of the side lengths is 2.}$$

$$\frac{2^{x \cdot \frac{1}{3}}}{2^{\frac{1}{3}}} = 2$$

Step 2 Use properties of exponents to simplify.

$$\frac{2^{\frac{x}{3}}}{2^{\frac{1}{3}}} = 2$$

> **STUDY TIP**
> To divide two powers with the same base, keep the common base and subtract the exponents.

$$2^{\frac{x}{3} - \frac{1}{3}} = 2 \qquad \text{Quotient of Powers Property}$$

$$2^{\frac{x-1}{3}} = 2$$

$$2^{\frac{x-1}{3}} = 2^1 \qquad \text{Write 2 with an exponent.}$$

Step 3 Equate the exponents and solve for x.

$$\frac{x-1}{3} = 1$$

$$x - 1 = 3$$

$$x = 4$$

The value of x is 4.

 Try It! **5.** What is the value of x if the side length of Terrarium A is four times the side length of Terrarium B?

CONCEPT SUMMARY Rational Exponents and Properties of Exponents

WORDS If the nth root of a is a real number and m is an integer, then

$$a^{\frac{1}{n}} = \sqrt[n]{a} \qquad\qquad a^{\frac{m}{n}} = \sqrt[n]{a^m} = (\sqrt[n]{a})^m$$

ALGEBRA Power of a Power	Power of a Product	Product of Powers	Quotient of Powers
$(a^m)^n = a^{mn}$	$(ab)^m = a^m \cdot b^m$	$a^m \cdot a^n = a^{m+n}$	$\dfrac{a^m}{a^n} = a^{m-n},\ a \neq 0$

NUMBERS

$\left(256^{\frac{1}{4}}\right)^{\frac{1}{2}} = 256^{\frac{1}{4} \cdot \frac{1}{2}}$	$(4 \times 9)^{\frac{1}{2}} = 4^{\frac{1}{2}} \cdot 9^{\frac{1}{2}}$	$16^{\frac{1}{4}} \times 16^{\frac{1}{4}} = 16^{\frac{1}{4}+\frac{1}{4}}$	$\dfrac{8^{\frac{2}{3}}}{8^{\frac{1}{3}}} = 8^{\frac{2}{3}-\frac{1}{3}}$
$= 256^{\frac{1}{8}}$	$= 2 \cdot 3$	$= 16^{\frac{2}{4}}$	$= 8^{\frac{1}{3}}$
$= 2$	$= 6$	$= 16^{\frac{1}{2}}$	$= 2$
		$= 4$	

☑ Do You UNDERSTAND?

1. **?** **ESSENTIAL QUESTION** What are the properties of rational exponents and how are they used to solve problems?

2. **Communicate Precisely** A square has an area of 15 ft^2. What are two ways of expressing its side length?

3. **Look for Relationships** If $3^x = 3^y$, what is the relationship between x and y?

4. **Error Analysis** Corey wrote $\sqrt[3]{4^2}$ as $4^{\frac{3}{2}}$. What error did Corey make?

5. **Reason** When is it useful to have rational exponents instead of radicals?

6. **Vocabulary** How are *rational exponents* different than whole number exponents? How are they the same?

Do You KNOW HOW?

Write each radical using rational exponents.

7. $\sqrt{7}$

8. $\sqrt{15}$

9. $\sqrt[3]{6^4}$

10. $\sqrt[3]{2^3}$

11. $\sqrt[4]{2^4}$

12. $\sqrt{8^3}$

Solve each equation.

13. $\left(2^{\frac{x}{3}}\right)\left(2^{\frac{x}{2}}\right) = 2^5$

14. $\left(4^{\frac{x}{2}}\right)\left(4^{\frac{x}{5}}\right) = 4^8$

15. $64^{x+1} = 4^{x+7}$

16. $16^{(x-3)} = 2^{(x-6)}$

17. $\left(\dfrac{1}{243}\right)^{-\frac{x}{3}} = \left(\dfrac{1}{9}\right)^{-\frac{x}{2}+1}$

18. $\left(\dfrac{1}{36}\right)^{(x-4)} = \left(\dfrac{1}{216}\right)^{x+1}$

PRACTICE & PROBLEM SOLVING

UNDERSTAND

19. Make Sense and Persevere Describe two ways to express the edge length of a cube with a volume shown.

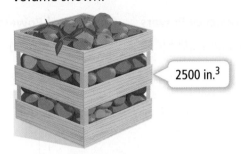

2500 in.^{3}

20. Construct Arguments Explain why $5^{\frac{4}{3}}$ must be equal to $\sqrt[3]{5^4}$ if the Power of a Power Property holds for rational exponents.

21. Error Analysis Describe and correct the error a student made when starting to solve the equation $8^{x+3} = 2^{2x-5}$.

$$8^{x+3} = 2^{2x-5}$$
$$(2^3)^{x+3} = 2^{2x-5}$$
$$2^{3x+3} = 2^{2x-5}$$
$$\vdots \qquad ✗$$

22. Construct Arguments The Power of a Quotient rule is $\left(\frac{a}{b}\right)^m = \frac{a^m}{b^m}$, $b \neq 0$. Will this rule work with rational exponents if $\frac{a}{b}$ is a positive number? Give an example to support your argument.

23. Higher Order Thinking The Zero Exponent Property is $a^0 = 1$, $a \neq 0$.

  a. How could you use properties of exponents to explain why $a^0 = 1$?

  b. How could the Zero Exponent Property be applied when solving equations with rational exponents?

24. Use Structure Consider the expression $\sqrt{\sqrt{625}}$.

  a. Write the radical using rational exponents.

  b. Describe two different ways to evaluate the expression.

  c. Simplify the expression from part (b).

PRACTICE

Write each radical using rational exponents.
SEE EXAMPLE 1

25. $\sqrt{3}$

26. $\sqrt[3]{7}$

27. $\sqrt[5]{3^2}$

28. $\sqrt[4]{2^{-5}}$

29. $\sqrt[3]{a^2}$

30. $\sqrt{b^a}$

Solve each equation. SEE EXAMPLES 2–5

31. $\left(5^{\frac{x}{3}}\right)\left(5^{\frac{x}{4}}\right) = 5^5$

32. $\left(2^{\frac{x}{2}}\right)\left(4^{\frac{x}{2}}\right) = 2^6$

33. $\left(3^{\frac{x}{2}+1}\right) = \left(3^{-\frac{5x}{2}}\right)$

34. $625^{2x-3} = 25^{3x-2}$

35. $\left(\frac{1}{243}\right)^{-\frac{x}{3}} = \left(\frac{1}{9}\right)^{-\frac{x}{2}+1}$

36. $8^{\frac{-x}{3}} = 4$

37. $49^{\frac{x}{4}-1} = 343^{\frac{x}{3}}$

38. $3 = \left(5^{\frac{1}{2}}\right)\left(x^{\frac{1}{2}}\right)$

39. $2 = \left(4^{\frac{1}{3}}\right)\left(2^{\frac{x}{3}}\right)$

40. $\dfrac{27^{\frac{1}{4}}}{3^{\frac{x}{4}}} = 1$

41. $5^{-\frac{2}{3}} = \dfrac{125^{\frac{x}{3}}}{25^{\frac{4}{3}}}$

42. $\dfrac{6^{\frac{1}{4}}}{36^{-\frac{x}{2}}} = 1$

For each partial solution, identify the property of exponents that is used. SEE EXAMPLES 2–4

43.

$$36^{\frac{x}{3}+3} = 216^{\frac{x}{5}}$$
$$(6^2)^{\frac{x}{3}+3} = (6^3)^{\frac{x}{5}}$$
$$6^{\frac{2x}{3}+6} = 6^{\frac{3x}{5}}$$
$$\vdots$$

44.

$$\vdots$$
$$\dfrac{3^{\frac{3x}{4}}}{3^{\frac{1}{4}}} = 3^{-\frac{3}{4}}$$
$$3^{\frac{3x}{4}-\frac{1}{4}} = 3^{-\frac{3}{4}}$$
$$\vdots$$

APPLY

45. Use Appropriate Tools The formula for the volume V of a sphere is $\frac{4}{3}\pi r^3$. What is the radius of the basketball shown?

$V = 392$ in.^{3}

46. Use Structure A singing contest eliminates contestants after each round. To find the number of contestants in the next round, raise the number of contestants in the current round to the power of $\frac{6-n}{7-n}$, where n is the number of the current round. The number of contestants in Round 2 is 243. How many contestants will be in Round 5?

47. Make Sense and Persevere Photos A, B, and C are all square photos. The area of Photo C is the same as a rectangular photo whose length is the side length of Photo A and whose width is the side length of Photo B. Use the properties of rational exponents to write and solve an equation to find the side length of Photo A to two decimal places.

Photo A	Photo B	Photo C
Area = x cm^2	Area = 72 cm^2	Area = 110 cm^2

ASSESSMENT PRACTICE

48. Match each expression with its equivalent expression.

I. $\sqrt[4]{2^5}$ **A.** $2^{\frac{1}{5}}$

II. $\sqrt{5}$ **B.** $2^{\frac{5}{4}}$

III. $\sqrt[5]{2^4}$ **C.** $2^{\frac{4}{5}}$

IV. $\sqrt[5]{2}$ **D.** $5^{\frac{1}{2}}$

49. SAT/ACT What is the value of x in $27^{\frac{x}{2}} = 3^{x-1}$?

Ⓐ -3

Ⓑ -2

Ⓒ $\frac{1}{3}$

Ⓓ 2

Ⓔ 3

50. Performance Task It is possible to write any positive integer as the sum of powers of 2 with whole number exponents. For example, you can write 75 in the following manner.

$$2^0 + 2^1 + 2^3 + 2^6 = 75$$

Part A Use the equation above to write 75 as the sum of powers of 8, using rational exponents. What are possible values for a, b, c and d?

$$8^a + 8^b + 8^c + 8^d = 75$$

Part B How can you modify the equation you wrote in part A to express 75 as sum of powers of 16?

$$16^a + 16^b + 16^c + 16^d = 75$$

Part C Given that a, b, c, and d are rational numbers, for what types of integer values of x is the following equation true? Explain your answer.

$$x^a + x^b + x^c + x^d = 75$$

1-3

Exponential Models

 PearsonRealize.com

I CAN... write exponential models in different ways to solve problems.

VOCABULARY
- compound interest formula
- continuously compounded interest formula
- natural base e

EXPLORE & REASON

Juan is studying exponential growth of bacteria cultures. Each is carefully controlled to maintain a specific growth rate. Copy and complete the table to find the number of bacteria cells in each culture.

Culture	Initial Number of Bacteria	Growth Rate per Day	Time (days)	Final Number of Bacteria
A	10,000	8%	1	
B	10,000	4%	2	
C	10,000	2%	4	
D	10,000	1%	8	

A. What is the relationship between the daily growth rate and the time in days for each culture?

B. **Look for Relationships** Would you expect a culture with a growth rate of $\frac{1}{2}\%$ and a time of 16 days to have more or fewer cells than the others in the table? Explain.

? ESSENTIAL QUESTION

How can you develop exponential models to represent and interpret situations?

EXAMPLE 1   Rewrite an Exponential Function to Identify a Rate

In 2015, the population of a small town was 8,000. The population is increasing at a rate of 2.5% per year. Rewrite an exponential growth function to find the monthly growth rate.

Write an exponential growth function using the annual rate to model the town's population y, in t years after 2015.

initial population   annual growth rate

$$y = 8,000(1 + 0.025)^t$$

years after 2015

$$y = 8,000(1.025)^t$$

To identify the monthly growth rate, you need the exponent to be the number of months in t years, or $12t$.

$$y = 8,000(1.025)^{\frac{12t}{12}}$$

Multiply the exponent by $\frac{12}{12}$ so that $12t$ represents the number of months.

$$y = 8,000(1.025^{\frac{1}{12}})^{12t}$$

$$y \approx 8,000(1.00206)^{12t}$$

Applying the Power of a Power rule helps to reveal the monthly growth rate by producing an expression with the exponent $12t$.

COMMON ERROR
Dividing the annual growth rate by 12 does not give the exact monthly growth rate. This Example shows how to find an expression for the exact monthly rate: $1.025^{\frac{1}{12}} - 1$.

The monthly growth rate is about $1.00206 - 1 = 0.00206$. The population is increasing about 0.206% per month.

☑ Try It!   1. The population in a small town is increasing annually by 1.8%. What is the quarterly rate of population increase?

CONCEPT Compound Interest

When interest is paid monthly, the interest earned after the first month becomes part of the new principal for the second month, and so on. Interest is earned on interest already earned. This is compound interest.

The **compound interest formula** is an exponential model that is used to calculate the value of an investment when interest is compounded.

$$A = P\left(1 + \frac{r}{n}\right)^{nt}$$

P = the initial principal invested

r = annual interest rate, written as a decimal

n = number of compounding periods per year

A = the value of the account after t years

EXAMPLE 2 Understand Compound Interest

Tamira invests $5,000 in an account that pays 4% annual interest. How much will there be in the account after 3 years if the interest is compounded annually, semi-annually, quarterly, or monthly?

Use the Compound Interest formula to find the amount in Tamira's account after 3 years.

	Compound Interest Formula	Amount After 3 Years ($)
Annually	$A = 5000\,(1 + \frac{0.04}{1})^{3(1)}$	5,624.32
Semi-Annually	$A = 5000\,(1 + \frac{0.04}{2})^{3(2)}$	5,630.81
Quarterly	$A = 5000\,(1 + \frac{0.04}{4})^{3(4)}$	5,634.13
Monthly	$A = 5000\,(1 + \frac{0.04}{12})^{3(12)}$	5,636.36

REASON
The more frequently interest is added to the account, the earlier that interest generates more interest. This reasoning supports the trend shown in the table.

As the number of compounding periods increases, the amount in the account also increases.

Try It! 2. $3,000 is invested in an account that earns 3% annual interest, compounded monthly.

 a. What is the value of the account after 10 years?

 b. What is the value of the account after 100 years?

CONCEPTUAL
UNDERSTANDING

👆 **EXAMPLE 3** **Understanding Continuously Compounded Interest**

Consider an investment of \$1 in an account that pays a 100% annual interest rate for one year. The equation $A = 1\left(1 + \frac{1}{n}\right)^{n(1)} = \left(1 + \frac{1}{n}\right)^{n}$ gives the amount in the account after one year for the number of compounding periods n. Find the value of the account for the number of periods given in the table.

Number of Periods, n	Value of $\left(1 + \frac{1}{n}\right)^{n}$
1	$\left(1 + \frac{1}{1}\right)^{1} = 2$
10	$\left(1 + \frac{1}{10}\right)^{10} = 2.59374246$
100	$\left(1 + \frac{1}{100}\right)^{100} = 2.704813829$
1000	$\left(1 + \frac{1}{1,000}\right)^{1,000} = 2.716923932$
10000	$\left(1 + \frac{1}{10,000}\right)^{10,000} = 2.718145927$
100000	$\left(1 + \frac{1}{100,000}\right)^{100,000} = 2.718268237$

Notice that as n continues to increase, the value of the account remains very close to 2.718. This special number is called the *natural base*.

The **natural base e** is defined as the value that the expression $\left(1 + \frac{1}{x}\right)^{x}$ approaches as $x \to +\infty$. The number e is an irrational number.

$$e = 2.718281828459\ldots$$

The number e is the base in the **continuously compounded interest formula**.

$A = Pe^{rt}$ P = the initial principal invested
    e = the natural base
    r = annual interest rate, written as a decimal
    A = the value of the account after t years

✅ **Try It!** **3.** If you continued the table for $n = 1,000,000$, would the value in the account increase or decrease? How do you know?

👆 **EXAMPLE 4** **Find Continuously Compounded Interest**

Regina invests \$12,600 in an account that earns 3.2% annual interest, compounded continuously. What is the value of the account after 12 years? Round your answer to the nearest dollar.

Use the continuously compounded interest formula with $P = 12,600$, $r = 0.032$, and $t = 12$.

COMMON ERROR
Be sure that when you evaluate $e^{0.032(12)}$ you either simplify $0.032(12)$ as 0.384 first, or use parentheses to ensure that e is raised to the entire product, rather than just the first factor.

$A = Pe^{rt}$

$= 12,600e^{0.032(12)}$

$= 12,600e^{0.384}$

$\approx 18,498.63$

To evaluate $e^{0.384}$, use the e^x key on your calculator.

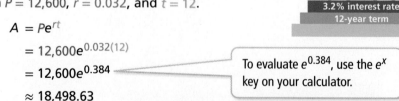
3.2% interest rate
12-year term

To the nearest dollar, the value of the account after 12 years is \$18,499.

CONTINUED ON THE NEXT PAGE

Try It! **4.** You invest $125,000 in an account that earns 4.75% annual interest, compounded continuously.

 a. What is the value of the account after 15 years?

 b. What is the value of the account after 30 years?

APPLICATION  **EXAMPLE 5** Use Two Points to Find an Exponential Model

Tia knew that the number of e-mails she sent was growing exponentially. She generated a record of the number of e-mails she sent each year since 2009. What is an exponential model that describes the data?

Write an exponential model in the form $y = a \cdot b^x$, with y equal to the number of e-mails in hundreds and x equal to the number of years since 2009. Use the data to find the values of the constants a and b.

COMMON ERROR
Remember that the growth factor $(1 + r)$ is different from the growth rate (r). In this example, the growth factor is 1.4 while the growth rate is 0.4, or 40%.

The growth factor for Tia's e-mails in the two consecutive years was $\frac{14}{10}$, or 1.4.

> When data points have consecutive x-values, the growth factor, b, is the ratio of their y-values.

Use the value of b and one of the data points to find the initial value, a.

$y = a \cdot b^x$ .... Write an exponential growth equation.

$14 = a(1.4)^7$ .... Substitute 1.4 for b, 7 for x, and 14 for y.

$\frac{14}{(1.4)^7} = a$ .... Division Property of Equality

$1.33 \approx a$ .... Simplify.

So, the function $y = 1.33(1.4)^x$ models the number of e-mails (in hundreds) Tia sends x years after 2009.

 Try It! **5.** A surveyor determined the value of an area of land over a period of several years since 1950. The land was worth $31,000 in 1954 and $35,000 in 1955. Use the data to determine an exponential model that describes the value of the land.

APPLICATION ⟶   👆 **EXAMPLE 6** ⟩ **Use Regression to Find an Exponential Model**

Randy is making soup. The soup reaches
the boiling point and then, as shown
by the data, begins to cool off. Randy
wants to serve the soup when it is
about 80°F, or about 10 degrees above
room temperature (68°F).

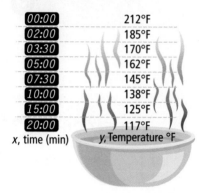

00:00	212°F
02:00	185°F
03:30	170°F
05:00	162°F
07:30	145°F
10:00	138°F
15:00	125°F
20:00	117°F

x, time (min)   *y*, Temperature °F

**A. Explain why the temperature might
follow an exponential decay curve
as it approaches room temperature.**

A scatter plot of the data shows
the soup cooling toward room
temperature. The graph is not
a line.

The rate of cooling appears to slow as the
graph approaches room temperature, around
68° F. This indicates exponential decay toward
an asymptote of $y = 68$.

**B. Find an exponential model for the data. Use your model to determine
when Randy should serve the soup.**

Step 1 Enter the data as lists in a graphing calculator. Because the
temperature values approach 68°F, subtract 68 from each
temperature value.

Most graphing calculators will only
calculate exponential regressions for
data values that approach 0.
You can subtract 68 so your data will
approach 0. Then you can undo the
adjustment in **Step 3** below.

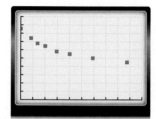

L₁	L₂	L₃ 2
2	117	
3.5	102	
5	94	
7.5	77	
10	70	
15	57	
20	49	

L₂(8)=49

Step 2 Use the calculator to find an exponential regression equation.
The exponential model that best fits the data is $y = 126.35(0.9492)^x$.

Step 3 Translate this function up vertically
by 68 units.

The translated model is
$y = 126.35(0.9492)^x + 68$.

Use the translated model to find when
the soup has a temperature of about 80°F.

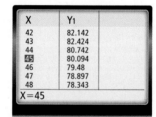

X	Y₁
42	82.142
43	82.424
44	80.742
45	80.094
46	79.48
47	78.897
48	78.343

X=45

The soup has a temperature of about 80°F after 45 minutes.

So, Randy should serve the soup about 45 minutes after it begins to cool.

☑ **Try It!** **6.** According to the model in Example 6, what was the
approximate temperature 35 minutes after cooling started?

 CONCEPT SUMMARY **Writing Exponential Models**

	General Exponential Model	Compound Interest	Continuously Compounded Interest
ALGEBRA	$y = a \cdot b^x$	$A = P\left(1 + \frac{r}{n}\right)^{nt}$	$A = Pe^{rt}$
NUMBERS	A necklace costs $250 and increases in value by 2% per year. $a = $ initial amount $250 $b = $ growth factor 1.02 $x = $ number of years $y = 250(1.02)^x$	A principal of $3,000 is invested at 5% annual interest, compounded monthly, for 4 years. $P = 3,000$ $r = 5\%$ $n = 12$ compounding periods per year $t = 4$ years $A = 3000\left(1 + \frac{0.05}{12}\right)^{(12)(4)}$	A principal of $3,000 is invested at 5% continuously compounded interest for 4 years. $P = 3,000$ $r = 5\%$ $t = 4$ years $A = 3000e^{(0.05)(4)}$

Do You UNDERSTAND?

1. **ESSENTIAL QUESTION** Why do you develop exponential models to represent and interpret situations?

2. **Error Analysis** The exponential model $y = 5,000(1.05)^t$ represents the amount Yori earns in an account after t years when $5,000 is invested. Yori said the monthly interest rate of the exponential model is 5%. Explain Yori's error.

3. **Vocabulary** Explain the similarities and differences between compound interest and continuously compounded interest.

4. **Communicate Precisely** Kylee is using a calculator to find an exponential regression model. How would you explain to Kylee what the variables in the model $y = a \cdot b^x$ represent?

Do You KNOW HOW?

The exponential function models the annual rate of increase. Find the monthly and quarterly rates.

5. $f(t) = 2,000(1.03)^t$

6. $f(t) = 500(1.055)^t$

Find the total amount of money in an account at the end of the given time period.

7. compounded monthly, $P = \$2,000$, $r = 3\%$, $t = 5$ years

8. continuously compounded, $P = \$1,500$, $r = 1.5\%$, $t = 6$ years

Write an exponential model given two points.

9. (3, 55) and (4, 70)

10. (7, 12) and (8, 25)

11. Paul invests $6,450 in an account that earns continuously compounded interest at an annual rate of 2.8%. What is the value of the account after 8 years?

UNDERSTAND

12. Error Analysis Suppose $6,500 is invested in an account that earns interest at a rate of 2% compounded quarterly for 10 years. Describe and correct the error a student made when finding the value of the account.

$$A = 6500 \left(1 + \frac{0.02}{12}\right)^{12(10)}$$

$$A = 7937.80 \qquad \text{✗}$$

13. Communicate Precisely The points (2, 54.61) and (4, 403.48) are points on the graph of an exponential model in the form $y = a \cdot e^x$.

a. Explain how to write the exponential model, and then write the model.

b. How can you use the exponential model to find the value of y when $x = 8$?

14. Model with Mathematics Use the points listed in the table for years 7 and 8 to find an exponential model. Then use a calculator to find an exponential model for the data. Explain how to find each model. Predict the amount in the account after 15 years.

Time (yr)	Amount ($)
1	3,225
2	3,500
3	3,754
4	4,042
5	4,368
6	4,702
7	5,063
8	5,456

15. Higher Order Thinking A power model is a type of function in the form $y = a \cdot x^b$. Use the points (1, 4), (2, 8), (3, 16) and (4, 64) and a calculator to find an exponential model and a power model for the data. Then use each model to predict the value of y when $x = 6$. Graph the points and models in the same window. What do you notice?

PRACTICE

Find the amount in the account for the given principal, interest rate, time, and compounding period. SEE EXAMPLES 2 AND 4

16. $P = 800$, $r = 6\%$, $t = 9$ years; compounded quarterly

17. $P = 3,750$, $r = 3.5\%$, $t = 20$ years; compounded monthly

18. $P = 2,400$, $r = 5.25\%$, $t = 12$ years; compounded semi-annually

19. $P = 1,500$, $r = 4.5\%$, $t = 3$ years; compounded daily

20. $P = \$1,000$, $r = 2.8\%$, $t = 5$ years; compounded continuously

21. $P = \$16,000$, $r = 4\%$, $t = 25$ years; compounded continuously

Write an exponential model given two points.
SEE EXAMPLE 5

22. (9, 140) and (10, 250)

23. (6, 85) and (7, 92)

24. (10, 43) and (11, 67)

25. In 2012, the population of a small town was 3,560. The population is decreasing at a rate of 1.7% per year. How can you rewrite an exponential growth function to find the quarterly decay rate? SEE EXAMPLE 1

26. Selena took a pizza out of the oven and it started to cool to room temperature (68°F). She will serve the pizza when it reaches 150°F. She took the pizza out of the oven at 5:00 P.M. When can she serve it? SEE EXAMPLE 6

Time (min)	Temperature (°F)
5	310
8	264
10	238
15	202
20	186
25	175

APPLY

27. Reason Adam invests $8,000 in an account that earns 1.25% interest, compounded quarterly for 20 years. On the same date, Jacinta invests $8,000 in an account that earns continuous compounded interest at a rate of 1.25% for 20 years. Who do you predict will have more money in their account after 20 years? Explain your reasoning.

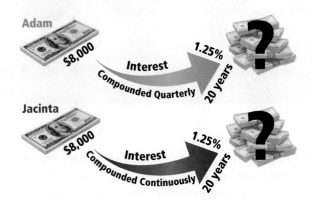

28. Make Sense and Persevere A blogger found that the number of visits to her Web site increases 5.6% annually. The Web site had 80,000 visits this year. Write an exponential model to represent this situation. By what percent does the number of visits increase daily? Explain how you found the daily rate.

29. Use Structure Jae invested $3,500 at a rate of 2.25% compounded continuously in 2010. How much will be in the account in 2025? How much interest will the account have earned by 2025?

30. Model with Mathematics A scientist is conducting an experiment with a pesticide. Use a calculator to find an exponential model for the data in the table. Use the model to determine how much pesticide remains after 180 days.

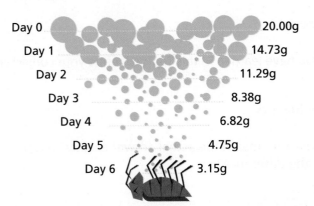

Day 0	20.00g
Day 1	14.73g
Day 2	11.29g
Day 3	8.38g
Day 4	6.82g
Day 5	4.75g
Day 6	3.15g

ASSESSMENT PRACTICE

31. The table shows the account information of five investors. Which of the following are true, assuming no withdrawals are made? Select all that apply.

Employee	P	r	t(years)	Compound
Anna	4000	1.5%	12	Quarterly
Nick	2500	3%	8	Monthly
Lori	7200	5%	15	Annually
Tara	2100	4.5%	6	Continuously
Steve	3800	3.5%	20	Semi-annually

Ⓐ After 12 years, Anna will have about $4,788.33 in her account.

Ⓑ After 8 years, Nick will have about $3,177.17 in his account.

Ⓒ After 15 years, Lori will have about $15,218.67 in her account.

Ⓓ After 6 years, Tara will have about $2,750.93 in her account.

Ⓔ After 20 years, Steve will have about $7,629.00 in his account.

32. SAT/ACT Rick invested money in a continuous compound account with an interest rate of 3%. How long will it take Rick's account to double?

Ⓐ about 2 years

Ⓑ about 10 years

Ⓒ about 23 years

Ⓓ about 46 years

Ⓔ about 67 years

33. Performance Task Cassie is financing a $2,400 treadmill. She is going to use her credit card for the purchase. Her card charges 17.5% interest compounded monthly. She is not required to make minimum monthly payments.

Part A How much will Cassie pay in interest if she waits a full year before paying the full balance?

Part B How much additional interest will Cassie pay if she waits two full years before paying the full balance?

Part C If both answers represent a single year of interest, why is the answer in B greater than the answer in A?

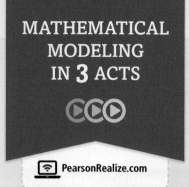

MATHEMATICAL MODELING IN 3 ACTS

PearsonRealize.com

Video

▶ Edgy Tiles

For more than 3,000 years, people have glazed ceramics and other materials to make decorative tile patterns. Tiles used to be used only in important buildings or by the very rich, but now you can find tiles in almost any house.

Before you start tiling a wall, floor, or other surface, it's important to plan out how your design will look. Think about this during the Mathematical Modeling in 3 Acts lesson.

Scan for Multimedia

ACT 1 ▷ Identify the Problem

1. What is the first question that comes to mind after watching the video?

2. Write down the main question you will answer about what you saw in the video.

3. Make an initial conjecture that answers this main question.

4. Explain how you arrived at your conjecture.

5. What information will be useful to know to answer the main question? How can you get it? How will you use that information?

ACT 2 ▷ Develop a Model

6. Use the math that you have learned in this Topic to refine your conjecture.

ACT 3 ▷ Interpret the Results

7. Did your refined conjecture match the actual answer exactly? If not, what might explain the difference?

1-4

The Square Root Function

I CAN... describe the key features of the square root function.

VOCABULARY
• square root function

EXPLORE & REASON

One of the strangest mysteries in archaeology was discovered in the Diquís Delta of Costa Rica. Hundreds of sphere-shaped stones were found.

A great circle is the circle with the greatest diameter that can be drawn on any given sphere.

A. The formula for the surface area of a sphere is $SA = 4\pi r^2$. What is the surface area of the stone in terms of the circumference of the great circle?

B. The circumferences of the great circles of spheres range in size from about 6 cm to 6 m. Make a graph that represents circumference as a function of surface area.

C. Look for Relationships What similarities and differences do you notice about the graph from Part B and the graph of a quadratic function?

? ESSENTIAL QUESTION

What key features are shared among the square root function and translations of the square function.

CONCEPTUAL UNDERSTANDING

EXAMPLE 1 Key Features of the Square Root Function

What are the key features of $f(x) = \sqrt{x}$?

The function $f(x) = \sqrt{x}$ is the **square root function**.

Make a table and graph the function.

COMMON ERROR
Recall that $\sqrt{x}$ is equal to the *positive* square root of x.

x	$f(x) = \sqrt{x}$
0	0
1	1
4	2
9	3
16	4

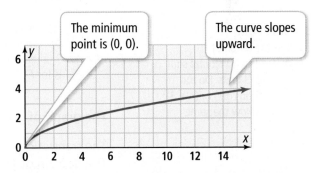

The minimum point is (0, 0).

The curve slopes upward.

The domain is restricted to $x \geq 0$, because only nonnegative numbers have a real square root. Since the square root of a number cannot be negative, the range is $f(x) \geq 0$.

For $f(x) = \sqrt{x}$, the x- and y-intercepts of the graph of the function are both 0. The graph is increasing for all values in the domain of f.

 Try It! **1.** Graph each function. What are the intercepts, domain, and range of the function?

a. $p(x) = -\sqrt{x}$ **b.** $q(x) = \sqrt{\dfrac{x}{10}}$

EXAMPLE 2   **Translations of the Square Root Function**

A. How does the graph of $g(x) = \sqrt{x} + 3$ compare to the graph of $f(x) = \sqrt{x}$?

Graph each function.

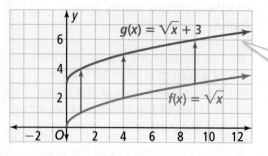

For each x-value, the corresponding y-value is 3 units greater for g than it is for f.

The graph of $g(x) = \sqrt{x} + 3$ is a vertical translation of $f(x) = \sqrt{x}$.

The translation is a result of adding a constant to the output of a function. The domain for both functions is $x \geq 0$. The range for function f is $y \geq 0$, so the range for function g is $y \geq 3$.

B. How does the graph of $g(x) = \sqrt{x + 3}$ compare to the graph of $f(x) = \sqrt{x}$?

Graph each function.

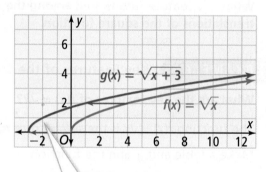

For each y-value, the corresponding x-value is 3 units less for g than it is for f.

USE STRUCTURE
Notice that the graph of $g(x) = \sqrt{x + 3}$ is a horizontal shift of $f(x) = \sqrt{x}$ left 3 units. Do the quadratic functions $g(x) = (x + 3)^2$ and $f(x) = x^2$ follow the same pattern?

The graph of $g(x) = \sqrt{x + 3}$ is a horizontal translation of $f(x) = \sqrt{x}$.

The translation is the result of adding a constant to the input of a function. The domain of f is $x \geq 0$, and the domain of g is $x \geq -3$. The range for both functions is $y \geq 0$.

 Try It!   **2.** How does each graph compare to the graph of $f(x) = \sqrt{x}$?

    a. $g(x) = \sqrt{x} - 4$

    b. $p(x) = \sqrt{x - 10}$

👆 **EXAMPLE 3** **Rate of Change of the Square Root Function**

For the function $f(x) = \sqrt{x}$, how does the average rate of change from $x = 0$ to $x = 0.3$ compare to the average rate of change from $x = 0.3$ to $x = 0.6$?

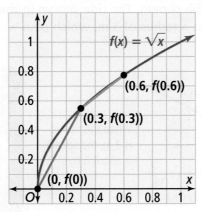

Step 1 Evaluate the function for the x–values that correspond to the endpoints of each interval.

$$f(0) = \sqrt{0}$$

$$= 0$$

$$f(0.3) = \sqrt{0.3}$$

$$\approx 0.548$$

$$f(0.6) = \sqrt{0.6}$$

$$\approx 0.775$$

Step 2 Find the average rate of change over each interval.

From $x = 0$ to $x = 0.3$:

$$\frac{f(0.3) - f(0)}{0.3 - 0} \approx \frac{0.548 - 0}{0.3 - 0}$$

$$= \frac{0.548}{0.3}$$

$$\approx 1.83$$

From $x = 0.3$ to $x = 0.6$:

$$\frac{f(0.6) - f(0.3)}{0.6 - 0.3} \approx \frac{0.775 - 0.548}{0.6 - 0.3}$$

$$= \frac{0.227}{0.3}$$

$$\approx 0.757$$

The average rate of change over the interval $0 \leq x \leq 0.3$ is greater than the average rate of change over the interval $0.3 \leq x \leq 0.6$.

LOOK FOR RELATIONSHIPS
You can see the difference in the average rates of change in the graph. The line through $(0, f(0))$ and $(0.3, f(0.3))$ is steeper than the line through $(0.3, f(0.3))$ and $(0.6, f(0.6))$.

☑ **Try It!** **3.** For the function $h(x) = \sqrt{2x}$, find $h(8)$, $h(10)$, and $h(12)$. Then find the average rate of change of the function over each interval.

a. $8 \leq x \leq 10$

b. $10 \leq x \leq 12$

APPLICATION 👆 **EXAMPLE 4** **Compare Functions**

Two plans are being considered to determine the speed of a theme park ride with a circular wall that spins. Plan A is represented by the function with the graph shown. The ride shown in the photo is an example of Plan B. If the ride has a radius of 3 m, which plan would result in a greater speed for the ride?

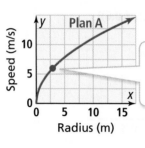

When the radius is 3 m, the speed is about 6 m/s.

USE APPROPRIATE TOOLS
How could you determine the radius in meters for both plans given a corresponding speed of 7.5 m/s?

Plan B is represented by the function $f(r) = 5\sqrt{r}$, where r is the radius of the ride, and $f(r)$ is the speed.

Compare the plans.

| Plan A | OR | Plan B |

Plan A

The graph of Plan A shows that the corresponding speed at a radius of 3 meters is about 6 m/s.

Plan B

Evaluate $f(r) = 5\sqrt{r}$ for $r = 3$.

$$f(3) = 5\sqrt{(3)}$$
$$\approx 8.7$$

The ride using Plan B has a speed of about 8.7 m/s when the radius is 3 m.

With a radius of 3 m, the speed of the ride using Plan A is 6 m/s, and the speed of the ride using Plan B is about 8.7 m/s.

So, the ride using Plan B has a greater speed for a radius of 3 m.

 Try It!   **4.** To the nearest thousandth, evaluate each function for the given value of the variable.

a. $v(x) = \frac{\sqrt{x}}{10}$; $x = 17$

b. $w(x) = \sqrt{\frac{x}{10}}$; $x = 17$

CONCEPT SUMMARY Translations of the Square Root Function

ALGEBRA $g(x) = \sqrt{x - h} + k$

- domain: $x \geq h$
- range: $y \geq k$
- minimum point: (h, k)

NUMBERS $g(x) = \sqrt{x - 2} + 4$

- domain: $x \geq 2$
- range: $y \geq 4$
- minimum point: $(2, 4)$

GRAPH

a vertical translation of 4 units up

a horizontal translation of 2 units right

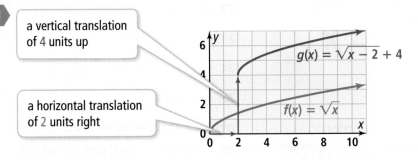

Do You UNDERSTAND?

1. **ESSENTIAL QUESTION** What key features are shared among the square root function and translations of the square function.

2. **Use Structure** Explain why each function is, or is not, a translation of the square root function $f(x) = \sqrt{x}$.

   a. $h(x) = 2\sqrt{x + 1}$

   b. $g(x) = \sqrt{x + 2} - 3$

3. **Error Analysis** A student identified $(6, 12)$ and $(9, 27)$ as points on the graph of the function $f(x) = \sqrt{3x}$. What error did the student make?

4. **Reason** What is the domain of $f(x) = \sqrt{x + 3}$?

Do You KNOW HOW?

How does the graph of each function compare to the graph of $f(x) = \sqrt{x}$?

5. $g(x) = \sqrt{x} - 2$

6. $h(x) = \sqrt{x - 5}$

7. $p(x) = 5 + \sqrt{x}$

8. $q(x) = \sqrt{7 + x}$

For the given function, find the average rate of change to the nearest hundredth over the given interval.

9. $f(x) = \sqrt{x + 7}$; $2 \leq x \leq 10$

10. $g(x) = \sqrt{x + 7}$; $-3 \leq x \leq 5$

11. $h(x) = \sqrt{2x}$; $0 \leq x \leq 10$

UNDERSTAND

12. **Use Appropriate Tools** Use a graphing calculator to graph $f(x) = -\sqrt{x + 7}$. Describe the domain and range of the function.

13. **Error Analysis** Describe and correct the error a student made when comparing the graph of $g(x) = \sqrt{x + 3}$ to the graph of $f(x) = \sqrt{x}$.

1. The expression under the radical in $g(x)$ is $x + 3$.
2. $x + 3$ is to the right of x, so the graph of g is a translation of the graph of f by 3 units to the right.

14. **Higher Order Thinking** Write a function involving a square root expression with domain $x \geq \frac{7}{2}$ and range $y \leq 2$.

15. **Mathematical Connections** Consider the two functions $f(x) = \sqrt{x}$ and $g(x) = -\sqrt{x}$.

   a. What is the average rate of change for each function from $x = 4$ to $x = 9$?

   b. How are the two values in part (a) related to each other?

   c. Suppose the average rate of change for $f(x)$ between two values of x is 0.32. What is the rate of change for $g(x)$ between the same two values of x?

16. **Use Structure** For a function of the form $f(x) = a\sqrt{x - h} + k$, why are some real numbers excluded from the domain and the range?

17. **Communicate Precisely** Explain the steps of each calculation.

   a. Find $f(10)$ if $f(x) = \frac{\sqrt{2x}}{7}$.

   b. Find $f(10)$ if $f(x) = \sqrt{\frac{2x}{7}}$.

PRACTICE

Find the *x*- and *y*-intercepts of each function. If there is no intercept, write *Does not exist.*
SEE EXAMPLE 1

18. $f(x) = \sqrt{x} - 2$

19. $g(x) = \sqrt{x - 9}$

20. $h(x) = \sqrt{x + 9}$

21. $k(x) = \sqrt{x + 4} - 9$

How does each graph compare to the graph of $f(x) = \sqrt{x}$? SEE EXAMPLE 2

22. $q(x) = \sqrt{x} + 11$

23. $r(x) = \sqrt{x + 11}$

24. $s(x) = \sqrt{x - 2} + 5$

25. $t(x) = \sqrt{x + 3} - 6$

Write an expression for each function. SEE EXAMPLE 2

26. a translation by 6 units up of $f(x) = \sqrt{x}$.

27. a translation by $\frac{1}{2}$ unit to the right of $f(x) = \sqrt{x}$.

28. a translation by 2 units down and 1 unit to the left of $f(x) = \sqrt{x}$.

Find the value of the given function at each end of the range of values of the variable. Then calculate the average rate of change of the function between the two values of the variable.
SEE EXAMPLES 3 AND 4

29. $p(x) = \sqrt{15x}$; $0.01 \leq x \leq 1.01$

30. $q(x) = \sqrt{x + 11}$; $-3 \leq x \leq 0$

31. $r(x) = \sqrt{2x - 7}$; $5 \leq x \leq 10$

32. $t(x) = \sqrt{\frac{x - 4}{2}}$; $4 \leq x \leq 8$

Describe the domain and range for each function. SEE EXAMPLE 1

33. Function p from Exercise 29

34. Function q from Exercise 30

35. Function r from Exercise 31

36. function t from Exercise 32

PRACTICE & PROBLEM SOLVING

APPLY

37. Model With Mathematics A teacher adjusts the grades of an exam using a curve. If a student's raw score on a test is x, the score based on the curve is given by the function $c(x) = 10\sqrt{x}$.

Five students received raw scores of 49, 42, 55, and 72. What are their scores according to the curve?

38. Make Sense and Persevere A group of campers leave Camp 2 and hike x miles along the path to Camp 3. The distance d between the group of campers and Camp 1 is given by $d(x) = \sqrt{x^2 + 1}$.

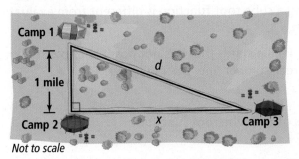

Not to scale

a. Use the function to find the distance d of the campers when $x = 1, 10, 15, 18.5, 25,$ and 50.

b. When the campers have hiked 5 miles from Camp 2, their distance from Camp 1 is $\sqrt{5^2 + 1} = \sqrt{26} \approx 5.1$ miles. How much farther do they need to hike until they double their distance from Camp 1? Show your work.

39. Communicate Precisely The distance to the horizon is a function of height above sea level. If the height h above sea level is measured in feet and the distance d to the horizon is measured in miles, then $d(h) \approx 1.22\sqrt{h}$.

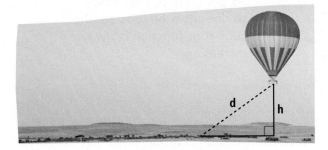

On a hot-air balloon ride, a passenger looks out from 54 ft above sea level. What is the distance from the passenger to the horizon?

ASSESSMENT PRACTICE

40. Which of the following functions are vertical translations of $f(x) = \sqrt{x}$? Select all that apply.
- Ⓐ $g(x) = \sqrt{x} - 4$
- Ⓑ $h(x) = 3 + \sqrt{x}$
- Ⓒ $k(x) = \sqrt{-5 + x}$
- Ⓓ $m(x) = \sqrt{5x}$
- Ⓔ $n(x) = -7 + \sqrt{x}$

41. SAT/ACT For the square root function $p(x) = \sqrt{x}$, the average rate of change between $x = 13$ and $x = a$ is 0.155. What is the value of a?
- Ⓐ −4
- Ⓑ 0
- Ⓒ 5
- Ⓓ 8
- Ⓔ 11

42. Performance Task The relationship between the surface area A and the diameter D of each glass sphere can be described using the equation shown.

$D = \sqrt{\dfrac{A}{\pi}}$

PART A Find the average rate of change in the diameter for surface areas between 20 in.^{2} and 10 in.^{2}.

PART B Find the average rate of change in the diameter when the surface area decreases from 16 in.^{2} to 14 in.^{2}.

PART C Find the average rate of change in D when A increases from 14.9 to 15.1 in.^{2}, and find the average rate of change in D when A increases from 14.99 to 15.01 in.^{2}.

PART D Describe a pattern in parts A, B, and C.

1-5

The Cube Root Function

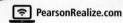
PearsonRealize.com

I CAN... identify the key features of the cube root function.

VOCABULARY
• cube root function

CRITIQUE & EXPLAIN

Emilia wrote several radical expressions on the whiteboard.

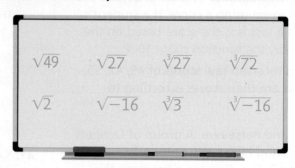

$\sqrt{49}$ $\sqrt{27}$ $\sqrt[3]{27}$ $\sqrt[3]{72}$

$\sqrt{2}$ $\sqrt{-16}$ $\sqrt[3]{3}$ $\sqrt[3]{-16}$

A. Evaluate each expression, and explain how to plot each value on a real number line.

B. Explain how evaluating a cube root function is different from evaluating a square root function.

C. Construct Arguments Emilia states that it is not possible to plot either $\sqrt{-16}$ or $\sqrt[3]{-16}$ on the real number line. Do you agree? Explain.

ESSENTIAL QUESTION

What are the key features of the cube root function?

CONCEPTUAL UNDERSTANDING

EXAMPLE 1   Key Features of the Cube Root Function

A. What are the key features of $f(x) = \sqrt[3]{x}$?

The function $f(x) = \sqrt[3]{x}$ is the **cube root function**.

Make a table of values.

LOOK FOR STRUCTURE
How does the cube root affect the domain and range of the function?

x	−8	−1	0	1	8
$f(x)$	−2	−1	0	1	2

$(-2)^3 = -8$, so $\sqrt[3]{-8} = -2$.

Since $x^3 = 0$ only when $x = 0$, the origin is the only point where the graph of $f(x) = \sqrt[3]{x}$ intercepts both the x- and y-axes.

Now graph the function.

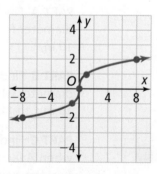

As the value of x increases, so does its cube root. So, the cube root function is always increasing.

There are no restrictions on the x- or y-values, so the domain and range are all real numbers.

CONTINUED ON THE NEXT PAGE

EXAMPLE 1 CONTINUED

B. What are the maximum and minimum values for $f(x) = \sqrt[3]{x}$ over the interval $-8 \le x \le 8$?

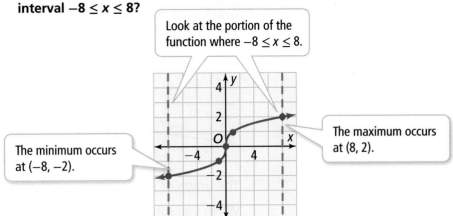

Look at the portion of the function where $-8 \le x \le 8$.

The minimum occurs at $(-8, -2)$.

The maximum occurs at $(8, 2)$.

GENERALIZE

Will this strategy—using the end points of the domain to find the maximum and minimum values of a cube root function—work for all functions?

The maximum value for $f(x) = \sqrt[3]{x}$ when $-8 \le x \le 8$ is 2, and the minimum value is -2.

Since the function is always increasing, the maximum and minimum values of the function occur at the endpoints of the given interval.

 Try It! **1.** What are the maximum and minimum values for $f(x) = \sqrt[3]{x}$ over the interval $-27 \le x \le 27$?

EXAMPLE 2 **Translations of the Cube Root Function**

A. How does the graph of $g(x) = \sqrt[3]{x} + 4$ compare to the graph of $f(x) = \sqrt[3]{x}$?

Graph each function.

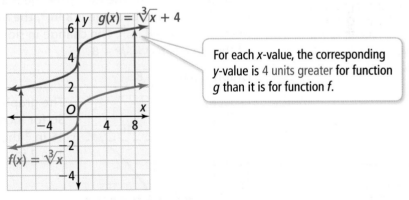

$g(x) = \sqrt[3]{x} + 4$

For each x-value, the corresponding y-value is 4 units greater for function g than it is for function f.

$f(x) = \sqrt[3]{x}$

The graph of $g(x) = \sqrt[3]{x} + 4$ is a vertical translation of the graph of $f(x) = \sqrt[3]{x}$.

As with other functions you have studied, when you add a constant to the output of the cube root function $f(x) = \sqrt[3]{x}$, the graph of the resulting function, $g(x) = \sqrt[3]{x} + k$, is a vertical translation of the graph of f. The domain and the range for both functions are all real numbers.

CONTINUED ON THE NEXT PAGE

EXAMPLE 2 CONTINUED

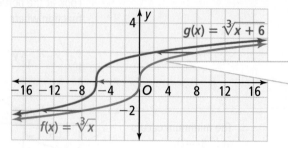

B. How does the graph of $g(x) = \sqrt[3]{x + 6}$ compare to the graph of $f(x) = \sqrt[3]{x}$?

Graph each function.

$g(x) = \sqrt[3]{x + 6}$

$f(x) = \sqrt[3]{x}$

For each y-value, the corresponding x-value is 6 units less for function g than it is for function f.

The graph of $g(x) = \sqrt[3]{x + 6}$ is a horizontal translation of $f(x) = \sqrt[3]{x}$.

When you subtract a constant from the input of the cube root function $f(x) = \sqrt[3]{x}$, the graph of the resulting function, $g(x) = \sqrt[3]{x - h}$, is a horizontal translation of the graph of f. The domain and the range for both functions are all real numbers.

 Try It! **2.** Compare the graph of each function to the graph of $f(x) = \sqrt[3]{x}$.

a. $g(x) = \sqrt[3]{x} - 2$ **b.** $p(x) = \sqrt[3]{x + 1}$

APPLICATION   **EXAMPLE 3**   **Model a Problem Using the Cube Root Function**

Creative Clays is increasing the package size for its art clay. Designers are considering different sizes. Assume that the new package will be a cube with volume x in.^{3}. For what increases in volume would the side length increase between 1 in. and 2 in.?

MODEL WITH MATHEMATICS
Mathematics has many industrial and commercial applications, such as the development of product packaging. Modeling before production begins can prevent expensive mistakes.

Since the volume of the new package is x in.^{3} and the volume of old package is 8 in.^{3}, the increase in volume is $x - 8$ in.^{3}. The change in side length of the cube is $f(x) = \sqrt[3]{x - 8}$.

Each orginal clay cube contains 8 in.^{3} of clay.

Graph $f(x) = \sqrt[3]{x - 8}$.

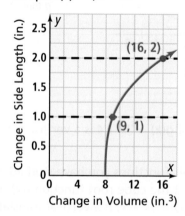

The graph shows that $f(9) = 1$ and $f(16) = 2$. So for increases in volume between 9 and 16 in.^{3} the side length would increase by 1 to 2 in.

 Try It! **3.** A cube has a volume of 10 cm^3. A larger cube has a volume of x cm^3. Consider the function $f(x) = \sqrt[3]{x - 10}$. What do the values $f(14)$ and $f(19)$ represent?

EXAMPLE 4 Compare Rates of Change of a Function

For the function $f(x) = \sqrt[3]{x} - 1$, how does the average rate of change from $x = 1$ to $x = 5$ compare to the average rate of change from $x = 5$ to $x = 9$?

Step 1 Evaluate the function for the x-values that correspond to the endpoints of each interval.

Interval: $1 \le x \le 5$

$f(1) = \sqrt[3]{1} - 1 \qquad f(5) = \sqrt[3]{5} - 1$
$= 0 \qquad\qquad \approx 1.59$

Interval: $5 \le x \le 9$

$f(5) = \sqrt[3]{5} - 1 \qquad f(9) = \sqrt[3]{9} - 1$
$\approx 1.59 \qquad\qquad = 2$

Step 2 Find the average rate of change over each interval.

$$\frac{f(5) - f(1)}{5 - 1} \approx \frac{1.59 - 0}{5 - 1}$$
$$\approx 0.40$$

$$\frac{f(9) - f(5)}{9 - 5} \approx \frac{2 - 1.59}{9 - 5}$$
$$\approx 0.10$$

The average rate of change of the function $f(x) = \sqrt[3]{x} - 1$ appears to decrease when $x \ge 1$ and as the x-values corresponding to the endpoints of the interval increase. This is consistent with the curve becoming less steep when $x \ge 1$ and x increases.

☑ **Try It!** 4. Compare the average rates of change for $f(x) = 2\sqrt[3]{x} - 3$ over the intervals $-12 \le x \le -8$ and $-4 \le x \le 0$.

EXAMPLE 5 Compare Rates of Change of Two Functions

The graph and table represent translations of the cube root function $f(x) = \sqrt[3]{x}$. Values in the table are rounded to the nearest hundredth. Which function has a greater average rate of change over the interval $2 \le x \le 4$?

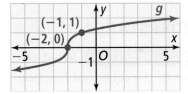

x	h(x)
0	1.22
1	2.22
2	2.48
3	2.66
4	2.81

COMMON ERROR
You may be tempted to express calculated values to a higher precision. This is misleading with estimated data. For reasonable comparisons, express both values in the same level of precision.

The function g is f translated to the left 2 units, so $g(x) = \sqrt[3]{x + 2}$. Use this function to find the average rate of change in the interval $2 \le x \le 4$.

$$\frac{g(4) - g(2)}{4 - 2} \approx \frac{1.82 - 1.59}{4 - 2}$$
$$= 0.115$$

To find the average rate of change for $h(x)$, use the values in the table directly.

$$\frac{h(4) - h(2)}{4 - 2} \approx \frac{2.81 - 2.48}{4 - 2}$$
$$= 0.165$$

The average rate of change of $h(x)$ is greater than the average rate of change of $g(x)$ on the interval $2 \le x \le 4$.

CONTINUED ON THE NEXT PAGE

EXAMPLE 5 CONTINUED

  Concept Summary Assess

Try It! **5.** Which function has the greater average rate of change over the interval $-5 \leq x \leq 0$: the translation of $f(x) = \sqrt[3]{x}$ to the right 1 unit and up 2 units, or the function $r(x) = \sqrt[3]{x} + 3$?

 CONCEPT SUMMARY The Cube Root Function $f(x) = \sqrt[3]{x}$.

GRAPH

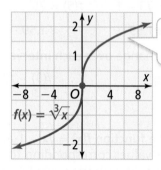

f is increasing over its whole domain.

$f(x) = \sqrt[3]{x}$

KEY FEATURES
- **x-intercept**   0
- **y-intercept**   0
- **domain**   all real numbers
- **range**   all real numbers

 Do You UNDERSTAND?

1. **ESSENTIAL QUESTION** What are the key features of the cube root function?

2. **Error Analysis** Timothy uses his calculator to investigate the domain and range of $f(x) = \sqrt[3]{x}$. He estimates the range as $-2 \leq y \leq 2$. What is the error that Timothy made?

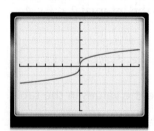

3. **Look for Relationships** Explain how the graph of $f(x) = \sqrt[3]{x}$ is related to the graph of $g(x) = -\sqrt[3]{x}$.

Do You KNOW HOW?

4. Identify the domain and range of $s(x) = \sqrt[3]{3x}$.

5. Describe how the graph of $g(x) = \sqrt[3]{x} - 3$ is related to the graph of $f(x) = \sqrt[3]{x}$.

6. Find the maximum and minimum values of $f(x) = \sqrt[3]{x - 1}$ for $-2 \leq x \leq 9$.

7. Calculate the average rate of change of $g(x) = \sqrt[3]{x} + 3$ for $4 \leq x \leq 7$.

8. Describe how the graph of $g(x) = \sqrt[3]{x - 4}$ is related to the graph of $f(x) = \sqrt{x}$.

UNDERSTAND

9. **Reason** Explain why the x- and y-intercepts of $f(x) = \sqrt[3]{x}$ are the same.

10. **Look for Relationships** Compare the average rates of change for $f(x) = \sqrt[3]{x}$ and $f(x) = \sqrt[3]{x} + 5$ for $0 \le x \le 4$.

11. **Error Analysis** Hugo calculated that the average rate of change of $f(x) = \sqrt[3]{3x}$ for $0 \le x \le 5$ is 1.026. Explain the error that Hugo made.

$$\frac{\sqrt[3]{3(5)} - \sqrt[3]{3(0)}}{5 - 0}$$

$$= \frac{3\left(\sqrt[3]{5} - \sqrt[3]{0}\right)}{5 - 0}$$

$$\approx 1.026 \quad \textbf{X}$$

12. **Use Appropriate Tools** Find the average rate of change of $f(x) = \sqrt[3]{x}$ for $0 \le x \le 4$. Use the symmetry of the function to predict its average rate of change for $-4 \le x \le 0$.

13. **Reason** Which gives a better approximation of the rate of change of $f(x) = \sqrt[3]{x}$ near $x = 1$: the average rate of change for $-1 \le x \le 3$ or for $\frac{1}{2} \le x \le \frac{3}{2}$? Explain your reasoning.

14. **Higher Order Thinking** Consider the function $f(x) = x^3$. How can you find two different intervals that have the same average rate of change? Explain how you can generalize your statement.

15. **Use Structure** For each condition, describe a translation or pair of translations of $f(x) = \sqrt[3]{x}$ that results in the graph of function g.

   a. The y-intercept of the graph of g is -2.

   b. The graph of g passes through the point $(3, 5)$.

   c. The x-intercept of the graph of g is -1.

PRACTICE

For each function, identify domain, range, and intercepts. SEE EXAMPLE 1

16. $f(x) = \sqrt[3]{x - 3}$

17. $f(x) = \sqrt[3]{2x}$

18. $f(x) = \sqrt[3]{x} - 1$

19. $f(x) = \sqrt[3]{x + 2}$

Describe translations that transform the graph of $f(x) = \sqrt[3]{x}$ into the graph of the given function. SEE EXAMPLE 2

20. $g(x) = \sqrt[3]{x - 3}$

21. $p(x) = \sqrt[3]{x} + 2$

22. $p(x) = \sqrt[3]{x} - 10$

23. $q(x) = \sqrt[3]{x + 7}$

24. $j(x) = \sqrt[3]{x + 4} - 8$

25. $k(x) = \sqrt[3]{\frac{1}{2} + x} - \frac{3}{4}$

Graph each function. Use the graph to estimate the values of x that satisfy each condition. SEE EXAMPLE 3

26. $f(x) = \sqrt[3]{x}$; $1 \le f(x) \le 2$

27. $g(x) = \sqrt[3]{x - 2}$; $1 \le g(x) \le 2$

28. $p(x) = \sqrt[3]{x - 1} + 3$; $2 \le p(x) \le 5$

Calculate the average rate of change for each function over the given interval. SEE EXAMPLE 4

29. $f(x) = \sqrt[3]{x}$ for $3 \le x \le 10$

30. $g(x) = \sqrt[3]{x} + 2$ for $-4 \le x \le 0$

31. $p(x) = \sqrt[3]{4x + 5}$ for $-1 \le x \le 1$

Let $f(x) = \sqrt[3]{x}$. The function g is shown in the graph. For each function, use $<$, $>$, or $=$ to complete each of the statements. SEE EXAMPLE 5

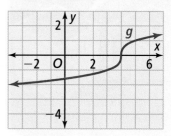

32. $f(3)$ _____ $g(3)$

33. x-intercept of f _____ x-intercept of g

34. y-intercept of f _____ y-intercept of g

APPLY

35. Model With Mathematics Tamika's Auto Sales opened recently. Weekly sales are shown in the table.

Week	1	2	3	4	5	6
Cars Sold	9	13	14	15	17	18

Plot the sales on a graph and write a cube root function that approximately models the sales. Explain what the features of the cube root function mean for the dealer's sales in the long run.

36. Communicate Precisely Max Wax Company packages colored wax to make homemade candles in cube-shaped containers. The production line needs to plan sizes of the containers based on the associated costs. Write a cube root function that tells the side lengths of the container, x, in inches for a given cost, C.

The cost of filling a container is $3 per cubic foot.

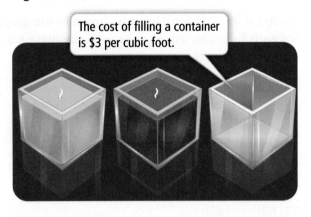

37. Mathematical Connections A cube has the same volume as a box that is 4 ft 5 in. long, 3 ft 2 in. wide, and 4 ft 3 in. deep.

  a. Write an expression that models the length of one side of the cube.

  b. Find the side length of the cube.

  c. Does the cube or the box have a greater surface area? How much greater?

ASSESSMENT PRACTICE

38. Analyze the key features of $g(x) = \sqrt[3]{x - 8} + 4$. Which of the following are true? Select all that apply.

  Ⓐ The domain of g is $x \geq 8$.

  Ⓑ The range of g is the set of all real numbers.

  Ⓒ As x approaches infinity, $g(x)$ approaches infinity.

  Ⓓ The graph of g is a translation of the graph of $f(x) = \sqrt[3]{x}$ left 8 units and up 4 units.

  Ⓔ The function has an absolute minimum at $x = 8$.

39. SAT/ACT Which shows the average rate of change of $f(x) = \sqrt[3]{x} - 2$ over $1 \leq x \leq 4$?

  Ⓐ 0.47

  Ⓑ 0.20

  Ⓒ −0.20

  Ⓓ −0.47

  Ⓔ −1.53

40. Performance Task Paul is filling spherical water balloons for an experiment. It is important that each balloon holds exactly the same volume of water, but Paul does not have a good instrument for measuring capacity.

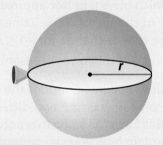

Part A Write a cube root function that allows Paul to predict the radius associated with a given volume using $V = \frac{4}{3}\pi r^3$.

Part B Describe a reasonable domain and range.

Part C If each balloon should have a volume of 72 in.³, what radius should the balloon have?

Topic Review

? TOPIC ESSENTIAL QUESTION

1. How do you use exponential, square root, and cube root functions to model situations and solve problems?

Vocabulary Review

Choose the correct term to complete each sentence.

2. Any of the distinct objects of a set is called a(n) _____.

3. If each element of *B* is also an element of *A*, *B* is a(n) _____ of *A*.

4. A well-defined collection of elements is a(n) _____.

5. The _____ is the function $f(x) = \sqrt[3]{x}$.

6. The _____ is the function $f(x) = \sqrt{x}$.

- cube root function
- element
- set
- square root function
- subset

Concepts & Skills Review

LESSON 1-1 **Operations on Real Numbers**

Quick Review

Sums, differences, and products of rational numbers are rational. Quotients of rational numbers (when they are defined) are rational.

The sum and difference of a rational number and an irrational number are irrational. The product and quotient (when defined) of a rational number and an irrational number are irrational, *except* when the rational number is 0.

Example

Let *a*, *b*, *c*, and *d* be integers, with $b \neq 0$ and $d \neq 0$. Is the sum of $\frac{a}{b}$ and $\frac{c}{d}$ rational or irrational? Is their product rational or irrational?

$$\frac{a}{b} + \frac{c}{d} = \frac{ad + bc}{bd} \qquad \frac{a}{b} \cdot \frac{c}{d} = \frac{ac}{bd}$$

The sum and product are both rational.

Practice & Problem Solving

7. Give an example of two irrational numbers whose product is rational.

For each number, determine whether it is an element of the real numbers, irrational numbers, rational numbers, integers, or whole numbers. List all that apply.

8. 13.9　　　9. $\sqrt{49}$　　　10. -48

Order from least to greatest.

11. $0.\overline{36}$, $\sqrt{15}$, $\sqrt{\frac{17}{3}}$　　　12. $\frac{29}{12}$, 2.4, $\sqrt{5.65}$

13. **Make Sense and Persevere** Taylor uses tape to mark a square play area in the basement for her daughter. The area measures 28 ft². Is the side length of the square rational or irrational? Explain.

LESSON 1-2 Rational Exponents and Properties of Exponents

Quick Review

If the nth root of a is a real number and m is an integer, then $a^{\frac{1}{n}} = \sqrt[n]{a}$ and $a^{\frac{m}{n}} = (\sqrt[n]{a})^m$.

Power of a Power: $(a^m)^n = a^{mn}$

Power of a Product: $(a \cdot b)^m = a^m b^m$

Product of Powers: $a^m \cdot a^n = a^{m+n}$

Quotient of Powers: $\frac{a^m}{a^n} = a^{m-n}$, $a \neq 0$

Example

How can you use the Power of a Power Property to solve $64^{x-3} = 16^{2x-1}$?

Rewrite the equation so both expressions have the same base.

$64^{x-3} = 16^{2x-1}$

$(2^6)^{x-3} = (2^4)^{2x-1}$

$2^{6x-18} = 2^{8x-4}$

$6x - 18 = 8x - 4$

$-18 = 2x - 4$

$-14 = 2x$

$-7 = x$

The solution is -7.

Practice & Problem Solving

Write each radical using rational exponents.

14. $\sqrt{8}$

15. $\sqrt[3]{12}$

Solve each equation.

16. $\left(6^{\frac{x}{2}}\right)\left(6^{\frac{x}{3}}\right) = 6^6$

17. $36^{4x-1} = 6^{x+2}$

18. **Make Sense and Persevere** Describe two ways to express the edge length of a cube with a volume of 64 cm³.

19. **Model With Mathematics** Use rational exponents to express the relationship between the dollar values of two prizes in a contest.

Prize	Value
Bicycle	$256
Luxury vehicle	$65,536

LESSON 1-3 Exponential Models

Quick Review

Interest may be compounded over different time periods, such as quarterly, monthly, or daily. The formula $A = P\left(1 + \frac{r}{n}\right)^{nt}$ is used to calculate the amount of money available after it has been invested for an amount of time. The formula $A = Pe^{rt}$ is used to calculate the amount of money available in an account that is compounded continuously. The calculator can be used to find an exponential model for a set of data.

Example

Jenny invests $2,500 in an account that pays 2.4% interest annually. The interest is compounded quarterly. How much will Jenny have in the account after 6 years?

Use the formula $A = P\left(1 + \frac{r}{n}\right)^{nt}$.

$A = 2,500\left(1 + \frac{0.024}{4}\right)^{4(6)}$ ⋯⋯ Substitute for A, P, n, and r.

$A = 2,500(1.006)^{24}$ ⋯⋯ Simplify.

$A = 2,885.97$ ⋯⋯ Use a calculator.

Jenny will have about $2,885.97.

Practice & Problem Solving

Find the total amount of money in the account after the given amount of time.

20. Compounded monthly, $P = \$5,000$, $r = 2.4\%$, $t = 8$ years

21. Continuously compounded, $P = \$7,500$, $r = 1.6\%$, $t = 10$ years

Write an exponential model given two points.

22. (12, 256) and (13, 302)

23. (3, 54) and (4, 74)

24. **Model With Mathematics** Jason's parents invested some money for Jason's education when Jason was born. The table shows how the account has grown.

Number of Years	Amount ($)
1	2,250
7	4,400
13	9,250

Predict how much will be in the account after 18 years.

Quick Review

The **square root function** is $f(x) = \sqrt{x}$.

Example

How does $g(x) = \sqrt{x} - 4$ compare to $f(x) = \sqrt{x}$?

For each y-value, the corresponding x-value is 4 units more for function g than it is for function f.

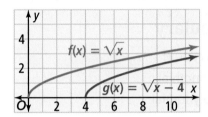

The graph of $g(x) = \sqrt{x} - 4$ is a horizontal translation of $f(x) = \sqrt{x}$ 4 units to the right. The domain for f is $x \geq 0$, and the domain for g is $x \geq 4$. The range is the same, $y \geq 0$.

Practice & Problem Solving

How does each graph compare to the graph of $f(x) = \sqrt{x}$?

25. $g(x) = \sqrt{x} + 4$ **26.** $g(x) = \sqrt{x - 8}$

27. $g(x) = \sqrt{x - 1} - 5$ **28.** $g(x) = \sqrt{x + 2} - 8$

Write an expression that represents each function.

29. $g(x)$, which is a translation 5 units down of $f(x) = \sqrt{x}$

30. $h(x)$, which is a translation 2 units left of $f(x) = \sqrt{x}$

31. Communicate Precisely The maximum speed of a sailboat is measured in knots and is estimated using the equation $s(\ell) = 1.34\sqrt{\ell}$, where ℓ is the length of the sailboat in feet. What is the approximate speed of a sailboat that has a length of 45 ft?

Quick Review

The **cube root function** is $f(x) = \sqrt[3]{x}$.

Example

For the function $f(x) = \sqrt[3]{x + 2}$, how does the average rate of change from $2 \leq x \leq 4$ compare to the average rate of change from $6 \leq x \leq 8$?

Evaluate the function for each x-value.

Interval: $2 \leq x \leq 4$

$f(2) = \sqrt[3]{2 + 2} \approx 1.59$ $f(4) = \sqrt[3]{4 + 2} \approx 1.82$

Interval: $6 \leq x \leq 8$

$f(6) = \sqrt[3]{6 + 2} = 2$ $f(8) = \sqrt[3]{8 + 2} \approx 2.15$

Find the average rate of change over each interval.

From $2 \leq x \leq 4$:   From $6 \leq x \leq 8$:

$\dfrac{1.82 - 1.59}{4 - 2} \approx 0.12$ $\dfrac{2.15 - 2}{8 - 6} \approx 0.08$

The average rate of change of the function $f(x) = \sqrt[3]{x + 2}$ decreases as the x-values of the interval increase.

Practice and Problem Solving

Describe translations that transform the graph of $f(x) = \sqrt[3]{x}$ into the graph of the given function.

32. $g(x) = \sqrt[3]{x + 5}$ **33.** $h(x) = \sqrt[3]{x} + 4$

34. $j(x) = \sqrt[3]{x - 1} + 2$ **35.** $p(x) = \sqrt[3]{x + 1.5} - 2.5$

Calculate the average rate of change for each function over the given interval.

36. $f(x) = \sqrt[3]{x}$ for $5 \leq x \leq 9$

37. $g(x) = \sqrt[3]{x + 6}$ for $-3 \leq x \leq 0$

38. Look for Relationships Compare the average rates of change for $f(x) = \sqrt[3]{x}$ and $g(x) = \sqrt[3]{x - 3}$ for $-2 \leq x \leq 2$.

39. Communicate Precisely A fish store needs more cube-shaped fish tanks for its display shelves. Each fish requires 1 ft^3 of water, and it costs \$5 per ft^3 for the tanks. Write a cube root function that gives the side lengths of the container x in inches for a given cost C.

TOPIC 1 REVIEW

? TOPIC ESSENTIAL QUESTION

How do you work with polynomials to rewrite expressions and solve problems?

Topic Overview

enVision® STEM Project:
Make Business Decisions

Topic Vocabulary

- Closure Property
- degree of a monomial
- degree of a polynomial
- difference of two squares
- monomial
- perfect-square trinomial
- polynomial
- standard form of a polynomial

Digital Experience

INTERACTIVE STUDENT EDITION Access online or offline.

ACTIVITIES Complete *Explore & Reason, Model & Discuss*, and *Critique & Explain* activities. Interact with Examples and Try Its.

ANIMATION View and interact with real-world applications.

PRACTICE Practice what you've learned.

 Go online | **PearsonRealize.com**

MATHEMATICAL MODELING IN **3** ACTS ⊕⊙⊕

▶ Who's Right?

People often approach a problem in different ways. Sometimes their solutions are the same, but other times different approaches lead to very different, but still valid, solutions.

Suppose you had to solve a system of linear equations. You might solve it by graphing while a classmate might use substitution. Is one way of solving a problem always better than another? Think about this during the Mathematical Modeling in 3 Acts lesson.

VIDEOS Watch clips to support *Mathematical Modeling in 3 Acts Lessons* and **enVision® STEM Projects**.

CONCEPT SUMMARY Review key lesson content through multiple representations.

ASSESSMENT Show what you've learned.

 GLOSSARY Read and listen to English and Spanish definitions.

 TUTORIALS Get help from *Virtual Nerd*, right when you need it.

 MATH TOOLS Explore math with digital tools and manipulatives.

Video

Did You Know?

Businesses can use functions to estimate their revenue and expenses, and then use that information to set sales targets and prices.

For every **100 new products** introduced each year, only **5 succeed**.

The biggest advertiser on TV
COMMUNICATION COMPANIES

The second biggest
CARS

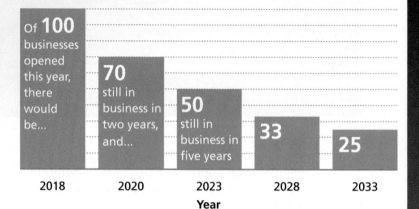

Of **100** businesses opened this year, there would be...

70 still in business in two years, and...

50 still in business in five years

33

25

2018   2020   2023   2028   2033
Year

About **543,000 new businesses** are started every month in the United States.

▶ Your Task: Make Business Decisions

You and your classmates will choose a business to model. You will suggest and defend choices for the number of items to make and the price(s) at which to sell them. Then, you will research ways that your decisions could change based on market factors.

2-1

Adding and Subtracting Polynomials

PearsonRealize.com

I CAN... combine like terms to simplify polynomials.

VOCABULARY
- Closure Property
- degree of a monomial
- degree of a polynomial
- monomial
- polynomial
- standard form of a polynomial

EXPLORE & REASON

Each year the Student Council conducts a food drive. At the end of the drive, the members report on the items collected.

A. Describe two different ways that the students can sort the items that were collected.

B. Model With Mathematics Write two expressions to represent the number and type of items collected.

C. Share your expression with classmates. How are the expressions similar? How are they different? Why are they different?

ESSENTIAL QUESTION How does adding or subtracting polynomials compare to adding or subtracting integers?

CONCEPTUAL UNDERSTANDING

EXAMPLE 1   Understand Polynomials

A. Why does a constant have a degree of 0?

A **monomial** is a real number, a variable, or the product of a real number and one or more variables with whole number exponents.

The **degree of a monomial** is the sum of the exponents of the variables of a monomial.

STUDY TIP
Remember to find the sum of the exponents of the variables in each term, not just the greatest exponent of any variable.

> The variable has an exponent of 2, so the degree is 2.

$15x^2$

$\frac{1}{2}x^5y^2$

> The sum of the variable exponents is 7, so the degree is 7.

A constant has no variable. However, any number to the 0 power is 1, so you can multiply a constant by x^0 without changing the value of the constant.

$$7 \longrightarrow 7x^0$$
$$= 7(1)$$
$$= 7$$

> The exponent of the variable is 0, so the degree of this monomial is 0.

So, the degree of a constant is 0.

CONTINUED ON THE NEXT PAGE

EXAMPLE 1 CONTINUED

B. Why is $5x^3 - 4$ called a cubic binomial?

A **polynomial** is a monomial or the sum or difference of two or more monomials, called terms.

Polynomials are named according to their degree. The **degree of a polynomial** is the greatest degree of any term of the polynomial.

Polynomial	Degree	Name Based on Degree
7	0	Constant
$4x$	1	Linear
$3x^2 + 2x + 1$	2	Quadratic
$-5x^2y$	3	Cubic
$4x^2y^2 + 5x - 2y + 6$	4	Fourth Degree

> Polynomials with a degree greater than 3 are named by their degree—fourth degree, fifth degree, and so on.

Polynomials are also named according to how many terms they have.

Polynomial	Number of Terms	Name Based on Number of Terms
$4x$	1	Monomial
$x + 7$	2	Binomial
$-5x^2y + x^2 + x$	3	Trinomial
$4x^2y^2 + 5x - 2y + 6$	4	Polynomial

> Polynomials with more than 3 terms do not have special names.

$5x^3 - 4$ is called a cubic binomial because it has a degree of 3 and two terms.

 Try It! **1.** Name each polynomial based on its degree and number of terms.

  a. $-2xy^2$ **b.** $6xy - 3x + y$

EXAMPLE 2   **Write Polynomials in Standard Form**

What is the standard form of the polynomial $7x - 5 - x^3 + 6x^4 - 3x^2$?

The **standard form of a polynomial** is the form of a polynomial in which the terms are written in descending order according to their degree.

LOOK FOR RELATIONSHIPS
Why is writing polynomials in standard form important? How will it be useful?

Rewrite the polynomial in standard form.

  $7x - 5 - x^3 + 6x^4 - 3x^2$ ⟵ $6x^4$ has the greatest degree, 4, so write it first.

  $6x^4 - x^3 - 3x^2 + 7x - 5$

The standard form of the polynomial is $6x^4 - x^3 - 3x^2 + 7x - 5$.

 Try It! **2.** Write each polynomial in standard form.

  a. $7 - 3x^3 + 6x^2$ **b.** $2y - 3 - 8y^2$

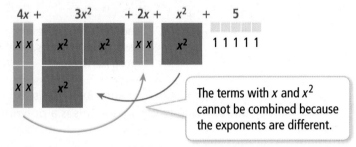

EXAMPLE 3 Add and Subtract Monomials

VOCABULARY
Remember, *like terms* are terms with exactly the same variable factors in an expression.

LOOK FOR RELATIONSHIPS
Which terms in a polynomial are like terms? How does combining them change the polynomial?

How can you use the properties of operations to combine like terms and write the expression $4x + 3x^2 + 2x + x^2 + 5$ in standard form?

Use algebra tiles to model the expression.

$4x + \quad 3x^2 \quad + 2x + \quad x^2 \quad + \quad 5$

| x x | x^2 | x^2 | x x | x^2 | 1 1 1 1 1 |
| x x | x^2 | | | | |

The terms with x and x^2 cannot be combined because the exponents are different.

Rearrange the tiles to group like terms together.

$3x^2 \quad + \quad x^2 \quad + 4x + 2x + \quad 5$

| x^2 | x^2 | x^2 | | x x | x x | 1 1 1 1 1 |
| x^2 | | | | x x | | |

$4x^2 \qquad + \quad 6x \quad + \quad 5$

The expression $4x + 3x^2 + 2x + x^2 + 5$ written in standard form is $4x^2 + 6x + 5$.

You can also rewrite the expression in standard form using the properties of operations.

$$4x + 3x^2 + 2x + x^2 + 5$$
$$= (3x^2 + x^2) + (4x + 2x) + 5$$
$$= 4x^2 + 6x + 5$$

You can apply the same properties of operations for real numbers to operations with monomials.

 Try It! **3.** Combine like terms and write each expression in standard form.

    a. $4x^2 - 3x - x^2 + 3x$ **b.** $7y^3 - 3y + 5y^3 - 2y + 7$

EXAMPLE 4 Add Polynomials

A. How is adding polynomials like adding whole numbers?

Consider the expressions $123 + 405$ and $(x^2 + 2x + 3) + (4x^2 + 5)$.

$$\begin{array}{r} 123 \\ + 405 \\ \hline 528 \end{array}$$
Only like place values can be added.

Only like terms can be added.
$$\begin{array}{r} x^2 + 2x + 3 \\ + 4x^2 \qquad + 5 \\ \hline 5x^2 + 2x + 8 \end{array}$$

Before you add polynomials, the terms must be aligned with like terms. This is similar to how, before adding whole numbers, the numbers must be aligned according to their place value.

CONTINUED ON THE NEXT PAGE

EXAMPLE 4 CONTINUED

B. What is the sum of $(4x^2 + 2x - 3)$ and $(3x^2 + 6)$?

To add two polynomials, combine like terms.

Method 1: Add vertically.

$$4x^2 + 2x - 3$$
$$+3x^2 \quad\quad + 6$$
$$\overline{7x^2 + 2x + 3}$$

Align like terms.

Use the Commutative and Associative Properties to group like terms.

Method 2: Add horizontally.

$$(4x^2 + 2x - 3) + (3x^2 + 6)$$
$$= (4x^2 + 3x^2) + (2x) + (-3 + 6)$$
$$= 7x^2 + 2x + 3$$

The sum of $(4x^2 + 2x - 3)$ and $(3x^2 + 6)$ is $7x^2 + 2x + 3$.
The sum of these two polynomials is a polynomial.

 Try It! 4. Simplify. Write each answer in standard form.

     a. $(3x^2 + 2x) + (-x + 9)$ **b.** $(-2x^2 + 5x - 7) + (3x + 7)$

EXAMPLE 5   **Subtract Polynomials**

What is the difference $(6x^2 + 3x - 2) - (3x^2 + 5x - 8)$?

To subtract two polynomials subtract like terms.

Method 1: Subtract vertically by lining up like terms.

Line up like terms. Then subtract.

$$6x^2 + 3x - 2$$
$$-(3x^2 + 5x - 8)$$

Distribute –1 to each term.

$$6x^2 + 3x - 2$$
$$-3x^2 - 5x + 8$$
$$\overline{3x^2 - 2x + 6}$$

Method 2: Subtract horizontally.

$$(6x^2 + 3x - 2) - (3x^2 + 5x - 8)$$

Distribute –1 to each term in the subtracted expression.

$$= 6x^2 + 3x - 2 - 3x^2 - 5x + 8$$

$$= (6x^2 - 3x^2) + (3x - 5x) + (-2 + 8)$$

Use the Commutative and Associative Properties to combine like terms. Then simplify.

$$= 3x^2 - 2x + 6$$

The difference of $(6x^2 + 3x - 2)$ and $(3x^2 + 5x - 8)$ is $3x^2 - 2x + 6$.
The difference of these two polynomials is also a polynomial.

In Examples 4 and 5, the result of adding or subtracting two polynomials is another polynomial. The **Closure Property** states that polynomials are closed under addition or subtraction because the result of these operations is another polynomial.

 Try It! 5. Simplify. Write each answer in standard form.

     a. $(3x^2 + 4x + 2) - (-x + 4)$ **b.** $(-5x - 6) - (4x^2 + 6)$

APPLICATION   👆 **EXAMPLE 6**   **Apply Polynomials**

An engineer is reviewing the layout of a solar farm. The solar farm shown has 4 small panels, 33 medium panels, and 32 large panels. What is the total area of the farm's solar panels?

The total area of the large solar panels is represented by $32x^2 + 384x$.

The total area of the small solar panels is represented by $4x^2 + 24x$.

The total area of the medium solar panels is represented by $33x^2 + 272x$.

USE STRUCTURE
How could you use what you know about polynomial addition to find an expression for the area of each small solar panel?

Write an expression to represent the total area of the solar panels.

Total area = Total area of + Total area of + Total area of
                large panels   medium panels   small panels

$= (32x^2 + 384x)\ +\ (33x^2 + 272x)\ +\ (4x^2 + 24x)$

$= (32x^2 + 33x^2 + 4x^2) + (384x + 272x + 24x)$

$= 69x^2 + 680x$

Use the Commutative and Associative Properties to group like terms. Then add.

The total area of the solar panels is modeled by the expression $69x^2 + 680x$, where x is the width, in meters, of each solar panel.

 Try It! **6.** What expression models the difference between the total area of the large solar panels and the total area of the small solar panels?

🔍 CONCEPT SUMMARY Adding and Subtracting Polynomials

STANDARD FORM ▶ **Standard Form of a Polynomial:** $3x^4 - 3x^2 + 4x - 2$ ← In standard form the monomial terms are written in descending order according to their degree.

NAMING POLYNOMIALS ▶ Polynomials can be named according to the number of terms and their degree.

$12x^3 + 6xy - 5$ ← There are 3 terms, so it is a trinomial.

The highest degree is 3, so it is cubic.

So $12x^3 + 6xy - 5$ is a cubic trinomial.

POLYNOMIAL OPERATIONS ▶

Adding Polynomials

$(-2x^3 + 4x^2 - 5) + (4x^3 + 2x^2 - x + 8)$

$= (-2x^3 + 4x^3) + (4x^2 + 2x^2) + (-x) + (-5 + 8)$

$= 2x^3 + 6x^2 - x + 3$

Subtracting Polynomials

$(3x^2 - 2x + 4) - (-3x^2 - x + 6)$

$= 3x^2 - 2x + 4 + 3x^2 + x - 6$

$= (3x^2 + 3x^2) + (-2x + x) + (4 - 6)$

$= 6x^2 - x - 2$

Add or subtract like terms just like you add or subtract digits with the same place value.

✓ Do You UNDERSTAND?

1. ❓ **ESSENTIAL QUESTION** ▶ How does adding or subtracting polynomials compare to adding or subtracting integers?

2. **Communicate Precisely** How does the definition of the prefixes *mono-*, *bi-*, and *tri-* help when naming polynomials?

3. **Vocabulary** Describe the relationship between the *degree of a monomial* and *the standard form of a polynomial*.

4. **Use Structure** Explain why the sum $x + x$ is equal to $2x$ instead of x^2.

5. **Error Analysis** Rebecca says that all monomials with the same degree are like terms. Explain Rebecca's error.

Do You KNOW HOW?

Name each polynomial based on its degree and number of terms.

6. $\frac{x}{4} + 2$

7. $7x^3 + xy - 4$

Write each polynomial in standard form.

8. $2y - 3 - y^2$

9. $3x^2 - 2x + x^3 + 6$

Simplify each expression.

10. $(x^2 + 2x - 4) + (2x^2 - 5x - 3)$

11. $(3x^2 - 5x - 8) - (-4x^2 - 2x - 1)$

12. A square prism has square sides with area $x^2 + 8x + 16$ and rectangular sides with area $2x^2 + 15x + 28$. What expression represents the surface area of the square prism?

UNDERSTAND

13. Reason How is it possible that the sum of two quadratic trinomials is a linear binomial?

14. Error Analysis Describe and correct the error a student made when naming the polynomial.

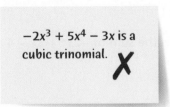

$-2x^3 + 5x^4 - 3x$ is a cubic trinomial. ✗

15. Error Analysis Describe and correct the error a student made when subtracting the polynomials.

$(-5x^2 + 2x - 3) - (3x^2 - 2x - 6)$
$-5x^2 + 2x - 3 - 3x^2 - 2x - 6$
$-8x^2 - 9$ ✗

16. Reason What is the missing term in the equation?

a. $(\_\_ + 7) + (2x - 6) = -4x + 1$

b. $(a^2 + \_\_ + 1) - (\_\_ + 5a + \_\_) = 4a^2 - 2a + 7$

17. Higher Order Thinking Describe each statement as *always, sometimes,* or *never* true.

a. A linear binomial has a degree of 0.

b. A trinomial has a degree of 2.

c. A constant has a degree of 1.

d. A cubic monomial has a degree of 3.

18. Make Sense and Persevere Consider the set of linear binomials $ax + b$, where a and b are positive integers, $a > 0$ and $b > 0$.

a. Does the set have closure for addition? Explain.

b. Does the set have closure for subtraction? Explain.

PRACTICE

Find the degree of each monomial. SEE EXAMPLE 1

19. $\frac{x}{4}$

20. $-7xy$

21. 21

22. $4x^2y$

Name each polynomial based on its degree and number of terms. SEE EXAMPLE 1

23. $17yx^2 + xy - 5$

24. $5x^3 + 2x - 8$

25. $100x^2 + 3$

26. $-9x^4 + 8x^3 - 7x + 1$

Simplify each expression. Write the answer in standard form. SEE EXAMPLES 2 AND 3

27. $3x + 2x^2 - 4x + 3x^2 - 5x$

28. $5 + 8y^2 - 12y^2 + 3y$

29. $3z - 7z^2 - 5z + 5z^2 + 2z^2$

30. $7 - 2x + 3 + 5x + 4x^2$

Add or subtract. Write each answer in standard form. SEE EXAMPLES 4 AND 5

31. $(3b - 8) + (7b + 4)$

32. $(2x^2 - 7x^3 + 8x) + (-8x^3 - 3x^2 + 4)$

33. $(5y^2 - 2y + 1) - (y^2 + y + 3)$

34. $(-7a^4 - a + 4a^2) - (-8a^2 + a - 7a^4)$

35. $(4m^2 - 2m + 4) + (2m^2 + 2m - 5)$

Write an expression to represent each situation. SEE EXAMPLE 6

36. Find the perimeter of the rectangle.

$3x - 1$

$x + 1$

37. A cube has square sides with area $x^2 + 24x + 144$. What expression represents the surface area of the cube?

38. A rectangle has a length of $5x + 2$ in. and a width of $4x + 6$ in. What is the perimeter of the rectangle?

APPLY

39. Mathematical Connections The perimeters of the two figures are equal.

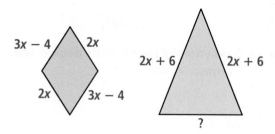

What expression represents the missing side length?

40. Make Sense and Persevere The owners of a house want to knock down the wall between the kitchen and family room.

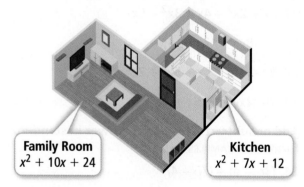

Family Room
$x^2 + 10x + 24$

Kitchen
$x^2 + 7x + 12$

What expression represents the area of the new combined open space?

41. Reason Polynomial A has degree 2; Polynomial B has degree 4. What can you determine about the name and degree of the sum of the polynomials and the difference of the polynomials if

a. Polynomial A is a binomial and Polynomial B is a monomial?

b. Both Polynomial A and Polynomial B are binomials?

42. Model With Mathematics A large indoor market is set up with 4 rows of booths. There are large booths with an area of x^2 sq. units, medium booths with an area of x sq. units, and small booths with an area of 1 sq. unit. In the marketplace, two of the rows contain 7 large booths, 6 medium booths, and 5 small booths each. The other two rows each contain 3 large booths, 5 medium booths, and 10 small booths. What is the total area of the booths in the marketplace?

ASSESSMENT PRACTICE

43. Which expression is equivalent to $(x^2 + 3x - 5) - (4x^2 + 3x - 6)$?

Ⓐ $5x^2 + 6x - 11$

Ⓑ $-3x^4 + 6x^2 + 1$

Ⓒ $-3x^2 + 1$

Ⓓ $-3x^2 + 6x - 11$

44. SAT/ACT What is the sum of $-2x^2 + 3x - 4$ and $3x^2 - 4x + 6$?

Ⓐ $x^4 - x^2 + 2$

Ⓑ $5x^4 + 7x^2 + 10$

Ⓒ 2

Ⓓ $x^2 - x + 2$

Ⓔ $2x^6$

45. Performance Task A room has the dimensions shown below. Molding was installed around the edge of the ceiling.

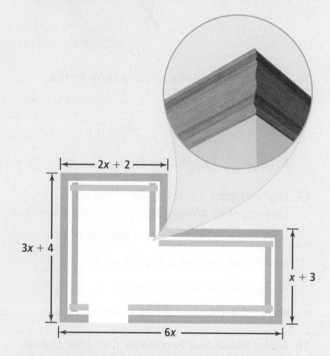

Part A Write an expression to represent the amount of molding needed.

Part B Sam used 80 feet of molding. What is the measurement of each edge of the ceiling?

2-2
Multiplying Polynomials

📶 **PearsonRealize.com**

I CAN... multiply two polynomials.

👆 **MODEL & DISCUSS**

Samantha makes the abstract painting shown using vertical and horizontal lines and four colors.

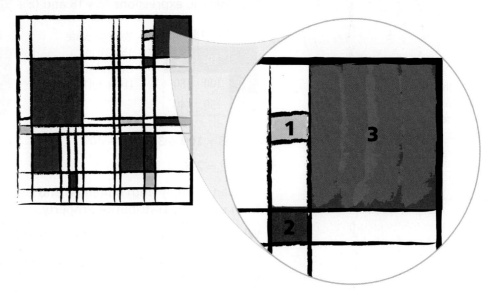

A. How can you use mathematics to describe the areas of Rectangle 1 and Rectangle 2?

B. Look for Relationships How can you use mathematics to describe the area of Rectangle 3?

❓ **ESSENTIAL QUESTION**   How does multiplying polynomials compare to multiplying integers?

👆 **EXAMPLE 1**   Multiply a Monomial and a Trinomial

What is the product of $-4x^3$ and $(x^2 + 3x - 4)$?

Use the Distributive Property. The Distributive Property works for polynomials in the same way that it works for real numbers.

$$-4x^3(x^2 + 3x - 4) = -4x^3(x^2) + -4x^3(3x) + -4x^3(-4)$$
$$= -4x^5 - 12x^4 + 16x^3$$

> Distribute $-4x^3$ to each term of the trinomial.

The product is $-4x^5 - 12x^4 + 16x^3$.

Notice that the product of these two polynomials is a polynomial.

COMMON ERROR
You may incorrectly state that $-4x^3(x^2)$ is $-4x^6$. Recall that when multiplying terms with exponents, you add the exponents of like bases.

 Try It!   **1.** Find each product.

   a. $-2x^2(x^2 + 3x + 4)$ **b.** $-4x(2x^2 - 3x + 5)$

CONCEPTUAL
UNDERSTANDING

EXAMPLE 2 Use a Table to Find the Product of Polynomials

A. How is multiplying binomials like multiplying two-digit numbers?

Multiply the expressions 15 • 18 and $(x + 5)(x + 8)$ using a table.

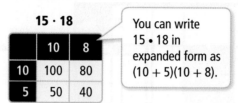

You can write 15 • 18 in expanded form as $(10 + 5)(10 + 8)$.

$15 • 18 = 100 + 80 + 50 + 40$

$= 270$

$(x + 5)(x + 8) = x^2 + 8x + 5x + 40$

$= x^2 + 13x + 40$

You can multiply both binomials and two-digit numbers in expanded form using the Distributive Property.

B. What is the area of the green rectangle?

The area of the green rectangle is represented by the expression $(2x + 1)(x + 3)$.

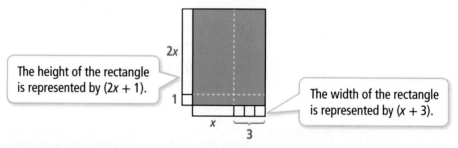

The height of the rectangle is represented by $(2x + 1)$.

The width of the rectangle is represented by $(x + 3)$.

Use a table to find the area of each section of the rectangle.

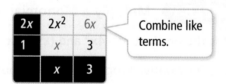

Combine like terms.

The area of the green rectangle is $2x^2 + 7x + 3$. Again, the product of these two polynomials is a polynomial.

 Try It! 2. Find the area of each green rectangle.

a.
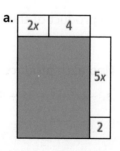

b.
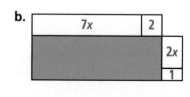

Go Online | PearsonRealize.com

EXAMPLE 3 Multiply Binomials

How can you use the Distributive Property to rewrite $(2x + 4)(x - 5)$ as a polynomial?

Distribute each term in the first binomial to each term in the second binomial.

$(2x + 4)(x - 5) = 2x(x - 5) + 4(x - 5)$ ·········· Distribute $2x$ and 4 to the second binomial.

$= 2x(x) + 2x(-5) + 4(x) + 4(-5)$ ··· Distribute $2x$ and 4 to each term in the second binomial.

$= 2x^2 - 10x + 4x - 20$ ·········· Multiply.

$= 2x^2 - 6x - 20$ ·········· Combine like terms.

The product of $(2x + 4)$ and $(x - 5)$ is $2x^2 - 6x - 20$.

Again, the product of these two polynomials is a polynomial.

GENERALIZE
Compare the factors and the final product. What generalizations can you make from this example?

Try It! 3. Find each product.

  a. $(5x - 4)(2x + 1)$ **b.** $(3x - 5)(2x + 4)$

EXAMPLE 4 Multiply a Trinomial and a Binomial

A. How can you use a table to find the product of $(x^2 + 2x - 1)$ and $(3x + 4)$?

Write the terms for each polynomial in the first row and column of the table. Multiply to find each product.

$3x + 4$

	x^2	$2x$	-1
$3x$	$3x^3$	$6x^2$	$-3x$
4	$4x^2$	$8x$	-4

$x^2 + 2x - 1$

Combine the like terms.

	x^2	$2x$	-1
$3x$	$3x^3$	$6x^2$	$-3x$
4	$4x^2$	$8x$	-4

$(x^2 + 2x - 1)(3x + 4) = 3x^3 + 6x^2 + 4x^2 + 8x + (-3x) + (-4)$

$= 3x^3 + 10x^2 + 5x - 4$

So $(x^2 + 2x - 1)(3x + 4) = 3x^3 + 10x^2 + 5x - 4$. When you multiply a trinomial by a binomial, the result is six individual products. Using a table is one method you can use to help organize these products.

CONTINUED ON THE NEXT PAGE

EXAMPLE 4 CONTINUED

B. How is multiplying a trinomial by a binomial like multiplying a three-digit number by a two-digit number?

Consider the products $312 \cdot 24$ and $(3x^2 + x + 2)(2x + 4)$.

> Multiply each place of the three-digit number by 4 ones and 2 tens. Then find the sum.

> Multiply each term of the trinomial by $+4$ and $2x$. Then combine like terms.

$$
\begin{array}{r}
3 \quad 1 \quad 2 \\
\times \qquad 2 \quad 4 \\
\hline
1, \quad 2 \quad 4 \quad 8 \\
+ \quad 6, \quad 2 \quad 4 \quad 0 \\
\hline
7, \quad 4 \quad 8 \quad 8
\end{array}
$$

$$
\begin{array}{r}
3x^2 + x + 2 \\
\times \qquad 2x + 4 \\
\hline
12x^2 + 4x + 8 \\
+\ 6x^3 + 2x^2 + 4x \\
\hline
6x^3 + 14x^2 + 8x + 8
\end{array}
$$

STUDY TIP
As you multiply, remember to line up like terms so combining them in the last step will be easier.

When multiplying a trinomial by a binomial, you multiply each term of the trinomial by each term of the binomial. This is similar to how, when multiplying a three-digit number by a two-digit number, you multiply by each place value of the two-digit number.

Try It!   **4.** Find each product.

    a. $(2x - 5)(-3x^2 + 4x - 7)$ **b.** $(-3x^2 + 1)(2x^2 + 3x - 4)$

 EXAMPLE 5   **Closure and Multiplication**

Why is the operation of multiplication closed over the set of polynomials?

For each example in this lesson, you have found the product of two polynomials. In each case the product has also been a polynomial.

Consider the first example: $-4x^3(x^2 + 3x - 4)$.

$-4x^3(x^2 + 3x - 4) = -4x^3(x^2) + -4x^3(3x) + -4x^3(-4)$

                      $= -4x^5 - 12x^4 + 16x^3$

> x^3, x^2, and x have whole number exponents, so the product will also have whole number exponents.

When you multiply two polynomials, the result is the sum or difference of terms. Each term is a real number coefficient multiplied by a variable raised to a whole number exponent. Each term is a monomial and the sum or difference of monomials is a polynomial. So polynomials are closed under multiplication.

Try It!   **5.** Why is it important that the product of two polynomials have only whole number exponents?

APPLICATION

EXAMPLE 6 **Apply Multiplication of Binomials**

A smartphone has a screen that has a width of x and a height that is 1.8 times the width. The outer dimensions of the phone are shown.

Write an expression for the portion of the phone that is not occupied by the screen. Assume that the phone is rectangular.

1.8x + 3 cm

x + 1 cm

Formulate ◀ Write expressions to represent the area of the screen and the area of the phone.

Area of screen = $x(1.8x)$

Area of phone = $(x + 1)(1.8x + 3)$

Compute ◀ Express each area in standard form.

Area of screen = $x(1.8x) = 1.8x^2$

Area of phone = $(x + 1)(1.8x + 3)$

$= x(1.8x + 3) + 1(1.8x + 3)$

$= 1.8x^2 + 3x + 1.8x + 3$

$= 1.8x^2 + 4.8x + 3$

Subtract the area of the screen from the area of the phone.

Non-screen Area = Area of Phone − Area of Screen

$= (1.8x^2 + 4.8x + 3) - 1.8x^2$

$= 4.8x + 3$

Interpret ◀ The expression $4.8x + 3$ represents the portion of the phone's surface not occupied by the screen.

 Try It! 6. Suppose the height of the phone in Example 6 were 1.9 times the width but all of the other conditions were the same. What expression would represent the area of the phone's surface not occupied by the screen?

CONCEPT SUMMARY Multiplying Polynomials

There are different methods that can be used to multiply polynomials. The methods used for multiplying polynomials are similar to the methods used for multiplying multi-digit numbers.

Binomial × Binomial	**Binomial × Trinomial**

ALGEBRA

Multiply Horizontally

$(x + 3)(x - 2)$

$= x(x - 2) + 3(x - 2)$

$= x^2 - 2x + 3x - 6$

$= x^2 + x - 6$

Multiply Horizontally

$(x + 3)(x^2 + 4x - 2)$

$= x(x^2 + 4x - 2) + 3(x^2 + 4x - 2)$

$= x^3 + 4x^2 - 2x + 3x^2 + 12x - 6$

$= x^3 + 7x^2 + 10x - 6$

Multiply Vertically

$$
\begin{array}{r}
x - 2 \\
\times \quad x + 3 \\
\hline
3x - 6 \\
+ \quad x^2 - 2x \\
\hline
x^2 + x - 6
\end{array}
$$

Multiply Vertically

$$
\begin{array}{r}
x^2 + 4x - 2 \\
\times \quad x + 3 \\
\hline
3x^2 + 12x - 6 \\
+ \, x^3 + 4x^2 - 2x \\
\hline
x^3 + 7x^2 + 10x - 6
\end{array}
$$

DIAGRAMS

	x	3
x	x^2	$3x$
-2	$-2x$	-6

$x^2 + x - 6$

	x	3
x^2	x^3	$3x^2$
$4x$	$4x^2$	$12x$
-2	$-2x$	-6

$x^3 + 7x^2 + 10x - 6$

Do You UNDERSTAND?

1. **ESSENTIAL QUESTION** How does multiplying polynomials compare to multiplying integers?

2. **Use Appropriate Tools** When multiplying two variables, how is using the Distributive Property similar to using a table?

3. **Error Analysis** Mercedes states that when multiplying $4x^3(x^3 + 2x^2 - 3)$ the product is $4x^9 + 8x^6 - 12x^3$. What was Mercedes's error?

4. **Use Structure** When multiplying polynomials, why is the degree of the product different from the degree of the factors?

Do You KNOW HOW?

Find each product.

5. $-2x^3(3x^2 - 4x + 7)$

6. $(2x + 6)(x - 4)$

7. $(x - 2)(3x + 4)$

8. $(5y - 2)(4y^2 + 3y - 1)$

9. $(3x^2 + 2x - 5)(2x - 3)$

10. Find the area of the rectangle.

$2x + 4$

$4x - 2$

Go Online | PearsonRealize.com

✎ PRACTICE & PROBLEM SOLVING

UNDERSTAND

11. **Make Sense and Persevere** The area of a rectangle is given. Identify the missing terms in the length and width.

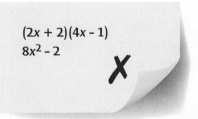

$(x + \underline{\quad})$

$x^2 + 11x + 28$ $(\underline{\quad} + 4)$

12. **Use Structure** The table shows the product when multiplying two binomials. What is the relationship between the numbers in the factors and the terms in the product?

Binomials	Products
$(x + 3)(x + 4)$	$x^2 + 7x + 12$
$(x + 2)(x - 5)$	$x^2 - 3x - 10$
$(x - 3)(x - 5)$	$x^2 - 8x + 15$

13. **Error Analysis** Describe and correct the error a student made when multiplying two binomials.

$(2x + 2)(4x - 1)$
$8x^2 - 2$

✗

14. **Use Appropriate Tools** Use a table to find the product of $(3x + 4)(x^2 + 3x - 2)$. How are the like terms in a table arranged?

15. **Higher Order Thinking** Is it possible for the product of a monomial and trinomial to be a binomial? Explain.

16. **Mathematical Connections** A triangle has a height of $2x + 6$ and a base length of $x + 4$. What is the area of the triangle?

17. **Communicate Precisely** Explain how to find the combined volume of the two rectangular prisms described. One has side lengths of $3x$, $2x + 1$, and $x + 3$. The other has side lengths of $5x - 2$, $x + 9$, and 8.

PRACTICE

Find each product. SEE EXAMPLE 1

18. $6x(x^2 - 4x - 3)$

19. $-y(-3y^2 + 2y - 7)$

20. $3x^2(-x^2 + 2x - 4)$

21. $-5x^3(2x^3 - 4x^2 + 2)$

Use a table to find each product. SEE EXAMPLE 2

22. $(x - 6)(3x + 4)$

23. $(2x + 1)(4x + 1)$

Use the Distributive Property to find each product.
SEE EXAMPLE 3

24. $(x - 6)(x + 3)$

25. $(3x - 4)(2x + 5)$

26. $(x - 8)(2x + 3)$

Find each product. SEE EXAMPLE 4

27. $(y + 3)(2y^2 - 3y + 4)$

28. $(2x - 7)(3x^2 - 4x + 1)$

29. $(2x^2 - 3x)(-3x^2 + 4x - 2)$

30. $(-2x^2 + 1)(2x^2 - 3x - 7)$

31. $(x^2 + 3x)(3x^2 - 2x + 4)$

32. Find the area of the shaded region.
SEE EXAMPLE 6

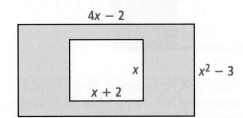

$4x - 2$

x

$x + 2$

$x^2 - 3$

33. A rectangular park is $6x + 2$ ft long and $3x + 7$ ft wide. In the middle of the park is a square turtle pond that is 8 ft wide. What expression represents the area of the park not occupied by the turtle pond? SEE EXAMPLE 6

APPLY

34. Model With Mathematics The volume of a cube is calculated by multiplying the length, width, and height. What is the volume of this cube?

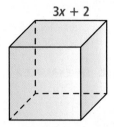

$3x + 2$

35. Reason The product of the binomial and the trinomial shown is a polynomial with four terms. Change one of the terms of the binomial or the trinomial so the product is also a trinomial.

$(2x + 2)(x^2 + 2x - 4) = 2x^3 + 7x^2 - 2x - 12$

36. Make Sense and Persevere What is the area of the painting shown?

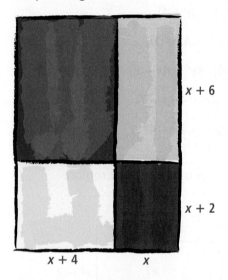

$x + 6$

$x + 2$

$x + 4$ x

37. Make Sense and Persevere A dance teacher wants to expand her studio to fit more classes. What is the combined area of Studio A and Studio B?

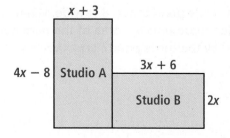

$x + 3$

$4x - 8$ Studio A

$3x + 6$

Studio B $2x$

ASSESSMENT PRACTICE

38. Write an expression for the product of $(x + 4)(2x + 1) - [(x - 5)(x + 3)] + 3x^2$.

39. SAT/ACT What is the product of $(-2x + 2)(x - 5)$?

Ⓐ $-2x^2 - 10$

Ⓑ $-2x^2 + 12x - 10$

Ⓒ $-x - 3$

Ⓓ $-2x^2 - 12x - 10$

40. Performance Task The net of a rectangular box and its dimensions are shown.

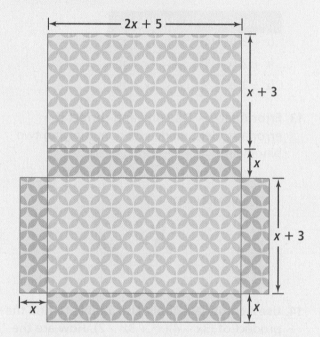

$2x + 5$

$x + 3$

x

$x + 3$

x x

Part A Write an expression for the surface area of the box in terms of x.

Part B Evaluate the polynomial expression you found in Part A. What integer value of x would give the prism a surface area of about 600 cm²?

2-3

Multiplying Special Cases

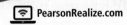 PearsonRealize.com

I CAN... use patterns to multiply binomials.

VOCABULARY
• difference of two squares

EXPLORE & REASON

The table gives values for *x* and *y* and different expressions.

x	y	(x − y)(x + y)	x²	y²	(x² − y²)
7	4				
6	2				
3	9				

A. Copy and complete the table.

B. Describe any patterns you notice.

C. **Use Structure** Try substituting variable expressions of the form 7*p* and 4*q* for *x* and *y*. Does the pattern still hold? Explain.

ESSENTIAL QUESTION

What patterns are there in the product of the square of a binomial and the product of a sum and a difference?

CONCEPTUAL UNDERSTANDING

EXAMPLE 1   Determine the Square of a Binomial

A. Why is $(a + b)^2$ considered a special case when multiplying polynomials?

Use the Distributive Property.

$$(a + b)^2 = (a + b)(a + b)$$
$$= a(a + b) + b(a + b)$$
$$= a^2 + ab + ba + b^2$$
$$= a^2 + 2ab + b^2$$

Use a visual model.

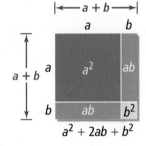

$$a^2 + 2ab + b^2$$

first term squared

twice the product of the first and last terms

last term squared

GENERALIZE
When squaring a binomial, think about how you can use the terms in the binomial to quickly determine the product. What generalizations about terms can you make?

The square of a binomial follows the pattern $(a + b)^2 = a^2 + 2ab + b^2$.

B. What is the product $(5x - 3)^2$?

Use the pattern you found in Part A to find the square of a difference.

$$(5x - 3)^2 = [5x + (-3)]^2 \quad \text{..........} \quad \text{Rewrite the difference as a sum.}$$

$$= (5x)^2 + 2(5x)(-3) + (-3)^2 \quad \text{..........} \quad \text{Substitute } 5x \text{ and } -3 \text{ into } a^2 + 2ab + b^2.$$

$$= 25x^2 - 30x + 9 \quad \text{..........} \quad \text{Simplify.}$$

You can write the product $(5x - 3)^2$ as $25x^2 - 30x + 9$.

CONTINUED ON THE NEXT PAGE

EXAMPLE 1 CONTINUED

C. How can you use the square of a binomial to find the product 29^2?

Rewrite the product as a difference of two values whose squares you know, such as $(30 - 1)^2$. Then use the pattern for the square of a binomial to find its square.

$$(30 - 1)^2 = (30)^2 + 2(30)(-1) + (-1)^2$$

> $(30 - 1)$ is the same as 29.
> So, $(30 - 1)^2$ is the same as 29^2.

$$= 900 - 60 + 1$$

$$= 841$$

So, $29^2 = 841$. In general, you can use the square of a binomial to find the square of a large number by rewriting the number as the sum or difference of two numbers with known squares.

 Try It! **1.** Find each product.

    a. $(3x - 4)^2$ **b.** 71^2

EXAMPLE 2   **Find the Product of a Sum and a Difference**

A. What is the product $(a + b)(a - b)$?

Use the Distributive Property to find the product.

$$(a + b)(a - b) = a(a - b) + b(a - b)$$

$$= a^2 - ab + ba - b^2$$

> The middle terms drop out because they are opposites.

$$= a^2 - b^2$$

> first term squared

> last term squared

The product of two binomials in the form $(a + b)(a - b)$ is $a^2 - b^2$. The product of the sum and difference of the same two values results in the **difference of two squares**.

B. What is the product $(5x + 7)(5x - 7)$?

Use the pattern you found in Part A.

$$(5x + 7)(5x - 7) = (5x)^2 - (7)^2$$ .... Substitute $5x$ and 7 into $a^2 - b^2$.

$$= 25x^2 - 49$$ .... Simplify.

The product of $(5x + 7)(5x - 7)$ is $25x^2 - 49$. It is the difference of two squares, $(5x)^2 - 7^2$.

COMMON ERROR
Remember that the last terms of each binomial are opposites. So, the product of the last terms will always be negative.

CONTINUED ON THE NEXT PAGE

EXAMPLE 2 CONTINUED

C. How can you use the difference of two squares to find the product of 43 and 37?

Rewrite the product as the sum and difference of the same two numbers a and b.

> 43 and 37 are each 3 units from 40.

$$(40 + 3)(40 - 3) = (40)^2 - (3)^2$$
$$= 1{,}600 - 9$$
$$= 1{,}591$$

> $(40 + 3)(40 - 3)$ is of the form $(a + b)(a - b)$, so it is equivalent to the difference of two squares.

You can use the difference of two squares to mentally find the product of large numbers when the numbers are the same distance from a known square.

USE APPROPRIATE TOOLS
What types of practical limitations are there on using the product of a sum and difference to find the product of two numbers?

Try It! 2. Find each product.

a. $(2x - 4)(2x + 4)$ b. $56 \cdot 44$

APPLICATION   **EXAMPLE 3** Apply the Square of a Binomial

A graphic designer is developing images for icons. The square pixelated image is placed inside a border that is 2 pixels wide on all sides. If the area of the border of the image is 176 square pixels, what is the area of the image?

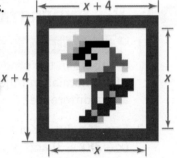

> Let x represent the length and width of the image.

Formulate ◀ The area of the image and the border is represented by the expression $(x + 4)^2$.

Total area	–	Area of Image	=	Area of Border
$(x + 4)^2$	–	x^2	=	176

Compute ◀
$$(x + 4)^2 - x^2 = 176$$
$$x^2 + 8x + 16 - x^2 = 176$$
$$8x + 16 = 176$$
$$8x = 160$$
$$x = 20$$

> Find the product of the squared binomial first.

Interpret ◀ The image will be 20 pixels by 20 pixels. The area of the image is $20 \cdot 20$, or 400 square pixels.

Try It! 3. What is the area of the square image if the area of the border is 704 square pixels and the border is 4 pixels wide?

CONCEPT SUMMARY Multiplying Special Cases

Square of a Binomial	Product of a Sum and Difference
WORDS	
The square of a binomial, $(a + b)^2$, always follows the same pattern: the square of the first term, plus twice the product of the first and last term, plus the square of the last term.	The product of two binomials in the form $(a + b)(a - b)$ results in the difference of two squares.
ALGEBRA	
$(a + b)^2 = a^2 + 2ab + b^2$ or $(a - b)^2 = a^2 - 2ab + b^2$	$(a + b)(a - b) = a^2 - b^2$ difference of two squares
NUMBERS	
$(x + 4)^2 = (x + 4)(x + 4)$ $= x^2 + 4x + 4x + 16$ $= x^2 + 8x + 16$	$(x - 7)(x + 7) = x^2 - 7x + 7x - 49$ $= x^2 - 49$

Do You UNDERSTAND?

1. **ESSENTIAL QUESTION** What patterns are there in the product of the square of a binomial and the product of a sum and a difference?

2. **Error Analysis** Kennedy multiplies $(x - 3)(x + 3)$ and gets an answer of $x^2 - 6x - 9$. Describe and correct Kennedy's error.

3. **Vocabulary** The product $(x + 6)(x - 6)$ is equivalent to an expression that is called the *difference of two squares*. Explain why the term *difference of two squares* is appropriate.

4. **Use Structure** Explain why the product of two binomials in the form $(a + b)(a - b)$ is a binomial instead of a trinomial.

Do You KNOW HOW?

Write each product in standard form.

5. $(x - 7)^2$

6. $(2x + 5)^2$

7. $(x + 4)(x - 4)$

8. $(3y - 5)(3y + 5)$

Use either the square of a binomial or the difference of two squares to find the area of each rectangle.

9.

54 cm

54 cm

10.

24 in.

36 in.

PRACTICE & PROBLEM SOLVING

UNDERSTAND

11. **Generalize** Find each product.

- $(x + 9)(x + 9)$
- $(x - 7)(x - 7)$
- $(2x - 1)^2$

a. What do all products of the square of a binomial have in common?

b. Will the third term of the square of a binomial always be positive? Explain.

c. What is the relationship between the sign of the binomial and the sign of the second term in the product?

d. What is true about the exponents representing perfect square variables?

12. **Look for Relationships** Find a value for m or n to make a true statement.

a. $mx^2 - 36 = (3x + 6)(3x - 6)$

b. $(mx + ny)^2 = 4x^2 + 12xy + 9y^2$

13. **Error Analysis** Describe and correct the error a student made when squaring $(x + 5)$.

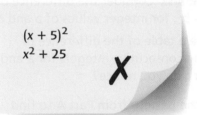

$(x + 5)^2$
$x^2 + 25$

14. **Use Structure** The expression $96^2 - 95^2$ is a difference of two squares. How can you use the factors $(96 - 95)(96 + 95)$ to make it easier to simplify this expression?

15. **Construct Arguments** Jacob makes the following conjectures. Is each conjecture correct? Provide arguments to support your answers.

a. The product of any two consecutive even numbers is 1 less than a perfect square.

b. The product of any two consecutive odd numbers is 1 less than a perfect square.

PRACTICE

Write each product in standard form. SEE EXAMPLE 1

16. $(y + 9)(y + 9)$ 17. $(5x - 3)(5x - 3)$

18. $(a + 11)(a + 11)$ 19. $(x - 13)(x - 13)$

20. $(p + 15)^2$ 21. $(3k + 8)^2$

22. $(x - 4y)^2$ 23. $(2a + 3b)^2$

24. $\left(\frac{2}{5}x + \frac{1}{5}\right)^2$ 25. $(0.4x + 1.2)^2$

Use the square of a binomial to find each product.
SEE EXAMPLE 1

26. 56^2 27. 72^2

Write each product in standard form.
SEE EXAMPLE 2

28. $(x - 12)(x + 12)$ 29. $(2x + 5)(2x - 5)$

30. $(3a - 4b)(3a + 4b)$ 31. $(x^2 - 2y)(x^2 + 2y)$

32. $\left(\frac{1}{4}x - \frac{2}{3}\right)\left(\frac{1}{4}x + \frac{2}{3}\right)$ 33. $(x + 2.5)(x - 2.5)$

Use the product of sum and difference to find each product. SEE EXAMPLE 2

34. $32 \cdot 28$ 35. $83 \cdot 97$

36. Consider the figure shown. SEE EXAMPLE 3

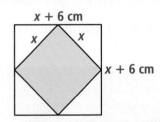

$x + 6$ cm

$x + 6$ cm

a. What expression represents the total area of the four white triangles?

b. If the length of each side of the shaded square is 12 cm, what is the total area of the four white triangles?

37. What is the area of the shaded region?
SEE EXAMPLE 3

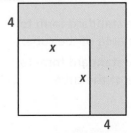

APPLY

38. **Mathematical Connections** The radius of the inner circle of a tile pattern shown is x inches. Write a polynomial in standard form to represent the area of the space between the inner and outer circle.

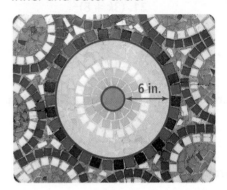

6 in.

39. **Make Sense and Persevere** In the figure shown, the darker square is removed.

a. Divide the remaining figure into two rectangles. What are the dimensions of each rectangle?

b. What is the area of each rectangle?

c. What is the total area of the remaining figure? How does this figure represent the difference of two squares?

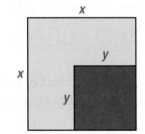

40. **Higher Order Thinking** The sculpture shown contains a large cube.

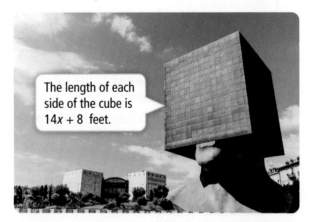

The length of each side of the cube is $14x + 8$ feet.

a. Write a polynomial in standard form to represent the surface area of the cube.

b. Write a polynomial in standard form to represent the volume of the cube.

ASSESSMENT PRACTICE

41. Consider each expression. Can you use the expression to find the product 53^2? Select *Yes* or *No* in each row.

	Yes	No
$(50 + 3)^2$	❑	❑
$(50 - 3)^2$	❑	❑
$(60 + 7)^2$	❑	❑
$(60 - 7)^2$	❑	❑
$(50 + 3)(50 - 3)$	❑	❑

42. **SAT/ACT** What is the product of $(3x^2 - 4y)(3x^2 + 4y)$?

Ⓐ $9x^4 - 24x^2y - 16y^2$

Ⓑ $3x^2 - 4y^2$

Ⓒ $9x^4 - 16y^2$

Ⓓ $3x^2 + 14x^2y - 4y$

43. **Performance Task** Consider the difference of squares $a^2 - b^2$, for integer values of a and b.

Part A Make a table of the difference of squares using consecutive integers for a and b. What pattern do you notice?

Part B Use the pattern from Part A to find pair of consecutive integers that generates a difference of squares of −45.

Part C Make a table of the difference of squares using consecutive even integers for a and b. What pattern do you notice?

Part D Use the pattern from Part C to find a pair of consecutive even integers that generates a difference of squares of −100.

2-4
Factoring Polynomials

 PearsonRealize.com

I CAN... factor a polynomial.

MODEL & DISCUSS

A catering company has been asked to design meal boxes for entrees and side dishes.

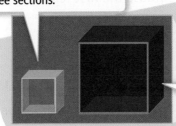

The sections for the side dishes are half the length and width of the entree sections.

The sections for the entrees must be square.

A. Design a meal box that meets each of these requirements:

    a. Equal numbers of sections for entrees and side dishes

    b. More sections for entrees than for side dishes

    c. More sections for side dishes than for entrees

B. Use Structure For each meal box from Part A, write an algebraic expression to model the area of the meal boxes.

? ESSENTIAL QUESTION

How is factoring a polynomial similar to factoring integers?

EXAMPLE 1   Find the Greatest Common Factor

What is the greatest common factor (GCF) of the terms of $12x^5 + 8x^4 - 6x^3$?

Step 1 Write the prime factorization of the coefficient for each term to determine if there is a greatest common factor other than 1.

    12   **8**   **6**

    $2 \cdot 2 \cdot 3$ $2 \cdot 2 \cdot 2$ $2 \cdot 3$

> One instance of 2 is the only common factor of the numbers, so the GCF of the coefficients of this trinomial is 2.

STUDY TIP
Recall that finding the prime factorization of a number is expressing the number as a product of only prime numbers.

Step 2 Determine the greatest common factor for the variables of each term.

    x^5 x^4 x^3

    $x \cdot x \cdot x \cdot x \cdot x$ $x \cdot x \cdot x \cdot x$ $x \cdot x \cdot x$

> Three instances of x are the only common factors of the terms, so the GCF of the variables is x^3.

The greatest common factor of the terms $12x^5 + 8x^4 - 6x^3$ is $2x^3$.

Try It!   1. Find the GCF of the terms of each polynomial.

    a. $15x^2 + 18$ **b.** $-18y^4 + 6y^3 + 24y^2$

CONCEPTUAL
UNDERSTANDING

 EXAMPLE 2 ▶ **Factor Out the Greatest Common Factor**

Why is it helpful to factor out the GCF from a polynomial?

Consider the polynomial $-12x^3 + 18x^2 - 27x$.

Step 1 Find the GCF of the terms of the polynomial, if there is one.

Because the first term is negative, it is helpful to factor out -1.

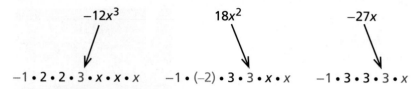

$$-12x^3 \qquad\qquad 18x^2 \qquad\qquad -27x$$

$$-1 \cdot 2 \cdot 2 \cdot 3 \cdot x \cdot x \cdot x \qquad -1 \cdot (-2) \cdot 3 \cdot 3 \cdot x \cdot x \qquad -1 \cdot 3 \cdot 3 \cdot 3 \cdot x$$

The greatest common factor is $-3x$.

Step 2 Factor the GCF out of each term of the polynomial.

$$-3x(4x^2 - 6x + 9)$$

Factoring out the greatest common factor results in a polynomial with smaller coefficients and/or smaller exponents of the variable(s). This makes it easier to analyze the polynomial or factor it further.

> **COMMON ERROR**
> Remember to include the negative sign when factoring out the GCF of negative terms. Also, factoring out a -1 from a positive term generates two negative factors.

 Try It! **2.** Factor out the GCF from each polynomial.

    a. $x^3 + 5x^2 - 22x$ **b.** $-16y^6 + 28y^4 - 20y^3$

APPLICATION

 EXAMPLE 3 ▶ **Factor a Polynomial Model**

Alani is in charge of marketing for a travel company. She is designing a brochure that will have 6 photos. The photos can be arranged on the page in a number of ways.

> There are 2 main square photos which have a length of x in. on each side.

> There are 4 narrower photos that are each 1 in. by x in.

A. What is the total area of the photos?

First, find the area of each type of photo.

Area = area of square photos + area of narrower photos

$$= \qquad 2(x^2) \qquad + \qquad 4(1x)$$

$$= 2x^2 + 4x$$

> There are 2 square photos, each with an area of x^2 in.^{2}.
> There are 4 narrower photos, each with an area of $1x$ in.^{2}.

The total area of the photos is $2x^2 + 4x$ in.^{2}.

CONTINUED ON THE NEXT PAGE

EXAMPLE 3 CONTINUED

B. Find a rectangular arrangement for the photos. What factored expression represents the area of the arrangement?

Try placing the photos in one row.

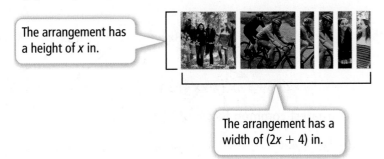

The arrangement has a height of x in.

The arrangement has a width of $(2x + 4)$ in.

The factored form that represents the area of the arrangement is $x(2x + 4)$.

C. Factor out the GCF from the polynomial. What does the GCF represent in this situation?

The GCF of $2x^2$ and $4x$ is $2x$. So you can rewrite the expression as $2x(x + 2)$.

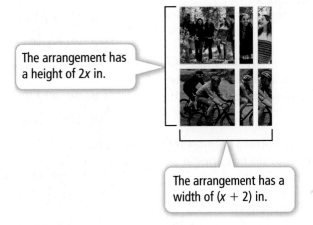

The arrangement has a height of $2x$ in.

The arrangement has a width of $(x + 2)$ in.

The GCF represents the height of one possible arrangement of the photos.

D. Which of these two arrangements is a more practical use of the space on a page of the brochure?

The arrangement based on the GCF is more practical because the arrangement with the photos in one line will likely be too wide for a page.

MODEL WITH MATHEMATICS
Think about how to represent this situation mathematically. How is the GCF useful in solving this problem?

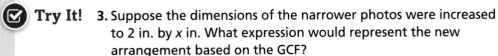

Try It! 3. Suppose the dimensions of the narrower photos were increased to 2 in. by x in. What expression would represent the new arrangement based on the GCF?

CONCEPT SUMMARY Factoring Polynomials

WORDS Determine if a polynomial can be factored. If the polynomial can be factored, find the greatest common factor of the terms and factor it out.

ALGEBRA

$$18x^3y^2 + 12x^2y + 15x$$ — Find the GCF of the terms.

$$2 \cdot 3 \cdot 3 \cdot x \cdot x \cdot x \cdot y \cdot y \qquad 2 \cdot 2 \cdot 3 \cdot x \cdot x \cdot y \qquad 3 \cdot 5 \cdot x$$

The greatest common factor of $18x^3y^2 + 12x^2y + 15x$ is $3x$.

$$3x(6x^2y^2 + 4xy + 5)$$ — Identify the remaining factors of the polynomial after factoring out the GCF, then write it in factored form.

Do You UNDERSTAND?

1. **ESSENTIAL QUESTION** How is factoring a polynomial similar to factoring integers?

2. **Look for Relationships** Why does the GCF of the variables of a polynomial have the *least* exponent of any variable term in the polynomial?

3. **Reason** What is the greatest common factor of two polynomials that do not appear to have any common factors?

4. **Error Analysis** Andrew factored $3x^2y - 6xy^2 + 3xy$ as $3xy(x - 2y)$. Describe and correct his error.

5. **Error Analysis** Wendell says that the greatest common factor of x^6 and x^8 is x^2, since the greatest common factor of 6 and 8 is 2. Is Wendell correct? Explain.

Do You KNOW HOW?

Find the GCF of each pair of monomials.

6. $10x$ and 25

7. x^3y^2 and x^5y

8. $8a^2$ and $28a^5$

9. $4x^3$ and $9y^5$

10. $12a^5b$ and $16a^4b^2$

11. $14x^{10}y^8$ and $15x^6y^9$

Factor out the GCF from each polynomial.

12. $10a^2b + 12ab^2$

13. $-3x^4 + 12x^3 - 21x^2$

14. $15x^3y - 10x^2y^3$

15. $x^{10} + x^9 - x^8$

16. $3x^3y^2 - 9xz^4 + 8y^2z$

17. $100a^7b^5 - 150a^8b^3$

UNDERSTAND

18. **Use Structure** What term and $12x^2y$ have a GCF of $4xy$? Write an expression that shows the monomial factored out of the polynomial.

19. **Look for Relationships** Write a trinomial that has a GCF of $4x^2$.

20. **Error Analysis** Describe and correct the error a student made when factoring $10a^3b - 5a^2b^2 - 15ab$.

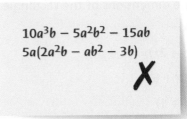

$10a^3b - 5a^2b^2 - 15ab$
$5a(2a^2b - ab^2 - 3b)$

✗

21. **Make Sense and Persevere** Write the difference in factored form.

$(24x^4 - 15x^2 + 6x) - (10x^4 + 5x^2 - 4x)$

22. **Higher Order Thinking** In the expression $ax^2 + b$, the coefficients of a and b are multiples of 2. The coefficients c and d in the expression $cx^2 + d$ are multiples of 3. Will the GCF of $ax^2 + b$ and $cx^2 + d$ *always*, *sometimes*, or *never* be a multiple of 6? Explain.

23. **Make Sense and Persevere** What is the GCF in the expression $x(x + 5) - 3x(x + 5) + 4(x + 5)$?

24. **Look for Relationships** Find the greatest common factor of the terms $x^{n+1}y^n$ and $x^n y^{n-2}$, where n is a whole number greater than 2. How can you factor the expression $x^{n+1}y^n + x^n y^{n-2}$?

25. **Mathematical Connections** consider the following set of monomials.

$A = \{2x, 3x, 4x, 5xy, 7x, 9y, 12xy, 13x, 15x\}$

The GCF the elements in subset $B = \{2x, 3x\}$ is x. Create 6 different subsets of A, such the GCFs of the elements are 1, 2x, 3, 4x, 5x, and y.

PRACTICE

Find the GCF of each group of monomials.

SEE EXAMPLE 1

26. $8y^3$ and $28y$

27. $9a^2b^3$, $15ab^2$, and $21a^4b^3$

28. $18m^2$ and 25

29. x^2y^3 and x^3y^5

Factor out the GCF from each polynomial.

SEE EXAMPLE 2

30. $12x^2 - 15x$

31. $-4y^4 + 6y^2 - 14y$

32. $3m^2 - 10m + 4$

33. $24x^3y^2 - 30x^2y^3 + 12x^2y^4$

The areas of the rectangles are given. Use factoring to find expressions for the missing dimensions.

SEE EXAMPLE 3

34.

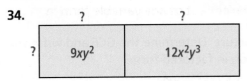

35.

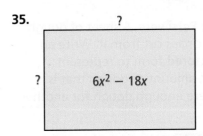

36.

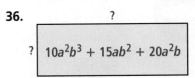

37. A farmer wants to plant three rectangular fields so that the widths are the same. The areas of the fields, in square yards, are given by the expressions $12x^2y$, $9xy^2$, and $21xy$. What is the width of the fields if $x = 3$ and $y = 4$?

SEE EXAMPLE 3

APPLY

38. Model With Mathematics Write an expression in factored form to represent the volume in the canister not occupied by the tennis balls. Assume the canister is cylinder with volume $V = \pi r^2 h$.

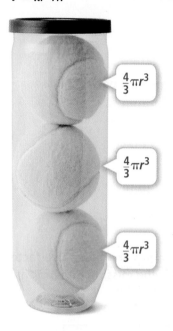

$\frac{4}{3}\pi r^3$

$\frac{4}{3}\pi r^3$

$\frac{4}{3}\pi r^3$

39. Use Structure Determine the GCF and write the expression in factored form.

$(6x^2 + 4x) + (4x^2 - 8x)$

40. Make Sense and Persevere A sheet of dough has six identical circles cut from it. Write an expression in factored form to represent the approximate amount of dough that is remaining. Is there enough dough for another circle?

x

ASSESSMENT PRACTICE

41. Fill in the blanks to find the factor pairs for $18x^4 + 12x^3 - 24x^2$.

■	$6x^2 + 4x - 8$
$2x$	■x■ $+$ ■x■ $-$ ■x
x■	$18x^2 + 12x - 24$
■x■	$3x^2 + 2x - 4$

42. SAT/ACT The area of a rectangle is $12x^3 - 18x^2 + 6x$. The width is equal to the GCF. What could the dimensions of the rectangle be?

Ⓐ $6x(2x^2 - 3x)$

Ⓑ $3(4x^3 - 6x^2 + 2x)$

Ⓒ $x(12x^2 - 18x + 6)$

Ⓓ $6x(2x^2 - 3x + 1)$

43. Performance Task Camilla is designing a platform for an athletic awards ceremony. The areas for two of the three faces of a platform are given.

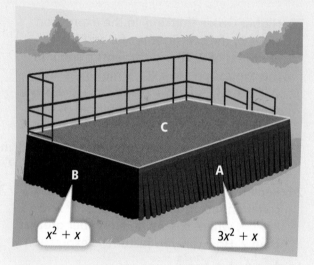

C

B

A

$x^2 + x$

$3x^2 + x$

Part A What are the dimensions of each face of the platform?

Part B What is the area of the top of the platform?

Part C What expression represents the surface area of the entire platform, including the bottom?

Part D What expression represents the volume of the platform?

2-5

Factoring
$x^2 + bx + c$

PearsonRealize.com

I CAN... factor a quadratic trinomial.

 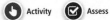
EXPLORE & REASON

Consider the following puzzles.

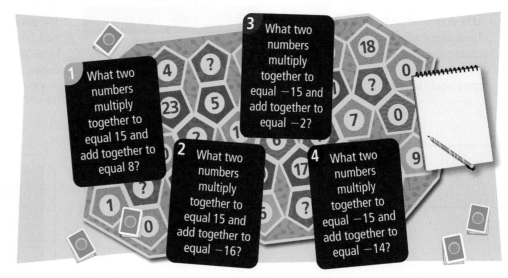

A. Find the solutions to the four puzzles shown.

B. **Look for Relationships** Write a set of four number puzzles of your own that have the same structure as these four. Describe the pattern.

? ESSENTIAL QUESTION

How does recognizing patterns in the signs of the terms help you factor polynomials?

CONCEPTUAL UNDERSTANDING

EXAMPLE 1   Understand Factoring a Trinomial

A. How does factoring a trinomial relate to multiplying binomials?

Consider the binomial product $(x + 2)(x + 3)$ and the trinomial $x^2 + 5x + 6$.

> The product of the second terms of the binomials is equal to the last term of the trinomial.

$$(x + 2)(x + 3) = x^2 + 3x + 2x + 6$$
$$= x^2 + 5x + 6$$

> The sum of the second terms of the binomials is equal to the coefficient of the second term of the trinomial.

LOOK FOR RELATIONSHIPS
How does factoring a trinomial relate to the Distributive Property?

When factoring a trinomial, you work backward to try to find the related binomial factors whose product equals the trinomial.

You can factor a trinomial of the form $x^2 + bx + c$ as $(x + p)(x + q)$ if $pq = c$ and $p + q = b$.

CONTINUED ON THE NEXT PAGE

EXAMPLE 1 CONTINUED

B. What is the factored form of $x^2 + 5x + 6$?

Identify a factor pair of 6 that has a sum of 5.

USE APPROPRIATE TOOLS
Think about different ways you could organize the factors and their sums. What organizational tools would be useful?

Factors of 6	Sum of Factors
1 and 6	7
2 and 3	5 ✓

The second term of each binomial is a factor of 6. These two factors add to 5.

If you factor using algebra tiles, the correct factor pair will form a rectangle.

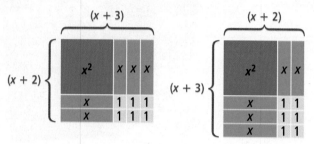

The factored form of $x^2 + 5x + 6$ is $(x + 2)(x + 3)$.

Check $(x + 2)(x + 3) = x^2 + 3x + 2x + 6$

$= x^2 + 5x + 6$ ✓

The first term of each binomial is x, since $x \cdot x = x^2$.

 Try It! **1.** Write the factored form of each trinomial.

a. $x^2 + 13x + 36$ **b.** $x^2 + 11x + 28$

👆 **EXAMPLE 2** **Factor $x^2 + bx + c$, When $b < 0$ and $c > 0$**

What is the factored form of $x^2 - 11x + 18$?

Identify a factor pair of 18 that has a sum of -11.

Because b is negative and c is positive, inspect only negative factors.

Factors of 18	Sum of Factors
-1 and -18	-19
-2 and -9	-11

Even though there are more factor pairs for 18, there is no need to continue once you find the correct sum.

The factored form of $x^2 - 11x + 18$ is $(x - 2)(x - 9)$.

Check $(x - 2)(x - 9) = x^2 - 9x - 2x + 18$

$= x^2 - 11x + 18$ ✓

 Try It! **2.** Write the factored form of each trinomial.

a. $x^2 - 8x + 15$ **b.** $x^2 - 13x + 42$

EXAMPLE 3 Factor $x^2 + bx + c$, When $c < 0$

What is the factored form of $x^2 + 5x - 6$?

Identify a factor pair of -6 that has a sum of 5.

COMMON ERROR
You may think that the pairs of factors 1, −6 and −1, 6 are the same. However, the sums of the two factors are different.

> Because c is negative, the factors will have opposite signs.

Factors of −6	Sum of Factors
1 and −6	−5
−1 and 6	5

The factored form of $x^2 + 5x - 6$ is $(x - 1)(x + 6)$.

☑ **Try It!** 3. Write the factored form of each trinomial.

    a. $x^2 - 5x - 14$ **b.** $x^2 + 6x - 16$

 EXAMPLE 4 **Factor a Trinomial With Two Variables**

A. How does multiplying binomials in two variables relate to factoring trinomials?

Consider the following binomial products.

$$(x + 2y)(x + 4y) = x^2 + 6xy + 8y^2$$

$$(x - 3y)(x + 5y) = x^2 + 2xy - 15y^2$$

$$(x - 7y)(x - 9y) = x^2 - 16xy - 63y^2$$

Each trinomial has the form $x^2 + bxy + cy^2$. Trinomials of this form are factorable when there is a factor pair of c that has a sum of b.

B. What is the factored form of $x^2 + 10xy + 24y^2$?

Identify a factor pair of 24 that has a sum of 10.

Factors of 24	Sum of Factors
3 and 8	11
4 and 6	10

STUDY TIP
When factoring a trinomial with two variables, make sure the factors contain both variables. Check your answer to determine whether you factored correctly.

The factored form of $x^2 + 10xy + 24y^2$ is $(x + 4y)(x + 6y)$.

Check $(x + 4y)(x + 6y) = x^2 + 6xy + 4xy + 24y^2$
$$= x^2 + 10xy + 24y^2 ✓$$

☑ **Try It!** 4. Write the factored form of each trinomial.

    a. $x^2 + 12xy + 32y^2$ **b.** $x^2 - 10xy + 21y^2$

APPLICATION   👆 EXAMPLE 5 Apply Factoring Trinomials

Benjamin is designing a new house. The bedroom closet will have one wall that contains a closet system using three different-sized storage units. The number and amount of wall space needed for each of the three types of storage units is shown. What are the dimensions of the largest amount of wall space that will be needed?

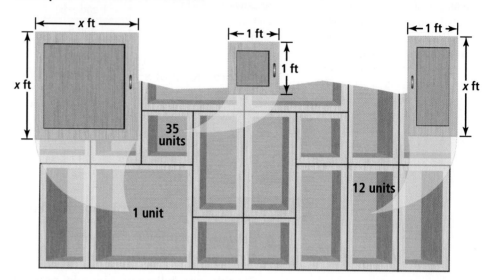

Formulate ◀ The largest possible closet storage system will use all of the units. Write an expression that represents the wall area of the closet in terms of the storage units.

$$x^2 + 12x + 35$$

Compute ◀ Because the area of a rectangle is the product of the length and width, factor the expression to find binomials that represent the length and width of the closet wall.

Factors of 35	Sum of Factors
1 and 35	36
5 and 7	12

$$x^2 + 12x + 35 = (x + 5)(x + 7)$$

Interpret ◀ The dimensions of the largest amount of wall space that will be needed are $(x + 7)$ ft by $(x + 5)$ ft.

☑ **Try It!** 5. What would be the dimensions of the largest wall area you would need if you used 11 of the 1 ft-by-1 ft units while keeping the other units the same?

 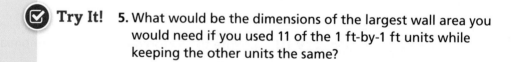

🔍 CONCEPT SUMMARY Factoring $x^2 + bx + c$

To factor a trinomial of the form $x^2 + bx + c$, find a factor pair of c that has a sum of b. Then use the factors you found to write the binomials that have a product equal to the trinomial.

	b and c are positive.	**b is negative and c is positive.**	**c is negative.**
WORDS	When the values of both b and c are positive, the second terms of the binomials are both positive.	When the value of b is negative and that of c is positive, the second terms of the binomials are both negative.	When the value of c is negative, the second terms of the binomials have opposite signs.
NUMBERS	b and c are positive.	b is negative and c is positive.	c is negative.
	$x^2 + 9x + 14$ $= (x + 2)(x + 7)$	$x^2 - 9x + 14$ $= (x - 2)(x - 7)$	$x^2 - 5x - 14$ $= (x + 2)(x - 7)$

☑ Do You UNDERSTAND?

1. **ESSENTIAL QUESTION** How does recognizing patterns in the signs of the terms help you factor polynomials?

2. **Error Analysis** A student says that since $x^2 - 5x - 6$ has two negative terms, both factors of c will be negative. Explain the error the student made.

3. **Reason** What is the first step to factoring any trinomial? Explain.

4. **Communicate Precisely** To factor a trinomial $x^2 + bx + c$, why do you find the factors of c and not b? Explain.

Do You KNOW HOW?

List the factor pairs of c for each trinomial.

5. $x^2 + 17x + 16$ 6. $x^2 + 4x - 21$

For each trinomial, tell whether the factor pairs of c will be both positive, both negative, or opposite signs.

7. $x^2 - 11x + 10$ 8. $x^2 + 9x - 10$

9. Copy and complete the table for factoring the trinomial $x^2 - 7x + 12$.

Factors of 12	Sum of Factors
−1 and −12	?
?	−7
−2 and −6	−8

✎ PRACTICE & PROBLEM SOLVING

UNDERSTAND

10. Mathematical Connections Explain how factoring a trinomial is like factoring a number. Explain how it is different.

11. Use Appropriate Tools How can you use algebra tiles to factor a trinomial? How do you determine the binomial factors from an algebra tile model?

12. Look for Relationships How are the binomial factors of $x^2 + 7x - 18$ and $x^2 - 7x - 18$ similar? How are they different?

13. Error Analysis Describe and correct the error a student made in making a table in order to factor the trinomial $x^2 - 11x - 26$.

Factors	Sum of Factors
−1 and 11	10
1 and −11	−10

The trinomial $x^2 - 11x - 26$ is not factorable because no factors of b sum to c.

✗

14. Higher Order Thinking Given that the trinomial $x^2 + bx + 8$ is factorable as $(x + p)(x + q)$, with p and q being integers, what are four possible values of b?

15. Reason What is missing from the last term of the trinomial $x^2 + 5xy + 4$ so that it is factorable as the product of binomials?

16. Look for Structure How does the sign of the last term of a trinomial help you know what type of factors you are looking for?

17. Reason A rectangle has an area of $x^2 + 7x + 12$ in.². Use factoring to find possible dimensions of the rectangle. Explain why you can use factoring to find the answer.

PRACTICE

Factor each trinomial represented by the algebra tiles. SEE EXAMPLE 1

18.

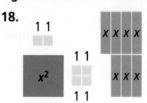

19.

Complete the table to factor each trinomial.
SEE EXAMPLES 1 AND 3

20. $x^2 + 9x + 20$

Factors of c	Sum of Factors
?	?
?	9
?	?

21. $x^2 + 9x - 22$

Factors of c	Sum of Factors
?	?
?	?
?	9
?	?

Write the factored form of each trinomial.
SEE EXAMPLES 1, 2, 3, 4, AND 5

22. $x^2 + 15x + 44$ **23.** $x^2 - 11x + 24$

24. $x^2 + 2x - 15$ **25.** $x^2 - 13x + 30$

26. $x^2 + 9x + 18$ **27.** $x^2 - 2x - 8$

28. $x^2 + 7xy + 6y^2$ **29.** $x^2 - 12x + 27$

30. $x^2 + 10x + 16$ **31.** $x^2 - 16xy + 28y^2$

32. $x^2 - 10xy - 11y^2$ **33.** $x^2 + 16x + 48$

34. $x^2 - 13x - 48$ **35.** $x^2 + 15xy + 54y^2$

APPLY

36. Make Sense and Persevere The volume of a rectangular box is represented by $x^3 + 3x^2 + 2x$. Use factoring to find possible dimensions of the box. How are the dimensions of the box related to one another?

37. Model with Mathematics A lake has a rectangular area roped off where people can swim under a lifeguard's supervision. The swimming section has an area of $x^2 + 3x - 40$ square feet, with the long side parallel to the lake shore.

a. What are possible dimensions of the roped-off area? Use factoring.

b. How much rope is needed for the three sides that are not along the beach? Explain.

c. The rope used to mark the swimming area is 238 ft long. What is x when the total length of rope is 238 ft?

38. Make Sense and Persevere
Sarah has a large square piece of foam for an art project. The side lengths of the square are x in. To fit her project, Sarah cuts a section of foam from two of the sides so she now has a rectangle. How much foam does Sarah cut from each of the two sides?

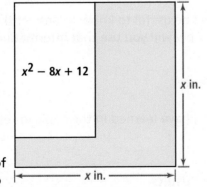

ASSESSMENT PRACTICE

39. Match each trinomial with its factored form.

   I. $x^2 + 13x + 30$ **A.** $(x - 10)(x + 3)$

   II. $x^2 + x - 30$ **B.** $(x - 6)(x + 5)$

   III. $x^2 - 7x - 30$ **C.** $(x - 5)(x + 6)$

   IV. $x^2 - x - 30$ **D.** $(x + 10)(x + 3)$

40. SAT/ACT What is the factored form of $4x^3 - 24x^2 - 28x$?

  Ⓐ $4x(x - 7)(x + 1)$

  Ⓑ $4x(x - 1)(x + 7)$

  Ⓒ $x(x - 7)(x + 4)$

  Ⓓ $x(x - 4)(x + 7)$

  Ⓔ $4(x - 7)(x - 1)$

41. Performance Task A city is designing the layout of a new park. The park will be divided into several different areas, including a field, a picnic area, and a recreation area. One design of the park is shown below.

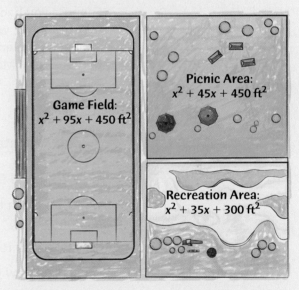

Game Field: $x^2 + 95x + 450$ ft^2

Picnic Area: $x^2 + 45x + 450$ ft^2

Recreation Area: $x^2 + 35x + 300$ ft^2

Part A Use factoring to find the dimensions of each of the three areas of the park shown

Part B Describe two different ways to find the total area of the park.

Part C What are the dimensions of the entire park?

Part D Can you find the value of x? Explain.

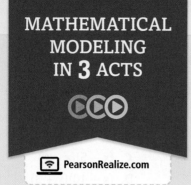

▶ Who's Right?

People often approach a problem in different ways. Sometimes their solutions are the same, but other times different approaches lead to very different, but still valid, solutions.

Suppose you had to solve a system of linear equations. You might solve it by graphing, while a classmate might use substitution. Is one way of solving a problem always better than another? Think about this during the Mathematical Modeling in 3 Acts lesson.

Scan for Multimedia

ACT 1   Identify the Problem

1. What is the first question that comes to mind after watching the video?

2. Write down the main question you will answer about what you saw in the video.

3. Make an initial conjecture that answers this main question.

4. Explain how you arrived at your conjecture.

5. What information will be useful to know to answer the main question? How can you get it? How will you use that information?

ACT 2   Develop a Model

6. Use the math that you have learned in this topic to refine your conjecture.

ACT 3   Interpret the Results

7. Did your refined conjecture match the actual answer exactly? If not, what might explain the difference?

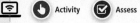
2-6

Factoring $ax^2 + bx + c$

PearsonRealize.com

I CAN... factor a quadratic trinomial when $a \neq 1$.

EXPLORE & REASON

A website design company resizes rectangular photos so they fit on the screens of various devices.

Area: $x^2 + 7x + 12$

A. What expression represents the width of the photo?

B. Write three possible lengths and corresponding widths of the photo by substituting different values for x.

C. **Make Sense and Persevere** Why would the company use an expression to represent the area? Explain.

? ESSENTIAL QUESTION

How is factoring a quadratic trinomial when $a \neq 1$ similar to factoring a quadratic trinomial when $a = 1$?

EXAMPLE 1   Factor Out a Common Factor

What is the factored form of $3x^3 + 15x^2 - 18x$?

Before factoring the trinomial into two binomials, look for any common factors that you can factor out.

$$3x^3 \quad + \quad 15x^2 \quad - \quad 18x$$

$$3 \cdot x \cdot x \cdot x \quad + \quad 3 \cdot 5 \cdot x \cdot x \quad - \quad 2 \cdot 3 \cdot 3 \cdot x$$

> There is a common factor of $3x$.

So, $3x^3 + 15x^2 - 18x = 3x(x^2 + 5x - 6)$.

Then factor the resulting trinomial, $x^2 + 5x - 6$.

VOCABULARY
The answer $3x(x - 1)(x + 6)$, is $3x^3 + 15x^2 - 18x$ factored completely. There are other ways you can factor the polynomial, but only one way to factor it completely.

> Because c is negative in the trinomial $x^2 + 5x - 6$, the factors will have opposite signs.

Factors of -6	Sum of Factors
1 and -6	-5
-1 and 6	5

The factored form of $x^2 + 5x - 6$ is $(x - 1)(x + 6)$, so the factored form of $3x^3 + 15x^2 - 18x$ is $3x(x - 1)(x + 6)$.

Try It!   1. Factor each trinomial.

     a. $5x^2 - 35x + 50$ b. $6x^3 + 30x^2 + 24x$

CONCEPTUAL
UNDERSTANDING

👆 **EXAMPLE 2**   **Understand Factoring by Grouping**

A. If $ax^2 + bx + c$ is a product of binomials, how are the values of a, b, and c related?

Consider the product $(3x + 4)(2x + 1)$.

$$(3x + 4)(2x + 1) = (3x)(2x) + (3x)(1) + (4)(2x) + (4)(1)$$
$$= 6x^2 + 3x + 8x + 4$$
$$= 6x^2 + 11x + 4$$

The product is $6x^2 + 11x + 4$. Notice that $ac = (6)(4)$ or $(3)(2)(4)(1)$, which is the product of all of the coefficients and constants from $(3x + 4)(2x + 1)$.

In the middle step, the coefficients of the x-terms, 3 and 8, add to form $b = 11$. They are composed of pairs of the coefficients and constants from the original product; $3 = (3)(1)$ and $8 = (4)(2)$.

If $ax^2 + bx + c$ is the product of binomials, there is a pair of factors of ac that have a sum of b.

STUDY TIP
To speed up your search, when looking for a factor pair that has a sum of b, you can rule out factor pairs with sums that are obviously far from the target.

B. How can you factor $ax^2 + bx + c$ by grouping?

Consider the trinomial $6x^2 + 11x + 4$, $a = 6$ and $c = 4$, so $ac = 24$.

Find the factor pair of 24 with a sum of 11.

Factors of 24	Sum of Factors
2 and 12	14
3 and 8	11

Rewrite $11x$ as $3x$ and $8x$.

USE STRUCTURE
Common factors are not limited to monomials. Here the common factors are monomials and binomials.

$6x^2 + 11x + 4 = 6x^2 + 3x + 8x + 4$

$$= (6x^2 + 3x) + (8x + 4) \quad \text{·········· Group as two binomials.}$$
$$= 3x(2x + 1) + 4(2x + 1) \quad \text{·········· Factor out the GCF of each binomial.}$$
$$= (3x + 4)(2x + 1) \quad \text{·········· Use the Distributive Property.}$$

The factored form of $6x^2 + 11x + 4$ is $(3x + 4)(2x + 1)$.

Check $(3x + 4)(2x + 1) = 6x^2 + 3x + 8x + 4$
$$= 6x^2 + 11x + 4 \checkmark$$

 Try It!   **2.** Factor each trinomial.

        a. $10x^2 + 17x + 3$ **b.** $2x^2 + x - 21$

EXAMPLE 3   **Factor a Trinomial Using Substitution**

How can you use substitution to help you factor $ax^2 + bx + c$ as the product of two binomials?

Consider the trinomial $3x^2 - 2x - 8$.

STEP 1 Multiply $ax^2 + bx + c$ by a to transform x^2 into $(ax)^2$.

$$3[3x^2 - 2x - 8]$$

> Multiply the entire trinomial by 3. The new trinomial is not equivalent to the original. Remember to divide by 3 as a last step.

$$= 3(3)x^2 - 2(3)x - 8(3)$$
$$= (3x)^2 - 2(3x) - 24$$

$$ax = 3x$$

STEP 2 Replace ax with a single variable. Let $p = ax$.

$$= p^2 - 2p - 24$$

> Substitute p for $3x$.

STEP 3 Factor the trinomial.

$$= (p - 6)(p + 4)$$

STEP 4 Substitute ax back into the product. Remember $p = 3x$. Factor out common factors if there are any.

$$= (3x - 6)(3x + 4)$$

> Substitute $3x$ for p.

$$= 3(x - 2)(3x + 4)$$

STEP 5 Since you started by multiplying the trinomial by a, you must divide by a to get a product that is equivalent to original trinomial.

$$(x - 2)(3x + 4)$$

> This product is equivalent to the original trinomial.

The factored form of $3x^2 - 2x - 8$ is $(x - 2)(3x + 4)$. In general, you can use substitution to help transform $ax^2 + bx + c$ with $a \neq 1$ to a simpler case in which $a = 1$, factor it, and then transform it back to an equivalent factored form.

STUDY TIP
Because you multiplied the original expression by a new factor, the answer will not be equivalent unless you divide out the same factor at the end of your computations.

 Try It!   3. Factor each trinomial using substitution.

a. $2x^2 - x - 6$ b. $10x^2 + 3x - 1$

CONCEPT SUMMARY Factoring $ax^2 + bx + c$

Factor by Grouping	**Factor Using Substitution**

ALGEBRA

To factor a trinomial of the form $ax^2 + bx + c$, find a factor pair of ac that has a sum of b. Rewrite bx as a sum of those factors. Then factor out the GCFs from the expression twice to factor the original trinomial as the product of two binomials.

To factor a trinomial of the form $ax^2 + bx + c$, multiply the trinomial by a. Rewrite the first two terms using ax. Substitute a single variable for ax. Factor the trinomial. Substitute ax back in for the variable. Divide by a.

NUMBERS

$3x^2 + 22x + 7$

$= 3x^2 + 21x + 1x + 7$

$= 3x(x + 7) + 1(x + 7)$

$= (3x + 1)(x + 7)$

$3x^2 - 20x - 7$

$3[3x^2 - 20x - 7]$

$= (3x)^2 - 20(3x) - 21$

$= p^2 - 20p - 21$

$= (p - 21)(p + 1)$

$= (3x - 21)(3x + 1)$

$= 3(x - 7)(3x + 1)$

$= (x - 7)(3x + 1)$

✓ Do You UNDERSTAND?

1. **ESSENTIAL QUESTION** How is factoring a quadratic trinomial when $a \neq 1$ similar to factoring a quadratic trinomial when $a = 1$?

2. **Error Analysis** A student says that for $ax^2 + bx + c$ to be factorable, b must equal $a + c$. Explain the error in the student's thinking.

3. **Reason** Suppose you can factor $ax^2 + bx + c$ as $(px + q)(sx + t)$, where $p, q, s,$ and t are integers. If $c = 1$, what do you know about the two binomial factors?

4. **Reason** When factoring $ax^2 + bx + c$ by substitution, why is it acceptable to multiply the polynomial by a to start?

5. **Construct Arguments** Felipe is factoring the expression $2x^2 - x - 28$. He knows $-x$ should be rewritten as $7x$ plus $-8x$, but he is not sure which order to place the terms in the expression. Explain to Felipe why it does not matter what order the terms are in.

Do You KNOW HOW?

List the factor pairs of ac for each trinomial.

6. $2x^2 + 7x + 4$

7. $12x^2 - 5x - 2$

Tell whether the terms of each trinomial share a common factor other than 1. If there is a common factor, identify it.

8. $15x^2 - 10x - 5$

9. $3x^3 - 2x^2 - 1$

Rewrite the x-term in each trinomial to factor by grouping.

10. $35x^2 + 17x + 2$

11. $12x^2 + 20x + 3$

Factor each trinomial to find possible dimensions of each rectangle.

12.
$A = 5x^2 + 17x + 6$

13.
$A = 6x^2 + 7x - 5$

Scan for Multimedia

Practice   Tutorial

Additional Exercises Available Online

UNDERSTAND

14. Mathematical Connections How is factoring a common factor out of a trinomial like factoring common factors out of the numerator and denominator of a fraction? How is it different?

15. Make Sense and Persevere What are all possible values of b for which $7x^2 + bx + 3$ is factorable, if the factors have integer coefficients and constants?

16. Look for Relationships Can you factor the trinomial $3x^2 + 5x + 3$ into linear factors with integer coefficients? Explain.

17. Error Analysis Describe and correct the error a student made in factoring $2x^2 + 11x + 15$.

$ac = 2 \times 15 = 30; b = 11$

Factors of 30	Sum of Factors
1×30	$1 + 30 = 31$
2×15	$2 + 15 = 17$
3×10	$3 + 10 = 13$
5×6	$5 + 6 = 11$

$2x^2 + 11x + 15 = (x + 5)(x + 6)$

18. Higher Order Thinking Can you factor the trinomial $6x^2 + 7x - 6$ as $(px + q)(sx + t)$, where $p, q, s,$ and t are integers? Explain why or why not.

19. Reason Use factoring to arrange the following algebra tiles first into one rectangle and then into two rectangles of equal size.

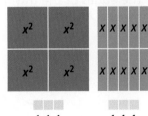

1 1 1   1 1 1

20. Use Structure What is the factored form of $pqx^2 + (mp + qn)x + mn$?

PRACTICE

Factor the trinomial represented by the algebra tiles.

21.

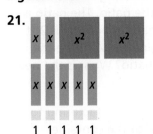

1 1 1 1 1

22.

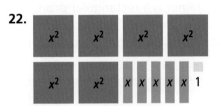

Factor each trinomial.   SEE EXAMPLE 1

23. $4x^2 + 16x + 12$ **24.** $2x^2 - 16x + 30$

25. $3x^2 + 12x - 63$ **26.** $6x^2 + 12x - 48$

Identify the factor pairs of ac you could use to rewrite b to factor each trinomial by grouping.
SEE EXAMPLE 2

27. $7x^2 + 9x + 2$ **28.** $6x^2 + 11x - 2$

29. $8x^2 - 2x - 1$ **30.** $10x^2 + 19x + 6$

31. $15x^2 - 16x - 7$ **32.** $12x^2 + 11x + 2$

Factor each trinomial completely.
SEE EXAMPLES 1, 2, AND 3

33. $4x^2 + 13x + 3$ **34.** $6x^2 - 25x - 14$

35. $2x^2 + 7x - 4$ **36.** $12x^2 + 13x + 3$

37. $6x^3 + 9x^2 + 3x$ **38.** $8x^2 - 10x - 3$

39. $12x^2 + 16x + 5$ **40.** $16x^3 + 32x^2 + 12x$

41. $21x^2 - 35x - 14$ **42.** $16x^2 + 22x - 3$

43. $9x^2 + 46x + 5$ **44.** $24x^3 - 10x^2 - 4x$

Factor each trinomial completely.

45. $3x^2 + xy - 2y^2$ **46.** $2x^2 + 9xy + 10y^2$

47. $5x^2 - 4xy - y^2$ **48.** $2x^2 + 10xy + 12y^2$

APPLY

49. Reason A rectangular patio has an area of $2x^2 + 13x - 24$ ft^2. Use factoring to find possible dimensions of the patio. The patio is to be enlarged so that each dimension is 2 ft greater than it was originally. What are the new dimensions of the patio? What is the new area of the patio?

50. Make Sense and Persevere Use factoring to find possible dimensions of the container shown. The container is a rectangular prism. What are the dimensions of the container if $x = 3$? What is the volume of the container if $x = 4$?

$V = 4x^3 + 10x^2 + 4x$ ft^3

51. Model With Mathematics A photographer is placing photos in a mat for a gallery show. Each mat she uses is x in. wide on each side. The total area of each photo and mat is shown.

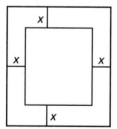

Area $= 4x^2 + 36x + 80$

a. Factor the total area to find possible dimensions of a photo and mat.

b. What are the dimensions of the photos in terms of x?

c. Explain why the photographer might use x to represent the width of the mat.

ASSESSMENT PRACTICE

52. The trinomial $ax^2 + bx + c$ is factorable when factors of _?_ have a sum of _?_.

53. SAT/ACT What is the factored form of $3x^2 - 5x - 12$?

Ⓐ $(x - 4)(3x + 1)$

Ⓑ $(x - 3)(3x + 4)$

Ⓒ $(x + 4)(3x - 9)$

Ⓓ $3(x + 2)(x - 3)$

Ⓔ $3(x - 4)(x + 1)$

54. Performance Task A paint tray has an area of $42x^2 + 135x + 108$ in.^{2}. The square paint compartments that are all the same size and spaced evenly, though the space along the edge of the tray is twice as wide as the space between squares.

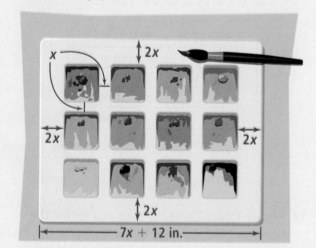

Part A What is the width of the paint tray?

Part B What is the area of each of the paint compartments in the tray?

Part C How wide are the edges of the tray if the width of the paint tray is 45 in.?

2-7
Factoring Special Cases

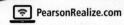
PearsonRealize.com

I CAN... factor special trinomials.

VOCABULARY
• perfect-square trinomial

Activity   Assess

CRITIQUE & EXPLAIN

Seth and Bailey are given the polynomial $8x^2 + 48x + 72$ to factor.

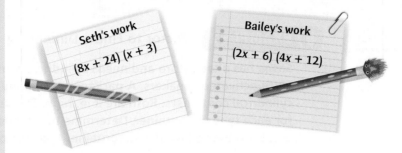

Seth's work

$(8x + 24)(x + 3)$

Bailey's work

$(2x + 6)(4x + 12)$

A. Analyze each factored expression to see if both are equivalent to the given polynomial.

B. How can the product of different pairs of expressions be equivalent?

C. Look for Relationships Find two other pairs of binomials that are different, but whose products are equal.

ESSENTIAL QUESTION

What special patterns are helpful when factoring a perfect-square trinomial and the difference of two squares?

CONCEPTUAL UNDERSTANDING

EXAMPLE 1   Understand Factoring a Perfect Square

What is the factored form of a perfect-square trinomial?

A **perfect-square trinomial** results when a binomial is squared.

$(a + b)(a + b) = (a + b)^2 = a^2 + 2ab + b^2$
$(a - b)(a - b) = (a - b)^2 = a^2 - 2ab + b^2$

> The first and last terms are perfect squares. The middle term is twice the product of the first and last terms of the binomial.

A. What is the factored form of $x^2 + 14x + 49$?

Write the last term as a perfect square.

$x^2 + 14x + 49 = x^2 + 14x + 7^2$

$= x^2 + 2(7)x + 7^2$

> $2ab = 2(7)x = 14x$, so the trinomial fits the pattern.

$= (x + 7)(x + 7) = (x + 7)^2$

COMMON ERROR
Be careful to identify the correct values for a and b when factoring special cases. The value of a can be different from x.

B. What is the factored form of $9x^2 - 30x + 25$?

Write the first and last terms as a perfect square.

$9x^2 - 30x + 25 = (3x)^2 - 30x + 5^2$

$= (3x)^2 - 2(3x)(5) + 5^2$

> $2ab = 2(3x)(5) = 30x$, so the trinomial fits the pattern.

$= (3x - 5)(3x - 5) = (3x - 5)^2$

The factored form of a perfect-square trinomial is $(a + b)^2$ when the trinomial fits the pattern $a^2 + 2ab + b^2$, and $(a - b)^2$ when the trinomial fits the pattern $a^2 - 2ab + b^2$.

CONTINUED ON THE NEXT PAGE

EXAMPLE 1 CONTINUED

Try It!   **1.** Factor each trinomial.

a. $4x^2 + 12x + 9$ b. $x^2 - 8x + 16$

APPLICATION   **EXAMPLE 2** **Factor to Find a Dimension**

Sasha has a tech store and needs cylindrical containers to package her voice-activated speakers. A packaging company makes two different cylindrical containers. Both are 3 in. high. The volume information is given for each type of container. Determine the radius of each cylinder. How much greater is the radius of one container than the other?

Volume:
$3\pi x^2$ in.^{3}

Volume:
$\pi(3x^2 + 30x + 75)$ in.^{3}

Formulate ◄ The formula for the volume of a cylinder is $V = \pi r^2 h$, where r is the radius and h is the height of the cylinder. The height of both containers is 3 in., so both expressions will have 3π in common.

> Factor 3 out of the trinomial

$$3\pi x^2 = 3\pi(x^2)$$ $$\pi(3x^2 + 30x + 75) = 3\pi(x^2 + 10x + 25)$$

Factor the expressions to identify the radius of each cylinder.

Compute ◄ The expression $x^2 = x \cdot x$, so the radius of the first cylinder is x in.

Factor the expression $x^2 + 10x + 25$ to find the radius of the second cylinder.

$$x^2 + 10x + 25 = x^2 + 2(5)x + 5^2$$

> Rewrite the first and last terms as squares.

$$= (x + 5)^2$$

The radius of the second cylinder is $(x + 5)$ in.

Find the difference between the radii.

$$(x + 5) - x = 5$$

Interpret ◄ The larger cylinder has a radius that is 5 in. greater than the smaller one.

Try It!   **2.** What is the radius of a cylinder that has a height of 3 in. and a volume of $\pi(27x^2 + 18x + 3)$ in.^{3}?

EXAMPLE 3 Factor a Difference of Two Squares

How can you factor the difference of squares using a pattern?

Recall that a binomial in the form $a^2 - b^2$ is called the difference of two squares.

$$(a - b)(a + b) = a^2 - ab + ab - b^2 = a^2 - b^2$$

A. What is the factored form of $x^2 - 9$?

Write the last term as a perfect square.

> **REASON**
> Determine whether the factoring rule for a difference of two squares makes sense by working backward.

$$x^2 - 9 = x^2 - 3^2$$
$$= (x + 3)(x - 3)$$

> $a = x$ and $b = 3$, so the binomial fits the pattern.

B. What is the factored form of $4x^2 - 81$?

Write the first and last terms as perfect squares.

$$4x^2 - 81 = (2x)^2 - 9^2$$
$$= (2x + 9)(2x - 9)$$

> $a = 2x$ and $b = 9$, so the binomial fits the pattern.

The difference of two squares is a factoring pattern when one perfect square is subtracted from another. If a binomial follows that pattern, you can factor it as a sum and difference.

☑ **Try It!** 3. Factor each expression.

    a. $x^2 - 64$

    b. $9x^2 - 100$

 EXAMPLE 4 Factor Out a Common Factor

What is the factored form of $3x^3y - 12xy^3$?

Factor out a greatest common factor of the terms if there is one. Then factor as the difference of squares.

$$3x^3y - 12xy^3 = 3xy(x^2 - 4y^2)$$ ⋯⋯⋯ Factor out the GCF, $3xy$.

$$= 3xy[x^2 - (2y)^2]$$ ⋯⋯⋯ Write each term in the brackets as a perfect square.

$$= 3xy(x + 2y)(x - 2y)$$ ⋯⋯ Use the difference of squares pattern.

The factored form of $3x^3y - 12xy^3$ is $3xy(x + 2y)(x - 2y)$.

☑ **Try It!** 4. Factor each expression completely.

    a. $4x^3 + 24x^2 + 36x$

    b. $50x^2 - 32y^2$

CONCEPT SUMMARY Factoring Special Cases of Polynomials

	Factoring a Perfect-Square Trinomial	**Factoring a Difference of Two Squares**
ALGEBRA	$a^2 + 2ab + b^2 = (a + b)^2$ $a^2 - 2ab + b^2 = (a - b)^2$	$a^2 - b^2 = (a + b)(a - b)$
WORDS	Use this pattern when the first and last terms are perfect squares and the middle term is twice the product of the expressions being squared.	Use this pattern when a binomial can be written as a difference of two squares. Both terms must be perfect squares.
NUMBERS	$x^2 + 16x + 64 = x^2 + 2(8)x + 8^2$ $\qquad = (x + 8)^2$ $x^2 - 16x + 64 = x^2 - 2(8)x + 8^2$ $\qquad = (x - 8)^2$	$x^2 - 36 = x^2 - 6^2$ $\qquad = (x + 6)(x - 6)$ $2x^2 - 72 = 2(x^2 - 36)$ $\qquad = 2(x^2 - 6^2)$ $\qquad = 2(x + 6)(x - 6)$

Do You UNDERSTAND?

1. **ESSENTIAL QUESTION** What special patterns are helpful when factoring a perfect-square trinomial and the difference of two squares?

2. **Error Analysis** A student says that to factor $x^2 - 4x + 2$, you should use the pattern of a difference of two squares. Explain the error in the student's thinking.

3. **Vocabulary** How is a perfect square trinomial similar to a perfect square number? Is it possible to have a perfect square binomial? Explain.

4. **Communicate Precisely** How is the pattern for factoring a perfect-square trinomial like the pattern for factoring the difference of two squares? How is it different?

5. **Construct Arguments** Why is it important to look for a common factor before factoring a trinomial?

Do You KNOW HOW?

Identify the pattern you can use to factor each expression.

6. $4x^2 - 9$

7. $x^2 + 6x + 9$

8. $9x^2 - 12x + 4$

9. $5x^2 - 30x + 45$

10. $100 - 16y^2$

11. $3x^2 + 30x + 75$

Write the factored form of each expression.

12. $49x^2 - 25$

13. $36x^2 + 48x + 16$

14. $3x^3 - 12x^2 + 12x$

15. $72x^2 - 32$

16. What is the side length of the square shown below?

Area = $x^2 + 22x + 121$

PRACTICE & PROBLEM SOLVING

UNDERSTAND

17. Mathematical Connections How could you use special factoring patterns to quickly rewrite the difference $50^2 - 45^2$ as a product? Explain.

18. Reason Is the expression $x^2 - 50$ factorable? Explain why or why not.

19. Look for Relationships What is the completely factored form of the expression $16x^4 - y^4$? Describe the method(s) of factoring you used.

20. Error Analysis Describe and correct the error a student made in factoring $x^2 - 36$.

> Use the perfect-square trinomial pattern to factor $x^2 - 36$ because both terms are perfect squares.
>
> $x^2 - 36 = (x - 6)(x - 6)$

21. Higher Order Thinking Use the visual shown as a starting point. Describe how you can use diagrams to show that $a^2 - b^2 = (a + b)(a - b)$.

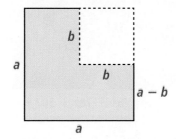

22. Make Sense and Persevere Describe the steps you would use to factor the expression $x^4 - 8x^2 + 16$.

23. Reason A rectangle has a width that is twice the length. If the area of the rectangle is represented by the expression $18x^2 + 48x + 32$, what expression represents the length of the rectangle? Explain.

24. Communicate Precisely How can you determine if a binomial of the form $x^2 - \frac{a}{b}$ is factorable using rational constants?

PRACTICE

Identify the value of c that would make the trinomial factorable using the perfect-square pattern. SEE EXAMPLE 1

25. $x^2 + 24x + c$ **26.** $x^2 - 10x + c$

27. $6x^2 - 36x + c$ **28.** $3x^2 + 24x + c$

Given the area of each square, factor to find the side length. SEE EXAMPLES 1 AND 2

29. Area $= 36x^2 + 120x + 100$

30. Area $= 144x^2 - 24x + 1$

Factor each expression completely.
SEE EXAMPLES 1, 3, and 4

31. $x^2 + 16x + 64$ **32.** $x^2 - 25$

33. $x^2 - 18x + 81$ **34.** $x^2 - 14x + 49$

35. $100x^2 - 36$ **36.** $16x^2 + 40x + 25$

37. $8x^2 - 32x + 32$ **38.** $16x^2 - 81y^2$

39. $2x^3 + 32x^2 + 128x$ **40.** $7x^3y - 63xy^3$

41. $49x^3 - 16xy^2$ **42.** $121x^2 + 110x + 25$

43. $-3x^3 + 18x^2 - 27x$ **44.** $64x^2y^2 - 144z^2$

Factor each expression as the product of binomials.

45. $x^2 - \frac{1}{4}$ **46.** $x^2 - \frac{1}{9}$

47. $p^2 - \frac{49}{100}$ **48.** $x^2 + x + \frac{1}{4}$

APPLY

49. Reason In front of a school are several gardens in rectangular raised beds. For each of the areas of a rectangular garden given, use factoring to find possible dimensions. Could the garden be square? If so, explain why.

a. $x^2 + 32x + 256$

b. $x^2 - 4y^2$

c. $x^2 - 20x + 100$

50. Make Sense and Persevere The area of a rectangular rug is $49x^2 - 25y^2$ in.^{2}. Use factoring to find possible dimensions of the rug. How are the side lengths related? What value would you need to subtract from the longer side and add to the shorter side for the rug to be a square?

51. Model With Mathematics A furniture company created an L-shaped table by removing part of a square table.

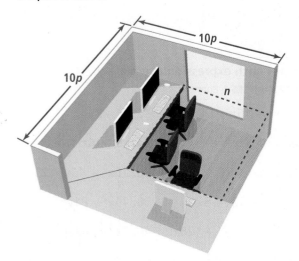

10p

10p

n

a. Write an expression that represents the area of the L-shaped table.

b. What are all the side lengths of the L-shaped table?

c. The furniture company decides to create another table with the same area, but needs this table to be rectangular. What are the possible dimensions of the rectangular table? Explain.

ASSESSMENT PRACTICE

52. Match each expression with its factored form.

I. $25m^2 - 9n^2$ A. $(5m + 3n)^2$

II. $25m^2 - 30mn + 9n^2$ B. $(5m - 3n)^2$

III. $25m^2 - 30mn - 9n^2$ C. $(5m + 3n)(5m - 3n)$

IV. $25m^2 + 30mn + 9n^2$ D. does not factor

53. SAT/ACT What is the factored form of $6x^2 - 60x + 150$?

Ⓐ $6(x - 25)^2$

Ⓑ $6(x - 5)(x - 10)$

Ⓒ $6(x - 5)^2$

Ⓓ $6(x - 5)(x + 5)$

54. Performance Task Two pieces of fabric are being used for clothing designs for a fashion show at school Expressions for the areas of the rectangular pieces are shown.

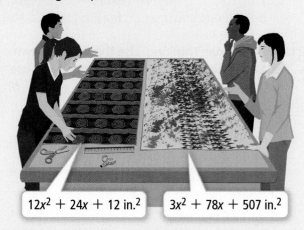

$12x^2 + 24x + 12$ in.^{2} $3x^2 + 78x + 507$ in.^{2}

Part A Factor the expressions for the areas completely.

Part B Using the factorings from Part A, write all of the possible dimensions of the pieces of fabric as binomials with integer coefficients.

Part C Assume that the table is about 6 ft long. Using integer values for x, which set of binomials yields to most reasonable dimensions based on the picture?

Part D Using your result from Part C what are the dimensions in inches of the two pieces of fabric?

Topic Review

1. How do you work with polynomials to rewrite expressions and solve problems?

Vocabulary Review

Choose the correct term to complete each sentence.

2. The _____ states that polynomials are closed under addition or subtraction because the result of these operations is another polynomial.

3. A(n) _____ results when a binomial is squared.

4. A(n) _____ is a real number, a variable, or the product of a real number and one or more variables with whole number exponents.

5. The product of two binomials in the form $(a + b)(a - b)$ is $a^2 - b^2$, which is called the _____.

6. The _____ is a an expression in which the terms are written in descending order according to their degree.

- Closure Property
- degree of a monomial
- degree of a polynomial
- difference of two squares
- monomial
- perfect-square trinomial
- polynomial
- standard form of a polynomial

Concepts & Skills Review

| LESSON 2-1 | Adding and Subtracting Polynomials |

Quick Review

A **polynomial** is a monomial or the sum or difference of two or more monomials, called terms. Polynomials are named according to their degree. The **degree of a polynomial** is the greatest degree of any term of the polynomial. The **standard form of a polynomial** is a polynomial in which terms are written in descending order according to their degree.

Example

What is the difference $(5x^2 + 3x - 5) - (2x^2 + 8)$?

$(5x^2 + 3x - 5) - (2x^2 + 8)$

$= 5x^2 + 3x - 5 - 2x^2 - 8$ · · · · Apply subtraction to each term in the second expression.

$= (5x^2 - 2x^2) + (3x) +$ · · · · Use the Commutative and
$(-5 - 8)$ Associative Properties to group like terms.

$= 3x^2 + 3x - 13$ · · · · · · · Simplify.

The difference is $3x^2 + 3x - 13$.

Practice & Problem Solving

Name each monomial based on its degree.

7. $2xy$ 8. -6 9. $3x^2y$

Add or subtract to simplify each expression. Write your final answer in standard form.

10. $(5x - 1) + (2x - 3)$

11. $(2x^2 - 4x - 1) - (3x^2 + 8x - 4)$

12. $(5b^4 - 2 + 3b^2) + (5b^2 - 4 + 3b^4)$

13. **Reason** What is the missing term in the equation? $(\_\_ + 5) + (3x - 2) = 8x + 3$. Explain.

14. **Make Sense and Persevere** A garden center has $(3x^2 + 12x + 18)$ sq. ft of sod. One week, they receive $(4x^2 + 16x + 60)$ sq. ft of sod, and sell $(2x^2 + 9x + 27)$ sq. ft of sod. What expression represents the area of the remaining sod?

LESSON 2-2   Multiplying Polynomials

Quick Review

Use the Distributive Property to multiply polynomials as you would when multiplying integers numbers. Distribute the first polynomial to each term in the second polynomial.

Example

How can you use the Distributive Property to rewrite $(3x - 5)(4x - 9)$ as a polynomial?

Distribute the first binomial to each term in the second binomial.

$(3x - 5)(4x - 9)$

$= 3x(4x - 9) - 5(4x - 9)$ Distribute $3x$ and -5 to the second binomial.

$= 3x(4x) + 3x(-9) - 5(4x)$ Distribute $3x$ and -5 to
$\quad - 5(-9)$ each term in the second binomial.

$= 12x^2 - 27x - 20x + 45$ Multiply.

$= 12x^2 - 47x + 45$ Combine like terms.

The product is $12x^2 - 47x + 45$.

Practice & Problem Solving

Use the Distributive Property to find each product.

15. $(x + 7)(x - 5)$ 16. $(2x - 5)(3x + 1)$

Use a table to find each product.

17. $(4x - 3y)(5x + y)$ 18. $(x + 4)(x^2 - 3x - 1)$

19. **Make Sense and Persevere** Identify the missing terms in the quotient and divisor.

     $(\underline{} + 3)(x + \underline{}) = x^2 + 11x + 24$

20. **Model With Mathematics** The volume of a cube is calculated by multiplying the length, width and height. What is the volume of this cube in standard form?

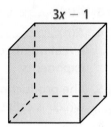

LESSON 2-3   Multiplying Special Cases

Quick Review

The square of a binomial always follows the same pattern, $a^2 + 2ab + b^2$. The product of two binomials in the form $(a + b)(a - b)$ is $a^2 - b^2$. This is called the **difference of two squares**.

Example

What is the product $(4x - 9)(4x + 9)$?

Use the pattern.

$(4x - 9)(4x + 9)$

$= (4x)^2 - (9)^2$ Substitute $4x$ and 9 and for a and b in $a^2 - b^2$.

$= 16x^2 - 81$ Simplify.

The product is $16x^2 - 81$.

Practice & Problem Solving

Write each product in standard form.

21. $(b + 12)(b + 12)$ 22. $(4x + 1)(4x + 1)$

23. $(6x - 9)(6x + 9)$ 24. $(3x - 4y)(3x + 4y)$

25. $(1.5x + 2)(1.5x - 2)$ 26. $(3a - 5b)^2$

27. **Look for Relationships** Find a value for m to make a true statement.

     $mx^2 - 64 = (5x + 8)(5x - 8)$

28. **Modeling With Mathematics** Write polynomials in standard form to represent the surface area and volume of the cube.

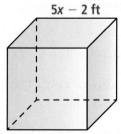

Go Online | PearsonRealize.com

Quick Review

To factor a common monomial factor out of a polynomial, first write the prime factorization of the coefficient for each term to determine if there is a greatest common factor other than 1. Then determine the greatest common factor for the variables of each term.

Example

What is the GCF of the terms of $16x^6 - 8x^4 + 4x^3$?

First, write the prime factorization of the coefficients for each term.

$16 = 2 \cdot 2 \cdot 2 \cdot 2$	Each number has a common
$8 = 2 \cdot 2 \cdot 2$	coefficient of 4, so the GCF of
$4 = 2 \cdot 2$	the coefficients is 4.

Next, determine the GCF of the variables for each term.

$x^6 = x \cdot x \cdot x \cdot x \cdot x \cdot x$	Each term has the common
$x^4 = x \cdot x \cdot x \cdot x$	factor of x^3, so the GCF of the
$x^3 = x \cdot x \cdot x$	variables is x^3.

The GCF of $16x^6 - 8x^4 + 4x^3$ is $4x^3$.

Practice & Problem Solving

Find the GCF of each group of monomials.

29. $6x^2$, $21x$

30. bc^2, b^3c

31. $14x^2y^2$, $84x^3y^5$, $21xy^3$

32. $24a^2$, 18

Factor out the GCF from each polynomial.

33. $15x^3 - 42x$

34. $6y^5 - 42y^3 + 18y$

35. $12a^3 + 18a^2 - 36a$

36. $49a^5b^3 - 14a^2b^2 + 35ab$

37. **Look for Relationships** Write a trinomial that has a GCF of $3x$.

38. **Use Structure** Determine the GCF and write the expression in factored form.

$$(8x^2 - 12x) + (6x^2 - 4x)$$

Quick Review

To factor $x^2 + bx + c$, find the factor pair of c that has a sum of b. Then use those factors to write the binomial factors of the trinomial.

Example

What is the factored form of $x^2 - 9x + 14$?

Identify a factor pair of 14 that has a sum of −9.

Factors of 14	Sum of Factors
−1 and −14	−15
−2 and −7	−9

The factored form of $x^2 - 9x + 14$ is $(x - 2)(x - 7)$.

Practice & Problem Solving

Complete the table to factor the trinomial

39. $x^2 + 7x - 18$

Factors of c	Sum of Factors
■	■
■	■
■	7

Write the factored form of each trinomial.

40. $x^2 + 12x + 32$

41. $x^2 + 3x - 28$

42. $x^2 - 13x - 48$

43. $x^2 + 18xy + 45y^2$

44. **Look for Relationships** How are the binomial factors of $x^2 + 4x - 21$ and $x^2 - 4x - 21$ similar? How are they different?

Factoring $ax^2 + bx + c$

Quick Review

To factor a trinomial of the form $ax^2 + bx + c$, find the factor pair of ac that has a sum of b. Then use the factors you found to write the binomials that have a product equal to the trinomial.

Example

What is the factored form of $2x^2 + 9x - 5$?

For the trinomial $2x^2 + 9x - 5$, $a = 2$ and $c = -5$, so $ac = -10$. Find the factor pair of -10 that has a sum of 9.

Factors of -10	Sum of Factors
-2 and 5	3
2 and -5	-3
-1 and 10	9

Since -1 and 10 are the correct factor pair, rewrite $9x$ as $-1x$ and $10x$.

$2x^2 + 9x - 5$

$$= 2x^2 + 10x - 1x - 5 \quad \text{Rewrite.}$$
$$= (2x^2 + 10x) + (-1x - 5) \quad \text{Group as two binomials.}$$
$$= 2x(x + 5) - 1(x + 5) \quad \text{Factor out the GCFs.}$$
$$= (2x - 1)(x + 5) \quad \text{Distributive Property}$$

The factored form of $2x^2 + 9x - 5$ is $(2x - 1)(x + 5)$.

Practice & Problem Solving

Identify all of the factor pairs of ac you could use to rewrite b in order to factor each trinomial by grouping.

45. $5x^2 + 9x + 4$

46. $2x^2 + x - 15$

Write the factored form of each trinomial.

47. $3x^2 + 10x + 8$

48. $4x^2 - 3x - 10$

49. $5x^2 + 7x - 6$

50. $6x^2 + 13x + 6$

51. $10x^2 + 3x - 4$

52. $12x^2 + 22x + 6$

53. **Make Sense and Persevere** What are all the possible values of b for which $3x^2 + bx - 8$ is factorable using only integer coefficients and constants?

54. **Reason** A parking lot has an area of $2x^2 + 9x - 5$ square meters. Use factoring to find possible dimensions of the parking lot. The parking lot is to be enlarged so that each dimension is 5 meters greater than it was originally. What are the new dimensions of the parking lot? What is the new area of the parking lot?

Quick Review

A **perfect-square trinomial** results when a binomial is squared.

Factor a perfect-square trinomial:

$a^2 + 2ab + b^2 = (a + b)^2$

$a^2 - 2ab + b^2 = (a - b)^2$

Use these patterns when the first and last terms are perfect squares and the middle term is twice the product of the numbers being squared.

Factor a difference of two squares:

$a^2 - b^2 = (a + b)(a - b)$

Use this pattern when a binomial can be written as a difference of two squares.

Example

What is the factored form of $9x^2 - 121$?

Write the first and last term as a perfect square.

$9x^2 - 121 = (3x)^2 - 11^2$

$\qquad\qquad = (3x - 11)(3x + 11)$

Practice & Problem Solving

Identify the value of c that would make each trinomial factorable using the perfect-square pattern.

55. $x^2 + 16x + c$ **56.** $2x^2 - 28x + c$

Write the factored form of each expression.

57. $x^2 + 10x + 25$ **58.** $x^2 - 121$

59. $x^2 - 18x + 81$ **60.** $9x^2 - 49y^2$

61. $3x^2 + 18x + 27$ **62.** $4x^2 - 56x + 196$

63. Reason Is the expression $3x^2 - 49$ factorable using only integer coefficients and constants? Explain why or why not.

64. Make Sense and Persevere The area of a playground is $36x^2 - 16y^2$ square feet. Without removing common factors, factor to find possible dimensions of the playground. How are the side lengths related? What value would you need to subtract from the longer side and add to the shorter side for the playground to be a square?

TOPIC 3

Quadratic Functions

? TOPIC ESSENTIAL QUESTION

How can you use sketches and equations of quadratic functions to model situations and make predictions?

Topic Overview

Topic Vocabulary

- parabola
- quadratic parent function
- quadratic regression
- standard form of a quadratic function
- vertex form of a quadratic function
- vertical motion model

Digital Experience

 INTERACTIVE STUDENT EDITION
Access online or offline.

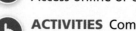 **ACTIVITIES** Complete *Explore & Reason, Model & Discuss*, and *Critique & Explain* activities. Interact with Examples and Try Its.

 ANIMATION View and interact with real-world applications.

 PRACTICE Practice what you've learned.

 Go online | **PearsonRealize.com**

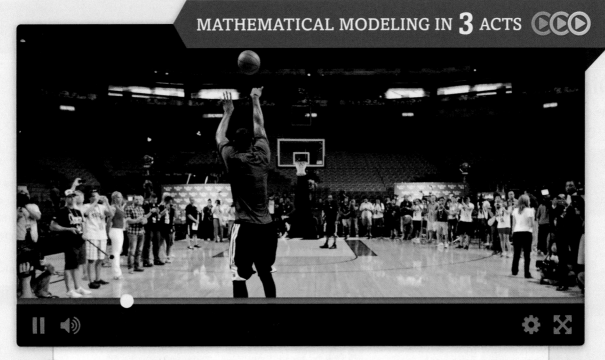

MATHEMATICAL MODELING IN **3** ACTS

▶ The Long Shot

Have you ever been to a basketball game where they hold contests at halftime? A popular contest is one where the contestant needs to make a basket from half court to win a prize. Contestants often shoot the ball in different ways. They might take a regular basketball shot, a hook shot, or an underhand toss.

What's the best way to shoot the basketball and make a basket? In the Mathematical Modeling in 3 Acts lesson, you decide!

VIDEOS Watch clips to support *Mathematical Modeling in 3 Acts Lessons* and enVision® *STEM Projects.*

CONCEPT SUMMARY Review key lesson content through multiple representations.

ASSESSMENT Show what you've learned.

 GLOSSARY Read and listen to English and Spanish definitions.

 TUTORIALS Get help from *Virtual Nerd*, right when you need it.

 MATH TOOLS Explore math with digital tools and manipulatives.

Did You Know?

The **goal of a business** owner is to **maximize profits**. Businesses have to consider many things to set the best price for their products.

A typical small business has a net profit margin of around 10%. This means 90% of its revenue is spent on costs, such as rent, labor, and raw materials.

FOUND IT *on* BLACK FRIDAY

HALF PRICE — ALL DESIGNER DRESSES WOMENSWEAR

HALF PRICE — ALL FORMAL SHIRTS MENSWEAR

HALF PRICE

FREE TEA OR COFF with any purchase up to 11am

The day after Thanksgiving is known as Black Friday because that is the day many retailers begin to **turn a profit** for the year. Being "in the black" is an accounting term for "making a profit."

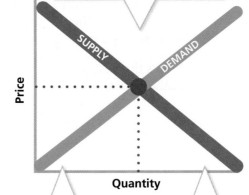

Market equilibrium is when supply = demand.

SUPPLY | DEMAND

Price / Quantity

Demand is how much of a product people want to buy. The **higher the demand, the higher** producers can price the product.

Supply is how much of a product is available. The **higher the supply, the lower the** price producers can charge.

▶ Your Task: Make Business Decisions

You and your classmates will pick an industry, then suggest and defend your choice of the number of an item to make and the price at which to sell the item.

3-1

Key Features of a Quadratic Function

PearsonRealize.com

I CAN... identify key features of the graph of the quadratic parent function.

VOCABULARY
• parabola
• quadratic parent function

👆 **EXPLORE & REASON**

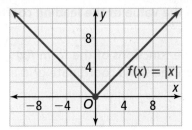

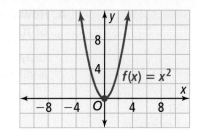

A. Look for Relationships How is the graph of $f(x) = |x|$ similar to the graph of $f(x) = x^2$? How is it different?

B. What do you notice about the axis of symmetry in each graph?

❓ **ESSENTIAL QUESTION** What is the quadratic parent function and how can you recognize the key features of its graph?

👆 **EXAMPLE 1**   **Identify a Quadratic Parent Function**

What is a quadratic parent function and what are its characteristics?

The **quadratic parent function** is $f(x) = x^2$. It is the simplest function in the quadratic function family. The graph of the function is a curve called a **parabola**.

x	$f(x) = x^2$	(x, y)
−2	4	(−2, 4)
−1	1	(−1, 1)
0	0	(0, 0)
1	1	(1, 1)
2	4	(2, 4)

> The vertex is the lowest (or highest) point on the graph of a quadratic function.

> The axis of symmetry is $x = 0$.

The parabola opens up.

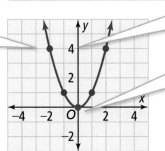

> The vertex is (0, 0). It is the turning point of the graph.

LOOK FOR RELATIONSHIPS
Think about how the features of a quadratic function compare and contrast to those of a linear function.

The axis of symmetry intersects the vertex, and divides the parabola in half.

 Try It!   **1.** When are the values of $f(x)$ positive and when are they negative?

👆 **EXAMPLE 2** ▶ **Understand the Graph of $f(x) = ax^2$**

A. How does the value of the leading coefficient, a, affect the graph of $f(x) = ax^2$?

Graph some functions of the form $f(x) = ax^2$ with different positive a-values on the same coordinate grid and compare them.

COMMON ERROR
You may think that an a value with an absolute value less than 1 would decrease the width of the parabola. However, it increases the width of the parabola.

The graph of $f(x) = 0.5x^2$ is wider than the graph of $f(x) = 2x^2$.

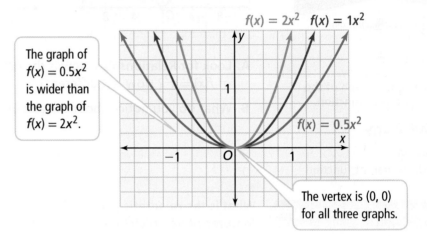

$f(x) = 2x^2$ $f(x) = 1x^2$

$f(x) = 0.5x^2$

The vertex is (0, 0) for all three graphs.

For $0 < |a| < 1$, the shape of the parabola is wider than the parent function. For $|a| > 1$, the shape of the parabola is narrower than the parent function.

B. How does the sign of a affect the graph of $f(x) = ax^2$?

Graph two functions of the form $f(x) = ax^2$ with opposite a-values on the same coordinate grid, and compare them.

LOOK FOR RELATIONSHIPS
Consider whether the value of a has an effect on the location of the vertex of the graph of $f(x) = ax^2$.

When $a > 0$, the y-coordinate of the vertex is the minimum value of the function. When $a < 0$, it is the maximum.

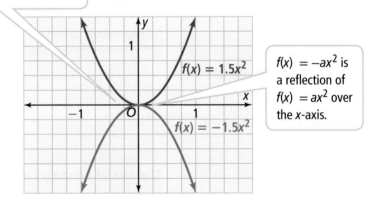

$f(x) = 1.5x^2$

$f(x) = -1.5x^2$

$f(x) = -ax^2$ is a reflection of $f(x) = ax^2$ over the x-axis.

When $a > 0$, the parabola opens upward.
When $a < 0$, the parabola opens downward.

 Try It!   **2.** How does the sign of a affect the domain and range of $f(x) = ax^2$?

 EXAMPLE 3 **Interpret Quadratic Functions from Tables**

Over what interval is $f(x) = 4x^2$ increasing? Over what interval is it decreasing?

Use the function to make a table of values.

> The function values are decreasing.

x	$f(x) = 4x^2$	(x, y)
-2	16	$(-2, 16)$
-1	4	$(-1, 4)$
0	0	$(0, 0)$
1	4	$(1, 4)$
2	16	$(2, 16)$

> The vertex $(0, 0)$ is the turning point of the function, where it changes from decreasing to increasing.

> The function values are increasing.

STUDY TIP
Remember that since the function has a minimum value, the parabola opens upward. If the function has a maximum value, the parabola opens downward.

The function is decreasing over the interval $x < 0$ and increasing over the interval $x > 0$.

 **Try It!** **3.** A function of the form $g(x) = ax^2$ increases over the interval $x < 0$ and decreases over the interval $x > 0$. What is a possible value for a? Explain.

APPLICATION **EXAMPLE 4** **Apply Quadratic Functions**

The owner of a new dance studio is installing wooden floors in all of the dance rooms. How much should the owner expect to spend on flooring for a square room with 15-ft side lengths?

Write a function that can be used to determine the cost of the flooring.

$c(x)$ = price per ft^2 of flooring • area of dance floor in ft^2

$c(x) = $ 8.75   • x^2

Find the value of the function when $x = 15$.

$c(x) = 8.75x^2$
$c(15) = 8.75(15)^2$ ⋯⋯⋯⋯⋯ Substitute 15 for x.
$c(15) = 1,968.75$ ⋯⋯⋯⋯⋯ Simplify.

The cost for a new floor for a square dance floor with sides of 15 ft is $1,968.75.

 Try It! **4.** By how much will the cost increase if the side length of the dance floor is increased by 2 ft?

LESSON 3-1 Key Features of a Quadratic Function **105**

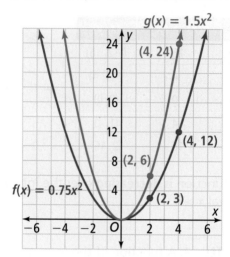
EXAMPLE 5 Compare the Rate of Change

A. How do the average rates of change for $f(x) = 0.75x^2$ and $g(x) = 1.5x^2$ over the interval $2 \leq x \leq 4$ compare?

Step 1 Graph the two functions.

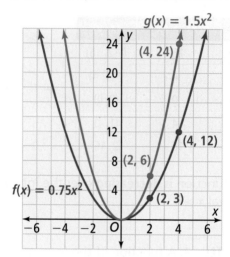

Step 2 Find the value of each function at the endpoints of the interval.

$f(2) = 0.75(2)^2 = 3$

$f(4) = 0.75(4)^2 = 12$

$g(2) = 1.5(2)^2 = 6$

$g(4) = 1.5(4)^2 = 24$

STUDY TIP
Use what you know about finding rates of change for linear functions. Think about the differences for quadratic functions.

Step 3 Find the slope of the line that passes through each pair of points.

$f(x)$: $\dfrac{12 - 3}{4 - 2} = \dfrac{9}{2} = 4.5$

$g(x)$: $\dfrac{24 - 6}{4 - 2} = \dfrac{18}{2} = 9$

> The rate of change for function g is twice the rate of change for function f.

On average, the values of function f increase by 4.5 units and the values of function g increase by 9 units for each unit increase in x over the interval $2 \leq x \leq 4$.

B. How do the rates of change relate to the values of a in the functions?

For positive intervals, the greater the value of a, the greater the average rate of change. In this case the ratio of the a-values in the two functions is the same as the ratio of the average rates of change.

Try It! **5.** How do the average rates of change for $f(x) = -0.5x^2$ and $g(x) = -1.5x^2$ over the interval $-5 \leq x \leq -2$ compare?

$f(x) = x^2$ $f(x) = ax^2$

GRAPHS

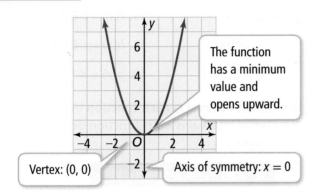

The function has a minimum value and opens upward.

Vertex: (0, 0)   Axis of symmetry: $x = 0$

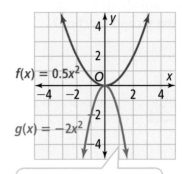

$f(x) = 0.5x^2$

$g(x) = -2x^2$

When $a < 0$, the parabola opens downward.

WORDS

The function $f(x) = x^2$ is the same as $f(x) = 1x^2$. It is the quadratic parent function. The function decreases over the interval $x < 0$ and increases over the interval $x > 0$.

When $0 < |a| < 1$, the graph of $f(x) = ax^2$ is wider than the graph of $f(x) = x^2$. When $|a| > 1$, graph of $f(x) = ax^2$ is narrower than the graph of $f(x) = x^2$.

☑ **Do You UNDERSTAND?**

1. **ESSENTIAL QUESTION** What is the quadratic parent function and how can you recognize the key features of its graph?

2. **Communicate Precisely** How is the graph of $f(x) = ax^2$ similar to the graph of $f(x) = x^2$? How is it different?

3. **Vocabulary** Make a conjecture about why the term *quadratic parent function* includes the word "parent."

4. **Error Analysis** Abby graphed the function $f(x) = -13x^2$ by plotting the point (–2, 52). Explain the error Abby made in her graph.

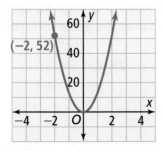

(–2, 52)

Do You KNOW HOW?

How does the value of a in each function affect its graph when compared to the graph of the quadratic parent function?

5. $g(x) = 4x^2$

6. $h(x) = 0.8x^2$

7. $j(x) = -5x^2$

8. $k(x) = -0.4x^2$

9. Given the function $f(x) = 2.5x^2 + 3$, find the average rate of change over the interval $0 \le x \le 4$. What does the average rate of change tell you about the function?

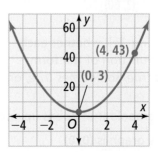

(4, 43)

(0, 3)

UNDERSTAND

10. Generalize The graph of the parent quadratic function $f(x) = x^2$ and that of a second function of the form $g(x) = ax^2$ are shown. What conclusion can you make about the value of a in the equation of the second function?

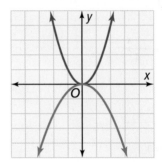

11. Error Analysis Describe and correct the error a student made in finding the average rate of change for $f(x) = 0.5x^2$ over the interval $-4 \leq x \leq -2$.

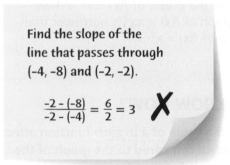

Find the slope of the line that passes through $(-4, -8)$ and $(-2, -2)$.

$$\frac{-2 - (-8)}{-2 - (-4)} = \frac{6}{2} = 3 \quad ✗$$

12. Use Structure Use the table shown below to describe the intervals over which $f(x) = 15x^2$ is increasing and decreasing.

x	$f(x) = 15x^2$	(x, y)
-2	60	$(-2, 60)$
-1	15	$(-1, 15)$
0	0	$(0, 0)$
1	15	$(1, 15)$
2	60	$(2, 60)$

13. Higher Order Thinking Tell whether each statement about a function of the form $f(x) = ax^2$ is *always true, sometimes true,* or *never true.*

a. The graph is a parabola that opens upward.

b. The vertex of the graph is $(0, 0)$.

c. The axis of symmetry of the graph is $x = 0$.

PRACTICE

How does the value of a in each function affect its graph when compared to the graph of the quadratic parent function? SEE EXAMPLES 1 AND 2

14. $g(x) = 6x^2$

15. $f(x) = 0.6x^2$

16. $f(x) = -7x^2$

17. $h(x) = -0.15x^2$

18. $C(x) = 0.04x^2$

19. $g(x) = 4.5x^2$

Over what interval is each function increasing and over what interval is each function decreasing? SEE EXAMPLE 3

20.

x	$f(x) = -0.3x^2$	(x, y)
-2	-1.2	$(-2, -1.2)$
-1	-0.3	$(-1, -0.3)$
0	0	$(0, 0)$
1	-0.3	$(1, -0.3)$
2	-1.2	$(2, -1.2)$

21.

x	$f(x) = 13x^2$	(x, y)
-2	52	$(-2, 52)$
-1	13	$(-1, 13)$
0	0	$(0, 0)$
1	13	$(1, 13)$
2	52	$(2, 52)$

Write a quadratic function for the area of each figure. Then find the area for the given value of x. SEE EXAMPLE 4

22. $x = 13$

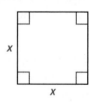

23. $x = 2.5$

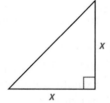

How do the average rates of change for each pair of functions compare over the given interval? SEE EXAMPLE 5

24. $f(x) = 0.1x^2$
$g(x) = 0.3x^2$
$1 \leq x \leq 4$

25. $f(x) = -2x^2$
$g(x) = -4x^2$
$-4 \leq x \leq -2$

APPLY

26. **Reason** Some students can plant 9 carrots per square foot in the community garden shown. Write a function f that can be used to determine the number of carrots the students can plant. Give a reasonable domain for the function. How many carrots can the students plant in a garden that is square with 4-ft side lengths?

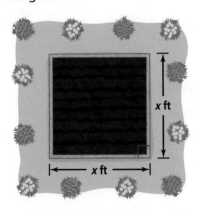

x ft

x ft

27. **Make Sense and Persevere** A burrito company uses the function $C(x) = 1.74x^2$ to calculate the number of calories in a tortilla with a diameter of x inches.

   a. Find the average rates of change for the function over the intervals $6 < x < 8$ and $9 < x < 11$.

   b. Interpret the average rates of change.

   c. What does the difference in the average rates of change mean in terms of the situation?

28. **Reason** An architect uses a computer program to design a skateboard ramp. The function $f(x) = ax^2$ represents the shape of the ramp's cross section. A portion of the design is shown. The scale of each axis is 1 unit per grid line. On the ramp, a person can skateboard from point A through point B and over to a point C. If point C is the same distance above the x-axis as point B, what are its coordinates? Explain.

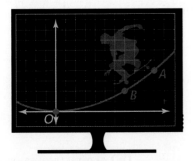

ASSESSMENT PRACTICE

29. The total cost, in dollars, of a square carpet can be determined by using $f(x) = 15x^2$, where x is the side length in yards. Which of the following are true? Select all that apply.

   Ⓐ The cost of a carpet increases and then decreases as the side length increases.

   Ⓑ The cost of the carpet is $15 per square yard.

   Ⓒ The cost of a carpet with a side length of 3 yd is $135.

   Ⓓ The cost of a carpet with 6-yd sides is twice the cost of a carpet with 3-yd sides.

   Ⓔ The cost of a carpet increases at a constant rate as the side length increases.

30. **SAT/ACT** The graph of $f(x) = ax^2$ opens downward and is narrower than the graph of the quadratic parent function. Which of the following could be the value of a?

   Ⓐ −2   Ⓑ −0.5   Ⓒ 0.5   Ⓓ 1   Ⓔ 2

31. **Performance Task** A manufacturer has two options for making cube-shaped boxes. The cost is calculated by multiplying the surface area of the box by the cost per square inch of the cardboard.

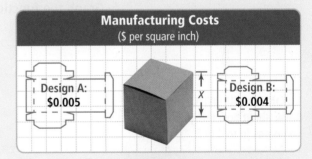

Manufacturing Costs
($ per square inch)

Design A: $0.005   Design B: $0.004

Part A Write a quadratic function of the form $f(x) = ax^2$ for each design that can be used to determine the total cardboard cost for cubes with any side length. Interpret the value of a in each function.

Part B How do the average rates of change for the designs compare for cubes with side lengths greater than 6 in., but less than 8 in.?

Part C Make a conjecture about the packaging costs for each design when the side length of the cube is greater than 36 in. Explain your conjecture.

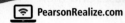
3-2

Quadratic Functions in Vertex Form

📶 PearsonRealize.com

I CAN... graph quadratic functions using the vertex form.

VOCABULARY
• vertex form of a quadratic function

👆 **CRITIQUE & EXPLAIN**

Allie states that the two graphs shown may look different, but they are actually the same figure. Esteban disagrees, stating that they are different figures because they look different.

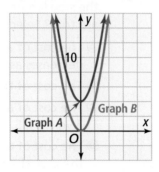

A. Give one mathematical argument to support Esteban's thinking.

B. Give one mathematical argument to support Allie's thinking.

C. Reason Who do you agree with? What argument can you give to justify your reasoning?

? ESSENTIAL QUESTION How can the vertex form of a quadratic function help you sketch the graph of the function?

👆 **EXAMPLE 1** Understand the Graph of $g(x) = x^2 + k$

How does the graph of $g(x) = x^2 - 4$ compare to that of $f(x) = x^2$?

Graph the function g and the parent function f.

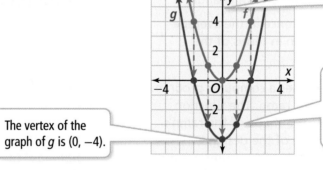

The two graphs have the same axis of symmetry: $x = 0$.

Each point $(x, f(x))$ is translated down 4 units to the corresponding point $(x, g(x))$.

The vertex of the graph of g is $(0, -4)$.

LOOK FOR RELATIONSHIPS
Think about how the graph of g compares to that of f.

The value of k in $g(x) = x^2 + k$ translates the graph of the parent function f, vertically k units. The vertex of the graph of g is at $(0, k)$, in this case $(0, -4)$. The value of k does not affect the axis of symmetry.

 Try It!   **1.** How does the graph of each function compare to the graph of $f(x) = x^2$?

   a. $h(x) = x^2 + 3$ **b.** $j(x) = x^2 - 2$

EXAMPLE 2 Understand the Graph of $g(x) = (x - h)^2$

How does the graph of $g(x) = (x - 3)^2$ compare to that of $f(x) = x^2$?

Graph the function g and the parent function f.

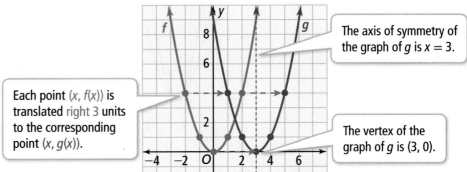

The axis of symmetry of the graph of g is $x = 3$.

Each point $(x, f(x))$ is translated right 3 units to the corresponding point $(x, g(x))$.

The vertex of the graph of g is $(3, 0)$.

COMMON ERROR
You may think that the graph of $g(x) = (x - 3)^2$ would be a horizontal translation of the graph of $f(x) = x^2$ to the left in the negative direction along the x-axis. However, the translation is to the right in the positive direction.

The value of h in $g(x) = (x - h)^2$ translates the graph of the parent function horizontally h units. The vertex of the graph of g is at $(h, 0)$, in this case $(3, 0)$. The value of h also translated the axis of symmetry horizontally.

 Try It!   **2.** How does the graph of each function compare to the graph of $f(x) = x^2$?

  a. $h(x) = (x + 1)^2$ **b.** $j(x) = (x - 5)^2$

CONCEPTUAL
UNDERSTANDING

EXAMPLE 3 Understand the Graph of $f(x) = a(x - h)^2 + k$

 A. What information do the values of h and k provide about the graph of $f(x) = (x - h)^2 + k$?

Graph several functions of the form $f(x) = (x - h)^2 + k$. Look at the location of the vertex of each graph.

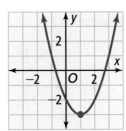   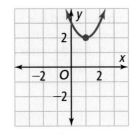   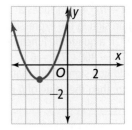

$f(x) = (x - 1)^2 - 3$ $f(x) = (x - 1)^2 + 2$ $f(x) = (x + 2)^2 - 1$
vertex: $(1, -3)$ vertex: $(1, 2)$ vertex: $(-2, -1)$

USE STRUCTURE
Consider $f(x) = (x - 1)^2 - 3$ to be in the form $f(x) = a(x - h)^2 + k$. What is the a-value of this function?

The values of h and k determine the location of the vertex and the axis of symmetry of the parabola. The vertex of the graph of $f(x) = (x - h)^2 + k$ is at (h, k). The axis of symmetry is $x = h$.

CONTINUED ON THE NEXT PAGE

EXAMPLE 3 CONTINUED

B. How does the value of *a* affect the graph of $f(x) = a(x - h)^2 + k$?

Graph each of the functions shown in part A. Then graph a new function with a different value of *a* to see how it affects the graph.

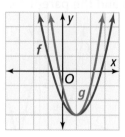   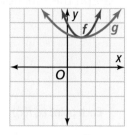   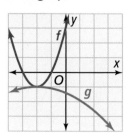

$f(x) = (x - 1)^2 - 3$ $f(x) = (x - 1)^2 + 2$ $f(x) = (x + 2)^2 - 1$
$g(x) = 2(x - 1)^2 - 3$ $g(x) = 0.25(x - 1)^2 + 2$ $g(x) = -0.1(x + 2)^2 - 1$

The value of *a* does not affect the location of the vertex. The sign of *a* affects the direction of the parabola. The absolute value of *a* affects the width of the parabola.

The function $f(x) = a(x - h)^2 + k$, where $a \neq 0$ is called the **vertex form of a quadratic function**. The vertex of the graph is (h, k). The graph of $f(x) = a(x - h)^2 + k$ is a translation of the function $f(x) = ax^2$ that is translated *h* units horizontally and *k* units vertically.

> **STUDY TIP**
> Notice that when $0 < |a| < 1$, the shape of the parabola is wider than the parent function. When $|a| > 1$, the shape of the parabola is narrower than the parent function.

✓ **Try It!**   **3.** How does the graph of $f(x) = -3(x - 5)^2 + 7$ compare to the graph of the parent function?

👆 **EXAMPLE 4**   **Graph Using Vertex Form**

How can you use the vertex form of a quadratic function to sketch the graph of the function?

Graph $f(x) = -2(x + 1)^2 + 5$.

> This is the same as
> $f(x) = -2(x - (-1))^2 + 5$

$h = -1$ and $k = 5$, so the vertex is $(-1, 5)$, and the axis of symmetry is $x = -1$.

> **COMMON ERROR**
> Recall that vertex form $f(x) = a(x - h)^2 + k$ includes a subtraction sign in the expression "$(x - h)$". If a quadratic function such as $f(x) = 3(x + 7)^2 - 6$ has an addition sign within that expression, then the value of *h* is negative.

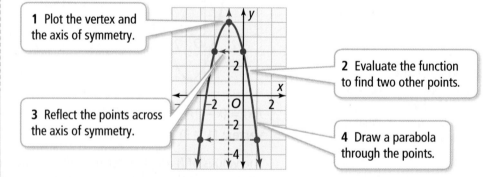

1 Plot the vertex and the axis of symmetry.

2 Evaluate the function to find two other points.

3 Reflect the points across the axis of symmetry.

4 Draw a parabola through the points.

✓ **Try It!**   **4.** Find the vertex and axis of symmetry, and sketch the graph of the function.

a. $g(x) = -3(x - 2)^2 + 1$ **b.** $h(x) = (x + 1)^2 - 4$

APPLICATION　👆 **EXAMPLE 5**　Use Vertex Form to Solve Problems

Deshawn and Chris are playing soccer. Chris takes a shot on goal. Deshawn is 3 ft in front of the goal and can reach the top of the 8-ft goal when standing directly beneath it. Can he block the shot from his current position without moving or jumping?

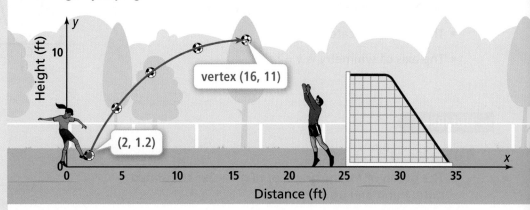

vertex (16, 11)

(2, 1.2)

Height (ft)

Distance (ft)

Formulate ◀　You can describe the parabolic path of the soccer ball using a quadratic function. The vertex of parabola is given, so write the function in vertex form.

$$f(x) = a(x - h)^2 + k$$

$$f(x) = a(x - 16)^2 + 11$$ ·········· Substitute $h = 16$ and $k = 11$.

Compute ◀　Use another point on the path of the ball to find the value of a.

The point (2, 1.2) represents the point where Chris's foot makes contact with the ball.

$$1.2 = a(2 - 16)^2 + 11$$ ·········· Substitute $x = 2$ and $f(x) = 1.2$.

$$1.2 = 196a + 11$$ ·········· Simplify.

$$-9.8 = 196a$$ ·········· Simplify.

$$\frac{-9.8}{196} = \frac{196a}{196}$$ ·········· Divide each side by 196.

$$a = -0.05$$

$$f(x) = -0.05(x - 16)^2 + 11$$ ·········· Substitute $a = -0.05$ into the function.

Use the function to find the altitude of the ball at Deshawn's position.

Deshawn is 3 ft in front of the goal, so his position is 25 ft − 3 ft = 22 ft.

$$f(22) = -0.05(22 - 16)^2 + 11$$ ····· Substitute $x = 22$ into the function.

$$\approx 9.2$$

Interpret ◀　When the ball reaches Deshawn it will be about 9.2 ft above the ground, which is above his 8-ft reach.

Deshawn cannot block Chris's shot from his current position without jumping or moving.

☑ **Try It!**　5. If Deshawn does not block Chris's shot, will it be a goal? Explain.

CONCEPT SUMMARY Vertex Form of a Quadratic Function

ALGEBRA

$f(x) = a(x - h)^2 + k$

- The graph of f is the graph of $g(x) = ax^2$ translated horizontally h units and vertically k units.
- The vertex is located at (h, k).
- The axis of symmetry is $x = h$.

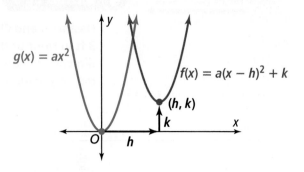

NUMBERS

$f(x) = -2(x - 1)^2 + 3$

- The graph of f is the graph of $g(x) = -2x^2$ translated right 1 unit and up 3 units.
- The vertex is located at $(1, 3)$.
- The axis of symmetry is $x = 1$.

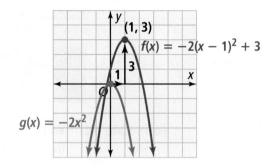

Do You UNDERSTAND?

1. **ESSENTIAL QUESTION** How can the vertex form of a quadratic function help you sketch the graph of the function?

2. **Reason** A table of values for the quadratic function g is shown. Do the graphs of the functions g and $f(x) = 3(x - 1)^2 + 2$ have the same axis of symmetry? Explain.

x	g(x)
-4	8
-2	3
0	0
6	3

3. **Use Structure** How are the form and the graph of $f(x) = (x - h)^2 + k$ similar to the form and graph of $f(x) = |x - h| + k$? How are they different?

4. **Error Analysis** Sarah said the vertex of the function $f(x) = (x + 2)^2 + 6$ is $(2, 6)$. Is she correct? Explain your answer.

Do You KNOW HOW?

Graph each function.

5. $g(x) = x^2 + 5$

6. $f(x) = (x - 2)^2$

7. $h(x) = -2(x + 4)^2 + 1$

8. Write a function in vertex form for the parabola shown below.

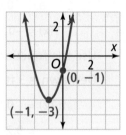

9. The height of a ball thrown into the air is a quadratic function of time. The ball is thrown from a height of 6 ft above the ground. After 1 second, the ball reaches its maximum height of 22 ft above the ground. Write the equation of the function in vertex form.

UNDERSTAND

10. Make Sense and Persevere
How can you determine the values of h and k from the graph shown? Write the function for the parabola.

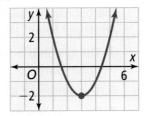

11. Reason To graph the function $f(x) = (x - 5)^2 - 8$, a student translates the graph of the quadratic parent function 5 units right and 8 units down. Can a student produce the graph of $f(x) = 2(x + 3)^2 - 5$ by simply translating the quadratic parent function? Explain.

12. Error Analysis A student used the steps shown to graph $f(x) = (x - 1)^2 + 6$. Describe and correct the student's error.

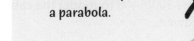

1. Plot the vertex at $(-1, 6)$.
2. Graph points at $(-2, 15)$ and $(-3, 22)$.
3. Reflect the points across the axis of symmetry $x = -1$.
4. Connect the points with a parabola. ✗

13. Mathematical Connections The graph shown is a translation of the graph of $f(x) = 2x^2$. Write the function for the graph in vertex form.

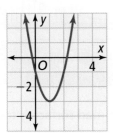

14. Higher Order Thinking The graph of h is the graph of $g(x) = (x - 2)^2 + 6$ translated 5 units left and 3 units down.

a. Describe the graph of h as a translation of the graph of $f(x) = x^2$.

b. Write the function h in vertex form.

PRACTICE

Identify the vertex and the axis of symmetry for each function. SEE EXAMPLES 1 AND 2

15. $f(x) = x^2 + 2$ **16.** $f(x) = x^2 - 5$

17. $g(x) = x^2 - 1$ **18.** $h(x) = x^2 + 0.5$

19. $f(x) = x^2 - 2.25$ **20.** $f(x) = x^2 + 50$

21. $h(x) = x^2 + 7$ **22.** $g(x) = (x - 1)^2$

23. $g(x) = (x + 2)^2$ **24.** $f(x) = (x - 6)^2$

25. $f(x) = (x - 0.5)^2$ **26.** $g(x) = (x - 4)^2$

Each graph shown is a translation of the graph of $f(x) = x^2$. Write each function in vertex form. SEE EXAMPLE 3

27.    **28.**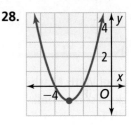

Identify the vertex, axis of symmetry, and direction of the graph of each function. Compare the width of the graph to the width of the graph of $f(x) = x^2$. SEE EXAMPLE 3

29. $f(x) = 2(x + 1)^2 + 4$

30. $g(x) = (x - 3)^2 - 3$

31. $g(x) = -0.75(x - 5)^2 + 6$

32. $h(x) = -3(x + 2)^2 - 5$

Sketch the graph of each function. SEE EXAMPLE 4

33. $f(x) = 2(x - 1)^2 + 4$ **34.** $g(x) = -2(x - 0.5)^2 + 1$

35. $f(x) = 0.5(x + 2)^2 + 2$ **36.** $h(x) = -2(x - 2)^2 - 2$

Each graph represents a quadratic function. Write each function in vertex form. SEE EXAMPLE 5

37. 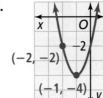   **38.**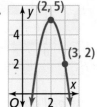

APPLY

39. Make Sense and Persevere A computer game designer uses the function $f(x) = 4(x - 2)^2 + 6$ to model the path of the fish. The horizontal path of the squid intersects the path of the fish. At what other point does the squid's path intersect the path of the fish?

(5, 42)

40. Model With Mathematics Suppose a goalie kicks a soccer ball. The ball travels in a parabolic path from point (0, 0) to (57, 0).

a. Consider a quadratic function in vertex form for the path of the ball. Which values can you determine? What values are you unable to determine? Explain.

b. Technology Use a graphing calculator to explore the undetermined values. Find a set of values that generates a realistic graph. Explain how the key features of the graph correspond to the situation.

41. Construct Arguments The function $f(x) = -(x - 1)^2 + 8$ models the path of a volleyball. The height of the net is 7 ft 4 in.

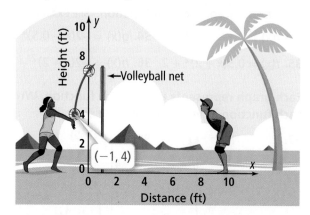

Volleyball net

(−1, 4)

Distance (ft)

Will the ball go over if the player is 2 ft from the net? 4 ft, from the net? Explain.

ASSESSMENT PRACTICE

42. The function $f(x) = 2(x - 3)^2 + 9$ is graphed in the coordinate plane. Which of the following are true? Select all that apply.

Ⓐ The graph is a parabola that opens downward.

Ⓑ The vertex of the graph is (−3, 9).

Ⓒ The axis of symmetry of the graph is $x = 3$.

Ⓓ The y-intercept of the graph is 9.

Ⓔ The minimum of the function is 9.

43. SAT/ACT The graph of $g(x) = x^2$ is translated right 2 units and down 10 units. Which of the following is the function of the new graph?

Ⓐ $f(x) = (x + 2)^2 - 10$

Ⓑ $f(x) = (x - 2)^2 - 10$

Ⓒ $f(x) = 2x^2 - 10$

Ⓓ $f(x) = -2x^2 - 10$

Ⓔ $f(x) = -2(x - 10)^2$

44. Performance Task An engineer is designing a suspension bridge with a center cable. The cable is shaped like a parabola and is attached to stability towers on both ends at the same height. For simplicity she assumes a quadratic function, and uses $f(x) = 0.0006(x - 300)^2 + 6$ to model the cable between the towers.

60 m

Part A How high above the road surface is the lowest point of the cable?

Part B How far apart are the two towers? Explain.

3-3

Quadratic Functions in Standard Form

📶 **PearsonRealize.com**

I CAN... graph quadratic functions using standard form.

VOCABULARY

• standard form of a quadratic function

Three functions of the form $f(x) = ax^2 + bx$ are graphed for $a = 2$ and different values of b.

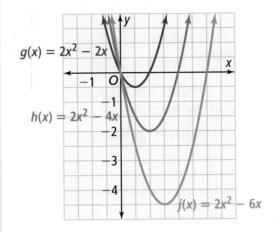

$g(x) = 2x^2 - 2x$
$h(x) = 2x^2 - 4x$
$j(x) = 2x^2 - 6x$

A. What do the graphs have in common? In what ways do they differ?

B. What do you notice about the *x*-intercepts of each graph? What do you notice about the *y*-intercepts of each graph?

C. **Look for Relationships** Look at the ratio $\frac{b}{a}$ for each function and compare it to its graph. What do you notice?

❓ **ESSENTIAL QUESTION** How is the standard form of a quadratic function different from the vertex form?

CONCEPTUAL UNDERSTANDING

👆 **EXAMPLE 1** ⟩ Relate *c* to the Graph of $f(x) = ax^2 + bx + c$

What information does *c* provide about the graph of $f(x) = ax^2 + bx + c$?

Graph several functions of the form $f(x) = ax^2 + bx + c$. Look for a connection between the graphs and the value of *c* for each function.

GENERALIZE
Consider the graphs of quadratic functions with the same *c*-values but different *a*- and *b*-values from those shown in the example.

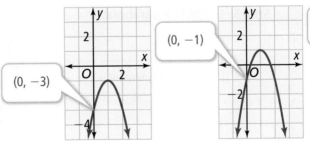

(0, −3)

(0, −1)

(0, 1)

$f(x) = -2x^2 + 4x - 3$ $f(x) = -2x^2 + 4x - 1$ $f(x) = -2x^2 + 4x + 1$

$c = -3$ $c = -1$ $c = 1$

The value of *c* corresponds to the *y*-intercept of the graph of $f(x) = ax^2 + bx + c$.

☑ **Try It!**   **1.** Evaluate $f(x) = ax^2 + bx + c$ for $x = 0$. How does $f(0)$ relate to the result in Example 1?

CONCEPT Standard Form of a Quadratic Equation

The **standard form of a quadratic function** is $f(x) = ax^2 + bx + c$, where $a \neq 0$. The value c is the y-intercept of the graph. The axis of symmetry of the graph is the line $x = -\frac{b}{2a}$ and the x-coordinate of the vertex is $-\frac{b}{2a}$.

EXAMPLE 2 Graph a Quadratic Function in Standard Form

Graph $f(x) = 2x^2 + 4x + 3$. What are the axis of symmetry, vertex, and y-intercept of the function?

Step 1 Find the axis of symmetry.

$$x = -\frac{b}{2a} = -\frac{4}{2(2)} = -1$$

> The x-coordinate of the vertex is also -1.

The axis of symmetry is $x = -1$.

Step 2 Plot the vertex.

Use the x-coordinate of the vertex to find the y-coordinate.

$f(x) = 2x^2 + 4x + 3$

$f(-1) = 2(-1)^2 + 4(-1) + 3$ ········ Substitute -1 for x.

$\qquad = 1$ ···························· Simplify.

USE STRUCTURE
Consider Step 3. Is there a situation where following this procedure would not yield two points on the parabola?

The y-coordinate of the vertex is 1. So, plot the vertex $(-1, 1)$.

Step 3 Plot the y-intercept and its reflection.

$f(x) = 2x^2 + 4x + 3$

> The value of c is the y-intercept.

Plot $(0, 3)$ and its reflection across the axis of symmetry $(-2, 3)$.

Step 4 Plot another point and its reflection.

Evaluate the function for another x-value. For $x = 1$, $f(1) = 9$. The reflection of $(1, 9)$ across the axis of symmetry is $(-3, 9)$. Plot $(1, 9)$ and $(-3, 9)$.

Step 5 Graph the parabola.

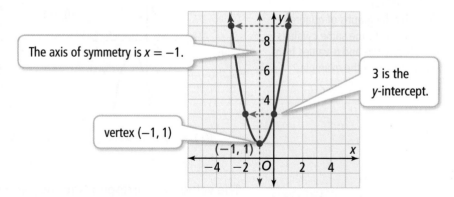

The axis of symmetry is $x = -1$.

3 is the y-intercept.

vertex $(-1, 1)$

CONTINUED ON THE NEXT PAGE

Try It! **2.** Graph each function. What are the *y*-intercept, the axis of symmetry, and the vertex of each function?

    a. $f(x) = x^2 + 2x + 4$ **b.** $g(x) = -0.75x^2 + 3x - 4$

APPLICATION   **EXAMPLE 3**   **Compare Properties of Quadratic Functions**

The trajectory of the water from Fountain A is represented by a function in standard form while the trajectory of the water from Fountain B is represented by a table of values. Compare the vertex of each function. Which trajectory reaches a greater height in feet?

Fountain A:
$f(x) = -x^2 + 2x + 8$

Fountain B:

x	y
−6	5
−5	8
−4	10
−3	8
−2	5

COMMON ERROR
You may incorrectly state that the *x*-coordinate of the vertex is −1. Remember that the formula is $-\frac{b}{2a}$. Make sure to include the negative in your calculations.

Find the vertex of each function.

Fountain **A**

Find the *x*-coordinate.

$$-\frac{b}{2a} = -\frac{2}{2(-1)} = 1$$

Find the *y*-coordinate.

$$f(1) = -(1)^2 + 2(1) + 8 = 9$$

The vertex is (1, 9).

Fountain **B**

Find the vertex.

x	y
−6	5
−5	8
−4	10
−3	8
−2	5

The vertex is (−4, 10).

Fountain **A** reaches a height of 9 ft.   Fountain **B** reaches a height of 10 ft.

The water from Fountain B reaches a greater height.

CONTINUED ON THE NEXT PAGE

EXAMPLE 3 CONTINUED

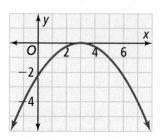

Try It! 3. Compare $f(x) = -0.3x^2 - 0.6x - 0.2$ to function g, shown in the graph. What are the maximum values? Which function has the greater maximum value?

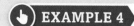

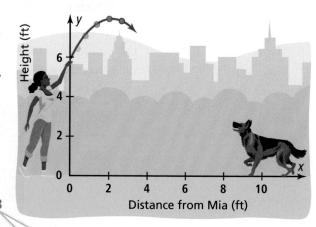

EXAMPLE 4 Analyze the Structure of Different Forms

Mia tosses a ball to her dog. The function $f(x) = -0.5(x - 2)^2 + 8$ represents the ball's path.

A. What does the vertex form of the function tell you about the situation?

$$f(x) = a(x - h)^2 + k$$

$$f(x) = -0.5(x - 2)^2 + 8$$

$a = -0.5$. Since $a < 0$, the parabola opens downward.

$h = 2$ and $k = 8$, so the vertex is $(2, 8)$.

The vertex form tells you the vertex of the graph of the function, which is $(2, 8)$. The ball reaches a maximum height of 8 ft above the ground, 2 ft away from where Mia releases it.

B. What does the standard form of a function tell you about the situation?

Rewrite the function in standard form.

$$f(x) = -0.5(x - 2)^2 + 8$$
$$= -0.5(x^2 - 4x + 4) + 8 \quad \text{Expand } (x - 2)^2.$$
$$= -0.5x^2 + 2x + 6 \quad \text{Use the Distributive Property and simplify.}$$
$$f(x) = ax^2 + bx + c$$

The y-intercept is 6.

$$f(x) = -0.5x^2 + 2x + 6$$

The standard form tells you the y-intercept of the graph of the function, which is $(0, 6)$. The ball was 6 ft above the ground when Mia threw it.

MAKE SENSE AND PERSEVERE
Think about the reasonableness of the domain and range when you graph the function. Do both positive and negative values makes sense?

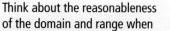

Try It! 4. Suppose the path of the ball in Example 4 is $f(x) = -0.25(x - 1)^2 + 6.25$. Find the ball's initial and maximum heights.

Go Online | PearsonRealize.com

CONCEPT SUMMARY Standard Form of a Quadratic Function

ALGEBRA Standard form: $f(x) = ax^2 + bx + c$, where $a \neq 0$.

y-intercept: c

Axis of symmetry: $x = -\dfrac{b}{2a}$

x-coordinate of the vertex: $-\dfrac{b}{2a}$

y-coordinate of the vertex: $f\left(-\dfrac{b}{2a}\right)$

Vertex: $\left(-\dfrac{b}{2a}, f\left(-\dfrac{b}{2a}\right)\right)$

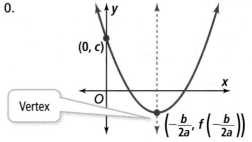

NUMBERS Standard form: $f(x) = 2x^2 + 8x + 5$.

y-intercept: 5

Axis of symmetry: $x = -\dfrac{8}{2(2)} = -2$

x-coordinate of the vertex: $-\dfrac{8}{2(2)} = -2$

y-coordinate of the vertex: $f(-2) = -3$

Vertex: $(-2, -3)$

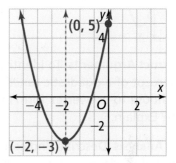

Do You UNDERSTAND?

1. **ESSENTIAL QUESTION** How is the standard form of a quadratic function different from the vertex form?

2. **Communicate Precisely** How are the form and graph of $f(x) = ax^2 + bx + c$ similar to the form and graph of $g(x) = ax^2 + bx$? How are they different?

3. **Vocabulary** How can you write a quadratic function in *standard form*, given its vertex form?

4. **Error Analysis** Sage began graphing $f(x) = -2x^2 + 4x + 9$ by finding the axis of symmetry $x = -1$. Explain the error Sage made.

Do You KNOW HOW?

Graph each function. For each, identify the axis of symmetry, the y-intercept, and the coordinates of the vertex.

5. $f(x) = 2x^2 + 8x - 1$

6. $f(x) = -0.5x^2 + 2x + 3$

7. $f(x) = -3x^2 - 6x - 5$

8. $f(x) = 0.25x^2 - 0.5x - 6$

9. A water balloon is tossed into the air. The function $h(x) = -0.5(x - 4)^2 + 9$ gives the height, in feet, of the balloon from the surface of a pool as a function of the balloon's horizontal distance from where it was first tossed. Will the balloon hit the ceiling 12 ft above the pool? Explain.

UNDERSTAND

10. Make Sense and Persevere The graph of the function $f(x) = 2x^2 - bx - 6$ is shown. What is the value of b? Explain.

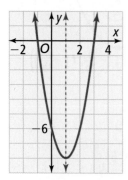

11. Construct Arguments To identify the y-intercept of a quadratic function, would you choose to use vertex form or standard form? Explain.

12. Error Analysis Describe and correct the error a student made when writing the quadratic function $f(x) = 2(x + 3)^2 - 4$ in standard form.

$$f(x) = 2(x + 3)^2 - 4$$
$$f(x) = 2x^2 + 6x + 9 - 4$$
$$f(x) = 2x^2 + 6x + 5 \quad ✗$$

13. Communicate Precisely Estimate the coordinates of the vertex of the graph of $f(x) = 1.25x^2 - 2x - 1$ below. Then explain how to find the exact coordinates.

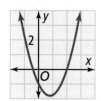

14. Higher Order Thinking Points $(2, -1)$, $(-2, 7)$, $(1, -2)$, $(0, -1)$, and $(4, 7)$ lie on the graph of a quadratic function.

a. What is the axis of symmetry of the graph?

b. What is the vertex?

c. What is the y-intercept?

d. Over what interval does the function increase?

PRACTICE

What is the y-intercept of each function?
SEE EXAMPLE 1

15. $f(x) = 2x^2 - 4x - 6$ **16.** $f(x) = 0.3x^2 + 0.6x - 0.7$

17. $f(x) = -2x^2 - 8x - 7$ **18.** $f(x) = 3x^2 + 6x + 5$

19. $f(x) = -x^2 - 2x + 3$ **20.** $f(x) = -0.5x^2 + x + 2$

Find the y-intercept, the axis of symmetry, and the vertex of the graph of each function. SEE EXAMPLE 2

21. $f(x) = 2x^2 + 8x + 2$ **22.** $f(x) = -2x^2 + 4x - 3$

23. $f(x) = 0.4x^2 + 1.6x$ **24.** $f(x) = -x^2 - 2x - 5$

25. $f(x) = 5x^2 + 5x + 12$ **26.** $f(x) = 4x^2 + 12x + 5$

27. $f(x) = x^2 - 6x + 12$ **28.** $f(x) = -2x^2 + 16x + 40$

Compare each function to function f, shown in the table. Which function has a lesser minimum value? Explain. SEE EXAMPLE 3

x	$(x, f(x))$
1	$(1, 0)$
2	$(2, -3)$
3	$(3, -4)$
4	$(4, -3)$
5	$(5, 0)$

29. $g(x) = 2x^2 + 8x + 3$ **30.** $h(x) = x^2 + x - 3.5$

Compare each function to function f, shown in the graph below. Which function has a greater maximum value? SEE EXAMPLE 3

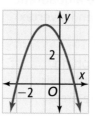

31. $g(x) = -2x^2 - 4x + 3$ **32.** $h(x) = -1.5x^2 - 4.5x + 1$

Write each function in standard form. SEE EXAMPLE 4

33. $f(x) = 4(x + 1)^2 - 3$ **34.** $f(x) = 0.1(x - 2)^2 - 0.1$

35. $f(x) = -2(x - 9)^2 + 15$ **36.** $f(x) = -(x + 3)^2 + 8$

APPLY

37. Use Structure Two balls are tossed up into the air. The function $f(x) = -4.9x^2 + 14.7x + 0.975$ models the path of Ball A. The path of Ball B over time is shown in the table. Which ball reaches a greater height? How much greater? Explain how you can answer without graphing either function.

Time (s)	Height (m)
x	g(x)
0	1.975
1	11.775
1.5	13
2	11.775
2.5	1.975

38. Use Structure The position of a ball after it is kicked can be determined by using the function $f(x) = -0.11x^2 + 2.2x + 1$, where y is the height, in feet, above the ground and x is the horizontal distance, in feet, of the ball from the point at which it was kicked. What is the height of the ball when it is kicked? What is the highest point of the ball in the air?

39. Reason A banner is hung for a party. The distance from a point on the bottom edge of the banner to the floor can be determined by using the function $f(x) = 0.25x^2 - x + 9.5$, where x is the distance, in feet, of the point from the left end of the banner. How high above the floor is the lowest point on the bottom edge of the banner? Explain.

ASSESSMENT PRACTICE

40. An object is launched at 64 ft per second from an elevated platform. The function $f(x) = -16x^2 + 64x + 6$, models its trajectory over time, x. Which of the following are true? Select all that apply.

Ⓐ The height of the platform is 6 ft.

Ⓑ The object reaches its maximum height after 2 seconds.

Ⓒ The maximum height of the object is 70 ft.

Ⓓ The object will be lower than 40 feet at 1 second.

Ⓔ The height of the object increases and then decreases.

41. SAT/ACT What is the maximum value of $f(x) = -4x^2 + 16x + 12$?

Ⓐ 12   Ⓑ 16   Ⓒ 24   Ⓓ 28   Ⓔ 64

42. Performance Task Two models are used to predict monthly revenue for a new sports drink. In each model, x is the number of $1-price increases from the original $2 per bottle price.

Model A $f(x) = -12.5x^2 + 75x + 200$

Model B

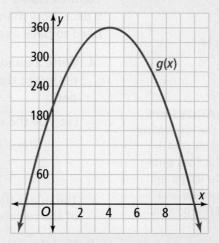

Part A Identify the price you would set for each model to maximize monthly revenue. Explain.

Part B A third model includes the points (9, 605), (8, 600), (10, 600), (7, 585), and (11, 585). What price maximizes revenue according to this model? Explain.

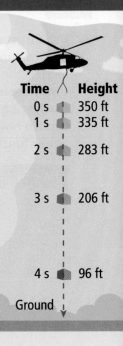
3-4

Modeling With Quadratic Functions

PearsonRealize.com

I CAN... use quadratic functions to model real-world situations.

VOCABULARY
• quadratic regression
• vertical motion model

👆 **MODEL & DISCUSS**

The graphic shows the heights of a supply package dropped from a helicopter hovering above ground.

A. Model With Mathematics Would a linear function be a good model for the data? Explain.

B. Would a quadratic function be a good model for the data? Explain.

Time	Height
0 s	350 ft
1 s	335 ft
2 s	283 ft
3 s	206 ft
4 s	96 ft
Ground	

? ESSENTIAL QUESTION What kinds of real-world situations can be modeled by quadratic functions?

APPLICATION 👆 **EXAMPLE 1** Use Quadratic Functions to Model Area

A company offers rectangular pool sizes with dimensions as shown. Each pool includes a deck around it. If Carolina wants a 15-ft wide pool with a deck, how many square feet will she need to have available in her yard?

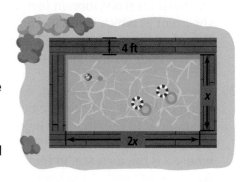

A. Write a quadratic function to represent the area of the pool and deck.

Let x be the width of the pool.

$f(x) = (2x + 8)(x + 8)$ ← Area = Length × Width

$= 2x^2 + 24x + 64$

LOOK FOR RELATIONSHIPS
To write the function, think about how the length of the pool is related to its width. Then write expressions for the length and width of the rectangular area that contains both the pool and the deck.

The quadratic function $f(x) = 2x^2 + 24x + 64$ can be used to find the area of the rectangular pool and the deck.

B. Find the area of the pool and the deck.

$f(15) = 2(15)^2 + 24(15) + 64$ ← Substitute 15 for x.

$= 874$

Carolina needs 874 ft² to build a 15-ft wide pool with deck.

✓ **Try It!** 1. Suppose the length of the pool in Example 1 is 3 times the width. How does the function that represents the combined area of the pool and the deck change? Explain.

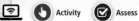

CONCEPT Vertical Motion Model

The equation $h(t) = -16t^2 + v_0t + h_0$ is the **vertical motion model**. The variable h represents the height of an object, in feet, t seconds after it is launched into the air. The term v_0 is the object's initial vertical velocity and h_0 is its initial height.

CONCEPTUAL UNDERSTANDING

 **EXAMPLE 2** Model Vertical Motion

A diver jumps off a high platform at an initial vertical velocity of 16 ft/s.

A. What quadratic function represents the height h of the diver after t seconds of the dive?

Use the vertical motion model to write the quadratic function.

$$h(t) = -16t^2 + v_0t + h_0$$

$$h(t) = -16t^2 + 16t + 30$$

Initial vertical velocity is 16 ft/s.

height of the platform is 30 ft.

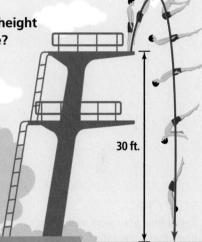

30 ft.

B. How many feet above the platform will the diver be at the highest point of his dive?

Find the maximum value of the graph described by $h(t) = -16t^2 + 16t + 30$.

$$t = -\frac{b}{2a}$$

The maximum value is located at t-value of the axis of symmetry.

$$t = -\frac{16}{2(-16)}$$

$$= \frac{1}{2}$$

$$h\left(\frac{1}{2}\right) = -16\left(\frac{1}{2}\right)^2 + 16\left(\frac{1}{2}\right) + 30$$

Substitute the t-value into the function to find $h(t)$, the y-value of the vertex.

$$= 34$$

The vertex is $\left(\frac{1}{2}, 34\right)$.

The platform is at a height of 30 ft and the vertex is at 34 ft. So the diver will be about $34 - 30$, or 4 feet above the platform.

USE STRUCTURE

What do you notice about the structure of the vertical motion model and the standard form of a quadratic function? How are they similar?

 Try It! 2. Find the diver's maximum height above the water if he dives from a 20-ft platform with an initial velocity of 8 ft/s.

Activity   Assess

APPLICATION

EXAMPLE 3 **Assess the Fit of a Function by Analyzing Residuals**

Each year, for the past five years, ticket prices for a school play have increased by $1. The director used the function $f(x) = -7x^2 + 90x + 750$ to represent the relationship between the number of price increases and the average predicted revenue per show, shown in the table. How well does the function represent the actual revenue data?

Step 1 Use the function to find the predicted values for each price increase. Subtract the predicted from the actual revenues to find the residuals.

Ticket Price ($)	Price Increase x	Actual Revenue ($)	Predicted Revenue f(x)	Residual
5	0	745	750	−5
6	1	846	833	+13
7	2	910	902	+8
8	3	952	957	−5
9	4	1008	988	+10

Step 2 Make a scatterplot of the data and graph the function on the same coordinate grid.

Step 3 Make a residual plot to show the fit of the function to the data.

STUDY TIP
Recall from your work with trend lines, that a good model would have roughly equal numbers of positive and negative residuals.

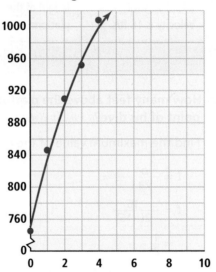

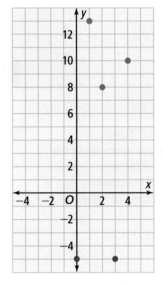

Step 4 Assess the fit of the function using the residual plot.

The residual plot shows both positive and negative residuals, which indicates a generally good model.

 Try It! 3. Make a scatterplot of the data and graph the function $f(x) = -8x^2 + 95x + 745$. Make a residual plot and describe how well the function fits the data.

Price Increase ($)	0	1	2	3	4
Sales ($)	730	850	930	951	1010

APPLICATION

EXAMPLE 4   Fit a Quadratic Function to Data

The theater director at the high school wants to find the most accurate quadratic model for ticket sales based on the data in Example 3. How would the revenue be affected if the prices increase one more time?

STUDY TIP
You may recall that *linear regression* fits a line to the data. For *quadratic regression*, you will fit a parabola to data.

Quadratic regression is a method used to find the quadratic function that best fits a data set.

Step 1   Use a graphing calculator. Enter the price increase, x, and average revenue, y, as lists.

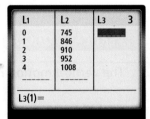

L_1 shows the number of price increases. L_2 shows the revenues.

Step 2   Use the Quadratic Regression feature.

The closer R^2 is to 1, the better the equation matches the given data points.

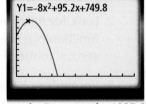

Use the values for a, b, and c to write an equation for the function.

The function $f(x) = -8x^2 + 95.2x + 749.8$ is a good model of the relationship between the number of \$1 increases and the predicted revenue per show.

Step 3   Graph the data and quadratic regression. Use the Trace function to determine the predicted revenue after the fifth \$1 price increase, so find $f(x)$ when $x = 5$.

Y1=-8x²+95.2x+749.8

$f(5) = -8(5)^2 + 95.2(5) + 749.8 = 1{,}025.8$

x scale: 5   y scale: 1025.8

REASON
Since tickets for this year are \$10 each, the predicted value of \$1,025.80 will not be the actual sales. You can reason that the actual sales will be a multiple of \$10.

If the price of a ticket increases to \$10, the predicted revenue will be \$1,025.80.

 Try It!   4. Use the model in Example 4 to determine the predicted revenue after the 6th and 7th price increases. What do you notice?

CONCEPT SUMMARY Modeling With Quadratic Functions

AREA

When the length and width of rectangle are each variable expressions, a quadratic function can be used to model the rectangle's area.

$$A = (3x + 4)(x - 2)$$
$$= 3x^2 - 2x - 8$$

$x - 2$

$3x + 4$

VERTICAL MOTION

The vertical motion model gives the height h, in feet, of an object t seconds after launch.

$$h(t) = -16t^2 + v_0 t + h_0$$

v_0 is the initial velocity

h_0 is the initial height

DATA

Quadratic regression finds the best model for a set of quadratic data.

For any model, analyzing the residuals determines how well the model fits the data.

Residual = Data value − Predicted value

Do You UNDERSTAND?

1. **ESSENTIAL QUESTION** What kinds of real-world situations can be modeled by quadratic functions?

2. **Look for Relationships** How is the function $h(t) = -16t^2 + bt + c$ related to vertical motion?

3. **Vocabulary** What does it mean in a real-world situation when the *initial velocity* is 0?

4. **Error Analysis** Chen uses $h(t) = -16t^2 + 6t + 16$ to determine the height of a ball t seconds after it is thrown at an initial velocity of 16 ft/s from an initial height of 6 ft. Describe the error Chen made.

Do You KNOW HOW?

Write a vertical motion model in the form $h(t) = -16t^2 + v_0 t + h_0$ for each situation presented. For each situation, determine how long, in seconds, it takes the thrown object to reach maximum height.

5. Initial velocity: 32 ft/s; initial height: 20 ft

6. Initial velocity: 120 ft/s; initial height: 50 ft

7. A rectangular patio has a length four times its width. It also has a 3-ft wide brick border around it. Write a quadratic function to determine the area of the patio and border.

8. The data are modeled by $f(x) = -2x^2 + 16.3x + 40.7$. What does the graph of the residuals tell you about the fit of the model?

x	y
1	55.0
2	65.3
3	71.6
4	73.9
5	72.2

UNDERSTAND

9. **Make Sense and Persevere** For each vertical motion model, identify the maximum height reached by the object and the amount of time for the object to reach the maximum height.

   a. $h(t) = -16t^2 + 200t + 25$

   b. $h(t) = -16t^2 + 36t + 4$

10. **Reason** When a student uses quadratic regression on a graphing calculator to model data, the value of R^2 is 0.2. Make a conjecture about the fit of the model.

11. **Error Analysis** Describe and correct the error a student made when interpreting the graph of the vertical motion model $h(t) = -at^2 + bt + c$.

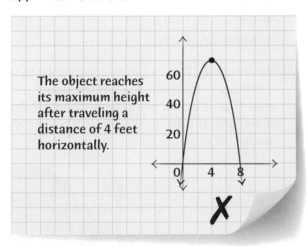

The object reaches its maximum height after traveling a distance of 4 feet horizontally.

12. **Look for Relationships** In the graph of a vertical motion model shown, how is the initial velocity related to the vertex of the parabola?

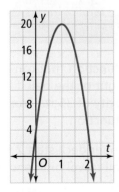

13. **Higher Order Thinking** The function $f(x) = x^2 + 3x - 10$ models the area of a rectangle.

   a. Describe the length and width of the rectangle in terms of x.

   b. What is a reasonable domain and range for the situation? Explain.

PRACTICE

Use a quadratic function to model the area of each rectangle. Graph the function. Evaluate each function for $x = 8$. SEE EXAMPLE 1

14.
$2x + 4$

$x + 3$

15.
$3x - 9$

$x + 2$

Write a function h to model the vertical motion for each situation, given $h(t) = -16t^2 + v_0t + h_0$. Find the maximum height. SEE EXAMPLE 2

16. initial vertical velocity: 32 ft/s initial height: 75 ft

17. initial vertical velocity: 200 ft/s initial height: 0 ft

18. initial vertical velocity: 50 ft/s initial height: 5 ft

19. initial vertical velocity: 48 ft/s initial height: 6 ft

Make a scatterplot of the data and graph the function on the same coordinate grid. Calculate the residuals and make a residual plot. Describe the fit of the function to the data. SEE EXAMPLE 3

20. $f(x) = 2x^2 - x + 1$

x	y
-2	13
-1	8
0	6
1	9
2	12

21. $f(x) = -x^2 + 3x + 2$

x	y
-2	-6
-1	-1
0	3
1	4
2	3

Use a graphing calculator to find a quadratic regression for each data set. Round values to the nearest ten-thousandth. SEE EXAMPLE 4

22.

x	y
0	15.50
1	11.21
2	8.43
3	5.67
4	3.43

23.

x	y
100	567.3
500	443.2
900	362.3
1,300	312.2
1,700	307.3

APPLY

24. Model With Mathematics A student drops a rock over the edge of the well and hears it splash into water after 3 seconds. Write a function in the form $h(t) = -16t^2 + v_0t + h_0$ to determine the height of the rock above the bottom of the well t seconds after the student drops the rock. What is the distance from the surface of the water to the bottom of the well?

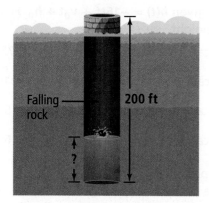

25. Construct Arguments The table below shows profits for a new model of headphones as a function of price x. The manufacturer says the price should be set at $15 to maximize profits. Do you agree? Justify your answers.

Price ($)	Profit ($ thousands)
16	240
17	223
18	200
19	173
20	140

26. Mathematical Connections Dakota bought 120 ft of wire fencing at $0.50/ft to enclose a rectangular playground. The playground surface will be covered with mulch at a cost of $1.25/ft². Write a quadratic function that can be used to determine the total cost of fencing and mulch for a playground with side length x. What is the cost if one side is 20 ft?

ASSESSMENT PRACTICE

27. The function $h(t) = -16t^2 + 96t + 10$ models the path of a projectile.

By inspecting the function you can tell that the initial height of the projectile is _____ ft, and the initial velocity is _____ ft/s.

The projectile reaches a maximum height of _____ ft at time _____ s.

28. SAT/ACT A basketball is thrown straight up into the air from a height of 2.1 ft with an initial velocity of 7 ft/s. Which function models the height of the ball after t seconds?

Ⓐ $h(t) = -16t^2 + 2.1t + 7$

Ⓑ $h(t) = -16t^2 - 2.1t + 7$

Ⓒ $h(t) = -16t^2 + 2.1t - 7$

Ⓓ $h(t) = -16t^2 + 7t + 2.1$

Ⓔ $h(t) = -16t^2 - 7t + 2.1$

29. Performance Task A baseball player is standing 1.5 ft away from the edge of the upper deck that is 20 ft above the baseball field. He throws a ball into the air for the fans sitting in the upper deck.

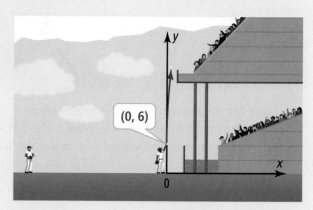

Part A Write a quadratic function that can be used to determine the height of the ball if it is thrown at an initial velocity of 35 ft/s from a height of 6 ft. Graph the function.

Part B The seats for the upper deck start 2 ft from the edge. Will the ball travel high enough to land on the upper deck?

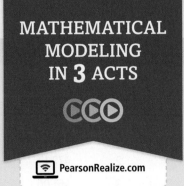

PearsonRealize.com

The Long Shot

Have you ever been to a basketball game where they hold contests at halftime? A popular contest is one where the contestant needs to make a basket from half court to win a prize. Contestants often shoot the ball in different ways. They might take a regular basketball shot, a hook shot, or an underhand toss.

What is the best way to shoot the basketball to make a basket? Think about this during this Mathematical Modeling in 3 Acts lesson.

Scan for
Multimedia

ACT 1 ▶ **Identify the Problem**

1. What is the first question that comes to mind after watching the video?

2. Write down the Main Question you will answer.

3. Make an initial conjecture that answers this Main Question.

4. Explain how you arrived at your conjecture.

ACT 2 ▶ **Develop a Model**

5. Use the math that you have learned in the topic to refine your conjecture.

ACT 3 ▶ **Interpret the Results**

6. Did your refined conjecture match the actual answer exactly? If not, what might explain the difference?

3-5

Linear, Exponential, and Quadratic Models

I CAN... determine whether a linear, exponential, or quadratic function best models a data set.

🖑 MODEL & DISCUSS

Jacy and Emma use different functions to model the value of a bike x years after it is purchased. Each function models the data in the table.

Jacy's function: $f(x) = -14.20x + 500$

Emma's function: $f(x) = 500(0.85)^x$

Time (yr)	Value ($)
0	500.00
1	485.20
2	472.13
3	461.00
4	452.10

A. Make Sense and Persevere Why did Jacy and Emma not choose a quadratic function to model the data?

B. Whose function do you think is a better model? Explain.

C. Do you agree with this statement? Explain why or why not.

> To ensure that you are finding the best model for a table of data, you need to find the values of the functions for the same values of x.

❓ ESSENTIAL QUESTION

How can you determine whether a linear, exponential, or quadratic function best models data?

CONCEPTUAL UNDERSTANDING

🖑 EXAMPLE 1 Determine Which Function Type Represents Data

A. How can you determine whether the data in the table can be modeled by a linear function?

First, confirm that the differences in the x-values are constant. Then analyze the *first differences*.

GENERALIZE
Look at the data in the table. What do you notice about the differences between consecutive y-values?

x	y	1st Differences
-2	-1	
-1	1	$1 - (-1) = 2$
0	3	$3 - 1 = 2$
1	5	$5 - 3 = 2$
2	7	$7 - 5 = 2$

(+1 between each x-value)

> The differences between consecutive y-values are the first differences.

A linear function best models the data when the first differences are constant.

CONTINUED ON THE NEXT PAGE

B. How can you determine whether the data in the table can be modeled by a quadratic function?

Analyze the *second differences*.

x	y	1st Differences	2nd Differences
0	3		
1	9	9 − 3 = 6	
2	19	19 − 9 = 10	10 − 6 = 4
3	33	33 − 19 = 14	14 − 10 = 4
4	51	51 − 33 = 18	18 − 14 = 4

First differences are not constant. Check the second differences.

The differences between consecutive first differences are called the *second differences*.

A quadratic function best models the data when the second differences are constant.

C. How can you determine whether the data in the table can be modeled by an exponential function?

The first differences and second differences are not constant. Find and analyze the ratios of consecutive *y*-values.

x	y	1st Differences	2nd Differences	Ratios of y-Values
0	1			
1	2	2 − 1 = 1		$\frac{2}{1} = 2$
2	4	4 − 2 = 2	2 − 1 = 1	$\frac{4}{2} = 2$
3	8	8 − 4 = 4	4 − 2 = 2	$\frac{8}{4} = 2$
4	16	16 − 8 = 8	8 − 4 = 4	$\frac{16}{8} = 2$

The first differences and second differences are not constant, so the data do not represent a linear or quadratic function.

The ratios of consecutive *y*-values are the same.

An exponential function best models the data when the ratios of consecutive *y*-values are the same.

 Try It!   **1.** Does a linear, quadratic, or exponential function best model the data? Explain.

a.

x	0	1	2	3	4
y	−2	−5	−14	−29	−50

b.

x	−2	−1	0	1	2
y	4	12	36	108	324

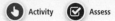
APPLICATION   🖱 **EXAMPLE 2**   **Choose a Function Type for Real-World Data**

The owner of a framing store tracks the cost of bubble wrap for packing pictures like the one shown. How can you use the data to estimate the cost of the bubble wrap for a picture with a length of 75 in.?

Length (in.)	Bubble Wrap Cost ($)
6	0.10
12	0.31
18	0.62
24	1.04
30	1.57

|← ———— 75 in. ———— →|

Step 1 Determine whether a linear, exponential, or quadratic function model best represents the data.

Analyze at the differences or ratios to determine which model best fits the data.

Length (in.) x	Bubble Wrap Cost ($) y	1st Differences	2nd Differences
6	0.10		
12	0.31	$0.31 - 0.10 = 0.21$	
18	0.62	$0.62 - 0.31 = 0.31$	$0.31 - 0.21 = 0.10$
24	1.04	$1.04 - 0.62 = 0.42$	$0.42 - 0.31 = 0.11$
30	1.57	$1.57 - 1.04 = 0.53$	$0.53 - 0.42 = 0.11$

The first differences are not constant.

The second differences are roughly constant.

A quadratic model best represents the data.

Step 2 Write a quadratic function that represents the data.

Use a graphing calculator to find a quadratic regression. Enter the data as lists, and use the quadratic regression feature.

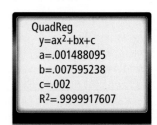

QuadReg
y=ax²+bx+c
a=.001488095
b=.007595238
c=.002
R²=.9999917607

STUDY TIP
You can find a quadratic regression for any set of data whether it is quadratic or not. Because the R^2 value is so close to 1, the quadratic equation generated by the calculator is a good model for the data.

Step 3 Substitute $x = 75$ into the equation.

Enter function
$y = 0.0015x^2 + 0.0076x + 0.002$ and evaluate for $x = 75$.

The cost of bubble wrap for a 75-in. picture is about $9.01.

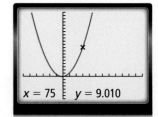

x = 75   y = 9.010

CONTINUED ON THE NEXT PAGE

EXAMPLE 2 CONTINUED

 Try It! **2.** Determine whether a linear, quadratic, or exponential function best models the data. Then, use regression to find the function that models the data.

x	0	1	2	3	4
y	100	89.5	78.9	68.4	57.8

EXAMPLE 3 **Compare Linear, Exponential, and Quadratic Growth**

The graph shows population models for three cities, based on data over a five-year period. If the populations continue to increase in the same ways, when will the population of City C exceed the populations of the other two cities?

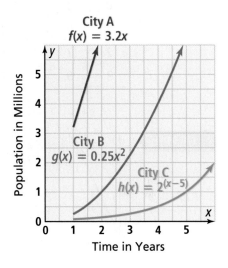

Method 1 Use the table of values.

x	$f(x)$	$g(x)$	$h(x)$
4	12.8	4.0	0.5
5	16.0	6.25	1
6	19.2	9.0	2
7	22.4	12.25	4
8	25.6	16.0	8
9	28.8	20.25	16
10	32.0	25.0	32
11	35.2	30.25	64

The population of City C is greater than those of City A and City B.

Method 2 Use a graphing calculator to determine the points of intersection.

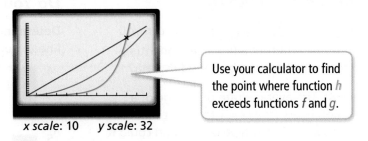

x scale: 10 *y scale:* 32

Use your calculator to find the point where function h exceeds functions f and g.

USE STRUCTURE
Look at the structure of each of the graphs. Notice that a quantity that increases exponentially will eventually exceed a quantity that increases linearly or quadratically.

After 10 years, the population of City C will exceed the populations of City A and City B. It will continue to outgrow the other cities because it is growing exponentially.

 Try It! **3.** Compare the functions $f(x) = 3x + 2$, $g(x) = 2x^2 + 3$, and $h(x) = 2^x$. Show that as x increases, $h(x)$ will eventually exceed $f(x)$ and $g(x)$.

CONCEPT SUMMARY Linear, Quadratic, and Exponential Functions

	Linear	Quadratic	Exponential
WORDS	The 1st differences are constant.	The 2nd differences are constant.	The ratios of consecutive y-values are constant.

TABLES

$f(x) = 2x + 3$

x	y	1st Differences
0	3	
1	5	2
2	7	2
3	9	2

$f(x) = 0.25x^2 + 0.5x + 0.25$

		Differences	
x	y	1st	2nd
0	0.25		
1	1.00	0.75	
2	2.25	1.25	0.5
3	4.00	1.75	0.5

$f(x) = 2^{x-3}$

x	y	Ratios
0	0.125	
1	0.25	$\frac{0.25}{0.125} = 2$
2	0.5	$\frac{0.5}{0.25} = 2$
3	1.00	$\frac{1}{0.5} = 2$

GRAPHS

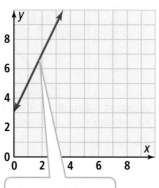

The rate of change is constant.

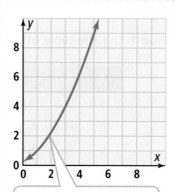

The rate of change in this function increases as the value of x increases.

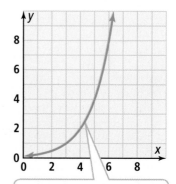

The rate of change in this function increases by equal factors as the value of x increases.

✓ Do You UNDERSTAND?

1. **ESSENTIAL QUESTION** How can you determine whether a linear, exponential, or quadratic function best models data?

2. **Reason** The average rate of change of a function is less from $x = 1$ to $x = 4$ than from $x = 5$ to $x = 8$. What type of function could it be? Explain.

3. **Error Analysis** Kiyo used a quadratic function to model data with constant first differences. Explain the error Kiyo made.

Do You KNOW HOW?

Determine whether the data are best modeled by a linear, quadratic, or exponential function.

4.

x	0	1	2	3	4
y	−2	1	10	25	46

5.

x	−2	−1	0	1	2
y	2	7	12	17	22

6. A company's profit from a certain product is represented by $P(x) = -5x^2 + 1{,}125x - 5{,}000$, where x is the price of the product. Compare the growth in profits from $x = 120$ to $x = 140$ and from $x = 140$ to $x = 160$. What do you notice?

UNDERSTAND

7. Communicate Precisely Create a flow chart to show the process to determine whether a given data set represents a function that is linear, quadratic, exponential, or none of these.

8. Generalize Calculate the 2nd differences for data in each table. Use a graphing calculator to find the quadratic regression for each data set. Make a conjecture about the relationship between the a values in the quadratic models and the 2nd differences of the data.

x	y
0	0
1	3
2	12
3	27
4	48

x	y
1	0.5
2	2
3	4.5
4	8
5	12.5

x	y
0	4
1	16
2	36
3	64
4	100

x	y
3	58.5
5	162.5
7	318.5
9	526.5
11	786.5

9. Error Analysis What is the error in the student's reasoning below? Describe how to correct the statement.

The data can be modeled with a linear function because the first differences are constant.

x	y
-3	-8
-1	-2
0	4
1	10
3	16

✗

10. Higher Order Thinking A savings account has a balance of $1. Savings Plan A will add $1,000 to an account each month, and Plan B will double the amount each month.

a. Which plan is better in the short run? For how long? Explain.

b. Which plan is better in the long run? Explain.

PRACTICE

Determine whether a linear, quadratic, or exponential function is the best model for the data in each table. SEE EXAMPLE 1

11.

x	y
0	1
1	3
2	9
3	27
4	81

12.

x	y
0	1
1	2
2	7
3	16
4	29

13.

x	y
0	56
1	57
2	50
3	35
4	12

14.

x	y
0	-6
1	-3
2	0
3	3
4	6

Do the data suggest a linear, quadratic, or an exponential function? Use regression to find a model for each data set. SEE EXAMPLE 2

15.

x	0	1	2	3	4
y	-20	-17.5	-15.1	-12.5	-10

16.

x	6	7	8	9	10
y	-19	-12	-7	-4	-3

17. Use the functions shown. SEE EXAMPLE 3

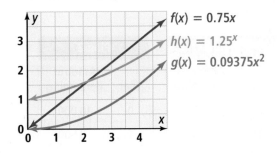

$f(x) = 0.75x$

$h(x) = 1.25^x$

$g(x) = 0.09375x^2$

a. Evaluate each function for $x = 6$, $x = 8$ and $x = 12$.

b. When will function h exceed function f and function g?

APPLY

18. Model With Mathematics The data in the table show the population of a city for the past five years. A new water plant will be built when the population exceeds 1 million. Will the city need a new water plant in the next ten years? Use a function model to justify your answer.

Year	2016	2017	2018	2019	2020
Population	794,000	803,000	814,000	822,000	830,000

19. Construct Arguments The graphic shows costs for rectangular lots of different widths. Each lot is twice as long as it is wide.

Parking Lot

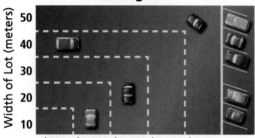

$250 $1,090 $2,450 $4,300 $6,750
Cost of Reflective Coating

To coat a parking lot 300 m long and 150 m wide, a developer budgeted $20,220, or three times the cost of a lot 50 m wide. Will the budget be sufficient? Justify your answers using a function model.

20. Construct Arguments Carmen is considering two plans to pay off a $10,000 loan. The tables show the amount remaining on the loan after x years.

Plan A		Plan B	
Year	Amount Remaining	Year	Amount Remaining
0	10,000	0	10,000
1	9,000	1	9,500
2	8,100	2	9,000
3	7,290	3	8,500
4	6,561	4	8,000

Which plan should Carmen use to pay off the loan as soon as possible? Justify your answer using a function model.

ASSESSMENT PRACTICE

21. Function f has constant second differences. Which of the following are true? Select all that apply.

Ⓐ The graph of f is a parabola.

Ⓑ The graph of f is a straight line.

Ⓒ The ratios of the y-values increase as x increases.

Ⓓ The function f is an exponential function.

Ⓔ The function f has constant first differences.

22. SAT/ACT At what point will $f(x) = 3^x$ exceed $g(x) = 2x + 5$ and $h(x) = x^2 + 4$?

Ⓐ (1, 7)

Ⓑ (1.8, 7.3)

Ⓒ (2, 9)

Ⓓ (2.4, 9.8)

23. Performance Task Ella wrote three different computer apps to analyze some data. The tables show the time in milliseconds y for each app to analyze data as a function of the number of data items x.

App A		App B		App C	
x	y	x	y	x	y
4	81	4	4,042	4	4,400
5	243	5	5,040	5	5,375
6	729	6	6,038	6	6,550
7	2,187	7	7,036	7	7,925
8	6,561	8	8,034	8	9,500

Part A Use regression on a graphing calculator to find a function that models each data set. Explain your choice of model.

Part B Make a conjecture about which app will require the most time as the number of data items gets very large. How could you support your conjecture?

Topic Review

1. How can you use sketches and equations of quadratic functions to model situations and make predictions?

Vocabulary Review

Choose the correct term to complete each sentence.

2. The graph of a quadratic function is a(n) _____.

3. The function $f(x) = x^2$ is called the _____.

4. To model the height of an object launched into the air t seconds after it is launched, you can use the _____.

5. The _____ is $f(x) = ax^2 + bx + c$.

6. A(n) _____ is a method used to find a quadratic function that best fits a data set.

- parabola
- quadratic parent function
- quadratic regression
- standard form of a quadratic function
- vertex form of a quadratic function
- vertical motion model

Concepts & Skills Review

LESSON 3-1 **Key Features of Quadratic Functions**

Quick Review

The graph of $f(x) = ax^2$ is a **parabola** with **vertex** (0, 0) and **axis of symmetry** $x = 0$. When $a > 0$, the parabola opens upward and the function has a minimum at the vertex. When $a < 0$, the parabola opens downward and the function has a maximum at the vertex.

Example

Compare the graph of $g(x) = -0.2x^2$ with the graph of $f(x) = x^2$.

The graph of g opens downward and is wider than the graph of f. For both graphs, the axis of symmetry is $x = 0$ and the vertex is (0, 0).

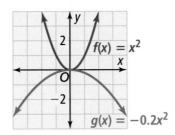

Practice and Problem Solving

Compare the graph of each function with the graph of $f(x) = x^2$.

7. $g(x) = 1.5x^2$

8. $h(x) = -9x^2$

9. **Communicate Precisely** Explain how you can you tell whether a function of the form $f(x) = ax^2$ has a minimum or a maximum value and what that value is.

10. **Model With Mathematics** Artificial turf costs $15/sq ft to install, and sod costs $0.15/sq ft to install. Write a quadratic function that represents the cost of installing artificial turf on a square plot with a side length of x feet, and a second quadratic function that represents the cost of installing sod on the same plot. How do the graphs of the two functions differ?

LESSON 3-2   Quadratic Functions in Vertex Form

Quick Review

The **vertex form of a quadratic function** is $f(x) = a(x - h)^2 + k$. The vertex of the graph is at (h, k) and the axis of symmetry is $x = h$.

Example

Graph the function $f(x) = (x + 1)^2 - 1$.

The vertex is $(-1, -1)$ and the axis of symmetry is $x = -1$.

Use the points $(0, 0)$ and $(1, 3)$ to find two other points. Reflect each point across the axis of symmetry.

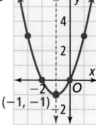

Practice and Problem Solving

11. Look for Relationships Graph the functions below. How are the graphs alike? How are the graphs different from each other?

$$f(x) = -5(x - 3)^2 + 2$$
$$g(x) = -2(x - 3)^2 + 2$$

Identify the vertex and axis of symmetry of the graph of each function.

12. $g(x) = (x + 8)^2 + 1$ **13.** $h(x) = (x - 5)^2 - 2$

14. An astronaut on the moon throws a moon rock into the air. The rock's height, in meters, above the moon's surface x seconds after it is thrown can be determined by the function $h(x) = -1.6(x - 2.5)^2 + 15$. What is the maximum height of the rock above the moon's surface? How many seconds after being thrown does the rock reach this height?

LESSON 3-3   Quadratic Functions in Standard Form

Quick Review

The **standard form of a quadratic function** is $f(x) = ax^2 + bx + c$, where $a \neq 0$. The y-intercept is c and the axis of symmetry, which is also the x-coordinate of the vertex, is $x = -\frac{b}{2a}$.

Example

Graph the function $f(x) = 3x^2 - 6x + 2$.

The y-intercept is 2.

Find the axis of symmetry.

$$x = -\frac{b}{2a} = -\frac{-6}{2(3)} = 1$$

Find the y-coordinate of the vertex.

$$f(1) = 3(1)^2 - 6(1) + 2 = -1$$

Plot the vertex $(1, -1)$ and identify the axis of symmetry.

Plot the y-intercept $(0, 2)$. Reflect that point across the axis of symmetry.

Practice and Problem Solving

Identify the y-intercept, axis of symmetry, and vertex of the graph of each function.

15. $g(x) = -x^2 + 4x + 5$ **16.** $h(x) = -3x^2 + 7x + 1$

17. When given a function in standard form, how can you determine if the parabola has a minimum or maximum value?

18. Graph the function $f(x) = -3x^2 + 12x + 5$.

19. Reason A ball is tossed into the air. The function $f(x) = -16x^2 + 4x + 5$ represents the height in feet of the ball x seconds after it is thrown. At what height was the ball tossed into the air?

TOPIC 3 Quadratic Functions

Modeling With Quadratic Functions

Quick Review

Quadratic functions can model situations. For example, the vertical motion model is a quadratic function.

Example

Alberto launches an emergency flare at an initial velocity of 64 ft/s from an initial height of 6 ft. The flare must reach a height of 100 ft to be seen by a rescue team. Is Alberto's launch successful?

Substitute 64 for v_0 and 6 for h_0 in the vertical motion model.

$$h(t) = -16t^2 + 64t + 6$$

Find the vertex $(t, h(t))$.

$$t = -\frac{b}{2a} = -\frac{64}{2(-16)} = 2$$
$$h(2) = -16(2)^2 + 64(2) + 6 = 70$$

The vertex is (2, 70).

The flare will reach a maximum height of 70 ft, so Alberto's launch is not successful.

Practice and Problem Solving

Write a function h to model the vertical motion for each situation, given $h(t) = -16t^2 + v_0t + h_0$. Find the maximum height.

20. initial velocity: 54 ft/s
     initial height: 7 ft

21. initial velocity: 18 ft/s
     initial height: 9 ft

Write a quadratic function to represent the area of each rectangle. Graph the function. Interpret the vertex and intercepts. Identify a reasonable domain and range.

22.
$x + 5$ / $2x - 1$

23.
$2x - 3$ / $x + 1$

24. **Make Sense and Persevere** Given a vertical motion model, how can you identify the amount of time an object is in the air before it reaches the ground?

Linear, Exponential, and Quadratic Models

Quick Review

To determine which function best models a data set, analyze the differences and ratios between consecutive y-values when the differences in consecutive x-values are constant.

Example

Determine whether the function below is linear, quadratic, or exponential.

x	y	1st Diff.	2nd Diff.	Ratios
0	1			
1	3	2		3
2	9	6	4	3
3	27	18	12	3

Since the ratio between the y-values is constant, the function is exponential.

Practice and Problem Solving

25. **Make Sense and Persevere** What is the first step in determining whether a table shows a linear, quadratic, or exponential function?

Determine whether the data in the tables represent a linear, quadratic, or exponential function.

26.

x	0	1	2	3	4
y	3	7	19	39	67

27.

x	−2	0	2	4	6
y	−20	−6	8	22	36

Solving Quadratic Equations

How do you use quadratic equations to model situations and solve problems?

Topic Overview

enVision® STEM Project:
Designing a T-Shirt Launcher

Mathematical Modeling in 3 Acts:
Unwrapping Change

Topic Vocabulary

- linear-quadratic system
- Product Property of Square Roots
- quadratic equation
- standard form of a quadratic equation
- Zero-Product Property
- zeros of a function

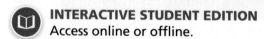

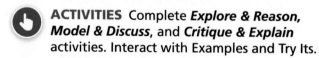

Digital Experience

INTERACTIVE STUDENT EDITION
Access online or offline.

ACTIVITIES Complete *Explore & Reason*, *Model & Discuss*, and *Critique & Explain* activities. Interact with Examples and Try Its.

ANIMATION View and interact with real-world applications.

PRACTICE Practice what you've learned.

Go online | **PearsonRealize.com**

⏸ 🔊   ⚙ ⛶

▶ Unwrapping Change

When you arrange a group of objects in different ways, it seems like the space they take up has changed. But, the number of objects didn't change!

We use coin wrappers to store coins in an efficient way. How much more efficient is it than the alternative? Think about this during the Mathematical Modeling in 3 Acts lesson.

TOPIC 4

▶ **VIDEOS** Watch clips to support *Mathematical Modeling in 3 Acts Lessons* and **enVision®** *STEM Projects.*

CONCEPT SUMMARY Review key lesson content through multiple representations.

☑ **ASSESSMENT** Show what you've learned.

A-Z **GLOSSARY** Read and listen to English and Spanish definitions.

⏻ **TUTORIALS** Get help from *Virtual Nerd*, right when you need it.

🔧 **MATH TOOLS** Explore math with digital tools and manipulatives.

Did You Know?

Objects launched or thrown into the air follow a **parabolic path**. The force of gravity and the horizontal and vertical velocities determine a quadratic function for an object's path.

The **weaker the gravity**, the higher an object will **fly** and the longer it will remain airborn.

Gravity

Earth:
9.8 m/s²

Mars
3.7 m/s²

Moon
1.6 m/s²

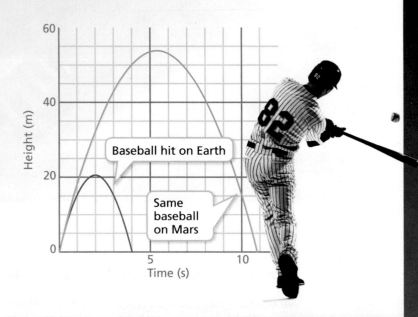

Baseball hit on Earth

Same baseball on Mars

T-shirt launchers are used at sporting events to send shirts to fans high in the stands. Some t-shirts can travel as far as **400 feet**.

▶ Your Task: Designing a T-Shirt Launcher

You and your classmates will design a t-shirt launcher and determine possible heights and distances on Earth and other planets.

4-1

Solving Quadratic Equations Using Graphs and Tables

PearsonRealize.com

I CAN... use graphs and tables to find solutions of quadratic equations.

VOCABULARY
- quadratic equation
- zeros of a function

EXPLORE & REASON

The path of a golf ball hit from the ground resembles the shape of a parabola.

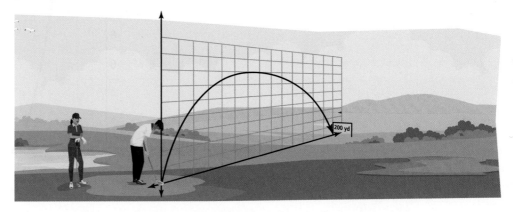

A. What point represents the golf ball before it is hit off the ground?

B. What point represents the golf ball when it lands on the ground?

C. Look for Relationships Explain how the points in Part A and B are related to the ball's distance from the ground.

❓ ESSENTIAL QUESTION

How can graphs and tables help you solve quadratic equations?

CONCEPTUAL UNDERSTANDING

👆 EXAMPLE 1   Recognize Solutions of Quadratic Equations

Why are the *x*-intercepts of the graph of a quadratic function important to the solution of a related equation?

A. Find the solutions of the quadratic equation $x^2 - 16 = 0$.

A **quadratic equation** is an equation of the second degree. The related function of a quadratic equation with 0 on one side is the quadratic expression given on the other side.

Graph the related function, $f(x) = x^2 - 16$.

CONSTRUCT ARGUMENTS
Think about the connection between the graph of the function and the solutions to the quadratic equation. What evidence can you give that the *x*-intercept is the solution of the quadratic equation?

The solutions of a quadratic equation are the value or values that make the equation true.

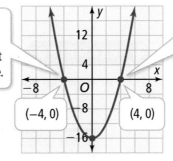

The *x*-intercepts of *f* occur where $x^2 - 16 = 0$ and represent the solutions of the equation.

$(-4, 0)$ $(4, 0)$

The graph of the function has two *x*-intercepts, so the equation has two real solutions. The solutions of the equation $x^2 - 16 = 0$ are $x = -4$ and $x = 4$. Solutions to an equation of the form $f(x) = 0$, are called the **zeros of a function.** The zeros of a function correspond to the *x*-intercepts of the function.

CONTINUED ON THE NEXT PAGE

EXAMPLE 1 CONTINUED

B. Find the solutions of $x^2 - 14x + 49 = 0$.

Graph the related function $f(x) = x^2 - 14x + 49$.

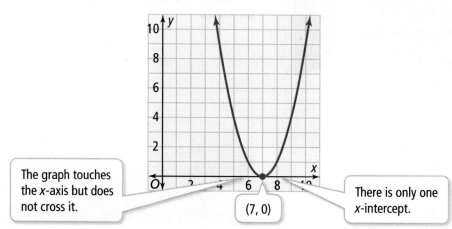

> The graph touches the x-axis but does not cross it.

(7, 0)

> There is only one x-intercept.

The graph of the function has only one x-intercept, so the equation has only one real solution, $x = 7$.

C. Find the solutions of $x^2 + 3x + 7 = 0$.

Graph the related function $f(x) = x^2 + 3x + 7$.

The graph of the function has no x-intercepts, so the equation has no real solutions.

STUDY TIP
A quadratic equation can have 0, 1, or 2 real solutions.

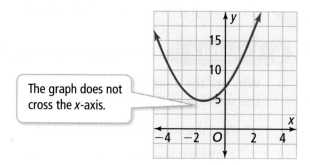

> The graph does not cross the x-axis.

✓ **Try It!** **1.** What are the solutions of each equation?

    a. $x^2 - 36 = 0$ **b.** $x^2 + 6x + 9 = 0$

👆 **EXAMPLE 2**   **Solve Quadratic Equations Using Tables**

A. How can you use a table to find the solutions of $x^2 - 7x + 6 = 0$?

Enter the function $y = x^2 - 7x + 6$ into a graphing calculator.

LOOK FOR RELATIONSHIPS
How would the solutions of this quadratic equation appear in a graph?

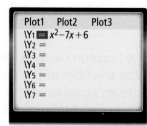

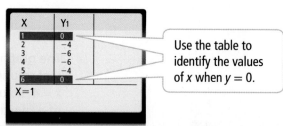

> Use the table to identify the values of x when $y = 0$.

There are two real solutions, $x = 1$ and $x = 6$.

CONTINUED ON THE NEXT PAGE

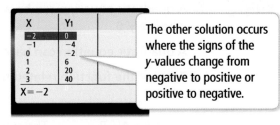

EXAMPLE 2 CONTINUED

B. How can you use a table to estimate the solutions of $3x^2 + 5x - 2 = 0$?

USE APPROPRIATE TOOLS
The solution may not always appear in a table when $y = 0$. Would a graph be more useful in finding the solution for this quadratic equation?

Enter the function $y = 3x^2 + 5x - 2$ into a graphing calculator.

The table shows one solution, $x = -2$.

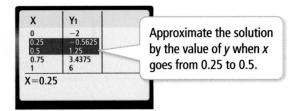

The other solution occurs where the signs of the y-values change from negative to positive or positive to negative.

Refine the table settings to find the other solution of the equation. Change the table settings to show steps of 0.25.

The other solution is between 0.25 and 0.5.

Using a table has limitations. When the corresponding x-values for $y = 0$ are not shown in the table, you can estimate the solution.

Approximate the solution by the value of y when x goes from 0.25 to 0.5.

✓ **Try It!** 2. Find the solutions for $4x^2 + 3x - 7 = 0$ using a table. If approximating, give the answer to the nearest tenth.

APPLICATION ▶ 👆 **EXAMPLE 3** **Use Approximate Solutions**

Anastasia hits her golf ball off the tee. The height of the golf ball is modeled by the function $f(x) = -5x^2 + 25x + 1$, where x is the number of seconds after the golf ball is hit. How long is the golf ball in the air?

Graph $f(x) = -5x^2 + 25x + 1$ to find when $y = 0$.

The graph of the function shows the x-intercept at 5.04. This means the golf ball was in the air about 5 seconds before it hit the ground.

CONSTRUCT ARGUMENTS
What are the benefits of using a graph to approximate a solution? When is a table more useful than a graph?

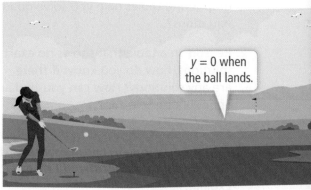

$y = 0$ when the ball lands.

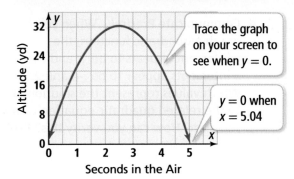

Trace the graph on your screen to see when $y = 0$.

$y = 0$ when $x = 5.04$

✓ **Try It!** 3. At the next tee, a golf ball was hit and modeled by $-16x^2 + 11x + 6 = 0$. When will the golf ball hit the ground?

LESSON 4-1 Solving Quadratic Equations Using Graphs and Tables   147

CONCEPT SUMMARY Solving Quadratic Equations Using Graphs and Tables

WORDS A quadratic equation can be written in standard form $ax^2 + bx + c = 0$, where $a \neq 0$.

A quadratic equation can have 0, 1, or 2 real solutions.

Zeros of the function related to a quadratic equation are the solutions of the equation.

ALGEBRA $x^2 + 5x + 4 = 0$ The solutions are $x = -4$ and $x = -1$.

GRAPH $f(x) = x^2 + 5x + 4$

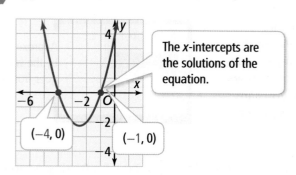

The x-intercepts are the solutions of the equation.

$(-4, 0)$ $(-1, 0)$

TABLE

x	y
−5	4
−4	0
−3	−2
−2	−2
−1	0

The solutions are the x-values when the y-values are 0.

Do You UNDERSTAND?

1. **ESSENTIAL QUESTION** How can graphs and tables help you solve quadratic equations?

2. **Reason** In a table that shows no exact solutions, how do you know if there are any solutions? How can you find an approximate solution?

3. **Error Analysis** Eli says that the solutions to $x^2 + 100 = 0$ are −10 and 10 because 10^2 is 100. What is the error that Eli made? Explain.

4. **Communicate Precisely** When you graph a quadratic function, the y-intercept appears to be 1, and the x-intercepts appear to be −4 and 2.5. Which values represent the solution(s) to the related quadratic equation of the function? How can you verify this? Explain.

Do You KNOW HOW?

Use each graph to find the solution of the equation.

5. $-x^2 + 2x - 1 = 0$ 6. $x^2 + x - 6 = 0$

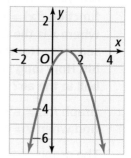 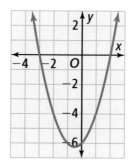

Solve each quadratic equation by graphing the related function.

7. $x^2 - 2x - 3 = 0$ 8. $x^2 + x + 1 = 0$

Find the solutions of each equation using a table. Round approximate solutions to the nearest tenth.

9. $x^2 + 3x - 4 = 0$ 10. $3x^2 - 2x + 1 = 0$

11. What are the solutions of $-5x^2 + 10x + 2 = 0$? Round approximate solutions to the nearest tenth.

PRACTICE & PROBLEM SOLVING

UNDERSTAND

12. Communicate Precisely Consider the quadratic equation $x^2 + 2x - 24 = 0$.

  a. How could you solve the equation using a graph? Explain.

  b. How could you solve the equation using a table? Explain.

13. Generalize For an equation of the form $ax^2 + bx + c = 0$, where the graph crosses the y-axis once and does not intersect the x-axis. Describe the solution(s) of the equation.

14. Error Analysis Describe and correct the error a student made in stating the number of solutions of a quadratic equation. Explain.

> A quadratic equation has either two solutions or no solution. ✗

15. Higher Order Thinking Infinitely many quadratic equations of the form $ax^2 + bx + c = 0$ can have the same two solutions. Sketch the graphs of two quadratic functions on the same grid to show how this could be true.

16. Communicate Precisely How many zeros does the function shown have? Explain.

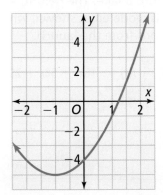

17. Mathematical Connections If a quadratic function has a maximum value that is greater than 0, how many zeros does the function have? Explain.

PRACTICE

Use each graph to find the solution of the related equation. SEE EXAMPLE 1

18. $x^2 - 2x + 2 = 0$

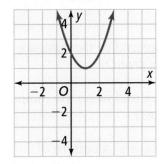

19. $-x^2 - x + 6 = 0$

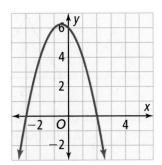

Solve each quadratic equation by graphing the related function. Round approximate solutions to the nearest tenth. SEE EXAMPLES 1 AND 3

20. $x^2 - 121 = 0$ **21.** $x^2 - 4x + 4 = 0$

22. $x^2 + 3x + 7 = 0$ **23.** $x^2 - 5x = 0$

24. $-x^2 + 6x + 7 = 0$ **25.** $-x^2 + 8x - 7 = 0$

26. $x^2 - 2 = 0$ **27.** $2x^2 - 11x + 12 = 0$

28. $-3x^2 + 5x + 7 = 0$ **29.** $-16x^2 + 70 = 0$

Find the solutions for each equation using a table. Round approximate solutions to the nearest tenth. SEE EXAMPLE 2

30. $x^2 - 16 = 0$ **31.** $x^2 + 8x + 16 = 0$

32. $x^2 + 3x + 1 = 0$ **33.** $x^2 + 4x + 6 = 0$

APPLY

34. Model With Mathematics A small company shows the profits from their business with the function $P(x) = -0.01x^2 + 60x + 500$, where x is the number of units they sell and P is the profit in dollars.

a. How many units are sold by the company to earn the maximum profit?

b. How many units are sold when the company starts showing a loss?

35. Make Sense and Persevere A pattern of triangular numbers is shown. The first is 1, the second is 3, the third is 6, and so on.

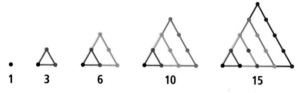

1   3   6   10   15

The formula $0.5n^2 + 0.5n$ can be used to find the nth triangular number. Is 50 a triangular number? Explain.

36. Make Sense and Persevere The equation $-16x^2 + 10x + 15 = 0$ represents the height, in feet, of a flotation device above the water after x seconds. The linear term represents the initial velocity. The constant term represents the initial height.

a. If the initial velocity is 0, when should the flotation device land in the water?

b. If the initial height is 0, when does the flotation device land in the water?

ASSESSMENT PRACTICE

37. Does each quadratic equation have two solutions? Select *Yes* or *No*.

	Yes	No
$0 = 2x^2 + 1$	☐	☐
$0 = 2x^2 + 5x + 1$	☐	☐
$0 = 2x^2 + 5x$	☐	☐
$0 = 4x^2 - 4x + 1$	☐	☐
$0 = 4x^2 - 4x - 1$	☐	☐

38. SAT/ACT What are the solutions of $x^2 + 2x - 15 = 0$ using the graph shown?

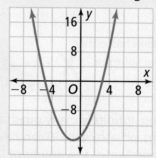

Ⓐ $-3, 3$ Ⓑ $-5, 3$

Ⓒ $-8, 5$ Ⓓ $-16, 0$

39. Performance Task A human catapult is used to launch a person into a lake. The height, in feet, of the person is modeled as shown, where x is the time in seconds from the launch.

$f(x) = -16x^2 + 50x + 20$

Part A What equation can you use to find when the person touches the lake? Find the solution.

Part B Are your solutions the same for the equation and problem? Why or why not?

Part C What is the greatest height reached?

4-2

Solving Quadratic Equations by Factoring

PearsonRealize.com

I CAN... find the solution of a quadratic equation by factoring.

VOCABULARY
• standard form of a quadratic equation
• Zero-Product Property

MODEL & DISCUSS

An artist has started a mosaic tile design on a wall. She needs to cover the entire wall.

4 ft

6 ft

X

X

A. Write expressions to represent the length of the wall and width of the wall.

B. Use Structure What expression represents the area of the entire wall? Explain.

C. How can you determine the area of the part of the wall that the artist has not yet covered?

? ESSENTIAL QUESTION

How does factoring help you solve quadratic equations?

EXAMPLE 1 Use the Zero-Product Property

How can you find the solution of the equation $(x - 9)(5x + 2) = 0$?

The **Zero-Product Property** states that for all real numbers a and b, if $ab = 0$, then either $a = 0$ or $b = 0$.

Set each factor of the equation equal to zero to find the solution.

$(x - 9) = 0$ or $(5x + 2) = 0$

$x = 9$ Either $(x - 9)$ or $(5x + 2)$ is equal to 0 according to the Zero-Product Property. $x = -\frac{2}{5}$

LOOK FOR RELATIONSHIPS
Think about solving this equation using a table and graph. How would the solutions appear in a table? In a graph?

Check each solution.

Substitute 9 for x.

$(9 - 9)(5(9) + 2) = 0$

$(0)(47) = 0$

$0 = 0$ ✓

Substitute $-\frac{2}{5}$ for x.

$\left(-\frac{2}{5} - 9\right)\left(5\left(-\frac{2}{5}\right) + 2\right) = 0$

$\left(-9\frac{2}{5}\right)(0) = 0$

$0 = 0$ ✓

The solutions of $(x - 9)(5x + 2) = 0$ are $x = 9$ and $x = -\frac{2}{5}$.

 Try It! **1.** Solve each equation.

a. $(2x - 1)(x + 3) = 0$

b. $(2x + 3)(3x - 1) = 0$

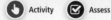
CONCEPTUAL
UNDERSTANDING

 EXAMPLE 2 Solve by Factoring

How can you use factoring to solve $x^2 + 9x = -20$?

The **standard form of a quadratic equation** is $ax^2 + bx + c = 0$, where $a \neq 0$.

Step 1 Write the equation in standard form.

$$x^2 + 9x = -20$$
$$x^2 + 9x + 20 = 0$$

> When solving a quadratic equation by factoring, always begin by writing the equation in standard form.

Step 2 Make a table to find the set of factors to solve $x^2 + 9x + 20 = 0$. The set of factors that have a product of 20 and a sum of 9 can be used to solve the equation.

Factors of 20	Sum of Factors
1, 20	21
2, 10	12
4, 5	9

> The factors 4 and 5 have a product of **20** and a sum of **9.**

STUDY TIP
If you can factor the standard form of the equation then you can find the solution.

Step 3 Rewrite the standard form of the equation in factored form.

$$(x + 4)(x + 5) = 0$$

Step 4 Use the Zero-Product Property to solve the equation.

$$(x + 4) = 0 \qquad \text{or} \qquad (x + 5) = 0$$
$$x = -4 \qquad\qquad\qquad x = -5$$

The solutions of $x^2 + 9x + 20 = 0$ are $x = -4$ and $x = -5$.

✓ **Try It!** **2.** Solve each equation by factoring.

    a. $x^2 + 16x + 64 = 0$ **b.** $x^2 - 12x = 64$

APPLICATION

👆 **EXAMPLE 3** Use Factoring to Solve a Real-World Problem

A museum vault has an outer steel wall with a uniform width of x. The area of the museum vault ceiling and the outer steel wall is 1,664 ft². What is the width of the outer steel wall?

20 ft   40 ft   x

Formulate ◄ Write an equation to represent the area of the vault.

$$(2x + 20)(2x + 40) = 1,664$$

> length × width = area

Compute ◄ Use the Distributive Property. Write the equation in standard form.

$$(2x + 20)(2x + 40) = 1,664$$
$$4x^2 + 120x - 864 = 0$$
$$\frac{4x^2}{4} + \frac{120x}{4} - \frac{864}{4} = \frac{0}{4}$$

> Divide each term by 4 to simplify the equation.

$$x^2 + 30x - 216 = 0$$
$$(x - 6)(x + 36) = 0$$

CONTINUED ON THE NEXT PAGE

EXAMPLE 3 CONTINUED

Interpret ◀ The solutions of the equation are $x = 6$ and $x = -36$.

The length of the wall cannot be negative. Therefore -36 cannot be a solution. The width of the wall is 6 ft.

Check the solution.

Substitute 6 for x in the original equation.

$$[2(6) + 20] \ [2(6) + 40] = 1{,}664$$

$$(32)(52) = 1{,}664 \ \checkmark$$

✓ **Try It!** **3.** A picture inside a frame has an area of 375 cm².

What is the width of the frame?

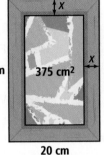

30 cm   375 cm²   ↕ x   ↔ x

20 cm

👆 **EXAMPLE 4** **Use Factored Form to Graph a Quadratic Function**

How can you use factoring to graph the function $f(x) = x^2 - 2x - 8$?

Step 1 Factor the related quadratic equation.

$$x^2 - 2x - 8 = 0$$
$$(x + 2)(x - 4) = 0$$

Step 2 Determine the solutions of the equation.

$$(x + 2) = 0 \qquad \text{or} \qquad (x - 4) = 0$$
$$x = -2 \qquad\qquad\qquad x = 4$$

STUDY TIP
A parabola is symmetrical so the vertex is halfway between the two x-intercepts.

Step 3 Find the coordinates of the vertex. Find the average of the x-intercepts 4 and -2.

$$\frac{4 + (-2)}{2} = 1$$

The x-coordinate of the vertex is 1.

Find the y-coordinate of the vertex.

Substitute the x-coordinate in the quadratic function.

$$f(x) = (1)^2 - 2(1) - 8 = -9$$

The vertex is $(1, -9)$.

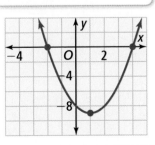

Step 4 Plot the vertex and the x-intercepts.

Use the vertex and x-intercepts to sketch the graph.

✓ **Try It!** **4.** Use factoring to graph the function $f(x) = 2x^2 + 5x - 3$.

 EXAMPLE 5 Write the Factored Form of a Quadratic Function

How can you write the factored form of the quadratic function related to a graph?

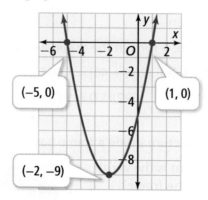

(−5, 0)

(1, 0)

(−2, −9)

Step 1 Find the *x*-intercepts.

The *x*-intercepts are −5 and 1.

Step 2 Write a quadratic equation in factored form.

Use the *x*-intercepts, which are also the solutions of the quadratic equation, as the factors.

$$a(x - p)(x - q) = 0$$
$$a[x - (-5)]\ [x - (1)] = 0$$
$$a(x + 5)(x - 1) = 0$$

> Substitute the *x*-intercepts for *p* and *q*.

STUDY TIP
There are an infinite number of parabolas that pass through (−5, 0) and (1, 0). You will need to determine the value of *a* to find the one parabola that also passes through (−2, −9).

Step 3 Write the function in factored form.

Use a third point to solve for *a*.

$$f(x) = a(x + 5)(x - 1)$$
$$-9 = a(-2 + 5)(-2 - 1)$$
$$a = 1$$

> Use the vertex. Substitute −2 for *x* and −9 for *f(x)*.

The factored form of the quadratic function is $f(x) = 1(x + 5)(x - 1)$ or $f(x) = (x + 5)(x - 1)$.

✓ **Try It!** **5.** What is the factored form of the function?

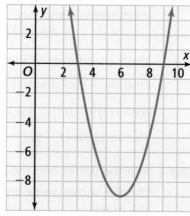

📶 **Go Online** | PearsonRealize.com

CONCEPT SUMMARY Solving Quadratic Equations by Factoring

WORDS ▸ The **Zero-Product Property** states that for all real numbers a and b, if $ab = 0$, then either $a = 0$ or $b = 0$. You can apply the Zero-Product Property to a factored quadratic equation to help you find the x-intercepts of the graph of the related function.

ALGEBRA ▸ $x^2 + 2x - 3 = 5$

$$x^2 + 2x - 8 = 0$$

$$(x + 4)(x - 2) = 0$$

> Write the equation in standard form and factor.

$$(x + 4) = 0 \qquad \text{or} \qquad (x - 2) = 0$$

$$x = -4 \qquad\qquad\qquad x = 2$$

The solutions of the quadratic equation are $x = -4$ and $x = 2$.

GRAPH ▸ $f(x) = x^2 + 2x - 8$

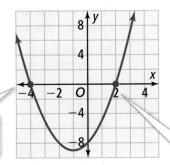

The x-intercepts are −4 and 2.

The x-intercepts of the graph correspond to the zeros of the function.

✓ Do You UNDERSTAND?

1. **ESSENTIAL QUESTION** How does factoring help you solve quadratic equations?

2. **Use Structure** Compare the solutions of $2x^2 + 5x - 7 = 0$ and $4x^2 + 10x - 14 = 0$. What do you notice? Explain.

3. **Vocabulary** What is the *Zero-Product Property*? When can you use it to solve a quadratic equation? Explain.

4. **Generalize** If a perfect-square trinomial has a value of 0, how many solutions does the equation have? Explain.

Do You KNOW HOW?

Solve each equation.

5. $(x - 10)(x + 20) = 0$

6. $(3x + 4)(x - 4) = 0$

Solve each equation by factoring.

7. $x^2 + 18x + 32 = 0$

8. $x^2 - 4x - 21 = 0$

Solve each equation.

9. $x^2 + 2x = -1$

10. $x^2 - 8x = 9$

11. $2x^2 + x = 15$

12. $5x^2 - 19x = -18$

13. Write a quadratic equation, in factored form, whose solutions correspond to the x-intercepts of the quadratic function shown at the right.

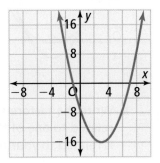

14. Factor the equation $x^2 - 6x + 5 = 0$.
Find the coordinates of the vertex of the related function, and graph the function $y = x^2 - 6x + 5$.

UNDERSTAND

15. Reason One solution of a quadratic equation is 8. What do you know about the quadratic equation? What are two ways you would know if a quadratic equation could have this solution?

16. Communicate Precisely Write a quadratic equation for each condition below. Explain your reasoning.

   a. The equation has solutions that are opposites.

   b. The equation has one solution.

17. Error Analysis Describe and correct the error a student made in factoring.

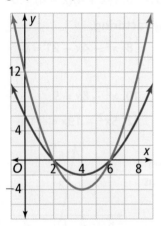

$$x^2 + 2x - 3 = 5$$
$$(x - 1)(x + 3) = 5$$
$$x - 1 = 5 \text{ or } x + 3 = 5$$
$$x = 6 \text{ or } x = 2$$

18. Make Sense and Persevere Explain how you would factor $2x^2 + 8x + 6 = 0$.

19. Higher Order Thinking Both parabolas are graphs of quadratic functions.

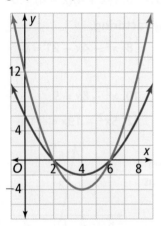

   a. Write the factored form of the equation related to one of the functions. Which curve is related to your function?

   b. Use a constant factor to find the equation related to the other function.

   c. What relationship do you see between the two functions? How are these reflected in the constant?

PRACTICE

Solve each equation. SEE EXAMPLE 1

20. $(x - 5)(x + 2) = 0$ **21.** $(2x - 5)(7x + 2) = 0$

22. $3(x + 2)(x - 2) = 0$ **23.** $(3x - 8)^2 = 0$

Solve each equation by factoring.
SEE EXAMPLES 2 AND 3

24. $x^2 + 2x + 1 = 0$ **25.** $x^2 - 5x - 14 = 0$

26. $x^2 + 7x = 0$ **27.** $2x^2 - 5x + 2 = 0$

28. $2x^2 + 3x = 5$ **29.** $5x^2 + 16x = -3$

Write an equation to represent the shaded area. Then find the value of x. SEE EXAMPLE 3

30. Total area = 198 cm²

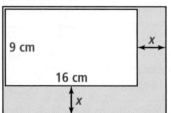

9 cm

16 cm

x

x

31.

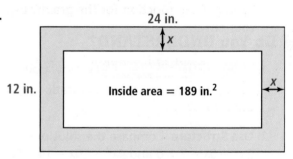

24 in.

12 in.

Inside area = 189 in.²

x

x

Factor, find the coordinates of the vertex of the related function, then graph. SEE EXAMPLE 4

32. $x^2 - 2x - 63 = 0$ **33.** $x^2 + 16x + 63 = 0$

Write the factored form for the quadratic function. SEE EXAMPLE 5

34.

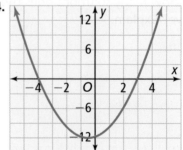

PRACTICE & PROBLEM SOLVING

APPLY

35. Mathematical Connections A streamer is launched 3 s after a fuse is lit and lands 8 s after it is lit.

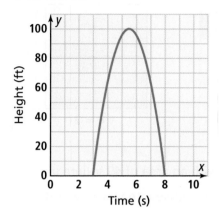

a. What is a quadratic equation in factored form that models the situation?

b. What is the vertex of the function related to your equation? How does this compare with the vertex of the graph?

c. What can you multiply your factored form by to get the function for the graph? Explain your answer.

36. Use Structure A 15 ft long cable is connected from a hook to the top of a pole that has an unknown height. The distance from the hook to the base of the pole is 3 ft shorter than the height of the pole.

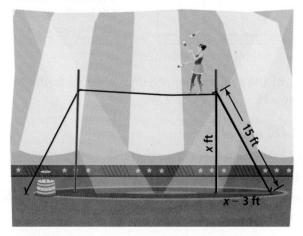

a. What can you use to find the height of the pole?

b. Write and solve a quadratic equation to find the height of the pole.

c. How far is the hook from the base of the pole?

ASSESSMENT PRACTICE

37. Match each equation with one or more factors of its standard form.

I. $x^2 + 6x = -8$ A. $2x - 3$

II. $2x^2 + x = 6$ B. $x + 4$

III. $x^2 + 2x = 8$ C. $x - 4$

IV. $2x^2 + 5x = 12$ D. $x + 2$

V. $2x^2 - 11x = -12$ E. $x - 2$

38. SAT/ACT A quadratic equation of the form $x^2 + bx + c = 0$ has a solution of −2. Its related function has a vertex at (2.5, −20.25). What is the other solution to the equation?

Ⓐ −11

Ⓑ −4.5

Ⓒ 0.5

Ⓓ 7

Ⓔ 9

39. Performance Task An engineer is designing a water fountain that starts 1 ft off of the edge of a 10 ft wide pool. The water from the fountain needs to project into the center of the pool. The path of the water from the fountain is in the shape of a parabola.

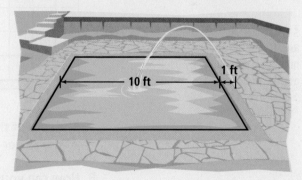

Part A Let the the point (1, 0) be the location of the starting point of the water. Write a quadratic equation to model the path of the water.

Part B What is the maximum height of the water? Use your equation from Part A.

Part C What is the equation for the path of the water if the maximum height of the water must be 4 ft?

4-3

Rewriting Radical Expressions

 PearsonRealize.com

I CAN... write equivalent radical expressions.

VOCABULARY
- Product Property of Square Roots

EXPLORE & REASON

The table shows the relationship between the area of a square, the side length of the square, and the square root of the area. A square with an area of 4 and a side length of 2 is shown at the right.

Area of Square (square units)	$s = \sqrt{\text{area}}$	Side Length, s (units)
1	$s = \sqrt{1}$	1
4	$s = \sqrt{4}$	2
9	$s = \sqrt{9}$	3
16	$s = \sqrt{16}$	4
25	$s = \sqrt{25}$	5

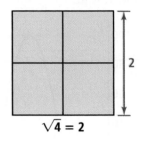

$\sqrt{4} = 2$

A. What is the side length of a square with an area of 49 square units?

B. Use Structure Between what two consecutive integers is $\sqrt{20}$? How do you know?

C. Think of three squares that have a side length between 3 and 4. What is the area of each square?

ESSENTIAL QUESTION How does rewriting radicals in different forms help you communicate your answers?

CONCEPTUAL UNDERSTANDING

EXAMPLE 1   Use Properties to Rewrite Radical Expressions

A. How can you visually show $\sqrt{16}$ is equivalent to $2\sqrt{4}$?

STUDY TIP
Recall that the square root is a number you multiply by itself to get the radicand.

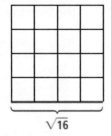

$\sqrt{16}$

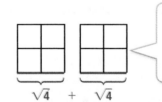

$\sqrt{4}$ + $\sqrt{4}$

Draw squares using grid paper that have side lengths equal to the two radicals.

The sum of the lengths of the two smaller red lines is equal to the length of the larger red line, so $\sqrt{16} = \sqrt{4} + \sqrt{4}$ or $2\sqrt{4}$.

B. How can you compare $\sqrt{20}$ and $2\sqrt{5}$?

The **Product Property of Square Roots** states that $\sqrt{ab} = \sqrt{a} \cdot \sqrt{b}$ when both a and b are greater than or equal to 0.

Use properties of square roots to show an equivalent expression for $\sqrt{20}$.

Write $\sqrt{20}$ as a product of square roots.

$\sqrt{20} = \sqrt{4} \cdot \sqrt{5}$

$\quad\quad = \sqrt{2 \cdot 2} \cdot \sqrt{5}$

$\quad\quad = 2\sqrt{5}$

A perfect square factor of 20 is 4.

The radical expression $\sqrt{20}$ is equivalent to $2\sqrt{5}$.

CONTINUED ON THE NEXT PAGE

EXAMPLE 1 CONTINUED

 Try It!   **1.** Compare each pair of radical expressions.

   a. $\sqrt{36}$ and $3\sqrt{6}$ **b.** $6\sqrt{2}$ and $\sqrt{72}$

EXAMPLE 2   **Write Equivalent Radical Expressions**

What is an equivalent expression for $\sqrt{63}$?

$$\sqrt{63} = \sqrt{9 \cdot 7}$$

> Write a factorization of 63 using as many perfect squares as possible. Note that 9 is a perfect square.

$$= \sqrt{3 \cdot 3} \cdot \sqrt{7}$$

$$= 3\sqrt{7}$$

The expression $\sqrt{63}$ is equivalent to $3\sqrt{7}$.

 Try It!   **2.** Rewrite each expression to remove perfect square factors other than 1 in the radicand.

   a. $\sqrt{44}$ **b.** $3\sqrt{27}$

EXAMPLE 3   **Write Equivalent Radical Expressions With Variables**

What is an equivalent expression for $\sqrt{63x^9}$?

Rewrite the expressions to remove perfect square factors in the radicand.

USE STRUCTURE
Think about the exponents of variables in terms that are perfect squares. How does the exponent of a variable determine when there is a perfect square factor of the expression?

$$\sqrt{63x^9} = \sqrt{9 \cdot 7 \cdot x^9}$$

$$= \sqrt{9 \cdot 7 \cdot x^4 \cdot x^4 \cdot x}$$

> Rewrite x^9 as $x^4 \cdot x^4 \cdot x$ to show the perfect square factors.

$$= \sqrt{3 \cdot 3} \cdot \sqrt{7} \cdot \sqrt{x^4 \cdot x^4} \cdot \sqrt{x}$$

$$= 3x^4\sqrt{7x}$$

The expression $\sqrt{63x^9}$ is equivalent to $3x^4\sqrt{7x}$.

 Try It!   **3.** Rewrite each expression to remove perfect square factors other than 1 in the radicand.

   a. $\sqrt{25x^3}$ **b.** $5\sqrt{4x^{17}}$

EXAMPLE 4   **Multiply Radical Expressions**

How can you write an expression for the product of $3\sqrt{5x} \cdot 2\sqrt{15x^3}$ without any perfect square factors in the radicand?

Find the product.

$$3\sqrt{5x} \cdot 2\sqrt{15x^3}$$

$$= 3 \cdot 2\sqrt{5x \cdot 15x^3}$$ Use the Product Property of Square Roots to multiply the radicands.

$$= 6\sqrt{5 \cdot 3 \cdot 5 \cdot x^4}$$

$$= 6 \cdot \sqrt{5 \cdot 5} \cdot \sqrt{3} \cdot \sqrt{x^2 \cdot x^2}$$ Rewrite to show the perfect-square factors.

$$= 6 \cdot 5 \cdot x^2 \cdot \sqrt{3}$$

$$= 30x^2\sqrt{3}$$

The expression $3\sqrt{5x} \cdot 2\sqrt{15x^3}$ is equivalent to $30x^2\sqrt{3}$.

STUDY TIP
When rewriting the product under the radicand, it is easier to find perfect squares by replacing each number with its factors. Instead of writing 5 • 15 as 75, write the factors, 5 • 3 • 5.

✓ Try It!   **4.** Write an expression for each product without perfect square factors in the radicand.

a. $\frac{1}{2}\sqrt{21x^3} \cdot 4\sqrt{7x^2}$ b. $2\sqrt{12x^9} \cdot \sqrt{18x^5}$

APPLICATION   **EXAMPLE 5**   **Write a Radical Expression**

A light fixture in an ice cream shop is in the shape of an ice cream cone and the cone has a height that is 7 times the radius. The expression for the slant height is $\sqrt{r^2 + h^2}$, where r is the radius and h is the height of the cone. The slant height should be no longer than 24 in. to fit on the wall. What is the slant height of the cone with the radius shown?

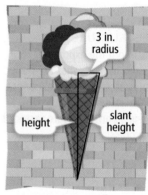

3 in. radius

height   slant height

Formulate ◀   Let r = radius and $7r$ = height.

$$\sqrt{r^2 + h^2} = \sqrt{r^2 + (7r)^2}$$

Compute ◀

$$= \sqrt{r^2 + 49r^2}$$ Substitute the values into the slant height expression

$$= \sqrt{50r^2}$$

$$= \sqrt{5 \cdot 5 \cdot 2 \cdot r^2}$$

$$= 5r\sqrt{2}$$

Interpret ◀   To determine the slant height of the cone, evaluate the expression for $r = 3$.

$$5 \cdot 3\sqrt{2} \approx 21.2$$

The slant height is about 21 in. so it will fit on the wall.

✓ Try It!   **5.** Another cone has a slant height s that is 5 times the radius. What is the simplified expression for the height in terms of the radius?

CONCEPT SUMMARY Rewriting Radical Expressions

| **WORDS** | A radical expression is written in the simplest form when there are no perfect square factors other than 1 in the radicand. |

| **ALGEBRA** | Product Property of Square Roots |

$\sqrt{ab} = \sqrt{a} \cdot \sqrt{b}$ when $a \geq 0$ and $b \geq 0$

NUMBERS

$$\sqrt{63} = \sqrt{9 \cdot 7}$$
$$= \sqrt{3 \cdot 3 \cdot 7}$$
$$= 3\sqrt{7}$$

> Use the same properties when there are variables under the radical.

$$\sqrt{28x^3} = \sqrt{4 \cdot 7 \cdot x^2 \cdot x}$$
$$= \sqrt{2 \cdot 2 \cdot 7 \cdot x \cdot x \cdot x}$$
$$= 2x\sqrt{7x}$$

$$4\sqrt{3} \cdot 6\sqrt{6} = 4 \cdot 6\sqrt{3 \cdot 6}$$
$$= 24\sqrt{3 \cdot 3 \cdot 2}$$
$$= 24 \cdot 3\sqrt{2}$$
$$= 72\sqrt{2}$$

$$5\sqrt{3x^2} \cdot 2\sqrt{6x} = 5 \cdot 2\sqrt{3 \cdot 6 \cdot x^2 \cdot x}$$
$$= 10\sqrt{3 \cdot 3 \cdot 2 \cdot x^2 \cdot x}$$
$$= 10 \cdot 3 \cdot x\sqrt{2x}$$
$$= 30x\sqrt{2x}$$

☑ Do You UNDERSTAND?

1. **ESSENTIAL QUESTION** How does rewriting radicals in different forms help you communicate your answer?

2. **Vocabulary** State the *Product Property of Square Roots* in your own words.

3. **Communicate Precisely** Write an expression for $\sqrt{32}$ without any perfect square factors in the radicand. Explain your steps.

4. **Error Analysis** Rikki says that the product $\sqrt{3x^3} \cdot \sqrt{x}$ is $3x^2$. Explain Rikki's error and write the correct product.

5. **Construct Arguments** Is $\sqrt{45}$ in simplest form? Explain.

6. **Make Sense and Persevere** Describe how you would simplify an expression so that there are no perfect square factors in the radicand.

Do You KNOW HOW?

Factor each radicand using the Product Property of Square Roots.

7. $\sqrt{80}$

8. $\sqrt{x^7}$

9. $\sqrt{40x^4}$

10. $\sqrt{11x^5}$

11. $\sqrt{200}$

12. $8\sqrt{8}$

Write an expression for each product without a perfect square factor other than 1 in the radicand.

13. $4\sqrt{3x^3} \cdot 3\sqrt{2x^2}$

14. $x\sqrt{2x^5} \cdot 2x\sqrt{8x}$

15. $\sqrt{7x} \cdot 3\sqrt{10x^7}$

Compare each pair of radical expressions by writing each expression as a product of square roots in simplest form.

16. $\sqrt{72}$ and $2\sqrt{50}$

17. $5\sqrt{28}$ and $\sqrt{119}$

Write each expression so there are no perfect square factors other than 1 in the radicand.

18. $\sqrt{100x^8}$

19. $4x^2y\sqrt{2x^4 y^6}$

UNDERSTAND

20. Use Structure For $\sqrt{x^n}$, consider rewriting this expression without a perfect square factor in the radicand for even and odd values of n, where n is a positive integer.

a. What is the expression when n is even?

b. What is the expression when n is odd?

21. Error Analysis Describe and correct the error a student made in multiplying $2\sqrt{7x^2}$ by $2\sqrt{14x^3}$.

$$2\sqrt{7x^2} \cdot 2\sqrt{14x^3}$$
$$= 2\cdot2\sqrt{7x^2 \cdot 14x^3}$$
$$= 4\sqrt{7 \cdot 2 \cdot 7 \cdot x \cdot x \cdot x \cdot x \cdot x}$$
$$= 8 \cdot 7\sqrt{x^2 \cdot x^2 \cdot x}$$
$$= 56x^2\sqrt{x}$$

✗

22. Use Structure Find $\sqrt{591x^{15}\,y^3} \cdot \sqrt{591x^{15}\,y^3}$ without calculating or simplifying.

23. Communicate Precisely Why do the multiplication properties of exponents apply to radicals? Explain.

24. Make Sense and Persevere How many perfect squares are under each radical?

Radical	Perfect squares
$\sqrt{8}$	
$\sqrt{18}$	
$\sqrt{32x^6}$	
$\sqrt{50x}$	
$\sqrt{72}$	

25. Higher Order Thinking Can you use the Product Property of Square Roots to find equivalent expressions for each radical? Explain.

a. $\sqrt[3]{24x^8}$

b. $\sqrt[4]{3^9\,x^{13}}$

PRACTICE

Compare each pair of radical expressions.
SEE EXAMPLE 1

26. $6\sqrt{3}$ and $\sqrt{108}$

27. $2\sqrt{21}$ and $4\sqrt{5}$

28. $40\sqrt{42}$ and $42\sqrt{40}$

29. $\frac{1}{2}\sqrt{120}$ and $\sqrt{30}$

30. $\sqrt{68}$ and $2\sqrt{18}$

31. $\sqrt{96}$ and $3\sqrt{15}$

Write each expression so the radicand has no perfect squares other than 1. SEE EXAMPLES 2 AND 3

32. $\sqrt{210}$ **33.** $\sqrt{250}$

34. $\sqrt{108}$ **35.** $2\sqrt{21}$

36. $\sqrt{98x^8}$ **37.** $\sqrt{200x^3}$

38. $\sqrt{32x^4\,y^3}$ **39.** $4x\sqrt{\frac{1}{4}x^6}$

Write each expression so the radicand has no perfect squares other than 1. SEE EXAMPLE 4

40. $\sqrt{12x} \cdot \sqrt{3x}$

41. $\sqrt{2x^9} \cdot \sqrt{26x^6}$

42. $\sqrt{27m} \cdot \sqrt{6m^{20}}$

43. $\sqrt{2x^3} \cdot \sqrt{25x^2y}$

44. $\sqrt{9x^9} \cdot \sqrt{18x^3}$

45. $\sqrt{32x} \cdot \sqrt{72x^{18}}$

Write an expression in simplest form for the missing side length. Then find the side lengths of each triangle to the nearest tenth when $x = 15$.
SEE EXAMPLE 5

46.

47.

PRACTICE & PROBLEM SOLVING

APPLY

48. Use Structure The time it takes a planet to revolve around the sun in Earth years can be modeled by $t = \sqrt{d^3}$, where d is the average distance from the sun in astronomical units (AU).

9.5 AU

a. Write an equivalent equation for the function.

b. How long does it take Saturn, pictured above, to orbit the sun? Show that both expressions give the same value.

49. Model With Mathematics A baseball "diamond" is a square that measures 90 ft on each side.

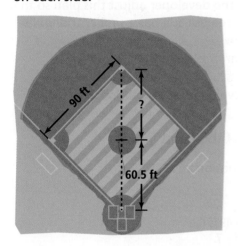

90 ft

?

60.5 ft

a. Write an expression for the distance from 2nd base to home plate in feet. What is this distance to the nearest tenth?

b. The pitcher standing on the pitcher's mound is about to throw to home plate but turns around and throws to 2nd base. How much farther is the throw? Explain.

50. Model With Mathematics A framed television has a ratio of width to height of about 1.732 : 1.

a. For a television with a height of h inches, what is an equivalent expression for the length of the diagonal? Justify your answer.

b. Write an expression for the perimeter.

51. Copy and complete the table. Find the product of each row and column without a perfect square factor in the radicand and enter it in the appropriate cell.

	$\sqrt{48}$	$5x\sqrt{6x^3}$
$\sqrt{12}$	▪	▪
$2x\sqrt{6x}$	▪	▪
$4x^2\sqrt{2x^5}$	▪	▪

52. SAT/ACT A car skidded s ft when traveling on a damp paved road. The expression $r = \sqrt{18s}$ is an estimate of the car's rate of speed in ft/s.

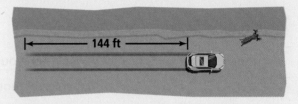

144 ft

Which expression represents the speed of the car in feet per second?

Ⓐ $24\sqrt{6}$

Ⓑ $12\sqrt{6}$

Ⓒ $36\sqrt{2}$

Ⓓ $24\sqrt{3}$

Ⓔ $48\sqrt{2}$

53. Performance Task Copy the figure. Center it on a large piece of paper so you can expand it.

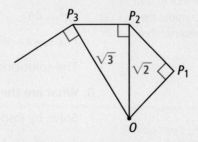

P_3 P_2

$\sqrt{3}$ $\sqrt{2}$ P_1

O

Part A Use the pattern to complete the triangle on the left. Label the side lengths.

Part B Continue using the pattern to add triangles while labeling side lengths.

Part C Are equivalent expressions of the square roots appropriate? Explain your reasoning.

4-4

Solving Quadratic Equations Using Square Roots

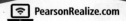 PearsonRealize.com

I CAN... solve quadratic equations by taking square roots.

🖐 EXPLORE & REASON

A developer is building three square recreation areas on a parcel of land. He has not decided what to do with the enclosed triangular area in the center.

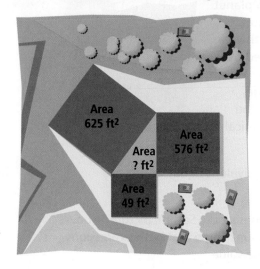

Area 625 ft²

Area 576 ft²

Area ? ft²

Area 49 ft²

A. How can you determine the side lengths of the enclosed triangle?

B. What relationships do you notice among the areas of the squares?

C. Look for Relationships How can the developer adjust this plan so that each recreation area covers less area but still has a similar triangular section in the middle? Explain.

❓ ESSENTIAL QUESTION

How can square roots be used to solve quadratic equations?

🖐 EXAMPLE 1 ▶ Solve Equations of the Form $x^2 = a$

A. What are the solutions of the equation $x^2 = 49$?

Solve by inspection.

$$x^2 = 49$$
$$x = \pm 7$$

> Remember that 49 is the square of 7 and −7.

The solutions of the equation are 7 and −7.

B. What are the solutions of the equation $x^2 = -121$?

Solve by inspection.

$$x^2 = -121$$
$$\sqrt{x^2} = \sqrt{-121}$$

There is no real number that can be multiplied by itself to produce a negative number. A negative radicand indicates that there is no real solution to an equation of the form $x = \sqrt{a}$.

STUDY TIP
When taking a square root to solve an equation, always consider the positive and negative square root solutions.

☑ Try It! 1. Solve each equation by inspection.

a. $x^2 = 169$

b. $x^2 = -16$

EXAMPLE 2 · Solve Equations of the Form $ax^2 = c$

A. What are the solutions of the equation $7x^2 = 112$?

Isolate the variable using properties of equality.

$$7x^2 = 112$$

$$\frac{7x^2}{7} = \frac{112}{7}$$

$$x^2 = 16$$

16 is a perfect square.

$$\sqrt{x^2} = \sqrt{16}$$

$$x = \pm 4$$

B. What are the solutions of the equation $-3x^2 = -24$?

Isolate the variable using properties of equality.

$$-3x^2 = -24$$

$$\frac{-3x^2}{-3} = \frac{-24}{-3}$$

$$x^2 = 8$$

Take the square root of both sides to solve for x.

$$x = \pm\sqrt{8}$$

REASON
You could rewrite $\pm\sqrt{8}$ as $\pm 2\sqrt{2}$. What is the advantage of using $\pm\sqrt{8}$? What would be the advantage of using $\pm 2\sqrt{2}$?

Try It! **2.** What are the solutions for each equation? If the solution is not a perfect square, state what two integers the solution is between.

a. $5x^2 = 125$

b. $-\frac{1}{2}x^2 = -36$

CONCEPTUAL UNDERSTANDING

EXAMPLE 3 · Solve Equations of the Form $ax^2 + b = c$

How can you solve the quadratic equation $3x^2 - 5 = 22$?

Rewrite the equation in the form $x^2 = a$.

$$3x^2 - 5 = 22$$

$$3x^2 = 27$$

$$x^2 = 9 \quad \cdots\cdots \text{Write in the form } x^2 = a, \text{ where } a \text{ is a real number.}$$

$$\sqrt{x^2} = \sqrt{9} \quad \cdots\cdots \text{Take the square root of each side of the equation.}$$

$$x = \pm 3$$

LOOK FOR RELATIONSHIPS
Compare the steps to solve a quadratic equation to those of solving a linear equation. How are the steps similar? How are they different?

You can use the properties of equality to write the equation $3x^2 - 5 = 22$ in the form $x^2 = a$. Since a is a perfect square there are two integer answers. The solutions of this quadratic equation are -3 and 3.

Try It! **3.** Solve the quadratic equations.

a. $-5x^2 - 19 = 144$

b. $3x^2 + 17 = 209$

APPLICATION 👆 **EXAMPLE 4** **Determine a Reasonable Solution**

A cell phone tower has a guy-wire for support as shown. The height of the tower and the distance from the tower to where the guy-wire is secured on the ground are the same distance. What is the height of the tower?

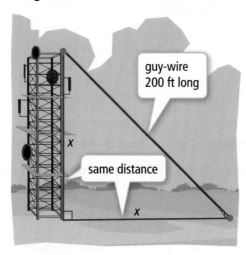

guy-wire 200 ft long

x

same distance

x

Formulate ◀ Write an equation that relates the lengths of the sides of the triangle formed by the guy-wire, the tower, and the distance on the ground from the tower to where the guy-wire is secured.

Let x represent the height of the tower and the distance on the ground.

$$x^2 + x^2 = 200^2$$

Use x in the Pythagorean Theorem for the side lengths since the two lengths are the same.

Compute ◀ Solve the equation for x.

$$x^2 + x^2 = 200^2$$
$$2x^2 = 40,000$$
$$x^2 = 20,000$$
$$\sqrt{x^2} = \sqrt{20,000}$$
$$x = \sqrt{2 \cdot 100 \cdot 100}$$

Rewrite 20,000 using 100 as a factor.

$$x = \pm 100\sqrt{2}$$

Interpret ◀ The height of the tower must be positive, so the solution is $100\sqrt{2} \approx 141$.

The height of the cell phone tower is approximately 141 ft.

☑ **Try It!** **4.** Find the distance from the base of the tower to the midpoint of the guy-wire.

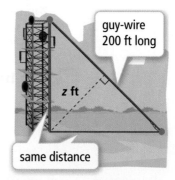

guy-wire 200 ft long

z ft

same distance

CONCEPT SUMMARY Solving Quadratic Equations Using Square Roots

WORDS To solve a quadratic equation using square roots, isolate the variable, and take the square root of both sides of the equation.

NUMBERS $x^2 = 25$

$x = \pm 5$

Solve by inspection. Remember that 25 is the square of 5 and -5.

Use $\pm$ to indicate there are two solutions, one positive and one negative.

$5x^2 - 8 = 12$

$5x^2 = 20$

$x^2 = 4$

$\sqrt{x^2} = \sqrt{4}$

$x = \pm 2$

$2x^2 + 9 = 1$

$2x^2 = -8$

$x^2 = -4$

$\sqrt{x^2} = \sqrt{-4}$

$x = \sqrt{-4}$

A negative radicand has no solution.

No solution

Do You UNDERSTAND?

1. **ESSENTIAL QUESTION** How can square roots be used to solve quadratic equations?

2. **Construct Arguments** How many solutions does $ax^2 = c$ have if a and c have different signs? Explain.

3. **Reason** How do you decide when to use the $\pm$ symbol when solving a quadratic equation?

4. **Error Analysis** Trey solved $2x^2 = 98$ and said that the solution in 7. Is he correct? Why or why not?

5. **Communicate Precisely** How is solving an equation in the form $ax^2 = c$ similar to solving an equation in the form $ax^2 + b = c$? How are they different?

Do You KNOW HOW?

Solve each equation by inspection.

6. $x^2 = 400$

7. $x^2 = -25$

Solve each equation.

8. $3x^2 = 400$

9. $-15x^2 = -90$

10. $2x^2 + 7 = 31$

11. $2x^2 - 7 = 38$

12. $-4x^2 - 1 = 48$

13. $-4x^2 + 50 = 1$

14. $3x^2 + 2x^2 = 150$

15. $3x^2 + 18 = 5x^2$

Solve for x.

16.

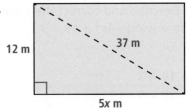

12 m, 37 m, 5x m

17.

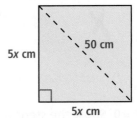

5x cm, 50 cm, 5x cm

Scan for Multimedia

Practice   Tutorial

Additional Exercises Available Online

UNDERSTAND

18. **Make Sense and Persevere** Where will the parabola intersect the line? What equation did you solve to find the intersection?

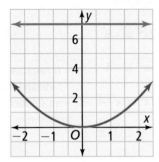

19. **Use Appropriate Tools** When solving an equation of the form $ax^2 + b = c$, what does the error message indicate? What situation may cause this error?

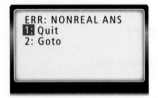

20. **Communicate Precisely** When does solving a quadratic equation of the form $ax^2 = c$ yield the given result?

   a. a rational solution

   b. an irrational solution

   c. one solution

   d. no solutions

21. **Error Analysis** Describe and correct the errors a student made in solving $-4x^2 + 19 = 3$.

$$-4x^2 + 19 = 3$$
$$-4x^2 + 19 - 19 = 3 - 19$$
$$-4x^2 = -16$$
$$-2x = -4 \quad ✗$$
$$x = 2$$

22. **Higher Order Thinking**

   a. Solve $(x - 5)^2 - 100 = 0$. Show the steps for your solution.

   b. Explain how you could solve an equation of the form $(x - d)^2 - c = 0$ for x.

PRACTICE

Solve each equation by inspection. SEE EXAMPLE 1

23. $x^2 = 256$

24. $x^2 = 144$

25. $x^2 = -20$

26. $x^2 = -27$

27. $x^2 = 91$

28. $x^2 = 0.25$

Solve each equation. SEE EXAMPLE 2

29. $12x^2 = 300$

30. $-x^2 = 0$

31. $0.1x^2 = 100$

32. $227x^2 = 1,816$

33. $-36x^2 = -36$

34. $-16x^2 = 200$

Solve each equation. SEE EXAMPLE 3

35. $x^2 + 65 = 90$

36. $x^2 - 65 = 90$

37. $3x^2 + 8 = 56$

38. $3x^2 - 8 = 56$

39. $\frac{4x^2 + 10}{2} = 5$

40. $\frac{8x^2 - 40}{4} = 470$

Solve each equation. Approximate irrational solutions to the nearest hundredth. SEE EXAMPLE 4

41. $6x^2 + 2x^2 = 80$

42. $6x^2 + (2x)^2 = 80$

Solve for x. Then find the side lengths of each triangle to the nearest tenth. SEE EXAMPLE 4

43.   44.

200 ft
2x ft
6x ft

6x ft
2x ft
200 ft

45. Use two methods to solve $x^2 - 900 = 0$. Explain.

46. At a certain time of day, the sun shines on a large flagpole causing a shadow that is twice as long as the flagpole is tall. What is the height of the flagpole to the nearest tenth of a foot?

210 ft

Go Online | PearsonRealize.com

PRACTICE & PROBLEM SOLVING

APPLY

47. A mannequin is dropped from the top of a fire department training tower. Use $-16t^2$ for the change in height per second.

67 ft

3 ft

a. Write an equation to determine the time it takes for the mannequin to drop on to the trampoline.

b. How long does it take before the mannequin is caught by the trampoline? Explain.

48. Make Sense and Persevere Calculate the distance in miles between the two points shown on the map.

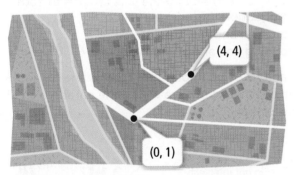

(4, 4)

(0, 1)

49. Make Sense and Persevere The evacuation slide from an aircraft is shown. If the slide is 73 feet long, what is its height at the top in feet?

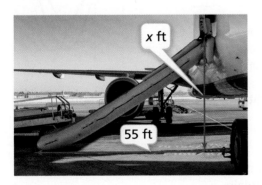

x ft

55 ft

ASSESSMENT PRACTICE

50. Fill in the solutions of $2{,}900 - 5x^2 = 840$.

+ _____ and − _____

51. SAT/ACT A park has an area of 280 m². A rectangular region with a length three times its width will be added to give the park a total area of 435 m². Which equation can be solved to find the width of the region?

Ⓐ $x + 3x + 280 = 435$

Ⓑ $(x \cdot 3x) + 280 = 435$

Ⓒ $(x^2 + 3x) + 280 = 435$

Ⓓ $x^2 + (3x)^2 + 280 = 435$

52. Performance Task A CEO flies to three different company locations. The flight times for two of her legs are shown.

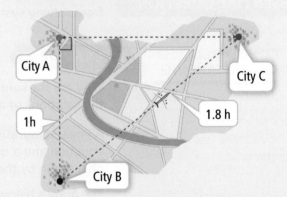

City A

City C

1h

1.8 h

City B

Part A The plane travels at an average speed of 120 mph. Find the distance between City A and City B and the distance between City B and City C.

Part B Write and solve a quadratic equation that can be used to find the distance between City A and City C.

Part C How long will the flight between City C and City A last?

4-5
Solving Systems of Linear and Quadratic Equations

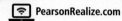 PearsonRealize.com

I CAN... solve a system of equations with linear and quadratic equations.

VOCABULARY
• linear-quadratic system

👍 MODEL & DISCUSS

An architect is designing an archway for a building that has a 9 ft ceiling. She is working with the constraints shown at the right.

A. Find a quadratic model for the arches if the highest point of the arch touches the ceiling.

B. Use Structure Describe how to change the model so that the highest point of the arch does not touch the ceiling.

7 ft

5 ft

❓ ESSENTIAL QUESTION

How is solving linear-quadratic systems of equations similar to and different from solving systems of linear equations?

CONCEPTUAL UNDERSTANDING

👍 EXAMPLE 1   Understand Linear-Quadratic Systems of Equations

Why are the solutions of a linear-quadratic system of equations related to the solutions of a quadratic equation?

A **linear-quadratic system** of equations includes a linear equation and a quadratic equation and is represented on a graph by their corresponding line and parabola.

$$y = mx + b$$
$$y = ax^2 + bx + c$$

The graphs below of a line and three parabolas show that a line can intersect a parabola at 0, 1, or 2 points. The solutions are where the parabola and the purple line of each system intersect.

REASON
A line can intersect a parabola a maximum of two times because setting a quadratic equation equal to a linear equation results in a quadratic equation.

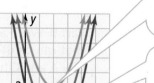

No solution: the green parabola and purple line do not intersect

1 solution: only 1 point where blue parabola and purple line intersect

2 solutions: 2 points where red parabola and purple line intersect

A linear-quadratic system of equations, just like a quadratic equation, can have 0, 1, or 2 real solutions.

☑ Try It!   1. How many solutions does the system of equations at the right have? Explain.

$$y = x$$
$$y = x^2$$

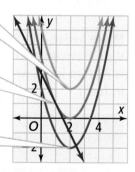

     Go Online | PearsonRealize.com

👆 **EXAMPLE 2**   **Solve a Linear-Quadratic Equation by Graphing**

How can you use graphs to find the solutions of the equation $5 - x^2 = x + 3$?

Set each side of the equation $5 - x^2 = x + 3$ equal to y, and write the equations as a linear-quadratic system of equations.

$$y = 5 - x^2$$
$$y = x + 3$$

Graph the equations in the system on the same coordinate plane.

USE APPROPRIATE TOOLS
A graphing calculator can be used to calculate intersection points when the equations are defined in its function editor.

Both graphs pass through the point $(-2, 1)$.

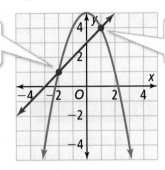

Both graphs pass through the point $(1, 4)$.

The solutions of the system appear to be $(1, 4)$ and $(-2, 1)$ where the two graphs intersect.

Check that each x-value is a solution of the equation $5 - x^2 = x + 3$.

$$5 - (1)^2 = (1) + 3 \qquad 5 - (-2)^2 = (-2) + 3$$
$$4 = 4 \checkmark \qquad\qquad 1 = 1 \checkmark$$

The solutions of the equation are $x = 1$ and $x = -2$.

 Try It!   **2.** What are the solutions of each of the equations? Rewrite each as a system of equations, and graph to solve.

   a. $x^2 + 1 = x + 3$ **b.** $5 - 0.5x^2 = -0.5x + 2$

👆 **EXAMPLE 3**   **Solve Systems of Equations Using Elimination**

What are the solutions of the system of equations below?
$$y = x^2 - 6x + 8$$
$$y = 2x - 4$$

Step 1 Use subtraction to eliminate a variable in the system of equations.

COMMON ERROR
Remember to subtract all like terms in the second equation from a like term in the first equation.

$$\begin{array}{r} y = x^2 - 6x + 8 \\ -(y = 2x - 4) \\ \hline 0 = x^2 - 8x + 12 \end{array}$$

Subtract the linear equation from the quadratic equation to eliminate the y-variable. Line up like terms.

Solve the resulting equation by factoring.

$$(x - 6)(x - 2) = 0$$

$$x - 6 = 0 \qquad \text{or} \qquad x - 2 = 0$$
$$x = 6 \qquad\qquad\qquad x = 2$$

CONTINUED ON THE NEXT PAGE

EXAMPLE 1 CONTINUED

Step 2 Substitute $x = 6$ and $x = 2$ in $y = 2x - 4$, and determine the corresponding values of y.

$$y = 2(6) - 4 \qquad\qquad y = 2(2) - 4$$

$$y = 12 - 4 \qquad\qquad y = 4 - 4$$

$$y = 8 \qquad\qquad\qquad y = 0$$

> Use the linear equation $y = 2x - 4$ to solve for y since it requires fewer steps.

The solutions of the system of equations are (6, 8) and (2, 0).

☑ **Try It!** **3.** Use elimination to solve each system of equations.

a. $\begin{aligned} y &= -x + 4 \\ y &= x^2 - 2 \end{aligned}$

b. $\begin{aligned} y &= -x^2 + 4x + 2 \\ y &= 2 - x \end{aligned}$

APPLICATION ➤ 👆 **EXAMPLE 4** Solve Systems Using Substitution

A phone company launches the sale of two phones in the same week. The phone on the right is an upgraded version of the other phone. During what week are the sales projected to be the same for both phones, in thousands? What will the weekly sales of each phone be for that week?

> Projected sales, in thousands, modeled by $y = -2x^2 + 60x$

> Projected sales, in thousands, modeled by $y = 20x$

Formulate ◀ Model the projected sales by writing a system of equations. Let x represent the number of weeks since the launch.

$$y = 20x$$

$$y = -2x^2 + 60x$$

Compute ◀ Solve the system of equations using substitution.

$$20x = -2x^2 + 60x$$

> Substitute $20x$ for y in the second equation.

$$0 = -2x^2 + 40x$$

$$0 = -2x(x - 20)$$

> Factor the binomial, then set each factor equal to 0 and solve.

$$-2x = 0 \qquad\qquad x - 20 = 0$$

$$x = 0 \qquad\qquad\quad x = 20$$

$$y = 20(20) \qquad\quad y = -2(20)^2 + 60(20)$$

$$y = 400 \qquad\qquad y = 400$$

> Projected sale of 400,000 for both phones.

Interpret ◀ The models project that both phones will have weekly sales of 400,000 phones at 20 weeks after the launch.

CONTINUED ON THE NEXT PAGE

EXAMPLE 4 CONTINUED

Try It! 4. Could you have used elimination or graphing to solve this linear-quadratic system of equations? Explain.

CONCEPT SUMMARY Solving Linear-Quadratic Systems of Equations

WORDS A system of equations composed of a linear equation and a quadratic equation has 0, 1, or 2 solutions. The system of equations can be solved using elimination, substitution, or graphing.

$$y = mx + b$$
$$y = ax^2 + bx + c$$

	Elimination	Substitution	Graphing

ALGEBRA

Elimination:
$$y = x^2 + x$$
$$y = x - 1$$

$$y = x^2 + x$$
$$-y = -x + 1$$
$$0 = x^2 + 1$$
$$x^2 = -1$$

No solution

Substitution:
$$y = -2x + 3$$
$$y = -x^2 + 2$$

$$-2x + 3 = -x^2 + 2$$
$$x^2 - 2x + 1 = 0$$
$$(x - 1)^2 = 0$$
$$x - 1 = 0$$
$$x = 1$$

$$y = -2(1) + 3 = 1$$
Solution is (1, 1)

Graphing:
$$y = \frac{1}{2}x + 1$$
$$y = -x^2 - 8x - 14$$

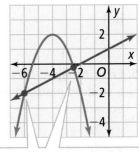

The solutions are where the line and parabola intersect at (−6, −2) and (−2.5, −0.25).

Do You UNDERSTAND?

1. **ESSENTIAL QUESTION** How is solving linear-quadratic systems of equations similar to and different from solving systems of linear equations?

2. **Error Analysis** A student claims that a linear-quadratic system of equations has three solutions. Explain the error the student made.

3. **Vocabulary** What are the characteristics of a *linear-quadratic system* of equations?

4. **Reason** What system of equations could you use to solve the equation $x^2 - 3 = 7$? Explain.

Do You KNOW HOW?

Rewrite each equation as a system of equations.

5. $3 = x^2 + 2x$

6. $x = x^2 - 5$

7. $2x^2 - 5 = x + 7$

8. $x^2 - 2x + 3 = x + 4$

Find the solution of each system of equations.

9. $\begin{cases} y = x^2 + 3x + 1 \\ y = -x + 1 \end{cases}$

10. $\begin{cases} y = x^2 + 1 \\ y = -2x \end{cases}$

11.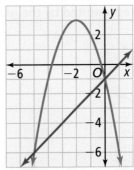

UNDERSTAND

12. **Mathematical Connections** How is the graph of a linear-quadratic system of equations different from the graph of a linear system of equations? How are the graphs similar?

13. **Look for Relationships** What does the graph of the system of equations tell you about its solution?
$$y = 3x^2 - 4x + 2$$
$$y = 8x - 10$$

14. **Higher Order Thinking** Given the equation $y = x^2 + 3x + 2$, write an equation for a line that intersects the parabola the given number of times.

a. 0

b. 1

c. 2

15. **Error Analysis** Describe and correct the error a student made in solving the system of equations.
$$y = 2x^2 + 3$$
$$y = 3x + 1$$

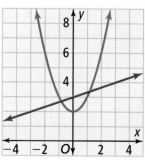

$$y = 2x^2 + 3$$
$$- (y = 3x + 1)$$
$$0 = -x^2 + 2$$
$$x^2 = 2$$
$$x = \pm\sqrt{2} \approx \pm 1.41 \quad ✗$$

16. **Use Appropriate Tools** How do you select the appropriate method for solving a linear-quadratic system? Describe when you would use graphing, elimination, and substitution.

17. **Use Structure** Write the linear-quadratic system of equations that is represented by the graph.

PRACTICE

Rewrite each equation as a system of equations, and then use a graph to solve. SEE EXAMPLES 1 AND 2

18. $\frac{1}{3}x^2 + 2 = -x + 8$

19. $2x^2 - 3x = -2x + 1$

20. $5x^2 = 3x - 7$

21. $x^2 - 2x = 2x - 4$

Rewrite each equation as a system of equations and graph to solve. SEE EXAMPLE 2

22. $x^2 - 4 = x + 2$

23. $-2x + 4 = -0.5x^2 + 4$

Find the solution of each system of equations.
SEE EXAMPLES 1–4

24. $y = x^2 + 3x - 2$
$y = 2x$

25. $y = -4x^2 + x + 1$
$y = -7x + 1$

26. $y = 0.5x^2 - 8x + 13$
$y = x - 3$

27. $y = 7x^2 + 12$
$y = 14x + 5$

28. $y = -x^2 - 2x + 9$
$y = 3x + 20$

29. $y = -5x^2 + 6x - 3$
$y = -4x - 3$

30. $y = 0.75x^2 + 4x - 5$
$y = 4x - 5$

31. $y = -2x^2 + 6x + 7$
$y = 13 - 2x$

32. A ropes course facility offers two types of courses, a low ropes course and a high ropes course. The price of a high ropes adventure is five times as much as a low ropes adventure. Eight members of the high school adventure club choose to participate in the low ropes course, and 15 members choose the high ropes course. The total cost is $1,411. What is the price of each type of ropes course adventure?

APPLY

33. Make Sense and Persevere An equation that models the height of an object dropped from the top of a building is $y = -16x^2 + 30$ where x is time in sec. Another equation $y = 14$ models the path of a bird flying in the air. Write a system of equations and then solve to find how many seconds the object is in the air before it crosses the bird's path.

34. Reason A car accelerates after being completely stopped at a stop sign and enters the highway. The distance the car has traveled in miles after x minutes is represented by $y = 0.5x^2$. A truck is traveling in the same direction at a constant speed so that its distance in miles from the same stop sign after x minutes is represented by $y = x + 4$. After how many minutes will the car pass the truck? Explain.

35. Model With Mathematics At the beginning of a month, the number of people rock climbing increases and then decreases by the end of the month. The number of people zip-lining steadily increases throughout the same month. The models show the number of people y for each type of activity based on the number of days x since the beginning of the month.

$y = -\frac{1}{7}x^2 + 2x + 10$ $y = 2x + 3$

a. Write a system of equations that represents this situation.

b. On what day or days were the same number of people rock climbing and zip-lining?

c. How many people were participating in each activity on that day or days?

ASSESSMENT PRACTICE

36. What is the solution of the system of equations?

$y = x^2 - 5x - 8$

$y = -2x - 4$

37. SAT/ACT What is the solution of the system of equations?

$y = 6x^2 + 3x - 11$

$y = 3x - 5$

Ⓐ $(1, -2), (-1, -8)$

Ⓑ $(1, -1)$

Ⓒ $(-2, 1), (-8, -1)$

Ⓓ $(-1, -8)$

38. Performance Task A music streaming service tracks the number of times songs are played. Two different songs are released on the same day. The functions model the number of times y, in thousands, each song is played x days following their release.

Song A is modeled by $y = 0.25x^2 + 3$.

Song B is modeled by $y = 0.5x + 5$.

Part A Write and solve a system of equations to find the number of days since the release when both songs are played the same number of times.

Part B How many solutions are there? Explain.

Part C A third song is released on the same day as the other two. The number of times this song is played is modeled by $y = 0.5x + 2$. Is there a day when the same number of people listen to the third song and the first song? Explain.

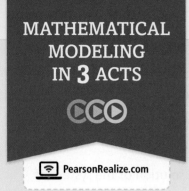

Video

▶ Unwrapping Change

When you arrange a group of objects in different ways, it seems like the space they take up has changed. But, the number of objects didn't change!

We use coin wrappers to store coins in an efficient way. How much more efficient is it than the alternative? Think about this during the Mathematical Modeling in 3 Acts lesson.

Scan for Multimedia

ACT 1 ▷ Identify the Problem

1. What is the first question that comes to mind after watching the video?

2. Write down the main question you will answer about what you saw in the video.

3. Make an initial conjecture that answers this main question.

4. Explain how you arrived at your conjecture.

5. What information will be useful to know to answer the main question? How can you get it? How will you use that information?

ACT 2 ▷ Develop a Model

6. Use the math that you have learned in this Topic to refine your conjecture.

ACT 3 ▷ Interpret the Results

7. Did your refined conjecture match the actual answer exactly? If not, what might explain the difference?

Topic Review

? TOPIC ESSENTIAL QUESTION

1. How do you use quadratic equations to model situations and solve problems?

Vocabulary Review

Choose the correct term to complete each sentence.

2. The _____ is $ax^2 + bx + c = 0$, where $a \neq 0$.

3. An equation of the second degree is called a _____.

4. The x-intercepts of the graph of the function are also called the _____.

5. The _____ states that $\sqrt{ab} = \sqrt{a} \cdot \sqrt{b}$, where both a and b are greater than or equal to 0.

6. The _____ states that for all real numbers a and b, if $ab = 0$, then either $a = 0$ or $b = 0$.

- Product Property of Square Roots
- quadratic equation
- standard form of a quadratic equation
- Zero-Product Property
- zeros of a function

Concepts & Skills Review

LESSON 4-1 · Solving Quadratic Equations Using Graphs and Tables

Quick Review

A **quadratic equation** is an equation of the second degree. A quadratic equation can have 0, 1 or 2 solutions, which are known as the **zeros of the related function**.

Example

Find the solutions of $0 = x^2 + x - 2$.

The x-intercepts of the related function are −2, and 1, so the equation has two real solutions.

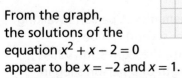

From the graph, the solutions of the equation $x^2 + x - 2 = 0$ appear to be $x = -2$ and $x = 1$.
It is important to verify those solutions by substituting into the equation.

$(-2)^2 + (-2) - 2 = 0 \qquad 1^2 + 1 - 2 = 0$
$\qquad\qquad 0 = 0 \qquad\qquad\qquad 0 = 0$

Practice & Problem Solving

Solve each quadratic equation by graphing.

7. $x^2 - 16 = 0$ 8. $x^2 - 6x + 9 = 0$

9. $x^2 + 2x + 8 = 0$ 10. $2x^2 - 11x + 5 = 0$

Find the solutions for each equation using a table. Round to the nearest tenth.

11. $x^2 - 64 = 0$ 12. $x^2 - 6x - 16 = 0$

13. **Model With Mathematics** A video game company uses the profit model $P(x) = -x^2 + 14x - 39$, where x is the number of video games sold, in thousands, and $P(x)$ is the profit earned in millions of dollars. How many video games would the company have to sell to earn a maximum profit? How many video games would the company have to sell to not show a profit?

LESSON 4-2 — Solving Quadratic Equations by Factoring

Quick Review

The **standard form of a quadratic equation** is $ax^2 + bx + c = 0$, where $a \neq 0$. The **Zero-Product Property** states that for all real numbers a and b, if $ab = 0$, then either $a = 0$ or $b = 0$. The solutions of a quadratic equation can often be determined by factoring.

Example

How can you use factoring to solve $x^2 + 4x = 12$?

First write the equation in standard form.

$x^2 + 4x - 12 = 0$

Then, rewrite the standard form of the equation in factored form.

$(x - 2)(x + 6) = 0$

Use the Zero-Product Property. Set each factor equal to zero and solve.

$x - 2 = 0$ or $x + 6 = 0$

    $x = 2$ $x = -6$

The solutions of $x^2 + 4x - 12 = 0$ are $x = 2$ and $x = -6$.

Practice & Problem Solving

Solve each equation by factoring.

14. $x^2 + 6x + 9 = 0$ 15. $x^2 - 3x - 10 = 0$

16. $x^2 - 12x = 0$ 17. $2x^2 - 7x - 15 = 0$

Factor, find the coordinates of the vertex of the related function, and then graph it.

18. $x^2 - 12x + 20 = 0$ 19. $x^2 - 8x + 15 = 0$

20. **Error Analysis** Describe and correct the error a student made in factoring.

$$2x^2 - 8x + 8 = 0$$
$$2(x^2 - 4x + 4) = 0$$
$$2(x - 2)(x - 2) = 0$$
$$x = -2$$

LESSON 4-3 — Rewriting Radical Expressions

Quick Review

A radical expression in simplest form has no perfect square factors other than 1 in the radicand. The **Product Property of Square Roots** states that $\sqrt{ab} = \sqrt{a} \cdot \sqrt{b}$, when $a \geq 0$ and $b \geq 0$.

Example

Write an expression for $5\sqrt{3x} \cdot 2\sqrt{12x^3}$ without any perfect squares in the radicand.

$5\sqrt{3x} \cdot 2\sqrt{12x^3}$ .... Multiply the constants, and use the Product Property of Square Roots to multiply the radicands.

$= 5 \cdot 2\sqrt{3x \cdot 12x^3}$

$= 10\sqrt{36x^4}$ .... Simplify.

$= 10 \cdot 6 \cdot x^2$ .... Simplify.

$= 60x^2$

The expression $5\sqrt{3x} \cdot 2\sqrt{12x^3}$ is equivalent to $60x^2$.

Practice & Problem Solving

Write an equivalent expression without a perfect square factor in the radicand.

21. $\sqrt{420}$

22. $4\sqrt{84}$

23. $\sqrt{35x} \cdot \sqrt{21x}$

24. $\sqrt{32x^5} \cdot \sqrt{24x^7}$

Compare each pair of radical expressions.

25. $2x^2\sqrt{21x}$ and $\sqrt{84x^5}$

26. $3xy\sqrt{15xy^2}$ and $\sqrt{135x^4y^3}$

27. **Model With Mathematics** A person's walking speed in inches per second can be approximated using the expression $\sqrt{384\ell}$, where ℓ is the length of a person's leg in inches. Write the expression in simplified form. What is the walking speed of a person with a leg length of 31 in.

Solving Quadratic Equations Using Square Roots

Quick Review

To solve a quadratic equation using square roots, isolate the variable and find the square root of both sides of the equation.

Example

Use the properties of equality to solve the quadratic equation $4x^2 - 7 = 57$.

Rewrite the equation in the form $x^2 = a$.

$4x^2 - 7 = 57$

$4x^2 = 64$ ·········· Rewrite using the form $x^2 = a$, where a is a real number.

$x^2 = 16$
$\sqrt{x^2} = \sqrt{16}$ ·········· Take the square root of each side of the equation.

$x = \pm 4$

Since 16 is perfect square, there are two integer answers. The solutions of the quadratic equation $4x^2 - 7 = 57$ are $x = -4$ and $x = 4$.

Practice & Problem Solving

Solve each equation by inspection.

28. $x^2 = 289$

29. $x^2 = -36$

30. $x^2 = 155$

31. $x^2 = 0.64$

Solve each equation.

32. $5x^2 = 320$

33. $x^2 - 42 = 358$

34. $4x^2 - 18 = 82$

35. Higher Order Thinking Solve $(x - 4)^2 - 81 = 0$. Explain the steps in your solution.

36. Communicate Precisely Use the equation $d = \sqrt{(12 - 5)^2 + (8 - 3)^2}$ to calculate the distance between the points (3, 5) and (8, 12). What is the distance?

Solving Systems of Linear and Quadratic Equations

Quick Review

A **linear-quadratic system** of equations includes a linear equation and a quadratic equation.

$y = mx + b$
$y = ax^2 + bx + c$

Example

What are the solutions of the system of equations?

$y = x^2 - 5x + 4$
$y = x - 4$

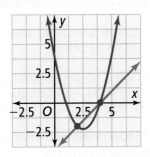

The solutions are where the parabola and the line intersect, which appear be at the points (2, −2) and (4, 0).

Practice & Problem Solving

Rewrite each equation as a system of equations, and then use a graph to solve.

37. $4x^2 = 2x - 5$ **38.** $2x^2 + 3x = 2x + 1$

39. $x^2 - 6x = 2x - 16$

40. $0.5x^2 + 4x = -12 - 1.5x$

Find the solution(s) of each system of equations.

41. $y = x^2 + 6x + 9$
$y = 3x$

42. $y = x^2 + 8x + 30$
$y = 5 - 2x$

43. $y = 3x^2 + 2x + 1$
$y = 2x + 1$

44. $y = 2x^2 + 5x - 30$
$y = 2x + 5$

45. Make Sense and Persevere Write an equation for a line that does not intersect the graph of the equation $y = x^2 + 6x + 9$.

? TOPIC ESSENTIAL QUESTION

How do you use quadratic equations and complex numbers to model situations and solve problems?

Topic Overview

Topic Vocabulary

- Binomial Theorem
- completing the square
- complex conjugates
- complex number
- discriminant
- identity
- imaginary number
- imaginary unit i
- Pascal's Triangle
- Quadratic Formula

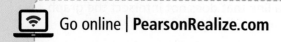

Digital Experience

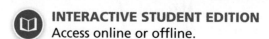

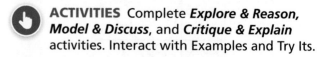

INTERACTIVE STUDENT EDITION Access online or offline.

ACTIVITIES Complete *Explore & Reason, Model & Discuss*, and *Critique & Explain* activities. Interact with Examples and Try Its.

ANIMATION View and interact with real-world applications.

PRACTICE Practice what you've learned.

Go online | PearsonRealize.com

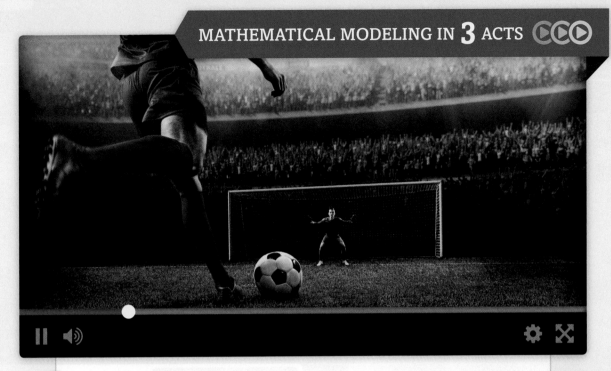

▶ Swift Kick

Whether you call it soccer, football, or fùtbol, it's the most popular sport in the world by far. Even if you don't play soccer, you probably know several people who do.

There are many ways to kick a soccer ball: you can use any part of either foot. If you want the ball to end up in the goal, you also need to try different amounts of spin and power. You'll see one person's effort in the Mathematical Modeling in 3-Acts lesson.

TOPIC 5

VIDEOS Watch clips to support *Mathematical Modeling in 3 Acts Lessons* and enVision® *STEM Projects.*

CONCEPT SUMMARY Review key lesson content through multiple representations.

ASSESSMENT Show what you've learned.

 GLOSSARY Read and listen to English and Spanish definitions.

 TUTORIALS Get help from *Virtual Nerd*, right when you need it.

 MATH TOOLS Explore math with digital tools and manipulatives.

:enVision® STEM

Did You Know?

Cameras and RADAR precisely track everything that happens in a professional baseball game, including the speed and launch angle of every batted ball.

If a baseball player hits a 90-mph pitch with more than 8,000 pounds of force, the ball leaves the bat at a speed of 110 mph.

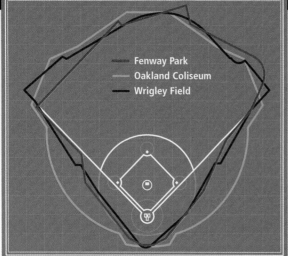

Fenway Park
Oakland Coliseum
Wrigley Field

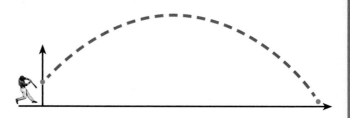

Each baseball park has unique features that help determine whether a hit will be a home run.

You can model the flight of a hit baseball with a parabola. The initial vertical and horizontal speed of the ball can be found using right triangle trigonometry and the launch angle of the hit.

▶ Your Task: Hit a Home Run

You and your classmates will design a ballpark and determine what it would take to hit a home run at that park.

5-1

Complex Numbers and Operations

PearsonRealize.com

I CAN... solve problems with complex numbers.

VOCABULARY
- complex conjugates
- complex number
- imaginary number
- imaginary unit i

👆 EXPLORE & REASON

A math class played a game called "Solve It, You're Out." At the start of each round, students chose a card from a deck marked with integers from −5 to 5. When an equation is shown, any student whose card states the solution to the equation is eliminated. Five students remain.

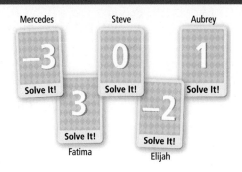

Mercedes   Steve   Aubrey
−3   0   1
Solve It!   Solve It!   Solve It!
3   −2
Solve It!   Solve It!
Fatima   Elijah

A. The next equation presented was $x^2 = 9$. Which student(s) was eliminated? Explain.

B. Construct Arguments In the next round, the equation presented was $x^2 = -4$. Elijah thought he was eliminated, but this is not the case. Explain why Elijah was incorrect.

C. What is true about solutions to $x^2 = a$ when a is a positive number? When a is a negative number? What about when $a = 0$?

❓ ESSENTIAL QUESTION

How can you represent and operate on numbers that are not on the real number line?

👆 EXAMPLE 1   Solve a Quadratic Equation Using Square Roots

How can you use square roots to solve each equation?

A. $x^2 = 16$

Notice that each side of the equation involves a perfect square.

$$x^2 = 16$$
$$x = \pm\sqrt{16}$$
$$= \pm 4$$

> What numbers can you square that result in 16?

STUDY TIP
You can also solve this equation by subtracting 16 from both sides, then factoring the expression.

The solutions of the equation $x^2 = 16$ are 4 and −4.

B. $x^2 = -9$

There are no real numbers that you can square that result in −9. However, you can simplify the expression by extending the properties of radicals.

$$x^2 = -9$$
$$x = \pm\sqrt{-9}$$
$$x = \pm\sqrt{9}\sqrt{-1}$$
$$x = \pm 3\sqrt{-1}$$

The solutions of the equation $x^2 = -9$ are not real numbers but are part of a number system called the complex numbers. The number $\sqrt{-1}$ is called the **imaginary unit i**. Replacing $\sqrt{-1}$ with i allows you to write the solutions to the equation $x^2 = -9$ as $3i$ and $-3i$.

☑ Try It!

1. Use square roots to solve each equation. Write your solutions using the imaginary unit, i.

a. $x^2 = -5$

b. $x^2 = -72$

CONCEPT Complex Numbers

The imaginary unit, i, is the principal square root of -1. Then $i^2 = -1$.

An **imaginary number** is any number, bi, where b is a non-zero real number and i is the square root of -1.

Complex numbers are numbers that can be written in the form $a + bi$, where a and b are real numbers and i is the square root of -1. They include all real and imaginary numbers, as well as the sum of real and imaginary numbers.

For example:

$$-6 + 4i \quad (a = -6, b = 4)$$
$$7 - i\sqrt{2} \quad (a = 7, b = -\sqrt{2})$$
$$0.5i \quad (a = 0, b = 0.5)$$

 EXAMPLE 2 **Add and Subtract Complex Numbers**

How can you add and subtract complex numbers?

A. What is the sum of $(4 - 7i)$ and $(-11 + 9i)$?

When adding (or subtracting) two numbers in the form $a + bi$, combine the real parts and then combine the imaginary parts. The sum (or difference) may include both a real and imaginary part and can be written in the form $a + bi$.

$$(4 - 7i) + (-11 + 9i) = (4 + -11) + (-7i + 9i)$$
$$= -7 + 2i$$

STUDY TIP
Combine real parts and imaginary parts of complex numbers as you would combine like terms.

B. What is the difference of $(6 + 8i)$ and $(2 - 5i)$?

$$(6 + 8i) - (2 - 5i) = (6 + 8i) + (-2 + 5i)$$

Remember to distribute the negative over the complex number.

$$= (6 + -2) + (8i + 5i)$$
$$= 4 + 13i$$

✓ **Try It!** **2.** Find the sum or difference.

    a. $(-4 + 6i) + (-2 - 9i)$

    b. $(3 - 2i) - (-4 + i)$

👆 **EXAMPLE 3** **Multiply Complex Numbers**

How can you write each product in the form $a + bi$?

A. $-2.5i(8 - 9i)$

$$-2.5i(8 - 9i) = -2.5i(8) - 2.5i(-9i) \quad \text{Use the Distributive Property.}$$

$$= -20i + 22.5i^2 \quad \text{Multiply.}$$

$$= -20i + 22.5(-1) \quad \text{Simplify using the definition of } i^2.$$

$$= -22.5 - 20i \quad \text{Write in the form } a + bi.$$

The product is $-22.5 - 20i$.

> **COMMON ERROR**
> Recall that $i^2 = -1$, so the product of 22.5 and i^2 is -22.5, not 22.5.

B. $(3 - 2i)(3 + 2i)$

$$(3 - 2i)(3 + 2i) = 3(3 + 2i) - 2i(3 + 2i) \quad \text{Use the Distributive Property.}$$

$$= 9 + 6i - 6i - 4i^2 \quad \text{Use the Distributive Property.}$$

$$= 9 + 6i - 6i - 4(-1) \quad \text{Simplify using the definition of } i^2.$$

$$= 13 \quad \text{Simplify.}$$

The product is 13.

☑ **Try It!**   **3.** Write each product in the form $a + bi$.

a. $\frac{2}{5}i\left(10 - \frac{5}{2}i\right)$

b. $\left(\frac{1}{2} + 2i\right)\left(\frac{1}{2} - 2i\right)$

CONCEPT Complex Conjugates

Complex conjugates are complex numbers with equivalent real parts and opposite imaginary parts. Their product is a real number.

For example:

$7 - 8i, 7 + 8i$ $-2 + i, -2 - i$

$(a + bi)(a - bi)$

$a^2 - abi + abi - b^2i^2$

$a^2 - b^2(-1)$

$a^2 + b^2$

👆 **EXAMPLE 4** **Simplify a Quotient With Complex Numbers**

How can you write the quotient $\frac{10}{2 - i}$ in the form $a + bi$?

When the denominator has an imaginary component, you can create an equivalent fraction with a real denominator by multiplying by its complex conjugate.

> **STUDY TIP**
> Multiplying the denominator by its complex conjugate will result in a new denominator that is a real number.

$$\frac{10}{2 - i} = \frac{10}{2 - i} \times \frac{2 + i}{2 + i} \quad \begin{array}{l}\text{Use the complex conjugate of the} \\ \text{denominator to multiply by 1.}\end{array}$$

$$= \frac{10(2 + i)}{4 + 2i - 2i - i^2} \quad \text{Use the Distributive Property.}$$

$$= \frac{10(2 + i)}{4 + 2i - 2i - (-1)} \quad \text{Simplify using the definition of } i^2.$$

$$= \frac{10(2 + i)}{5} \quad \text{Simplify.}$$

$$= 2(2 + i) \quad \text{Simplify.}$$

$$= 4 + 2i \quad \text{Write in the form } a + bi.$$

CONTINUED ON THE NEXT PAGE

EXAMPLE 4 CONTINUED

 Try It! **4.** Write each quotient in the form $a + bi$.

a. $\dfrac{80}{2 - 6i}$ b. $\dfrac{4 - 3i}{-1 + 2i}$

CONCEPTUAL
UNDERSTANDING

 EXAMPLE 5 Factor a Sum of Squares

How can you use complex numbers to factor the sum of two squares?

A. How can you factor the expression $x^2 + y^2$?

Rewrite $x^2 + y^2$ as a difference of two squares: $x^2 - (-y^2)$.

You can think of $(-y^2)$ as $(-1)(y^2)$.

> *How can $(-y^2)$ be a perfect square?*

Since $-1 = i^2$, $(-1)(y^2) = (i^2)(y^2) = (yi)^2$.

So $x^2 + y^2 = x^2 - (yi)^2$

$\quad\quad\quad = (x + yi)(x - yi)$

> *Factor as the difference of two squares.*

The factors of $x^2 + y^2$ are $(x + yi)$ and $(x - yi)$.

STUDY TIP
The product of complex conjugates $(a + bi)$ and $(a - bi)$ will always be equal to $a^2 + b^2$, which is the sum of two squares.

B. How can you factor the expression $12x^2 + 3$?

$12x^2 + 3 = 3(4x^2 + 1)$ .... Factor out the GCF.

$\quad\quad\quad = 3(4x^2 - i^2)$ .... Rewrite as a difference of squares.

$\quad\quad\quad = 3(2x + i)(2x - i)$ .... Factor the difference of squares.

The factors of $12x^2 + 3$ are 3, $(2x + i)$, and $(2x - i)$.

 Try It! **5.** Factor each expression.

a. $4x^2 + 25$ b. $8y^2 + 18$

 EXAMPLE 6 Solve a Quadratic Equation With Complex Solutions

How can you solve $x^2 + 4 = 0$ using factoring?

$\quad\quad x^2 + 4 = 0$ .... Write the original equation.

$\quad\quad x^2 - (2i)^2 = 0$ .... Rewrite as a difference of squares.

$(x + 2i)(x - 2i) = 0$ .... Factor the difference of squares.

$x + 2i = 0 \quad x - 2i = 0$ .... Set each factor equal to 0.

$x = -2i \quad\quad x = 2i$ .... Solve.

The solutions are $x = -2i$ and $x = 2i$.

LOOK FOR RELATIONSHIPS
In Example 1, you solved a similar problem by taking the square root of both sides. This example provides an alternative method that utilizes factoring.

 Try It! **6.** Find the value(s) of x that will solve each equation.

a. $x^2 + 49 = 0$ b. $9x^2 + 25 = 0$

🔍 CONCEPT SUMMARY Complex Numbers and Operations

The imaginary unit i is the number whose square is equal to -1: $\sqrt{-1} = i$, so $i^2 = -1$.

Complex numbers are written in the form $a + bi$.

real numbers   imaginary unit

The four basic operations can be applied to complex numbers, such as $2 + 3i$ and $5 - i$.

ADDITION

Add as you would with binomials with like terms.

$(2 + 3i) + (5 - i) = 7 + 2i$

SUBTRACTION

Subtract as you would with binomials with like terms.

$(2 + 3i) - (5 - i) = -3 + 4i$

MULTIPLICATION

Distribute as you would with binomials.

$(2 + 3i)(5 - i) = 10 - 2i + 15i - 3i^2 = 13 + 13i$

DIVISION

Simplify so that the denominator is a real number. Multiply the numerator and denominator by the conjugate of the denominator.

$\frac{2 + 3i}{5 - i} = \frac{(2 + 3i)(5 + i)}{(5 - i)(5 + i)} = \frac{7 + 17i}{26} = \frac{7}{26} + \frac{17}{26}i$

☑ Do You UNDERSTAND?

1. **❓ ESSENTIAL QUESTION** How can you represent and operate on numbers that are not on the real number line?

2. **Vocabulary** How do you form the *complex conjugate* of a complex number $a + bi$?

3. **Error Analysis** Helena was asked to write the quotient $\frac{4}{3-i}$ in the form $a + bi$. She began this way: $\frac{4}{3-i} \times \frac{3-i}{3-i} = \frac{4(3-i)}{3^2 + 1^2} = \frac{12 - 4i}{10}$. Explain the error Helena made.

4. **Look for Relationships** The quadratic equation $x^2 + 9 = 0$ has solutions $x = 3i$ and $x = -3i$. How many times will the graph of $f(x) = x^2 + 9$ cross the x-axis? Explain.

Do You KNOW HOW?

Write each of the following in the form $a + bi$.

5. $(2 + 5i) - (-6 + i)$

6. $(2i)(6 + 3i)$

Solve each equation.

7. $x^2 + 16 = 0$

8. $y^2 = -25$

9. **Model With Mathematics** The total source voltage in the circuit is $6 - 3i$ V. What is the voltage at the middle source?

$(2 + 6i)V$ + E_1 −

$(a + bi)V$ + E_2 −

$(2 - 5i)V$ + E_3 −

UNDERSTAND

10. Construct Arguments Tamara says that raising the number i to any integer power results in either -1 or 1 as the result, since $i^2 = -1$. Do you agree with Tamara? Explain.

11. Error Analysis Describe and correct the error a student made when dividing complex numbers.

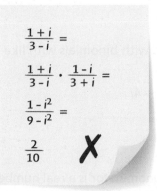

$$\frac{1+i}{3-i} =$$

$$\frac{1+i}{3-i} \cdot \frac{1-i}{3+i} =$$

$$\frac{1-i^2}{9-i^2} =$$

$$\frac{2}{10} \quad \text{✗}$$

12. Higher Order Thinking Label the diagram with the following sets of numbers:

1. complex numbers

2. real numbers

3. imaginary numbers

4. integers

5. rational numbers

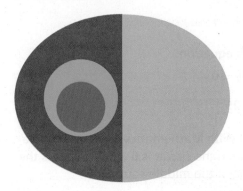

Include an example of each type of number in the diagram.

13. Generalize Write an explicit formula, in standard form, to find the quotient of two complex numbers. Use the numbers $a + bi$ and $c + di$.

PRACTICE

Use square roots to solve each equation over the complex numbers. SEE EXAMPLE 1

14. $x^2 = -5$

15. $x^2 = -0.01$

16. $x^2 = -18$

17. $x^2 = (-1)^2$

Add or subtract. Write the answer in the form $a + bi$. SEE EXAMPLE 2

18. $(3 - 2i) - (-9 + i)$

19. $(5 + 1.2i) + (-6 + 0.8i)$

20. $(2i) - (2i - 11)$

21. $13 + 2i - 4 - 8i$

22. $\frac{3-i}{4} - \frac{2+i}{3}$

23. $4.5i - 4.5 + 3.5i + 2.5$

Write each product in the form $a + bi$. SEE EXAMPLE 3

24. $(11i)(3i)$

25. $(3i)(5 - 4i)$

26. $(5 - 2i)(5 + 2i)$

27. $(8 + 3i)(8 + 3i)$

28. $\frac{1}{3}i(3 + 6i)$

29. $(-2i + 7)(7 + 2i)$

Write each quotient in the form $a + bi$.
SEE EXAMPLE 4

30. $\frac{12}{1-i}$

31. $\frac{5}{6+2i}$

32. $\frac{6+12i}{3i}$

33. $\frac{4-4i}{1+3i}$

Factor the sums of two squares. SEE EXAMPLE 5

34. $4x^2 + 49$

35. $x^2 + 1$

36. $36 + 100a^2$

37. $18y^2 + 8$

38. $\frac{1}{4}b^2 + 25$

39. $x^2 + y^2$

Solve each equation. SEE EXAMPLE 6

40. $x^2 + 81 = 0$

41. $25x^2 + 9 = 0$

42. $x^2 = -16$

43. $4 + 49y^2 = 0$

44. $y^2 + 1 = 0$

45. $x^2 + \frac{1}{4} = 0$

PRACTICE & PROBLEM SOLVING

Practice   Tutorial

Mixed Review Available Online

APPLY

46. Model With Mathematics The two resistors shown in the circuit are referred to as *in parallel*. The total resistance of the resistors is given by the formula $\frac{1}{R_T} = \frac{1}{R_1} + \frac{1}{R_2}$.

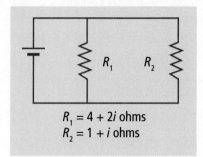

$R_1 = 4 + 2i$ ohms
$R_2 = 1 + i$ ohms

a. Find the total resistance. Write your answer in the form $a + bi$.

b. Show that the total resistance is equivalent to the expression $\frac{R_1 R_2}{R_1 + R_2}$.

c. Change the value of R_2 so that the total resistance is a real number. Explain how you chose the value.

47. Use Structure The complex number $a + bi$ can be represented on a coordinate plane as the point (a, b). You can use multiplication by i to rotate a point about the origin in the coordinate plane.

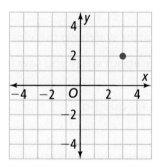

a. Write the point (x, y) on the graph as the complex number $x + yi$.

b. Multiply the complex number by i. Interpret the new value as a new point in the plane.

c. Repeat the steps above for two other points. How does multiplication by i rotate a point?

ASSESSMENT PRACTICE

48. Complete the table by classifying each number as real, imaginary, or complex. Use the most specific classification. For example, all real numbers are also complex numbers, so it is more specific to classify a number as real.

Number	R, I, C
$2 + i$	C
$5 - 0i$	R
$2i$	I
$(3 - i)^2$	
$i^2 + 1$	
$3i$	
$(3 - i)(3 + i)$	
$(3 + i) - (2 + i)$	
$\sqrt{-14}$	
$i(4 + i) - 3i$	

49. SAT/ACT Which of the following is a solution to the equation $3x^2 = -12$?

Ⓐ $-4i$ Ⓑ $-2i$ Ⓒ -2 Ⓓ 2 Ⓔ $4i$

50. Performance Task Abby wants to write the square root of i in the form $a + bi$. She begins by writing the equation $\sqrt{i} = a + bi$.

Part A Square both sides of the equation. Then use the fact that the real part and imaginary part on each side of the equation are equal to write a system of equations involving the variables a and b.

Part B Solve the system to find b. Then find a.

Part C List the possible solutions for a and b.

Part D Square each of the possible solutions. What are the two square roots of i?

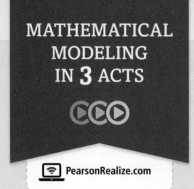

MATHEMATICAL
MODELING
IN **3** ACTS

PearsonRealize.com

Video

▶ Swift Kick

Whether you call it soccer, football, or fùtbol, it's the most popular sport in the world by far. Even if you don't play soccer, you probably know several people who do.

There are many ways to kick a soccer ball: you can use any part of either foot. If you want the ball to end up in the goal, you also need to try different amounts of spin and power. You'll see one person's effort in the Mathematical Modeling in 3-Acts lesson.

Scan for Multimedia

ACT 1 ▶ Identify the Problem

1. What is the first question that comes to mind after watching the video?

2. Write down the main question you will answer about what you saw in the video.

3. Make an initial conjecture that answers this main question.

4. Explain how you arrived at your conjecture.

5. What information will be useful to know to answer the main question? How can you get it? How will you use that information?

ACT 2 ▶ Develop a Model

6. Use the math that you have learned in this Topic to refine your conjecture.

ACT 3 ▶ Interpret the Results

7. Did your refined conjecture match the actual answer exactly? If not, what might explain the difference?

5-2

Completing the Square

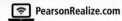
I CAN... solve quadratic equations by completing the square.

VOCABULARY
• completing the square

CRITIQUE & EXPLAIN

Hana and Enrique used different methods to solve the equation $x^2 - 6x + 9 = 16$.

Hana	Enrique
$x^2 - 6x + 9 = 16$	$x^2 - 6x + 9 = 16$
$x^2 - 6x - 7 = 0$	$(x - 3)^2 = 16$
$(x - 7)(x + 1) = 0$	I can square 4 or -4 to get 16.
$x - 7 = 0$ OR $x + 1 = 0$	$x - 3 = 4$ OR $x - 3 = -4$
$x = 7$ OR $x = -1$	$x = 7$ OR $x = -1$
The solutions are 7 and -1.	The solutions are 7 and -1.

A. Does Hana's method work? If her method is valid, explain the reasoning she used. If her method is not valid, explain why not.

B. Does Enrique's method work? If his method is valid, explain the reasoning he used. If his method is not valid, explain why not.

C. Use Structure Can you use either Hana's or Enrique's method to solve the equation $x^2 + 10x + 25 = 3$? Explain.

? ESSENTIAL QUESTION

How can you solve a quadratic equation by completing the square?

EXAMPLE 1   Use Square Roots to Solve Quadratic Equations

What are the solution(s) of $25 = x^2 + 14x + 49$?

Previously, you solved a simple quadratic equation by finding the square root of both sides. You can use a similar method to solve more complicated quadratic equations.

$25 = x^2 + 14x + 49$	Write the original equation.
$25 = x^2 + 2(7)x + 7^2$	Recognize that the quadratic expression is a perfect square trinomial.
$25 = (x + 7)^2$	Factor the perfect square trinomial.
$\sqrt{25} = \sqrt{(x + 7)^2}$	Take the square root of each side of the equation.
$5 = |x + 7|$	Apply the definition of principal square root.
$\pm 5 = x + 7$	Apply the definition of absolute value.

COMMUNICATE PRECISELY
The principal square root returns only positive values, but you can square either 5 or -5 to get 25. How does the absolute value account for this?

$5 = x + 7$	or	$-5 = x + 7$
$-2 = x$	or	$-12 = x$

The solutions of $25 = x^2 + 14x + 49$ are $x = -2$ and $x = -12$.

 Try It!   **1.** Find the solution(s) to the equations.

a. $81 = x^2 + 12x + 36$ **b.** $9 = x^2 - 16x + 64$

CONCEPTUAL UNDERSTANDING

EXAMPLE 2 Understand the Process of Completing the Square

How can you complete the square to write an expression as a perfect square?

A. How can you rewrite the expression $x^2 + bx$ in the form $(x + p)^2$?

Not every quadratic expression is a perfect square trinomial. **Completing the square** is the process of finding the constant to add to $x^2 + bx$ to create a perfect square trinomial.

The model below depicts the process of completing the square.

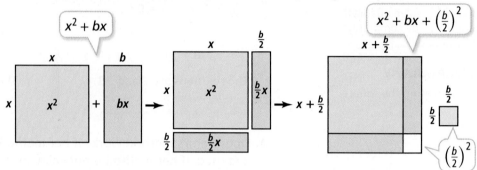

To create a perfect square trinomial, add $\left(\frac{b}{2}\right)^2$ to the variable expression.

$$x^2 + bx + \left(\frac{b}{2}\right)^2 = \left(x + \frac{b}{2}\right)^2$$

B. Write $x^2 + 8x + 5 = 0$ in the form $(x + p)^2 = q$

$x^2 + 8x + 5 = 0$	Write the original equation.
$x^2 + 8x = -5$	Isolate the variable expression.
$x^2 + 8x + 16 = -5 + 16$	Determine the constant needed to complete the square: $\left(\frac{b}{2}\right)^2 = \left(\frac{8}{2}\right)^2 = 16$.
$(x + 4)^2 = 11$	Write the left side of the equation as a perfect square.

The equation $x^2 + 8x + 5 = 0$ can be rewritten as $(x + 4)^2 = 11$.

Try It! **2.** How can you write the equation $x^2 - 6x - 11 = 0$ in the form $(x - p)^2 = q$?

EXAMPLE 3 Solve a Quadratic Equation by Completing the Square

How can you solve $0 = x^2 - 2x + 3$ by completing the square?

$0 = x^2 - 2x + 3$	Write the original equation.
$-3 = x^2 - 2x$	Subtract 3 from each side.
$-3 + 1 = x^2 - 2x + 1$	Add $\left(\frac{-2}{2}\right)^2$ to both sides of the equation.
$-2 = (x - 1)^2$	Write the right side of the equation as a perfect square.
$\pm i\sqrt{2} = x - 1$	Take the square root of each side of the equation.
$1 \pm i\sqrt{2} = x$	Solve.

The solutions of $0 = x^2 - 2x + 3$ are $x = 1 + i\sqrt{2}$ and $x = 1 - i\sqrt{2}$.

CONTINUED ON THE NEXT PAGE

EXAMPLE 3 CONTINUED

☑ **Try It!**   **3.** Solve the following equations by completing the square.

a. $0 = x^2 + 4x + 8$ **b.** $0 = x^2 - 8x + 17$

APPLICATION ➤   👆 **EXAMPLE 4**   **Complete the Square to Solve a Real-World Problem**

Libby plans to create a rectangular pasturing enclosure. She has 340 m of fencing available for the enclosure's perimeter and wants it to have an area of 6,000 m². What dimensions should Libby use?

6,000 m²

w   ℓ

Formulate ◀   Let ℓ and w represent the length and width of the enclosure.

The perimeter is $2\ell + 2w = 340$, so:

$$2w = 340 - 2\ell$$

$$w = 170 - \ell$$

Libby wants the area to be 6,000 m². Write this as an equation:

$$A = \ell w$$

$$6,000 = \ell(170 - \ell)$$ —— Substitute for A and w.

Compute ◀

$$6,000 = 170\ell - \ell^2$$

$$\ell^2 - 170\ell = -6,000$$

$$\ell^2 - 170\ell + 7,225 = -6,000 + 7,225$$ —— Find the number to complete the square: $\frac{-170}{2} = -85$ and $(-85)^2 = 7,225$.

$$(\ell - 85)^2 = 1,225$$

$$\ell - 85 = \pm 35$$

$$\ell = 85 \pm 35$$

$$\ell = 120 \text{ or } \ell = 50$$

Interpret ◀   When $\ell = 120$, then $w = 170 - 120$, or 50.

When $\ell = 50$, then $w = 170 - 50$, or 120.

In each case, there is $2(120) + 2(50)$, or 340 m, of fencing used.

Likewise, the area is $(120)(50)$, or 6,000 m².

Libby should make two sides of the enclosure 120 m long and the other two sides 50 m long.

CONTINUED ON THE NEXT PAGE

EXAMPLE 4 CONTINUED

 Try It! **4.** The relationship between the time since a ball was thrown and its height can be modeled by the equation $h = 32t - 16t^2 + 4$, where h is the height of the ball after t seconds. Complete the square to find how long it will take the ball to reach a height of 20 ft.

 EXAMPLE 5 **Write a Quadratic Equation in Vertex Form**

Write the equation $y = -2x^2 + 10x + 1$ in vertex form and graph it. What is the maximum or minimum value of the graph of the equation?

$$y = -2x^2 + 10x + 1 \quad \cdots\cdots\cdots \text{Write the original equation.}$$

$$y - 1 = -2x^2 + 10x \quad \cdots\cdots\cdots \text{Subtract 1 from each side.}$$

$$y - 1 = -2(x^2 - 5x) \quad \cdots\cdots\cdots \text{Factor out the } x^2 \text{ coefficient, } -2.$$

$$y - 1 - (2)(6.25) = -2(x^2 - 5x + 6.25) \quad \cdots\cdots\cdots \text{Complete the square:}$$
$$\left(\tfrac{b}{2}\right)^2 = \left(\tfrac{-5}{2}\right)^2 = 6.25.$$

$$y - 13.5 = -2(x - 2.5)^2 \quad \cdots\cdots\cdots \text{Simplify and factor.}$$

$$y = -2(x - 2.5)^2 + 13.5 \quad \cdots\cdots \text{Write in vertex form.}$$

COMMON ERROR
You may think that you have to add 6.25 to both sides; on the right side, 6.25 was added **with −2 already factored out**. So add −2(6.25), or −12.5, to the left side of the equation.

The vertex of the parabola is (2.5, 13.5).

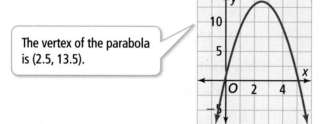

The graph of this equation is a parabola that opens downward, so it has a maximum of $y = 13.5$, at $x = 2.5$.

 Try It! **5.** Write each equation in vertex form. Identify the maximum or minimum value of the graph of each equation.

a. $y = -3x^2 - 9x + 7$ **b.** $y = 2x^2 + 12x + 9$

🔑 **CONCEPT SUMMARY Key Features of Completing the Square**

GEOMETRIC MODEL ▸ The rectangles showing $x^2 + 10x$ are arranged into a square.

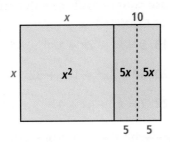 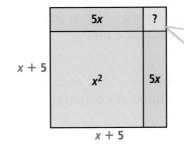

The green section represents the part of the square that has to be added in order to "complete" the square.

The square has side length $x + 5$, so the number needed to complete the square is 25.

ALGEBRAIC MODEL ▸ The number needed to complete the square is half the coefficient of the middle term, squared: the middle term coefficient is 10, half of 10 is 5, and $5^2 = 25$.

To solve $x^2 + 10x = 3$, add 25 to both sides of the equation, take the square root of both sides and solve for x:

$$x^2 + 10x + 25 = 3 + 25$$

$$(x + 5)^2 = 28$$

$$x + 5 = \pm 2\sqrt{7}$$

$$x = -5 \pm 2\sqrt{7}$$

✓ **Do You UNDERSTAND?**

1. ❓ **ESSENTIAL QUESTION** How can you solve a quadratic equation by completing the square?

2. **Error Analysis** Paula said that only quadratic equations with leading coefficients of 1 can be solved by completing the square. Is Paula correct? Explain.

3. **Generalize** Given the expression $x^2 + bx$, describe how to find c so that $x^2 + bx + c$ is a perfect square trinomial.

4. **Make Sense and Persevere** How can you complete the square to find the vertex of a parabola?

Do You KNOW HOW?

Solve each equation by completing the square.

5. $0 = x^2 + 12x + 11$

6. $27 = 3x^2 + 12x$

7. $0 = 2x^2 + 6x - 14$

Write the equation in vertex form, and identify the maximum or minimum value of the graph of the function.

8. $y = x^2 + 6x - 6$

9. $y = -2x^2 + 20x - 42$

10. The daily profit, P, for a company is modeled by the function $p(x) = -0.5x^2 + 40x - 300$, where x is the number of units sold. How many units does the company need to sell each day to maximize profits?

UNDERSTAND

11. Use Appropriate Tools How could you use a graphing calculator to determine whether you have correctly solved a quadratic equation by completing the square?

12. Error Analysis Describe and correct the error a student made in solving a quadratic equation by completing the square.

$$0 = x^2 + 16x - 5$$
$$5 = x^2 + 16x + 64$$
$$5 = (x + 8)^2$$
$$x = -8 \pm \sqrt{5}$$ ✗

13. Higher Order Thinking What number do you need to add to $x^2 + \frac{7}{2}x$ in order to create a perfect square trinomial? Explain.

14. Reason Does the geometric model hold for finding the number that completes the square of the expression $x^2 - 12x$? Explain.

15. Error Analysis When given the equation $-23 = x^2 + 8x$, a student says that you can add 64 to each side of the equation to complete the square. Is the student correct? If not, describe and correct the error.

16. Construct Arguments Explain why you should not try to complete the square when solving $0 = x^2 - 4$.

17. Use Structure Jacob completed the square to rewrite the equation $f(x) = -2x^2 + 12x - 13$ as $f(x) = -2(x - 3)^2 + 5$. Which form of the equation is more helpful for identifying the key features of the graph? Explain.

PRACTICE

Use square roots to solve the quadratic equations.
SEE EXAMPLE 1

18. $9 = x^2 + 2x + 1$

19. $16 = x^2 - 10x + 25$

20. $50 = 2x^2 + 16x + 32$

21. $5 = 3x^2 - 36x + 108$

22. $7 = x^2 + 4x + 4$

23. $-4 = x^2 + 14x + 49$

Rewrite the equations in the form $(x - p)^2 = q$.
SEE EXAMPLE 2

24. $0 = x^2 - 18x + 64$

25. $x^2 + 22x + 120.5 = 0$

26. $x^2 + 3x - \frac{27}{4} = 0$

27. $0 = 4x^2 + 4x - 14$

28. $0 = x^2 - \frac{3}{2}x - \frac{70}{8}$

29. $x^2 + 0.6x - 19.1 = 0$

Solve the following quadratic equations by completing the square. SEE EXAMPLES 3 AND 4

30. $x^2 + 8x + 60 = 0$

31. $x^2 + 14x = 51$

32 $4x^2 + 16x - 65 = 0$

33. $7x^2 + 56x - 22 = 0$

34. $3x^2 - 6x + 13 = 0$

35. $x^2 - 0.4x - 1.2 = 0$

36. $x^2 + 6x = 59$

37. $8x^2 + 16x = 42$

38. $5x^2 - 25 = 10x$

39. $-2x^2 - 12x + 18 = 0$

40. $-3x^2 - 24x - 19 = 0$

41. $17 - x^2 - 18x = 0$

42. What is the length and width of the skate park?

1,029.1 ft² area

141.4 ft perimeter

Write the equation in vertex form. Identify the maximum or minimum value of the graph of the equation. SEE EXAMPLE 5

43. $y = x^2 + 4x - 13$

44. $y = x^2 - 14x + 71$

45. $y = -2x^2 - 20x - 58$

46. $y = -3x^2 + 36x - 93$

47. $y = 6x^2 - 42x + 74.5$

48. $y = 0.5x^2 + 0.5x + 2.125$

APPLY

49. Make Sense and Persevere Keenan launches a model helicopter. The height of the helicopter, in feet, is given by the equation $h = -16t^2 + 64t + 190$, where t is the time in seconds. To the nearest hundredth, how many seconds will it take the helicopter to hit the ground? What is the maximum height of the helicopter?

$h(t) = -16t^2 + 64t + 190$

50. Use Structure The decreasing population, p, of owls in a national park is being monitored by ecologists and is modeled by the equation $p = -0.4 t^2 + 128t + 1,200$, where t is the number of months since the ecologists started observing the owls.

a. If this model is accurate, when will the population reach its maximum?

b. What is the maximum population? Round to the nearest whole number.

c. Use the equation to determine in how many months the population of owls will disappear.

51. Make Sense and Persevere Between 2000 and 2005, the number of skateboarders s in the United States, in millions, can be approximated by the equation $s = 0.33t^2 + 2.27t + 3.96$, where t represents the number of years since 2000. If this model is accurate, in what year did 9.8 million people skateboard?

ASSESSMENT PRACTICE

52. The roots of $f(x) = -2x^2 + 8x + 13$ are _____ and _____. The vertex of the parabola is at _____.

53. SAT/ACT Solve $x^2 + 2x - 5 = 0$.
Ⓐ −5, 1
Ⓑ $-1 \pm \sqrt{5}$
Ⓒ $-1 \pm \sqrt{6}$
Ⓓ $1 \pm \sqrt{5}$
Ⓔ −3, 1

$x^2 + 2x = 5$
$(x^2 + 2x + 1) = 5 + 1$
$(x+1)^2 = 6$
$x + 1 = \pm\sqrt{6}$
$x = -1 \pm \sqrt{6}$

54. Performance Task Yumiko has a rectangular-shaped patio. She wants to double the area of the patio by increasing the length and width by the same amount.

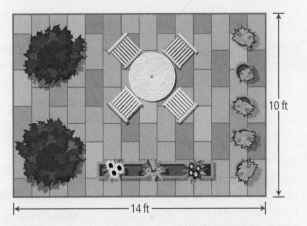

10 ft

14 ft

Part A Write a function to calculate the number of feet Yumiko would need to add to the length and width. Explain your reasoning.

Part B To the nearest hundredth, what are the new dimensions of the patio?

5-3

The Quadratic Formula

PearsonRealize.com

I CAN... solve quadratic equations using the Quadratic Formula.

VOCABULARY
- discriminant
- Quadratic Formula

Activity Assess

👆 EXPLORE & REASON

You can complete the square to solve the general quadratic equation, $ax^2 + bx + c = 0$.

A. Construct Arguments Justify each step in this general solution.

B. What must be true of the value of $b^2 - 4ac$ if the equation $ax^2 + bx + c = 0$ has two non-real solutions? If it has just one solution?

$$ax^2 + bx + c = 0$$
$$ax^2 + bx = -c$$
$$x^2 + \left(\frac{b}{a}\right)x = -\frac{c}{a}$$
$$x^2 + \left(\frac{b}{a}\right)x + \left(\frac{b}{2a}\right)^2 = -\frac{c}{a} + \left(\frac{b}{2a}\right)^2$$
$$\left(x + \frac{b}{2a}\right)^2 = \frac{b^2}{4a^2} - \frac{c}{a}$$
$$\left(x + \frac{b}{2a}\right)^2 = \frac{b^2 - 4ac}{4a^2}$$
$$x + \frac{b}{2a} = \pm\sqrt{\frac{b^2 - 4ac}{4a^2}}$$
$$x = \frac{-b \pm \sqrt{b^2 - 4ac}}{2a}$$

❓ ESSENTIAL QUESTION

How can you use the Quadratic Formula to solve quadratic equations or to predict the nature of their solutions?

👆 EXAMPLE 1 Solve Quadratic Equations

What are the solutions to the equation?

USE APPROPRIATE TOOLS
The Quadratic Formula is a useful tool for finding solutions, particularly when an equation cannot be easily factored.

A. $3x^2 - 4x - 9 = 0$

The **Quadratic Formula**, $x = \frac{-b \pm \sqrt{b^2 - 4ac}}{2a}$, provides the solutions of the quadratic equation $ax^2 + bx + c = 0$, for $a \neq 0$.

$$x = \frac{-b \pm \sqrt{b^2 - 4ac}}{2a} \quad \text{Write the Quadratic Formula.}$$

$$= \frac{-(-4) \pm \sqrt{(-4)^2 - 4(3)(-9)}}{2(3)} \quad \begin{array}{l}\text{Substitute 3 for } a, -4 \text{ for } b, \\ \text{and } -9 \text{ for } c.\end{array}$$

$$= \frac{4 \pm \sqrt{124}}{6} \quad \text{Simplify.}$$

$$= \frac{4 \pm 2\sqrt{31}}{6}$$

$$= \frac{2 \pm \sqrt{31}}{3}$$

The solutions are
$$x = \frac{2 + \sqrt{31}}{3} \text{ and } x = \frac{2 - \sqrt{31}}{3}.$$

CONTINUED ON THE NEXT PAGE

198 TOPIC 5 Quadratic Equations and Complex Numbers

Go Online | PearsonRealize.com

EXAMPLE 1 CONTINUED

B. How can you use the Quadratic Formula to solve $x^2 - 9x + 27 = 0$?

$$x = \frac{-b \pm \sqrt{b^2 - 4ac}}{2a}$$ ⟶ Write the Quadratic Formula.

$$= \frac{-(-9) \pm \sqrt{(-9)^2 - 4(1)(27)}}{2(1)}$$ ⟶ Substitute 1 for a, −9 for b, and 27 for c.

$$= \frac{9 \pm \sqrt{-27}}{2}$$ ⟶ Simplify.

$$= \frac{9 \pm i\sqrt{27}}{2}$$ ⟶ $\sqrt{-1} = i$

$$= \frac{9 \pm 3i\sqrt{3}}{2}$$ ⟶ Simplify.

The solutions are $x = \frac{9 + 3i\sqrt{3}}{2}$ and $x = \frac{9 - 3i\sqrt{3}}{2}$.

GENERALIZE
Look for relationships between the coefficients of a quadratic equation and its solutions. If $a = 1$, then the sum of the solutions is the opposite of the x-coefficient, b, and their product is the constant coefficient, c.

Try It! **1.** Solve using the Quadratic Formula.

  a. $2x^2 + 6x + 3 = 0$ **b.** $3x^2 - 2x + 7 = 0$

EXAMPLE 2 **Choose a Solution Method**

Solve the equation $6x^2 - 7x - 20 = 0$ using two different methods. Which do you prefer and why?

STUDY TIP
When you substitute a negative number into a formula, such as the Quadratic Formula, use parentheses to help keep track of the effect of the sign.

Using the Quadratic Formula:

Let $a = 6$, $b = -7$, and $c = -20$

$$x = \frac{-(-7) \pm \sqrt{(-7)^2 - 4(6)(-20)}}{2(6)}$$

$$= \frac{7 \pm \sqrt{49 + 480}}{12}$$

$$= \frac{7 \pm \sqrt{529}}{12}$$

$$= \frac{7 \pm 23}{12}$$

$$x = \frac{7 + 23}{12} = \frac{30}{12} = \frac{5}{2}, \text{ and}$$

$$x = \frac{7 - 23}{12} = -\frac{16}{12} = -\frac{4}{3}$$

Factoring by Grouping:

$$6x^2 - 7x - 20 = 0$$

$$6x^2 - 15x + 8x - 20 = 0$$

$$3x(2x - 5) + 4(2x - 5) = 0$$

$$(3x + 4)(2x - 5) = 0$$

$$x = -\frac{4}{3} \text{ and } x = \frac{5}{2}$$

> You may also find the factorization through trial and error.

Both solution methods give the same result. Factoring may be more efficient, but the Quadratic Formula *always works*, regardless of whether the function has real or imaginary roots.

Try It! **2.** Solve the equation $6x^2 + x - 15 = 0$ using the Quadratic Formula and another method.

CONCEPTUAL
UNDERSTANDING

EXAMPLE 3 Identify the Number of Real-Number Solutions

How can you determine the number and type of roots for a quadratic equation?

Graph each equation. Then use the quadratic formula to find the roots.

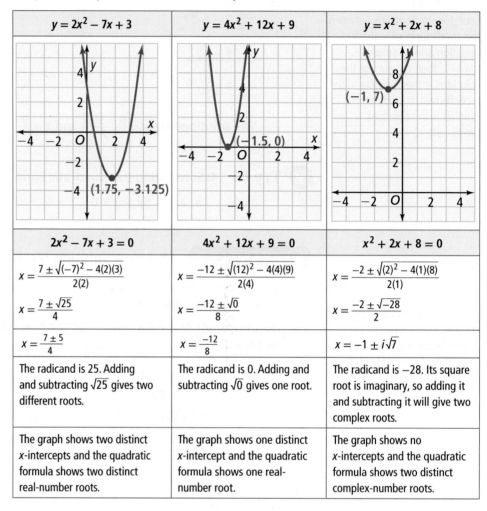

$y = 2x^2 - 7x + 3$	$y = 4x^2 + 12x + 9$	$y = x^2 + 2x + 8$
$2x^2 - 7x + 3 = 0$	$4x^2 + 12x + 9 = 0$	$x^2 + 2x + 8 = 0$
$x = \dfrac{7 \pm \sqrt{(-7)^2 - 4(2)(3)}}{2(2)}$	$x = \dfrac{-12 \pm \sqrt{(12)^2 - 4(4)(9)}}{2(4)}$	$x = \dfrac{-2 \pm \sqrt{(2)^2 - 4(1)(8)}}{2(1)}$
$x = \dfrac{7 \pm \sqrt{25}}{4}$	$x = \dfrac{-12 \pm \sqrt{0}}{8}$	$x = \dfrac{-2 \pm \sqrt{-28}}{2}$
$x = \dfrac{7 \pm 5}{4}$	$x = \dfrac{-12}{8}$	$x = -1 \pm i\sqrt{7}$
The radicand is 25. Adding and subtracting $\sqrt{25}$ gives two different roots.	The radicand is 0. Adding and subtracting $\sqrt{0}$ gives one root.	The radicand is -28. Its square root is imaginary, so adding it and subtracting it will give two complex roots.
The graph shows two distinct x-intercepts and the quadratic formula shows two distinct real-number roots.	The graph shows one distinct x-intercept and the quadratic formula shows one real-number root.	The graph shows no x-intercepts and the quadratic formula shows two distinct complex-number roots.

The radicand in the quadratic formula is what determines the nature of the roots.

The **discriminant** of a quadratic equation in the form $ax^2 + bx + c = 0$ is the value of the radicand, $b^2 - 4ac$.

If $b^2 - 4ac > 0$, then $ax^2 + bx + c = 0$ has two real roots.

If $b^2 - 4ac = 0$, then $ax^2 + bx + c = 0$ has one real root.

If $b^2 - 4ac < 0$, then $ax^2 + bx + c = 0$ has two non-real roots.

 Try It! **3.** Describe the nature of the solutions for each equation.

        a. $16x^2 + 8x + 1 = 0$ **b.** $2x^2 - 5x + 6 = 0$

APPLICATION →   ● **EXAMPLE 4**   **Interpret the Discriminant**

Rachel is about to serve and tosses a tennis ball straight up into the air. The height, h, of the ball, in meters, at time t, in seconds is given by $h(t) = -5t^2 + 5t + 2$. Will the ball reach a height of 4 meters?

$h = -5t^2 + 5t + 2$

To see if $h = 4$ for some value of t, set the quadratic expression for h equal to 4, and solve.

$$-5t^2 + 5t + 2 = 4$$

Rewrite the equation in standard form:

$$-5t^2 + 5t - 2 = 0$$

$$a = -5, b = 5, c = -2$$

The discriminant is: $(5)^2 - 4(-5)(-2)$
$$= 25 - 40$$

$$25 - 40 = -15$$

$$-15 < 0$$

So the equation $h = 4$ does not have a real solution. Therefore, the ball does not reach 4 m.

 Try It!   **4.** According to the model of Rachel's serve, will the ball reach a height of 3 meters?

● **EXAMPLE 5**   **Use the Discriminant to Find a Particular Equation**

What value(s) of b will cause $2x^2 + bx + 18 = 0$ to have one real solution?

For this equation, $a = 2$ and $c = 18$.

The equation will have a single rational solution when the discriminant is equal to 0.

$$b^2 - 4ac = 0$$

$$b^2 - 4(2)(18) = 0$$

$$b^2 - 144 = 0$$

$$b^2 = 144$$

$$b = \pm 12$$

There are two possible equations: $2x^2 + 12x + 18 = 0$ and $2x^2 - 12x + 18 = 0$.

STUDY TIP
Note that the equation $2x^2 + bx + 18 = 0$ will have two real solutions if $b > 12$ or $b < -12$. It will have two non-real solutions if $-12 < b < 12$.

 Try It!   **5.** Determine the value(s) of b that ensure $5x^2 + bx + 5 = 0$ has two non-real solutions.

CONCEPT SUMMARY   Key Features of the Quadratic Formula

QUADRATIC FORMULA

$$x = \frac{-b \pm \sqrt{b^2 - 4ac}}{2a}$$

This formula is used to solve any quadratic equation: $ax^2 + bx + c = 0$, where $a \neq 0$.

USING THE DISCRIMINANT

Predict the number and type of solutions using the discriminant, $b^2 - 4ac$.

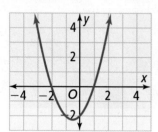

$x^2 + x - 2 = 0$

$b^2 - 4ac > 0$

Two real solutions

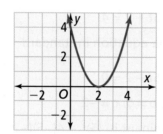

$x^2 - 4x + 4 = 0$

$b^2 - 4ac = 0$

One real solution

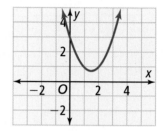

$x^2 - 3x + 3 = 0$

$b^2 - 4ac < 0$

Two non-real solutions

Do You UNDERSTAND?

1. **ESSENTIAL QUESTION** How can you use the Quadratic Formula to solve quadratic equations or to predict the nature of their solutions?

2. **Vocabulary** Why is the discriminant a useful tool to use when solving quadratic equations?

3. **Error Analysis** Rick claims that the equation $x^2 + 5x + 9 = 0$ has no solution. Jenny claims that there are two solutions. Explain how Rick could be correct, and explain how Jenny could be correct.

4. **Use Appropriate Tools** What methods can you use to solve quadratic equations?

Do You KNOW HOW?

5. Describe the number and type of solutions of the equation $2x^2 + 7x + 11 = 0$.

6. Use the Quadratic Formula to solve the equation $x^2 + 6x - 10 = 0$.

7. At time t seconds, the height, h, of a ball thrown vertically upward is modeled by the equation $h = -5t^2 + 33t + 4$. About how long will it take for the ball to hit the ground?

8. Use the Quadratic Formula to solve the equation $x^2 - 8x + 16 = 0$. Is this the only way to solve this equation? Explain.

UNDERSTAND

9. **Look for Relationships** How can you use the Quadratic Formula to factor a quadratic equation?

10. **Error Analysis** Describe and correct the error a student made in solving an equation.

$$x^2 - 5x + 5 = 0$$
$$a = 1, b = -5, c = 5$$
$$x = \frac{-5 \pm \sqrt{(-5)^2 - 4(1)(5)}}{2(1)}$$
$$= \frac{-5 \pm \sqrt{25 - 20}}{2}$$
$$= \frac{-5}{2} \pm \frac{\sqrt{5}}{2} \quad ✗$$

11. **Mathematical Connections** What does the Quadratic Formula tell you about the graph of a quadratic function?

12. **Communicate Precisely** Explain your process for choosing a method for solving quadratic equations.

13. **Higher Order Thinking** Kelsey wants to use the Quadratic Formula to solve the equation $x^4 + 5x^2 - 5 = 0$. Is this possible? If so, describe the steps she should follow.

14. **Construct Arguments** Explain why the graph of the quadratic function $f(x) = x^2 + x + 5$ crosses the y-axis but does not cross the x-axis.

15. **Construct Arguments** Sage said that the Quadratic Formula does not always work. Sage used it to solve the equation $x^2 - 3x - 2 = -4$, with $a = 1$, $b = -3$, and $c = -2$. The formula gave $x = \frac{3 \pm \sqrt{17}}{2}$ as the solutions to the equation. When Sage checked, neither one of them satisfied the equation. How could you convince Sage that the Quadratic Formula does always work?

PRACTICE

Use the Quadratic Formula to solve each equation. SEE EXAMPLE 1

16. $x^2 - 10x + 25 = 0$ 17. $x^2 + 2x + 2 = 0$

18. $5x^2 - 8x + 4 = 0$ 19. $x^2 + 9x - 1 = 3x - 10$

20. $3x^2 - 20x - 7 = 0$ 21. $-x^2 + 3x - 8 = 0$

Use the discriminant to identify the number and type of solutions for each equation. SEE EXAMPLE 3

22. $25x^2 - 20x + 4 = 0$ 23. $x^2 + 7x + 11 = 0$

24. $3x^2 - 8x - 10 = 0$ 25. $2x^2 + 9x + 14 = 0$

Deon throws a ball into the air. The height, h, of the ball, in meters, at time t seconds is modeled by the function $h(t) = -5t^2 + t + 4$. SEE EXAMPLE 4

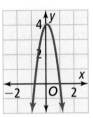

26. When will the ball hit the ground?

27. Will the ball reach a height of 5 meters?

Use any method to solve the equation. SEE EXAMPLE 2

28. $4x^2 + 7x - 11 = 0$ 29. $x^2 + 4x + 4 = 100$

30. $3x^2 + x + 7 = x^2 + 10$ 31. $6x^2 + 2x + 3 = 0$

Find the value(s) of k that will cause the equation to have the given number and type of solutions. SEE EXAMPLE 5

32. $5x^2 + kx + 5 = 0$, 1 real solution

33. $3x^2 + 12x + k = 0$, 2 real solutions

34. $kx^2 - 3x + 4 = 0$, 2 real solutions

APPLY

35. Model With Mathematics The table shows the average cost of tuition and fees at a public four-year college for an in-state student in recent years.

Academic Year	Tuition and Fees
2012–13	$9,006
2013–14	$9,077
2014–15	$9,161
2015–16	$9,410

a. Write an equation that can be used to find the average cost, C, of tuition after x years.

b. Use the model to predict when tuition will exceed $10,000.

36. Make Sense and Persevere The first astronaut on Mars tosses a rock straight up. The height, h, measured in feet after t seconds, is given by the function $h(t) = -6t^2 + 24t + 6$.

$h(t) = -6t^2 + 24t + 6$

a. After how many seconds will the rock be 30 feet above the surface?

b. After how many seconds will the rock be 10 feet above the surface?

c. How many seconds will it take for the rock to return to the surface?

d. The same action on Earth is modeled by the equation $g(t) = -16t^2 + 24t + 6$. On Earth, how many seconds would it take for the rock to hit the ground?

ASSESSMENT PRACTICE

37. Which of the following equations has two real solutions? Select *Yes* or *No*.

	Yes	No
a. $x^2 - 8x - 2 = 0$	❑	❑
b. $2x^2 + 10x + 17 = 0$	❑	❑
c. $4x^2 - 28x + 49 = 0$	❑	❑
d. $x^2 + 10x - 25 = 4x + 2$	❑	❑
e. $2x^2 + x + 10 = 5 - 4x - x^2$	❑	❑

38. SAT/ACT Which expression can be simplified to find the solution(s) of the equation $2x^2 - x - 15 = 0$?

Ⓐ $-1 \pm \dfrac{\sqrt{1 - 4(2)(-15)}}{2(2)}$

Ⓑ $\dfrac{1 \pm \sqrt{1 - 4(2)(-15)}}{2(2)}$

Ⓒ $\dfrac{1 \pm \sqrt{-1 - 4(2)(-15)}}{2(2)}$

Ⓓ $\dfrac{1 \pm \sqrt{1 - 4(2)(15)}}{2(2)}$

Ⓔ $\dfrac{1 \pm \sqrt{1 + 4(2)(-15)}}{2(2)}$

39. Performance Task Four congruent squares are cut from a rectangular piece of cardboard.

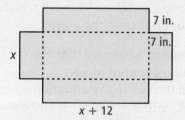

Part A. If the resulting flaps are folded up and taped together to make a box, write a function to represent the volume of the box in terms of the width of the original piece of cardboard.

Part B. What are the dimensions of the original cardboard, to the nearest tenth, if the volume of the box is 434 in.^{3}

5-4

Linear-Quadratic Systems

 PearsonRealize.com

I CAN... solve linear-quadratic systems.

EXPLORE & REASON

Draw a rough sketch of a parabola and a line on the coordinate plane.

A. Count the number of points of intersection between the two graphs.

B. Sketch another parabola on a coordinate plane. Use a straightedge to investigate the different ways that a line and a parabola intersect. What conjectures can you make?

C. Construct Arguments How many different numbers of intersection points are possible between a quadratic function and a linear function? Justify that you have found all of the possibilities.

ESSENTIAL QUESTION How can you solve a system of two equations or inequalities in which one is linear and one is quadratic?

CONCEPTUAL UNDERSTANDING

EXAMPLE 1 **Determine the Number of Solutions**

How many solutions can there be for a linear-quadratic system?

COMMUNICATE PRECISELY
A solution to a system of equations is an ordered pair that produces a true statement in all the equations of the system. In the graph, the solutions are the coordinates of the intersection points.

A. How many real solutions does the system $\begin{cases} y = x^2 \\ y = 2x \end{cases}$ **have?**

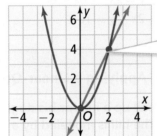

The graph seems to show that the quadratic function and linear function intersect at two points.

This system has two real solutions.

B. How does modifying the linear function in the system $\begin{cases} y = x^2 \\ y = 2x + b \end{cases}$ **affect the number of solutions?**

Test values for b to determine when the system has different numbers of solutions.

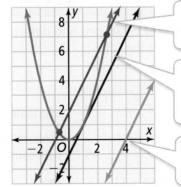

When $b = 2$, there are two solutions. The graphs intersect at two points.

When $b = -1$, there is one solution. The graph of $y = 2x - 1$ is tangent to the graph of $y = x^2$.

When $b = -8$, there are no solutions. The graph of $y = 2x - 8$ does not intersect the graph of $y = x^2$.

Visually inspecting the graph suggests that there is no way for a line to cross a parabola more than twice. Thus, the system of a linear function and a quadratic function may have 0, 1, or 2 solutions.

 Try It! **1.** Determine the number of real solutions of the system $\begin{cases} y = 3x^2 \\ y = 3x - 2 \end{cases}$.

EXAMPLE 2 **Solve a Linear-Quadratic System Using Substitution**

USE STRUCTURE
As with a system of linear equations, you can use substitution and elimination to find the values of x and y that make the system true. In this case, substitution yields a new quadratic equation to solve.

How can you use substitution to solve this system? $\begin{cases} y = 3x^2 + 3x - 5 \\ 2x - y = 3 \end{cases}$

The first equation provides an expression for y in terms of x. Substitute this expression in the second equation.

$2x - (3x^2 + 3x - 5) = 3$ .... Substitute $3x^2 + 3x - 5$ for y in the second equation.

$2x - 3x^2 - 3x + 5 = 3$ .... Distribute -1 to remove parentheses.

$3x^2 + x - 2 = 0$ .... Simplify.

$(x + 1)(3x - 2) = 0$ .... Factor.

So $x = -1$ and $x = \frac{2}{3}$ are solutions of this quadratic equation.

> If the graphs of the equations have two solutions, there are two points of intersection for the graphs of the equations.

When $x = -1$, $y = 2(-1) - 3$, or -5. When $x = \frac{2}{3}$, $y = 2\left(\frac{2}{3}\right) - 3$, or $-\frac{5}{3}$.
The solutions of the system are $(-1, -5)$ and $\left(\frac{2}{3}, -\frac{5}{3}\right)$.

Try It! 2. Solve each system by substitution.

a. $\begin{cases} y = 2x^2 - 6x - 8 \\ 2x - y = 16 \end{cases}$ b. $\begin{cases} y = -3x^2 + x + 4 \\ 4x - y = 2 \end{cases}$

APPLICATION

EXAMPLE 3 **Applying a Linear-Quadratic System**

Andrew kicks a ball up a hill for his dog, Laika, to chase. The hill is modeled by a line through the origin. The path of the ball is modeled by the quadratic function shown. How far does the ball travel horizontally? How far must Laika run up the hill to catch it?

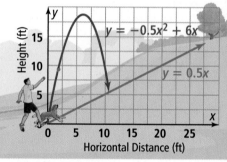

Create a system of equations and determine where the path of the ball intersects the hill.

$\begin{cases} y = -0.5x^2 + 6x \\ y = 0.5x \end{cases}$

$0.5x = -0.5x^2 + 6x$ .... Substitute for y.

$0 = -0.5x^2 + 5.5x$ .... Subtract $0.5x$ from both sides.

$0 = -0.5x(x - 11)$ .... Factor.

$-0.5x = 0$ and $x - 11 = 0$ ..... Set each factor equal to 0 and solve.

$x = 0$ and $x = 11$

CONTINUED ON THE NEXT PAGE

EXAMPLE 3 CONTINUED

The solution $x = 0$ represents the horizontal distance, in feet, when Andrew kicks the ball. The solution $x = 11$ represents the horizontal distance, in feet, when the ball lands on the hill. So the ball travels 11 ft horizontally.

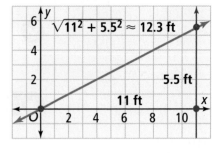

$\sqrt{11^2 + 5.5^2} \approx 12.3$ ft

5.5 ft

11 ft

The route Laika runs can be modeled as the hypotenuse of a right triangle.

So Laika runs approximately 12.3 ft to get the ball.

COMMON ERROR
Make sure to answer every part of the question. After solving this equation, you still need to find the distance that Laika ran.

✓ **Try It!**   **3.** Revenue for the high school band concert is given by the function $y = -30x^2 + 250x$, where x is the ticket price, in dollars. The cost of the concert is given by the function $y = 490 - 30x$. At what ticket price will the band make enough revenue to cover their costs?

👆 **EXAMPLE 4**   **Solve a Linear-Quadratic System of Inequalities**

How can you solve this system of inequalities? $\begin{cases} y < -2x^2 + 12x - 10 \\ 4x + y > 4 \end{cases}$

Graphing an inequality is similar to graphing an equation. You start in the same manner, but later you have to consider whether to sketch the graph as a solid or dotted and how to shade the graph.

Graph the quadratic inequality:

Complete the square to write the inequality in vertex form.

$$y + 10 < -2(x^2 - 6x)$$
$$y + 10 - 18 < -2(x^2 - 6x + 9)$$
$$y - 8 < -2(x - 3)^2$$
$$y < -2(x - 3)^2 + 8$$

The parabola has vertex (3, 8).

Find two symmetric points on either side of the vertex:

$x = 2, y = 6 \rightarrow (2, 6)$ $x = 4, y = 6 \rightarrow (4, 6)$

Sketch the graph of the quadratic inequality using these three points.

Graph the linear inequality:

Solve the inequality for y to write in slope-intercept form:

Sketch the graph of the linear inequality using the slope and y-intercept.

$$y > -4x + 4$$

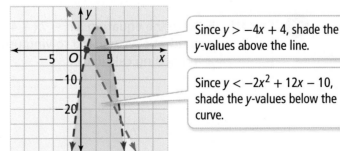

Since $y > -4x + 4$, shade the y-values above the line.

Since $y < -2x^2 + 12x - 10$, shade the y-values below the curve.

The region where the two shaded areas overlap holds the solutions to the system.

CONTINUED ON THE NEXT PAGE

EXAMPLE 4 CONTINUED

 Try It! 4. Solve the system of inequalities $\begin{cases} y > x^2 + 6x - 12 \\ 3x - y \geq -8 \end{cases}$ using shading.

EXAMPLE 5 Using a System to Solve an Equation

Solve the equation $x^2 + 9x - 5 = 4 - 3x$ by writing a linear-quadratic system and using the intersection feature of a graphing calculator to solve it.

STUDY TIP
If you graph both of these equations on your calculator, you can use the TRACE or INTERSECTION function to approximate the solution as a check.

Graph the system $\begin{cases} y = x^2 + 9x - 5 \\ y = 4 - 3x \end{cases}$.

The graphing calculator shows the curve and line intersect at $x \approx 0.71$ and $x \approx -12.71$.

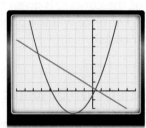

x scale: 2   y scale: 10

Check: Substitute the values into the original equation to verify the solutions. Because the values are approximations, one side of the equation should be approximately equal to the other.

$$x^2 + 9x - 5 = 4 - 3x$$
$$(0.71)^2 + 9(0.71) - 5 \overset{?}{=} 4 - 3(0.71)$$
$$0.5041 + 6.39 - 5 \overset{?}{=} 4 - 2.13$$
$$1.8941 \approx 1.87$$

$$x^2 + 9x - 5 = 4 - 3x$$
$$(-12.71)^2 + 9(-12.71) - 5 \overset{?}{=} 4 - 3(-12.71)$$
$$161.5441 - 114.39 - 5 \overset{?}{=} 4 + 38.13$$
$$42.1541 \approx 42.13$$

The equations show that the approximate solutions are reasonable.

 Try It! 5. Solve the equation $3x^2 - 7x + 4 = 9 - 2x$ by writing a linear-quadratic system and solving using the intersection feature of a graphing calculator.

CONCEPT SUMMARY Key Features of Linear-Quadratic Systems

Linear-Quadratic Systems of Equations

WORDS Use substitution or elimination to solve the system.

GRAPHS

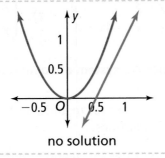

no solution

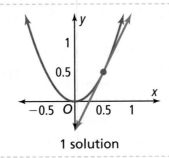

1 solution

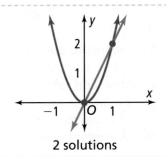

2 solutions

Linear-Quadratic Systems of Inequalities

WORDS Graph linear and quadratic inequalities, considering whether the graph is solid or dotted. Use shading to identify the solution region.

GRAPH

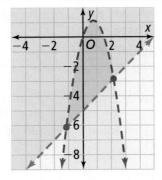

✓ Do You UNDERSTAND?

1. **? ESSENTIAL QUESTION** How can you solve a system of two equations or inequalities in which one is linear and one is quadratic?

2. **Error Analysis** Dyani was asked to use substitution to solve this system:

$$\begin{cases} y = 2x^2 - 6x + 4 \\ x - y = 7 \end{cases}$$

She began as follows, to find the x-coordinate(s) to the solution(s) of the system:

$x + 2x^2 - 6x + 4 = 7$	Substitute for y.
$2x^2 - 5x - 3 = 0$	Simplify.
$(2x + 1)(x - 3) = 0$	Factor.
$x = -\dfrac{1}{2},\ x = 3$	Set each factor equal to 0, solve for x. **✗**

But Dyani has already made an error. What was her mistake?

Do You KNOW HOW?

Determine the number of solutions for the system of equations.

3. $\begin{cases} y = \dfrac{2}{5}x^2 \\ y = x - 2 \end{cases}$

4. $\begin{cases} y = -x - 1 \\ 3x^2 + 2y = 4 \end{cases}$

Use substitution to solve the system of equations.

5. $\begin{cases} y = 3x^2 + 7x - 10 \\ y - 19x = 22 \end{cases}$

6. $\begin{cases} y = 3x^2 \\ y - 3x = -2 \end{cases}$

(handwritten notes):
$2x \quad x^{5} \quad 5$
$\dfrac{2}{5}x^2 = x - 2$
$2x^2 = 5x - 10$
$2x^2 - 5x + 10 = 0$
$\dfrac{5 \pm \sqrt{25 - 80}}{4} \quad \dfrac{5 \pm i\sqrt{55}}{4}$

Scan for Multimedia

Practice Tutorial

Additional Exercises Available Online

UNDERSTAND

7. Construct Arguments Nora and William are asked to solve the system of equations
$$\begin{cases} y - 1 = 3x \\ y = 2x^2 - 4x + 9 \end{cases}$$ without graphing.

Nora wants to use substitution, inserting $2x^2 - 4x + 9$ in place of y in the upper equation and solving. William wants to rewrite $y - 1 = 3x$ as $y = 3x + 1$ and begin by setting $3x + 1$ equal to $2x^2 - 4x + 9$, and then solving. Which student is correct, and why?

8. Error Analysis Chris was given the system of equations $$\begin{cases} y = -x^2 \\ y = 2x + b \end{cases}$$ and asked to use graphing to test the number of solutions of the system for different values of b. He graphed the system as shown, and concluded that the system could have one solution or no solutions depending on the value of b. What was Chris's error?

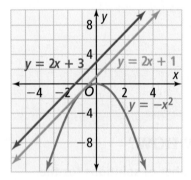

9. Reason You are given the following system of equations: $$\begin{cases} y = x^2 \\ y = -1 \end{cases}$$. Without graphing or performing any substitutions, can you see how many solutions the system must have? Describe your reasoning.

10. Construct Arguments Can a system of equations with one linear and one quadratic equation have more than two solutions? Give at least two arguments for your answer.

PRACTICE

Determine how many solutions each system of equations has by graphing them. SEE EXAMPLE 1

11. $$\begin{cases} y = 3 \\ y = x^2 - 4x + 7 \end{cases}$$

12. $$\begin{cases} y = 3x^2 - 2x + 7 \\ y + 5 = \frac{1}{2}x \end{cases}$$

Consider the system of equations $$\begin{cases} y = x^2 \\ y = mx + b \end{cases}$$.
SEE EXAMPLE 1

13. Find values for m and b so that the system has two solutions.

14. Find values for m and b so that the system has no solutions.

15. Find values for m and b so that the system has one solution.

Use substitution to solve the system of equations.
SEE EXAMPLE 2

16. $$\begin{cases} y = 5 \\ y = 2x^2 - 16x + 29 \end{cases}$$

17. $$\begin{cases} y = 3x^2 - 4x \\ 27 + y = 14x \end{cases}$$

18. LaToya throws a ball from the top of a bridge. Her throw is modeled by the equation $y = -0.5x^2 + 3x + 10$, and the bridge is modeled by the equation $y = -0.2x + 7$. About how far does the ball travel horizontally before its first bounce? SEE EXAMPLE 3

Solve each system of inequalities using shading.
SEE EXAMPLE 4

19. $$\begin{cases} y > x^2 \\ 5 > y \end{cases}$$

20. $$\begin{cases} -5 < y - x \\ y < -3x^2 + 6x + 1 \end{cases}$$

Solve each equation by writing a linear-quadratic system and solving using the intersection feature of a graphing calculator. SEE EXAMPLE 5

21. $6x^2 - 15x + 8 = 17 - 4x$

22. $7x^2 - 28x + 32 = 4$

23. $-\frac{5}{2}x - 10 = -2x^2 - x - 3$

Go Online | PearsonRealize.com

APPLY

24. **Model With Mathematics** A boulder is flung out of the top of a 3,000 m tall volcano. The boulder's height, y, in meters, is a function of the horizontal distance it travels, x, in meters. The slope of the line representing the volcano's hillside is $-\frac{5}{3}$. At what height above the ground will the boulder strike the hillside? How far will it have traveled horizontally when it crashes?

$y = -\frac{1}{1,000}x^2 - \frac{1}{6}x + 3,000$

slope $= -\frac{5}{3}$

25. **Use Structure** You are given the system of equations:

$$\begin{cases} y = x + 1 \\ y^2 + x^2 = 25 \end{cases}$$

Solve the system using any of the methods you have learned in this lesson. Explain why you selected the method you used.

26. **Reason** A football player punts the football, whose path is modeled by the equation $h = -4.9t^2 + 18.24t + 0.8$ for h, in meters, and t, in seconds. The height of a blocker's hands for the same time, t, is modeled as $h = -1.43t + 4.26$. Is it possible for the blocker to knock down the ball? What else would you have to know to be sure?

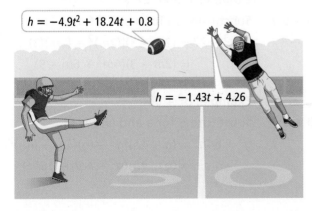

$h = -4.9t^2 + 18.24t + 0.8$

$h = -1.43t + 4.26$

27. Classify each function as having *exactly one* or *no* points of intersection with the function $y = x^2 + 8x + 11$.

   a. $y = 2x - 12$

   b. $y = 12x + 7$

   c. $y = -5$

   d. $y = 11 + 8x$

   e. $y = -6$

28. **SAT/ACT** How many solutions does the following system of equations have?

$$\begin{cases} y = 16x - 19 \\ y = 3x^2 + 4x - 7 \end{cases}$$

   Ⓐ two solutions

   Ⓑ no solutions

   Ⓒ an infinite number of solutions

   Ⓓ one solution

   Ⓔ The number of solutions cannot be determined.

29. **Performance Task** A golfer accidentally hits a ball toward a water hazard that is downhill from her current position on the fairway. The hill can be modeled by a line through the origin with slope $-\frac{1}{8}$. The path of the ball can be modeled by the function $y = -\frac{1}{100}x^2 + \frac{3}{2}x$.

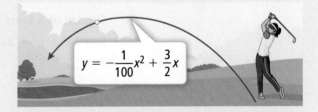

$y = -\frac{1}{100}x^2 + \frac{3}{2}x$

   Part A If the golfer stands at the origin, and the water hazard is 180 yd away, will the golfer's ball bounce or splash?

   Part B How far did the ball land from the edge of the water hazard?

   Part C Does it matter whether you measure the 180 yd horizontally or along the hill? Explain.

5-5

Polynomial Identities

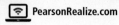
PearsonRealize.com

I CAN... prove and use polynomial identities.

VOCABULARY
• Binomial Theorem
• identity
• Pascal's Triangle

👆 **EXPLORE & REASON**

Look at the following triangle.

Each number is the sum of the two numbers diagonally above. If there is not a second number, think of it as 0.

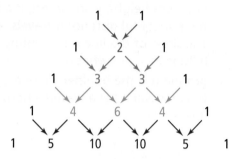

A. Write the numbers in the next three rows.

B. **Look for Relationships** What other patterns do you see?

C. Find the sum of the numbers in each row of the triangle. Write a formula for the sum of the numbers in the nth row.

❓ **ESSENTIAL QUESTION**   How can you use polynomial identities to rewrite expressions efficiently?

CONCEPT Polynomial Identities

A mathematical statement that equates two polynomial expressions is an **identity** if one side can be transformed into the other side using mathematical operations. These polynomial identities are helpful tools used to multiply and factor polynomials.

Difference of Squares
$a^2 - b^2 = (a + b)(a - b)$

Example: $25x^2 - 36y^2$
Substitute $5x$ for a and $6y$ for b.
$25x^2 - 36y^2 = (5x + 6y)(5x - 6y)$

Square of a Sum
$(a + b)^2 = a^2 + 2ab + b^2$

Example: $(3x + 4y)^2$
Substitute $3x$ for a and $4y$ for b.
$(3x + 4y)^2 = (3x)^2 + 2(3x)(4y) + (4y)^2$
$= 9x^2 + 24xy + 16y^2$

Difference of Cubes
$a^3 - b^3 = (a - b)(a^2 + ab + b^2)$

Example: $8m^3 - 27$
Substitute $2m$ for a and 3 for b.
$8m^3 - 27 = (2m - 3)[(2m)^2 + (2m)(3) + 3^2]$
$= (2m - 3)(4m^2 + 6m + 9)$

Sum of Cubes
$a^3 + b^3 = (a + b)(a^2 - ab + b^2)$

Example: $g^3 + 64h^3$
Substitute g for a and $4h$ for b.
$g^3 + 64h^3 = (g + 4h)[g^2 - (g)(4h) + (4h)^2]$
$= (g + 4h)(g^2 - 4gh + 16h^2)$

EXAMPLE 1   Prove a Polynomial Identity

How can you prove the Sum of Cubes Identity, $a^3 + b^3 = (a + b)(a^2 - ab + b^2)$?

To prove an identity, start with the expression on one side of the equation and use properties of operations on polynomials to transform it into the expression on the other side.

USE STRUCTURE
Another way to establish the identity is to multiply each term of the second factor by $(a + b)$, and then combine like terms.

$(a + b)(a^2 - ab + b^2)$

$= a(a^2 - ab + b^2) + b(a^2 - ab + b^2)$ .... Use the Distributive Property.

$= a^3 - a^2b + ab^2 + a^2b - ab^2 + b^3$ .... Use the Distributive Property.

$= a^3 + (-a^2b + a^2b) + (ab^2 - ab^2) + b^3$ .... Group like terms.

$= a^3 + b^3$ .... Combine like terms.

So, $a^3 + b^3 = (a + b)(a^2 - ab + b^2)$.

✓ **Try It!**   **1.** Prove the Difference of Cubes Identity.

EXAMPLE 2   Use Polynomial Identities to Multiply

How can you use polynomial identities to multiply expressions?

A. $(2x^2 + y^3)^2$ — The sum is a binomial, and the entire sum is being raised to the second power.

COMMON ERROR
When finding $(a + b)^2$, recall that it is not sufficient to square the first term and square the second term. You must distribute the two binomials.

Use the Square of a Sum Identity to find the product:

$(a + b)^2 = a^2 + 2ab + b^2$

$(2x^2 + y^3)^2 = (2x^2)^2 + 2(2x^2)(y^3) + (y^3)^2$ .... Substitute $2x^2$ for a and y^3 for b.

$= 4x^4 + 4x^2y^3 + y^6$ .... Simplify.

So, $(2x^2 + y^3)^2 = 4x^4 + 4x^2y^3 + y^6$.

B. 41 • 39

Rewrite the expression in terms of a and b.

$41 • 39 = (a + b)(a - b)$

$= (40 + 1)(40 - 1)$

Use the Difference of Squares Identity:

$(40 + 1)(40 - 1) = 40^2 - 1^2$

$= 1,600 - 1$

$= 1,599$

So $41 • 39 = 1,599$.

✓ **Try It!**   **2.** Use polynomial identities to multiply the expressions.

a. $(3x^2 + 5y^3)(3x^2 - 5y^3)$ **b.** $(12 + 15)^2$

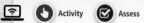
☝ **EXAMPLE 3** Use Polynomial Identities to Factor and Simplify

How can you use polynomial identities to factor polynomials and simplify numerical expressions?

A. $9m^4 - 25n^6$

$9m^4$ and $25n^6$ are both perfect squares.

> A square term includes an even exponent, not necessarily an exponent that is a perfect square.

$$9m^4 = (3m^2)^2$$
$$25n^6 = (5n^3)^2$$

Use the Difference of Squares Identity: $a^2 - b^2 = (a + b)(a - b)$.

$$9m^4 - 25n^6 = (3m^2)^2 - (5n^3)^2 \quad \text{Express each term as a square.}$$
$$= (3m^2 + 5n^3)(3m^2 - 5n^3) \quad \text{Write the factors.}$$

So, $9m^4 - 25n^6 = (3m^2 + 5n^3)(3m^2 - 5n^3)$.

B. $x^3 - 216$

x^3 and 216 are both perfect cubes.

$$x^3 = (x)^3$$
$$216 = 6^3$$

Use the Difference of Cubes Identity: $a^3 - b^3 = (a - b)(a^2 + ab + b^2)$.

$$x^3 - 216 = (x)^3 - (6)^3 \quad \text{Express each term as a cube.}$$
$$= (x - 6)(x^2 + 6x + 36) \quad \text{Write the factors.}$$

So, $x^3 - 216 = (x - 6)(x^2 + 6x + 36)$.

COMMON ERROR
The second factor is *almost* a Square of a Sum. Remember that the middle term of the Difference of Cubes Identity is the product ab, not $2ab$.

C. $11^3 + 5^3$

Use the Sum of Cubes Identity: $a^3 + b^3 = (a + b)(a^2 - ab + b^2)$.

$$11^3 + 5^3 = (11 + 5)(11^2 - 11(5) + 5^2)$$
$$= (16)(121 - 55 + 25)$$
$$= 16(91)$$
$$= 1{,}456$$

So, $11^3 + 5^3 = 1{,}456$.

 Try It! **3.** Use polynomial identities to factor each polynomial.

a. $m^8 - 9n^{10}$ **b.** $27x^9 - 343y^6$ **c.** $12^3 + 2^3$

CONCEPTUAL
UNDERSTANDING

 EXAMPLE 4 Expand a Power of a Binomial

How is $(x + y)^n$ obtained from $(x + y)^{n-1}$?

A. What are $(x + y)^3$ and $(x + y)^4$?

$$(x + y)^3 = (x + y)(x + y)^2$$
$$= (x + y)(x^2 + 2xy + y^2)$$

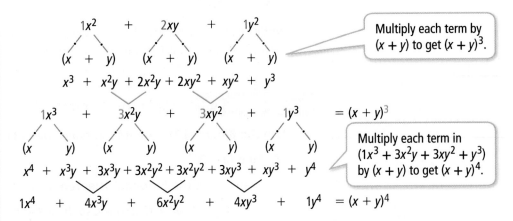

The coefficients of $(x + y)^n$ are produced by adding the coefficients of $(x + y)^{n-1}$, producing an array known as Pascal's Triangle. **Pascal's Triangle** is the triangular pattern of numbers where each number is the sum of the two numbers diagonally above it. If there is not a second number diagonally above in the triangle, think of the missing number as 0.

Row 0			1		1		$(x + y)^0$
Row 1		1	1		$1x + 1y$		$(x + y)^1$
Row 2	1	2	1		$1x^2 + 2xy + 1y^2$		$(x + y)^2$
Row 3	1	3	3	1	$1x^3 + 3x^2y + 3xy^2 + 1y^3$		$(x + y)^3$
Row 4	1	4	6	4	1	$1x^4 + 4x^3y + 6x^2y^2 + 4xy^3 + 1y^4$	$(x + y)^4$

You can obtain $(x + y)^n$ by adding adjacent pairs of coefficients from $(x + y)^{n-1}$.

B. Use Pascal's Triangle to expand $(x + y)^5$.

Add pairs of coefficients from Row 4 to complete Row 5.

Row 4   1   4   6   4   1

Row 5   1   5   10   10   5   1

Write the expansion. Use the coefficients from Row 5 with powers of x starting at 5 and decreasing to 0 and with powers of y starting at 0 and increasing to 5.

> The sum of the exponents in each term is equal to the exponent on the original binomial.

$$(x + y)^5 = 1x^5 + 5x^4y + 10x^3y^2 + 10x^2y^3 + 5xy^4 + 1y^5$$

STUDY TIP
Notice the patterns of the powers. The powers of x decrease from n to 0 and the powers of y increase from 0 to n when reading the terms from left to right.

Try It! 4. Use Pascal's Triangle to expand $(x + y)^6$.

CONCEPT Binomial Theorem

The **Binomial Theorem** states that, for every positive integer n,

$$(a + b)^n = C_0 a^n + C_1 a^{n-1}b + C_2 a^{n-2}b^2 + \ldots + C_{n-1}ab^{n-1} + C_n b^n.$$

The coefficients $C_0, C_1, C_2, \ldots, C_{n-1}, C_n$ are the numbers in Row n of Pascal's Triangle.

Notice that the powers of a are decreasing while the powers of b are increasing, and that the sum of the powers of a and b in each term is always n.

EXAMPLE 5 ▷ **Apply the Binomial Theorem**

Use the Binomial Theorem to expand the expressions.

A. Find $(x - 3)^4$.

Step 1 Use the Binomial Theorem to write the expansion when $n = 4$.

$$C_0 a^4 + C_1 a^3 b + C_2 a^2 b^2 + C_3 ab^3 + C_4 b^4$$

Step 2 Use Row 4 in Pascal's Triangle to write the coefficients.

$$a^4 + 4a^3 b + 6a^2 b^2 + 4ab^3 + b^4$$

Pascal's Triangle
```
          1
        1   1
      1   2   1
    1   3   3   1
  1   4   6   4   1
1   5   10  10  5   1
```

Step 3 Identify a and b.

$$a = x \text{ and } b = -3$$

> **COMMON ERROR**
> Remember that the base of $(a + b)^n$ in the Binomial Theorem is $(a + b)$. If the terms are being subtracted, use the opposite of b in the expansion.

Step 4 Substitute x for a and -3 for b in the pattern. Then simplify.

$$x^4 + 4x^3(-3) + 6x^2(-3)^2 + 4x(-3)^3 + (-3)^4$$

$$x^4 - 12x^3 + 54x^2 - 108x + 81$$

So $(x - 3)^4 = x^4 - 12x^3 + 54x^2 - 108x + 81$.

B. Find $(s^2 + 3)^5$.

The expansion of $(a + b)^5$ is $a^5 + 5a^4 b + 10a^3 b^2 + 10a^2 b^3 + 5ab^4 + b^5$.

Since $a = s^2$ and $b = 3$, the expansion is:

$$(s^2 + 3)^5 = (s^2)^5 + 5(s^2)^4(3) + 10(s^2)^3(3)^2 + 10(s^2)^2(3)^3 + 5(s^2)(3)^4 + (3)^5$$

$$= s^{10} + 15s^8 + 90s^6 + 270s^4 + 405s^2 + 243$$

So $(s^2 + 3)^5 = s^{10} + 15s^8 + 90s^6 + 270s^4 + 405s^2 + 243$.

 Try It! **5.** Use the Binomial Theorem to expand each expression.

a. $(x - 1)^7$

b. $(2c + d)^6$

CONCEPT SUMMARY Polynomial Identities

POLYNOMIAL IDENTITIES

Special polynomial identities can be used to multiply and factor polynomials.

Difference of Squares

$a^2 - b^2 = (a + b)(a - b)$

Difference of Cubes

$a^3 - b^3 = (a - b)(a^2 + ab + b^2)$

Square of a Sum

$(a + b)^2 = a^2 + 2ab + b^2$

Sum of Cubes

$a^3 + b^3 = (a + b)(a^2 - ab + b^2)$

BINOMIAL EXPANSION

The binomial expansion of $(a + b)^n$ has the following properties:

1) The expansion contains $n + 1$ terms.

2) The coefficients of each term are numbers from the nth row of Pascal's Triangle.

3) The exponent of a is n in the first term and decreases by 1 in each successive term.

4) The exponent of b is 0 in the first term and increases by 1 in each successive term.

5) The sum of the exponents in any term is n.

Row 0 ———————— 1 ———————————— 1 ———————— $(x + y)^0$

Row 1 ———— 1   1 ———————— $1x + 1y$ ———— $(x + y)^1$

Row 2 ———— 1   2   1 ———————— $1x^2 + 2xy + 1y^2$ ———— $(x + y)^2$

Row 3 ——— 1   3   3   1 ——— $1x^3 + 3x^2y + 3xy^2 + 1y^3$ ——— $(x + y)^3$

Row 4 —1   4   6   4   1 — $1x^4 + 4x^3y + 6x^2y^2 + 4xy^3 + 1y^4$ —— $(x + y)^4$

Do You UNDERSTAND?

1. **ESSENTIAL QUESTION** How can you use polynomial identities to rewrite expressions efficiently?

2. **Reason** Explain why the middle term of $(x + 5)^2$ is $10x$.

3. **Communicate Precisely** How are Pascal's Triangle and a binomial expansion, such as $(a + b)^5$, related?

4. **Use Structure** Explain how to use a polynomial identity to factor $8x^6 - 27y^3$.

5. **Make Sense and Persevere** What number does C_3 represent in the expansion $C_0a^5 + C_1a^4b + C_2a^3b^2 + C_3a^2b^3 + C_4ab^4 + C_5b^5$? Explain.

6. **Error Analysis** Dakota said the third term of the expansion of $(2g + 3h)^4$ is $36g^2h^2$. Explain Dakota's error. Then correct the error.

Do You KNOW HOW?

Use polynomial identities to multiply each expression.

7. $(2x + 8y)(2x - 8y)$

8. $(x + 3y^3)^2$

Use polynomial identities to factor each polynomial.

9. $36a^6 - 4b^2$

10. $8x^6 - y^3$ $(2x^3 - y)(4x^6 + 2x^3y + y^2)$
   $2x^3$ y

11. $m^9 + 27n^6$ $(m^3 + 3n^2)(m^6 - 3m^3n^2 + 9n^4)$
   m^3 $3n^2$

Find the term of the binomial expansion.

12. fifth term of $(x + y)^5$ $1x^5 + 5x^4y + 10x^3y^2 + 10x^2y^3 + 5xy^4 + y^5$

13. third term of $(a - 3)^6$ $a^6 + 6a^5(-3) + 15a^4(-3)^2 + 20a^3(-3)^3$
   $= 145a^4$

Use Pascal's Triangle to expand each expression.

14. $(x + 1)^5$ 15. $(a - b)^6$

Use the Binomial Theorem to expand each expression.

16. $(d - 1)^4$ 17. $(x + y)^7$

UNDERSTAND

18. Use Structure Expand $(3x + 4y)^3$ using Pascal's Triangle and the Binomial Theorem.

19. Error Analysis Emma factored $625g^{16} - 25h^4$. Describe and correct the error Emma made in factoring the polynomial.

$$625g^{16} - 25h^4$$
$$= (25g^4)^2 - (5h^2)^2$$
$$= (25g^4 + 5h^2)(25g^4 - 5h^2)$$
✗

20. Higher Order Thinking Use Pascal's Triangle and the Binomial Theorem to expand $(x + i)^4$. Justify your work.

21. Use Structure Expand the expression $(2x - 1)^4$. What is the sum of the coefficients?

22. Error Analysis A student says that the expansion of the expression $(-4y + z)^7$ has seven terms. Describe and correct the error the student may have made.

23. Reason The sum of the coefficients in the expansion of the expression $(a + b)^n$ is 64. Use Pascal's Triangle to find the value of n.

24. Use Structure Factor $x^3 - 125y^6$ in the form $(x - A)(x^2 + Bx + C)$. What are the values of A, B, and C?

25. Generalize How many terms will there be in the expansion of the expression $(x + 3)^n$? Explain how you know.

26. Make Sense and Persevere How could you use polynomial identities to factor the expression $x^6 - y^6$?

PRACTICE

27. Prove the polynomial identity.
$$x^4 - y^4 = (x - y)(x + y)(x^2 + y^2)$$
SEE EXAMPLE 1

Use polynomial identities to multiply the expressions. SEE EXAMPLE 2

28. $(x + 9)(x - 9)$ **29.** $(x + 6)^2$

30. $(3x - 7)^2$ **31.** $(2x - 5)(2x + 5)$

32. $(4x^2 + 6y^2)(4x^2 - 6y^2)$ **33.** $(x^2 + y^6)^2$

34. $(8 - x^2)(8 + x^2)$ **35.** $(6 - y^3)^2$

36. $18 \cdot 22$ **37.** $103 \cdot 97$

38. $(7 + 9)^2$ **39.** $(10 + 5)^2$

Use polynomial identities to factor the polynomials or simplify the expressions. SEE EXAMPLE 3

40. $x^8 - 9$ **41.** $x^9 - 8$

42. $8x^3 + y^9$ **43.** $x^6 - 27y^3$

44. $4x^2 - y^6$ **45.** $216 + 27y^{12}$

46. $64x^3 - 125y^6$ **47.** $\frac{1}{16}x^6 - 25y^4$

48. $9^3 + 6^3$ **49.** $10^3 + 5^3$

50. $10^3 - 3^3$ **51.** $8^3 - 2^3$

Use the Binomial Theorem to expand the expressions. SEE EXAMPLES 4 and 5

52. $(x + 3)^3$ **53.** $(2a - b)^5$

54. $\left(b - \frac{1}{2}\right)^4$ **55.** $(x^2 + 1)^4$

56. $\left(2x + \frac{1}{3}\right)^3$ **57.** $(x^3 + y^2)^6$

58. $(d - 3)^4$ **59.** $(2m + 2n)^6$

60. $(n + 5)^5$ **61.** $(3x - 0.2)^3$

62. $(4g + 2h)^4$ **63.** $\left(m^2 + \frac{1}{2}n\right)^3$

PRACTICE & PROBLEM SOLVING

APPLY

64. Reason A medium-sized shipping box with side length s units has a volume of s^3 cubic units.

a. A large shipping box has side lengths that are 3 units longer than the medium shipping box. Write a binomial expression for the volume of the large shipping box.

b. Expand the polynomial in part a to simplify the volume of the large shipping box.

c. A small shipping box has side lengths that are 2 units shorter than the medium shipping box. Write a binomial expression for the volume of the small shipping box.

d. Expand the polynomial in part c to simplify the volume of the small shipping box.

65. Use Structure The dimensions of a rectangle are shown. Write the area of the rectangle as a sum of cubes.

$x + 3$

$x^2 - 3x + 9$

66. A Pythagorean triple is a set of three positive integers a, b, and c that satisfy $a^2 + b^2 = c^2$. The identity $(x^2 - y^2)^2 + (2xy)^2 = (x^2 + y^2)^2$ can be used to generate Pythagorean triples. Use the identity to generate a Pythagorean triple when $x = 5$ and $y = 4$.

ASSESSMENT PRACTICE

67. Are the expressions below perfect square trinomials? Select *Yes* or *No*.

	Yes	No
$x^2 + 16x + 64$		
$4x^2 - 44x + 121$		
$9x^2 - 15x + 25$		

68. SAT/ACT How many terms are in the expansion of $(2x + 7y)^9$?

Ⓐ 2   Ⓑ 7   Ⓒ 8   Ⓓ 9   Ⓔ 10

69. Performance Task If an event has a probability of success p and a probability of failure q, then each term in the expansion of $(p + q)^n$ represents a probability. For example, if a basketball player makes 60% of his free throw attempts, $p = 0.6$ and $q = 0.4$. To find the probability the basketball player will make exactly h out of k free throws, find $C_{k-h}p^h q^{k-h}$, where C_{k-h} is a coefficient of row k of Pascal's Triangle, p is the probability of success, and q is the probability of failure.

Part A What is the probability the basketball player will make exactly 6 out of 10 free throws? Round to the nearest percent.

Part B Another basketball player makes 80% of her free throw attempts. Write an expression to find the probability of this basketball player making exactly 7 out of 10 free throws. Describe what each variable in the expression represents.

Part C Find the probability that the basketball player from Part B will make exactly 7 out of 10 free throws. Round to the nearest percent.

5-5a

The Fundamental Theorem of Algebra

 PearsonRealize.com

I CAN... use the Fundamental Theorem of Algebra to verify that I have found all complex roots of a quadratic equation.

VOCABULARY
• multiplicity of a root

? **ESSENTIAL QUESTION** How can you use the Fundamental Theorem of Algebra to verify that you have found all complex roots of a quadratic equation?

EXAMPLE 1 Find the Number of Complex Roots of an Equation

How many complex roots are there for the given equations?

A. $x^2 + 4x + 5 = 0$

Use the quadratic formula.

$$x = \frac{-4 \pm \sqrt{4^2 - 4 \cdot 1 \cdot 5}}{2 \cdot 1}$$

$$= \frac{-4 \pm \sqrt{-4}}{2}$$

> Since the discriminant is negative, the roots are nonreal.

$$= -2 \pm i$$

Because of the "$\pm$" symbol in the quadratic formula, there are two complex roots. The roots of the equation are $-2 - i$ and $-2 + i$.

B. $x^2 + 6x + 9 = 0$

The expression $x^2 + 6x + 9$ is a perfect square. Factor, then solve for x.

$$x^2 + 6x + 9 = 0$$

$$(x + 3)^2 = 0$$

$$x + 3 = 0$$

> -3 is a complex root of the form $a + bi$, where $a = -3$ and $b = 0$.

$$x = -3$$

When you can rewrite the equation $f(x) = 0$ as $g(x)^n \cdot h(x) = 0$, if $g(c) = 0$, then $f(c) = 0$, and the **multiplicity of the root** c is n.

The equation $x^2 + 6x + 9 = 0$ has one complex root, -3, with multiplicity 2.

☑ **Try It!** **1.** Find the number of complex roots of each equation. Indicate the multiplicity of each root.

   a. $x^2 + 4 = 0$

   b. $x^2 - 9 = 0$

CONCEPT The Fundamental Theorem of Algebra

You can generalize the results from Example 1 to polynomial equations of higher degree in the following theorem.

> The polynomial equation $p(x) = 0$, where $p(x)$ is a polynomial of degree $n \geq 1$, has exactly n complex roots, including any roots with multiplicity greater than 1.

Corollary to the Fundamental Theorem of Algebra

> The quadratic equation $ax^2 + bx + c = 0$ has exactly two complex roots, or one complex root with multiplicity 2.

Go Online | PearsonRealize.com

EXAMPLE 2 Prove the Fundamental Theorem of Algebra for Quadratics

Show that the equation $ax^2 + bx + c = 0$ has two complex roots, or one complex root of multiplicity 2.

You know that when the discriminant $b^2 - 4ac$ is positive, there are exactly two real roots. When the discriminant is 0, there is one real root, with multiplicity 2.

Now let the discriminant $b^2 - 4ac = d$ be negative.

USE STRUCTURE
Consider the discriminant $b^2 - 4ac$ as a single number, d.

$$\frac{-b \pm \sqrt{b^2 - 4ac}}{2a} = \frac{-b \pm \sqrt{d}}{2a}$$

Simplify the radical as the product of the imaginary unit i and a real number.

$$= \frac{-b \pm i\sqrt{|d|}}{2a}$$

$$= \frac{-b}{2a} \pm i\frac{\sqrt{|d|}}{2a}$$

There are two complex roots of the equation, namely $\frac{-b}{2a} + i\frac{\sqrt{d}}{2a}$ and $\frac{-b}{2a} - i\frac{\sqrt{d}}{2a}$.

Try It! **2.** Show that the equation has two complex roots.

    a. $x^2 - 2x + 3 = 0$

    b. $x^2 - 4x + 16 = 0$

CONCEPT SUMMARY Complex Roots of Quadratic Equations

The Fundamental Theorem of Algebra tells you that there are two complex roots for every quadratic equation, or one complex root with multiplicity 2.

DISCRIMINANT	$b^2 - 4ac > 0$	$b^2 - 4ac = 0$	$b^2 - 4ac < 0$
ROOTS	Two real roots	One real root with multiplicity 2.	Two nonreal roots

---

Do You UNDERSTAND?

1. **ESSENTIAL QUESTION** How can you use the Fundamental Theorem of Algebra to verify that you have found all complex roots of a quadratic equation?

2. **Error Analysis** Joe says the equation $x^2 - 4x + 5 = 0$ has no complex roots because the discriminant is negative. What is his error?

3. **Reason** Let $p(x)$ be a quadratic polynomial with one real root. What do you know about the other root?

Do You KNOW HOW?

Determine whether the equation has two real roots, two nonreal roots, or one real root with multiplicity 2.

4. $x^2 - 6x + 10 = 0$

5. $4x^2 - 12x + 9 = 0$

Find the complex roots for the equation.

6. $x^2 + 6x + 11 = 0$

7. $x^2 - 8x + 44 = 0$

8. $x^2 + 2x - 8 = 0$

9. **Generalize** Show that if $a + bi$ is a root of a quadratic equation with real coefficients, then $a - bi$ is the other root.

10. **Mathematical Connections** For each quadratic function, find the number of roots of the equation shown. Determine whether the roots are real or nonreal, and give their multiplicity.

a.

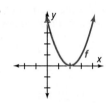

$$f(x) = 0$$

b.

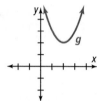

$$g(x) = 0$$

c.

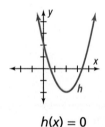

$$h(x) = 0$$

d.

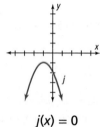

$$j(x) = 0$$

11. **Construct Arguments** Show that the equation $ax^3 + bx^2 + cx = 0$ has three complex roots.

12. **Reason** Can a quadratic equation with real coefficients have a single nonreal root with multiplicity 2? Explain.

13. **Higher Order Thinking** Let $q(x) = 0$ be a quadratic equation with real coefficients. Is it possible for it to have one root that is a real number and one root that is a nonreal number? Explain.

Determine the number of complex roots of the equation and the multiplicity of each root.

14. $x^2 + 2x + 1 = 0$ 15. $x^2 + 3x - 4 = 0$

16. $x^2 - 8$ 17. $x^2 + 8$

18. $x^2 - 2x + 10 = 0$ 19. $-x^2 + 4x - 8 = 0$

20. $2x^2 - 4x + 4 = 0$ 21. $x^2 - 6x + 13 = 0$

Find all complex roots of the equation.

22. $x^2 - 4x + 13 = 0$ 23. $x^2 - 2x - 3 = 0$

24. $4x^2 - 4x - 2 = 0$ 25. $4x^2 - 20x + 25 = 0$

26. An economist uses a quadratic model to describe the relationship between the number of items produced by a manufacturer, x, and the total revenue resulting from the sale of the items, $R(x)$. The graph of the model is shown.

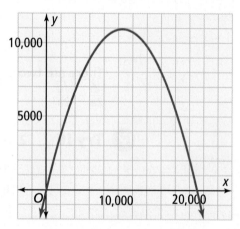

a. What equation can she use to determine when revenue is equal to 0?

b. She finds that revenue is equal to 0 when $x = 100$ and $x = 21,000$. Can she conclude that these are the only two values of x where the model predicts that the total revenue is 0? Explain.

27. An electrical engineer is solving a problem modeled by $P(x) \cdot Q(x) = 0$, where $P(x)$ and $Q(x)$ are each quadratic expressions. The graphs of P and Q are shown.

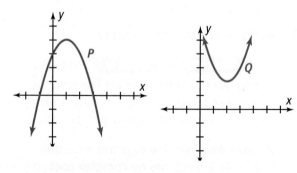

He concludes that he need to solve only $P(x) = 0$ to find all real solutions to $P(x) \cdot Q(x) = 0$. Is he correct? Explain.

Topic Review

1. How do you use quadratic equations and complex numbers to model situations and solve problems?

Vocabulary Review

Choose the correct term to complete each sentence.

2. The _____ of a quadratic function is the value of the radicand, $b^2 - 4ac$.

3. A number with both real and imaginary parts is called a _____.

4. _____ is a method used to rewrite an equation as a perfect square trinomial equal to a constant.

- completing the square
- complex number
- discriminant
- imaginary number

Concepts & Skills Review

LESSON 5-1 | **Complex Numbers and Operations**

Quick Review

The **imaginary unit** i is the number whose square is equal to -1. An **imaginary number** bi is the product of any real number b and the imaginary unit i. A **complex number** is a number that may be written in the form $a + bi$. **Complex conjugates** are complex numbers with equivalent real parts and opposite imaginary parts.

Example

Write the product of $3.5i(4 - 6i)$ in the form $a + bi$.

$3.5i(4 - 6i)$

$= 3.5i(4) + 3.5i(-6i)$ ········· Distribute.

$= 14i - 21i^2$ ········· Simplify.

$= 14i - 21(-1)$ ········· Substitute -1 for i.

$= 14i + 21$ ········· Write in the form $a + bi$.

The product is $14i + 21$.

Practice & Problem Solving

Write each product in the form $a + bi$.

5. $(5 - 3i)(2 + i)$

6. $(-3 + 2i)(2 - 3i)$

Divide. Write the answer in the form $a + bi$.

7. $\dfrac{5}{3 + i}$

8. $\dfrac{2 - 3i}{1 + 2i}$

9. **Error Analysis** Describe and correct the error a student made when multiplying complex numbers.

$(2 - 3i)(4 + i) = 2(4) + 2(i) - 3i(4) - 3i(i)$
$= 8 + 2i - 12i - 3i^2$
$= 8 - 10i - 3i^2$

10. **Model With Mathematics** The formula $E = IZ$ is used to calculate voltage, where E is voltage, I is current, and Z is impedance. If the voltage in a circuit is $35 + 10i$ volts and the impedance is $4 + 4i$ ohms, what is the current (in amps)? Write your answer in the form $a + bi$.

LESSON 5-2   Completing the Square

Quick Review

Completing the square is a method used to rewrite a quadratic equation as a perfect square trinomial equal to a constant. A perfect square trinomial with the coefficient of x^2 equal to 1 has the form $(x - p)^2$ which is equivalent to $x^2 - 2px + p^2$.

Example

Solve the equation $0 = x^2 - 2x + 4$ by completing the square.

$0 = x^2 - 2x + 4$ · · · Write the original equation.

$-4 = x^2 - 2x$ · · · · · · · Subtract 4 from both sides of the equation.

$1 - 4 = x^2 - 2x + 1$ · · · Complete the square

$-3 = (x - 1)^2$ · · · · · · · Write the right side of the equation as a perfect square.

$\pm\sqrt{-3} = x - 1$ · · · · · · · Take the square root of each side of the equation.

$1 \pm \sqrt{-3} = x$ · · · · · · · Add 1 to each side of the equation.

The solutions are $x = 1 \pm \sqrt{-3}$.

Practice & Problem Solving

Rewrite the equations in the form $(x - p)^2 = q$.

11. $0 = x^2 - 16x + 36$ 12. $0 = 4x^2 - 28x - 42$

Solve the following quadratic equations by completing the square.

13. $x^2 - 24x - 82 = 0$ 14. $-3x^2 - 42x = 18$

15. $4x^2 = 16x + 25$ 16. $12 + x^2 = 15x$

17. **Reason** The height, in meters, of a punted football with respect to time is modeled using the function $f(x) = -4.9x^2 + 24.5x + 1$, where x is time in seconds. You determine that the roots of the function $f(x) = -4.9x^2 + 24.5x + 1$ are approximately -0.04 and 5.04. When does the ball hit the ground? Explain.

18. **Make Sense and Persevere** A bike manufacturer can predict profits, P, from a new sports bike using the quadratic function $P(x) = -100x^2 + 46{,}000x - 2{,}100{,}000$, where x is the price of the bike. At what prices will the company make $0 in profit?

LESSON 5-3   The Quadratic Formula

Quick Review

The **Quadratic Formula**, $x = \dfrac{-b \pm \sqrt{b^2 - 4ac}}{2a}$, provides the solutions of the quadratic equation $ax^2 + bx + c = 0$ for $a \neq 0$. You can calculate the **discriminant** of a quadratic equation to determine the number of real roots.

$b^2 - 4ac > 0$: $ax^2 + bx + c = 0$ has 2 real roots.

$b^2 - 4ac = 0$: $ax^2 + bx + c = 0$ has 1 real root.

$b^2 - 4ac < 0$: $ax^2 + bx + c = 0$ has 2 non-real roots.

Example

How many real roots does $3x^2 - 8x + 1 = 0$ have?

Find the discriminant.

$b^2 - 4ac = (-8)^2 - 4(3)(1)$

$= 64 - 12$

$= 52$

Since $52 > 0$, the equation has two real roots.

Practice & Problem Solving

Use the Quadratic Formula to solve the equation.

19. $x^2 - 16x + 24 = 0$ 20. $x^2 + 5x + 2 = 0$

21. $2x^2 - 18x + 5 = 0$ 22. $3x^2 - 5x - 19 = 0$

Use the discriminant to identify the number and type of solutions for each equation.

23. $x^2 - 24x + 19 = 0$ 24. $3x^2 - 8x + 12 = 0$

25. Find the value(s) of k that will cause the equation $4x^2 - kx + 4 = 0$ to have one real solution.

26. **Construct Arguments** Why does the graph of the quadratic function $f(x) = x^2 + 4x + 5$ cross the y-axis but not the x-axis?

27. **Model With Mathematics** The function $C(x) = 0.0045x^2 - 0.47x + 139$ models the cost per hour of running a bus between two cities, where x is the speed in kilometers per hour. At what speeds will the cost of running the bus exceed $130?

LESSON 5-4 — Linear-Quadratic Systems

Quick Review

Solutions to a system of equations are points that produces a true statement for all the equations of the system. The solutions on a graph are the coordinates of the intersection points.

Example

Use substitution to solve the system of equations.

$$\begin{cases} y = 2x^2 - 5x + 4 \\ 5x - y = 4 \end{cases}$$

Substitute $2x^2 - 5x + 4$ for y in the second equation.

$$5x - (2x^2 - 5x + 4) = 4$$
$$-2x^2 + 10x - 8 = 0$$

Factor: $-2(x - 1)(x - 4) = 0$

So $x = 1$ and $x = 4$ are solutions.

When $x = 1$, $y = 2(1)^2 - 5(1) + 4 = 1$.

When $x = 4$, $y = 2(4)^2 - 5(4) + 4 = 16$.

The solutions of the system are $(1, 1)$ and $(4, 16)$.

Practice & Problem Solving

Determine the number of solutions of each system of equations.

28. $\begin{cases} y = x^2 - 5x + 9 \\ y = 3 \end{cases}$

29. $\begin{cases} y = 3x^2 + 4x + 5 \\ y - 4 = 2x \end{cases}$

Solve each system of equations.

30. $\begin{cases} y = x^2 + 4x + 3 \\ y - 2x = 6 \end{cases}$

31. $\begin{cases} y = x^2 + 2x + 7 \\ y = 7 + x \end{cases}$

32. **Model With Mathematics** An archer shoots an arrow to a height (meters) given by the equation $y = -5t^2 + 18t - 0.25$, where t is the time in seconds. A target sits on a hill represented by the equation $y = 0.75x - 1$. At what height will the arrow strike the target, and how long will it take?

LESSON 5-5 — Polynomial Identities

Quick Review

Polynomial identities can be used to factor or multiply polynomials.

Example

Use polynomial identities to factor $8x^3 + 27y^3$.

Use the Sum of Cubes Identity. Express each term as a square. Then write the factors.

$$a^3 + b^3 = (a + b)(a^2 - ab + b^2)$$
$$8x^3 + 27y^3 = (2x)^3 + (3y)^3$$
$$= (2x + 3y)(4x^2 - 6xy + 9y^2)$$

Practice & Problem Solving

Use polynomial identities to multiply each polynomial.

33. $(5x + 8)^2$

34. $(7x - 4)(7x + 4)$

Factor the polynomial.

35. $x^6 - 64$

36. $27x^3 + y^6$

Use Pascal's Triangle or the Binomial Theorem to expand the expressions.

37. $(x - 2)^4$

38. $(x + 5y)^5$

39. **Communicate Precisely** Explain why the set of polynomials is closed under subtraction.

40. **Reason** The length of a rectangle is represented by $3x^3 - 2x^2 + 10x - 4$, and the width is represented by $-x^3 + 6x^2 - x + 8$. What is the perimeter of the rectangle?

TOPIC 6

Working With Functions

? TOPIC ESSENTIAL QUESTION

What are some operations on functions that you can use to create models and solve problems?

Topic Overview

enVision® STEM Project:
Predict a Population

Topic Vocabulary

- absolute value function
- axis of symmetry
- ceiling function
- floor function
- inverse of a function
- piecewise-defined function
- step function
- vertex

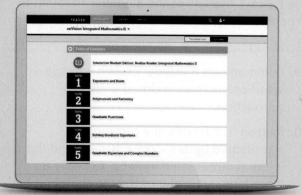

Digital Experience

 INTERACTIVE STUDENT EDITION
Access online or offline.

 ACTIVITIES Complete *Explore & Reason, Model & Discuss,* and *Critique & Explain* activities. Interact with Examples and Try Its.

 ANIMATION View and interact with real-world applications.

 PRACTICE Practice what you've learned.

 Go online | PearsonRealize.com

▶ The Mad Runner

People run in many different places: on the soccer field during a game, around the neighborhood, on the basketball court, on the street to catch a bus, in gym class.

Sometimes people run on flat ground and other times they run up or down hills or even up and down stairs. They also run on different surfaces, such as grass, pavement, sand, or a basketball court. Think about this during the Mathematical Modeling in 3 Acts lesson.

VIDEOS Watch clips to support *Mathematical Modeling in 3 Acts Lessons* and **enVision®** *STEM Projects.*

CONCEPT SUMMARY Review key lesson content through multiple representations.

ASSESSMENT Show what you've learned.

GLOSSARY Read and listen to English and Spanish definitions.

TUTORIALS Get help from *Virtual Nerd*, right when you need it.

MATH TOOLS Explore math with digital tools and manipulatives.

Did You Know?

Locusts are a species of grasshopper that are mostly solitary but sometimes band together in large numbers. Swarming locusts can fly great distances and consume large quantities of vegetation wherever they settle.

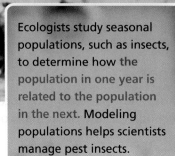

Ecologists study seasonal populations, such as insects, to determine how the population in one year is related to the population in the next. Modeling populations helps scientists manage pest insects.

Over 90% of the animals on Earth are insects.

Rest of animal population

The only place on Earth without insects is the ocean.

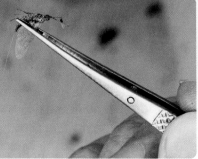

One of the largest cicada broods, Brood VI, has a periodic life cycle and spends 17 years underground between outbreaks. The brood is projected to surface in 2034.

▶ Your Task: Predict a Population

You and your classmates will analyze a model for population growth and determine how increases in the rate of reproduction affect an insect population.

6-1

The Absolute Value Function

PearsonRealize.com

I CAN... analyze functions that include absolute value expressions.

VOCABULARY
• absolute value function
• axis of symmetry
• vertex

✋ EXPLORE & REASON

Groups of students are hiking from mile markers 2, 6 and 8 to meet at the waterfall located at mile marker 5.

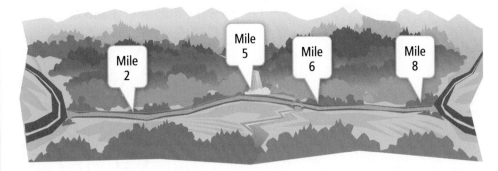

A. How can you use the mile marker to determine the number of miles each group of students needs to hike to the waterfall?

B. Model With Mathematics Make a graph that relates the position of each group on the trail to their distance from the waterfall.

C. How would the points in your graph from part B change as the groups of students approach the waterfall?

❓ ESSENTIAL QUESTION

What are the key features of the graph of the absolute value function?

✋ EXAMPLE 1   Graph the Absolute Value Function

What are the features of the graph of $f(x) = |x|$?

Make a table of values and graph the **absolute value function** $f(x) = |x|$.

x	$f(x) = |x|$	$(x, f(x))$
−2	2	(−2, 2)
−1	1	(−1, 1)
0	0	(0, 0)
1	1	(1, 1)
2	2	(2, 2)

The *vertex*, (0, 0), is the turning point of the graph.

LOOK FOR RELATIONSHIPS
How does the nature of absolute value contribute to the symmetric appearance of the graph?

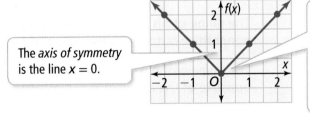

The *axis of symmetry* is the line $x = 0$.

The graph has a **vertex**, where the axis of symmetry intersects the graph. It represents the minimum value in the range.

The graph has an **axis of symmetry**, which intersects the vertex and divides the graph into two sections, or pieces, that are images of each other under a reflection.

✓ Try It!   1. What are the domain and range of $f(x) = |x|$?

CONCEPTUAL
UNDERSTANDING

 EXAMPLE 2 Transform the Absolute Value Function

A. How do the domain and range of $g(x) = 2|x|$ compare with the domain and range of $f(x) = |x|$?

Compare the graphs of g and f.

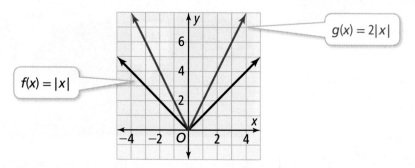

The domain of f and the domain of g are all real numbers.

Because the absolute value expression produces only nonnegative values, the range of f is $y \geq 0$. Multiplying $|x|$ by a positive factor, in this case, 2, yields nonnegative outputs, so the range of g is also $y \geq 0$.

The domain and range of the function g are the same as those of function f.

B. How do the domain and range of $h(x) = -1|x|$ compare with the domain and range of $f(x) = |x|$?

Compare the graphs of h and f.

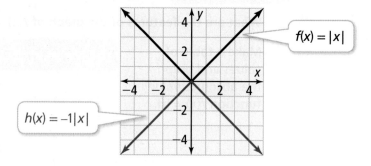

USE APPROPRIATE TOOLS
Why is it helpful to use both a graph and a table to explore the domain and range of functions that involve absolute value expressions?

The domain of f and the domain of h are all real numbers.

The range of f is $y \geq 0$. Multiplying $|x|$ by a negative factor, -1, yields nonpositive outputs, so the range of h is $y \leq 0$.

The domain of h is the same as the domain of f. The range of h is the opposite of the range of f.

✅ **Try It!** **2.** How do the domain and range of each function compare with the domain and range of $f(x) = |x|$?

a. $g(x) = \frac{1}{2}|x|$ b. $h(x) = -2|x|$

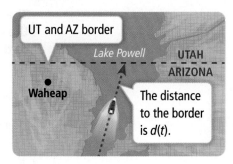
APPLICATION   👆 **EXAMPLE 3**   **Interpret the Graph of a Function**

Jay rides in a boat from his home to his friend's home in a neighboring state. The graph of the function $d(t) = 30\,|t - 1.5|$ shows the distance of the boat in miles from the state line at t hours. Assume the graph shows Jay's entire trip.

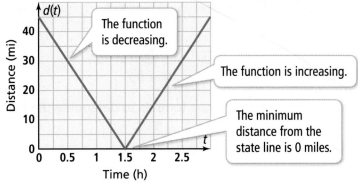

UT and AZ border

Lake Powell   UTAH
                ARIZONA
Waheap   The distance to the border is $d(t)$.

COMMON ERROR
Remember that a graph representing the motion of an object may not be a picture of its path.

The function is decreasing.

The function is increasing.

The minimum distance from the state line is 0 miles.

A. How far does Jay travel to visit his friend?

Jay began his trip 45 mi from the state line, traveled towards the state line, which he crossed after an hour and a half. He then traveled away from the state line and was 45 mi from the state line after 3 h. He traveled a total of 90 mi to visit his friend.

B. How does the graph relate to the domain and range of the function?

Since Jay's entire trip is 3 h, the domain of the function is $0 \le t \le 3$.

For the section of the domain $0 < t < 1.5$, his distance to the border is decreasing. For $1.5 < t < 3$ his distance from the border is increasing.

The maximum and minimum values on the graph are 45 and 0, so the range of the function is $0 \le d(t) \le 45$.

 Try It!   **3.** A cyclist competing in a race rides past a water station. The graph of the function $d(t) = \frac{1}{3}|t - 60|$ shows her distance from the water station at t minutes. Assume the graph represents the entire race. What does the graph tell you about her race?

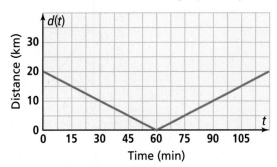

EXAMPLE 4 **Determine Rate of Change**

The graph shows Jay's boat ride across the state line from Example 3. What is the rate of change over the interval $2 \leq t \leq 2.5$? What does it mean in terms of the situation?

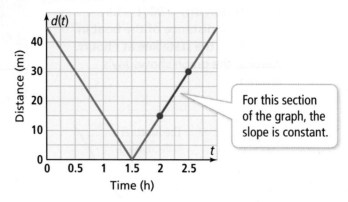

For this section of the graph, the slope is constant.

Use the slope formula to determine the rate of change from $t = 2$ to $t = 2.5$.

Use the points from (2, 15) and (2.5, 30).

$$m = \frac{y_2 - y_1}{x_2 - x_1}$$

$$= \frac{30 - 15}{2.5 - 2}$$

$$= \frac{15}{0.5}$$

$$= 30$$

MAKE SENSE AND PERSEVERE
The rate of change is a different constant value for each section of the graph. How does this relate to the situation?

The rate of change over this interval is 30.

The rate of change represents the speed of the boat in miles per hour. Since the rate of change is positive, Jay's distance from the border is increasing. The boat is traveling at 30 mi/h away from the border.

 Try It! 4. Kata gets on a moving walkway at the airport. Then, 8 s after she gets on, she taps Lisa, who is standing alongside the walkway. The graph shows Kata's distance from Lisa over time. Calculate the rate of change in her distance from Lisa from 6 s to 8 s, and then from 8 s to 12 s. What do the rates of change mean in terms of Kata's movement?

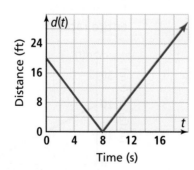

CONCEPT SUMMARY The Absolute Value Function

WORDS The graph of the absolute value function has a vertex, which represents the minimum value of the function. The axis of symmetry intersects the vertex and divides the graph into two sections that are images of each other under a reflection.

ALGEBRA $f(x) = |x|$

GRAPH

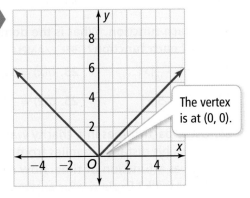

The vertex is at (0, 0).

The domain is all real numbers, the range is $y \geq 0$.

Do You UNDERSTAND?

1. **ESSENTIAL QUESTION** What are the key features of the graph of the absolute value function?

2. **Communicate Precisely** How do the domain and range of $g(x) = a|x|$ compare to the domain and range of $f(x) = |x|$ when $0 < a < 1$? Explain.

3. **Make Sense and Persevere** The graph of the function $g(x) = a|x|$ includes the point (1, 16). What is another point on the graph of the function? What is the value of a?

4. **Error Analysis** Janiece says that the vertex of the graph of $g(x) = a|x|$ always represents the minimum value of the function g. Explain her error.

Do You KNOW HOW?

Find the domain and range of each function.

5. $g(x) = 5|x|$

6. $h(x) = -2|x|$

Graph each function.

7. $g(x) = 1.5|x|$

8. $h(x) = -0.8|x|$

9. What is the rate of change over the interval $15 \leq x \leq 18$?

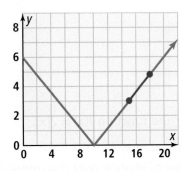

UNDERSTAND

10. Reason How does changing the sign of the constant a from positive to negative affect the domain and range of $f(x) = a|x|$?

11. Communicate Precisely Compare and contrast the graph of $f(x) = |x|$ and the graph of $f(x) = x$. How are they alike? How do they differ?

12. Error Analysis Describe and correct the error a student made in determining the relationship between the domain and range of $f(x) = 10|x|$ and $f(x) = |x|$.

> The domain of $f(x) = 10|x|$
> is the same as the domain of $f(x) = |x|$.
> The range of $f(x) = 10|x|$
> is 10 times the range of $f(x) = |x|$. ✗

13. Higher Order Thinking For which values of a would the graph of $f(x) = a|x|$ form a right angle at the vertex? Explain.

14. Use Structure The table shows selected values for the function $g(x) = a|x|$. Copy and complete the table. Write any unknown answers in terms of a and b.

x	$g(x) = a|x|$
-4	b
■	a
■	0
1	■
■	b
■	$2b$

15. Reason Consider the function $f(x) = 2|x|$.

a. Graph f over the domain $-4 \le x \le 4$.

b. What is the rate of change over the interval $0 \le x \le 4$?

c. How is the rate of change over this interval related to the form of the function?

PRACTICE

Tell whether each point is on the graph of $f(x) = |x|$. If it is, give the coordinates of another point with the same y value. SEE EXAMPLE 1

16. $(11, 11)$ **17.** $(-2.3, -2.3)$

18. $(0, 1)$ **19.** $(15, -15)$

20. $(-8, 8)$ **21.** $(1, 0)$

Graph each function. What is the domain and range of each function? SEE EXAMPLE 2

22. $g(x) = -\frac{1}{4}|x|$ **23.** $h(x) = 3.5|x|$

24. $p(x) = -5|x|$ **25.** $d(x) = \frac{1}{3}|x|$

26. Oscar participates in a charity walk. The graph shows his distance in miles from the water stop as a function of time. How many miles did Oscar walk? Explain your answer. SEE EXAMPLE 3

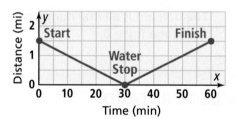

For the graph shown, find the rate of change over the interval. SEE EXAMPLE 4

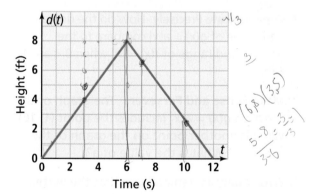

27. $3 \le t \le 6$ **28.** $7 \le t \le 10$

For each description, write a function in the form $g(x) = a|x|$.

29. vertex at $(0, 0)$; passes through $(1, 3)$

30. range is $y \le 0$; passes through $(-1, -4)$

APPLY

31. Model With Mathematics A game designer is looking for two functions to model the solid lines in the figure she constructed. What functions represent the solid lines?

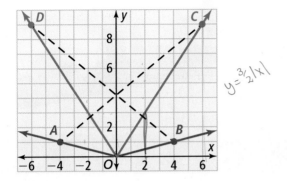

$y = \frac{3}{2}|x|$

32. Make Sense and Persevere The graph shows the distance between a bicyclist and a sandwich shop along her route. Estimate the rate of change over the highlighted interval. What does the rate mean in terms of the situation?

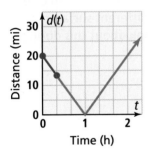

33. Make Sense and Persevere The function $h(x) = -|x| + 34$ models the height of the roof of a house, where x is the horizontal distance from the center of the house. If a raindrop falls from the end of the roof, how far from the center of the base does it land? Explain your solution.

16 ft

? ft

ASSESSMENT PRACTICE

34. The graph of $f(x) = -0.1|x|$ opens ____. The point (____, -10) is on the graph.

35. SAT/ACT For what domain is the range of $y = -x$ and $y = -|x|$ the same?

Ⓐ $\{x \mid x < 0\}$

Ⓑ $\{x \mid x \le 0\}$

Ⓒ $\{x \mid x > 0\}$

Ⓓ $\{x \mid x \ge 0\}$

Ⓔ all real numbers

36. Performance Task The position of a lizard in a video game is modeled on a coordinate plane. The lizard follows the path shown.

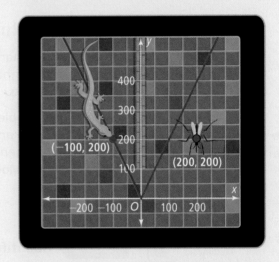

(-100, 200)

(200, 200)

Part A Write a function that includes an absolute value expression for the position of the lizard.

Part B Interpret the graph. Find the vertex and determine the intervals in which the function is increasing, decreasing; and any maximum or minimum values.

Part C Where would the function need to intersect the x-axis so that the lizard can eat the mosquito?

Part D Write a function for which the new vertex that you found in Part C is a solution to the function, and allows the lizard to eat the mosquito.

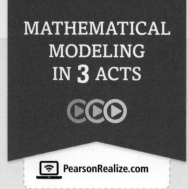

MATHEMATICAL MODELING IN 3 ACTS

PearsonRealize.com

Video

The Mad Runner

People run in many different places: on the soccer field during a game, around the neighborhood, on the basketball court, on the street to catch a bus, in gym class.

Sometimes people run on flat ground and other times they run up or down hills or even up and down stairs. They also run on different surfaces, such as grass, pavement, sand, or a basketball court. Think about this during the Mathematical Modeling in 3 Acts lesson.

Scan for Multimedia

ACT 1 ▶ Identify the Problem

1. What is the first question that comes to mind after watching the video?

2. Write down the main question you will answer about what you saw in the video.

ACT 2 ▶ Develop a Model

3. Make a graph that represents this situation.

ACT 3 ▶ Interpret the Results

4. Did your graph match the actual answer exactly? If not, what might explain the difference?

6-2

Piecewise-Defined Functions

 PearsonRealize.com

I CAN... graph and apply piecewise-defined functions.

VOCABULARY
• piecewise-defined function

👆 EXPLORE & REASON

In a relay race, each runner carries a baton for an equal distance before handing off the baton to the next runner.

A. Graph the distance traveled by the baton as a function of time. How is the speed of each runner represented in the graph?

B. Who is the fastest runner?

C. Communicate Precisely How is the graph of this function similar to the graph of a linear function? How is it different?

Path of the Baton		
	Time (min)	Total Distance (mi)
Start	0	0
Runner 1	3	0.25
Runner 2	5.75	0.50
Runner 3	9	0.75
Runner 4	11.50	1.00

❓ ESSENTIAL QUESTION   What are the key features of piecewise-defined functions?

CONCEPTUAL UNDERSTANDING

👆 EXAMPLE 1   Understand Piecewise-Defined Functions

How is $f(x) = 2|x|$ related to a linear function?

Inspect the graph of the function $f(x) = 2|x|$. The graph has two pieces that meet at the vertex. Each piece is part of a line.

Find the rule for each piece of the function.

When $x \geq 0$, the rule is $f(x) = 2x$.
When $x < 0$, the rule is $f(x) = -2x$.

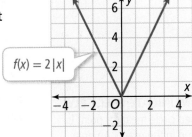

STUDY TIP
Recall that $|x| = x$, when $x \geq 0$ and $|x| = -x$ when $x < 0$.

You can write this function in terms of its pieces, each defined for a given domain.

$$f(x) = \begin{cases} 2x, & x \geq 0 \\ -2x, & x < 0 \end{cases}$$

The function f is a *piecewise-defined* function. A **piecewise-defined function** has different rules for different intervals of its domain.

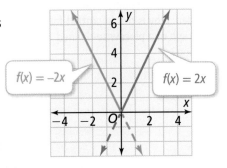

The function $f(x) = 2|x|$ has two pieces over two intervals of the domain. For each interval, the piece is a linear function.

☑ Try It!   1. Express $f(x) = -3|x|$ as a piecewise-defined function.

👆 **EXAMPLE 2** **Graph a Piecewise-Defined Function**

A. What is the graph of $f(x) = \begin{cases} x + 1, & x \le 2 \\ -\frac{3}{2}x + 6, & x > 2 \end{cases}$?

Graph each piece of the function for the given domain.

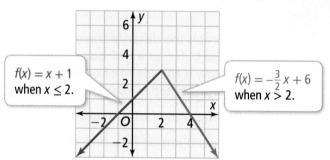

$f(x) = x + 1$ when $x \le 2$.

$f(x) = -\frac{3}{2}x + 6$ when $x > 2$.

COMMON ERROR
You might assume that the pieces of a piecewise-defined function must connect, but this is not necessarily the case.

B. Over what part of the domain is the function increasing? Decreasing?

The function f is increasing when $x \le 2$ and decreasing when $x > 2$.

✅ **Try It!** **2.** Graph the following function. $f(x) = \begin{cases} x - 2, & x \le 1 \\ -2x + 3, & x > 1 \end{cases}$

👆 **EXAMPLE 3** **Analyze the Graph of a Piecewise-Defined Function**

Cheyenne's mother is reviewing the monthly water bills from the summer. Each monthly bill includes a graph like the one shown, which reflects the different rates charged for water based on usage.

Several relatives visited Cheyenne's family in July and their water bill more than doubled. Assuming that the water consumption did not double that month, what is a possible explanation for the increase?

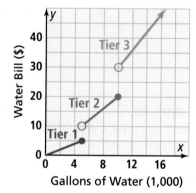

COMMUNICATE PRECISELY
A closed circle means a point is included in the graph. An open circle means the point is not included. Why is this important for the graph of a piecewise-defined function?

The graph shows three tiers of pricing for water consumption: from 0 to 5000 gal, from 5001 to 10,000 gal, and more than 10,000 gal.

The large increase in the bill probably resulted from the usage increasing across one boundary of the domain, from Tier 1 to Tier 2, or Tier 2 to Tier 3.

At the Tier 1–Tier 2 boundary 5,000 gal of usage results in a bill of $5 while using slightly more water results in a bill of at least $10.

✅ **Try It!** **3.** Make a conjecture about why a utility company might charge higher rates for greater levels of water consumption.

APPLICATION ▶ 🖐 **EXAMPLE 4** ▶ **Apply a Piecewise-Defined Function**

A gym owner wants to purchase custom wristbands for a marketing promotion. She thinks she will need about 75 bands. Her assistant insists that ordering over 100 wristbands will be less expensive than ordering 75. How can the assistant convince the gym owner?

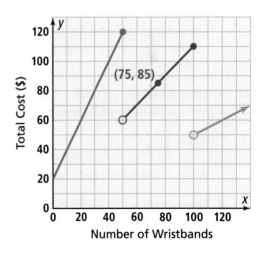

Cost of Custom Wristbands Order

0 to 50 wristbands............ $2.00 each + $20 Shipping
51 to 100 wristbands.........$1.00 each + $10 Shipping
over 100 wristbands..........$0.50 each + free Shipping

Formulate ◀ Write a rule to represent each price point.

Let x = number of wristbands

Let $f(x)$ = total cost

Number of wristbands	Price ($)	•	Wristbands	+	Shipping ($)
0–50	2.00	•	x	+	20
51–100	1.00	•	x	+	10
more than 100	0.50	•	x		

Write a piecewise-defined function to represent the situation.

$$f(x) = \begin{cases} 2x + 20, \ 0 \le x \le 50 & \text{0 to 50 wristbands} \\ x + 10, \ 50 < x \le 100 & \text{51 to 100 wristbands} \\ 0.5x, \qquad x > 100 & \text{over 100 wristbands} \end{cases}$$

Compute ◀ Evaluate the function for $f(75)$ and $f(101)$.

$f(75) = 75 + 10$

$\quad\quad = 85$

$f(101) = 0.5(101)$

$\quad\quad\quad = 50.5$

The cost for 75 wristbands is $85 and the cost for 101 wristbands is $50.50.

Interpret ◀ The gym owner will spend less if she orders more than 100 wristbands.

(75, 85)

Total Cost ($)

Number of Wristbands

Try It! **4.** What is the difference in cost between one order of 100 200 wristbands, two orders of 100²²⁰ wristbands each, and four orders of 50 wristbands each? 480

CONCEPT SUMMARY Piecewise-Defined Functions

WORDS Piecewise-defined functions are defined by different rules for different intervals of the domain.

ALGEBRA $f(x) = \begin{cases} -\frac{1}{3}x - 2, & x \le 3 \\ x + 1, & x > 3 \end{cases}$ ← The boundary is 3.

GRAPH

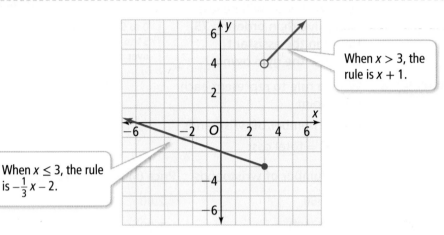

When $x > 3$, the rule is $x + 1$.

When $x \le 3$, the rule is $-\frac{1}{3}x - 2$.

Do You UNDERSTAND?

1. **ESSENTIAL QUESTION** What are the key features of piecewise-defined functions?

2. **Construct Arguments** If the domain of a piecewise-defined function f is all real numbers, must the range of f also be all real numbers? Explain.

3. **Error Analysis** Liz wrote the following piecewise-defined function:

   $f(x) = \begin{cases} x - 3, & x \le -3 \\ -2x - 4, & x \ge -3 \end{cases}$

   What is the error that Liz made?

4. **Reason** How many pieces does the absolute value function have? Explain.

Do You KNOW HOW?

Express each function as a piecewise-defined function. $5x, x \ge 0$

5. $f(x) = 5|x|$ $-5x, x < 0$ 6. $f(x) = -2|x|$

Graph each function.

7. $f(x) = \begin{cases} -3x + 1, & x \le 1 \\ x + 1, & x > 1 \end{cases}$

8. $f(x) = \begin{cases} 2x - 1, & x < 3 \\ -2x + 4, & x \ge 3 \end{cases}$

9. A function f is defined by the rule $-0.5x + 1$ for the domain $x < 1$ and by the rule x for the domain $x \ge 1$. Write the piecewise-defined function f using function notation.

Scan for Multimedia

Practice | Tutorial
Additional Exercises Available Online

UNDERSTAND

10. **Generalize** Describe two ways you could express the function $f(x) = |x|$.

11. **Look for Relationships** How are the pieces of a piecewise-defined function related to the domain? Explain.

12. **Error Analysis** Describe and correct the error a student made in expressing the function $f(x) = 3|x|$ as a piecewise-defined function.

$f(x) = 3|x|$

$f(x) = \begin{cases} 3x, & x \le 0 \\ -3x, & x > 0 \end{cases}$ ✗

13. **Communicate Precisely** A piecewise-defined f is shown. Use function notation to describe the function and determine the x- and y-intercepts.

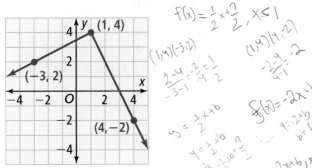

14. **Reason** A piecewise-defined function is shown.

$f(x) = \begin{cases} x - 1, & x < n \\ -x + 4, & x \ge n \end{cases}$

a. If $n = 5$, what is the range of f?

b. Does changing the value of n change the range? Explain.

15. **Higher Order Thinking** For a given piecewise-defined function, the pieces of the function are defined for intervals of the domain, $x \le 1$ and $x > 1$.

a. Explain how you could find the y-intercept for the intervals over the intervals $x \le 1$ and $x > 1$.

b. In general, how could you find the y-intercept for two pieces over the intervals $x \le n$ and $x > n$?

PRACTICE

Express each absolute value function as a piecewise-defined function. SEE EXAMPLE 1

16. $f(x) = 6|x|$

17. $f(x) = -|x|$

18. $f(x) = \frac{1}{2}|x|$

19. $f(x) = -1.5|x|$

Graph each function. Identify the intervals where the function is increasing, decreasing, or constant. SEE EXAMPLE 2

20. $f(x) = \begin{cases} x + 1, & x < 1 \\ -x - 3, & x \ge 2 \end{cases}$

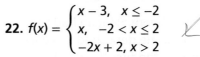

21. $f(x) = \begin{cases} -\frac{4}{3}x + 4, & x \le 6 \\ 2x - 8, & x > 6 \end{cases}$

22. $f(x) = \begin{cases} x - 3, & x \le -2 \\ x, & -2 < x \le 2 \\ -2x + 2, & x > 2 \end{cases}$

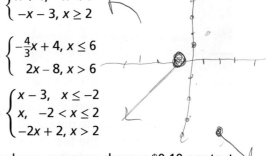

23. A cell phone company charges $0.10 per text message if a customer sends up to 100 messages per month. The company charges $0.08 per text if a customer sends between 101–200 messages, and $0.06 per text if the customer sends between 201–300 messages. Today is the last day of the month. Tamira has sent 200 text messages, is it worth it for her to send 1 more text message? Explain. SEE EXAMPLES 3 AND 4

Write a piecewise-defined function for each graph. SEE EXAMPLE 4

24.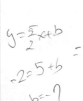

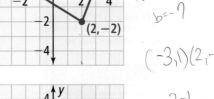

25.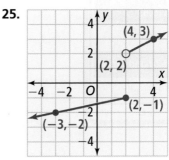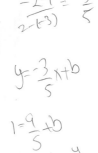

PRACTICE & PROBLEM SOLVING

Mixed Review Available Online

APPLY

26. Model With Mathematics Selena needs at least 22 subway rides for the month. She has two options for buying subway cards. Write a function that represents the situation. Can she buy more than 22 rides and save money? Explain.

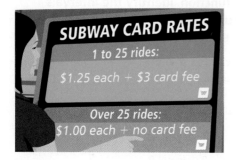

SUBWAY CARD RATES
1 to 25 rides:
$1.25 each + $3 card fee
Over 25 rides:
$1.00 each + no card fee

27. Make Sense and Persevere Reagan had $122 in his savings account. He deposited $70 each week from his job for the first five weeks of summer. In the sixth week, Reagan got a raise and increased his weekly deposits by $12.

a. Write a piecewise-defined function to represent his bank balance.

$f(x) \begin{cases} 122, x=1 \\ 122+70x, 0 \le x \le 5 \\ 122+82x, x \ge 6 \end{cases}$

b. Find $f(8)$.

c. What does $f(8) - 122$ mean in terms of the situation?

28. Make Sense and Persevere A group of friends eat at Jae's Cafe. They have an online coupon. The costs of their main courses, before applying the coupon, are $13.99, $16.99, $19.99, and $21.99. The total cost of their drinks is $12.00. What will their bill be before tax and tip?

Jae's Cafe Coupon
Main Course Discounts!
* From $15 to $19.99:
10% off!
* $20 and up:
15% off!

ASSESSMENT PRACTICE

29. The graph of function f is shown.

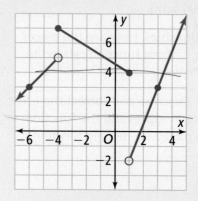

The domain of f is _____. The range of f is _____. There are _____ values in the domain where $f(x) = 4$ and $f(1) =$ _____.

30. SAT/ACT Which function has the same graph as $f(x) = 0.1|x|$?

Ⓐ $f(x) = \begin{cases} 0.1x, & x < 0 \\ -0.1x, & x > 0 \end{cases}$

Ⓑ $f(x) = \begin{cases} 0.1x, & x \le 0 \\ -0.1x, & x > 0 \end{cases}$

Ⓒ $f(x) = \begin{cases} 0.1x, & x > 0 \\ -0.1x, & x < 0 \end{cases}$

Ⓓ $f(x) = \begin{cases} 0.1x, & x \ge 0 \\ -0.1x, & x < 0 \end{cases}$

Ⓔ $f(x) = \begin{cases} -0.1x, & x \ge 0 \\ 0.1x, & x < 0 \end{cases}$

31. Performance Task Sue charges $15 for the first hour of babysitting and $10 for each additional hour, with each fraction of an hour counting as a whole hour. The rates that Vic charges for x hours of babysitting are modeled by the function shown.

$f(x) = \begin{cases} 12.5x, & 0 \le x < 4 \\ 10x, & 4 \le x < 8 \\ 9.5x, & x \ge 8 \end{cases}$

Part A Who will charge more to babysit for 10 hours? Justify your response.

Part B What is the rate of change for each function over the interval $7 \le x \le 11$?

Part C Which average rate of change is more meaningful? Explain.

242   TOPIC 6 Working With Functions

Go Online | PearsonRealize.com

6-3

Step Functions

PearsonRealize.com

I CAN... graph and apply step functions.

VOCABULARY
- ceiling function
- floor function
- step function

CRITIQUE & EXPLAIN

Students are told there is a function where decimals are the inputs and each decimal is rounded to the nearest whole number to get the output. Beth and Latoya each make a sketch of the graph of the function.

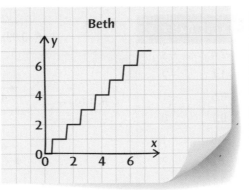

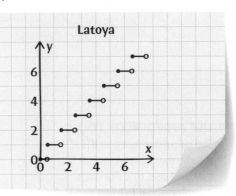

A. Make Sense and Persevere What is causing both students to create graphs that look like steps?

B. Which graph do you think is correct? Explain.

C. What does the graph of this function look like? Explain.

? ESSENTIAL QUESTION   How are step functions related to piecewise-defined functions?

CONCEPTUAL UNDERSTANDING

EXAMPLE 1   Understand Step Functions

A. What is the graph of the ceiling function?

A **step function** is a piecewise-defined function that consists of constant pieces. The graph resembles a set of steps.

COMMUNICATE PRECISELY
The symbol for ceiling is very similar to other related symbols. What clue can help you remember the meaning of the symbol?

The **ceiling function** is a kind of step function. It rounds numbers up to the nearest integer. It is notated as $f(x) = \text{ceiling}(x)$ or $f(x) = \lceil x \rceil$.

Make a table of values and graph.

x	$f(x) = \lceil x \rceil$
−2.4	−2
−1.4	−1
−0.5	0
0.7	1
1.8	2
2.1	3
3.1	4

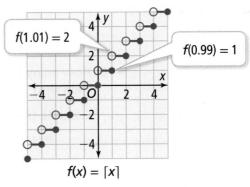

$f(1.01) = 2$

$f(0.99) = 1$

$f(x) = \lceil x \rceil$

The domain is all real numbers. The range is all integers.

CONTINUED ON THE NEXT PAGE

EXAMPLE 1 CONTINUED

B. What is the graph of the floor function?

The **floor function** is another kind of step function. It rounds numbers down to the nearest integer. It is notated as $f(x) = \text{floor}(x)$ or $f(x) = \lfloor x \rfloor$.

Make a table of values and graph.

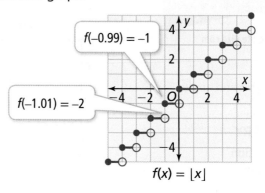

x	$f(x) = \lfloor x \rfloor$
-2.4	-3
-1.4	-2
-0.5	-1
0.7	0
1.8	1
2.1	2
3.1	3

$f(-0.99) = -1$

$f(-1.01) = -2$

$f(x) = \lfloor x \rfloor$

USE APPROPRIATE TOOLS
The calculator function INT returns the greatest integer less than or equal to x. For most calculators, the INT function is the same as floor(x). For others, it is the same only for $x > 0$.

The domain is is all real numbers. The range is all integers.

✅ **Try It!**   1. Evaluate each function for the given value.

   a. $f(x) = \lceil x \rceil$; $x = 2.65$ b. $f(x) = \text{floor}(x)$; $x = 2.19$

   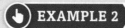

APPLICATION   ⏺ **EXAMPLE 2** **Use a Step Function to Represent a Real-World Situation**

Some students are planning a field trip. If there are 40 students and adults or fewer going on the field trip, they rent vans that hold 15 people. If there are more than 40 students and adults, they rent buses that hold 65 people.

A. What function can you use to represent this situation?

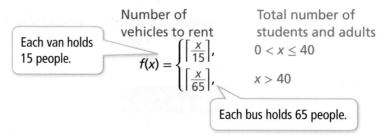

Each van holds 15 people.

Number of vehicles to rent

Total number of students and adults

$$f(x) = \begin{cases} \left\lceil \dfrac{x}{15} \right\rceil, & 0 < x \le 40 \\ \left\lceil \dfrac{x}{65} \right\rceil, & x > 40 \end{cases}$$

Each bus holds 65 people.

B. How many buses are needed if 412 students and adults are going on a field trip?

Evaluate the function for $f(412)$.

$$f(412) = \left\lceil \frac{412}{65} \right\rceil$$
$$= \lceil 6.34 \rceil$$
$$= 7$$

Seven buses are needed if 412 students and adults are going on a field trip.

✅ **Try It!**   2. The postage for a first-class letter weighing one ounce or less is $0.47. Each additional ounce is $0.21. The maximum weight of a first-class letter is $3\frac{1}{2}$ oz. Write a function to represent the situation.

APPLICATION   ☝ **EXAMPLE 3**   **Use a Step Function to Solve Problems**

Jamal and his brother plan to rent a karaoke machine for a class event. The graph shows the rental costs.

A. How much should they expect to spend if they rent the karaoke machine from 8:00 A.M. until 7:30 P.M.?

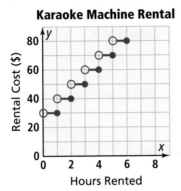
Karaoke Machine Rental

$30 first hour

$10 each hour after

> **COMMON ERROR**
> Even though the graph is not connected, the domain of the function is continuous because it includes all positive real numbers.

Step 1 Write a function to represent the rental costs.

$$f(x) = \begin{cases} 30\lceil x \rceil, & 0 < x \le 1 \\ 10\lceil x \rceil + 20, & x > 1 \end{cases}$$

$30 for the first hour, or any fraction of an hour

an additional $10 for each hour, or any fraction of an hour after the first hour

Step 2 Determine the duration of the rental.

8:00 A.M. to 7:30 P.M. is 11 h, 30 min or $11\frac{1}{2}$ h.

Step 3 Evaluate the function for $f(11.5)$.

$$f(11.5) = 10\lceil 11.5 \rceil + 20$$
$$= 10(12) + 20$$
$$= 140$$

The cost of the rental will be $140.

B. The class event ended early, so Jamal could return the machine by 7:05 P.M. How much money would he save if he returned the machine at 7:05 P.M.?

Jamal would save no money if he returned the machine at 7:05 P.M. He will be charged for the full hour.

☑ **Try It!**   **3.** You rent a karaoke machine at 1 P.M. and plan to return it by 4 P.M. Will you save any money if you return the machine 15 min early? Explain.

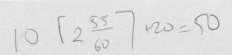

CONCEPT SUMMARY Step Functions

	Step Function	Ceiling Function	Floor Function
WORDS	A step function is a piecewise-defined function that consists of constant pieces and whose graph resembles a set of steps.	The least integer function, also called the ceiling function, returns the least integer greater than or equal to x.	The greatest integer function, also called the floor function, returns the greatest integer less than or equal to x.
ALGEBRA	$f(x) = \begin{cases} 4,\ 0 < x \le 2 \\ 8,\ 2 < x \le 5 \\ 12,\ 5 < x \le 8 \end{cases}$	$f(x) = \lceil x \rceil$	$f(x) = \lfloor x \rfloor$
GRAPHS	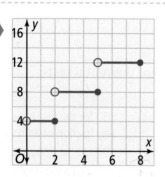	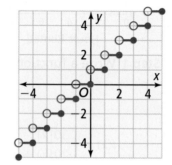	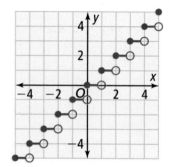

✓ Do You UNDERSTAND?

1. **ESSENTIAL QUESTION** How are step functions related to piecewise-defined functions?

2. **Vocabulary** How are the *ceiling function* and the *floor function* similar? How are they different?

3. **Error Analysis** Jason defined the following step function.

$$f(x) = \begin{cases} 5,\ \ 0 \le x \le 10 \\ 6,\ 10 \le x \le 20 \\ 7,\ 20 \le x \le 30 \end{cases}$$

   What is the error that Jason made?

4. **Reason** For the function that rounds numbers to the nearest whole number, what are the pieces of the domain for the interval from 0 to 4?

Do You KNOW HOW?

Evaluate the ceiling function for the given value.

5. $f(x) = \lceil x \rceil$; $x = 5.13$

6. $f(x) = $ ceiling(x); $x = 11.71$

Evaluate the floor function for the given value.

7. $f(x) = \lfloor x \rfloor$; $x = 9.37$

8. $f(x) = $ floor (x); $x = 5.49$

9. Graph the function f.

x	$f(x)$
$0 < x \le 1$	4
$1 < x \le 2$	5
$2 < x \le 3$	6
$3 < x \le 4$	7
$4 < x \le 5$	8
$5 < x \le 6$	9

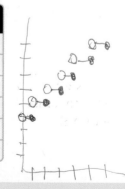

UNDERSTAND

10. Communicate Precisely
Many calculators use
an INT function which
returns the greatest
integer less than or
equal to *x*. The graph
of **Y1 = INT(X)** is shown.
How is this function like
the floor function? How is it different?

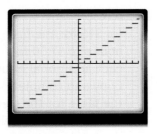

11. Look for Relationships How are the pieces
of a step function related to the domain of the
function? Justify your thinking.

12. Error Analysis Kenji wrote a step function to
round numbers up to nearest multiple of three.
Describe and correct the error he made.

$$f(x) = \begin{cases} 3, 3 < x \le 6 \\ 6, 6 < x \le 9 \\ 9, 9 < x \le 12 \\ 12, 12 < x \le 15 \end{cases} \quad ✗$$

13. Communicate Precisely
Explain how you can use
the graph shown below to
find the value of the step
function for *x* = 1. How is
this different from finding
the value for *x* = 1 when
the graph of a function is
a straight line?

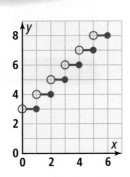

14. Higher Order Thinking Results of the **INT**
function are shown in the spreadsheet.

a. If *f*(*x*) = INT(*x*),
what is *f*(4.6), *f*(5),
and *f*(–6.5)?

b. Write *f*(*x*) = INT(*x*)
as a step function
for the domain
–4 ≤ *x* ≤ 4.

	A	B
1	−3.1	=INT(A1)
2	−2.4	−3
3	−1.8	−2
4	−0.9	−1
5	0	0
6	0.8	0
7	1.9	1
8	2.8	2

PRACTICE

Evaluate the function for the given value.
SEE EXAMPLE 1

15. $f(x) = \lceil x \rceil$; *x* = 0.1

16. $f(x) = \text{ceiling}(x)$; *x* = 5.15

17. $f(x) = \lfloor x \rfloor$; *x* = –4.01

18. $f(x) = \text{ceiling}(x)$; *x* = 13.20

19. $f(x) = \lfloor x \rfloor$; *x* = 7.06

20. $f(x) = \text{floor}(x)$; *x* = 33.7

21. $f(x) = \text{floor}(x)$; *x* = 23.2

22. $f(x) = \lfloor x \rfloor$; *x* = –8.4

**For each table, graph the step function and write
a rule for *f* using the ceiling or floor function.**
SEE EXAMPLES 2 AND 3

23.

x	f(x)
0 < x ≤ 1	5
1 < x ≤ 2	6
2 < x ≤ 3	7
3 < x ≤ 4	8
4 < x ≤ 5	9
5 < x ≤ 6	10

24.

x	f(x)
0 ≤ x < 2	3
2 ≤ x < 4	4
4 ≤ x < 6	5
6 ≤ x < 8	6
8 ≤ x < 10	7
10 ≤ x < 12	8

**Sketch the graph of each function over the
domain 0 < *x* ≤ 10.**

25. The function *g* returns the greatest integer *g*(*x*)
that is less than or equal to *x* + 2.

26. The function *f* returns the least integer *f*(*x*) that
is greater than 3*x*.

APPLY

27. Mathematical Connections There are 240 seniors in Kathryn's school. Her class is planning a trip, and is taking buses that hold a maximum of 50 passengers. Assume that the trip is optional.

a. Write a step function f that maps the number of students x, to the number of buses needed, $f(x)$. $\lceil \frac{x}{50} \rceil$

b. What assumptions do you need to make to write the function?

c. What is the average rate of change of the function over the interval from 40 to 60? From 60 to 80?

d. What do the average rates of change mean in terms of the situation? Explain.

28. Construct Arguments Amit parks his car for 144 h, and Nan parks her car for 145 h. Does Nan pay more? If so, how much more? Make a table and then graph a function to support your answer. $50 + 25\lceil x \rceil$

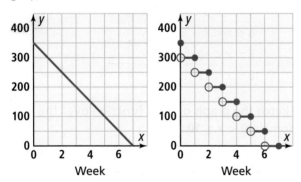

Airport Parking Rates ✈ P

$50 for first 24 hours plus $25 for each additional 24 hours.

Any fraction of a 24-hour period will be charged for the entire 24-hour period.

29. Model With Mathematics Mia has $350 in her bank account at the beginning of the school year. Every week she withdraws $50. Two graphs model the situation.

a. Write a function for each graph.

b. How do the graphs and the functions differ in how they represent the situation?

c. What are the advantages and disadvantages of each type of function?

ASSESSMENT PRACTICE

30. A resort rents skis for $15 for the first hour and $7.50 for each additional hour. Copy and complete the table for the step function that models the total cost, in dollars, of renting skis for x hours.

x	$f(x)$
$x \le 1$	15
$1 < x \le 2$	22.5
$2 < x \le 3$	30
$3 < x \le 4$	___
___	45
$5 < x \le 6$	___

31. SAT/ACT What is the value of $f(2) + f(4) + f(11) + f(12)$ for the function f?

$$f(x) = \begin{cases} 100, & 0 < x \le 4 \\ 95, & 4 < x \le 8 \\ 90, & 8 < x \le 12 \\ 95, & 12 < x \le 16 \end{cases}$$

$100 + 100 + 90 + 90$

Ⓐ 30   Ⓑ 280

Ⓒ 290   Ⓓ 380

Ⓔ 300

32. Performance Task Abdul and his family are traveling on a toll highway. The table shows the cost of using the highway as a function of distance.

Exit Number	Distance (mi)	Toll ($)
1	0	0.00
2	40	1.25
3	75	1.75
4	85	1.90
5	120	2.25
6	150	2.50

Part A Write a step function t to represent the cost of the tolls in terms of distance.

Part B Assume their car averages 30 mi/gal and gasoline costs $3.50/gal. Write a function g to represent the cost of the gas in terms of distance.

Part C Use functions t and g to determine the cost of Abdul's trip if his family leaves the highway at Exit 5.

6-4

Transformations of Piecewise-Defined Functions

PearsonRealize.com

I CAN... graph and analyze transformations of the piecewise-defined functions.

MODEL & DISCUSS

Cleo takes three 1-hour classes at a community college. The graph shows the time she spends in each class.

A. Next semester, each class will start an hour later. How will this change the graph?

B. How will the graph change if she takes two 90-minute classes, one starting at 8:30 A.M. and the second at 10:00 A.M.?

C. Construct Arguments Starting in the fall, Cleo will take three classes in a row with the first starting at 7:00 A.M. Cleo says that she can update the graph by moving all three steps one unit to the left. Do you agree? Justify your answer.

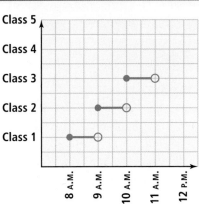

? ESSENTIAL QUESTION

How do the constants affect the graphs of piecewise-defined functions?

APPLICATION

EXAMPLE 1   Translate Step Functions

Uptown Sandwich Shop is increasing the number of bonus points by 2 in the shop's rewards program. How will the total points awarded for a $3.80 item change?

You can represent the two versions of the reward program with step functions. Use the INT function on a graphing calculator to graph the two functions.

STUDY TIP
Recall that the INT function, which returns the greatest integer less than or equal to x, is another name for the floor function.

Uptown Sandwich Shop Rewards Program
1 point for each $1 you spend plus 5 bonus points for each visit. No fractional points awarded.

Reward points	=	Dollar part of amount spent	+	Bonus points
Before:	$f(x)$ =	INT(x)	+	5
After:	$g(x)$ =	INT(x)	+	7

an increase of 2 points

Enter the functions.   Graph the functions.

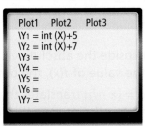

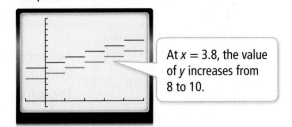

At $x = 3.8$, the value of y increases from 8 to 10.

The graph is translated up 2 units. The points for a $3.80 item increase from 8 to 10.

✓ **Try It!**   **1.** How will the total points awarded for a $1.25 juice drink change if the bonus points are decreased by 2 points?

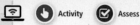

EXAMPLE 2 Vertical Translations of the Absolute Value Function

How does adding a constant to the output affect the graph of $f(x) = |x|$?

Compare the graphs of $h(x) = |x| - 4$ and $g(x) = |x| + 2$ with the graph of $f(x) = |x|$.

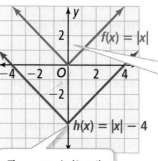

The graphs have the same axis of symmetry: $x = 0$.

The vertex is $(0, -4)$.

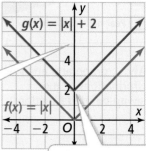

The vertex is $(0, 2)$.

Adding a constant, k, outside of the absolute value bars changes the value of $f(x)$, or the output. It does not change the input. The value of k, in $g(x) = |x| + k$, translates the graph of $f(x) = |x|$ vertically by k units. The axis of symmetry does not change.

 Try It! **2.** For each function, identify the vertex and the axis of symmetry.

a. $p(x) = |x| + 3$ b. $g(x) = |x| - 2$

EXAMPLE 3 Horizontal Translations of the Absolute Value Function

How does adding a constant to the input affect the graph of $f(x) = |x|$?

Compare the graph of $g(x) = |x - 4|$ with the graph of $f(x) = |x|$.

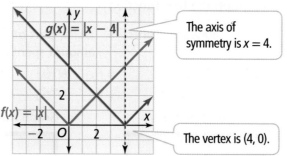

The axis of symmetry is $x = 4$.

The vertex is $(4, 0)$.

Adding a constant, h, inside the absolute value bars changes the value of x, the input, as well as the value of $f(x)$, the output.

The value of h, in $g(x) = |x - h|$ translates the graph of $f(x) = |x|$ horizontally by h units. If $h > 0$, the translation is to the right. If $h < 0$, the translation is to the left. Because the input is changed, the translation is horizontal, and the axis of symmetry also shifts.

 Try It! **3.** For each function, identify the vertex and the axis of symmetry.

a. $g(x) = |x - 3|$ b. $p(x) = |x + 5|$

CONCEPTUAL UNDERSTANDING

EXAMPLE 4   **Understand Vertical and Horizontal Translations**

What information do the constants *h* and *k* provide about the graph of $g(x) = |x - h| + k$**?**

Compare the graphs of $g(x) = |x - 4| - 2$ and $g(x) = |x + 5| + 1$ with the graph of $f(x) = |x|$.

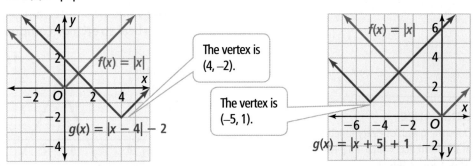

The vertex is (4, –2).

The vertex is (–5, 1).

USE STRUCTURE

If the function $g(x) = |x + 5| + 1$, is in the form $g(x) = |x - h| + k$, what are the values of *h* and *k*?

The value of *h* translates the graph horizontally and the value of *k* translates it vertically. The vertex of the graph $g(x) = |x - h| + k$ is at (h, k).

 Try It!   **4.** Find the vertex of the graph of each function.

    a. $g(x) = |x - 1| - 3$ **b.** $g(x) = |x + 2| + 6$

EXAMPLE 5   **Understand Vertical Stretches and Compressions**

How does the constant *a* affect the graph of $g(x) = a|x|$**?**

Compare the graphs of $g(x) = \frac{1}{2}|x|$ and $g(x) = -4|x|$ with the graph of $f(x) = |x|$.

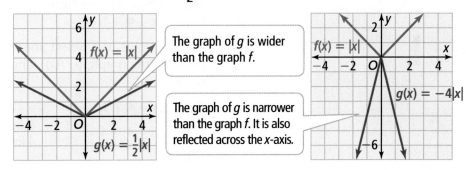

The graph of *g* is wider than the graph *f*.

The graph of *g* is narrower than the graph *f*. It is also reflected across the *x*-axis.

In $g(x) = a|x|$, the constant *a* multiplies the output of the function $f(x) = |x|$ by *a*.

- When $0 < |a| < 1$ the graph of $g(x) = a|x|$ is a vertical compression towards the *x*-axis of the graph of $f(x) = |x|$.
- When $|a| > 1$, the graph of $g(x) = a|x|$ is a vertical stretch away from the *x*-axis of the graph of $f(x) = |x|$.
- When $a < 0$, the graph of *g* is reflected across the *x*-axis.

The value of *a* stretches or compresses the graph vertically.

 Try It!   **5.** Compare the graph of each function with the graph of $f(x) = |x|$.

    a. $g(x) = 3|x|$ **b.** $g(x) = -\frac{1}{3}|x|$

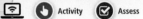

 EXAMPLE 6 Understand Transformations of the Absolute Value Function

A. How do the constants a, h, and k affect the graph of $g(x) = a|x - h| + k$?

Graph $g(x) = -2|x + 3| + 4$.

The values of h and k determine the location of the vertex and the axis of symmetry. The value of a determines the direction of the graph and whether it is a vertical stretch or compression of the graph of $f(x) = |x|$.

GENERALIZE
Does the graph of every function of the form $g(x) = a|x - h| + k$ have a y-intercept?

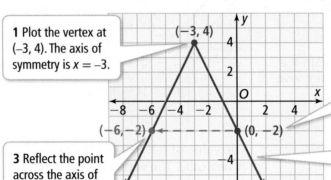

1 Plot the vertex at $(-3, 4)$. The axis of symmetry is $x = -3$.

2 Evaluate the function to find another point. $g(0) = -2$.

3 Reflect the point across the axis of symmetry.

4 Sketch the graph through the points.

Since $|a| > 1$ and a is negative the graph is a vertical stretch of the graph of $f(x) = |x|$ that is reflected across the x-axis.

B. How can you use the constants a, h, and k to write a function given its graph?

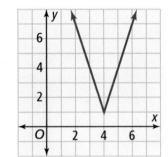

Step 1 Identify the vertex of the graph.

The vertex is $(4, 1)$, so $h = 4$ and $k = 1$.

The function has the form $f(x) = a|x - 4| + 1$.

Step 2 Find the value of a. Select another point on the graph, $(x, f(x))$, and solve for a.

$f(x) = a|x - 4| + 1$

$4 = a|5 - 4| + 1$ ⟵ Substitute 5 for x and 4 for $f(x)$.

$a = 3$

The graph represents the function $f(x) = 3|x - 4| + 1$.

✓ **Try It!** **6. a.** Write a function for the graph shown.

b. Write the function of the graph after a translation 1 unit right and 4 units up.

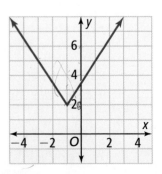

CONCEPT SUMMARY Transformations of the Absolute Value Function

WORDS The graph of $g(x) = a|x - h| + k$ is a transformation of the graph of the absolute value function, $f(x) = |x|$.

- Adding a constant, h, to the input translates the graph of f horizontally.
- Adding a constant, k, to the output translates the graph of f vertically.
- Multiplying the input by a constant, a, greater than 1 results in a vertical stretch of the graph of f.
- Multiplying the input by a constant, a, less than 1 but greater than 0 results in a vertical compression of the graph of f.
- When $a < 0$ the graph of the function is reflected across the x-axis.

ALGEBRA $g(x) = a|x - h| + k$

The vertex of the graph is (h, k).

NUMBERS $g(x) = -2|x + 3| + 4$

The vertex of the graph is $(-3, 4)$.

GRAPH

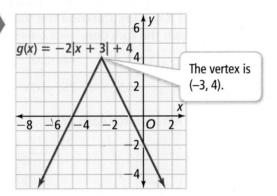

$g(x) = -2|x + 3| + 4$

The vertex is $(-3, 4)$.

Do You UNDERSTAND?

1. **ESSENTIAL QUESTION** How do the constants affect the graphs of piecewise-defined functions?

2. **Generalize** How do the constants a, h, and k affect the domain and range of $g(x) = a|x - h| + k$ when $a > 0$?

3. **Error Analysis** Jacy says that $f(x) = 4|x - 1|$ and $f(x) = |4x - 1|$ have the same graph. Is Jacy correct? Explain.

4. **Use Structure** How can you reflect the graph of $f(x) = 3|x + 2| + 1$ across the x-axis?

Do You KNOW HOW?

Find the vertex and graph each function.

5. $f(x) = |x| + 2.5$

6. $f(x) = |x + 2.5|$

7. $f(x) = |x - 2| + 4$

8. $f(x) = -3|x + 1| - 5$

9. Write a function for the graph.

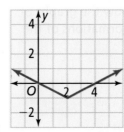

UNDERSTAND

PRACTICE

10. Model With Mathematics Give two examples of functions that include an absolute value expression and have a vertex of $(-1, 3)$.

11. Mathematical Connections Consider the function $f(x) = 2|x + 1| - 7$.

a. A linear function containing one branch of the function is $f(x) = 2(x + 1) - 7$. What linear function contains the other branch?

b. For the general function $f(x) = a|x - h| + k$, what are the two linear functions containing the branches?

12. Use Appropriate Tools Explain how you can write a second step function that translates the graph of the step function shown down 6 units.

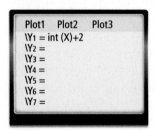

13. Error Analysis Describe and correct the errors a student made in describing the graph of the function $f(x) = -0.5|x + 1| + 3$.

The graph of $y = -0.5|x + 1| + 3$ compresses the graph of $y = |x|$ vertically toward the x-axis, and moves the vertex to $(1, 3)$. ✗

14. Higher Order Thinking Write each function Y1 through Y4. Explain how the graphs of Y2 through Y4 are transformations of the graph of Y1.

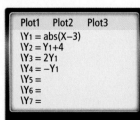

15. Describe the transformation for the pair of step functions. **SEE EXAMPLE 1**

Find the vertex and graph each function.
SEE EXAMPLES 2, 3, AND 4

16. $f(x) = |x| - 2$ **17.** $f(x) = |x| + 1$

18. $f(x) = |x + 0.5|$ **19.** $f(x) = |x - 1|$

20. $f(x) = |x + 7| - 2$ **21.** $f(x) = |x - 0.5| + 0.5$

Compare the graph of each function with the graph of $f(x) = |x|$. Describe the transformation, then graph the function. SEE EXAMPLES 4, 5, AND 6

22. $g(x) = \frac{1}{3}|x + 6| - 1$ **23.** $g(x) = -4|x - 2| - 1$

24. $g(x) = -|x + 3.5| + 4$ **25.** $g(x) = \frac{5}{4}|x - 2| + 7$

Write a function for each graph. SEE EXAMPLE 6

26. 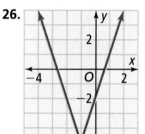   **27.**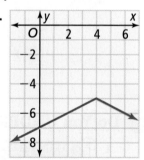

What function g describes the graph of f after the given transformations?

28. $f(x) = |x|$; translated 2 units up and 1 unit right

29. $f(x) = |x| + 1$; translated 3 units down and 2 units left

30. $f(x) = |x|$; reflected across the x-axis and translated 4 units up

31. $f(x) = |x|$; vertically stretched by a factor of 3 and reflected across the x-axis

APPLY

32. Model With Mathematics The rates for Carolina's dog boarding service are shown. Carolina plans on increasing the rate for the first hour by $5.

a. Make a graph that shows the step functions for the cost of boarding a dog before and after the rate increase.

b. How much will it cost to board a dog for 4 hours after the rate increase?

Welcome to Carolina's Dog House Retreat

$20 for the first hour plus $12 for each additional hour.

33. Model With Mathematics Emma wants to model the sides of a pyramid by using a function that includes an absolute value expression. Emma will place the pyramid on a coordinate grid as shown. What function should she use? For what domain?

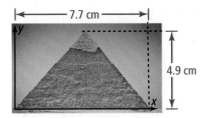

34. Make Sense and Persevere One part of a dog agility course is an obstacle called an A-frame. Assume that the left corner of the A-frame corresponds to the point (0, 0). What function that includes an absolute value expression could you use to model the obstacle? What is the domain of the function? Explain your reasoning.

ASSESSMENT PRACTICE

Fill in the blanks with the correct answer.

35. The graph of $g(x) = -|x + 15| - 7$, is a vertical translation of the graph of the _____ function, $f(x) = |x|$ by _____ units. The graph of g is a horizontal translation of the graph of f by _____ units. The vertex of the graph of g is _____. The y-intercept is _____, and there is/are _____ x-intercept(s).

36. SAT/ACT Which function has the same graph as $f(x) = 4|x - 2| + 2$?

Ⓐ $f(x) = 2|2x - 4| + 2$

Ⓑ $f(x) = 2|2x - 1| + 2$

Ⓒ $f(x) = 2|2x - 1| + 1$

Ⓓ $f(x) = 2|2x - 4| + 1$

Ⓔ none of these

37. Performance Task You are playing a ship trapping game. There are 4 of your opponent's red ships on the screen. You can send out 3 strikes from your blue ships through the red ships' positions to capture them. Each strike sends two lasers that resemble the graph of a function with an absolute value expression.

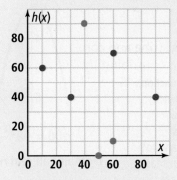

Part A How can symmetry help you find a path to capture two ships?

Part B Write three functions that represent strike paths to capture the ships. Show how each ship is captured by a function.

Part C For your function that captures two ships, can you write a different function from one of your other ships that represent strikes paths to capture these two ships? Explain.

6-5

Analyzing Functions Graphically

PearsonRealize.com

I CAN... identify the common features of a function when given an equation or graph.

👆 **MODEL & DISCUSS**

Each table represents part of a function.

x	f(x)
−2	1
−1	4
0	5
1	4
2	1

x	g(x)
−2	20
−1	10
0	5
1	2.5
2	1.25

x	h(x)
−2	11
−1	8
0	5
1	2
2	−1

x	j(x)
−2	2
−1	1
0	0
1	1
2	2

x	k(x)
−2	21
−1	11
0	5
1	3
2	5

A. Plot the points of each function on a graph. Describe what you know about each function.

B. Look for Relationships Which functions are related? Explain your reasoning.

ESSENTIAL QUESTION

What can you learn about a function by analyzing its graph?

EXAMPLE 1 ▶ Analyze Domain and Range

The graphs of three functions are shown. What are their domains and ranges?

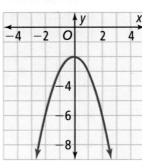

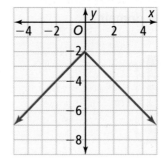

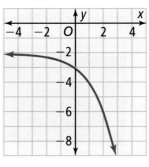

$g(x) = -x^2 - 2$

Domain: all real numbers

Range: $y \le -2$

$h(x) = -|x| - 2$

Domain: all real numbers

Range: $y \le -2$

$j(x) = -2^x - 2$

Domain: all real numbers

Range: $y < -2$

COMMON ERROR
Remember to extend the function, beyond the edges of the sketch when the domain is all real numbers. The graph of j, for example, continues down and to the right out of view as x increases.

To find the range of f, note that $x^2 \ge 0$ for all x. Therefore $-x^2 \le 0$, and $-x^2 - 2 \le -2$ for all x. So the range of f is $y \le -2$.

You can find the ranges of h and j in a similar way. The range of h is $y \le -2$. The range of j is $y < -2$.

✅ **Try It!** **1.** Explain how you can determine the ranges of h and j from the expressions that define them.

EXAMPLE 2   Analyze Maximum and Minimum Values

Which of these functions has a maximum value and/or a minimum value?

$$f(x) = 2x - 3 \qquad g(x) = -\left(\tfrac{1}{2}\right)^x + 4 \qquad h(x) = |x + 1| + 2$$

Consider the graphs of a linear function, an exponential function, and a translation of the absolute value function.

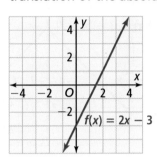

The graph of the linear function *f* increases at a constant rate. There is no maximum or minimum value.

The graph of the function *g* is a translation of an exponential function. It is bounded above by the asymptote $y = 4$ which means that $g(x) < 4$. However it has no maximum because it is always increasing.

The function *g* also has no minimum. As *x* decreases, $g(x)$ decreases.

> As the *x*-value increases the *y*-value approaches 4, but it never reaches 4.

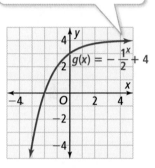

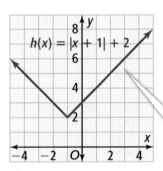

The graph of *h* is a translation of the absolute value function. It opens upward so the function has a minimum value of 2 at the vertex (−1, 2).

COMMUNICATE PRECISELY
The maximum or minimum value is a *y*-value of the function. What value tells you *where* the maximum or minimum is found?

> If the function were instead $h(x) = -|x + 1| + 2$, the absolute value function would open down. It would then have a maximum value instead of a minimum value.

 Try It!   2. Does each function have a maximum value and/or a minimum value? Sketch the graph of each function to help you.

     a. $f(x) = x^2 - 3x + 1$

     b. $g(x) = 2\sqrt{x + 1}$

     c. $h(x) = \sqrt[3]{8(x - 1)} + 5$

CONCEPTUAL UNDERSTANDING ➞   👆 **EXAMPLE 3**   **Understand Axes of Symmetry**

Which of the functions shown has an axis of symmetry?

STUDY TIP
If you fold a sketch of the graph along the axis of symmetry, the parts of the graph on either side of the axis of symmetry will coincide.

$f(x) = 3 - |x + 3|$	
x	**f(x)**
−6	0
−5	1
−4	2
−3	3
−2	2
−1	1
0	0

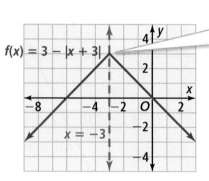

Translations of the absolute value function always have an axis of symmetry passing through the vertex.

$g(x) = (x - 2)^2$	
x	**g(x)**
−1	9
0	4
1	1
2	0
3	1
4	4
5	9

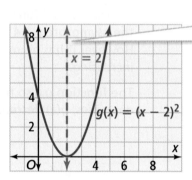

Quadratic functions always have a vertical axis of symmetry.

$h(x) = \sqrt{x} - 4$	
x	**h(x)**
4	0
5	1
8	2
13	3
20	4
29	5
40	6

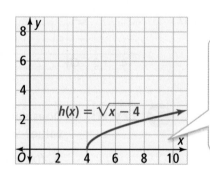

This function does not have an axis of symmetry. There is no way to fold the graph so that one side aligns with the other.

Quadratic functions and translations of the absolute value function have an axis of symmetry.

 Try It!   **3.** Does each function have an axis of symmetry? Sketch graphs to help you.

          a. $g(x) = 2^x$ **b.** $h(x) = \sqrt[3]{x + 4}$

👆 **EXAMPLE 4** **Analyze End Behaviors of Graphs**

What is the end behavior of each function?

End behavior describes what happens to the ends of the graph of a function as x approaches infinity or negative infinity (written as $x \to \infty$ and $x \to -\infty$).

LOOK FOR RELATIONSHIPS
You can determine end behavior of polynomial functions, such as a quadratic function, by looking at the leading term. The end behavior of $g(x) = ax^2$ is the same as the end behavior of $f(x) = ax^2 + bx + c$ when $a \neq 0$.

As $x \to \infty$, the values of $f(x)$ decrease without bound, or $f(x) \to -\infty$.
The same is true as $x \to -\infty$.

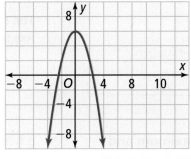

$$f(x) = -x^2 + 6$$

For this exponential function, there is a horizontal asymptote at $y = 0$. So as $x \to \infty$, the values of $g(x)$ approach 0. But as $x \to -\infty$, the values of $g(x)$ increase without bound, or $g(x) \to \infty$.

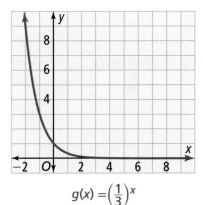

$$g(x) = \left(\frac{1}{3}\right)^x$$

As $x \to \infty$, the values of $h(x)$ grow less and less steeply, but they do not approach any asymptote, so $h(x) \to \infty$. As $x \to -\infty$, values of $h(x)$ decrease, and $h(x) \to -\infty$.

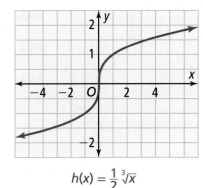

$$h(x) = \frac{1}{2}\sqrt[3]{x}$$

 Try It! **4.** Compare the end behaviors of the functions.

$$f(x) = 2^{x+2} \qquad g(x) = \left(\frac{1}{3}\right)^x + 4 \qquad h(x) = x^2 - 2x + 1$$

CONCEPT SUMMARY Common Features of Functions

WORDS		GRAPHS

Domain and Range

The domain of f is the set of all real numbers.

The range of f is the set of all real number less than or equal to 6.

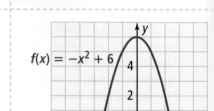

Maximum and Minimum Values

g has no maximum value.

The minimum value of g is 0, for $x = -3$.

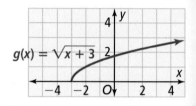

Axis of Symmetry

A vertical line that divides a function into mirror images is an axis of symmetry.

The line $x = 2$ is an axis of symmetry for h.

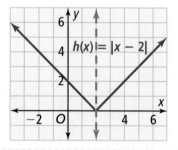

End Behavior

End behavior describes what happens to the ends of the graph.

As $x \to \infty$, $k(x) \to \infty$.

As $x \to -\infty$, $k(x) \to -2$.

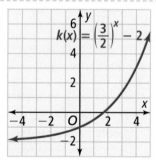

Do You UNDERSTAND?

1. **ESSENTIAL QUESTION** What can you learn about a function by analyzing its graph?

2. **Error Analysis** Kona states that the maximum value of $f(x) = -2^x$ is 0. Explain Kona's error.

3. **Look for Relationships** How are behaviors of quadratic functions like those of the absolute value function?

Do You KNOW HOW?

For each function identify the domain and range, state the maximum and minimum values, identify the axis of symmetry, if it exists, and describe the end behavior.

4. $f(x) = \sqrt{x - 5}$

5. $g(x) = x^2 + 2x + 1$

6. $h(x) = 2 - |x + 6|$

PRACTICE & PROBLEM SOLVING

UNDERSTAND

7. Look for Relationships Without sketching the graph, how can you identify the domain and range of $f(x) = 4 - \sqrt{2x - 5}$?

8. Mathematical Connections The function $f(x) = \sqrt[3]{x}$ has a domain of all real numbers and has neither a maximum nor a minimum value. How can you redefine the domain so that f has a maximum of 8 and a minimum of −8?

9. Error Analysis Describe and correct the error a student made in describing the end behavior of the function $y = 1,000,000 - x^2$.

> Every number that I enter for x gives a great big value for y, so as $x \to \infty$, $y \to \infty$.

10. Communicate Precisely Explain why the line $y = 3$ cannot be an axis of symmetry for a function.

11. Higher Order Thinking The domain of a function, f, is the set of all real numbers. Its axis of symmetry is the line $x = 4$. As x approaches infinity, y approaches infinity. Can the range of f be all real numbers? Explain your reasoning.

12. Error Analysis If a function is increasing throughout its domain, the y-values are greater and greater as x approaches infinity. Libby claims that any function that has all real numbers as its domain and is increasing everywhere must have all real numbers as its range as well. Is Libby correct? Explain why or why not.

13. Use Structure For what values of a and b would the graph of f have an axis of symmetry?

$$f(x) = \begin{cases} a\sqrt[3]{x}, & x \le b \\ \sqrt[3]{x}, & x > b \end{cases}$$

PRACTICE

Sketch the graph of each function and identify its domain and range. SEE EXAMPLE 1

14. $f(x) = x^2 - 2$ **15.** $f(x) = \sqrt{x - 3}$

16. $f(x) = 5^x$ **17.** $f(x) = 3 - |x - 4|$

Use the graph of each function to help you identify its maximum and minimum values, if they exist. SEE EXAMPLE 2

18. $f(x) = 3 - x^2$ **19.** $f(x) = \sqrt[3]{x}$

20. $f(x) = -2^x$ **21.** $f(x) = 5|x| - 8$

State the equation of the axis of symmetry for each function, if it exists. SEE EXAMPLE 3

22.

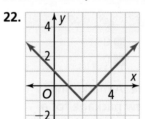

23.

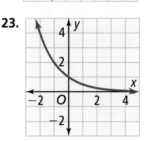

24.

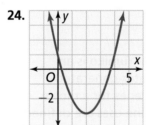

Describe the end behavior of each function. SEE EXAMPLE 4

25. $f(x) = 1 - 3x$ **26.** $f(x) = x^2 + 2$

27. $f(x) = -7^x$ **28.** $f(x) = |x + 2| - 8$

29. $f(x) = -3(x + 4)^2$ **30.** $f(x) = \sqrt{x} - 5$

PRACTICE & PROBLEM SOLVING

Practice   Tutorial

Mixed Review Available Online

31. Model With Mathematics The average high temperatures for four different cities, Anchorage, AK, Kansas City, MO, Miami, FL, and New York, NY, have been used to create the graph. Use information about maximum and minimum values to complete the legend for the graph. Explain your reasoning.

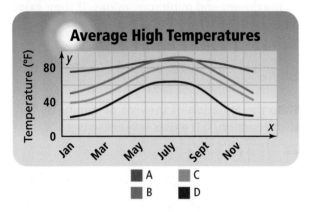

32. Make Sense and Persevere A marketing company is designing a new package for a box of cereal. They have determined that the function $C(x) = 4.5x^2$ models the cost of a box with side lengths as shown (measured in inches). Identify a reasonable domain and range for the function.

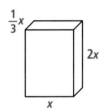

33. Model With Mathematics Yumiko is an animator. She uses computer-generated imagery (CGI) to create scenes for a movie. The shapes and features she uses are defined by functions. Which features of functions will be useful for Yumiko, and how can she use them in her work?

34. Analyze the behavior of $f(x) = x^2 - 2x + 5$. Which of the following are true? Select all that apply.

Ⓐ As x approaches infinity, y approaches infinity.

Ⓑ As x approaches negative infinity, y approaches negative infinity.

Ⓒ f has an axis of symmetry at $x = 1$.

Ⓓ The domain of f is the set of all real numbers.

Ⓔ The maximum value of f is 4, for $x = 1$.

35. SAT/ACT Which function has an axis of symmetry at $x = 1$ and a maximum value of 3?

Ⓐ $y = 1 - |x - 3|$

Ⓑ $y = |x - 1| + 3$

Ⓒ $y = |x + 1| - 3$

Ⓓ $y = 3 - |x - 1|$

Ⓔ $y = |x - 3| + 1$

36. Performance Task Jack started a small business recently, and he has been tracking his monthly profits, summarized in the table below.

Jan	$3	May	$100
Feb	$10	June	$180
Mar	$25	July	$415
Apr	$40	Aug	$795

Part A Create a graph to show Jack's profits over time. Determine the type of function that will best model Jack's profits based on data collected so far.

Part B Evaluate features of the function that will be relevant to Jack's business. Explain what those features mean in this context.

Part C Write an equation that models the growth of Jack's business. Use your function to predict Jack's profits for August of the following year. Is your prediction reasonable? Explain why or why not.

262   TOPIC 6 Working With Functions   Go Online | PearsonRealize.com

6-6

Translations of Functions

PearsonRealize.com

I CAN... graph and analyze transformations of functions.

CRITIQUE & EXPLAIN

The figure shows $f(x) = \sqrt{x}$ and $g(x) = \sqrt[3]{x}$. Venetta says that vertical translations will work in the same way for these functions as they do for quadratic and exponential functions. Tonya disagrees.

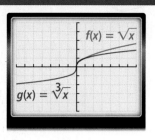

A. For $f(x) + c$ and $g(x) + c$, what translation do you expect when c is positive? When c is negative?

B. Generalize Which student is correct? Explain your answer.

? ESSENTIAL QUESTION

Do horizontal and vertical translations work in the same way for all types of functions?

EXAMPLE 1   Vertical Translations

How does adding a constant value to the output change the graph of a function?

Consider how the value of the constant changes the graph of each function shown.

You can write this operation as $g(x) = f(x) + k$. This means that for a value of x, g takes the output of f and adds the constant k.

LOOK FOR RELATIONSHIPS
Adding a negative constant k to a function decreases the function value by k, so it moves the graph down k units.

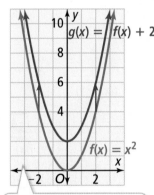

The graph of g is a translation of f up 2 units.

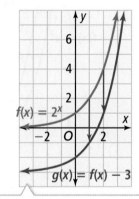

The graph of g is a translation of f down 3 units.

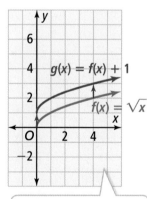

The graph of g is a translation of f up 1 unit.

Adding a positive constant translates the graph up, while adding a negative constant translates the graph down.

 Try It!   **1.** For each function $g(x) = f(x) + k$, how does the value of k affect the graph of function f?

a. $g(x) = f(x) + 7$ **b.** $g(x) = f(x) - 9$

👆 **EXAMPLE 2** ▸ **Analyze Horizontal Translations**

How does subtracting a constant from the input change the graph of a function?

Consider how the value of the constant changes the graph of each function shown.

You can write this operation generally as $g(x) = f(x - h)$. This means that g takes the input of f and subtracts the constant h before applying function f.

To see what happens to the graph when you subtract a constant from the input, consider what inputs for g you would need to get the same output as f for a given input x.

For example, if $g(x) = f(x + 2)$, you would need an input x_1 that is 2 units *less* than x for $g(x_1) = f(x)$. So the graph of g is the graph of f shifted 2 units to the *left*.

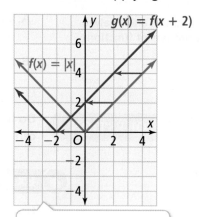

The graph of g is a translation of f left 2 units.

> **COMMON ERROR**
> The expression $x + 2$ in the function $f(x + 2)$ shifts the graph of $f(x)$ horizontally in the *negative* direction, not the positive direction. You can think of this as $f(x - (-2))$, so the constant is negative.

You can use the same reasoning to see how the graph changes for any function.

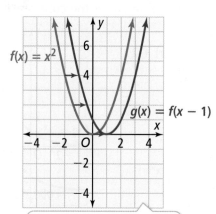

The graph of g is a translation of f right 1 unit.

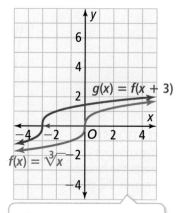

The graph of g is a translation of f left 3 units.

Subtracting a positive constant from x translates the graph to the right, while subtracting a negative constant from x translates the graph to the left.

 Try It! 2. For each function $g(x) = f(x - h)$, how does the value of h affect the graph of function f?

        a. $g(x) = f(x - 8)$ **b.** $g(x) = f(x + 7)$

CONCEPTUAL
UNDERSTANDING

EXAMPLE 3 **Combine Translations**

How does subtracting a constant value from the input and adding a constant value to the output change the graph of a function?

Graph $g(x) = f(x + 4) - 1$ for various types of functions f.

In the form $g(x) = f(x - h) + k$, $g(x) = f(x - (-4)) + (-1)$, so $h = -4$ and $k = -1$.

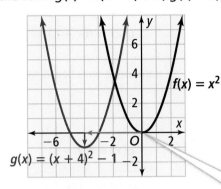

$f(x) = x^2$

$g(x) = (x + 4)^2 - 1$

Subtracting -4 from x translates the vertex 4 units left. Adding -1 translates the vertex 1 unit down.

REASON
For function graphs without a vertex, consider what points you can use as a reference points when you translate.

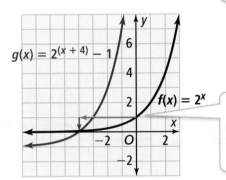

$g(x) = 2^{(x + 4)} - 1$

$f(x) = 2^x$

Subtracting -4 from x translates the reference point 4 units left. Adding -1 translates the point 1 unit down.

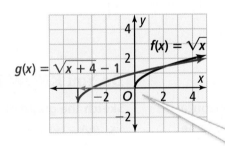

$f(x) = \sqrt{x}$

$g(x) = \sqrt{x + 4} - 1$

Subtracting -4 from x translates the reference point 4 units left. Adding -1 translates the point 1 unit down.

The combination of translations represented by $g(x) = f(x + 4) - 1$ affects the graph of these functions the same way. All points of graph f are translated left 4 units and down 1 unit.

The combined horizontal and vertical translations are independent of each other. Although they can be applied in either order, the horizontal one is applied first. Given $g(x) = f(x - h) + k$, the graph of function g is the graph of function f translated h units horizontally, then translated k units vertically.

 Try It! **3.** Graph f and $g(x) = f(x - 2) + 3$.

    a. $f(x) = x^2$ **b.** $f(x) = 2^x$ **c.** $f(x) = \sqrt{x}$

CONCEPT SUMMARY Translations of Functions

WORDS	Changes to the **output** translate the graph vertically.	Changes to the **input** translate the graph horizontally.
	$k > 0$: shifts $|k|$ units up	$h > 0$: shifts $|h|$ units right
	$k < 0$: shifts $|k|$ units down	$h < 0$: shifts $|h|$ units left

ALGEBRA $g(x) = f(x) + k$

translates k units vertically

$g(x) = f(x - h)$

translates h units horizontally

$g(x) = f(x - h) + k$

translates h units horizontally and k units vertically

NUMBERS $g(x) = f(x) - 2$

translates 2 units down

$g(x) = f(x + 3)$

translates 3 units left

$g(x) = f(x + 3) - 2$

translates 3 units left and 2 units down

GRAPHS

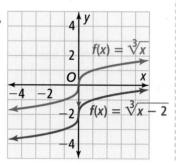

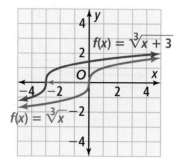

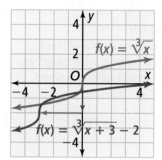

Do You UNDERSTAND?

1. **ESSENTIAL QUESTION** Do horizontal and vertical translations work in the same way for all types of functions?

2. **Use Structure** How can translations help you sketch the graph of $f(x) = x^2 + 8x + 16$?

3. **Error Analysis** Ashton says that $f(x) = \sqrt{x - 3}$ has domain $x \geq -3$. Is Ashton correct? Explain your reasoning.

4. **Construct Arguments** Explain why adding a number to the output of a function shifts its graph vertically.

Do You KNOW HOW?

Sketch the graph of each function.

5. $f(x) = |x| + 4$

6. $f(x) = (x - 2)^3$

7. $f(x) = \sqrt{x + 2}$

8. $f(x) = 3^x - 5$

9. $f(x) = (x - 1)^2 - 2$

10. $f(x) = \sqrt{x + 4} + 3$

11. What is the equation of the graph?

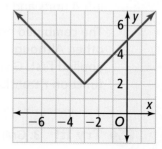

Scan for Multimedia

Practice   Tutorial

Additional Exercises Available Online

UNDERSTAND

12. Reason How does the graph of $f(x) = 5$ change for $g(x) = f(x - h) + k$, where h and k are constants?

13. Use Structure The graph of $g(x) = f(x - 2) + 1$ is shown. Sketch the graph of f.

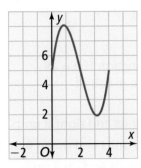

14. Error Analysis Victor is asked to explain how the graph of $g(x) = |x - 2| + 2$ relates to the graph of $f(x) = |x|$. His work is shown below. Is Victor correct? Explain why or why not.

$f(x) = |x - 2| + 2$
$= |x| + (-2 + 2)$
$= |x|$

Graph of $f(x) = |x - 2| + 2$ is the same as the graph of $f(x) = |x|$, with vertex at $(0, 0)$.   ✗

15. Use Structure Describe a combination of translations to apply to the floor function, $f(x) = \lfloor x \rfloor$, that leaves its graph appearing unchanged. Write the new equation.

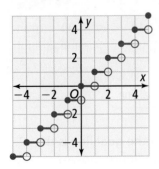

16. Higher Order Thinking Given $g(x) = f(x - 2) + 4$ and $j(x) = g(x + 5) - 3$, find the values of h and k in the equation $j(x) = f(x - h) + k$.

PRACTICE

Sketch the graph of each function.
SEE EXAMPLES 1 AND 2

17. $g(x) = |x| + 6$ **18.** $g(x) = x^2 - 3$

19. $g(x) = \frac{1}{3}x + 2$ **20.** $g(x) = \sqrt{x} - 8$

21. $g(x) = (x - 2)^2$ **22.** $g(x) = |x + 4|$

23. $g(x) = \sqrt{x + 3}$ **24.** $g(x) = \sqrt[3]{x - 5}$

Each graph is a translation of the given function. Write the function for the graph. SEE EXAMPLE 2

25. $f(x) = x^2$ **26.** $f(x) = \sqrt[3]{x}$

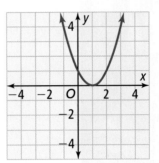   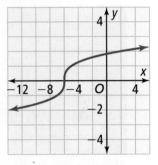

27. $f(x) = |x|$

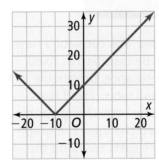

28. $f(x) = \sqrt{x}$

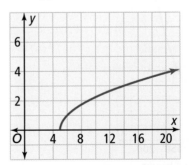

Sketch the graph of each function. SEE EXAMPLE 3

29. $g(x) = 2^{x+4} - 7$ **30.** $g(x) = |x + 4.3| - 2.7$

APPLY

31. Make Sense and Persevere The height, h, in meters of a Saturn V rocket t seconds after launch is modeled by the graph shown. Note that the graph is not the actual path of the rocket. A launch is delayed by 60 seconds by a technical problem. Describe the effect on $h(t)$ as a translation. Sketch the graph of the height of the rocket t seconds from the original launch time.

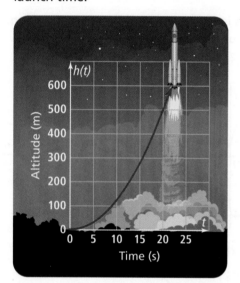

32. Mathematical Connections The costs for a new publishing company can be classified as fixed costs, such as rent and insurance, or variable costs, such as materials and labor. Fixed costs are constant, while variable costs change as the number of items produced changes. The graph shows the weekly variable costs based on the number of books produced.

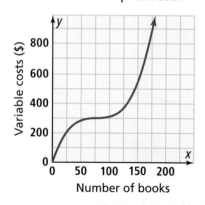

a. If weekly fixed costs are $300, sketch a graph showing total expenses for the week.

b. Find the total cost of producing 75 books in a week.

ASSESSMENT PRACTICE

33. Which is true about the graph of the function $f(x) = (x - 2)^2 - 3$? Select all that apply.

Ⓐ It is a parabola that opens upward.

Ⓑ It is a parabola that opens downward.

Ⓒ The vertex is (2, −3).

Ⓓ The vertex is (−2, −3).

Ⓔ The vertex is (2, 3).

34. SAT/ACT How is the function $f(x) = \sqrt{x}$ translated to obtain the graph of $g(x) = \sqrt{x + 5} + 6$?

Ⓐ Shift $f(x) = \sqrt{x}$ up 5 units and right 6 units.

Ⓑ Shift $f(x) = \sqrt{x}$ right 5 units and down 6 units.

Ⓒ Shift $f(x) = \sqrt{x}$ left 5 units and up 6 units.

Ⓓ Shift $f(x) = \sqrt{x}$ left 5 units and down 6 units.

Ⓔ Shift $f(x) = \sqrt{x}$ down 5 units and left 6 units.

35. Performance Task In a computer football game, you are attempting to kick a field goal. Every kick in the game can be modeled by a horizontal translation of the function shown. Assume the translations are to the nearest tenth of a yard. The goal post is 10 yards behind the goal line.

The center of the goal post crossbar is at $(-10, 3\frac{1}{3})$. $f(x) = -\frac{1}{100}(x - 10)^2 + 12$

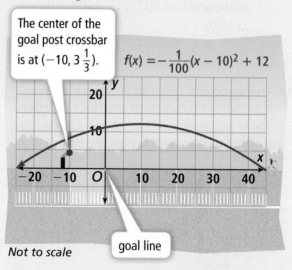

Not to scale goal line

Part A How far from the goal line is the football placed in the figure shown?

Part B What is the maximum distance from the goal line the football can be placed for the kick to clear the crossbar?

Part C Write the function for the kick in Part B.

6-7

Compressions and Stretches of Functions

 PearsonRealize.com

I CAN... change functions to compress or stretch their graphs.

👆 **EXPLORE & REASON**

The graphs of three quadratic functions *g*, *h*, and *j* all have a vertex of (0, 0). Additional points that lie on the graph of each function are shown.

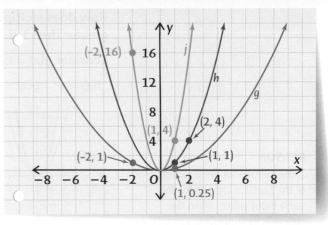

A. Write a quadratic function for each parabola.

B. Communicate Precisely How are these functions similar? How are they different?

C. Using your knowledge of compressions and stretches of other functions and your answers to parts A and B, describe how how to write a vertical stretch or compression of $f(x) = \sqrt{x}$.

❓ **ESSENTIAL QUESTION**   What change to a function will result in a vertical or horizontal stretch or compression of its graph?

👆 **EXAMPLE 1**   Analyze Reflections Across the *x*-Axis

How does multiplying the output by −1 change the graph of a function?

Consider $g(x) = -1f(x)$ for $f(x) = x^2$ and for $f(x) = \sqrt[3]{x}$.

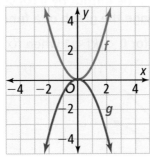

$$f(x) = x^2$$
$$g(x) = -x^2$$

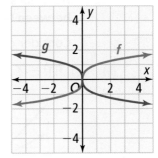

$$f(x) = \sqrt[3]{x}$$
$$g(x) = -\sqrt[3]{x}$$

LOOK FOR RELATIONSHIPS
Recall the transformations of other functions you have studied. How does the graph of a linear function change when the output is multiplied by −1?

The graph of $g(x) = -x^2$ is a reflection of $f(x) = x^2$ across the *x*-axis. The graph of $g(x) = -\sqrt[3]{x}$ is a reflection of $f(x) = \sqrt[3]{x}$ across the *x*-axis.

In general, if $g(x) = -1f(x)$, the graph of *g* is a reflection across the *x*-axis of the graph of *f*.

✓ **Try It!**   **1.** Write a function with a graph that is the reflection of the graph of *f* across the *x*-axis.

    a. $f(x) = x$ **b.** $f(x) = \sqrt{x}$

EXAMPLE 2   Analyze Vertical Stretches of Graphs

How does multiplying the output by a constant with an absolute value greater than 1 change the graph of a function?

Consider $g(x) = kf(x)$ for $|k| > 1$ when $f(x) = x^2$ and when $f(x) = \sqrt[3]{x}$.

$f(x) = x^2 \quad g(x) = 2x^2$ $f(x) = \sqrt[3]{x} \quad g(x) = 4\sqrt[3]{x}$

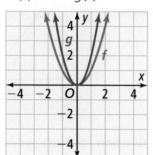 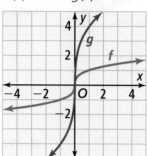

REASON
Think about how the y-values of the function change for the same input values when the output is multiplied by a constant greater than 1.

The graph of $g(x) = 2x^2$ is a vertical stretch of $f(x) = x^2$ away from the x-axis. The graph of $g(x) = 4\sqrt[3]{x}$ is a vertical stretch of $f(x) = \sqrt[3]{x}$ away from the x-axis.

In general, if $g(x) = kf(x)$ for $|k| > 1$, the graph of g is a vertical stretch away from the x-axis of the graph of f.

✓ **Try It!**   **2.** Write a function with a graph that is a vertical stretch of the graph of f, away from the x-axis.

      a. $f(x) = x$ **b.** $f(x) = \sqrt{x}$

EXAMPLE 3   Analyze Vertical Compressions of Graphs

How does multiplying the output by a constant with an absolute value between 0 and 1 change the graph of a function?

Consider $g(x) = kf(x)$ for $0 < |k| < 1$ when $f(x) = |x + 1|$ and when $f(x) = x^2$.

$f(x) = |x + 1| \quad g(x) = \frac{1}{2}|x + 1|$ $f(x) = x^2 \quad g(x) = \frac{1}{2}x^2$

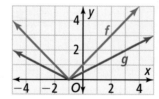 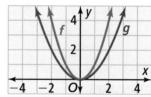

The graph of $g(x) = \frac{1}{2}|x + 1|$ is a vertical compression of $f(x) = |x + 1|$ toward the x-axis. The graph of $g(x) = \frac{1}{2}x^2$ is a vertical compression of $f(x) = x^2$ toward the x-axis.

In general, if $g(x) = kf(x)$ for $0 < |k| < 1$, the graph of g is a vertical compression toward the x-axis of the graph of f.

✓ **Try It!**   **3.** Write a function with a graph that is a vertical compression of the graph of f, toward the x-axis.

      a. $f(x) = \sqrt{x}$ **b.** $f(x) = |x|$

CONCEPTUAL
UNDERSTANDING

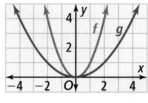 **EXAMPLE 4** **Analyze Horizontal Stretches of Graphs**

Why does multiplying the input of the function stretch the graph horizontally?

Consider $g(x) = f(kx)$ for $0 < k < 1$ when $f(x) = x^2$.

LOOK FOR RELATIONSHIPS
To get the same y-values from function g as from f, you must double the input x. The graph of g is a horizontal stretch of the graph of f away from y-axis by a scale factor of 2.

x	$f(x)$	$g(x)$
-2	4	1
-1	1	0.25
0	0	0
1	1	0.25
2	4	1

$g(-2) = f(-1)$

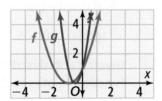

$f(x) = x^2 \qquad g(x) = \left(\tfrac{1}{2}x\right)^2$

Multiplying the input of $f(x) = x^2$ by the constant $\frac{1}{2}$ yields $g(x) = \left(\frac{1}{2}x\right)^2$. To get y-values from function g that are equal to those from function f you need to input x-values into g that are farther away from the y-axis than the x-values you input into f. So the graph of g is a horizontal stretch away from the y-axis of the graph of f.

 Try It!   **4.** Why is $g(x) = 0.2x + 2$ a horizontal stretch of $f(x) = x + 2$?

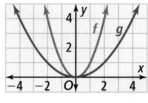 **EXAMPLE 5** **Analyze Horizontal Compressions of Graphs**

How does multiplying the input by a constant with an absolute value greater than 1 change the graph of a function?

Consider $g(x) = f(kx)$ for $|k| > 1$ when $f(x) = x^2 + 2$ and when $f(x) = |x + 1|$.

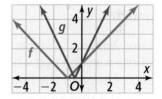

$f(x) = (x + 1)^2$ $f(x) = |x + 1|$

$g(x) = (2x + 1)^2$ $g(x) = |2x + 1|$

COMMON ERROR
You might think that as k increases the graph of the function $f(kx)$ would stretch horizontally. Instead, it compresses the graph horizontally as k increases.

The graph of $g(x) = (2x + 1)^2$ is a horizontal compression of $f(x) = (x + 1)^2$ toward the y-axis. The graph of $g(x) = |2x + 1|$ is a horizontal compression of $f(x) = |x + 1|$ toward the y-axis.

In general, when $g(x) = f(kx)$ for $|k| > 1$, the graph of g is a horizontal compression toward the y-axis of the graph of f.

 Try It!   **5.** Write a function with a graph that is a horizontal compression of the graph of f, toward the y-axis.

   a. $f(x) = \sqrt[3]{x}$ **b.** $f(x) = x^2$

CONCEPT SUMMARY Stretches and Compressions of Functions

	Vertical Stretch or Compression	Horizontal Stretch or Compression
WORDS	$g(x) = kf(x)$ stretches or compresses the graph of f vertically by a factor of k	$g(x) = f(kx)$ stretches or compresses the graph of f horizontally by a factor of k
ALGEBRA	$f(x) = \sqrt{x}$ $g(x) = 3\sqrt{x}$	$f(x) = x^2$ $g(x) = (0.6x)^2$
GRAPHS	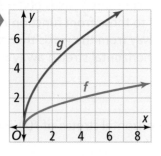	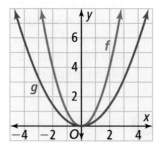

✅ Do You UNDERSTAND?

1. **? ESSENTIAL QUESTION** What change to a function will result in a vertical or horizontal stretch or compression of its graph?

2. **Error Analysis** A student says that the graph of the function $g(x) = 0.4f(x)$ is a horizontal compression of the function f. Explain the error the student made.

3. **Communicate Precisely** Compare and contrast a vertical stretch and a horizontal stretch.

4. **Reason** Given the function f and the constant k, write the general form for a horizontal stretch of the function. Make sure to include any constraints on k.

Do You KNOW HOW?

Tell whether the graph of g is a reflection across the x-axis of the graph of f.

5. $f(x) = 4x + 5$

   $g(x) = -4x - 5$

6. $f(x) = -3x^2 + 7$

   $g(x) = 3x^2 + 7$

Given $k = 8$, describe how the graph of each function relates to f.

7. $g(x) = f(kx)$

8. $g(x) = kf(x)$

9. Identify whether a horizontal stretch or compression was used to produce the graph of g given the graph of f shown below.

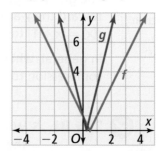

UNDERSTAND

10. Mathematical Connections Is the slope m of a line $y = mx + b$ related to vertical and horizontal compressions and stretches of the graph of the line? Explain.

11. Look for Relationships Graph $f(x) = \sqrt{x}$ and $g(x) = \sqrt{2x}$. Explain why you can consider the function g to be either a vertical stretch of f or a horizontal compression of f.

12. Make Sense and Persevere Two graphs of two quadratic functions $f(x)$ and $g(x) = f(kx)$ are shown below. What is the approximate value of k?

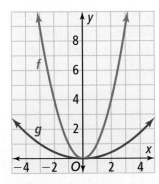

13. Error Analysis Describe and correct the error a student made in describing the relationship between the graphs of the two functions.

$f(x) = x^2 + 1$

$g(x) = (4x)^2 + 1$

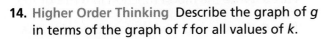

Because the input of f is being multiplied by a constant to get g, the graph of g is the graph of f being horizontally stretched or compressed The constant is 4, which is greater than 1, so it is a horizontal stretch. ✗

14. Higher Order Thinking Describe the graph of g in terms of the graph of f for all values of k.

a. $g(x) = kf(x)$ for $0 < |k| < 1$

b. $g(x) = kf(x)$ for $1 < |k|$

c. $g(x) = f(kx)$ for $0 < |k| < 1$

PRACTICE

Write a function with a graph that is the reflection of the graph of f across the x-axis. SEE EXAMPLE 1

15. $f(x) = x^2 - 3$

16. $f(x) = |2x + 5|$

17. $f(x) = -\sqrt{2x}$

18. $f(x) = -x + 4$

For each pair, tell whether the graph of g is a vertical or horizontal compression or stretch of the graph of f. SEE EXAMPLES 2, 3, 4 AND 5

19. $f(x) = |x + 3|$

$g(x) = 2|x + 3|$

20. $f(x) = x^2 - 4$

$g(x) = (0.5x)^2 - 4$

21. $f(x) = \sqrt{x + 1}$

$g(x) = 0.25\sqrt{x + 1}$

22. $f(x) = \sqrt[3]{x - 1}$

$g(x) = \sqrt[3]{2x - 1}$

23. $f(x) = x - 3$

$g(x) = 0.4x - 3$

24. $f(x) = |x - 2|$

$g(x) = \frac{2}{3}|x - 2|$

25. $f(x) = x^2 + 2$

$g(x) = 6x^2 + 12$

26. $f(x) = \sqrt{x}$

$g(x) = \sqrt{7x}$

For each graph, identify the transformation applied to f that results in g, and identify the value of k.

27.

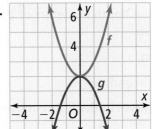

28.

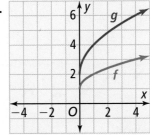

29. The graph of g is a reflection of the graph of $f(x) = \sqrt{x}$ across the x-axis and a vertical stretch of that graph by a factor of 3. Write the function g.

APPLY

30. Make Sense and Persevere A company's logo is modeled by the function $f(x) = -|x| + 2$. For a new design, the company wants the logo to be narrower. What are two ways the function f could be altered so that the graph of the new function gives a narrower logo? Explain.

31. Reason The area A of a square is given by $A = s^2$, where s is a side length of the square.

a. Graph the function $A = s^2$ on a grid. How does the graph change when you double the side length of the square? Describe the changes in terms of stretches and compressions.

b. Write a function that gives the side length of a square in terms of its area.

c. Graph your function from part (b).

d. How does this graph change when you double the side length of the square? Describe the changes in terms of stretches and compressions.

32. Model With Mathematics The speed of a wave in the ocean in meters per second can be determined using the function $f(x) = 3.13\sqrt{x}$, where x represents the depth in meters of the water under the wave.

a. Graph the function.

b. Identify the domain and range.

c. How fast are the waves in the figure moving over the water?

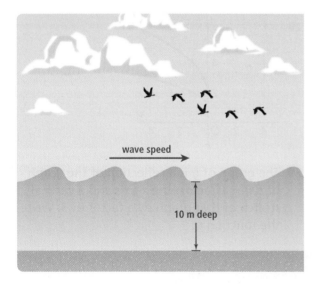

wave speed

10 m deep

ASSESSMENT PRACTICE

33. What is a function rule for g such that the graph of g is a reflection across the x-axis of the graph of $f(x) = |2x + 5|$?

34. SAT/ACT Which function has a graph that is a vertical stretch of the graph of $f(x) = 4x^2 - 1$?

Ⓐ $g(x) = 6(4x^2 - 1)$

Ⓑ $g(x) = 0.6(4x^2 - 1)$

Ⓒ $g(x) = 4(6x)^2 - 1$

Ⓓ $g(x) = -(4x^2 - 1)$

35. Performance Task The period, in seconds, of a pendulum's swing on Earth is given by the function $f(x) = 2\pi\sqrt{\frac{x}{9.8}}$, where x is the length of the pendulum in meters. On the moon, the equation that gives the period of the pendulum is $g(x) = 2\pi\sqrt{\frac{x}{1.6}}$.

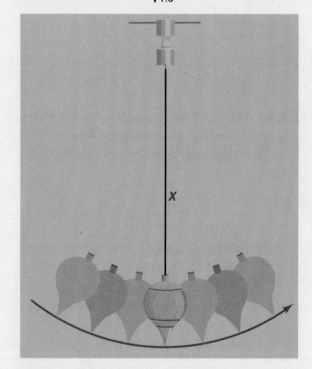

x

Part A Graph both functions on the same grid.

Part B Write the moon function in terms of $f(x)$.

Part C If $g(x) = kf(x)$, what does the value of k tell you about how a pendulum swings on the moon as compared to on Earth?

Part D Describe how the graph of g differs from the graph of f in terms of stretches and compressions.

6-8

Operations With Functions

PearsonRealize.com

I CAN... add, subtract, and multiply functions.

EXPLORE & REASON

The graphs of $f(x) = x^2$ and $g(x) = x^2 + 3$ are shown.

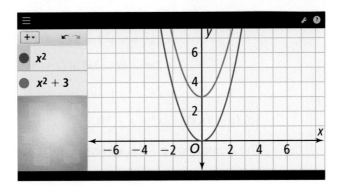

A. Compare the domain and range of each function.

B. Graph another function of the form $f(x) = x^2 + c$ using a different constant added to x^2.

C. **Look for Relationships** Does changing a function by adding a constant alter the domain of the function? Does changing a function by adding a constant alter the range of the function? Explain.

? ESSENTIAL QUESTION

How can you extend addition, subtraction, and multiplication from numbers to functions?

CONCEPTUAL UNDERSTANDING

EXAMPLE 1   Add and Subtract Functions

A. If $f(x) = 2x - 3$ and $g(x) = 2x^2 + x + 7$, what is $f + g$? How do the domain and range of $f + g$ compare with the domains and ranges of f and g?

Just as you can add numbers, expressions, and polynomials, you can also add functions. The sum of two functions f and g is another function called $f + g$. The function $f + g$ is defined as $(f + g)(x) = f(x) + g(x)$.

STUDY TIP
In $f + g$, the plus sign indicates the addition of functions. In $f(x) + g(x)$, the plus sign indicates the addition of numbers.

$f(x) + g(x) = (2x - 3) + (2x^2 + x + 7)$

$\qquad = 2x^2 + (2x + x) + (-3 + 7)$

$\qquad = 2x^2 + 3x + 4$

> When adding polynomials, you add the like terms.

So, $(f + g)(x) = 2x^2 + 3x + 4$.

Notice that f is a linear function and g and $f + g$ are quadratic functions. The domains of f, g, and $f + g$ are the same: all real numbers. The range of f is all real numbers. You can find the range of the quadratic functions graphically or algebraically. The range of g is $y \geq 6.875$ and the range of $f + g$ is $y \geq 2.875$.

In general, the domain and range of the combined functions may be different from the domain and range of the original functions. If a value is not in the domain of one of the functions, it is not in the domain of the sum or difference of the original functions either.

CONTINUED ON THE NEXT PAGE

EXAMPLE 1 CONTINUED

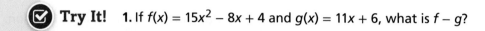

B. If $f(x) = 2x - 3$ and $g(x) = 2x^2 + x + 7$, what is $g - f$?

The difference of two functions $g - f$ is defined as $(g - f)(x) = g(x) - f(x)$.

$$g(x) - f(x) = (2x^2 + x + 7) - (2x - 3)$$
$$= 2x^2 + x + 7 - 2x + 3$$
$$= 2x^2 + (x - 2x) + (7 + 3)$$
$$= 2x^2 - x + 10$$

So, $(g - f)(x) = 2x^2 - x + 10$.

The domain of $g - f$ is all real numbers, and the range is $y \geq 9.875$.

> **COMMON ERROR**
> Recall that when subtracting a polynomial, every term in that polynomial must be subtracted.

☑ Try It! 1. If $f(x) = 15x^2 - 8x + 4$ and $g(x) = 11x + 6$, what is $f - g$?

✋ EXAMPLE 2 **Multiply Functions**

A. What is the product of the two functions $f(x) = 9x + 20$ and $g(x) = x + 5$?

The product of two functions $f \cdot g$ is defined as $(f \cdot g)(x) = f(x) \cdot g(x)$.

$$f(x) \cdot g(x) = (9x + 20)(x + 5)$$
$$= 9x(x) + 9x(5) + 20(x) + 20(5)$$
$$= 9x^2 + 45x + 20x + 100$$
$$= 9x^2 + 65x + 100$$

So, $(f \cdot g)(x) = 9x^2 + 65x + 100$.

> **USE STRUCTURE**
> Think about the properties you could use to simplify the product of the two functions.

B. Are the domain and range of functions f and g the same as the domain and range of $f \cdot g$?

Since f and g are both linear functions, the domain and range for both functions are all real numbers.

The product of f and g is a quadratic function, the domain is all real numbers, but the range is limited.

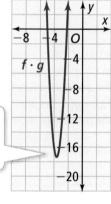

> The vertex is at $(-3.6, -17.4)$, and the graph opens up, so the range is $y \geq -17.4$.

The domain of $f \cdot g$ is the same as the domain of f and g, but the range is different.

☑ Try It! 2. Find the product of f and g. What are the domain and the range of the product?

    a. $f(x) = \sqrt{x}$ **b.** $f(x) = 3x^2 + 4$

       $g(x) = 2x - 1$ $g(x) = 2^x$

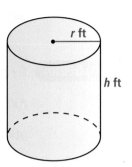
APPLICATION   ☝ **EXAMPLE 3**   Apply Function Operations

A cylinder has a height that is twice its radius. The cylinder is sealed at the top and bottom to form a container. Find a function for the total surface area of the container. What dimensions would yield a total surface area of about 120 ft²?

Formulate ◀ Write a function for the surface area of the top and bottom of the cylinder.

$$f(r) = 2 \cdot \text{area of the base}$$

$$= 2\pi r^2$$

Write a function for the lateral surface area of the cylinder. Recall that the lateral surface is the curved surface of the cylinder. Unrolled, it would form a rectangle.

$$g(r) = \text{height} \cdot \text{circumference}$$

$$= h \cdot 2\pi r$$

$$= 2r \cdot 2\pi r \quad \boxed{\text{The height is twice the radius.}}$$

$$= 4\pi r^2$$

Compute ◀ The total surface area is the sum of the area of the bases and the lateral surface area. Find $f + g$.

$$f(r) + g(r) = 2\pi r^2 + 4\pi r^2$$

$$= 6\pi r^2$$

Graph $(f + g)(r) = 6\pi r^2$ to find the value of r that corresponds to a total surface area of 120 ft².

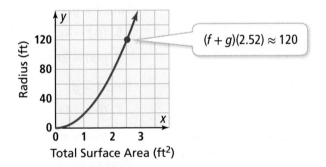

$(f + g)(2.52) \approx 120$

Radius (ft)

Total Surface Area (ft²)

Interpret ◀ When the radius is 2.52 ft, the total surface area of the cylinder is about 120 ft². The height of the cylinder would be twice the radius, or 5.04 ft.

 Try It!   3. Suppose the cylinder in Example 3 is not sealed, so the total surface area includes only the area of the bottom and the lateral surface area. What dimensions would yield a total surface area of about 120 ft²?

Adding Functions	Subtracting Functions	Multiplying Functions
ALGEBRA $f + g$	$f - g$	$f \cdot g$
$f(x) = x^2 + 3$	$f(x) = 3^x$	$f(x) = x + 1$
$g(x) = 2^x$	$g(x) = x + 2$	$g(x) = x - 4$
$f(x) + g(x) = (x^2 + 3) + (2^x)$	$f(x) - g(x) = (3^x) - (x + 2)$	$f(x) \cdot g(x) = (x + 1)(x - 4)$
$(f + g)(x) = x^2 + 3 + 2^x$	$(f - g)(x) = 3^x - x - 2$	$= x^2 - 4x + x - 4$
		$(f \cdot g)(x) = x^2 - 3x - 4$

GRAPHS

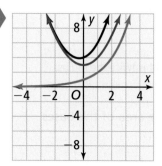 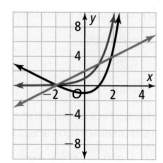 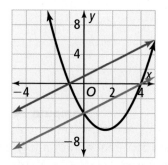

Do You UNDERSTAND?

1. **ESSENTIAL QUESTION** How can you extend addition, subtraction, and multiplication from numbers to functions?

2. **Use Structure** What property is useful when subtracting a function that has multiple terms?

3. **Use Appropriate Tools** Describe how you can use a graph to find the domain and range of two combined functions.

4. **Error Analysis** A student claimed that the functions $f(x) = \sqrt{x}$ and $g(x) = 2x - 5$ cannot be combined because there are no like terms. Explain the error the student made.

Do You KNOW HOW?

Find $f + g$.

5. $f(x) = 4x + 1$
   $g(x) = 2x^2 - 5x$

6. $f(x) = x^2$
   $g(x) = 3^x$

Find $f - g$.

7. $f(x) = 4x^2$
   $g(x) = x^2 + 2x + 7$

8. $f(x) = 6x + 5$
   $g(x) = \sqrt{2x}$

Find $f \cdot g$.

9. $f(x) = 3x^2 - 2$
   $g(x) = x^2 - 4x$

10. $f(x) = 6x$
    $g(x) = 8^x$

UNDERSTAND

11. **Mathematical Connections** How is adding functions like adding polynomials? How is it different?

12. **Look for Relationships** Write two functions that, when combined by adding, have a different domain than at least one of the original functions.

13. **Make Sense and Persevere** Given the graphs of f and g, sketch the graphs of $f + g$ and $f \cdot g$.

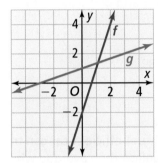

14. **Error Analysis** Describe and correct the error a student made in multiplying the two functions, $f(x) = x^3 + 3x^2 + 1$ and $g(x) = 2x - 1$.

$$(x^3 + 3x^2 + 1)(2x - 1)$$
$$= x^3(2x) + 3x^2(2x) + 2x$$
$$= 2x^4 + 6x^3 + 2x \quad ✗$$

15. **Higher Order Thinking** What two functions could you multiply to create the function shown in the graph? How do the domain and range of each of the functions compare to the domain and range of the graphed function?

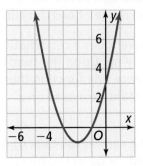

PRACTICE

Find $f + g$. SEE EXAMPLE 1

16. $f(x) = 6x^3 + 7x$
    $g(x) = x^2 - 3x + 2$

17. $f(x) = 3\sqrt{x}$
    $g(x) = -2x + 4$

Find $f - g$. SEE EXAMPLE 1

18. $f(x) = 2x^3 + 2x^2 - 3$
    $g(x) = 8x + 15$

19. $f(x) = 7^x$
    $g(x) = 5x^2 - 2x - 4$

Find $f \cdot g$. SEE EXAMPLE 2

20. $f(x) = 9x - 2$
    $g(x) = x^2 + 4x - 7$

21. $f(x) = 3x^2 + 8x + 2$
    $g(x) = -6x + 1$

22. $f(x) = 3^x$
    $g(x) = 5x^2 - 2$

23. $f(x) = \sqrt{5x}$
    $g(x) = 7x + 2$

Given the graphs of f and g, graph $f + g$. Compare the domain and range of $f + g$ to the domains and ranges of f and g.

24.

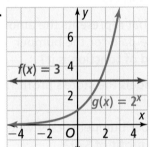

25.

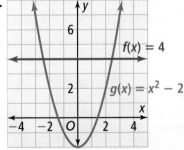

26. A florist charges $10 for delivery plus an additional $2 per mile from the flower shop. The florist pays the delivery driver $0.50 per mile and $5 for gas per delivery. If x is the number of miles a delivery location is from the flower shop, what expression models the amount of money the florist earns for each delivery? SEE EXAMPLE 3

APPLY

27. Make Sense and Persevere A laser tag center charges $50 to set up a party, and $75 per hour. The center pays its employees that work the party a total of $36 per hour.

 a. Write a function f that represents the amount of revenue from a party that runs for x hours.

 b. Write a function g that represents the expenses for a party that runs for x hours.

 c. Write a combined function that represents the amount of profit the laser tag center makes on a party that runs x hours.

28. Reason A store is selling bumper stickers in support of a local sports team. The function $h(x) = -20x^2 + 80x + 240$ models the revenue, in dollars, the store expects to make by increasing the price of a bumper sticker x dollars over the original price of $2. The store paid a total of $200 for the bumper stickers.

 a. Write a function that represents the amount of money the store paid for the bumper stickers. What kind of function is it?

 b. What function models the store's profit from the bumper stickers?

 c. What is the price per bumper sticker when the store makes a profit of $20?

29. Model With Mathematics The surface of a cylindrical tank is being painted. The total surface area of a cylindrical tank is the sum of two area functions.

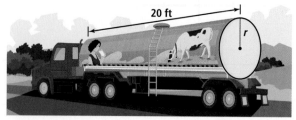

20 ft

r

 a. Write a function that gives the total area of the two circular ends as a function of radius.

 b. Write a function that gives the lateral surface area of the cylinder as a function of radius.

 c. Combine the functions from parts (a) and (b) to get the total surface area of the cylinder as a function of radius.

30. Given the functions $f(x) = x + 8$ and $g(x) = x^2 - 9$, which of the following are true statements about $f - g$? Select all that apply.

 Ⓐ It is a linear function.

 Ⓑ It is a quadratic function.

 Ⓒ The domain is all real numbers.

 Ⓓ The range is all real numbers.

 Ⓔ The range is $y \geq 17$.

31. SAT/ACT The function h is the sum of the functions $f(x) = 3x + 5$ and $g(x) = 2x^2 - 6x - 2$. Which represents h?

 Ⓐ $h(x) = 5x^2 - x - 2$

 Ⓑ $h(x) = 2x^2 - 3x + 3$

 Ⓒ $h(x) = 2x^2 + 9x + 7$

 Ⓓ $h(x) = -3x + 3$

32. Performance Task A fuel-efficient car can travel 6 miles further per gallon than average while driving on the highway, and about 4 miles less than average while in the city.

Gas tank holds about 13 gallons.

averages 28 mpg

Part A Write two functions to determine the distance the driver could travel in the city or on the highway, using x gallons of gasoline.

Part B Assuming that the car has full tank of gas, what is the domain and range of each function?

Part C Suppose the driver does a combination of city and highway driving. Using the functions you found in Part A, write one function that could represent the distance traveled on x gallons of gasoline.

Part D Assume that the car has full tank of gas, what is the domain and range of the function you found in Part C?

6-9
Inverse Functions

 PearsonRealize.com

I CAN... use inverse functions to solve problems.

VOCABULARY
• inverse of a function

🖐 **EXPLORE & REASON**

The tables of data show food orders for different parties.

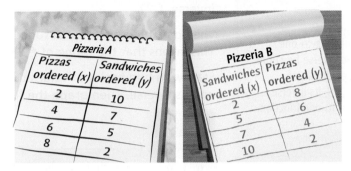

A. Graph the data points shown in the tables. Use a different color for each data set.

B. **Look for Relationships** What observations can you make about the graphs of the data in the two tables?

C. What similarities and differences do you notice about the data?

❓ **ESSENTIAL QUESTION** | How can you use inverse functions to help solve problems?

CONCEPTUAL UNDERSTANDING

🖐 **EXAMPLE 1** Understand Inverse Functions

What is the inverse of the function $f(x) = 2x + 6$?

The **inverse of a function** reverses the order of the outputs and inputs of a function. The inverse of a function f is usually written as f^{-1} (read "f inverse"). If $f(x) = y$, then $f^{-1}(y) = x$ for all x in the domain of f and all y in the range of f. A function f has an inverse function f^{-1} if and only if the original function f is one-to-one. The function f is also the inverse of f^{-1}.

VOCABULARY
Remember, a *one-to-one function* is a function for which each item in the range corresponds to exactly one item in the domain.

Make tables for the function and its inverse.

f	
x	**y**
0	6
1	8
2	10
3	12

Switch the x-values and the y-values to find the inverse.

f⁻¹	
x	**y**
6	0
8	1
10	2
12	3

The data in the table for the inverse function are linear. Write an equation for the inverse function.

$$m = \frac{1-0}{8-6}$$

Identify the slope and then use point-slope form.

$$= \frac{1}{2}$$

$$y - y_1 = m(x - x_1)$$

$$y - 0 = \frac{1}{2}(x - 6)$$

$$y = \frac{1}{2}x - 3$$

The inverse of the function is $f^{-1}(x) = \frac{1}{2}x - 3$.

✅ **Try It!** 1. How is the slope of f^{-1} related to the slope of f?

EXAMPLE 2   Graph Inverse Functions

What is the graph of $f(x) = x^2$ for $x \geq 0$? What is the graph of its inverse, f^{-1}?

The domain of the original function f is restricted to nonnegative values. This means that the range of f^{-1} will be restricted to nonnegative values.

Start with two tables of values to show points on the graph of the function and its inverse. Then graph the functions.

f	
x	**y**
0	0
1	1
2	4
3	9

Switch the x-values and the y-values to find points on the graph of the inverse.

f^{-1}	
x	**y**
0	0
1	1
4	2
9	3

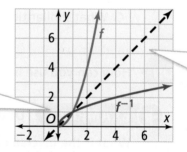

If the domain of the original function were not restricted, then the inverse would not be a function.

Notice that if the grid were folded along the line of the equation $y = x$, the original function and its inverse would coincide.

The graph of the inverse of a function is a reflection of the graph of the original function across the line representing the equation $y = x$.

 Try It!   2. Graph each function and its inverse.

    a. $f(x) = 3x - 2$ **b.** $f(x) = 2x^2, x \geq 0$

EXAMPLE 3   Find the Inverse of a Function Algebraically

How can you find the inverse function of $f(x) = 2x + 6$ algebraically?

Write the original function as an equation.

$$y = 2x + 6$$
$$x = 2y + 6$$

Switch x and y to switch domain and range. Then solve for y.

$$x - 6 = 2y$$
$$\tfrac{1}{2}x - 3 = y$$

The inverse function of $f(x) = 2x + 6$ is $f^{-1}(x) = \tfrac{1}{2}x - 3$.

 Try It!   3. Find the inverse of each function.

    a. $f(x) = 3x^2, x \geq 0$ **b.** $f(x) = x - 7$

APPLICATION

EXAMPLE 4   **Interpret Inverse Functions**

Keenan plans to fly 1,097 miles from Miami to New York City to help assemble a dinosaur exhibit at a museum. He wants to use the miles he earns from his credit card purchases to pay for his flight. How much will Keenan need to spend in order to earn enough miles for the flight from Miami to New York City?

Turn your purchases into airline miles.

Earn 1 mile for every $10 you spend.

BONUS!
500 miles on your first purchase!

Formulate   Find the function f that represents the balance of Keenan's airline miles.

miles balance = mile per dollar spent • amount spent + bonus miles

$$f(x) = \quad 0.1 \quad • \quad x \quad + \quad 500$$

Since Keenan earns 1 mile for every $10 he spends, he earns 0.1 mile for every $1 that he spends.

Find the inverse of the function.

$$y = 0.1x + 500$$

$$x = 0.1y + 500$$

Reverse the variables and solve for y to find the inverse function.

$$x - 500 = 0.1y$$

$$10(x - 500) = (0.1y)10$$

$$10x - 5{,}000 = y$$

The inverse function is $f^{-1}(x) = 10x - 5{,}000$. The inverse function represents the amount Keenan spends, $f^{-1}(x)$, to earn x miles.

Compute   Substitute 1,097 for x.

$$f^{-1}(1{,}097) = 10(1{,}097) - 5{,}000$$

$$= 10{,}970 - 5{,}000$$

$$= 5{,}970$$

Interpret   Keenan needs to spend $5,970 to earn enough miles for his trip.

☑ **Try It!**   **4.** Suppose the credit card company changes the program so Keenan earns 1 mile for every $8 he spends. How would that change the amount of money Keenan needs to spend to earn the miles for his trip?

CONCEPT SUMMARY Finding the Inverse of a Function

TABLES Switch the *x*-values and *y*-values in the table.

x	y
1	7
2	11
3	15

→

x	y
7	1
11	2
15	3

GRAPH Reflect the graph across the line represented by the equation $y = x$. If needed, restrict the domain of the original function so its inverse will also be a function.

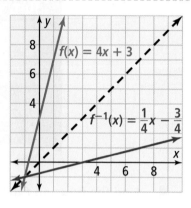

$f(x) = 4x + 3$

$f^{-1}(x) = \frac{1}{4}x - \frac{3}{4}$

ALGEBRA When the function is written as an equation, in terms of *x* and *y*, switch the variables and solve for *y*.

$y = 4x + 3$

$x = 4y + 3$

$x - 3 = 4y$

$\frac{x - 3}{4} = y$

$y = \frac{1}{4}x - \frac{3}{4}$

Do You UNDERSTAND?

1. **ESSENTIAL QUESTION** How can you use inverse functions to help solve problems?

2. **Error Analysis** A student claims that the graph of the inverse of a function is a reflection across the *x*-axis of the graph of the original function. Explain the error the student made.

3. **Vocabulary** Does every function have an inverse function? Explain.

4. **Reason** If the graph of a function crosses the *x*-axis twice, does the function have an inverse function? Explain.

Do You KNOW HOW?

Copy and complete each table of values for the function. Then make a table of values for the inverse of the function.

5. $y = -2x + 3$

x	y
0	■
1	■
2	■
3	■

6. $y = 8x$

x	y
0	■
1	■
2	■
3	■

Write the inverse of each function.

7. $f(x) = 2x + 11$

8. $f(x) = \sqrt{x}$

PRACTICE & PROBLEM SOLVING

Scan for
Multimedia

Practice   Tutorial

Additional Exercises Available Online

UNDERSTAND

9. Mathematical Connections How is the inverse of a function similar to inverse operations? How is it different? Explain.

10. Error Analysis Describe and correct the error a student made finding the inverse of $f(x) = -x + 4$.

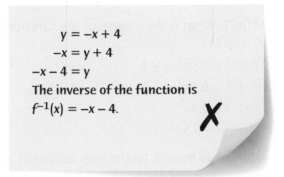

$$y = -x + 4$$
$$-x = y + 4$$
$$-x - 4 = y$$
The inverse of the function is
$$f^{-1}(x) = -x - 4.$$ ✗

11. Reason Does each function have an inverse function? If so, write the inverse function. If not, explain how you could restrict the domain so that function f does have an inverse function.

  a. $f(x) = 5x$

  b. $f(x) = 5x^2$

  c. $f(x) = |5x|$

12. Construct Arguments Can a relation that is not a function have a function as its inverse? Give an example to support your answer.

13. Use Structure What is the inverse of the function graphed below? Describe how you found your answer.

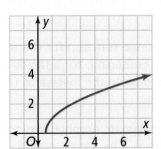

14. Higher Order Thinking What is the inverse of $f(x) = -x$? Use a graph of the function to support your answer.

PRACTICE

For each table, create a table of values for the inverse function. SEE EXAMPLE 1

15.

x	y
0	11
1	15
2	19
3	23

16.

x	y
0	3
1	4
2	7
3	12

Graph each function and its inverse. SEE EXAMPLE 2

17. $f(x) = -\frac{1}{3}x + 2$ **18.** $f(x) = \frac{3}{4}x - 1$

19. $f(x) = 0.25x^2, x \geq 0$ **20.** $f(x) = \sqrt{3x}$

Tell whether the functions f and g are inverses or not. SEE EXAMPLE 2

21.

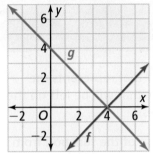

22.

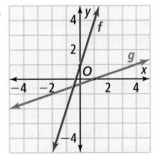

Find the inverse of each function. SEE EXAMPLE 3

23. $f(x) = -5x - 11$ **24.** $f(x) = 0.7x + 4$

25. $f(x) = 7x + 12$ **26.** $f(x) = 9x^2, x \geq 0$

27. $f(x) = x^2 + 7, x \geq 0$ **28.** $f(x) = \sqrt{4x + 1}$

29. Camilla has $100 in her savings account. She will put 25% of her salary in her account every time she gets paid at work. Camilla wants to save $1,250 to go on vacation this summer. Write and evaluate the inverse function to find the amount of money Camilla must earn at work to reach her savings goal. SEE EXAMPLE 4

APPLY

30. Reason The perimeter P of a square is given by the equation $P = 4s$, where s is a side length of the square. What is the inverse of $P = 4s$? What type of question could you answer by using the inverse function?

31. Model With Mathematics A raffle has a $50 gift card to a miniature golf course as a prize.

Only $4 per game!

a. Write a function f that represents the amount of money that will be left on the gift card after x games.

b. What is the inverse of the function from part (a)?

c. Graph the functions from parts (a) and (b) on the same grid. Label each graph.

d. Which function would you use to find how many games were played when $10 was left on the card? Explain.

32. Make Sense and Persevere The area A of a circle in terms of the circle's radius r is $A = \pi r^2$.

a. Explain the restrictions on the domain of the function $A = \pi r^2$ and the inverse function in this context.

b. Write the inverse function of $A = \pi r^2$.

c. Use the inverse function you wrote in part (b) to find the radius of a circle that has an area of 50.25 in.^{2}. Round your answer to the nearest inch.

ASSESSMENT PRACTICE

33. Match each function with its inverse.

I. $f(x) = 4x - 8$ 　　A. $f(x)^{-1} = \frac{1}{2}\sqrt{x}$

II. $f(x) = 0.25x - 2$ 　B. $f(x)^{-1} = 0.25x + 2$

III. $f(x) = 4x^2, x \geq 0$ 　C. $f(x)^{-1} = 4x + 8$

IV. $f(x) = 2x^2, x \geq 0$ 　D. $f(x)^{-1} = \sqrt{\frac{1}{2}x}$

34. SAT/ACT What is the inverse of the function $f(x) = -\sqrt{2x}$?

Ⓐ $f(x)^{-1} = 0.5x^2, x \geq 0$

Ⓑ $f(x)^{-1} = 0.5x^2, x \leq 0$

Ⓒ $f(x)^{-1} = 0.5x^2$

Ⓓ $f(x)^{-1} = -0.5x^2$

35. Performance Task A health club advertises a new family membership plan, as shown in the advertisement.

Family Plan:	Additional Members:
HEALTH CLUB	
$90 to join	$25 to join
$75 per month for the first member	$40 per month for each additional member

Part A Write two functions, one that gives the total cost of a membership for the first member and one that gives the total cost for each additional member. Write each function, y, in terms of the number of months, x, a member belongs to the health club.

Part B Write a combined function for the total cost on the family membership for a family of three members. Then write the inverse of the function.

Part C Find the approximate number of months that a family of three will be members of the health club if they spend a total of $1,380.

Topic Review

1. What are some operations on functions that you can use to create models and solve problems?

Vocabulary Review

Choose the correct term to complete each sentence.

2. The _____ intersects the vertex, and divides the graph into two congruent halves that are images of each other under a reflection.

3. The _____ rounds numbers up to the nearest integer.

4. The _____ has an algebraic expression with absolute value symbols.

5. A(n) _____ has different rules for different intervals of its domain.

- absolute value function
- axis of symmetry
- ceiling function
- floor function
- piecewise-defined function
- step function
- vertex

Concepts & Skills Review

| LESSON 6-1 | The Absolute Value Function |

Quick Review

The graph of the absolute value function, $f(x) = |x|$ has a **vertex** at $(0, 0)$ and an **axis of symmetry** $x = 0$.

Example

How do the domain and range of $g(x) = 0.5|x|$ compare with the domain and range of $f(x) = |x|$?

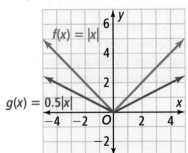

The domain of f and the domain of g are all real numbers. The range of both functions is $y \geq 0$.

Practice & Problem Solving

Tell whether each point is on the graph of $f(x) = |x|$. If it is, give the coordinates of another point with the same y-coordinate.

6. $(8, 8)$ 7. $(-5, 5)$ 8. $(-3.5, -3.5)$

Graph each function. What is the domain and range of each function?

9. $f(x) = -2.5|x|$ 10. $g(x) = \frac{1}{3}|x|$

For each function, find the vertex and tell whether it represents a maximum or minimum value of the function.

11. $g(x) = -6.3|x|$ 12. $g(x) = 7|x|$

13. **Look for Relationships** Find the domain, range, and vertex of the graphed function.

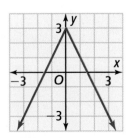

Quick Review

A **piecewise-defined function** has different rules for different intervals of the domain.

You can express functions of the form $g(x) = a|x|$ as piecewise-defined functions using a pair of linear rules with boundaries on the domain.

Example

What is the graph of $f(x) = \begin{cases} -x - 5, & x < 0 \\ \frac{1}{4}x + 2, & x \geq 0 \end{cases}$ **?**

Over what interval of the domain is the function increasing? Decreasing?

Graph each rule of the function for the given interval of the domain.

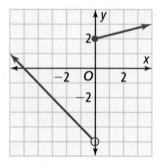

The function is decreasing when $x < 0$.
The function is increasing when $x \geq 0$.

Practice & Problem Solving

Express each function as a piecewise-defined function.

14. $f(x) = 4|x|$ **15.** $f(x) = -2|x|$

Graph each piecewise-defined function. Identify the intervals over which the function is increasing, decreasing, or constant.

16. $f(x) = \begin{cases} x + 1, & x < -1 \\ \frac{1}{2}x - 2, & -1 \leq x \end{cases}$

17. $f(x) = \begin{cases} -x + 4, & -2 < x \leq 3 \\ x - 5, & 3 < x \end{cases}$

18. Error Analysis Describe and correct the error a student made in expressing the function $f(x) = -5|x|$ as a piecewise-defined function.

$$f(x) = -5|x|, \; f(x) = \begin{cases} -5x, \; x < 0 \\ 5x, \; x > 0 \end{cases}$$

19. Write a piecewise-defined function that represents the graph.

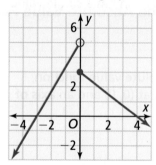

20. Model With Mathematics A jeweler sells rings for $35 each plus a flat fee of $5 for shipping for orders up to 10 rings. If customers order more than 10 rings, the cost is $30 per ring and shipping is free. Write a piecewise function to represent the situation.

Quick Review

Step functions are a type of piecewise-defined function that consists of constant pieces. The constant pieces of the function result in a graph that looks like the steps of a staircase.

The floor and ceiling functions are specific types of step functions. The **ceiling function** rounds numbers up to the nearest integer. The **floor function** rounds numbers down to the nearest integer.

Example

Graph the function f. What is the domain and range of the function?

x	f(x)
$0 < x \le 3$	4
$3 < x \le 6$	6
$6 < x \le 9$	8
$9 < x \le 12$	10

Each section of the domain has a single value assigned to it.

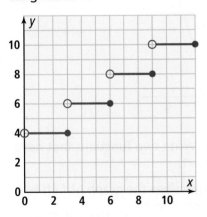

The domain of f is $0 < x \le 12$. The range is the set values {4, 6, 8, 10}.

Practice & Problem Solving

Evaluate the ceiling function for the given value.

21. $f(x) = \lceil x \rceil$; $x = 7.03$

22. $f(x) = \text{ceiling}(x)$; $x = 2.6$

Evaluate the floor function for the given value.

23. $f(x) = \lfloor x \rfloor$; $x = 6.1$

24. $f(x) = \text{floor}(x)$; $x = 0.08$

For each table, graph the step function and write a rule for f using a ceiling or floor function.

25.

x	f(x)
$1 < x \le 2$	7
$2 < x \le 3$	8
$3 < x \le 4$	9
$4 < x \le 5$	10
$5 < x \le 6$	11

26.

x	f(x)
$0 < x \le 2$	−2
$2 < x \le 4$	−3
$4 < x \le 6$	−4
$6 < x \le 8$	−5
$8 < x \le 10$	−6

Sketch the graph of each function over the domain $0 < x \le 10$.

27. The function g returns the greatest integer g(x) less than or equal to 2x.

28. The function f returns the least integer f(x) greater than x − 3.

29. Make Sense and Persevere Egg cartons hold a dozen eggs in each container. Write a step function that represents the number of egg cartons needed as a function of the number of eggs over the domain $0 < x \le 72$. Is the function a floor or a ceiling function? Explain.

Quick Review

The graph of $g(x) = a|x - h| + k$ is a transformation of the graph of $f(x) = |x|$ when $a \neq 1$, $h \neq 0$, or $k \neq 0$. The vertex of the graph is located at (h, k). The value of h indicates that the graph of g is a horizontal translation of h units of the graph of f. The value of k indicates that the graph of g is a vertical translation of k units of the graph of f.

When $|a| > 1$, the graph of g is a vertical stretch of the graph of f. When $0 \leq |a| \leq 1$, the graph is a vertical compression of the graph of f.

Example

For the function $g(x) = 2|x + 3| - 4$, find the vertex and graph the function. Describe the graph of g as a transformation of the graph of $f(x) = |x|$.

The vertex is located at (h, k), so the vertex of this graph is $(-3, -4)$.

Graph the function.

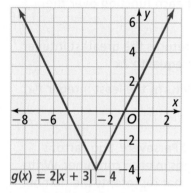

The graph of g is a translation of the graph of f horizontally, 3 units to the left, and vertically 4 units down. It is also a vertical stretch of the graph of f by a factor of 2.

Practice & Problem Solving

Find the vertex and graph each function.

30. $g(x) = |x| + 4$ **31.** $g(x) = |x - 2|$

32. $g(x) = |x + 1| - 2$ **33.** $g(x) = |x - 3| + 1$

Compare each function with $f(x) = |x|$. Describe the graph of g as transformation of the graph of f.

34. $g(x) = 2|x + 6| - 1$ **35.** $g(x) = -|x - 2| - 1$

36. $g(x) = -0.5|x| + 4$ **37.** $g(x) = \frac{3}{2}|x - 1| + 8$

Write the function that includes absolute value expressions for each graph.

38.

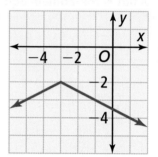

39.

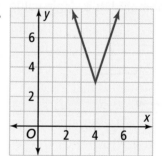

40. Use Structure Write two functions that have a vertex of $(2, -1)$.

What function g describes the graph of f after the given transformations?

41. $f(x) = |x| + 3$; translated 1 unit up and 5 units right

42. $f(x) = |x - 1| + 5$; translated 2 units down and 4 units left

43. Make Sense and Persevere A traffic cone is 18 in. tall and 12 in. wide. You want to sketch an image of the traffic cone on a coordinate grid with one edge at $(0, 0)$. What function that includes an absolute value expression could represent the traffic cone? What would be the domain of the function? Explain.

LESSON 6-5 — Analyzing Functions Graphically

Quick Review

If you know the algebraic structure of a function, you can often use its graph to determine key features of the function.

Example

For the function $f(x) = \sqrt{x - 5}$, identify the domain and range, maximum and minimum values, and axis of symmetry, and describe the end behavior.

First graph the function.

The domain is $x \geq 5$, and the range is $y \geq 0$.

The minimum is 0 when $x = 5$.

There is no axis of symmetry.

As $x \to \infty$, $f(x) \to \infty$, and as $x \to 5$, $f(x) \to 0$.

Practice & Problem Solving

Sketch the graph of each function and identify its domain and range.

44. $f(x) = x^2 + 6$

45. $g(x) = \sqrt{x + 5}$

Describe the end behavior of each function.

46. $j(x) = -5^x$

47. $d(x) = |x - 4| - 2$

48. Look for Relationships Without sketching the graph, how can you identify the end behavior of $f(x) = x^2 - 5x + 8$?

49. Model With Mathematics The height of a ball thrown from the top of a building is modeled by $h(t) = -16t^2 + 48t + 80$, where $h(t)$ is the height of the ball in feet after t seconds. The height of another ball hit by a bat on a small hill is modeled by $g(t) = -16t^2 + 98t + 20$. Give the maximum values and the axes of symmetry for both functions.

LESSON 6-6 — Translations of Functions

Quick Review

The graph of $g(x) = f(x) + k$ is the graph of f shifted up $|k|$ units when $k > 0$ or translated down $|k|$ units when $k < 0$.

The graph of $g(x) = f(x - h)$ is the graph of f shifted right $|h|$ units when $h > 0$ or translated left $|h|$ units when $h < 0$.

Example

Given $f(x) = 3^x$, how does the graph of g compare with the graph of f if $g(x) = f(x) + 4$?

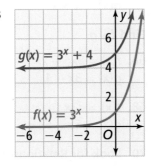

Graph both equations.

The graph of g translates the graph of f 4 units up.

Practice & Problem Solving

Sketch the graph of each function.

50. $g(x) = |x - 3|$

51. $g(x) = x^2 + 5$

52. The graph shown is a translation of the function $f(x) = x^2$. Write the function for the graph.

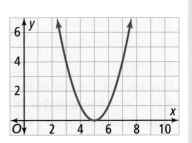

53. Reason Given $f(x) = -3$ and $g(x) = f(x - h) + k$, describe how the constants h and k affect the graph of g.

Compressions and Stretches of Functions

Quick Review

The graph of $g(x) = kf(x)$ is the graph of f stretched away from the x-axis when $|k| > 1$ and compressed toward the x-axis when $0 < |k| < 1$.

The graph of $g(x) = f(kx)$ is the graph of f stretched away from the y-axis when $0 < |k| < 1$ and compressed toward the y-axis when $|k| > 1$.

Example

Given $f(x) = \sqrt[3]{x+2}$, how does the graph of g compare with the graph of f if $g(x) = 2f(x)$?

Graph both functions.

The graph of g stretches the graph of f vertically away from the x-axis by a factor of 2.

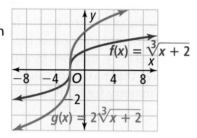

Practice & Problem Solving

Write a function with a graph that is the reflection of the graph of f across the x-axis.

54. $f(x) = x^2 + 5$ **55.** $f(x) = |2x - 1|$

For each pair, tell whether the graph of g is a vertical or horizontal compression or stretch of the graph of f.

56. $f(x) = |2x - 5|$ **57.** $f(x) = x^2 + 9$
$g(x) = 2|2x - 5|$ $g(x) = 0.25x^2 + 9$

58. $f(x) = \sqrt{x - 4}$ **59.** $f(x) = 2x - 9$
$g(x) = \sqrt{4x - 4}$ $g(x) = 6x - 27$

60. Look for Relationships Graph $f(x) = |x - 3|$ and $g(x) = 3|x - 3|$. Is the graph of g a vertical stretch or a horizontal compression of the graph of f? Explain.

61. Make Sense and Persevere A T-shirt designer uses the function $f(x) = x^2 - 3$ to sew parabolas on his clothing. What are two ways the function could be altered to make the parabolas wider? Explain.

Operations With Functions

Quick Review

You can add, subtract, and multiply functions to form new functions.

Example

What is the product of the two functions $f(x) = 3x - 5$ and $g(x) = 4x - 1$? Determine the domain and range of $f \cdot g$.

Use the Distributive Property when multiplying polynomials.

$f(x) \cdot g(x) = (3x - 5) \cdot (4x - 1)$

$\quad = 3x(4x) + 3x(-1) + (-5)(4x) + (-5)(-1)$

$\quad = 12x^2 - 3x - 20x + 5$

$(f \cdot g)(x) = 12x^2 - 23x + 5$

The domain and range of the original functions are all real numbers. The domain of $f \cdot g$ is all real numbers. The range of $f \cdot g$ is all real numbers greater than or equal to approximately -6.02.

Practice & Problem Solving

Find $f + g$.

62. $f(x) = 3x^2 + 5x$ **63.** $f(x) = 3x^2 - 5x + 1$
$g(x) = 2x - 8$ $g(x) = x^2 - 8x - 3$

64. $f(x) = \sqrt{2x}$ **65.** $f(x) = 4^x - 1$
$g(x) = 4 - x$ $g(x) = 2x^2 + 5x - 3$

Find $f \cdot g$.

66. $f(x) = 5x^2 + 2x$ **67.** $f(x) = x^2 + 2x - 5$
$g(x) = 3x - 1$ $g(x) = x - 4$

68. $f(x) = \sqrt{3x}$ **69.** $f(x) = 2^x$
$g(x) = 6x - 5$ $g(x) = 4x^2 - 3x - 8$

70. Look for Relationships Write two functions that, when combined by multiplying, have a different range than at least one of the functions.

Quick Review

The **inverse of a function** reverses the inputs and outputs of a function. A function f has an inverse function f^{-1} only if the original function f is one-to-one.

To graph the inverse of a function, switch the x- and y-values in the table, or reflect the graph across the line $y = x$. To create an inverse equation, switch the variables and solve for y.

Example

What is the inverse function of $f(x) = 3x - 8$?

Write the original function as an equation

$$y = 3x - 8$$

$$x = 3y - 8 \quad \cdots\cdots \text{Switch } x \text{ and } y \text{ and solve for } y.$$

$$x + 8 = 3y - 8 + 8 \quad \cdots\cdots \text{Add 8 to both sides.}$$

$$x + 8 = 3y \quad \cdots\cdots \text{Simplify.}$$

$$\frac{x + 8}{3} = \frac{3y}{3} \quad \cdots\cdots \text{Divide both sides by 3.}$$

$$\frac{x + 8}{3} = y \quad \cdots\cdots \text{Simplify.}$$

The inverse function of $f(x) = 3x - 8$ is $f^{-1}(x) = \frac{x+8}{3}$.

Practice & Problem Solving

For each table, create a table of values for the inverse function.

71.

x	y
0	3
1	5
2	8
3	11

72.

x	y
0	2
1	4
2	8
3	16

Find the inverse of each function.

73. $f(x) = 4x - 7$

74. $f(x) = 3x^2 - 8,\ x \geq 0$

75. $f(x) = \sqrt{2x - 3}$

76. $f(x) = 5 + 2x$

77. Error Analysis Describe and correct the error a student made finding the inverse of $f(x) = 2x^2 + 3$.

$$y = 2x^2 + 3$$
$$x = 2y^2 + 3$$
$$x + 3 = 2y^2$$
$$\frac{x + 3}{2} = y^2$$
$$\sqrt{\frac{x + 3}{2}} = y$$

The inverse of the function

is $f^{-1}(x) = \sqrt{\frac{x + 3}{2}}$.

78. Reason The surface area A of a cube is given by the equation $A = 6s^2$, where s is the side length of the cube. What is the inverse of $A = 6s^2$? What type of question could you answer by using the inverse function?

? TOPIC ESSENTIAL QUESTION

How are the sides, segments, and angles of triangles related?

Topic Overview

enVision® STEM Project
Find the Center of Mass

Topic Vocabulary

- altitude
- centroid
- circumcenter
- circumscribed
- concurrent
- equidistant
- incenter
- inscribed
- median
- orthocenter
- paragraph proof
- point of concurrency
- proof
- theorem
- two-column proof

Digital Experience

INTERACTIVE STUDENT EDITION
Access online or offline.

ACTIVITIES Complete *Explore & Reason,*
Model & Discuss, and *Critique & Explain*
activities. Interact with Examples and Try Its.

ANIMATION View and interact with
real-world applications.

PRACTICE Practice what
you've learned.

 Go online | **PearsonRealize.com**

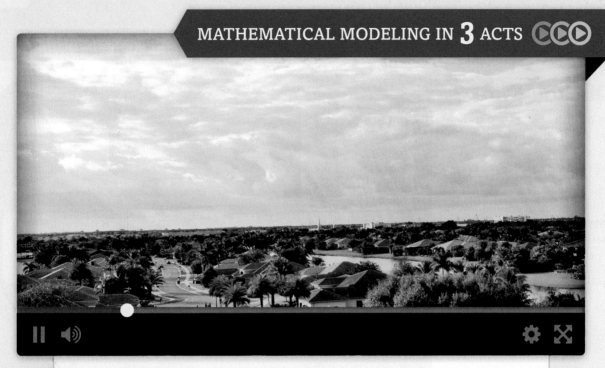

▶ Making it Fair

In rural areas, county planners often work with local officials from a number of small towns to establish a regional medical center to serve all of the nearby communities.

County planners might also establish regional medical evacuation centers to transport patients with serious trauma to larger medical centers. The locations of these regional centers are carefully planned. Think about this during the Mathematical Modeling in 3 Acts lesson.

VIDEOS Watch clips to support *Mathematical Modeling in 3 Acts Lessons* and **enVision®** *STEM Projects.*

CONCEPT SUMMARY Review key lesson content through multiple representations.

ASSESSMENT Show what you've learned.

GLOSSARY Read and listen to English and Spanish definitions.

TUTORIALS Get help from *Virtual Nerd*, right when you need it.

MATH TOOLS Explore math with digital tools and manipulatives.

Video

Did You Know?

An object's **center of mass** is the single point at which its mass is evenly dispersed and the object is in balance.

When an object is moving within Earth's gravitational field, the object's center of mass is sometimes called its *center of gravity*.

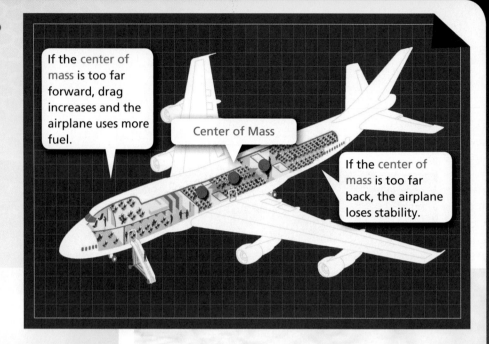

If the center of mass is too far forward, drag increases and the airplane uses more fuel.

Center of Mass

If the center of mass is too far back, the airplane loses stability.

Athletes adjust their **center of mass** to maximize performance.

▶ Your Task: Find the Center of Mass

In this project, you and your classmates will find the center of mass for a triangular object using mathematics. You will also find the center of mass for an irregular object through experimentation.

 Go Online | PearsonRealize.com

7-1

Writing Proofs

PearsonRealize.com

I CAN... use deductive reasoning to prove theorems.

VOCABULARY
- paragraph proof
- proof
- theorem
- two-column proof

CRITIQUE & EXPLAIN

William solved an equation for *x* and wrote justifications for each step of his solution.

$6(14 + x) = 108$	Given
$84 + 6x = 108$	Distributive Property
$6x = 108 - 84$	Subtraction Property of Equality
$6x = 24$	Simplify
$x = 4$	Multiplication Property of Equality

A. Make Sense and Persevere Are William's justifications valid at each step? If not, what might you change? Explain.

B. Can you justify another series of steps that result in the same solution for *x*?

? ESSENTIAL QUESTION

How is deductive reasoning used to prove a theorem?

THEOREM 7-1 Vertical Angles Theorem

Vertical angles are congruent.

If...

PROOF: SEE EXAMPLE 1.

Then... $\angle 1 \cong \angle 2$ and $\angle 3 \cong \angle 4$

CONCEPTUAL UNDERSTANDING

EXAMPLE 1   Write a Two-Column Proof

A **theorem** is a conjecture that is proven. Prove the Vertical Angles Theorem.

Given: $\angle 1$ and $\angle 2$ are vertical angles

Prove: $\angle 1 \cong \angle 2$

A **proof** is a convincing argument that uses deductive reasoning. A **two-column proof**, in which the statements and reasons are aligned in columns, is one way to organize and present a proof.

Statements	Reasons
1) $\angle 1$ and $\angle 2$ are vertical angles	1) Given
2) $m\angle 1 + m\angle 3 = 180$ and $m\angle 2 + m\angle 3 = 180$	2) Supplementary Angles
3) $m\angle 1 + m\angle 3 = m\angle 2 + m\angle 3$	3) Transitive Property of Equality
4) $m\angle 1 = m\angle 2$	4) Subtraction Property of Equality
5) $\angle 1 \cong \angle 2$	5) Definition of congruent angles

COMMON ERROR
You may think that the proof is complete by stating that the measures of the angles are equal. You must explicitly state that the angles are congruent in order to complete the proof.

EXAMPLE 1 CONTINUED

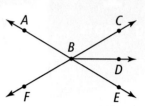

✓ Try It! 1. Write a two-column proof.

Given: $\overrightarrow{BD}$ bisects $\angle CBE$.

Prove: $\angle ABD \cong \angle FBD$

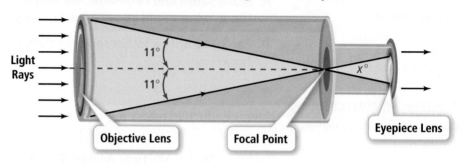

APPLICATION ● **EXAMPLE 2** **Apply the Vertical Angles Theorem**

The diagram shows how glass lenses change the direction of light rays passing through a telescope. What is the value of x, the angle formed by the crossed outermost light rays through the focal point?

Formulate ◀ Draw and label a diagram to represent the telescope.

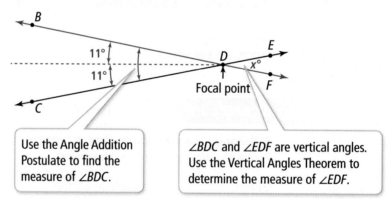

Use the Angle Addition Postulate to find the measure of $\angle BDC$.

$\angle BDC$ and $\angle EDF$ are vertical angles. Use the Vertical Angles Theorem to determine the measure of $\angle EDF$.

Compute ◀ $m\angle BDC = 11 + 11 = 22$ $m\angle EDF = m\angle BDC = 22$

Interpret ◀ The outermost light rays form a 22° angle as they leave the focal point, so the value of x is 22.

✓ Try It! 2. Find the value of x and the measure of each labeled angle.

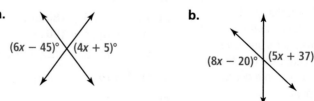

a. $(6x - 45)°$ $(4x + 5)°$

b. $(8x - 20)°$ $(5x + 37)°$

THEOREM 7-2 Congruent Supplements Theorem

If two angles are supplementary to congruent angles (or to the same angle), then they are congruent.

If... $m\angle 1 + m\angle 2 = 180$ and
$m\angle 3 + m\angle 2 = 180$

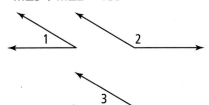

PROOF: SEE EXAMPLE 3.

Then... $\angle 1 \cong \angle 3$

THEOREM 7-3 Congruent Complements Theorem

If two angles are complementary to congruent angles (or to the same angle), then they are congruent.

If... $m\angle 1 + m\angle 2 = 90$ and
$m\angle 3 + m\angle 2 = 90$

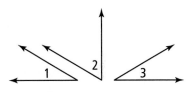

PROOF: SEE EXAMPLE 3 TRY IT.

Then... $\angle 1 \cong \angle 3$

PROOF

EXAMPLE 3 ▸ Write a Paragraph Proof

Write a paragraph proof of the Congruent Supplements Theorem.

Given: $\angle 1$ and $\angle 2$ are supplementary.
$\angle 2$ and $\angle 3$ are supplementary.

Prove: $\angle 1 \cong \angle 3$

STUDY TIP
It may be helpful to confirm that a paragraph proof is complete by underlining each statement and then circling the corresponding reason.

Another way to write a proof is a paragraph proof. In a **paragraph proof**, the statements and reasons are connected in sentences.

Proof: By the definition of supplementary angles, $m\angle 1 + m\angle 2 = 180$ and $m\angle 2 + m\angle 3 = 180$. Since both sums equal 180, $m\angle 1 + m\angle 2 = m\angle 2 + m\angle 3$. Subtract $m\angle 2$ from each side of this equation to get $m\angle 1 = m\angle 3$. By the definition of congruent angles, $\angle 1 \cong \angle 3$.

 Try It! **3.** Write a paragraph proof of the Congruent Complements Theorem.

Given: $\angle 1$ and $\angle 2$ are complementary.
$\angle 2$ and $\angle 3$ are complementary.

Prove: $\angle 1 \cong \angle 3$

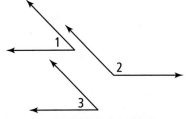

THEOREM 7-4

All right angles are congruent.

PROOF: SEE EXERCISE 9.

If...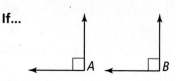

Then... $\angle A \cong \angle B$

THEOREM 7-5

If two angles are congruent and supplementary, then each is a right angle.

PROOF: SEE EXERCISE 11.

If... $\angle 1 \cong \angle 2$ and $m\angle 1 + m\angle 2 = 180$

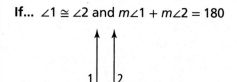

Then... $\angle 1$ and $\angle 2$ are right angles

THEOREM 7-6 Linear Pairs Theorem

The sum of the measures of a linear pair is 180.

PROOF: SEE EXERCISE 12.

If... $\angle 1$ and $\angle 2$ form a linear pair.

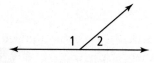

Then... $m\angle 1 + m\angle 2 = 180$

PROOF → ✋ **EXAMPLE 4** Write a Proof Using a Theorem

Write a two-column proof.

Given: $m\angle 1 = m\angle 2$, $m\angle 1 = 105$

Prove: $m\angle 3 = 75$

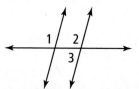

Statements	Reasons
1) $m\angle 1 = m\angle 2$	**1)** Given
2) $m\angle 1 = 105$	**2)** Given
3) $m\angle 2 = 105$	**3)** Transitive Property of Equality
4) $\angle 2$ and $\angle 3$ are a linear pair	**4)** Definition of a linear pair
5) $m\angle 2 + m\angle 3 = 180$	**5)** Linear Pairs Theorem
6) $105 + m\angle 3 = 180$	**6)** Substitution Property of Equality
7) $m\angle 3 = 75$	**7)** Subtraction Property of Equality

CONSTRUCT ARGUMENTS
Consider the logical flow for writing a proof. How can you be sure that each step in a proof follows logically from the preceding step or steps?

☑ **Try It!**   **4.** Write a two-column proof.

Given: $m\angle 4 = 35$, $m\angle 1 = m\angle 2 + m\angle 4$

Prove: $m\angle 3 = 70$

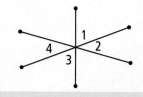 **Go Online** | PearsonRealize.com

CONCEPT SUMMARY Proofs

Proofs use given information and logical steps justified by **definitions, postulates, theorems,** and **properties** to reach a conclusion.

Given: ∠1 and ∠2 and are vertical angles

Prove: ∠1 ≅ ∠2

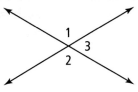

PROOF Two-Column Proof

Statements	Reasons
1) ∠1 and ∠2 are vertical angles	1) Given
2) $m\angle 1 + m\angle 3 = 180$ and $m\angle 2 + m\angle 3 = 180$	2) Supplementary Angles
3) $m\angle 1 + m\angle 3 = m\angle 2 + m\angle 3$	3) Subst. Prop. of Equality
4) $m\angle 1 = m\angle 2$	4) Subtr. Prop. of Equality
5) ∠1 ≅ ∠2	5) Def. ≅ angles

PROOF Paragraph Proof

By Supplementary Angles, $m\angle 1 + m\angle 3 = 180$ and $m\angle 2 + m\angle 3 = 180$. By the Substitution Property of Equality, $m\angle 1 + m\angle 3 = m\angle 2 + m\angle 3$. Subtracting $m\angle 3$ from each side of the equation gives $m\angle 1 = m\angle 2$. Then by the definition of congruent angles, ∠1 ≅ ∠2.

Do You UNDERSTAND?

1. **ESSENTIAL QUESTION** How is deductive reasoning used to prove a theorem?

2. **Error Analysis** Jayden states that based on the Congruent Supplements Theorem, if $m\angle 1 + m\angle 2 = 90$ and if $m\angle 1 + m\angle 3 = 90$, then ∠2 ≅ ∠3. What is the error in Jayden's reasoning?

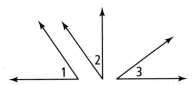

3. **Vocabulary** How is a theorem different from a postulate? How is a theorem different from a conjecture?

4. **Reason** If ∠2 and ∠3 are complementary, how could you use the Vertical Angles Theorem to find $m\angle 1$?

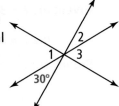

Do You KNOW HOW?

Use the figures to answer Exercises 5–7.

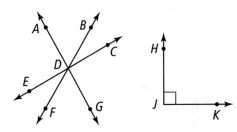

5. What statement could you write in a proof for $m\angle ADC$ using the Angle Addition Postulate as a reason?

6. Could you use the Vertical Angles Theorem as a reason in a proof to state $m\angle ADC = m\angle EDG$ or to state ∠ADC ≅ ∠EDG? Explain.

7. Given $m\angle ADC = 90$, what reason could you give in a proof to state ∠ADC ≅ ∠HJK?

8. The Leaning Tower of Pisa leans at an angle of about 4° from the vertical, as shown. What equation for the measure of x, the angle it makes from the horizontal, could you use in a proof?

UNDERSTAND

9. **Construct Arguments** Fill in the missing reasons for the proof of Theorem 7-4.

Given: ∠F and ∠G are right angles.

Prove: ∠F ≅ ∠G

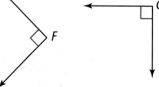

Statements	Reasons
1) ∠F and ∠G are right angles	1) Given
2) $m∠F = 90$ and $m∠G = 90$	2)
3) $m∠F = m∠G$	3)
4) ∠F ≅ ∠G	4)

10. **Error Analysis** A student uses the Vertical Angles Theorem and the definition of complementary angles to conclude $m∠PTR = 50$ in the figure. What mistake did the student make?

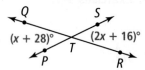

11. **Construct Arguments** Write a paragraph proof of Theorem 7-5. Given that ∠N and ∠M are congruent and supplementary, prove that ∠N and ∠M are right angles.

12. **Construct Arguments** Write a two-column proof of Theorem 7-6. Given that ∠ABC and ∠CBD are a linear pair, prove that ∠ABC and ∠CBD are supplementary.

13. **Higher Order Thinking** Explain how the Congruent Complements Theorem applies to the figure shown.

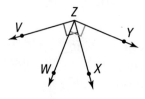

PRACTICE

Find the value of each variable and the measure of each labeled angle. SEE EXAMPLES 1 AND 2

14.
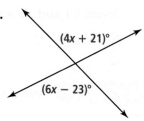
$(2x)°$ $(3x - 42)°$

15.
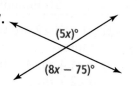
$(4x + 21)°$
$(6x - 23)°$

16.
$(3x - 47)°$ $(2x + 8)°$

17.
$(5x)°$
$(8x - 75)°$

18. Write a paragraph proof. SEE EXAMPLE 3

Given: $m∠ABC = 114$; $m∠DHE = 25$; $m∠EHF = 41$; ∠ABC and ∠GHF are supplementary.

Prove: $m∠DHF ≅ m∠GHF$

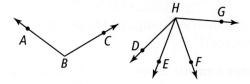

Write a two-column proof for each statement. SEE EXAMPLE 4

19. Given: ∠1 and ∠2 are complementary.

$m∠1 = 23$

Prove: $m∠3 = 113$

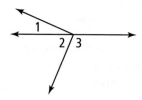

20. Given: $m∠2 = 30$

$m∠1 = 2m∠2$

Prove: $m∠3 + m∠4 = 90$

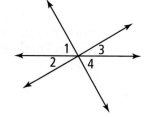

APPLY

21. Mathematical Connections The graph shows percentages of sales made by various divisions of a company in one year. What are the angles formed by the segments for each division? What are the missing percentages? Explain how you were able to determine each percentage.

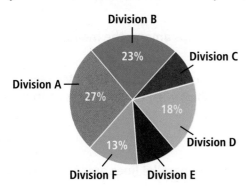

22. Use Structure A type of floor tiling is designed to give the illusion of a three-dimensional figure. Given that $m\angle 1 = 85$ and $m\angle 3 = 45$, what are the measures of the remaining angles?

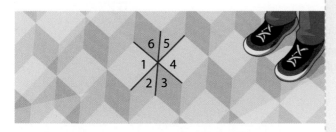

23. Reason Consider the angles formed by the garden gate. Using theorems from this lesson, what can you conclude from each of the following statements? State which theorem you applied to reach your conclusion.

a. $m\angle 1 = 90$ and $m\angle 2 = 90$.

b. $\angle 3$ and $\angle 4$ are vertical angles.

ASSESSMENT PRACTICE

24. Consider the figure shown.

Classify each of the following statements as *always true*, *sometimes true*, or *never true*.

- $m\angle 1 + m\angle 4 = 180$

- $m\angle 1 + m\angle 2 + m\angle 3 = 180$

- $m\angle 2 + m\angle 4 = 180$

- $\angle 2 \cong \angle 3$

- $\angle 2 \cong \angle 4$

- $m\angle 3 = m\angle 4$

25. SAT/ACT Given $\angle ABC$ and $\angle DEF$ are supplementary and $\angle ABC$ and $\angle GHJ$ are supplementary, what can you conclude about the angles?

Ⓐ $m\angle DEF = m\angle GHJ$

Ⓑ $m\angle DEF + m\angle GHJ = 90$

Ⓒ $m\angle DEF + m\angle GHJ = 180$

Ⓓ $m\angle ABC = m\angle DEF$ and $m\angle ABC = m\angle GHJ$

26. Performance Task The figure shows lines that divide a designer window into different parts.

Part A Copy the figure onto a sheet of paper. Label each of the inner angles. Use a protractor to measure any two of the inner angles in the figure. Using your measurements, determine the measurements of the other angles.

Part B Choose two of the inner angles that you did not actually measure. How do you know the angle measures for these two angles? Write a two-column proof to show how you know their measures are correct.

7-2

Parallel Lines

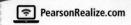
I CAN... use completing the square to solve quadratic equations and to write quadratic equations in vertex form.

VOCABULARY

• completing the square

👆 EXPLORE & REASON

The diagram shows two parallel lines cut by a transversal.

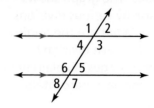

A. Look for Relationships What relationships among the measures of the angles do you see?

B. Suppose a different transversal intersects the parallel lines. Would you expect to find the same relationships with the measures of those angles? Explain.

? ESSENTIAL QUESTION

What angle relationships are created when parallel lines are intersected by a transversal?

👆 EXAMPLE 1   Identify Angle Pairs

Identify the pairs of angles of each angle type made by the snowmobile tracks.

∠4 and ∠8, ∠1 and ∠5, ∠2 and ∠6, and ∠3 and ∠7 are corresponding angles.

∠7 and ∠1, and ∠6 and ∠4 are alternate interior angles.

∠2 and ∠8, and ∠5 and ∠3 are alternate exterior angles.

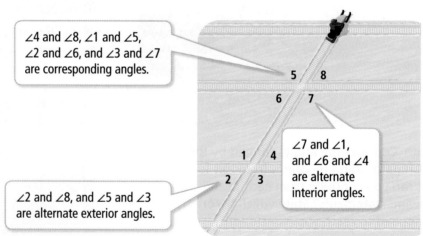

STUDY TIP

Transversals can intersect either parallel or nonparallel lines. The types of angle pairs remain the same.

✓ Try It!

1. Which angle pairs include the named angle?

   a. ∠4   b. ∠7

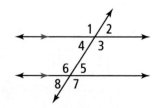

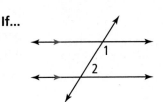

POSTULATE 7-1 Same-Side Interior Angles Postulate

If a transversal intersects two parallel lines, then same-side interior angles are supplementary.

If...

Then... $m\angle 1 + m\angle 2 = 180$

CONCEPTUAL UNDERSTANDING

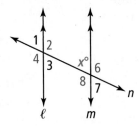

EXAMPLE 2 Explore Angle Relationships

How can you express each of the numbered angles in terms of x?

LOOK FOR RELATIONSHIPS
What patterns do you notice about the angles formed by two parallel lines cut by a transversal?

Angle 7 and the angle with measure x are vertical angles. Both $\angle 6$ and $\angle 8$ each form a linear pair with the angle with measure x and are therefore supplementary to it.

By Postulate 7-1 you know that $\angle 2$ and the angle with measure x are supplementary. From that you can make conclusions about $\angle 1$, $\angle 3$, and $\angle 4$ like you did with $\angle 6$, $\angle 7$, and $\angle 8$.

The angles equal to $x°$ are $\angle 1$, $\angle 3$, and $\angle 7$.
The angles that are supplementary to the angle with measure x have the measure $(180 - x)$. These are $\angle 2$, $\angle 4$, $\angle 6$, and $\angle 8$.

Try It! 2. If $\angle 4 = 118°$, what is the measure of each of the other angles?

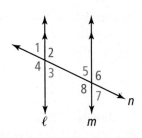

THEOREM 7-7 Alternate Interior Angles Theorem

If a transversal intersects two parallel lines, then alternate interior angles are congruent.

PROOF: SEE EXAMPLE 3.

If...

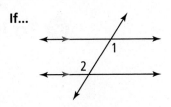

Then... $\angle 1 \cong \angle 2$

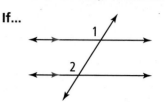

THEOREM 7-8 Corresponding Angles Theorem

If a transversal intersects two parallel lines, then corresponding angles are congruent.

PROOF: SEE EXAMPLE 3 TRY IT.

If...

Then... $\angle 1 \cong \angle 2$

THEOREM 7-9 Alternate Exterior Angles Theorem

If a transversal intersects two parallel lines, then alternate exterior angles are congruent.

PROOF: SEE EXERCISE 10.

If...

Then... $\angle 1 \cong \angle 2$

PROOF  **EXAMPLE 3**   **Prove the Alternate Interior Angles Theorem**

Prove the Alternate Interior Angles Theorem.

Given: $m \parallel n$

Prove: $\angle 1 \cong \angle 2$

Plan: Use the Same-Side Interior Angles Postulate to show $\angle 1$ is supplementary to $\angle 3$. Then show that angles 1 and 2 are congruent because they are both supplementary to the same angle.

Proof:

Statements	Reasons
1) $m \parallel n$	**1)** Given
2) $\angle 1$ and $\angle 3$ are supplementary	**2)** Same-Side Interior $\angle$s Postulate
3) $m\angle 1 + m\angle 3 = 180$	**3)** Def. of supplementary angles
4) $m\angle 2 + m\angle 3 = 180$	**4)** Angle Addition Postulate
5) $m\angle 1 + m\angle 3 = m\angle 2 + m\angle 3$	**5)** Transitive Property of Equality
6) $m\angle 1 = m\angle 2$	**6)** Subtraction Property of Equality
7) $\angle 1 \cong \angle 2$	**7)** Def. of congruence

COMMON ERROR
Remember that for the proof to be complete, the last statement of the proof must match what you are trying to prove.

 Try It!   **3.** Prove the Corresponding Angles Theorem.

           Given: $m \parallel n$

           Prove: $\angle 1 \cong \angle 2$

 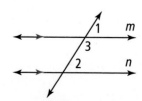

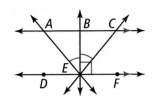

PROOF   **EXAMPLE 4**   **Use Parallel Lines to Prove an Angle Relationship**

Use the diagram to prove the angle relationship.

Given: $\overline{AC} \parallel \overline{DF}$, and $\overline{BE} \perp \overline{DF}$, $\angle AEB \cong \angle CEB$

Prove: $\angle BAE \cong \angle BCE$

Proof:

MAKE SENSE AND PERSEVERE
Look for relationships in the diagram not listed as given information. What angle relationships are shown in the diagram?

Statements	Reasons
1) $\overline{AC} \parallel \overline{DF}$, $\overline{AC} \perp \overline{BE}$	1) Given
2) $\angle BED$, $\angle BEF$ are rt. angles	2) Def. of perpendicular
3) $m\angle BED = m\angle BEF = 90$	3) Def. of rt. angles
4) $m\angle AED + m\angle AEB = 90$, $m\angle CEF + m\angle CEB = 90$	4) Angle Addition Postulate
5) $\angle AEB \cong \angle CEB$	5) Given
6) $\angle AED \cong \angle CEF$	6) Congruent Complements Thm.
7) $\angle BAE \cong \angle AED$, $\angle BCE \cong \angle CEF$	7) Alt. Interior $\angle$s Thm.
8) $\angle BAE \cong \angle BCE$	8) Transitive Prop. of Congruence

✓ Try It!   **4.** Given $\overline{AB} \parallel \overline{CD}$, prove that $m\angle 1 + m\angle 2 + m\angle 3 = 180$.

APPLICATION   **EXAMPLE 5**   **Find Angle Measures**

The white trim shown for the wall of a barn should be constructed so that $\overline{AC} \parallel \overline{EG}$, $\overline{JA} \parallel \overline{HB}$, and $\overline{JC} \parallel \overline{KG}$. What should $m\angle 1$ and $m\angle 3$ be?

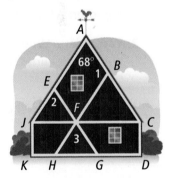

Formulate ◀ Look for relationships among the angles.

Compute ◀ By the Same-Side Interior Angles Postulate, $m\angle 1 + 68 = 180$.

$m\angle 1 = 180 - 68 = 112$

By the Corresponding Angles Theorem, $\angle EAB \cong \angle 2$ and $\angle 2 \cong \angle 3$, so $\angle 3 \cong \angle EAB$ by the Transitive Property of Congruence.

$m\angle 3 = 68$

Interpret ◀ So, $m\angle 1 = 112$ and $m\angle 3 = 68$.

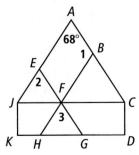

✓ Try It!   **5.** If $m\angle EJF = 56$, find $m\angle FHK$.

CONCEPT SUMMARY Parallel Lines and Angle Pairs

There are four special angle relationships formed when parallel lines are intersected by a transversal.

POSTULATE 7-1 ▸ Same-Side Interior Angles Postulate

If...

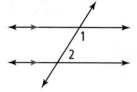

Then... $m\angle 1 + m\angle 2 = 180$

THEOREM 7-7 ▸ Alternate Interior Angles Theorem

If...

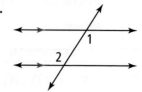

Then... $\angle 1 \cong \angle 2$

THEOREM 7-8 ▸ Corresponding Angles Theorem

If...

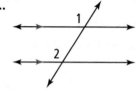

Then... $\angle 1 \cong \angle 2$

THEOREM 7-9 ▸ Alternate Exterior Angles Theorem

If...

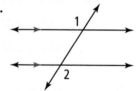

Then... $\angle 1 \cong \angle 2$

☑ Do You UNDERSTAND?

1. **ESSENTIAL QUESTION** What angle relationships are created when parallel lines are intersected by a transversal?

2. **Vocabulary** When a transversal intersects two parallel lines, which angle pairs are congruent?

3. **Error Analysis** What error did Leah make?

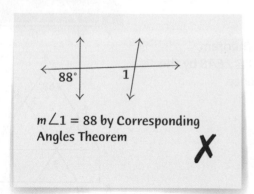

$m\angle 1 = 88$ by Corresponding Angles Theorem ✗

4. **Generalize** For any pair of angles formed by a transversal intersecting parallel lines, what are two possible relationships?

Do You KNOW HOW?

Use the diagram for Exercises 5–8.

Classify each pair of angles. Compare angle measures, and give the postulate or theorem that justifies it.

5. $\angle 2$ and $\angle 6$

6. $\angle 3$ and $\angle 5$

If $m\angle 1 = 71$, find the measure of each angle.

7. $\angle 5$

8. $\angle 7$

9. Elm St. and Spruce St. are parallel. What is $m\angle 1$?

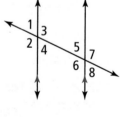

PRACTICE & PROBLEM SOLVING

UNDERSTAND

10. Construct Arguments Write a two-column proof of the Alternate Exterior Angles Theorem.

Given: $m \parallel n$

Prove: $\angle 1 \cong \angle 2$

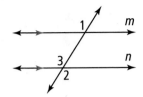

11. Higher Order Thinking Using what you know about angle pairs formed by parallel lines and a transversal, how are $\angle 1$, $\angle 2$, $\angle 3$, and $\angle 4$ related in the trapezoid? Explain.

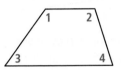

12. Error Analysis What error did Tyler make?

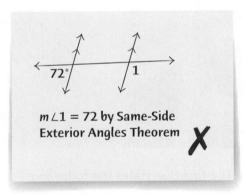

$m \angle 1 = 72$ by Same-Side Exterior Angles Theorem ✗

13. Generalize In the diagram shown, if $x + y = 180$, label the remaining angles as $x°$ or $y°$.

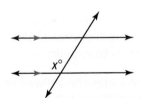

14. Mathematical Connections A transversal intersects two parallel lines. The measures of a pair of alternate interior angles are $5v$ and $2w$. The measures of a pair of same-side exterior angles are $10w$ and $5v$. What are the values of w and v?

PRACTICE

Identify a pair of angles for each type. SEE EXAMPLE 1

15. same-side interior

16. corresponding

17. alternate exterior

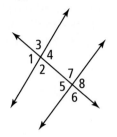

18. Which angles are supplementary to $\angle 1$? Which are congruent to $\angle 1$? SEE EXAMPLE 2

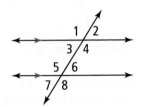

Find each angle measure. SEE EXAMPLE 3

19. $m \angle 1$

20. $m \angle 2$

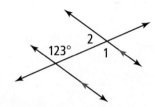

21. Opposite sides of a parallelogram are parallel. Prove that opposite angles of a parallelogram are congruent. SEE EXAMPLE 4

Given: $ABCD$ is a parallelogram

Prove: $\angle A \cong \angle C$, $\angle B \cong \angle D$

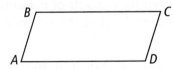

22. Three parallelograms are hinged at each vertex to create an arm that can extend and collapse for an exploratory spaceship robot. What is $m \angle 1$? Explain how you found the answer. SEE EXAMPLE 5

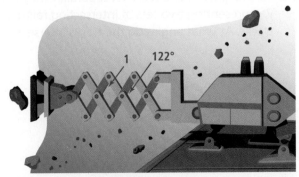

APPLY

23. **Model With Mathematics** A glazier is setting supports in parallel segments to prevent glass breakage during storms. What are the values of x and y? Justify your conclusions.

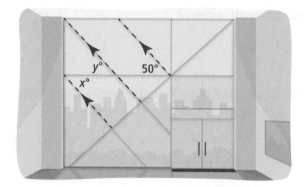

24. **Reason** In the parking lot shown, all of the lines for the parking spaces should be parallel. If $m\angle 3 = 61$, what should $m\angle 1$ and $m\angle 2$ be? Explain.

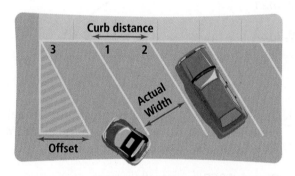

25. **Communicate Precisely** Margaret is in a boat traveling due west. She turned the boat 50° north of due west for a couple of minutes to get around a peninsula. Then she resumed due west again.

a. How many degrees would she turn the wheel to resume a due west course?

b. Name the pair of angles she used. Are the angles congruent or supplementary?

26. Parallel lines m and n intersect parallel lines x and y, representing two sets of intersecting railroad tracks. At what angles do the tracks intersect?

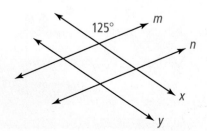

ASSESSMENT PRACTICE

27. Classify each angle as *congruent to ∠1* or *congruent to ∠2*.

∠3   ∠4

∠5   ∠6

∠7   ∠8

28. **SAT/ACT** In the diagram, a ∥ b. What is m∠1?

Ⓐ 28

Ⓑ 62

Ⓒ 90

Ⓓ 118

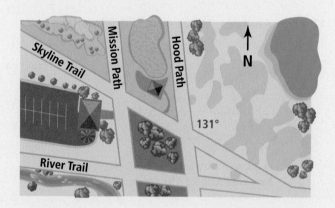

29. **Performance Task** Students on a scavenger hunt are given the map shown and several clues.

Part A The first clue states the following.

Skyline Trail forms a transversal with Hood Path and Mission Path. Go to the corners that form same side exterior angles north of Skyline Trail.

Which two corners does the clue mean? Use intersections and directions to explain.

Part B If the second clue states the following, what trail marker should they go to?

Hood and Mission Paths are parallel, and the northeast corner of Hood Path and Skyline Trail forms a 131° angle. The angle measure formed by the southwest corner of Skyline Trail and Mission Path is equal to the trail marker number on River Trail you must go to.

7-3

Perpendicular and Angle Bisectors

 **PearsonRealize.com**

I CAN... use perpendicular and angle bisectors to solve problems.

VOCABULARY
• equidistant

MODEL & DISCUSS

A new high school will be built for Brighton and Springfield. The location of the school must be the same distance from each middle school. The distance between the two middle schools is 18 miles.

A. Trace the points for the schools on a piece of paper. Locate a new point that is 12 mi from each school. Compare your point with the points of other students. Is there more than one location for the new high school? Explain.

B. Reason Can you find locations for the new high school that are the same distance from each middle school for any given distance? Explain.

? ESSENTIAL QUESTION   What is the relationship between a segment and the points on its perpendicular bisector? Between an angle and the points on its bisector?

CONCEPTUAL UNDERSTANDING

EXAMPLE 1 Find Equidistant Points

How can you find points that are equidistant from the endpoints of $\overline{AB}$? What do you notice about these points and their relationship with $\overline{AB}$?

A point that is the same distance from two points is **equidistant** from the points.

COMMON ERROR
Be sure not to change the compass setting when drawing each pair of intersecting arcs from each endpoint.

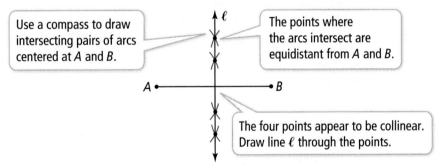

Use a compass to draw intersecting pairs of arcs centered at A and B.

The points where the arcs intersect are equidistant from A and B.

The four points appear to be collinear. Draw line ℓ through the points.

The points that are equidistant from A and B appear to lie on line ℓ. Line ℓ appears to be perpendicular to and bisect $\overline{AB}$ in the same plane as $\overline{AB}$. You can use a ruler and a protractor to support this hypothesis.

 Try It!   **1.** Draw a pair of fixed points, and find points that are equidistant from the two fixed points. Draw a line through the set of equidistant of points. Repeat this process for several pairs of fixed points. What conjecture can you make about points that are the same distance from a given pair of points?

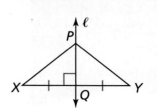

THEOREM 7-10 Perpendicular Bisector Theorem

If a point is on the perpendicular bisector of a segment, then it is equidistant from the endpoints of the segment.

If...

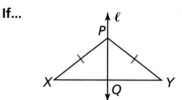

PROOF: SEE EXAMPLE 2.

Then... $PX = PY$

THEOREM 7-11 Converse of the Perpendicular Bisector Theorem

If a point is equidistant from the endpoints of a segment, then it is on the perpendicular bisector of the segment.

If...

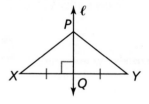

PROOF: SEE EXAMPLE 2 TRY IT.

Then... $XQ = YQ$ and $\overleftrightarrow{PQ} \perp \overline{XY}$

PROOF

EXAMPLE 2 Prove the Perpendicular Bisector Theorem

Prove the Perpendicular Bisector Theorem.

Given: ℓ is the perpendicular bisector of $\overline{XY}$.

Prove: $PX = PY$

Proof:

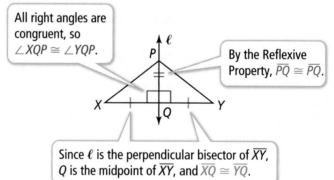

All right angles are congruent, so $\angle XQP \cong \angle YQP$.

By the Reflexive Property, $\overline{PQ} \cong \overline{PQ}$.

Since ℓ is the perpendicular bisector of $\overline{XY}$, Q is the midpoint of $\overline{XY}$, and $\overline{XQ} \cong \overline{YQ}$.

By SAS, $\triangle XQP \cong \triangle YQP$. Therefore, $\overline{PX} \cong \overline{PY}$ by CPCTC, so $PX = PY$.

STUDY TIP
Remember that if a line is a perpendicular bisector of a segment, you can conclude two things: the line is perpendicular to the segment, and it bisects the segment.

 Try It! 2. Prove the Converse of the Perpendicular Bisector Theorem.

APPLICATION

EXAMPLE 3 Use a Perpendicular Bisector

Mr. Lee wants to park his ice cream cart on Main Street so that he is equidistant from the entrances of the amusement park and the zoo. Where should Mr. Lee park? How can he determine where to park?

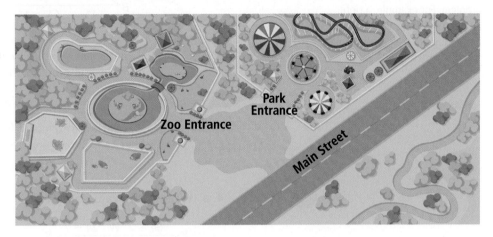

Mr. Lee can use the perpendicular bisector of the segment that connects the two entrances to find the location.

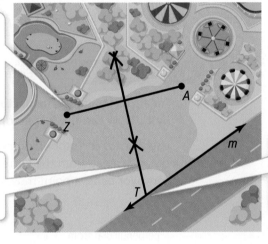

Step 1 Label the entrances of the amusement park and zoo as points A and Z, and draw line m for Main Street.

Step 2 Draw $\overline{AZ}$, and construct the perpendicular bisector.

Step 3 Mark point T where the perpendicular bisector and line m intersect.

STUDY TIP
You may need to extend a line to find the point where it intersects with another line.

Mr. Lee should park his cart at point T, because it is equidistant from both entrances.

 Try It! **3.** The entrances are 40 feet apart. Mr. Lee decides to move his cart off the street to the area between the Main Street and the entrances to the amusement park and the zoo. How can you find where Mr. Lee should park if he must be 30 feet from both entrances?

EXAMPLE 4   Apply the Perpendicular Bisector Theorem

STUDY TIP
Look for relationships in the diagram to help you solve a problem. For example, a right angle marker tells you that two line segments are perpendicular.

What is the value of *AD*?

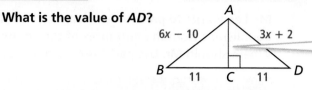

By definition, $\overline{AC}$ is the perpendicular bisector of $\overline{BD}$.

$$AB = AD$$
$$6x - 10 = 3x + 2$$
$$3x = 12$$
$$x = 4$$
$$AD = 3(4) + 2$$
$$AD = 14$$

The lengths are equal by the Perpendicular Bisector Theorem.

Evaluate the expression for *AD*.

☑ **Try It!** 4. a. What is the value of *WY*?   b. What is the value of *OL*?

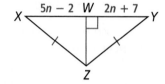

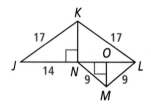

EXAMPLE 5   Find Equidistant Points from the Sides of an Angle

An airport baggage inspector needs to stand equidistant from two conveyor belts. How can the inspector determine where he should stand?

Use pairs of corresponding points on each conveyor belt that are the same distance away from the vertex of the angle. To be equidistant from the conveyor belts, a point must have the same distance from corresponding points.

USE APPROPRIATE TOOLS
Think about the tools you can use to make sure that segments are perpendicular. What tool would you use?

Draw the lines perpendicular from each pair of corresponding points.

The distance between a point and a line is the length of the segment perpendicular from the line to the point.

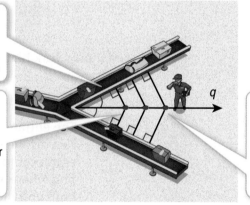

The points of intersection are equidistant from each belt and appear to be collinear.

Ray *q* appears to be the angle bisector. You can use a protractor to support this.

The inspector can determine where to stand by choosing a point on the angle bisector.

☑ **Try It!** 5. Consider two triangles that result from drawing perpendicular segments from where the inspector stands to the conveyor belts. How are the triangles related? Explain.

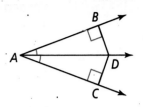

THEOREM 7-12 Angle Bisector Theorem

If a point is on the bisector of an angle, then it is equidistant from the two sides of the angle.

If...

Then... $BD = CD$

PROOF: SEE EXERCISE 9.

THEOREM 7-13 Converse of the Angle Bisector Theorem

If a point is equidistant from two sides of an angle, then it is on the angle bisector.

If...

Then... $m\angle BAD = m\angle CAD$

PROOF: SEE EXERCISE 10.

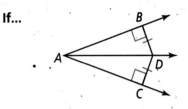

EXAMPLE 6 **Apply the Angle Bisector Theorem**

What is the value of _KL_?

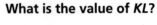

$\overrightarrow{JL}$ is the angle bisector of $\angle KJM$ since $m\angle KJL = m\angle MJL$.

$KL = ML$ The lengths are equal by the Angle Bisector Theorem.

$2x + 3 = 4x - 11$

$2x = 14$

$x = 7$

$KL = 2(7) + 3$ Evaluate the expression for _KL_.

$KL = 17$

STUDY TIP
To apply the Angle Bisector Theorem, be sure a diagram reflects the necessary conditions—angles are marked as congruent and right angles are marked to indicate that segments are perpendicular to the sides.

✓ **Try It!** **6.** Use the figure shown.

a. If $HI = .7$, $IJ = 7$, and $m\angle HGI = 25$, what is $m\angle IGJ$?

b. If $m\angle HGJ = 57$, $m\angle IGJ = 28.5$, and $HI = 12.2$, what is the value of _IJ_?

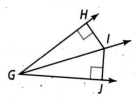

CONCEPT SUMMARY Perpendicular and Angle Bisectors

THEOREM 7-10 ▶ **Perpendicular Bisector Theorem**

If...

Then...

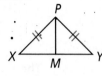

$XM = YM$ and $\overline{PM} \perp \overline{XY}$ $PX = PY$

THEOREM 7-11 ▶ **Converse of Perpendicular Bisector Theorem**

If...

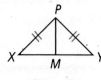

Then...

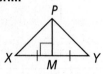

$PX = PY$ $XM = YM$ and $\overline{PM} \perp \overline{XY}$

THEOREM 7-12 ▶ **Angle Bisector Theorem**

If...

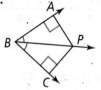

Then...

$\angle ABP \cong \angle CBP$ $AP = CP$

THEOREM 7-13 ▶ **Converse of Angle Bisector Theorem**

If...

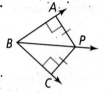

Then...

$AP = CP$ $\angle ABP \cong \angle CBP$

✓ Do You UNDERSTAND?

1. **ESSENTIAL QUESTION** What is the relationship between a segment and the points on its perpendicular bisector? Between an angle and the points on its bisector?

2. **Vocabulary** How can you determine if a point is *equidistant* from the sides of an angle?

3. **Error Analysis** River says that $\overrightarrow{KM}$ is the bisector of $\angle LKJ$ because $LM = MJ$. Explain the error in River's reasoning.

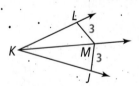

4. **Construct Arguments** You know that $\overline{AB}$ is the perpendicular bisector of $\overline{XY}$, and $\overline{XY}$ is the perpendicular bisector of $\overline{AB}$. What can you conclude about the side lengths of quadrilateral $AXBY$? Explain.

Do You KNOW HOW?

5. If $JL = 14$, $KL = 10$, and $ML = 7$, what is JK?

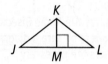

Use the figure shown for Exercises 6 and 7.

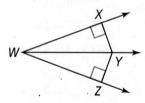

6. If $\angle XWY \cong \angle ZWY$ and $XY = 4$, what is YZ?

7. If $XY = ZY$ and $m\angle ZWY = 18$, what is $m\angle XWZ$?

8. What is an algebraic expression for the area of the square picture and frame?

$x - 2$ in.

PRACTICE & PROBLEM SOLVING

UNDERSTAND

9. Construct Arguments Write a two-column proof for the Angle Bisector Theorem.

10. Construct Arguments Write a paragraph proof for the Converse of the Angle Bisector Theorem.

11. Reason In the diagram below, $AB = BC$, $DF = EF$, and $m\angle BDF = m\angle BEF = 90°$. Is $\triangle ADF \cong \triangle CEF$? Justify your answer.

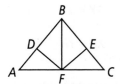

12. Error Analysis A student analyzed the diagram and incorrectly concluded that $AB = 2BC$. Explain the student's error.

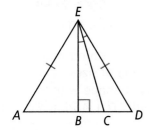

> $\overline{EB}$ is the perpendicular bisector of $\overline{AD}$, so $AB = BD$.
> $\angle BEC \cong \angle DEC$, so $BC = CD$.
> $BC + CD = BD = AB$, and $BC + CD = BC + BC = 2BC$, so $AB = 2BC$.
>

13. Higher Order Thinking Describe the process of constructing the bisector of an angle. Draw a diagram and explain how this construction can be related to the Angle Bisector Theorem.

PRACTICE

Use the figure shown for Exercises 14 and 15.
SEE EXAMPLES 1–3

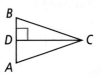

14. If $AD = 3$, $AC = 8$, and $BD = 3$, what is the perimeter of $\triangle ABC$?

15. If $BC = 10$, $AB = 7$, and the perimeter of $\triangle ABC$ is 27, what is the value of BD?

Use the figure shown for Exercises 16 and 17.
SEE EXAMPLE 4

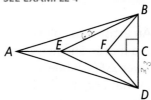

16. If $AD = 21$, $BF = 8$, and $DF = 8$, what is the value of AB?

17. If $EB = 6.2$, $CD = 3.3$, and $ED = 6.2$, what is the value of BD?

Use the figure shown for Exercises 18 and 19.
SEE EXAMPLES 5 AND 6

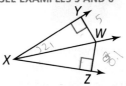

18. If $m\angle YXW = 21$, $YW = 5$, and $WZ = 5$, what is $m\angle ZXY$?

19. If $m\angle YXZ = 38$, $m\angle WXZ = 19$, and $WZ = 8.1$, what is the value of YW?

20. If $CD = 4$ and the perimeter of $\triangle ABC$ is 23, what is the perimeter of $\triangle ABE$?

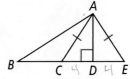

21. Given that $\angle ACF \cong \angle ECF$ and $m\angle ABF = m\angle EDF = 90$, write a two-column proof to show that $\triangle ABF \cong \triangle EDF$.

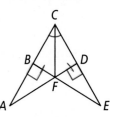

APPLY

22. Make Sense and Persevere A gardener wants to replace the fence along the perimeter of her garden. How much new fencing will be required?

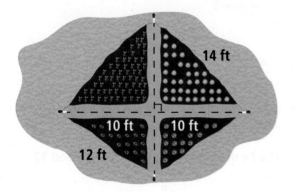

14 ft

10 ft   10 ft

12 ft

23. Look for Relationships An artist uses colored tape to divide sections of a mural. She needs to cut a piece of paper to cover △EFC while she works on other sections. What angles should she cut so she only covers the triangle?

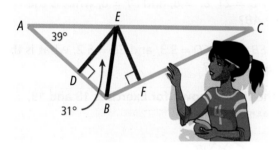

24. Mathematical Connections A surveyor took some measurements of a piece of land. The owner needs to know the area of the land to determine the value. What is the area of the piece of land?

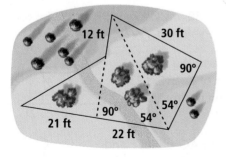

ASSESSMENT PRACTICE

25. $\overleftrightarrow{AB}$ is the perpendicular bisector of $\overline{XY}$. Point P is the midpoint of $\overline{XY}$. Is each statement always true? Select *Yes* or *No*.

	Yes	No
$AP = XP$	❑	❑
$AB = XY$	❑	❑
$AP = BP$	❑	❑
$XB = YB$	❑	❑
$AY = XB$	❑	❑
$XP = YP$	❑	❑

26. SAT/ACT Points G, J, and K are not collinear, and $GJ = GK$. If P is a point on $\overline{JK}$, which of the following conditions is sufficient to prove that $\overleftrightarrow{GP}$ is the perpendicular bisector of $\overline{JK}$?

Ⓐ $JG = PG$ Ⓒ $\angle GJK \cong \angle GKJ$

Ⓑ $m\angle GPJ = 90$ Ⓓ $PK = PG$

27. Performance Task A manufacturer makes roofing trusses in a variety of sizes. All of the trusses have the same shape with three supports, as shown, with $\overline{ED} \perp \overline{AB}$ and $\overline{FD} \perp \overline{BC}$.

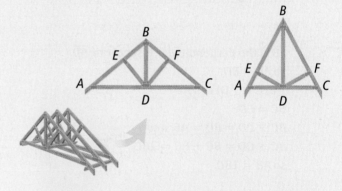

Part A One builder needs $\angle ABD$ and $\angle CBD$ to be congruent for a project. You need to check that a truss meets the builder's requirement. The only tools you have are a measuring tape and a steel square, which is a carpentry tool for measuring right angles. How can you use these tools to verify the angles are congruent?

Part B In addition to the requirement of the first builder, another builder also needs $\overline{AB}$ and $\overline{BC}$ to be congruent as well as $\overline{AD}$ and $\overline{DC}$. Using the same tools, how can you efficiently verify that all three pairs are congruent? Explain.

7-4

Bisectors in Triangles

PearsonRealize.com

I CAN... use triangle bisectors to solve problems.

VOCABULARY

• circumcenter
• circumscribed
• concurrent
• incenter
• inscribed
• point of concurrency

MODEL & DISCUSS

A sporting goods company has three stores in three different towns. They want to build a distribution center so that the distance from each store to the distribution center is as close to equal as possible.

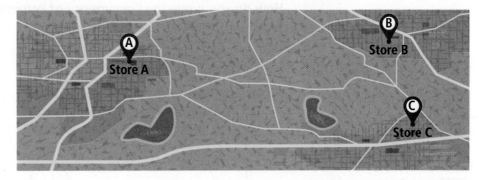

A. Points *A*, *B*, and *C* represent the locations of the three stores. Trace the points on a piece of paper. Locate a point *D* that appears to be the same distance from *A*, *B*, and *C* by sight only.

B. Communicate Precisely Measure the length from points *A*, *B*, and *C* to point *D* on your diagram. Are the lengths equal? If not, can you find a better location for point *D*? Explain.

C. What do you think is the quickest way to find the best point *D* in similar situations?

? ESSENTIAL QUESTION

What are the properties of the perpendicular bisectors in a triangle? What are the properties of the angle bisectors in a triangle?

The Concurrency of the Perpendicular Bisectors Theorem explains the relationship between the perpendicular bisectors of a triangle.

THEOREM 7-14 Concurrency of Perpendicular Bisectors

The perpendicular bisectors of the sides of a triangle are concurrent at a point equidistant from the vertices.

If...

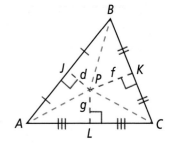

PROOF: SEE EXAMPLE 1.

Then... *d*, *f*, and *g* intersect at *P* and *PA = PB = PC*

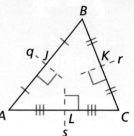
PROOF   **EXAMPLE 1**   **Prove Theorem 7-14**

When three or more lines intersect at one point, the lines are **concurrent**. The point where the lines intersect is called the **point of concurrency**. How do you prove the Concurrency of Perpendicular Bisectors Theorem?

Given: △*ABC* with midpoints *J*, *K*, and *L*, and perpendicular bisectors *q*, *r*, and *s*.

Prove: Lines *q*, *r*, and *s* are concurrent at a point that is equidistant from *A*, *B*, and *C*.

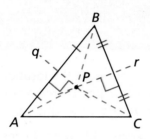
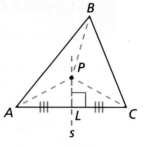
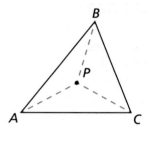

Let *P* be the point of intersection of *q* and *r*. By the Perpendicular Bisector Theorem, *PA* = *PB*, and *PB* = *PC*. Therefore *PA* = *PC*.

By the Converse of the Perpendicular Bisector Theorem, *P* also lies on the perpendicular bisector of $\overline{AC}$.

P is the point of concurrency of *q*, *r*, and *s*. Since *PA* = *PB* = *PC*, point *P* is equidistant from *A*, *B*, and *C*.

Try It!   1. Verify the Concurrency of Perpendicular Bisectors Theorem on acute, right, and obtuse triangles using a straightedge and compass or geometry software.

CONCEPTUAL UNDERSTANDING   **EXAMPLE 2**   **Investigate Circumscribed Circles**

How can you construct a circle that contains the three vertices of a given triangle?

The circle that contains all three vertices of a triangle is the **circumscribed** circle of the triangle.

All points on a circle are equidistant from the center of the circle.

The vertices of the triangle must be equidistant from the center of the circle.

By the Concurrency of Perpendicular Bisectors Theorem, the perpendicular bisectors intersect at a point that is equidistant from the vertices.

CONTINUED ON THE NEXT PAGE

EXAMPLE 2 CONTINUED

The point of concurrency of the perpendicular bisectors of a triangle is the **circumcenter**, so the circumcenter is the center of the circumscribed circle of the triangle.

COMMUNICATE PRECISELY
When you are learning a new concept, think about how to explain it in your own words. How would you explain the circumcenter of a triangle to another student?

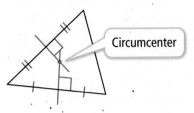

Circumcenter

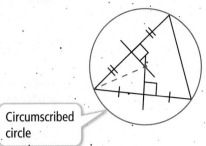

Circumscribed circle

First, construct two perpendicular bisectors to find the circumcenter.

Then construct the circle centered on the circumcenter passing through any vertex.

 Try It!   2. What conjecture can you make about the location of the circumcenter for acute, right, and obtuse triangles?

APPLICATION   **EXAMPLE 3**   **Use a Circumcenter**

A city manager wants to place a new emergency siren so that it is the same distance from the school, hospital, and recreation center. Where should the emergency siren be placed?

Step 1 Label S for the school, H for the hospital, and R for the recreation center. Connect the points to form a triangle.

Step 2 Construct the perpendicular bisectors of two of the sides.

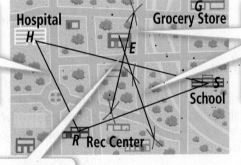

Step 3 Label point E where the perpendicular bisectors intersect.

The city manager should place the emergency siren at point E, because it is equidistant to the three locations.

 Try It!   3. If the city manager decided to place the siren so that it is the same distance from the hospital, school, and grocery store, how can she find the location?

Another kind of special segment in a triangle is the angle bisector. Like the perpendicular bisectors of a triangle, the angle bisectors of a triangle also have a point of concurrency.

THEOREM 7-15 Concurrency of Angle Bisectors

The angle bisectors of the angles of a triangle are concurrent at a point equidistant from the sides of the triangle.

If...

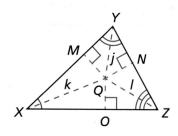

PROOF: SEE EXERCISE 10.

Then... j, k, and l intersect at Q and $QM = QN = QO$

EXAMPLE 4 Investigate Inscribed Circles

How can you construct a circle that intersects each side of a given triangle in exactly one point?

The circle that intersects each side of a triangle at exactly one point and has no points outside of the triangle is the **inscribed** circle of the triangle.

None of the points on the circle are outside the triangle.

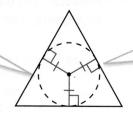

The sides of the triangle must be equidistant from the center of the circle.

STUDY TIP
The parts of the word *incenter* can help you remember what it means: it is the *center* of the circle that is *inside* the triangle.

By the Concurrency of Angle Bisectors Theorem, the angle bisectors of a triangle intersect at a point that is equidistant from the sides of the triangle. The point of concurrency of the angle bisectors of a triangle is the **incenter**, so the incenter is the center of the inscribed circle of the triangle.

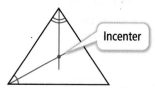

Incenter

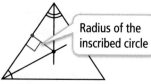

Radius of the inscribed circle

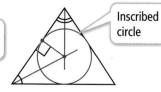

Inscribed circle

First, construct two angle bisectors to find the incenter.

Next, construct a perpendicular segment from the incenter to any side.

Finally, construct the circle centered on the incenter and passing through the point of intersection of the perpendicular segment and the side.

 Try It! 4. Do you think the incenter of a triangle can ever be located on a side of the triangle? Explain.

Go Online | PearsonRealize.com

EXAMPLE 5   **Identify and Use the Incenter of a Triangle**

If $QP = 3(x + 1)$ and $RP = 5x - 3$, what is the radius of the inscribed circle of $\triangle JKL$?

Since $\overline{KP}$ and $\overline{LP}$ are angle bisectors of $\triangle JKL$, P is the incenter of $\triangle JKL$. Therefore, $QP = RP$.

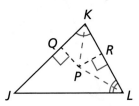

Step 1 Solve for x.

$$QP = RP$$
$$3(x + 1) = 5x - 3$$
$$3x + 3 = 5x - 3$$
$$6 = 2x$$
$$x = 3$$

STUDY TIP
Remember that $QP = RP$, so evaluating either expression for $x = 3$ gives the value of the radius. Select the expression that is easier to evaluate.

Step 2 Find the radius.

$$RP = 5x - 3 \qquad \text{The radius of the incircle is equal to } RP.$$
$$= 5(3) - 3$$
$$= 12$$

The radius of the inscribed circle is 12.

✓ **Try It!**   **5.** Use the figure shown.

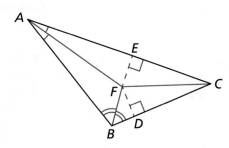

  a. If $m\angle BAF = 15$ and $m\angle CBF = 52$, what is $m\angle ACF$?

  b. If $EF = 3y - 5$ and $DF = 2y + 4$, what is the distance from F to $\overline{AB}$?

PROPERTIES › **Perpendicular Bisectors**

Perpendicular bisectors intersect at the circumcenter.

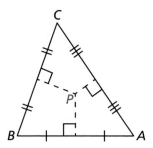

The circumcenter is equidistant from the vertices.

PROPERTIES › **Angle Bisectors**

Angle bisectors intersect at the incenter.

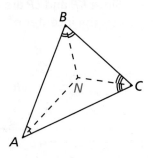

The incenter is equidistant from the sides.

✓ Do You UNDERSTAND?

1. **❓ ESSENTIAL QUESTION** What are the properties of the perpendicular bisectors in a triangle? What are the properties of the angle bisectors in a triangle?

2. **Error Analysis** Terrence constructed the circumscribed circle for △XYZ. Explain Terrence's error.

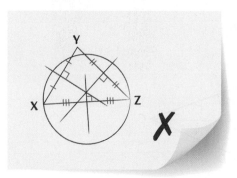

3. **Vocabulary** What parts of the triangle is the *circumcenter* equidistant from? What parts of the triangle is the *incenter* equidistant from?

4. **Reason** Is it possible for the circumscribed circle and the inscribed circle of a triangle to be the same? Explain your reasoning.

Do You KNOW HOW?

The perpendicular bisectors of △ABC are $\overline{PT}$, $\overline{QT}$, and $\overline{RT}$. Find each value.

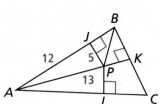

5. *AT*   6. *RC*

Two of the angle bisectors of △ABC are $\overline{AP}$ and $\overline{BP}$. Find each value.

7. *PK*

8. Perimeter of △APL

9. An artist will place a circular piece of stained glass inside the triangular frame so that the glass touches each side of the frame. What is the diameter of the stained glass? Round to the nearest tenth.

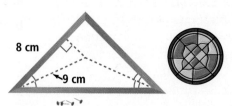

UNDERSTAND

10. **Construct Arguments** Write a Proof of Theorem 7–15: In △ABC, let the angle bisectors of ∠A and ∠B intersect at point P. Show that P is equidistant from each side of △ABC, and that $\overline{CP}$ bisects ∠C.

11. **Higher Order Thinking** A right triangle has vertices X(0, 0), Y(0, 2a), Z(2b, 0). What is the circumcenter of the triangle? Make a conjecture about the diameter of a circle that is circumscribed about a right triangle.

12. **Error Analysis** What is the error that a student made in finding the perimeter of △DTM? Correct the error.

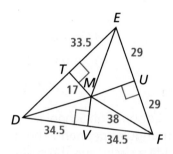

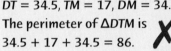

DT = 34.5, TM = 17, DM = 34.5.
The perimeter of △DTM is
34.5 + 17 + 34.5 = 86. ✗

13. **Mathematical Connections** A triangle with incenter P has side lengths x, y, and z. The distance from P to each side is a. Write an expression for the area of the triangle. Use the distributive property to factor your expression.

14. **Reason** In a right triangle with side lengths of 3, 4, and 5, what is the radius of the inscribed circle? Show your work. (Hint: Let r be the radius. Label the lengths of each segment formed by the perpendiculars to the sides.)

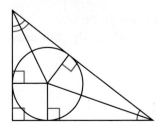

PRACTICE

15. The perpendicular bisectors of △JKL are $\overline{PT}$, $\overline{QT}$, and $\overline{RT}$. Name three isosceles triangles. SEE EXAMPLE 1

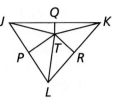

Use the diagram below for Exercises 16–18. Points D, E, and F are the midpoints of the sides of △ABC. SEE EXAMPLES 2 AND 4

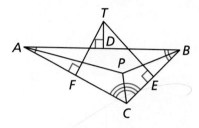

16. Which point is the center of a circle that contains A, B, and C?

17. Which point is the center of a circle that intersects each side of △ABC at exactly one point?

18. The perpendicular bisector of $\overline{AB}$ is m and the perpendicular bisector of $\overline{BC}$ is n. Lines m and n intersect at T. If TA = 8.2, what is TC? SEE EXAMPLE 3

Find the values. SEE EXAMPLE 5

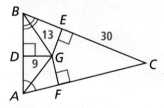

19. EG   20. GF

If XY = 24, XZ = 22, and JQ = 5, find the values. Round to the nearest tenth.

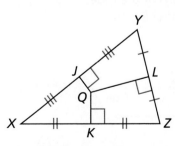

21. The radius of the circumscribed circle of △XYZ

22. QK

APPLY

23. Model With Mathematics A maintenance crew wants to build a shed at a location that is the same distance from each path. Where should the shed be located? Justify your answer with a diagram.

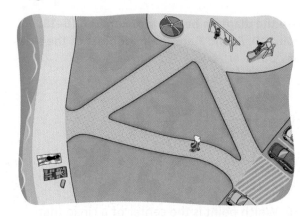

24. Reason What is the area of the patio **not** covered by the sunshade? Round to the nearest tenth, and explain how you found your answer.

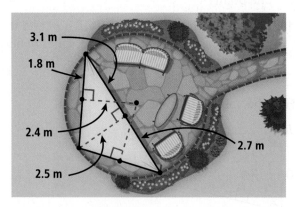

3.1 m
1.8 m
2.4 m
2.5 m
2.7 m

25. Make Sense and Persevere A ball manufacturer wants to stack three balls, each with an 8-centimeter diameter, in a box that is an equilateral triangular prism. The diagram shows the dimensions of the bases. Will the balls fit in the box? Explain how you know.

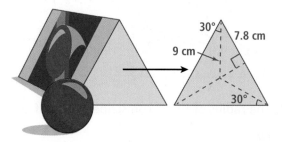

30°
7.8 cm
9 cm
30°

✅ ASSESSMENT PRACTICE

26. In $\triangle ABC$, $\overline{AB}$ has midpoint M, and ℓ is the perpendicular bisector of $\overline{AB}$ and the angle bisector of $\angle ACB$. Which of the following must be true? Select all that apply.

Ⓐ The radius of the inscribed circle of $\triangle ABC$ is AM.

Ⓑ $AC = CB$

Ⓒ Both the circumcenter and incenter of $\triangle ABC$ are on ℓ.

Ⓓ The circumcenter of $\triangle ABC$ is inside the triangle.

27. SAT/ACT Circle O intersects $\overline{AB}$ only at F, $\overline{BC}$ only at G, and $\overline{AC}$ only at H. Which equation is true?

Ⓐ $AH = AC$

Ⓑ $m\angle OFB = 90$

Ⓒ $OB = OC$

Ⓓ $OF = OC$

Ⓔ $\angle BAO \cong \angle ABO$

28. Performance Task Edison High School is designing a new triangular pennant. The school mascot will be inside a circle, and the circle must touch each side of the pennant. The circle should fill as much of the pennant as possible.

🐻 **Wildcats!**

Part A Using a straightedge and compass, draw at least 4 different types of triangles for the pennant. Construct an inscribed circle in each triangle.

Part B Make a table about your pennants. Include side lengths, type of triangle, circle radius and area, triangle area, and ratio of circle area to triangle area.

Part C What type of triangle do you recommend that they use? Justify your answer.

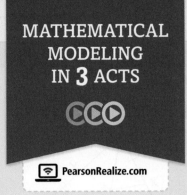

MATHEMATICAL MODELING IN 3 ACTS

PearsonRealize.com

Video

Making It Fair

In rural areas, county planners often work with local officials from a number of small towns to establish a regional medical center to serve all of the nearby communities.

County planners might also establish regional medical evacuation centers to transport patients with serious trauma to larger medical centers. The locations of these regional centers are carefully planned. Think about this during the Mathematical Modeling in 3 Acts lesson.

Scan for Multimedia

ACT 1 Identify the Problem

1. What is the first question that comes to mind after watching the video?

2. Write down the main question you will answer about what you saw in the video.

3. Make an initial conjecture that answers this main question.

4. Explain how you arrived at your conjecture.

5. What information will be useful to know to answer the main question? How can you get it? How will you use that information?

ACT 2 Develop a Model

6. Use the math that you have learned in this Topic to refine your conjecture.

ACT 3 Interpret the Results

7. Did your refined conjecture match the actual answer exactly? If not, what might explain the difference?

TOPIC 7 Mathematical Modeling in 3 Acts   327

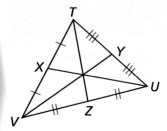
7-5

Medians and Altitudes

📶 PearsonRealize.com

I CAN... find the points of concurrency for the medians of a triangle and the altitudes of a triangle.

VOCABULARY

- altitude
- centroid
- median
- orthocenter

CRITIQUE & EXPLAIN

Aisha wrote the following explanation of the relationships in the triangle.

> I can see that ∠TVY ≅ ∠YVU, ∠VUX ≅ ∠XUT, and ∠UTZ ≅ ∠ZTV because $\overline{TZ}$, $\overline{VY}$, and $\overline{UX}$ bisect the sides opposite each vertex. By the Concurrency of Angle Bisectors Theorem, $\overline{VY}$, $\overline{UX}$, and $\overline{TZ}$ are concurrent.

A. Why is Aisha's explanation not correct?

B. Communicate Precisely What can you do in the future to avoid Aisha's mistake?

❓ **ESSENTIAL QUESTION**
What are the properties of the medians in a triangle? What are the properties of the altitudes in a triangle?

👆 EXAMPLE 1   Identify Special Segments in Triangles

What are the *altitude* and *median* that are shown in △ADC?

An **altitude** is a perpendicular segment from a vertex of a triangle to the line containing the side opposite the vertex. A **median** of a triangle is a segment that has endpoints at a vertex and the midpoint of the side opposite the vertex.

STUDY TIP
Recall that if congruence marks are not on a diagram, you cannot assume congruence.

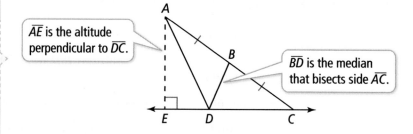

$\overline{AE}$ is the altitude perpendicular to $\overline{DC}$.

$\overline{BD}$ is the median that bisects side $\overline{AC}$.

✅ **Try It!**   1. Use the figure shown.

a. What are the altitude and median that are shown in △ABC?

b. Copy the triangle and draw the other altitudes and medians of the triangle.

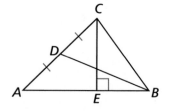

📶 Go Online | PearsonRealize.com

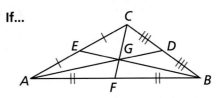

THEOREM 7-16 Concurrency of Medians

The medians of a triangle are concurrent at a point that is two-thirds the distance from each vertex to the midpoint of the opposite side.

PROOF: SEE LESSON 11-2.

If...

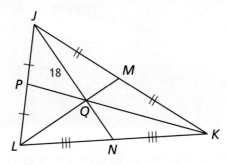

Then...

$$AG = \frac{2}{3}AD \quad BG = \frac{2}{3}BE \quad CG = \frac{2}{3}CF$$

✋ **EXAMPLE 2** Find the Length of a Median

What is the length of $\overline{JN}$ in the figure?

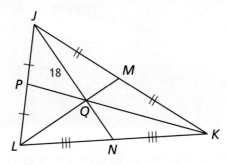

The medians of $\triangle JKL$ are $\overline{JN}$, $\overline{KP}$, and $\overline{LM}$. Point Q is the point of concurrency of the medians. The point of concurrency of the medians of a triangle is called the **centroid**.

COMMON ERROR
Be careful not to confuse which part is $\frac{1}{3}$ of the length of the median and which part is $\frac{2}{3}$ of the length.

$\frac{2}{3}JN = JQ$ ⟵ Use the Concurrency of Medians Theorem.

$\frac{2}{3}JN = 18$

$JN = 27$

☑ **Try It!** **2.** Find AD for each triangle.

a.

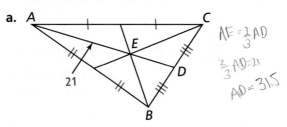

$AE = \frac{2}{3}AD$

$\frac{2}{3}AD = 21$

$AD = 31.5$

b.

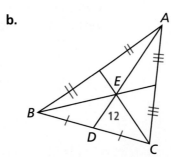

EXAMPLE 3 > Locate the Centroid

An artist wants to balance a triangular piece of wood at a single point so that the triangle is parallel to the ground. Where should he balance the triangle?

A triangle is balanced at its *center of gravity,* which is at the centroid of the triangle.

USE APPROPRIATE TOOLS
Think about what tools you can use to find the midpoint. What tool would you use?

Step 1 Find the midpoint of each side.

Step 2 Draw a median from each midpoint.

Step 3 Label the centroid point Q.

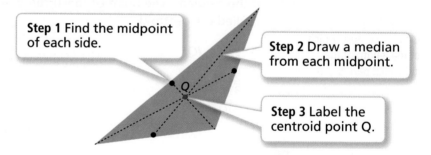

The artist should balance the triangle at point *Q*.

 Try It! 3. Copy the triangle shown.

    a. Use the medians of the triangle to locate its centroid.

    b. Use a ruler to verify the centroid is two-thirds the distance from each vertex to the midpoint of the opposite side.

THEOREM 7-17   Concurrency of Altitudes

The lines that contain the altitudes of a triangle are concurrent.

If...

PROOF: SEE LESSON 11-2.

Then... $\overleftrightarrow{KQ}$, $\overleftrightarrow{LN}$, and $\overleftrightarrow{MP}$ are concurrent at X.

CONCEPTUAL
UNDERSTANDING

 EXAMPLE 4   **Locate the Orthocenter**

The orthocenter is the point of concurrency of the lines containing the altitudes of a triangle. How does the type of triangle (obtuse, acute, right) relate to the location of its orthocenter?

Draw at least two of each type of triangle. Describe any relationship you notice between the type of triangle and the location of its orthocenter.

Obtuse triangles	Acute triangles	Right triangles

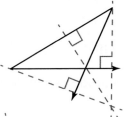  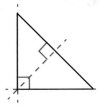

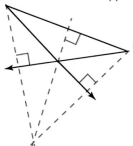 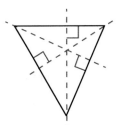 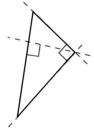

STUDY TIP
Recall that when you make a conjecture by observing a few examples, you are not actually proving the conjecture.

The orthocenter is outside an obtuse triangle and inside an acute triangle. For a right triangle, the orthocenter is at the vertex of the right angle.

✓ **Try It!**   **4.** What is the relationship between an isosceles triangle and the location of its orthocenter? Explain your answer.

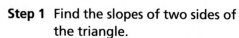
EXAMPLE 5 · Find the Orthocenter of a Triangle

Orthocenters can be found using constructions or coordinate geometry. Where is the orthocenter of △KLM?

Since the orthocenter is the point of concurrency of the altitudes, find the equations for two altitudes, and solve for the point of intersection.

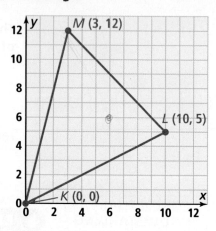

Step 1 Find the slopes of two sides of the triangle.

$$\text{slope of } \overline{KL} = \frac{5-0}{10-0} = \frac{1}{2}$$

$$\text{slope of } \overline{LM} = \frac{12-5}{3-10} = -1$$

Step 2 Use the point slope form, $y - y_1 = m(x - x_1)$, to write the equations of the altitudes perpendicular to $\overline{KL}$ and $\overline{LM}$.

Equation of the altitude perpendicular to $\overline{KL}$:

$$y - 12 = -2(x - 3)$$
$$y = -2x + 6 + 12$$
$$y = -2x + 18$$

> Point M is the vertex opposite $\overline{KL}$, and the slope of a line perpendicular to $\overline{KL}$ is -2.

Equation of the altitude perpendicular to $\overline{LM}$:

$$y - 0 = 1(x - 0)$$
$$y = x$$

> Point K is the vertex opposite $\overline{LM}$, and the slope of a line perpendicular to $\overline{LM}$ is 1.

STUDY TIP
Remember that since an altitude is perpendicular to a side of the triangle, you must find the reciprocal and reverse the sign of the slope of a side to find the slope of an altitude.

Step 3 Solve the system of equations to determine the coordinates of the point of intersection.

$$y = -2x + 18$$
$$y = -2(y) + 18$$
$$y + 2y = 18$$
$$3y = 18$$
$$y = 6$$

> Since $y = x$, substitute y in the equation $y = -2x + 18$. Then solve for y.

Since $y = x$, $x = 6$.

Since all three altitudes intersect at the orthocenter, the intersection of two altitudes is sufficient to determine the orthocenter. The orthocenter of △KLM is (6, 6).

✓ Try It! 5. Find the orthocenter of a triangle with vertices at each of the following sets of coordinates.

    a. (0, 0), (10, 4), (8, 9)   **b.** (0, 0), (6, 3), (8, 9)

CONCEPT SUMMARY Medians and Altitudes

MEDIANS

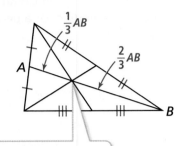

The **centroid** is the point of concurrency of the medians of a triangle.

ALTITUDES

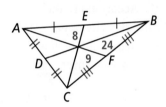

The **orthocenter** is the point of concurrency of the lines containing the altitudes of a triangle.

Do You UNDERSTAND?

1. **ESSENTIAL QUESTION** What are the properties of the medians in a triangle? What are the properties of the altitudes in a triangle?

2. **Vocabulary** The prefix *ortho-* means "upright" or "right." How can this meaning help you remember which segments of a triangle have a point of concurrency at the orthocenter?

3. **Error Analysis** A student labeled P as the centroid of the triangle. What error did the student make? Explain.

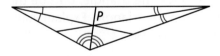

4. **Reason** Why is an orthocenter sometimes outside a triangle but a centroid is always inside?

5. **Look for Relationships** Consider the three types of triangles: acute, obtuse, and right. What is the relationship between the type of triangle and the location of the orthocenter? Does the type of triangle tell you anything about the location of the centroid?

6. **Generalize** For any right triangle, where is the orthocenter located?

Do You KNOW HOW?

7. Find the length of each of the medians of the triangle.

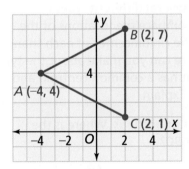

8. Where is the orthocenter of △ABC?

9. A crane operator needs to lift a large triangular piece of plywood. Copy the triangle and use its medians to locate the centroid.

UNDERSTAND

10. Make Sense and Persevere Describe the process for finding the orthocenter of a triangle that is on a coordinate plane.

11. Look for Relationships Given the midpoints of a triangle, which two points of concurrency can you locate? Which point of concurrency can you locate if you only know the angle bisectors? Which two points of concurrency can you locate by only drawing perpendicular segments?

12. Error Analysis A student uses the following explanation to identify the triangle's point of concurrency. Explain the student's error.

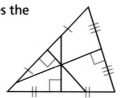

A perpendicular segment bisects each side of the triangle. According to the Concurrency of Altitudes Theorem, the segments are concurrent. The point of concurrency is the orthocenter. ✗

13. Reason Draw several different types of triangles and compare the locations of the centroid and the circumcenter of each triangle. What conjecture can you make about the type of triangle that has a common centroid and circumcenter? Explain.

14. Mathematical Connections Where is the centroid of △ABC?

- Locate the midpoints of any two sides.
- Find the equations of two medians using the vertex and the opposite midpoint.
- Solve the system of the two equations to find the coordinates of the centroid.

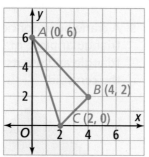

How can you verify that the coordinates you found are correct?

PRACTICE

15. Identify whether each segment is an altitude, an angle bisector, a median, or a perpendicular bisector. SEE EXAMPLE 1

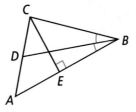

a. $\overline{BD}$ b. $\overline{FJ}$

c. $\overline{CE}$ d. $\overline{KL}$

16. What is the value of $\overline{KL}$? SEE EXAMPLE 2

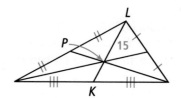

17. Copy the triangle and use its medians to locate the centroid. SEE EXAMPLE 3

18. State whether the orthocenter of each triangle is inside the triangle, outside the triangle, or on the triangle. Explain your reasoning. SEE EXAMPLE 4

a.   b.

c.   d.

19. Find the coordinates of the orthocenter of a triangle with vertices at each set of points on a coordinate plane. SEE EXAMPLE 5

a. (0, 0), (8, 4), (4, 22)

b. (3, 1), (10, 8), (5, 13)

APPLY

20. Model With Mathematics A large triangular-shaped table is supported by a single pole at the center of gravity. How far is vertex C from the center of gravity?

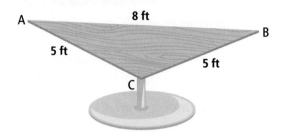

21. Reason To support a triangular kite, Hana attaches thin strips of wood from each vertex perpendicular to the opposite edge. She then attaches the kite's string at the point of concurrency. To calculate the point of concurrency, she determines the coordinates of each vertex on a coordinate plane. What are the coordinates where the wood strips cross? Round your answer to the nearest hundredth.

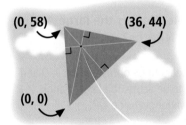

22. Higher Order Thinking A designer wants to place a fountain at the intersection of the shortest paths from each side to the opposite vertex. What mistake is made on her model? At what point of concurrency should the fountain be located?

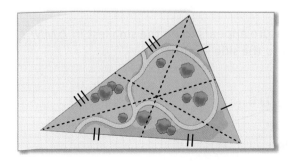

ASSESSMENT PRACTICE

23. Identify the segments and point in $\triangle ABC$.

The segment $\overline{AD}$ is a(n) ___?___ of the triangle. The segment $\overline{BE}$ is a(n) ___?___ of the triangle. The point X is the ___?___ of the triangle.

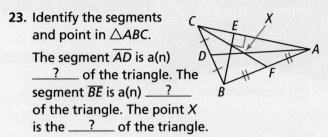

24. SAT/ACT A triangle with vertices at (3, 4) and (9, 17) has a centroid at (8, 16). What are the coordinates of the third vertex?

Ⓐ (10, 4)   Ⓒ (12, 14)

Ⓑ (10, 7)   Ⓓ (12, 27)

25. Performance Task Steve is designing a mobile with triangular pieces of wood, where each piece attaches to a wire at the center of gravity and hangs parallel to the ground. The side lengths of the triangles will be between 4 cm and 8 cm.

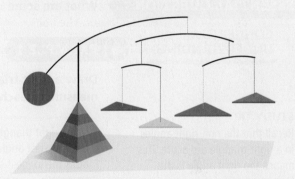

Part A Describe how Steve can find the center of gravity for any triangular piece. Then model this process by finding the center of gravity of a triangle with side lengths 5 cm, 5 cm, and 6 cm.

Part B Is it possible for a triangle attached at the orthocenter to hang so that it is parallel to the ground? If it is possible, describe the triangle. What are possible side lengths for such a triangle? If it is not possible, explain why not.

I CAN... use theorems to compare the sides and angles of a triangle.

👆 **EXPLORE & REASON**

Cut several drinking straws to the sizes shown.

A. Take your two shortest straws and your longest straw. Can they form a triangle? Explain.

B. Try different combinations of three straws to form triangles. Which side length combinations work? Which combinations do not work?

C. Look for Relationships What do you notice about the relationship between the combined lengths of the two shorter sides and the length of the longest side?

❓ **ESSENTIAL QUESTION**   What are some relationships between the sides and angles of any triangle?

CONCEPTUAL
UNDERSTANDING

👆 **EXAMPLE 1**   Investigate Side and Angle Relationships

Draw a right triangle and a non-right triangle. How is the largest angle measure of each triangle related to the side lengths?

STUDY TIP
Recall that the non-right angles in a right triangle are acute. This means the right angle is the largest angle.

In the right triangle, $\angle A$ is the largest angle and $\overline{BC}$ is the longest side.

Angle P appears to be obtuse, while $\angle Q$ and $\angle R$ appear to be acute. The largest angle $\angle P$ is across from longest side $\overline{QR}$.

A
5 m   12 m
C   13 m   B

P
6 in.   6 in.
R   10 in.   Q

The largest angle appears to be opposite the longest side.

✓ **Try It!**   **1.** Which angle measure appears to be the smallest in $\triangle MNP$? How is it related to the side lengths?

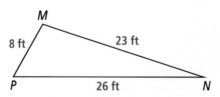

M
8 ft   23 ft
P   26 ft   N

THEOREM 7-18

If two sides of a triangle are not congruent, then the larger angle lies opposite the longer side.

PROOF: SEE EXERCISE 13.

If... $b > a$

Then... $m\angle B > m\angle A$

⤷ EXAMPLE 2 ▸ Use Theorem 7-18

To support a triangular piece of a float, a brace is placed at the largest angle and a guide wire is placed at the smallest angle. Which angle is the largest? Which angle is the smallest?

REASON
Think about the relationships between pairs of numbers. How can you use the relationships between pairs of numbers to order all the numbers?

Compare side lengths to find larger angle measures.

Since $12 > 10$, $m\angle A > m\angle B$.

Since $13 > 12$, $m\angle C > m\angle A$.

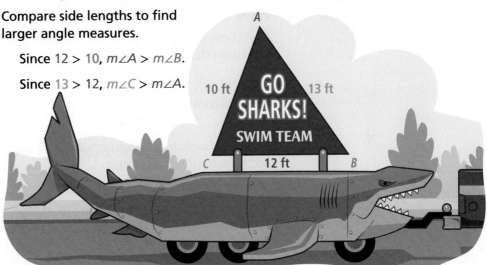

Combining the inequalities of the angle measures, $m\angle C > m\angle A > m\angle B$. Thus, the largest angle is $\angle C$ and the smallest angle is $\angle B$.

☑ **Try It!** 2. Lucas sketched a diagram for a garden box.

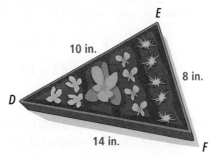

a. Which angle is the largest?

b. Which angle is the smallest?

THEOREM 7-19 Converse of Theorem 7-18

If two angles of a triangle are not congruent, then the longer side lies opposite the larger angle.	**If...** $m\angle B > m\angle A$
PROOF: SEE EXAMPLE 3.	**Then...** $b > a$

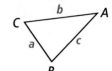

PROOF

🖐 **EXAMPLE 3** **Prove Theorem 7-19**

Use indirect reasoning to prove Theorem 7–19; assume that $GH \le HJ$. This means that $GH = HJ$ or $GH < HJ$.

Given: $m\angle J > m\angle G$

Prove: $GH > HJ$

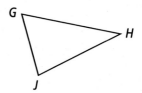

First show that assuming $GH = HJ$ leads to a contradiction of the given condition that $m\angle J > m\angle G$.

$$GH = HJ \longrightarrow \overline{GH} \cong \overline{HJ} \longrightarrow \triangle GHJ \text{ is isosceles.} \longrightarrow \angle J \cong \angle G$$

Assumption   Def. of congruent   Def. of isosceles   Isosceles Triangle Thm.

By the definition of congruence $m\angle J = m\angle G$, which contradicts $m\angle J > m\angle G$. So the assumption is false.

☑ **Try It!**   **3.** To complete the proof of Theorem 7-19, show that assuming $GH < HJ$ leads to a contradiction of the given condition that $m\angle J > m\angle G$.

🖐 **EXAMPLE 4** **Use Theorem 7-19**

Which side of △KLM is the longest?

By Theorem 7-19, the longest side of the triangle is across from the largest angle. Find the unknown angle measure.

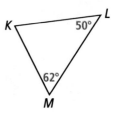

$$m\angle K + m\angle L + m\angle M = 180$$
$$m\angle K + 50 + 62 = 180$$
$$m\angle K = 68$$

Apply the Triangle Angle-Sum Theorem.

The largest angle in the triangle is $\angle K$, so the longest side is the side opposite $\angle K$. The longest side is $\overline{LM}$.

☑ **Try It!**   **4.** Identify the sides of △NOP.

     a. Which side is the longest?

     b. Which side is the shortest?

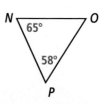

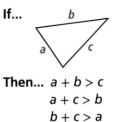
THEOREM 7-20 Triangle Inequality Theorem

The sum of the lengths of any two sides of a triangle is greater than the length of the third side.

PROOF: SEE EXERCISE 14.

If...

Then... $a + b > c$
$a + c > b$
$b + c > a$

👆 **EXAMPLE 5**   Use the Triangle Inequality Theorem

A. Which of the following sets of segments could be the sides of a triangle?

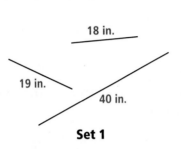

Set 1

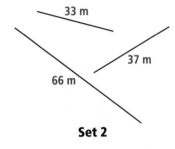

Set 2

> **COMMON ERROR**
> You may compare any two sides to a third side, but you must compare the shorter two sides to the longest side to determine whether a triangle is possible.

Determine if the sum of the two shorter side lengths is longer than the longest side length.

$18 + 19 = 37$

Since $37 < 40$, the segments in Set 1 cannot form a triangle.

$33 + 37 = 70$

Since $70 > 66$, the segments in Set 2 can form a triangle.

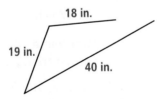

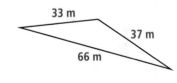

B. A triangle has sides that measure 11 cm and 16 cm. What are the possible lengths of the third side?

Apply the Triangle Inequality Theorem.

$x + 11 > 16$ $x + 16 > 11$ $11 + 16 > x$

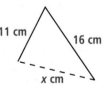

- If $x + 11 > 16$, then $x > 5$. So, x is greater than 5.
- The inequality $x + 16 > 11$ is true for all positive values of x, so this inequality only tells you that $x > 0$.
- If $11 + 16 > x$, then $27 > x$, so x is less than 27.

Therefore, $5 < x < 27$.

The third side of the triangle could be between 5 cm and 27 cm long.

 Try It!   **5. a.** Could a triangle have side lengths 16 m, 39 m, and 28 m?

        b. A triangle has side lengths that are 30 in. and 50 in. What are the possible lengths of the third side?

CONCEPT SUMMARY Inequalities in One Triangle

THEOREMS 7-18 AND 7-19

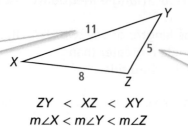

The longest side is opposite the largest angle.

The shortest side is opposite the smallest angle.

$$ZY < XZ < XY$$
$$m\angle X < m\angle Y < m\angle Z$$

THEOREM 7-20   Triangle Inequality Theorem

The sum of the lengths of any two sides is greater than the length of the third side.

$$5 + 8 > 11$$
$$5 + 11 > 8$$
$$8 + 11 > 5$$

Do You UNDERSTAND?

1. **ESSENTIAL QUESTION** What are some relationships between the sides and angles of any triangle?

2. **Reason** If a triangle has three different side lengths, what does that tell you about the measures of its angles?

3. **Error Analysis** Richard says that $\angle X$ must be the largest angle in $\triangle XYZ$. Explain his error.

4. **Use Structure** An isosceles triangle has base angles that each measure 50. How could you determine whether b or s is greater?

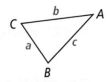

5. **Generalize** In $\triangle ABC$, $a < c < b$. List the angles in order from smallest to largest.

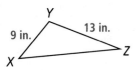

Do You KNOW HOW?

Identify the sides of $\triangle PQR$.

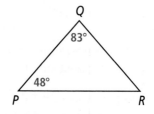

6. Which side is the longest?

7. Which side is the shortest?

Determine whether each set of lengths could form a triangle.

8. 5, 2, and 3

9. 55, 76, and 112

10. 102, 95, and 157

11. 17, 17, and 35

12. Kelsey is welding 3 metal rods to make a triangle. If the lengths of two of the rods are 15 in. and 22 in., what are the possible lengths of a third rod?

UNDERSTAND

13. Construct Arguments Fill in the missing reasons in the proof of Theorem 7-18. (Hint: The Comparison Property of Inequality states that if $a = b + c$ and $c > 0$, then $a > b$.)

Given: $AB > AC$, $\overline{AC} \cong \overline{AM}$

Prove: $m\angle ACB > m\angle B$

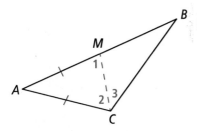

Statements	Reasons
1) $\overline{AC} \cong \overline{AM}$	1) Given
2) $m\angle 1 = m\angle 2$	2) Isosc. Triangle Thm.
3) $m\angle ACB = m\angle 2 + m\angle 3$	3)
4) $m\angle ACB > m\angle 2$	4)
5) $m\angle ACB > m\angle 1$	5)
6) $m\angle 1 = m\angle B + m\angle 3$	6) Ext. Angles Thm.
7) $m\angle 1 > m\angle B$	7)
8) $m\angle ACB > m\angle B$	8)

14. Construct Arguments Write a paragraph proof for Theorem 7-20. Use the figure shown and prove that $AB + CB > AC$.

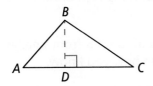

15. Error Analysis A student said that a triangle with side lengths of 3 ft and 4 ft could have a third side with a length of 7 ft. Explain why the student is incorrect. What is a correct statement about the third side of the triangle?

16. Error Analysis Tia says that $\angle Q$ must be the largest angle in $\triangle QRS$ because $150 > 70 > 1.7$. Explain Tia's error.

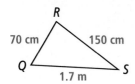

PRACTICE

17. Which angle measure appears to be the smallest in $\triangle JKL$? What can you conclude about the side opposite that angle? SEE EXAMPLE 1.

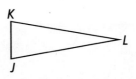

Identify the angles of $\triangle FGH$. SEE EXAMPLE 2.

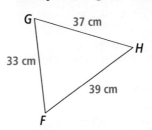

18. Which angle is the smallest?

19. Which angle is the largest?

Identify the sides of $\triangle NOP$. SEE EXAMPLES 3 AND 4.

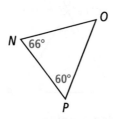

20. Which side is the longest?

21. Which side is the shortest?

Determine whether the side lengths could form a triangle. SEE EXAMPLE 5.

22. 13, 15, 9

23. 8, 15, 7

24. 35, 20, 11

25. 65, 32, 40

Given two sides of a triangle, determine the range of possible lengths of the third side. SEE EXAMPLE 5.

26. 10 in. and 12 in.

27. 5 ft and 10 ft

28. 200 m and 300 m

29. 90 km and 150 km

APPLY

30. Make Sense and Persevere It took Ines 2 hours to bicycle the perimeter shown at a constant speed of 10 miles per hour. Which two roads form the largest angle?

31. Reason A jewelry designer plans to make a triangular pendant out of gold wire. The wire costs $31.65 per centimeter. What is the possible range of costs for the wire?

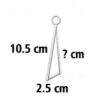

10.5 cm   ? cm
2.5 cm

32. Use Structure A stage manager must use tape to outline a triangular platform on the set. Order the sides of the platform from longest to shortest.

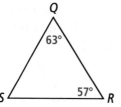

Q
63°
S   57° R

33. Make Sense and Persevere A dog running an agility course has difficulty making turns. The sharper the angle, the more difficult the turn. Which corner is most difficult for her to turn?

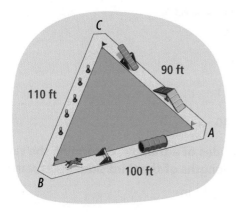

C
90 ft
110 ft
A
100 ft
B

ASSESSMENT PRACTICE

34. The lengths of two sides of a triangle are 13 and 20. What is the range of values for the length x of the third side?

35. SAT/ACT Look at △RST.

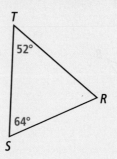

T
52°
R
64°
S

Which statement is false?

Ⓐ $TS = TR$

Ⓑ $m\angle STR < m\angle TRS$

Ⓒ $TR > SR$

Ⓓ $TS < SR$

Ⓔ $TS + TR > SR$

36. Performance Task Teo designed a skateboard ramp.

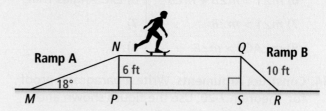

Ramp A   N   Q   Ramp B
6 ft   10 ft
18°
M   P   S   R

Part A List the sides of ramp A in order from shortest to longest.

Part B List the angles of ramp B from smallest to largest, and explain how you know.

Part C Ramp B cannot be steeper than 45°. Is it possible to build ramp B so that $\overline{SR}$ is shorter than 6 ft? Explain.

7-7

Inequalities in Two Triangles

PearsonRealize.com

I CAN... compare a pair of sides of two triangles when the remaining pairs of sides are congruent.

A woodworker uses a caliper to measure the widths of a bat to help him determine the widths for a new bat. The woodworker places the open tips of the caliper on the bat. The distance between the tips is a width of the bat.

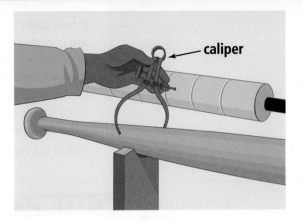
caliper

A. Suppose a caliper opens to an angle of 25° for one width of a bat and opens to an angle of 35° for another. What can you conclude about the widths of the bat?

B. Look for Relationships Next, suppose you use a caliper to measure the width of a narrow part of a bat and a wider part of the bat. What can you predict about the angle to which the caliper opens each time?

❓ ESSENTIAL QUESTION

When two triangles have two pairs of congruent sides, how are the third pair of sides and the pair of angles opposite the third pair of sides related?

CONCEPTUAL UNDERSTANDING

👆 **EXAMPLE 1** Investigate Side Lengths in Triangles

As a rider pedals a unicycle, how do the measure of ∠A and length *b* change? What does this suggest about the change in the triangle?

LOOK FOR RELATIONSHIPS
Consider how multiple diagrams are used to show the relationship between moving parts. What changes and what remains the same between diagrams?

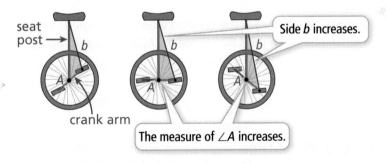

seat post →
Side *b* increases.
crank arm
The measure of ∠A increases.

If two sides of a triangle stay the same, but the measure of the angle between them increases, the length of the third side also increases.

☑ **Try It!** **1.** Compare the measure of ∠J and side length *k* for the triangles.

acute

obtuse

right

THEOREM 7-21 Hinge Theorem

If two sides of one triangle are congruent to two sides of another triangle, and the included angles are not congruent, then the longer third side is opposite the larger included angle.

PROOF: SEE EXERCISE 9.

If... $m\angle YWX > m\angle CAB$

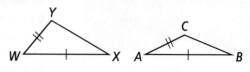

Then... $XY > BC$

APPLICATION

 EXAMPLE 2 **Apply the Hinge Theorem**

The tension in the exercise band varies proportionally with the stretch distance. The tension T is described by the function $T(x) = kx$, where k is a constant that depends on the elasticity of the band and x is the stretch distance. Which position shown in the figures has a greater tension in the band?

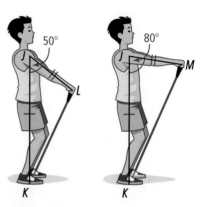

Formulate ◄ Model each figure with a triangle.

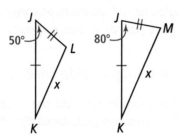

Compute ◄ $T(LK)$ is the tension when the angle is 50°, and $T(MK)$ is the tension when the angle is 80°. Since $m\angle MJK > m\angle LJK$, apply the Hinge Theorem.

$$MK > LK$$

$$\frac{T(MK)}{k} > \frac{T(LK)}{k}$$

Since the tension T is equal to the product of k and the stretch distance, we can substitute $\frac{T}{k}$ for each distance.

$$T(MK) > T(LK)$$

Interpret ◄ A larger angle corresponds to a larger distance from the man's hands to his feet. The larger distance corresponds to a higher tension.

The tension is greater when the man pulls higher on the tension band.

Try It! **2.** The man keeps his arms extended and the length of the tension band the same. If he wants to make the measure of $\angle L$ smaller, how would $\overline{JK}$ change?

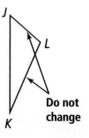

Do not change

THEOREM 7-22 Converse of the Hinge Theorem

If two sides of one triangle are congruent to two sides of another triangle, and the third sides are not congruent, then the larger included angle is opposite the longer third side.

If... $EF > UV$

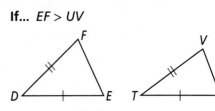

PROOF: SEE EXAMPLE 3.

Then... $m\angle D > m\angle T$

👆 **EXAMPLE 3**   **Prove the Converse of the Hinge Theorem**

Use indirect reasoning to prove the Converse of the Hinge Theorem.

Given: $\overline{DF} \cong \overline{TV}$; $\overline{DE} \cong \overline{TU}$; $EF > UV$

Prove: $m\angle FDE > m\angle VTU$

> **STUDY TIP**
> If you get stuck when writing a proof, make a list of things you know and what you want to prove.

Assume that $m\angle FDE$ is not greater than $m\angle VTU$, that is, that $m\angle FDE = m\angle VTU$, or $m\angle FDE < m\angle VTU$.

Assuming that $m\angle FDE = m\angle VTU$, $\angle FDE \cong \angle VTU$. Applying SAS, $\triangle DEF \cong \triangle TUV$, so by CPCTC, $\overline{EF} \cong \overline{UV}$ and $EF = UV$. But, this contradicts $EF > UV$.

☑ **Try It!**   **3.** To complete the proof of the Hinge Theorem, show that assuming $m\angle FDE < m\angle VTU$ leads to a contradiction of the given statement, $EF > UV$.

👆 **EXAMPLE 4**   **Apply the Converse of the Hinge Theorem**

What are the possible values of x?

Since $FG < CD$ and $CD < AB$, apply the Converse of the Hinge Theorem.

> **COMMON ERROR**
> Be careful to use the correct inequality sign when comparing triangles. After you write the inequality, check a second time to be sure it indicates that the larger angle is opposite the longer side.

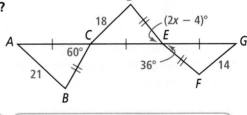

$$m\angle FEG < m\angle CED < m\angle ACB$$
$$36 < 2x - 4 < 60$$
$$40 < 2x < 64$$
$$20 < x < 32$$

Use the Converse of the Hinge Theorem.

The possible values for x are between 20 and 32.

☑ **Try It!**   **4.** What are the possible values of x for each diagram?

a.

b.

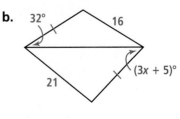

CONCEPT SUMMARY Inequalities in Two Triangles

THEOREM 7-21 ▶ **Hinge Theorem**

If... $\overline{WX} \cong \overline{AB}$, $\overline{WY} \cong \overline{AC}$, and $m\angle W > m\angle A$

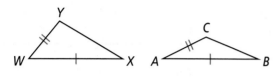

Then... $XY > BC$

THEOREM 7-22 ▶ **Converse of the Hinge Theorem**

If... $\overline{DF} \cong \overline{TV}$, $\overline{DE} \cong \overline{TU}$, and $EF > UV$

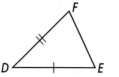

Then... $m\angle D > m\angle T$

Do You UNDERSTAND?

1. **ESSENTIAL QUESTION** When two triangles have two pairs of congruent sides, how are the third pair of sides and the pair of angles opposite the third pair of sides related?

2. **Error Analysis** Venetta applies the Converse of the Hinge Theorem to conclude that $m\angle EKF > m\angle HKG$ for the triangles shown. Is Venetta correct? Explain your answer.

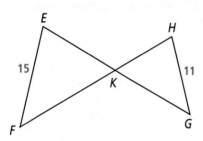

3. **Reason** Why must the angles described in the Hinge Theorem be between the congruent pairs of sides?

4. **Communicate Precisely** The Hinge Theorem is also known as the Side-Angle-Side Inequality Theorem or SAS Inequality Theorem. How are the requirements for applying the Hinge Theorem similar to the requirements for applying SAS? How are the requirements different?

Do You KNOW HOW?

5. Order AB, BC, and CD from least to greatest.

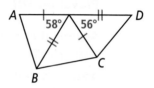

6. Order the measures of $\angle PTU$, $\angle SQT$, and $\angle QSR$ from least to greatest.

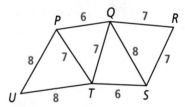

7. Kayak A and kayak B leave a dock as shown. Which kayak is closer to the dock?

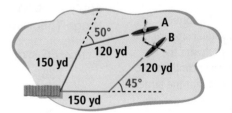

UNDERSTAND

8. Error Analysis Tonya has the scissors shown.

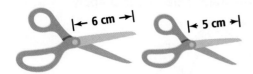

Tonya writes the following description of how she will use the Hinge Theorem with the scissors.

> If you open the right pair of scissors to an angle of 30° and open the left pair of scissors to an angle of 45°, then by the Hinge Theorem, the distance between the blade tips of the left pair of scissors will be larger. ✗

What is the mistake in her use of the Hinge Theorem?

9. Construct Arguments Write a paragraph proof of the Hinge Theorem.

Given: $\overline{WX} \cong \overline{AB}, \overline{WY} \cong \overline{AC}, m\angle W > m\angle A$

Prove: $XY > BC$

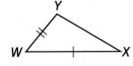 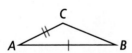

Use the following outline.
- Find a point D outside $\triangle ABC$ so $\overline{AD} \cong \overline{WY}$ and $\angle DAB \cong \angle YWX$.
- Show that $\triangle WXY \cong \triangle ABD$.
- Construct the angle bisector of $\angle CAD$. Let point E be the point where the angle bisector intersects $\overline{BD}$.

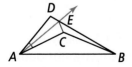

- Show that $\triangle ACE \cong \triangle ADE$ so $\overline{CE} \cong \overline{DE}$.
- Show that $DB = CE + EB$.
- Use the Triangle Inequality Theorem on $\triangle BCE$.

PRACTICE

10. Write an inequality describing the range of x for each pair of triangles. **SEE EXAMPLES 1 AND 2.**

a.

b.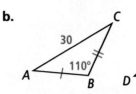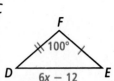

11. Write an inequality describing the possible values of x for each pair of triangles.
SEE EXAMPLES 3 AND 4.

a.

b.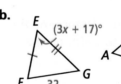

12. Write an inequality describing the possible values of x for each diagram.

a.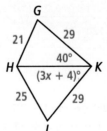

b.

APPLY

13. Reason Airplane A flies 300 miles due east of an airport and then flies 200 miles at 15° north of east. Airplane B flies 200 miles due north and then flies 300 miles at 20° west of north. Which airplane is closer to the airport? Explain how you know.

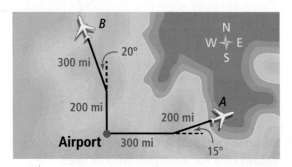

14. Model With Mathematics According to the Hinge Theorem, is the distance between the tips of the hands greater at 4:00 or at 7:00? Explain how the distance changes throughout a day.

15. Mathematical Connections Determine the shortest path from start to finish on the obstacle course.

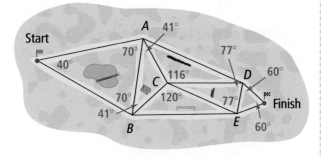

16. Higher Order Thinking When $m\angle 1 = 75$, $d = 43$ in., and when $m\angle 1 = 100$, $d = 54$ in. Neil wants to know how wide a sofa he can buy if he can open the door at most 85°. Using the Hinge Theorem or the Converse of the Hinge Theorem, can you determine the exact value of d when $m\angle 1 = 85$? If you can, explain the method. If not, explain what you can determine about the distance.

ASSESSMENT PRACTICE

17. Which of the following can you conclude from the diagram? Select all that apply.

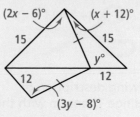

Ⓐ $x < 24$ Ⓒ $y < 12$

Ⓑ $x > 18$ Ⓓ $y > 4$

18. SAT/ACT Which of the following can you conclude from the diagram?

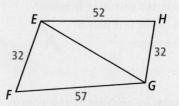

Ⓐ $m\angle EFG = m\angle GHE$ Ⓒ $m\angle GEF > m\angle EGH$

Ⓑ $m\angle FGE = m\angle HEG$ Ⓓ $m\angle FGE > m\angle EGH$

19. Performance Task Abby, Danielle, and Jacy walk from their campsite to get to the lake. The lake is located 3 miles away in the direction of 40° north of west.

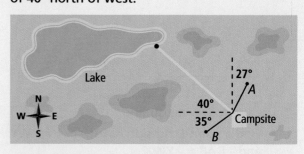

Part A Abby walks along a straight path in the direction of 27° east of north for 1 mile to point A. Using the Hinge Theorem, if Danielle walks along a straight path in the direction of 35° south of west for 1 mile to point B, who is closer to the lake?

Part B Jacy also walks for 1 mile from the campsite along a different straight path than Abby. Her straight-line distance to the lake is shorter than Abby's distance. What directions could Jacy have taken?

Topic Review

1. How are the sides, segments, and angles of triangles related?

Vocabulary Review

Choose the correct term to complete each sentence.

2. The _____ is the point of concurrency of the angle bisectors of a triangle.

3. Three or more lines that intersect at one point are _____.

4. The point of concurrency of the altitudes of a triangle is the _____.

5. A perpendicular segment from a vertex to the line containing the side opposite the vertex is a(n) _____ of a triangle.

6. A point that is the same distance from two points is _____ from the points.

7. A(n) _____ of a triangle has endpoints at a vertex and at the midpoint of the side opposite the vertex.

- altitude
- centroid
- circumcenter
- concurrent
- equidistant
- incenter
- median
- orthocenter

Concepts & Skills Review

| LESSON 7-1 | **Writing Proofs** |

Quick Review

A **proof** uses deductive reasoning to explain why a conjecture is true. A conjecture that has been proven is a **theorem**.

Example

Write a paragraph proof.

Given: $m\angle BDC + m\angle ADE = 180$

Prove: $\angle ADB \cong \angle BDC$

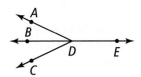

Proof: By definition of supplementary angles, $m\angle ADB + m\angle ADE = 180$. Since it is given that $m\angle BDC + m\angle ADE = 180$, by the Congruent Supplements Theorem, $\angle ADB \cong \angle BDC$.

Practice & Problem Solving

Find the value of each variable and the measure of each labeled angle.

8.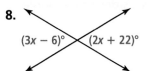
$(3x - 6)°$ $(2x + 22)°$

9.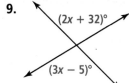
$(2x + 32)°$
$(3x - 5)°$

10. **Construct Arguments** Write a proof.

Given: $m\angle TUV = 90$

Prove: $x = 12$

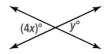
$(4x)°$ $y°$

Parallel Lines

Quick Review

When two **parallel lines** are intersected by a **transversal**, the angle pairs that are formed have special relationships. These angle pairs are either congruent or supplementary angles.

Example

Which angles are supplementary to ∠3?

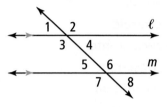

∠1, ∠4, ∠5, ∠8

Practice & Problem Solving

Use the figure for Exercises 11–13.

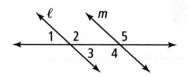

11. Suppose $\ell \parallel m$. What is the measure of each angle if $m\angle 2 = 138$?

    a. $m\angle 1$ **b.** $m\angle 3$ **c.** $m\angle 4$

12. If $m\angle 1 = 3x - 3$ and $m\angle 5 = 7x + 23$, for what value of x is $\ell \parallel m$?

13. Reason The transversal that intersects two parallel lines forms corresponding angles with measures $m\angle 1 = 3x - 7$ and $m\angle 2 = 2x + 12$. What is the measure of each angle?

Perpendicular and Angle Bisectors

Quick Review

Perpendicular bisectors and angle bisectors are related to the segments or angles they bisect:

- Any point on the perpendicular bisector of a segment is **equidistant** from the endpoints of the segment.

- Any point on the bisector of an angle is equidistant from the two sides of the angle.

Example

Find AB.

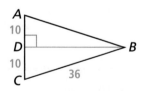

$\overline{DB}$ is the perpendicular bisector of $\overline{AC}$, so $AB = CB$. $AB = 36$.

Practice & Problem Solving

Use the given values to find each unknown.

14. If $PS = 36$, $PQ = 3x + 5$, $QR = 6x - 10$, and $RS = 36$, then $PR = \blacksquare$.

15. If $PS = 4x + 8$, $PQ = 29$, $RS = 5x - 3$, and $QR = 29$, then $PS = \blacksquare$.

16. If $JM = 12$, $LM = 12$, and $m\angle JMK = 25$, then $m\angle KML = \blacksquare$.

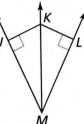

17. If $m\angle JML = 49$, $m\angle JMK = 24.5$, and $JK = 17$, then $KL = \blacksquare$.

18. Reason A point on a perpendicular bisector is 7 cm from each endpoint of the bisected segment and 5 cm from the point of intersection. To the nearest tenth, what is the length of the segment?

Bisectors in Triangles

Quick Review

The perpendicular bisectors of a triangle are concurrent at the point equidistant from the vertices of the triangle. This point is called the **circumcenter**.

The angle bisectors of a triangle are concurrent at a point equidistant from the sides of the triangle. This point is called the **incenter**.

Example

For △ABC, what is the radius of the inscribed circle?

$DF = EF$
$3x = 2x + 16$
$x = 16$

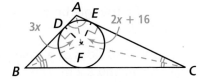

The radius is $DF = 3x = 3(16) = 48$.

Practice & Problem Solving

Identify each point of concurrency.

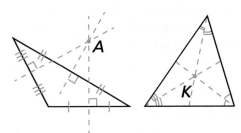

19. incenter

20. circumcenter

Use the diagram to find each unknown quantity.

21. If $m\angle GFL = 34$, and $m\angle GEL = 36$, what is $m\angle FGL$?

22. If $JL = 5$, what is the measure of KL?

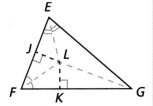

23. **Reason** The circumcenter of a triangle is on one side of the triangle. Explain how to find the area of the circumscribed circle of the triangle given the lengths of the sides.

Medians and Altitudes

Quick Review

A **median** of a triangle is a line segment from the midpoint of one side to the opposite vertex. The medians of a triangle are concurrent at the **centroid**. The distance from a vertex to the centroid is two-thirds the distance of the median from that vertex.

An **altitude** of a triangle is a line segment perpendicular to one side and ending at the opposite vertex. The lines containing the altitudes of a triangle are concurrent at the **orthocenter**.

Example

Q is the centroid of △XYZ. If DZ = 24, what is QZ?

$QZ = \frac{2}{3} DZ$
$QZ = \frac{2}{3} (24)$
$QZ = 16$

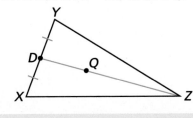

Practice & Problem Solving

Identify each segment type.

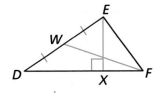

24. median

25. altitude

Find the orthocenter of each triangle with the given set of vertices.

26. (2, 0), (2, 12), (8, 6)   **27.** (7, 8), (9, 6), (5, 4)

28. **Reason** The orthocenter of △ABC is point B. What is the measure of ∠ABC?

29. A plastic triangle is suspended parallel to the ground by a string attached at the centroid. Copy the triangle and show where the string should be attached.

Quick Review

In a triangle, if two sides are not congruent, then the larger angle is opposite the longer side. If two angles are not congruent, then the longer side is opposite the larger angle.

$XY > XZ > YZ$

$m\angle Z > m\angle Y > m\angle X$

The sum of the lengths of any two sides of a triangle is greater than the length of the third side.

$4 + 5 > 7 \qquad 4 + 7 > 5 \qquad 5 + 7 > 4$

Example

Which side of △TUV is the longest?

$m\angle T + m\angle U + m\angle V = 180$

$\qquad 52 + 71 + m\angle V = 180$

$\qquad\qquad\qquad m\angle V = 57$

The largest angle is $\angle U$, so the longest side is $\overline{VT}$.

Practice & Problem Solving

Determine if the lengths can form a triangle.

30. 14, 32, 18   **31.** 14, 25, 29

32. 37, 22, 56   **33.** 87, 35, 41

Use the figure for Exercises 34 and 35.

34. Which angle has the least measure?

35. Which angle has the greatest measure?

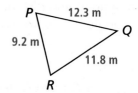

36. Use Structure Why must the sum of two sides of a triangle be greater than the third side?

37. Reason Two sides of a triangular garden are 6.4 m and 8.2 m. The gardener buys fencing for $29.25 per meter. What is the range of total cost of the fencing?

Quick Review

The Hinge Theorem states that if two triangles have two congruent sides, and the included angles are not congruent, then the longer third side is opposite the larger included angle.

Example

Order AC, DF, and GJ from greatest to least.

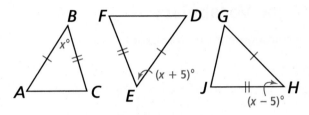

The triangles have two congruent sides.

$\overline{AB} \cong \overline{DE} \cong \overline{GH}$ and $\overline{BC} \cong \overline{EF} \cong \overline{HJ}$

The included angles are not congruent.

$x + 5 > x > x - 5$

Therefore, $DF > AC > GJ$.

Practice & Problem Solving

38. Write an inequality for the possible values of x.

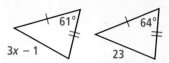

39. Write an inequality for the possible values of x.

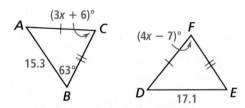

40. Construct Arguments Cameron incorrectly says the Converse of the Hinge Theorem proves that $m\angle S < m\angle W$. Explain his error.

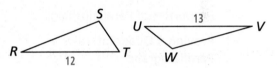

TOPIC
8

Quadrilaterals and Other Polygons

? TOPIC ESSENTIAL QUESTION

How are properties of parallelograms used to solve problems and to classify quadrilaterals?

Topic Overview

Topic Vocabulary

- midsegment of a trapezoid

Digital Experience

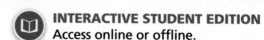

INTERACTIVE STUDENT EDITION Access online or offline.

ACTIVITIES Complete *Explore & Reason*, *Model & Discuss*, and *Critique & Explain* activities. Interact with Examples and Try Its.

ANIMATION View and interact with real-world applications.

PRACTICE Practice what you've learned.

Go online | PearsonRealize.com

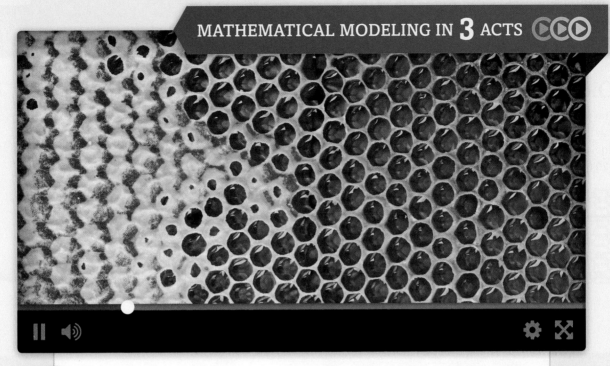

▶ The Mystery Sides

Have you ever looked closely at honeycombs? What shape are they? How do you know? Most often the cells in the honeycombs look like hexagons, but they might also look like circles. Scientists now believe that the bees make circular cells that become hexagonal due to the bees' body heat and natural physical forces.

What are some strategies you use to identify shapes? Think about this during the Mathematical Modeling in 3 Acts lesson.

TOPIC 8

▶ VIDEOS Watch clips to support *Mathematical Modeling in 3 Acts Lessons* and **enVision®** *STEM Projects.*

CONCEPT SUMMARY Review key lesson content through multiple representations.

ASSESSMENT Show what you've learned.

A-Z GLOSSARY Read and listen to English and Spanish definitions.

TUTORIALS Get help from *Virtual Nerd*, right when you need it.

MATH TOOLS Explore math with digital tools and manipulatives.

Video

Did You Know?

The rhinoceros beetle of Central and South America can lift up to **850 times** its own weight. That's equivalent to a 150-pound human lifting some 120,000 pounds, or **30 cars**.

Cargo bay

The world's largest cargo plane can carry more than half a million pounds. The cargo bay is 142 feet long, which is longer than the length of the first airplane *flight* by the Wright brothers, in 1903.

▶ Your Task: Design a Quadrilateral Lift

A 50,000-pound bus needs to be lifted 6 feet off the ground for engine repairs. You and your classmates will analyze quadrilaterals and design a hydraulic lift for a mechanic to use for those repairs.

📶 **Go Online** | PearsonRealize.com

8-1

The Polygon Angle-Sum Theorems

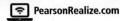 PearsonRealize.com

I CAN... find the sums of the measures of the exterior angles and interior angles of polygons.

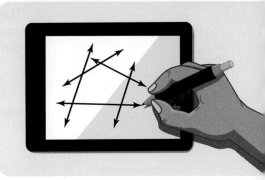

EXPLORE & REASON

Start by drawing a pentagon. Then, for each side of the pentagon, draw the line that includes the side. An example is shown.

A. Choose one pair of lines that intersect at a vertex of the pentagon. Is each of the four angles formed at the vertex an interior angle or an exterior angle of the pentagon?

B. Are the relationships the same for the angles formed by the other pairs of intersecting lines?

C. **Make Sense and Persevere** If you drew a hexagon and the lines that included the sides of the hexagon, would the relationships between the angles at each vertex be the same as those in the pentagon?

? ESSENTIAL QUESTION

How does the number of sides in convex polygons relate to the sums of the measures of the exterior and interior angles?

CONCEPTUAL UNDERSTANDING

EXAMPLE 1 Explore Polygon Interior Angle Sums

How does the number of sides of a convex polygon, *n*, relate to the sum of measures of its interior angles?

You know that the sum of the interior angle measures of a triangle is 180°. Decompose polygons into triangles and look for a pattern.

COMMON ERROR
Remember that *n* represents the number of sides of the polygon, not the number of triangles.

To decompose a convex polygon into triangles, construct all diagonals from one vertex.

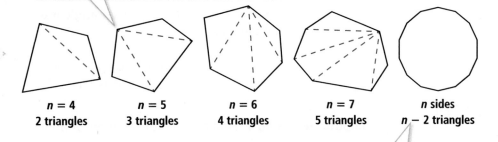

$n = 4$	$n = 5$	$n = 6$	$n = 7$	n sides
2 triangles	3 triangles	4 triangles	5 triangles	$n - 2$ triangles

There are $n - 2$ triangles in every n-sided polygon. Each triangle has an angle sum of 180.

Interior angle sum of an n-sided polygon $= 180 \cdot (n - 2)$

 Try It! **1. a.** How many triangles are formed by drawing diagonals from a vertex in a convex octagon?

b. What is the interior angle sum for a convex octagon?

THEOREM 8-1 Polygon Interior Angle-Sum Theorem

The sum of the measures of the interior angles of a convex *n*-gon is 180 · (*n* − 2).

PROOF: SEE EXERCISE 11.

If...

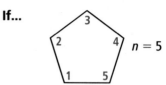

Then... $m\angle 1 + m\angle 2 + m\angle 3 + m\angle 4 + m\angle 5 + m\angle 6 + m\angle 7 = 180 \cdot (7 - 2) = 900$

COROLLARY to Theorem 8-1

The measure of an interior angle of a regular *n*-gon is $\frac{180 \cdot (n - 2)}{n}$.

If...

n = 5

Then... $m\angle 1 = \dfrac{180 \cdot (5 - 2)}{5} = 108$

APPLICATION   👆 **EXAMPLE 2**   **Apply the Polygon Interior Angle-Sum Theorem**

Jenna is building a corner cabinet to fit in a rectangular room. If she builds it with the angles shown, how can she determine whether the cabinet will fit?

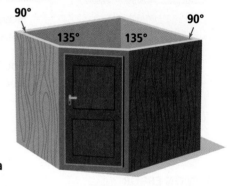

Formulate ◀   Draw a pentagon to represent the cabinet. Find the sum of interior angle measures of the pentagon and then subtract the known angle measures to determine whether the corner angle is a right angle.

To fit in the corner, this angle must be 90°.

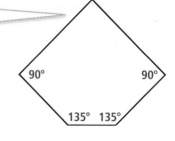

Compute ◀   **Step 1** Find the sum of the interior angles.

$$(n - 2) \cdot 180 = (5 - 2) \cdot 180$$
$$= 3 \cdot 180$$
$$= 540$$

Step 2 Find the missing angle measure.

$$540 - (90 + 135 + 135 + 90) = 90$$

Interpret ◀   The angle is 90°, so the cabinet will fit in the corner.

CONTINUED ON THE NEXT PAGE

EXAMPLE 2 CONTINUED

 Try It!   **2. a.** What is the interior angle sum of a 17-gon?

b. Each angle of a regular *n*-gon measures 172.8. How many sides does the *n*-gon have?

EXAMPLE 3 Understand Exterior Angle Measures of a Polygon

What is the sum of the exterior angle measures of a convex polygon?

You can use what you know about the sum of the interior angle measures of convex polygons to find the sum of the exterior angle measures.

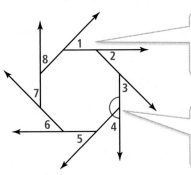

Remember, one side of the polygon and the extension of an adjacent side form an exterior angle.

Each interior and exterior angle pair forms a linear pair, which measures 180°.

GENERALIZE
How do you know that a polygon with *n* sides has *n* angle pairs?

The sum of the measures of *n* interior and exterior angle pairs is $180 \cdot n$.

sum of exterior angle measures	=	sum of interior and exterior angle measures	−	sum of interior angle measures
	=	$180n$	−	$180(n - 2)$

$$= 180n - 180n + 360$$

$$= 360$$

The sum of the exterior angle measures of any convex polygon is 360.

 Try It!   **3.** What is the sum of exterior angle measures of a convex 17-gon?

THEOREM 8-2 Polygon Exterior Angle-Sum Theorem

The sum of the measures of the exterior angles of a convex polygon, one at each vertex, is 360.

If...

Then... $m\angle 1 + m\angle 2 + m\angle 3 + m\angle 4 + m\angle 5 = 360$

PROOF: SEE EXERCISE 15.

EXAMPLE 4 Find an Exterior Angle Measure

Suppose ∠1 ≅ ∠3, m∠1 = 3x, and m∠2 = 2x. What is the measure of each exterior angle?

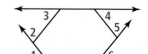

Step 1 Find x.

$$m\angle1 + m\angle2 + m\angle3 + m\angle4 + m\angle5 = 360$$

$$m\angle1 + m\angle2 + m\angle1 + 90 + 90 = 360$$

$$3x + 2x + 3x + 180 = 360$$

$$8x = 180$$

$$x = 22.5$$

> The exterior angle sum of a polygon is 360.

MAKE SENSE AND PERSEVERE
Think about how to verify your answers. What must be true if your answers are correct?

Step 2 Use the value of x to determine the measure of each exterior angle.

m∠1 = 3x	m∠2 = 2x	m∠3 = m∠1	m∠4 = 90
m∠1 = 3(22.5)	m∠2 = 2(22.5)	m∠3 = 67.5	m∠5 = 90
m∠1 = 67.5	m∠2 = 45		

 Try It! 4. Suppose ∠1 ≅ ∠3 ≅ ∠4 ≅ ∠6, ∠2 ≅ ∠5, and m∠3 = m∠2 + 30. What is m∠4?

EXAMPLE 5 Find the Measures of Interior Angles

What are the measures of the interior angles of the pentagon shown?

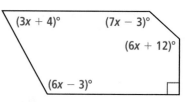

Step 1 Apply the Polygon Interior Angle-Sum Theorem and solve for x.

$$90 + (6x - 3) + (3x + 4) + (7x - 3) + (6x + 12) = 180 \cdot (5 - 2)$$

$$90 + 22x + 10 = 540$$

$$22x = 440$$

$$x = 20$$

Step 2 Substitute the value of x to find each angle measure.

6x − 3 = 6(20) − 3	3x + 4 = 3(20) + 4
= 117	= 64
7x − 3 = 7(20) − 3	6x + 12 = 6(20) + 12
= 137	= 132

The measures of the interior angles are 90, 117, 64, 137, and 132.

 Try It! 5. The measure of each interior angle of a regular 100-gon is (3x + 26.4). What is the value of x?

Go Online | PearsonRealize.com

CONCEPT SUMMARY Polygon Angle Sums

THEOREM 8-1 ▶ **Polygon Interior Angle-Sum Theorem**

The sum of the measures of the interior angles of a convex polygon is $180 \cdot (n - 2)$, where n is the number of sides of the polygon.

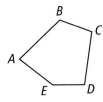

$m\angle A + m\angle B + m\angle C + m\angle D + m\angle E = 180(5 - 2)$
$= 540$

THEOREM 8-2 ▶ **Polygon Exterior Angle-Sum Theorem**

The sum of the measures of the exterior angles of a convex polygon, one at each vertex, is 360.

$m\angle 1 + m\angle 2 + m\angle 3 + m\angle 4 = 360$

☑ Do You UNDERSTAND?

1. ❓ **ESSENTIAL QUESTION** How does the number of sides in convex polygons relate to the sums of the measures of the exterior and interior angles?

2. **Error Analysis** In the calculation shown, what is Danielle's error?

> The sum of the measures of the exterior angles of a 25-gon is
> $180 \cdot (25 - 2) = 4{,}140$. ✗

3. **Make Sense and Persevere** What is the minimum amount of information needed to find the sum of the interior angles of a regular polygon?

4. **Reason** A convex polygon can be decomposed into 47 triangles. How many sides does the polygon have? Explain.

Do You KNOW HOW?

Use polygon A for Exercises 5 and 6.

5. What is the sum of the measures of the interior angles?

6. What is the sum of the measures of the exterior angles?

Polygon A

Use polygon B for Exercises 7 and 8.

7. What is the value of y?

8. What is the value of x?

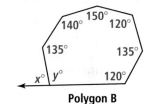

Polygon B

9. What are the measures of the exterior angles of the polygon shown?

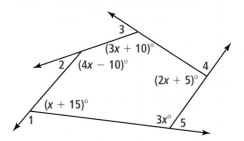

10. The sum of the interior angles of a regular n-gon is $6{,}120°$. What is the measure of each interior angle?

UNDERSTAND

11. **Construct Arguments** Write a proof of the Polygon Interior Angle-Sum Theorem.

12. **Make Sense and Persevere** What are the measures of the angles in the right triangles formed by the two regular pentagons shown?

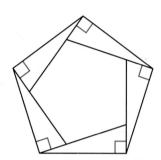

13. **Reason** Explain why a regular polygon cannot have an interior angle that is 40°.

14. **Error Analysis** Jayesh makes the calculation shown to find the measure of each interior angle of a regular nonagon. What is his error?

> Sum of measure of exterior angles:
> $180 \cdot 9 = 1,620$
> Sum of measure of interior angles:
> $1,620 \div 7 = 231$

15. **Construct Arguments** Write a proof of the Polygon Exterior Angle-Sum Theorem.

16. **Higher Order Thinking** The star shown is constructed by extending each side of a regular pentagon. Explain why the surrounding triangles are isosceles and congruent.

PRACTICE

For Exercises 17 and 18, find the sum of the interior angles and the measure of each angle for the given regular polygon. SEE EXAMPLES 1 AND 2

17. 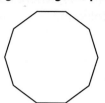   18.

19. How many sides does a regular polygon have if the measure of each interior angle is 160°? SEE EXAMPLES 1 AND 2

20. What is the measure of each exterior angle of a regular polygon with 72 sides? SEE EXAMPLE 3

21. How many sides does a regular polygon with an exterior angle measure of 60° have? SEE EXAMPLE 3

22. What is the value of x? What is the measure of each exterior angle? SEE EXAMPLE 4

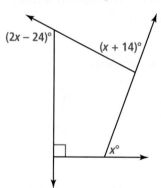

For Exercises 23 and 24, find the value of x and the measure of each interior angle. SEE EXAMPLE 5

23.
$(4x - 80)°$ $(4x - 80)°$
$(2x + 50)°$ $(2x + 50)°$
$(2x + 50)°$ $(2x + 50)°$
$(4x - 80)°$ $(4x - 80)°$

24.
$(3x - 20)°$ $(3x - 20)°$
$4x°$ $4x°$
$(3x - 20)°$ $(3x - 20)°$

APPLY

25. Model With Mathematics An airplane is navigating a polygon-shaped course. Each turn is labeled with the measure of the external angle at the striped post. What is $m\angle 1$?

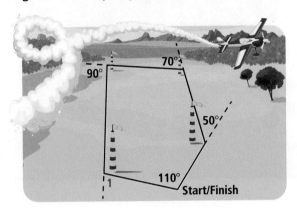

26. Use Structure A music producer needs to soundproof a wall with nonoverlapping foam panels consisting of regular polygons. When placed, there cannot be any space between the figures. Which of the regular polygons can she use? Explain.

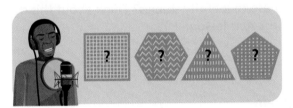

27. Mathematical Connections Ricardo wants to install two security cameras at point A so the parking lot from side $\overline{AE}$ to side $\overline{AB}$ of the building can be monitored. Can he use two cameras, both with a field of view of 110°, installed at point A? Explain. If not, what is the minimum field of view that each camera should have?

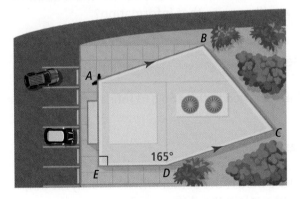

ASSESSMENT PRACTICE

28. Match the number of sides of a regular polygon with the measure of each interior angle.

I.   4   A. 120

II. 6   B. 157.5

III. 16   C. 160

VI. 18   D. 90

29. SAT/ACT Suppose the figure below is a regular polygon. What is the value of n? Round to the nearest whole number.

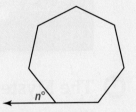

Ⓐ 45   Ⓑ 51   Ⓒ 129   Ⓓ 135

30. Performance Task The tables of a conference room are the same size, and all have the shape of a trapezoid. The conference coordinator wants to arrange the tables so they form a regular polygon.

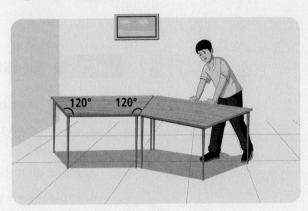

Part A Can the tables be arranged to form a regular polygon? Explain.

Part B If they can be arranged to form a regular polygon, how many tables are needed? If not, what should the measure of the 120° angle be changed to so that the tables can be arranged to form a regular polygon?

Part C What should the measures of the angles of the tables be if they can be arranged to form a regular pentagon?

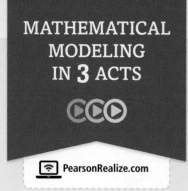
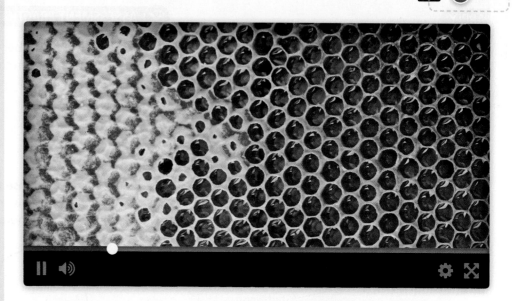

Video

▶ The Mystery Sides

Have you ever looked closely at honeycombs? What shape are they? How do you know? Most often the cells in the honeycombs look like hexagons, but they might also look like circles. Scientists now believe that bees make circular cells that become hexagonal due to the bees' body heat and natural physical forces.

What are some strategies you use to identify shapes? Think about this during the Mathematical Modeling in 3 Acts lesson.

Scan for
Multimedia

ACT 1 Identify the Problem

1. What is the first question that comes to mind after watching the video?

2. Write down the main question you will answer about what you saw in the video.

3. Make an initial conjecture that answers this main question.

4. Explain how you arrived at your conjecture.

5. What information will be useful to know to answer the main question? How can you get it? How will you use that information?

ACT 2 Develop a Model

6. Use the math that you have learned in this Topic to refine your conjecture.

ACT 3 Interpret the Results

7. Did your refined conjecture match the actual answer exactly? If not, how is it different? What might explain the difference?

8-2

Kites and Trapezoids

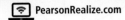
I CAN... use triangle congruence to understand kites and trapezoids.

VOCABULARY
• midsegment of a trapezoid

CRITIQUE & EXPLAIN

Manuel draws a diagram of kite *PQRS* with $\overleftrightarrow{QS}$ as the line of symmetry over a design of a kite-shaped key fob. He makes a list of conclusions based on the diagram.

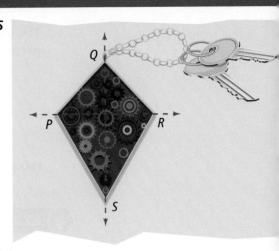

- $\overline{PR} \perp \overline{QS}$
- $\overline{QP} \cong \overline{QR}$
- $\overline{SP} \cong \overline{SR}$
- $\overline{PR}$ bisects $\overline{QS}$.
- $\triangle PQR$ is an equilateral triangle.
- $\triangle PSR$ is an isosceles triangle.

A. Which of Manuel's conclusions do you agree with? Which do you disagree with? Explain.

B. Use Structure What other conclusions are supported by the diagram?

? ESSENTIAL QUESTION

How are diagonals and angle measures related in kites and trapezoids?

CONCEPTUAL UNDERSTANDING

✋ EXAMPLE 1   Investigate the Diagonals of a Kite

How are the diagonals of a kite related?

A kite has two pairs of congruent adjacent sides.

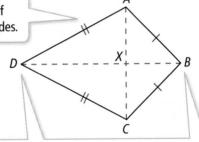

Point *B* is equidistant from the endpoints of $\overline{AC}$, as is *D*, so they lie on the perpendicular bisector of $\overline{AC}$.

STUDY TIP
Remember that you must show that both *B* and *D* are on the perpendicular bisector in order to show that one diagonal is the perpendicular bisector of the other. It is not sufficient to show that only one is on the perpendicular bisector.

The diagonals of a kite are perpendicular to each other. Exactly one diagonal bisects the other.

Try It!

1. a. What is the measure of $\angle AXB$?

b. If $AX = 3.8$, what is AC?

c. If $BD = 10$, does $BX = 5$? Explain.

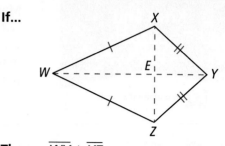
THEOREM 8-3

The diagonals of a kite are perpendicular.

PROOF: SEE EXERCISE 12.

If...

Then... $\overline{WY} \perp \overline{XZ}$

EXAMPLE 2 ☞ **Use the Diagonals of a Kite**

Quadrilateral *PQRS* is a kite with diagonals $\overline{QS}$ and $\overline{PR}$.

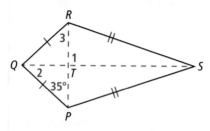

A. What is $m\angle 1$?

The diagonals of a kite are perpendicular, so $m\angle 1 = 90$.

B. What is $m\angle 2$?

The sum of the angles of $\triangle PQT$ is 180.

$$m\angle 2 + 35 + 90 = 180$$

$$m\angle 2 = 55$$

C. What is $m\angle 3$?

Since $\triangle PQR$ is an isosceles triangle, $\angle 3 \cong \angle QPT$.

So, $m\angle 3 = 35$.

COMMON ERROR
You may incorrectly assume angles are congruent just from their appearance. Always check that you can prove congruence first.

☑ **Try It!** 2. Quadrilateral *WXYZ* is a kite.

   a. What is $m\angle 1$?

   b. What is $m\angle 2$?

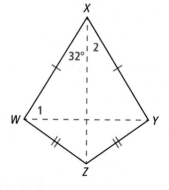

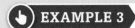

APPLICATION

EXAMPLE 3 Explore Parts of an Isosceles Trapezoid

Kiyo is designing a trapezoid-shaped roof. In order for the roof to be symmetric, the overlapping triangles $\triangle DAB$ and $\triangle ADC$ must be congruent. Will the roof be symmetric?

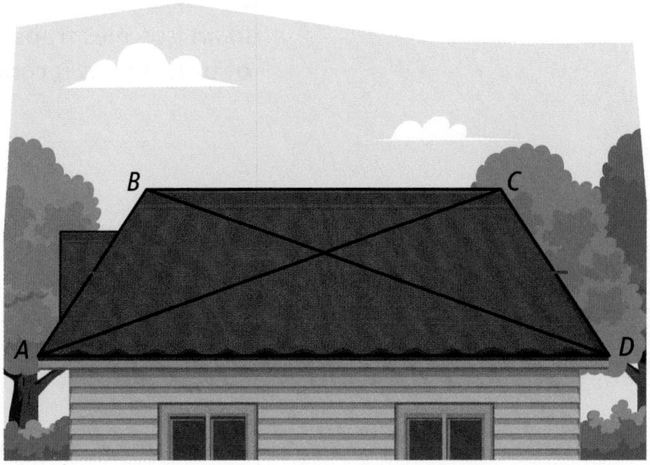
B
C
A
D

Step 1 Show $\triangle ABE \cong \triangle DCF$.

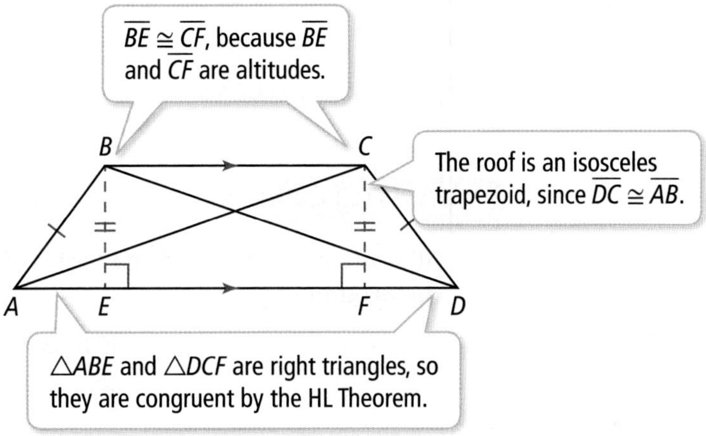
$\overline{BE} \cong \overline{CF}$, because $\overline{BE}$ and $\overline{CF}$ are altitudes.
The roof is an isosceles trapezoid, since $\overline{DC} \cong \overline{AB}$.
$\triangle ABE$ and $\triangle DCF$ are right triangles, so they are congruent by the HL Theorem.
B
C
A
E
F
D

GENERALIZE
How do the lengths of the diagonals and the way they intersect relate to the sides of a quadrilateral?

Step 2 Show $\triangle DAB \cong \triangle ADC$.

By CPCTC, $\angle DAB \cong \angle ADC$. By the Reflexive Property of Congruency, $\overline{AD} \cong \overline{DA}$. So, $\triangle DAB \cong \triangle ADC$ by SAS.

The overlapping triangles are congruent, so the roof is symmetric.

Try It! **3. a.** Given isosceles trapezoid $PQRS$, what are $m\angle P$, $m\angle Q$, and $m\angle S$?

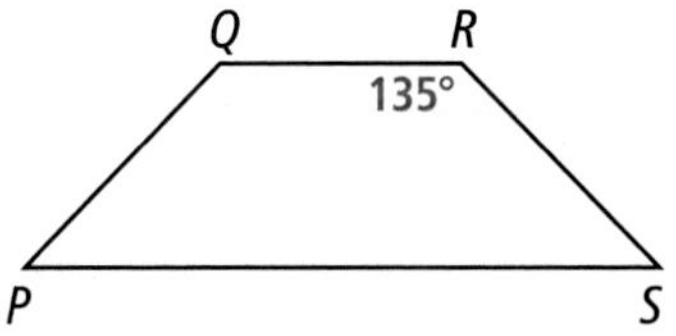
Q
R
135°
P
S

b. Given $\overline{ST} \parallel \overline{RU}$, what is the measure of $\angle TUR$?

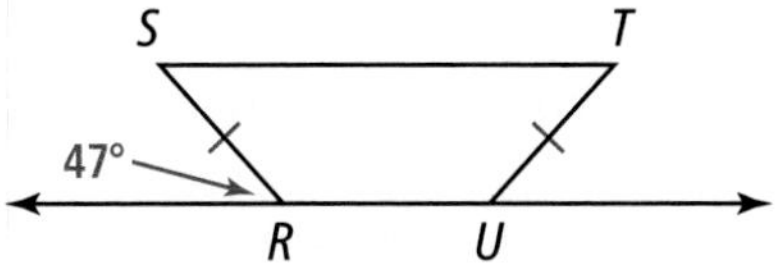
S
T
47°
R
U

THEOREM 8-4

In an isosceles trapezoid, each pair of base angles is congruent.

If...

PROOF: LESSON 6-3, EXERCISE 17.

Then... ∠BAD ≅ ∠CDA, ∠ABC ≅ ∠DCB

THEOREM 8-5

The diagonals of an isosceles trapezoid are congruent.

If...

PROOF: SEE EXERCISE 18.

Then... $\overline{AC} \cong \overline{DB}$

EXAMPLE 4   **Solve Problems Involving Isosceles Trapezoids**

All horizontal beams of the high-voltage transmission tower are parallel to the ground.

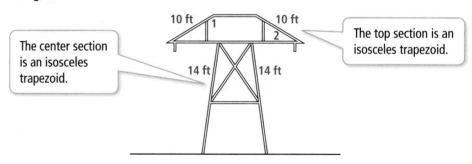

The center section is an isosceles trapezoid.

The top section is an isosceles trapezoid.

A. If $m\angle 1 = 138$, what is $m\angle 2$?

The sum of the interior angle measures of a quadrilateral is 360.

$$m\angle 1 + m\angle 1 + m\angle 2 + m\angle 2 = 360$$
$$138 + 138 + 2(m\angle 2) = 360$$
$$276 + 2(m\angle 2) = 360$$
$$2(m\angle 2) = 84$$
$$m\angle 2 = 42$$

The base angles are congruent.

The measure of ∠2 is 42.

CONTINUED ON THE NEXT PAGE

MAKE SENSE AND PERSEVERE
What other strategy might you use to solve this problem?

Go Online | PearsonRealize.com

EXAMPLE 4 CONTINUED

GENERALIZE
Why might this strategy work for isosceles trapezoids but not for trapezoids with noncongruent legs?

B. One cross support in the center of the tower measures $4c + 3$, and the other measures $6c - 5$. What is the length of each cross support?

The cross supports are diagonals of an isosceles trapezoid, so they are congruent.

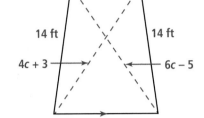

Step 1 Find the value of c.

$$4c + 3 = 6c - 5$$
$$8 = 2c$$
$$4 = c$$

Step 2 Find the lengths of the diagonals.

$$4c + 3 = 4(4) + 3$$
$$= 19$$
$$6c - 5 = 6(4) - 5$$
$$= 19$$

Each cross support measures 19 ft in length.

☑ **Try It!** **4.** Given isosceles trapezoid *MNOP* where the given expressions represent the measures of the diagonals, what is the value of a?

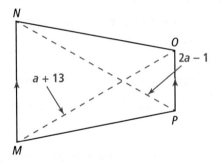

THEOREM 8-6 Trapezoid Midsegment Theorem

In a trapezoid, the segment containing the midpoints of the two legs is parallel to the bases, and its length is half the sum of the lengths of the bases.

If...

Then... $\overline{XY} \parallel \overline{AD}$, $\overline{XY} \parallel \overline{BC}$, and $XY = \frac{1}{2}(AD + BC)$

PROOF: SEE LESSON 11-2.

APPLICATION

🖐 **EXAMPLE 5** Apply the Trapezoid Midsegment Theorem

Paxton makes trapezoidal handbags for her friends. She stiches decorative trim along the top, middle, and bottom on both sides of the handbags. How much trim does she need for three handbags? Explain.

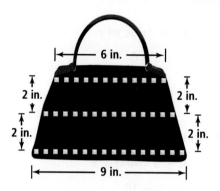

6 in.

2 in.   2 in.

2 in.   2 in.

9 in.

Formulate ◀ The top and bottom sides of the handbag are the bases of a trapezoid. The left and right sides are the legs. Since the middle segment divides both legs in half, it is the midsegment of the trapezoid. The **midsegment of a trapezoid** is the segment that connects the midpoints of the legs.

Let x represent the length of the midsegment in inches.

Compute ◀ **Step 1** Find the value of x.

$$x = \frac{1}{2}(6 + 9)$$

Apply the Trapezoid Midsegment Theorem with the base lengths 6 and 9.

$$x = 7.5$$

The length of the midsegment is 7.5 in.

Step 2 Find the amount of trim that she needs.

First, find the amount for one side.

$$6 + 9 + 7.5 = 22.5$$

Then, multiply by 2 for the number of sides per handbag and by 3 for the number of handbags.

$$22.5 \cdot 2 \cdot 3 = 135$$

Interpret ◀ Paxton needs 135 inches of trim.

☑ **Try It!** 5. Given trapezoid *JKLM*, what is *KL*?

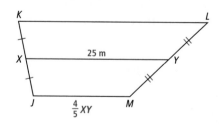

📱 Go Online | PearsonRealize.com

Concept Summary   ✓ Assess

WORDS	Kites	Trapezoids

Kites

A kite is a quadrilateral with two pairs of adjacent sides congruent and no pairs of opposite sides congruent. Exactly one diagonal is a perpendicular bisector of the other.

Trapezoids

A trapezoid is a quadrilateral with exactly one pair of parallel sides. The length of the midsegment is the average of the lengths of the two bases. A trapezoid with congruent legs is an isosceles trapezoid that has congruent base angles and congruent diagonals.

DIAGRAMS

Quadrilateral *ABCD* is a kite.

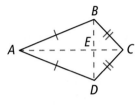

$$\overline{AC} \perp \overline{BD}$$
$$BE = ED$$

Quadrilateral *RSTU* is an isosceles trapezoid.

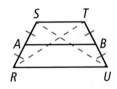

$$\overline{SU} \cong \overline{TR}$$
$$AB = \frac{1}{2}(ST + RU)$$

$$\overline{AB} \parallel \overline{ST} \parallel \overline{RU}$$
$$m\angle S = m\angle T$$
$$m\angle R = m\angle U$$

✓ Do You UNDERSTAND?

1. **ESSENTIAL QUESTION** How are diagonals and angle measures related in kites and trapezoids?

2. **Error Analysis** What is Reagan's error?

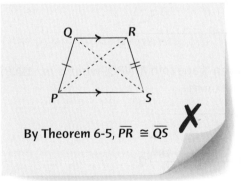

By Theorem 6-5, $\overline{PR} \cong \overline{QS}$ ✗

3. **Vocabulary** If $\overline{XY}$ is the midsegment of a trapezoid, what must be true about point *X* and point *Y*?

4. **Construct Arguments** Emaan says every kite is composed of 4 right triangles. Is he correct? Explain.

Do You KNOW HOW?

For Exercises 5–7, use kite *WXYZ* to find the measures.

5. $m\angle XQY$

6. $m\angle YZQ$

7. WY

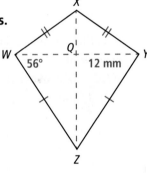

For Exercises 8–10, use trapezoid *DEFG* with $EG = 21$ ft and $m\angle DGF = 77$ to find each measure.

8. ED

9. DF

10. $m\angle DEF$

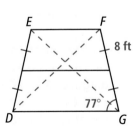

11. What is the length of $\overline{PQ}$?

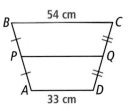

UNDERSTAND

12. Construct Arguments Write a two-column proof to show that the diagonals of a kite are perpendicular.

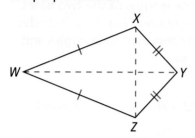

13. Prove that the perpendicular bisector of $\overline{BC}$ is also the perpendicular bisector of $\overline{AD}$. (*Hint:* Extend $\overline{BA}$ and $\overline{CD}$ to meet at point M, and show that the perpendicular bisector of $\overline{BC}$ contains M.)

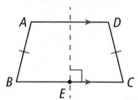

14. Error Analysis What is Emery's error?

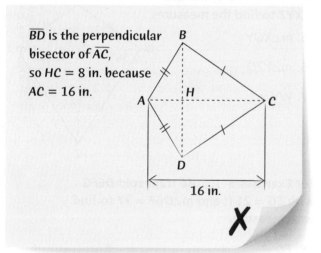

$\overline{BD}$ is the perpendicular bisector of $\overline{AC}$, so $HC = 8$ in. because $AC = 16$ in.

16 in.

✗

15. Higher Order Thinking Given kite *JKLM* with diagonal $\overline{KM}$, $JK < JM$, and $KL < LM$, prove that $\angle JMK$ is congruent to $\angle LMK$.

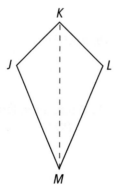

PRACTICE

16. Given kite *ABCD*, in which $AN = 4.6$ m, what is *AC*? SEE EXAMPLE 1

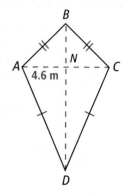

17. Given kite *RSTU*, what is $m\angle RUS$? SEE EXAMPLE 2

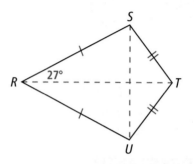

18. Write a two-column proof to show that the diagonals of an isosceles trapezoid are congruent. SEE EXAMPLES 3 AND 4

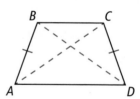

19. Given trapezoid *MNPQ*, what is $m\angle MNP$? SEE EXAMPLE 4

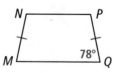

20. Given trapezoid *WXYZ*, what is *XY*? SEE EXAMPLE 5

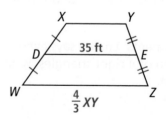

APPLY

21. Model With Mathematics Gregory plans to make a kite like the one shown. He has 1,700 square inches of plastic sheeting. Does Gregory have enough plastic to make the kite? Explain.

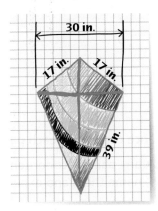

22. Reason Coach Murphy uses the map to plan a 2-mile run for the track team. How many times will the team run the route shown?

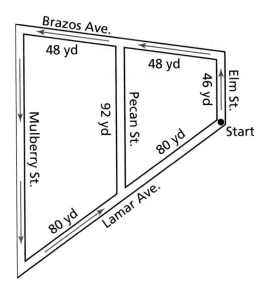

23. Use Structure Abby builds a bench with the seat parallel to the ground. She bends pipe to make the leg and seat supports. At what angles should she bend the pipe? Explain.

ASSESSMENT PRACTICE

24. The ___?___ of a kite are always ___?___.

25. SAT/ACT Given trapezoid $ABCD$, what is the length of $\overline{XY}$?

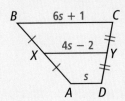

Ⓐ $3\frac{3}{5}$　Ⓑ $4\frac{2}{3}$　Ⓒ 5　Ⓓ 11　Ⓔ 18

26. Performance Task Cindy is a member of a volunteer group that built the play structure shown.

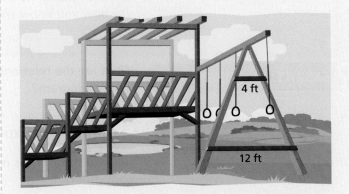

Part A Cindy wants to add three more boards evenly spaced between and parallel to the bottom and top boards of the triangular frame. Based on the lengths of the top and bottom boards shown, what will be the lengths of each of the three additional boards? Explain.

Part B How can Cindy determine where along to nail the new boards into the existing frame?

Part C What other measurements should Cindy find to be certain that the boards will fit exactly onto the triangular frame?

I CAN... use the properties of parallel lines, diagonals, and triangles to investigate parallelograms.

✋ CRITIQUE & EXPLAIN

Kennedy lists all the pairs of congruent triangles she finds in quadrilateral *ABCD*.

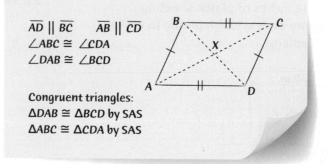

$\overline{AD} \parallel \overline{BC}$ $\overline{AB} \parallel \overline{CD}$
$\angle ABC \cong \angle CDA$
$\angle DAB \cong \angle BCD$

Congruent triangles:
$\triangle DAB \cong \triangle BCD$ by SAS
$\triangle ABC \cong \triangle CDA$ by SAS

A. Is Kennedy's justification for triangle congruence correct for each pair?

B. Look for Relationships Did Kennedy overlook any pairs of congruent triangles? If not, explain how you know. If so, name them and explain how you know they are congruent.

❓ ESSENTIAL QUESTION

What are the relationships of the sides, the angles, and the diagonals of a parallelogram?

CONCEPTUAL UNDERSTANDING

✋ EXAMPLE 1   Explore Opposite Sides of Parallelograms

How do the lengths of the opposite sides of a parallelogram compare to each other?

Quadrilateral *ABCD* is a parallelogram.

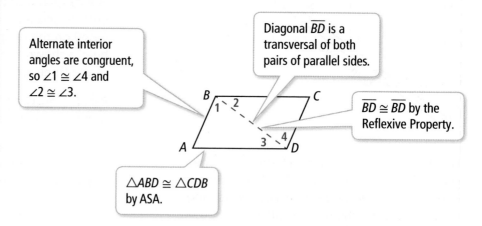

Alternate interior angles are congruent, so $\angle 1 \cong \angle 4$ and $\angle 2 \cong \angle 3$.

Diagonal $\overline{BD}$ is a transversal of both pairs of parallel sides.

$\overline{BD} \cong \overline{BD}$ by the Reflexive Property.

$\triangle ABD \cong \triangle CDB$ by ASA.

USE STRUCTURE
Can you use the same strategy to show other relationships in a parallelogram?

By CPCTC, $\overline{AD} \cong \overline{CB}$ and $\overline{AB} \cong \overline{CD}$, so the lengths of the opposite sides are congruent to each other.

✔ Try It!   1. Given parallelogram *WXYZ*, what is *YZ*?

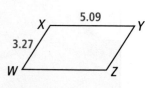

5.09
3.27

THEOREM 8-7

If a quadrilateral is a parallelogram, then its opposite sides are congruent.

PROOF: SEE EXERCISE 13.

If...

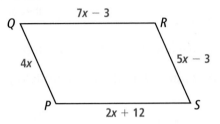

$\overline{WX} \parallel \overline{ZY}$
$\overline{WZ} \parallel \overline{XY}$

Then... $\overline{WX} \cong \overline{YZ}$
$\overline{WZ} \cong \overline{XY}$

 EXAMPLE 2 Use Opposite Sides of a Parallelogram

Quadrilateral *PQRS* is a parallelogram.

Q ——— 7x − 3 ——— R
4x   5x − 3
P ——— 2x + 12 ——— S

STUDY TIP
Remember there is often more than one way to solve a problem. You could also find the value of *x* by solving the equation $4x = 5x − 3$, since $\overline{QP}$ and $\overline{RS}$ are also opposite sides of the parallelogram.

A. What is the value of *x*?

$$7x − 3 = 2x + 12$$

$\overline{QR} \cong \overline{PS}$ because they are opposite sides of a parallelogram.

$$5x = 15$$

$$x = 3$$

B. What is the length of each side of *PQRS*?

$PQ = 4x$	$QR = 7x − 3$	$RS = 5x − 3$	$PS = 2x + 12$
$= 4(3)$	$= 7(3) − 3$	$= 5(3) − 3$	$= 2(3) + 12$
$= 12$	$= 21 − 3$	$= 15 − 3$	$= 6 + 12$
	$= 18$	$= 12$	$= 18$

✓ **Try It!** **2.** The 600-meter fence around City Park forms a parallelogram. The fence along Chaco Road is twice as long as the fence along Grover Lane. What is the length of the fence along Jones Road?

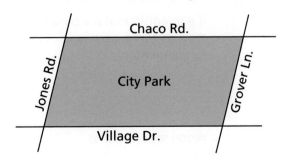

EXAMPLE 3   Explore Angle Measures in Parallelograms

A. How are consecutive angles in a parallelogram related?

You can use what you know about angle relationships formed when parallel lines are cut by a transversal.

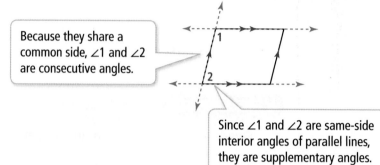

Because they share a common side, ∠1 and ∠2 are consecutive angles.

Since ∠1 and ∠2 are same-side interior angles of parallel lines, they are supplementary angles.

Consecutive angles ∠1 and ∠2 are supplementary.

B. How are opposite angles in a parallelogram related?

Consecutive angles ∠1 and ∠2 are supplementary.

Consecutive angles ∠2 and ∠3 are supplementary.

In the figure, ∠1 and ∠3 are opposite angles. Both angles are supplementary to ∠2, so opposite angles in a parallelogram are congruent.

 Try It!   **3. a.** Given parallelogram *ABCD*, what are *m∠A* and *m∠C*?

b. What is *m∠B*?

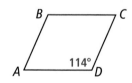

THEOREM 8-8

If a quadrilateral is a parallelogram, then its consecutive angles are supplementary.

If...

$\overline{AB} \parallel \overline{DC}$
$\overline{AD} \parallel \overline{BC}$

Then... $m\angle A + m\angle B = 180$
$m\angle B + m\angle C = 180$
$m\angle C + m\angle D = 180$
$m\angle D + m\angle A = 180$

PROOF: SEE EXERCISE 15.

THEOREM 8-9

If a quadrilateral is parallelogram, then opposite angles are congruent.

If...

$\overline{AB} \parallel \overline{DC}$
$\overline{AD} \parallel \overline{BC}$

Then... $\angle A \cong \angle C$
$\angle B \cong \angle D$

PROOF: SEE EXERCISE 23.

⏺ **EXAMPLE 4** **Use Angles of a Parallelogram**

The green shape in the fabric design is a parallelogram. The measure of ∠2 is twice the measure of ∠1. What are $m\angle 1$, $m\angle 2$, and $m\angle 3$?

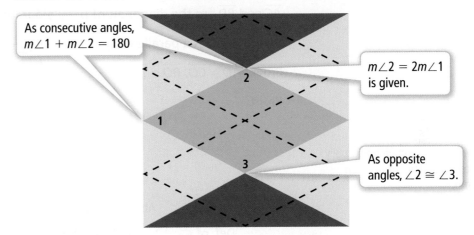

As consecutive angles, $m\angle 1 + m\angle 2 = 180$

$m\angle 2 = 2m\angle 1$ is given.

As opposite angles, $\angle 2 \cong \angle 3$.

COMMON ERROR
You may incorrectly write $m\angle 1 = 2m\angle 2$, but $m\angle 1 = 2m\angle 2$ means that $m\angle 1$ is twice $m\angle 2$.

Find $m\angle 1$.

$m\angle 1 + m\angle 2 = 180$

$m\angle 1 + 2m\angle 1 = 180$

$m\angle 1 = 60$

Find $m\angle 2$.

$m\angle 2 = 2m\angle 1$

$m\angle 2 = 2(60)$

$m\angle 2 = 120$

Find $m\angle 3$.

$m\angle 3 = m\angle 2$

$m\angle 3 = 120$

The measures of ∠1, ∠2, and ∠3 are 60, 120, and 120, respectively.

✅ **Try It!** **4.** Use the parallelogram shown.

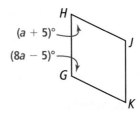

a. Given parallelogram *GHJK*, what is the value of *a*?

b. What are $m\angle G$, $m\angle H$, $m\angle J$, and $m\angle K$?

THEOREM 8-10

If a quadrilateral is a parallelogram, then its diagonals bisect each other.

PROOF: SEE EXAMPLE 5.

If...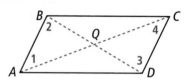

$\overline{WX} \parallel \overline{ZY}$
$\overline{WZ} \parallel \overline{XY}$

Then... $\overline{AW} \cong \overline{AY}$
$\overline{AX} \cong \overline{AZ}$

PROOF

EXAMPLE 5   **Explore the Diagonals of a Parallelogram**

How are the diagonals of a parallelogram related?

$\overline{AC}$ and $\overline{BD}$ are the diagonals of parallelogram *ABCD*.

Given: *ABCD* is a parallelogram.

Prove: $\overline{AQ} \cong \overline{CQ}, \overline{BQ} \cong \overline{DQ}$

Proof:

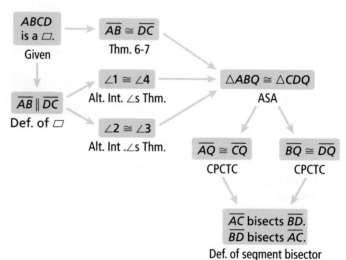

STUDY TIP
The given information is usually the best statement to begin a proof.

 Try It!   **5.** Use parallelogram *RSTU* with *SU* = 35 and *KT* = 19.

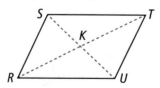

a. What is *SK*?

b. What is *RT*?

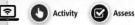

APPLICATION    **EXAMPLE 6**   **Find Unknown Lengths in a Parallelogram**

Corey stamps the orange and purple pattern shown on the front of a poster she is making. How many times will she need to stamp the design to make a row 60 cm wide along the dashed line?

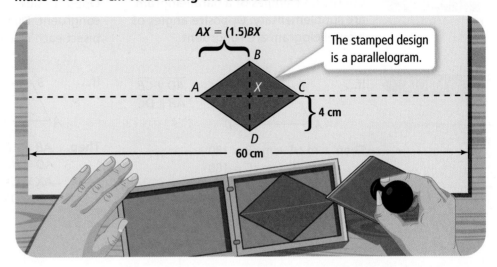

Formulate ◄ By Theorem 8-10, the diagonals $\overline{AC}$ and $\overline{BD}$ bisect each other. So $\overline{BX} \cong \overline{DX}$, and $\overline{AX} \cong \overline{CX}$.

Compute ◄ **Step 1** Determine the length of the diagonal, $\overline{AC}$.

$$BX = DX$$ ⟵ Diagonals bisect each other.

$$BX = 4$$

$$AX = 1.5\ BX$$ ⟵ Given

$$AX = 1.5(4)$$

$$AX = 6$$

$$AC = 2(AX)$$ ⟵ Diagonals bisect each other.

$$AC = 2(6)$$

$$AC = 12$$

Step 2 Find the number of times Corey needs to stamp.

$$60 \div 12 = 5$$

Interpret ◄ Corey will need to stamp the design 5 times to make a row 60 cm wide.

✓ **Try It!** **6.** Given parallelogram $GHJK$, if $PK = 4$ and $HK = \frac{2}{3}(GJ)$, what is GP?

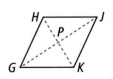

CONCEPT SUMMARY Properties of Parallelograms

Angles of Parallelograms	Sides and Diagonals of Parallelograms
WORDS Consecutive angles of a parallelogram are supplementary. Opposite angles of a parallelogram are congruent.	Opposite sides of a parallelogram are congruent. Diagonals of a parallelogram bisect each other.

SYMBOLS

If...

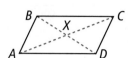

$\overline{AD} \parallel \overline{CB}$
$\overline{AB} \parallel \overline{DC}$

Then... $m\angle A + m\angle B = 180$
$m\angle B + m\angle C = 180$
$m\angle C + m\angle D = 180$
$m\angle D + m\angle A = 180$
$m\angle A = m\angle C$
$m\angle B = m\angle D$

If...

$\overline{AD} \parallel \overline{CB}$
$\overline{AB} \parallel \overline{DC}$

Then... $AB = CD$
$AD = BC$
$AX = CX$
$BX = DX$

Do You UNDERSTAND?

1. **ESSENTIAL QUESTION** What are the relationships of the sides, the angles, and the diagonals of a parallelogram?

2. **Error Analysis** What is Carla's error?

$\overline{PR} \cong \overline{QS}$

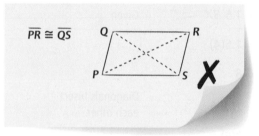

3. **Make Sense and Persevere** If you knew the length of $\overline{DF}$ in parallelogram *DEFG*, how would you find the length of $\overline{DK}$? Explain.

4. **Reason** Given parallelogram *JKLM*, what could the expression $180 - (3x + 8)$ represent? Explain.

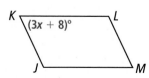

Do You KNOW HOW?

For Exercises 5 and 6, use parallelogram *ABCD* to find each length. The measure of $\overline{DE}$ is $x + 2$.

5. *BC*

6. *BD*

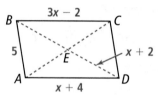

For Exercises 7 and 8, use parallelogram *WXYZ* to find each angle measure.

7. $m\angle WXY$

8. $m\angle XYZ$

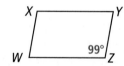

For Exercises 9 and 10, use parallelogram *EFGH* to find each length.

9. *EJ*

10. *FH*

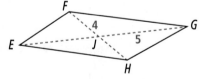

For Exercises 11 and 12, use parallelogram *MNPQ* to find each angle measure.

11. $m\angle NPQ$

12. $m\angle PQM$

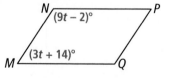

UNDERSTAND

13. Construct Arguments Write a proof of Theorem 8-7.

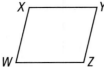

Given: $\overline{WX} \parallel \overline{ZY}$, $\overline{WZ} \parallel \overline{XY}$

Prove: $\overline{WX} \cong \overline{ZY}$, $\overline{WZ} \cong \overline{XY}$

14. Error Analysis In the statements shown, explain the student's error. What shape is the quadrilateral?

$\overline{JK} \cong \overline{KL}$ and $\overline{LM} \cong \overline{MJ}$.
$\angle MJK \cong \angle KLM$

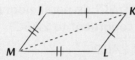

Therefore, $\triangle MJK \cong \triangle KLM$ by SAS. The triangular halves of JKLM are congruent, so JKLM must be a parallelogram. **X**

15. Construct Arguments Write a proof of Theorem 8-8.

Given: $\overline{AB} \parallel \overline{DC}$, $\overline{AD} \parallel \overline{BC}$

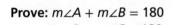

Prove: $m\angle A + m\angle B = 180$
$m\angle B + m\angle C = 180$
$m\angle C + m\angle D = 180$
$m\angle D + m\angle A = 180$

16. Use Appropriate Tools In a parallelogram, opposite sides are congruent, and opposite angles are congruent. If all sides in a parallelogram are congruent, are all angles congruent also? Draw a picture to explain your answer.

17. Prove that each pair of base angles of an isosceles trapezoid are congruent. *Hint:* Use the figure below and construct $\overline{AE}$ to be parallel to $\overline{DC}$.

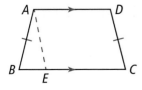

PRACTICE

18. What are the values of AB and DE in parallelogram ABCD? **SEE EXAMPLES 1 AND 2**

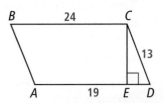

19. Quadrilateral EFGH is a parallelogram. What is $m\angle F$? **SEE EXAMPLES 3 AND 4**

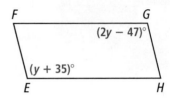

20. Quadrilateral MNPQ is a parallelogram. What is NQ? **SEE EXAMPLES 5 AND 6**

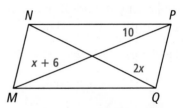

21. The figure below can be divided into two parallelograms. What is the angle measure of the point at the bottom?

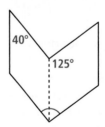

22. Find the perimeter of the parallelogram.

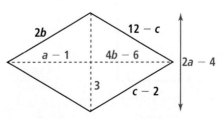

23. Write a proof of Theorem 8-9.

Given: $\overline{AB} \parallel \overline{DC}$, $\overline{AD} \parallel \overline{BC}$

Prove: $\angle A \cong \angle C$, $\angle B \cong \angle D$

APPLY

24. Model With Mathematics All four arms of a mechanical jack are the same length, and they form a parallelogram. Turning the crank pulls the arms together, raising the top of the jack. How high is the top of the jack when the crank is 5 inches off the ground? Explain.

25. Use Structure The handrails for a steel staircase form a parallelogram *ABCD*. Additional bars are needed one third and two thirds of the way up the stairs. Explain why the additional bars must be the same length as the end bars.

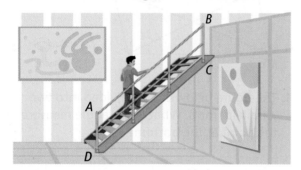

26. Higher Order Thinking Reagan designs a pattern consisting of large squares of the same size, small squares of the same size, and some parallelograms. She wants to replicate the pattern using tiles for her bathroom. Are the vertical and horizontal parallelograms congruent? Explain.

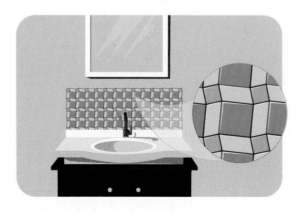

ASSESSMENT PRACTICE

27. Find the values of *a*, *b*, and *c* in the parallelogram.

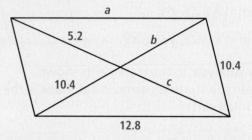

28. SAT/ACT In parallelogram *ABCD*, which angle is congruent to $\angle ABC$?

Ⓐ $\angle ABD$ Ⓒ $\angle BCD$

Ⓑ $\angle CDA$ Ⓓ $\angle DAB$

29. Performance Task A pipe at an amusement park sprays water onto visitors. A cross section of each pipe has the shape of a parallelogram.

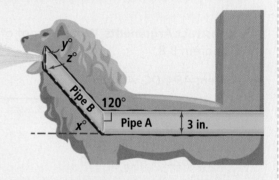

Part A Pipe A makes a 120° angle with Pipe B. What are the interior angles of parallelogram B? What is *x*, the measure of the angle that Pipe B makes with the horizontal? Explain.

Part B Park engineers fasten a circular cap onto the end of Pipe B. In the middle of the cap is a nozzle to turn the spray of water into a mist. If the diameter of Pipe A is 3 inches, what is the diameter of the circular cap? Explain.

Part C What are *y* and *z*, the angle measures that the cap makes with Pipe B? Explain.

8-4

Proving a Quadrilateral Is a Parallelogram

PearsonRealize.com

I CAN... use properties of sides, angles, and diagonals to identify a parallelogram.

EXPLORE & REASON

Sketch the quadrilaterals as described in the table. Include the diagonals.

	Parallel Sides	Congruent Sides
Quadrilateral 1	0 pairs	2 consecutive pairs
Quadrilateral 2	1 pair	exactly 1 nonparallel pair
Quadrilateral 3	2 pairs	2 opposite pairs

A. Measure the angles of each quadrilateral. How are the angle measures in Quadrilateral 1 related to each other? In Quadrilateral 2? In Quadrilateral 3?

B. Measure the diagonals of each quadrilateral. How are the diagonals in Quadrilateral 1 related to each other? In Quadrilateral 2? In Quadrilateral 3?

C. Communicate Precisely Compare the relationships among the angles and diagonals of Quadrilateral 3 to those of the other two quadrilaterals. Are there any relationships that make Quadrilateral 3 unique?

ESSENTIAL QUESTION

Which properties determine whether a quadrilateral is a parallelogram?

EXAMPLE 1   Investigate Sides to Confirm a Parallelogram

In quadrilateral $ABCD$, $\overline{AC}$ is a diagonal, $\overline{AB} \cong \overline{CD}$, and $\overline{AD} \cong \overline{BC}$. Is $ABCD$ a parallelogram? Explain.

STUDY TIP
Recall that any segment is congruent to itself by the Reflexive Property of Congruence.

$\triangle ABC \cong \triangle CDA$ by SSS.

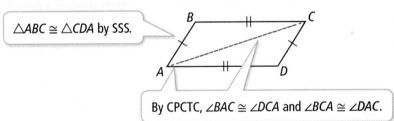

By CPCTC, $\angle BAC \cong \angle DCA$ and $\angle BCA \cong \angle DAC$.

By the Converse of the Alternate Interior Angles Theorem, $\overline{AB} \parallel \overline{CD}$ and $\overline{AD} \parallel \overline{BC}$. By definition, quadrilateral $ABCD$ is a parallelogram.

Try It!   1. Explain why you cannot conclude that $ABCD$ is a parallelogram.

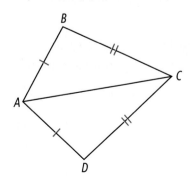

THEOREM 8-11 Converse of Theorem 8-7

If both pairs of opposite sides of a quadrilateral are congruent, then the quadrilateral is a parallelogram.

If...

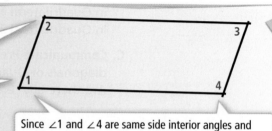

$\overline{AB} \cong \overline{CD}$

$\overline{AD} \cong \overline{BC}$

PROOF: SEE EXAMPLE 1.

Then... *ABCD* is a parallelogram.

CONCEPTUAL UNDERSTANDING

EXAMPLE 2 Explore Angle Measures to Confirm a Parallelogram

A. Teo sketches a design of a quadrilateral-shaped building. If ∠1 is supplementary to ∠2 and ∠4, is his design a parallelogram?

STUDY TIP
By definition, opposite sides of a parallelogram are parallel. Use theorems about parallel lines to show that a quadrilateral is a parallelogram.

Since ∠1 and ∠2 are same-side interior angles and supplementary, the top and bottom sides are parallel.

Since ∠1 and ∠4 are same side interior angles and supplementary, the left and right sides are parallel.

The quadrilateral has two pairs of parallel sides, so it is a parallelogram. The design is a parallelogram.

B. Teo sketches a second design in which ∠1 is congruent to ∠3, and ∠2 is congruent to ∠4. Is that design a parallelogram?

The sum of interior angles is 360.

$$m\angle 1 + m\angle 2 + m\angle 3 + m\angle 4 = 360$$

$$m\angle 1 + m\angle 2 + m\angle 1 + m\angle 2 = 360$$

$$2(m\angle 1 + m\angle 2) = 360$$

$$m\angle 1 + m\angle 2 = 180$$

Since ∠1 ≅ ∠3 and ∠2 ≅ ∠4, substitute *m*∠1 for *m*∠3 and *m*∠2 for *m*∠4.

Substitute *m*∠4 for *m*∠2.

$$m\angle 1 + m\angle 4 = 180$$

Because the edges form a quadrilateral with one angle supplementary to both consecutive angles and from the result in part A, the second design is also a parallelogram.

 Try It! **2. a.** Is *DEFG* a parallelogram? Explain.

b. Is *LMNO* a parallelogram? Explain.

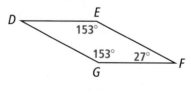

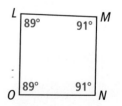

THEOREM 8-12 Converse of Theorem 8-8

If an angle of a quadrilateral is supplementary to both of its consecutive angles, then the quadrilateral is a parallelogram.

If...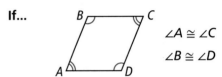

$m\angle A + m\angle B = 180$

$m\angle A + m\angle D = 180$

PROOF: SEE EXERCISE 12.

Then... ABCD is a parallelogram.

THEOREM 8-13 Converse of Theorem 8-9

If both pairs of opposite angles of a quadrilateral are congruent, then the quadrilateral is a parallelogram.

If...

$\angle A \cong \angle C$

$\angle B \cong \angle D$

PROOF: SEE EXERCISE 14.

Then... ABCD is a parallelogram.

👆 EXAMPLE 3   Find Values to Make Parallelograms

A. For what values of r and s is WXYZ a parallelogram?

Quadrilateral WXYZ is a parallelogram if both pairs of opposite sides are congruent.

$$7r + 1 = 4r + 7 \qquad 2s - 2 = s + 5$$

$$r = 2 \qquad\qquad s = 7$$

If $r = 2$ and $s = 7$, then WX and ZY are both 15, and XY and WZ are both 12. So WXYZ is a parallelogram.

GENERALIZE
Think about the properties of a parallelogram. What do you know about a quadrilateral that is a parallelogram?

B. For what values of a and b is RSTU a parallelogram?

Quadrilateral RSTU is a parallelogram if both pairs of opposite angles are congruent.

$$5a = 3a + 14 \qquad 4b + 1 = 3b + 37$$

$$2a = 14 \qquad\qquad b = 36$$

$$a = 7$$

If $a = 7$ and $b = 36$, then angles S and U are both 35° and angles T and R are both 145°. So RSTU is a parallelogram.

✓ Try It!

3. a. If $x = 25$ and $y = 30$, is PQRS a parallelogram?

b. If $g = 14$ and $h = 5$, is ABCD a parallelogram?

THEOREM 8-14 Converse of Theorem 8-10

If the diagonals of a quadrilateral bisect each other, then the quadrilateral is a parallelogram.

If...

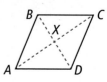

$\overline{AX} \cong \overline{CX}$
$\overline{BX} \cong \overline{DX}$

PROOF: SEE EXAMPLE 4.

Then... *ABCD* is a parallelogram.

THEOREM 8-15

If one pair of opposite sides of a quadrilateral is both congruent and parallel, then the quadrilateral is a parallelogram.

If...

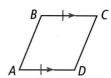

$\overline{AD} \cong \overline{BC}$
$\overline{AD} \parallel \overline{BC}$

PROOF: SEE EXERCISE 20.

Then... *ABCD* is a parallelogram.

PROOF ➡ 🖱 **EXAMPLE 4** **Investigate Diagonals to Confirm a Parallelogram**

Given: $\overline{AX} \cong \overline{CX}$ and $\overline{BX} \cong \overline{DX}$

Prove: *ABCD* is a parallelogram

Proof:

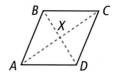

> **COMMON ERROR**
> Remember, noncongruent diagonals may bisect each other, just as congruent diagonals do.

Statements	Reasons
1) $\overline{AX} \cong \overline{CX}$ and $\overline{BX} \cong \overline{DX}$	1) Given
2) $\angle AXD \cong \angle CXB$ and $\angle AXB \cong \angle CXD$	2) Vertical Angles Theorem
3) $\triangle AXD \cong \triangle CXB$ and $\triangle AXB \cong \triangle CXD$	3) SAS
4) $\overline{AD} \cong \overline{CB}$ and $\overline{AB} \cong \overline{CD}$	4) CPCTC
5) *ABCD* is a parallelogram.	5) Theorem 8-11

☑ **Try It!** **4.** For what values of *p* and *q* is *ABCD* a parallelogram?

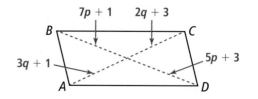

🖱 **EXAMPLE 5** **Identify a Parallelogram**

A. Is *PQRS* a parallelogram? Explain.

Same-side interior angles *Q* and *R* are supplementary, so $\overline{QP} \parallel \overline{RS}$.

PQRS is a parallelogram by Theorem 8-15.

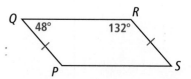

CONTINUED ON THE NEXT PAGE

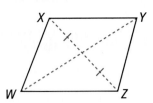
EXAMPLE 5 CONTINUED

B. Is WXYZ a parallelogram? Explain.

Although diagonal $\overline{WY}$ bisects $\overline{XZ}$, diagonal $\overline{XZ}$ does not necessarily bisect $\overline{WY}$. Quadrilateral WXYZ does not meet the conditions of Theorem 8-14, and so it is not necessarily a parallelogram.

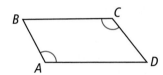

 Try It! **5. a.** Is ABCD a parallelogram? Explain.

b. Is EFGH a parallelogram? Explain.

APPLICATION 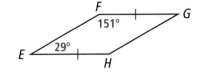 **EXAMPLE 6** **Verify a Parallelogram**

A mechanic raises a truck using a lift. For safety, the floor must be horizontal and the top of the lift must be parallel to the floor. Is the lift shown in a safe position? Explain.

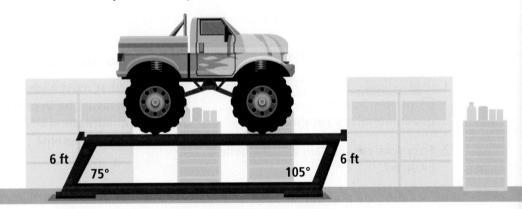

Formulate ◀ The lift and the floor form a quadrilateral. If the quadrilateral is a parallelogram, then the side holding the truck will be parallel to the floor and the lift will be safe.

Compute ◀ Find the sum of the given angles.

$$105 + 75 = 180$$

Since a pair of same-side alternate interior angles are supplementary, the 6-ft sides of the lift are parallel. The lift is a parallelogram by Theorem 8-15.

Interpret ◀ Opposite sides of a parallelogram are parallel, so the side of the lift holding the truck is parallel to the floor. The lift is in a safe position.

 Try It! **6.** A carpenter builds the table shown. If the floor is level, how likely is it that a ball placed on the table will roll off?

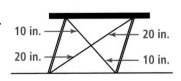

SIDES AND DIAGONALS

A quadrilateral is a parallelogram if

- two pairs of opposite sides are congruent

- one pair of opposite sides is congruent and parallel

- the diagonals bisect each other

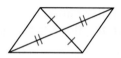

ANGLES

A quadrilateral is a parallelogram if

- one angle is supplementary to both consecutive angles

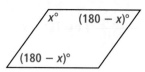

- two pairs of opposite angles are congruent

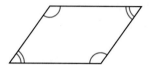

Do You UNDERSTAND?

1. ❓ ESSENTIAL QUESTION Which properties determine whether a quadrilateral is a parallelogram?

2. **Error Analysis** Explain why Rochelle is incorrect.

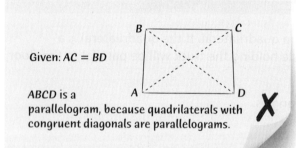

Given: $AC = BD$

ABCD is a parallelogram, because quadrilaterals with congruent diagonals are parallelograms. ✗

3. **Make Sense and Persevere** Is the information in the diagram enough to show WXYZ is a parallelogram? Explain.

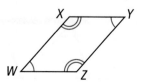

Do You KNOW HOW?

What must each angle measure be in order for quadrilateral DEFG to be a parallelogram?

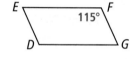

4. $m\angle D$ 5. $m\angle E$

What must each length be in order for quadrilateral JKLM to be a parallelogram?

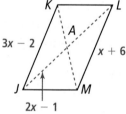

6. JK

7. JL

Use the diagram for Exercises 8 and 9.

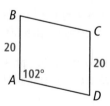

8. If $AB \parallel DC$, is ABCD a parallelogram? Explain.

9. If ABCD is a parallelogram, how does AC compare to BD? Explain.

PRACTICE & PROBLEM SOLVING

Scan for Multimedia

Practice   Tutorial

Additional Exercises Available Online

UNDERSTAND

10. **Use Appropriate Tools** If you are given a drawing of a quadrilateral, how can you determine whether or not it is a parallelogram? What tool or tools can you use?

11. **Error Analysis** Ahmed uses the following explanation to prove that a figure is a parallelogram. What is Ahmed's error?

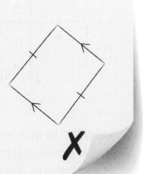

The quadrilateral has a pair of opposite sides congruent and a pair of opposite sides parallel. According to Theorem 6-15, the figure is a parallelogram.

✗

12. **Construct Arguments** Write a proof of Theorem 8-12.

Given: $m\angle F + m\angle G = 180$
$m\angle F + m\angle J = 180$

Prove: FGHJ is a parallelogram.

13. **Mathematical Connections** A rectangle is defined as a quadrilateral with four right angles. Which theorem or theorems from the lesson explain why a rectangle is a parallelogram? Explain how the theorem or theorems apply.

14. **Construct Arguments** Write a proof of Theorem 8-13.

Given: $\angle L \cong \angle N$, $\angle M \cong \angle O$

Prove: LMNO is a parallelogram.

15. **Higher Order Thinking** Describe rigid motions you can apply to $\triangle PQR$ to construct three different parallelograms by combining the preimage and image. Explain why the resulting figures are parallelograms.

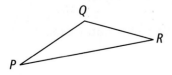

PRACTICE

16. Is each quadrilateral a parallelogram? Explain. SEE EXAMPLES 1 AND 2

a.

b.

17. In each figure, for what values of x and y is the figure a parallelogram? SEE EXAMPLE 3

a.
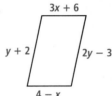

b.
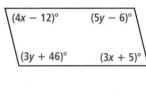

18. Given the lengths shown, for what values of w and z is the figure a parallelogram? SEE EXAMPLE 4

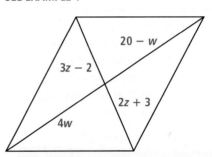

19. Is the figure below a parallelogram? Explain. SEE EXAMPLES 5 AND 6

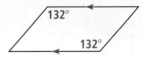

20. Write a proof of Theorem 8-15.

Given: $\overline{KL} \parallel \overline{JM}$, $\overline{KL} \cong \overline{JM}$

Prove: JKLM is a parallelogram.

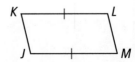

Hint: Construct diagonal $\overline{JL}$.

APPLY

21. Make Sense and Persevere A lamp on a wall is suspended from an extendable arm that allows the lamp to slide up and down. When it expands, does the shape shown remain a parallelogram? Explain.

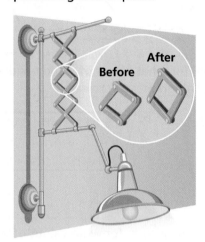

22. Model With Mathematics Simon wants to decorate a cake with a pattern of parallelograms. He first pipes two parallel lines that are 3 inches apart. He then makes a mark every $\frac{1}{2}$ inch along each line. He pipes a line from one mark to the next on the opposite side. Does this ensure that the lines will be parallel? Explain your answer.

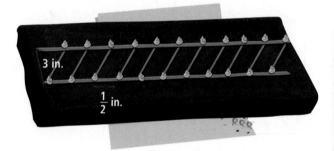

23. Communicate Precisely In the game shown, the arrangement of marbles on the board is called a *parallelogram formation*. Why is that name appropriate? Explain.

ASSESSMENT PRACTICE

24. Copy the graph and plot all possible coordinate pairs for point Q on the coordinate plane so that points P, Q, R, and S form the vertices of a parallelogram.

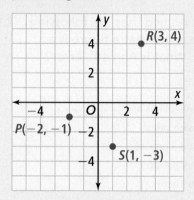

25. SAT/ACT In quadrilateral $ABCD$, $\angle A \cong \angle C$. Which additional statement can be used to show that $ABCD$ is a parallelogram?

Ⓐ $m\angle A + m\angle C = 180$ Ⓒ $m\angle B + m\angle D = 180$

Ⓑ $\overline{BD}$ bisects $\overline{AC}$ Ⓓ $\angle B \cong \angle D$

26. Performance Task Margaret helps her sister build a baby gate that is built from dowels hinged at the top and bottom, so the gate can open up against the wall along the stairs. They call it the parallelogram gate.

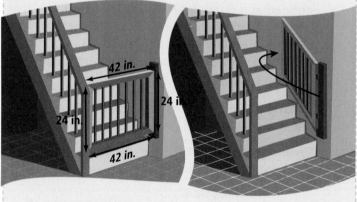

Part A Are they correct to call it a parallelogram gate? Explain.

Part B What are the measurements of the sides of the gate when the gate is open? Explain.

Part C Margaret's father suggests that they add two diagonal slats at the front of the baby gate. What would that do to the gate? Explain.

8-5

Properties of Special Parallelograms

📶 **PearsonRealize.com**

I CAN... use the properties of rhombuses, rectangles, and squares to solve problems.

👆 **EXPLORE & REASON**

Consider these three figures.

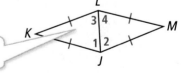

Figure 1   Figure 2   Figure 3

A. What questions would you ask to determine whether each figure is a parallelogram?

B. Communicate Precisely What questions would you ask to determine whether Figure 1 is a rectangle? What additional questions would you ask to determine whether Figure 2 is a square?

C. If all three figures are parallelograms, what is the most descriptive name for Figure 3? How do you know?

❓ **ESSENTIAL QUESTION**   What properties of rhombuses, rectangles, and squares differentiate them from other parallelograms?

CONCEPTUAL UNDERSTANDING

👆 **EXAMPLE 1**   Find the Diagonals of a Rhombus

A. Parallelogram *ABCD* is a rhombus. What are the measures of ∠1, ∠2, ∠3, and ∠4?

All four sides of a rhombus are congruent.

STUDY TIP
Recall that a rhombus is a parallelogram, so it has all the properties of parallelograms.

By the Converse of the Perpendicular Bisector Theorem, *B* and *D* are on the perpendicular bisector of $\overline{AC}$, so $\overline{AC} \perp \overline{BD}$.

All four angles formed by the intersection of the diagonals are right angles, so the measure of ∠1, ∠2, ∠3, and ∠4 is 90.

B. Parallelogram *JKLM* is a rhombus. How are ∠1, ∠2, ∠3, and ∠4 related?

By SSS, △*JKL* ≅ △*JML*, so ∠1 ≅ ∠2 and ∠3 ≅ ∠4.

$\overline{JL} \cong \overline{JL}$

The diagonals of a rhombus bisect the angles at each vertex.

✓ **Try It!**   **1. a.** What is *WY*?   **b.** What is *m∠RPS*?

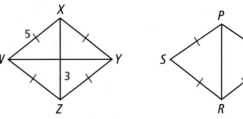

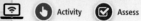
THEOREM 8-16

If a parallelogram is a rhombus, then its diagonals are perpendicular bisectors of each other.

If...

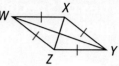

PROOF: SEE EXERCISE 14.

Then... $\overline{WY}$ and $\overline{XZ}$ are perpendicular bisectors of each other.

THEOREM 8-17

If a parallelogram is a rhombus, then each diagonal bisects a pair of opposite angles.

If...

PROOF: SEE EXERCISE 17.

Then... $\angle 1 \cong \angle 2$, $\angle 3 \cong \angle 4$, $\angle 5 \cong \angle 6$, and $\angle 7 \cong \angle 8$.

EXAMPLE 2 Find Lengths and Angle Measures in a Rhombus

A. Quadrilateral *ABCD* is a rhombus. What is $m\angle ADE$?

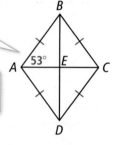

$\overline{AC}$ bisects $\angle BAD$, so $m\angle DAC = 53$.

$$m\angle DAE + m\angle AED + m\angle ADE = 180$$
$$53 + 90 + m\angle ADE = 180$$
$$m\angle ADE = 37$$

$\overline{AC} \perp \overline{BD}$, so $m\angle AED = 90$.

> **COMMON ERROR**
> You may incorrectly state that $m\angle ADE = m\angle DAE$. Remember that consecutive angles are not necessarily congruent.

B. Quadrilateral *GHJK* is a rhombus. What is *GH*?

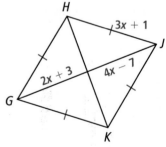

Step 1 Find *x*.
$$2x + 3 = 4x - 7$$
$$2x = 10$$
$$x = 5$$

Step 2 Use the value of *x* to find *GH*.
$$HJ = 3(5) + 1 = 16$$
$$GH = HJ$$
$$GH = 16$$

 Try It! **2.** Each quadrilateral is a rhombus.

a. What is $m\angle MNO$?

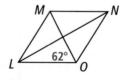

b. What is *QT*?

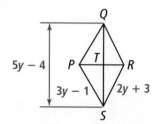

Go Online | PearsonRealize.com

THEOREM 8-18

If a parallelogram is a rectangle, then its diagonals are congruent.

If...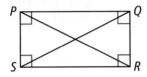

PROOF: SEE EXAMPLE 3.

Then... $\overline{AC} \cong \overline{BD}$

PROOF ➡ 🖑 **EXAMPLE 3** **Prove Diagonals of a Rectangle Are Congruent**

Write a proof for Theorem 8-18.

Given: *PQRS* is a rectangle.

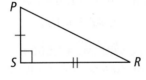

Prove: $\overline{PR} \cong \overline{QS}$

Plan: To show that the diagonals are congruent, find a pair of congruent triangles that each diagonal is a part of. Both △*PSR* and △*QRS* appear to be congruent. Think about how to use properties of rectangles to show they are congruent. Draw each triangle separately and label the congruent sides.

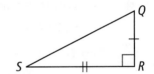

Proof:

Statements	Reasons
1) *PQRS* is a rectangle.	1) Given
2) *PQRS* is a parallelogram.	2) Def. of rectangle
3) $\overline{PS} \cong \overline{QR}$	3) Opposite sides of a parallelogram are congruent.
4) ∠*PSR* and ∠*QRS* are right angles.	4) Def. of rectangle
5) ∠*PSR* ≅ ∠*QRS*	5) All right angles are congruent.
6) $\overline{SR} \cong \overline{RS}$	6) Reflexive Prop. of Congruence
7) △*PSR* ≅ △*QRS*	7) SAS Triangle Congruence Thm.
8) $\overline{PR} \cong \overline{QS}$	8) CPCTC

STUDY TIP
When you see triangles in a diagram for a proof, you can often use congruent triangles and CPCTC to complete the proof.

 Try It! **3.** A carpenter needs to check the gate his apprentice built to be sure it is rectangular. The diagonals measure 52 inches and 53 inches. Is the gate rectangular? Explain.

APPLICATION **EXAMPLE 4**   **Find Diagonal Lengths of a Rectangle**

Paul is training his horse to run the course at a pace of 4 meters per second or faster. Paul rides his horse from *D* to *C* to *E* to *B* in 1 minute 30 seconds. The figure *ABCD* is a rectangle. Did he make his goal?

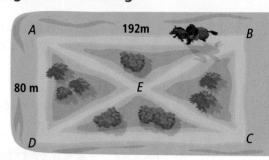

Formulate ◀ Use the Pythagorean Theorem to find *BD*. Then use properties of rectangles to find each segment length and the total distance. Finally, determine his speed.

Compute ◀
$$(BD)^2 = 80^2 + 192^2$$
$$(BD)^2 = 43{,}264$$
$$BD = 208$$

> Apply the Pythagorean Theorem.

Use the properties of rectangles to find the total distance.

$$CE = EB = 104$$
$$DC + CE + EB = 192 + 104 + 104 = 400$$

> Diagonals are congruent and bisect each other.

Determine the pace.

$$400 \div 90 \approx 4.4$$

Interpret ◀ Paul's horse ran at a pace of about 4.4 m/s, so he made his goal.

✓ **Try It!**   **4.** A rectangle with area 1,600 m² is 4 times as long as it is wide. What is the sum of the diagonals?

 EXAMPLE 5   **Diagonals and Angle Measures of a Square**

Figure *WXYZ* is a square. If *WY* + *XZ* = 92, what is the area of △*WPZ*?

Since the figure is also a rhombus, $\overline{WY} \perp \overline{XZ}$ and *WP* and *ZP* are the base and height of △*WPZ*.

Step 1 Find the lengths of the diagonals.

$$WY + XZ = 92$$
$$WY = XZ = 46$$

> *WXYZ* is a rectangle, so $\overline{WY} \cong \overline{XZ}$.

USE STRUCTURE
Consider the four triangles formed by the diagonals of a square. What observations do you make about these triangles?

Step 2 Find *WP* and *ZP*.

$$WP = \tfrac{1}{2}(WY) = 23$$
$$ZP = \tfrac{1}{2}(XZ) = 23$$

> *WXYZ* is a parallelogram, so *WY* and *XZ* bisect each other.

Step 3 Find the area of △*WPZ*.

$$\text{area}(\triangle WPZ) = \tfrac{1}{2}(23)(23) = 264.5$$

The area of △*WPZ* is 264.5 square units.

✓ **Try It!**   **5.** Square *ABCD* has diagonals $\overline{AC}$ and $\overline{BD}$. What is $m\angle ABD$? Explain.

CONCEPT SUMMARY Properties of Special Parallelograms

	Rectangle	Rhombus	Square
WORDS	If a parallelogram is a rectangle, then the diagonals are congruent.	If a parallelogram is a rhombus, then the diagonals are perpendicular and bisect each pair of opposite angles.	If a parallelogram is a square, the properties of both a rectangle and a rhombus apply.
DIAGRAMS	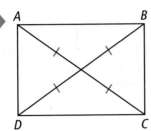	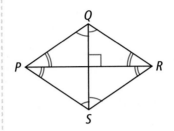	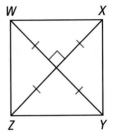
SYMBOLS	$\overline{AC} \cong \overline{BD}$	$\overline{PR} \perp \overline{QS}$	$\overline{WY} \cong \overline{XZ}$ $\overline{WY} \perp \overline{XZ}$

Do You UNDERSTAND?

1. **ESSENTIAL QUESTION** What properties of rhombuses, rectangles, and squares differentiate them from other parallelograms?

2. **Error Analysis** Figure QRST is a rectangle. Ramona wants to show that the four interior triangles are congruent. What is Ramona's error?

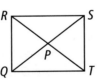

> Diagonals of a rectangle are congruent and bisect each other, so $\overline{RP} \cong \overline{TP} \cong \overline{QP} \cong \overline{SP}$. Because the diagonals are perpendicular bisectors, $\angle RPS$, $\angle SPT$, $\angle TPQ$, and $\angle QPR$ are right angles. Therefore, by SAS, $\triangle RPS \cong \triangle SPT \cong \triangle TPQ \cong \triangle PQR$.

3. **Construct Arguments** Is any quadrilateral with four congruent sides a rhombus? Explain.

Do You KNOW HOW?

Find each length and angle measure for rhombus DEFG. Round to the nearest tenth.

4. DF

5. $m\angle DFG$

6. EG

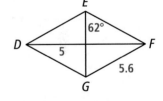

Find each length for rectangle MNPQ. Round to the nearest tenth.

7. MP

8. MQ

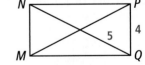

Find each length and angle measure for square WXYZ.

9. $m\angle YPZ$

10. $m\angle XWP$

11. XZ

12. What is the value of x?

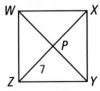

UNDERSTAND

13. Construct Arguments Write a proof of Theorem 8-16.

Given: *WXYZ* is a rhombus.

Prove: $\overline{WY}$ and $\overline{XZ}$ are perpendicular bisectors of each other.

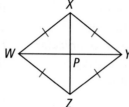

14. Error Analysis Figure *ABCD* is a rhombus. What is Malcolm's error?

Since *ABCD* is a rhombus, $\overline{AB} \cong \overline{CD}$. Since the diagonals of a rhombus bisect each other, $\overline{AE} \cong \overline{BE} \cong \overline{CE} \cong \overline{DE}$. So, by SSS, $\triangle ABE \cong \triangle CDE$.

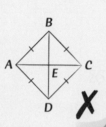

15. Mathematical Connections The area of rectangle *WXYZ* is 115.5 in.². What is the perimeter of $\triangle XYZ$? Explain your work.

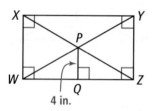
4 in.

16. Construct Arguments Write a proof of Theorem 8-17.

Given: *ABCD* is a rhombus.

Prove: $\angle 1 \cong \angle 2$, $\angle 3 \cong \angle 4$, $\angle 5 \cong 6$, $\angle 7 \cong \angle 8$

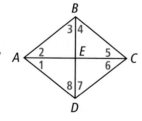

17. Higher Order Thinking A square is cut apart and reassembled into a rectangle as shown. Which figure has a greater perimeter? Explain.

PRACTICE

For Exercises 18–20, find each angle measure for rhombus *ABCD*. SEE EXAMPLES 1 AND 2

18. $m\angle ACD$

19. $m\angle ABC$

20. $m\angle BEA$

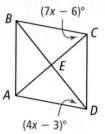

For Exercises 21–23, find each length for rhombus *PQRS*. Round to the nearest tenth. SEE EXAMPLES 1 AND 2

21. *TR*

22. *QS*

23. *PS*

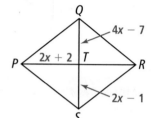

For Exercises 24–27, find each length and angle measure for rectangle *GHJK*. Round to the nearest tenth. SEE EXAMPLES 3 AND 4

24. $m\angle GHK$

25. $m\angle HLJ$

26. *GJ*

27. *HL*

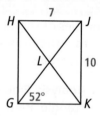

For Exercises 28–30, find each length and value for square *QRST*. Round to the nearest tenth. SEE EXAMPLE 5

28. *SV*

29. *RT*

30. perimeter of $\triangle RVS$

31. If *ABCD* is a square, what is *GC*?

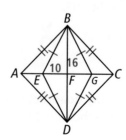

APPLY

32. Model With Mathematics Jordan wants a collapsible puppy pen that gives his puppy at least 35 square feet of area and at least 10 feet of diagonal length. Should Jordan buy the pen shown? Explain.

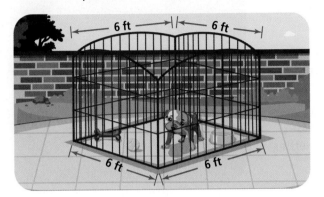

33. Make Sense and Persevere Luis is using different types of wood to make a rectangular inlay top for a chest with the pattern shown.

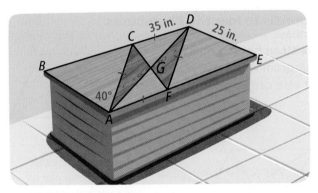

a. What angle should he cut for ∠CDG? Explain.

b. If he makes the table top correctly, what will the length of the completed top be?

34. Look for Relationships A carpenter is building a support for a stage. What should be the measures of ∠1, ∠2, ∠3, and ∠4? Explain your answers.

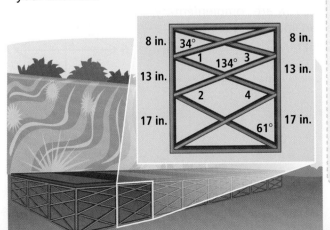

ASSESSMENT PRACTICE

35. Which statements are true about all rectangles? Select all that apply.

Ⓐ Diagonals bisect each other.

Ⓑ Adjacent sides are perpendicular.

Ⓒ Diagonals are perpendicular.

Ⓓ Consecutive angles are supplementary.

36. SAT/ACT Which expression gives $m\angle DBC$?

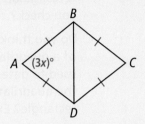

Ⓐ $\left(180 - \frac{3x}{2}\right)^\circ$ Ⓒ $\left(\frac{180 - 3x}{2}\right)^\circ$

Ⓑ $(180 - 3x)^\circ$ Ⓓ $\left(\frac{3x}{2} - 180\right)^\circ$

37. Performance Task At a carnival, the goal is to toss a disc into one of three zones to win a prize. Zone 1 is a square, zone 2 is a rhombus, and zone 3 is a rectangle. Some measurements have been provided.

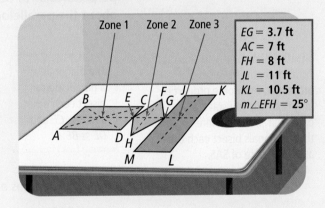

$EG = 3.7$ ft
$AC = 7$ ft
$FH = 8$ ft
$JL = 11$ ft
$KL = 10.5$ ft
$m\angle EFH = 25°$

Part A What are the lengths of the sides of each zone?

Part B What are the angle measures of each zone?

Part C What is the area of each zone?

LESSON 8-5 Properties of Special Parallelograms   397

8-6
Conditions of Special Parallelograms

💻 PearsonRealize.com

I CAN... identify rhombuses, rectangles, and squares by the characteristics of their diagonals.

👆 **MODEL & DISCUSS**

The sides of the lantern are identical quadrilaterals.

A. Construct Arguments How could you check to see whether a side is a parallelogram? Justify your answer.

B. Does the side appear to be rectangular? How could you check?

C. Do you think that diagonals of a quadrilateral can be used to determine whether the quadrilateral is a rectangle? Explain.

❓ **ESSENTIAL QUESTION**

Which properties of the diagonals of a parallelogram help you to classify a parallelogram?

CONCEPTUAL UNDERSTANDING

👆 **EXAMPLE 1** **Use Diagonals to Identify Rhombuses**

Information about diagonals can help to classify a parallelogram. In parallelogram $ABCD$, $\overline{AC}$ is perpendicular to $\overline{BD}$. What else can you conclude about the parallelogram?

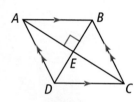

STUDY TIP
Parallelograms have several properties, and some properties may not help you solve a particular problem. Here, the fact that diagonals bisect each other allows the use of SAS.

The diagonals of a parallelogram bisect each other, so $\overline{AE} \cong \overline{CE}$ and $\overline{DE} \cong \overline{BE}$.

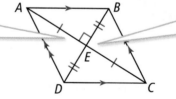

Any angle at E either forms a linear pair or is a vertical angle with $\angle AEB$, so all four angles are right angles.

The four triangles are congruent by SAS, so $\overline{AB} \cong \overline{CB} \cong \overline{CD} \cong \overline{AD}$.

Since $ABCD$ is a parallelogram with four congruent sides, $ABCD$ is a rhombus.

☑ **Try It!** **1.** If $\angle JHK$ and $\angle JGK$ are complementary, what else can you conclude about $GHJK$? Explain.

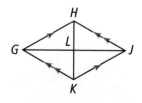

THEOREM 8-19 Converse of Theorem 8-16

If the diagonals of a parallelogram are perpendicular, then the parallelogram is a rhombus.

If...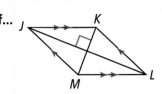

PROOF: SEE EXERCISE 9.

Then... $\overline{JK} \cong \overline{KL} \cong \overline{LM} \cong \overline{MJ}$

THEOREM 8-20 Converse of Theorem 8-17

If a diagonal of a parallelogram bisects two angles of the parallelogram, then the parallelogram is a rhombus.

If...

PROOF: SEE EXAMPLE 2.

Then... $\overline{AB} \cong \overline{BC} \cong \overline{CD} \cong \overline{DA}$

PROOF

EXAMPLE 2 Prove Theorem 8-20

Write a proof of Theorem 8-20.

Given: Parallelogram *FGHJ* with ∠1 ≅ ∠2 and ∠3 ≅ ∠4

Prove: *FGHJ* is a rhombus.

Proof:

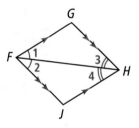

STUDY TIP
Drawing diagonals in parallelograms can help you see additional information that is useful in solving problems.

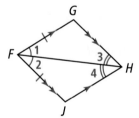 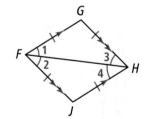

By ASA, △*FHJ* ≅ △*FHG*. Thus, $\overline{FJ} \cong \overline{FG}$.

By the Alternate Interior Angles Theorem, ∠1 ≅ ∠4, so ∠1 ≅ ∠2 ≅ ∠3 ≅ ∠4.

By the Converse of the Isosceles Triangle Theorem, $\overline{FG} \cong \overline{HG}$ and $\overline{FJ} \cong \overline{HJ}$.

Using the Transitive Property of Congruence, $\overline{FG} \cong \overline{HG} \cong \overline{FJ} \cong \overline{HJ}$. Since *FGHJ* is a parallelogram with congruent sides, it is a rhombus.

 Try It! 2. Refer to the figure *FGHJ* in Example 2. Use properties of parallelograms to show that if ∠1 ≅ ∠2 and ∠3 ≅ ∠4, then the four angles are congruent.

EXAMPLE 3 Use Diagonals to Identify Rectangles

Ashton measures the diagonals for his deck frame and finds that they are congruent. Will the deck be rectangular?

Since opposite sides are congruent, the supports form a parallelogram. To show that the structure is rectangular, show that the angles are right angles.

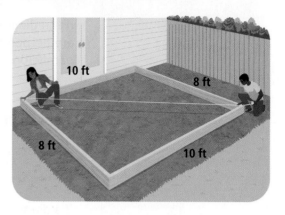

10 ft 8 ft 8 ft 10 ft

Opposite sides and the diagonals are congruent, so △ACD ≅ △BDC by SSS. Therefore, ∠ADC ≅ ∠BCD.

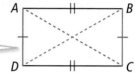

In a parallelogram, consecutive angles are supplementary. Angles that are congruent and supplementary are right angles. Similarly, ∠DAB and ∠CBA are also right angles.

The frame forms a parallelogram with four right angles, which is a rectangle.

 Try It! 3. If the diagonals of any quadrilateral are congruent, is the quadrilateral a rectangle? Justify your answer.

THEOREM 8-21 Converse of Theorem 8-18

If the diagonals of a parallelogram are congruent, then the parallelogram is a rectangle.

If...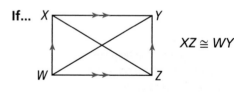

$XZ \cong WY$

PROOF: SEE EXERCISE 11.

Then... ∠XWZ, ∠WZY, ∠XYZ, and ∠WXY are right angles

EXAMPLE 4 Identify Special Parallelograms

Can you conclude whether each parallelogram is a rhombus, a square, or a rectangle? Explain.

A. Parallelogram *ABCD*

By SAS, △ABD ≅ △CBD.

∠ADB ≅ ∠CDB by CPCTC.

Diagonal $\overline{BD}$ bisects ∠ABC and ∠ADC, so parallelogram ABCD is a rhombus.

CONSTRUCT ARGUMENTS
There are often multiple ways to prove something. How could you use properties of parallelograms to show the figure is a rhombus without the congruent angles shown?

CONTINUED ON THE NEXT PAGE

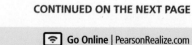

EXAMPLE 4 CONTINUED

B. Parallelogram **PQRS**

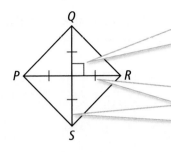

Diagonals are perpendicular, so PQRS is a rhombus.

Diagonals are congruent, so PQRS is a rectangle.

Since the parallelogram is a rhombus and a rectangle, it is a square.

 Try It! **4.** Is each parallelogram a rhombus, a square, or a rectangle? Explain.

a. 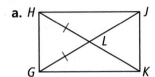 **b.**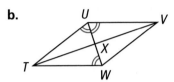

 EXAMPLE 5 **Use Properties of Special Parallelograms**

Quadrilateral **STUV** is a rhombus. What are the values of **x** and **y**?

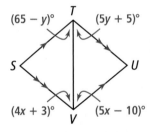

MAKE SENSE AND PERSEVERE
Consider the information given in the diagram. How can you determine whether $\overline{TV}$ bisects the angles?

If a parallelogram is a rhombus then each diagonal bisects opposite angles. So, $\overline{TV}$ bisects ∠SVU and ∠STU.

Solve for x.

$m∠SVT = m∠UVT$ ⟵ $\overline{TV}$ bisects ∠SVU and ∠STU. ⟶ Solve for y.

$m∠STV = m∠UTV$

$4x + 3 = 5x - 10$ $65 - y = 5y + 5$

$-x = -13$ $-6y = -60$

$x = 13$ $y = 10$

 Try It! **5.** In parallelogram ABCD, AC = 3w − 1 and BD = 2(w + 6). What must be true for ABCD to be a rectangle?

APPLICATION

EXAMPLE 6 **Apply Properties of Special Parallelograms**

A group of friends set up a kickball field with bases 60 ft apart. How can they verify that the field is a square?

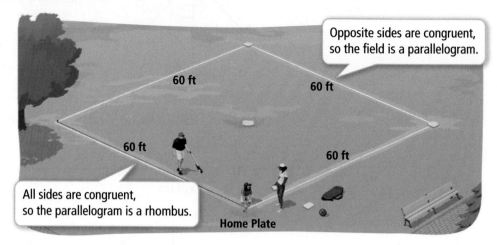

Opposite sides are congruent, so the field is a parallelogram.

60 ft 60 ft

60 ft 60 ft

All sides are congruent, so the parallelogram is a rhombus.

Home Plate

The field is a rhombus. To show that the rhombus is a square, show that it is also a rectangle.

A parallelogram is a rectangle if the diagonals are congruent.

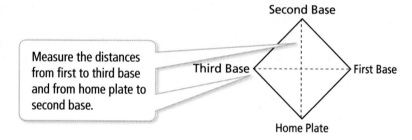

Second Base

Measure the distances from first to third base and from home plate to second base.

Third Base ←--------→ First Base

Home Plate

The group of friends can verify the field is a square if they find that the distances from first base to third base and from second base to home plate are equal.

 Try It! **6.** Is *MNPQ* a rhombus? Explain.

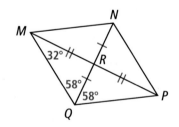

Go Online | PearsonRealize.com

CONCEPT SUMMARY Conditions of Special Parallelograms

RHOMBUS

A parallelogram is a rhombus if

- diagonals are perpendicular

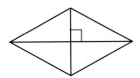

- a diagonal bisects angles

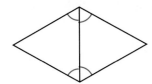

RECTANGLE

A parallelogram is a rectangle if

- diagonals are congruent

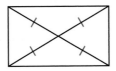

SQUARE

A parallelogram is a square if

- diagonals are perpendicular and congruent

- a diagonal bisects angles and diagonals are congruent

Do You UNDERSTAND?

1. **ESSENTIAL QUESTION** Which properties of the diagonals of a parallelogram help you to classify a parallelogram?

2. **Error Analysis** Sage was asked to classify *DEFG*. What was Sage's error?

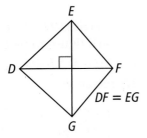

$DF = EG$

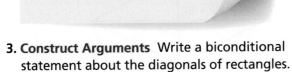

Since *DF* = *EG*, *DEFG* is a rectangle.
Since $\overline{EG} \perp \overline{DF}$, *DEFG* is also a rhombus.
Therefore, *DEFG* is a square. ✗

3. **Construct Arguments** Write a biconditional statement about the diagonals of rectangles. What theorems justify your statement?

4. **Use Appropriate Tools** Make a concept map showing the relationships among quadrilaterals, parallelograms, trapezoids, isosceles trapezoids, kites, rectangles, squares, and rhombuses.

Do You KNOW HOW?

For Exercises 5–8, is the parallelogram a rhombus, a square, or a rectangle?

5.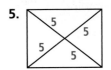

6.

7.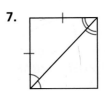

8.

9. What value of *x* will make the parallelogram a rhombus?

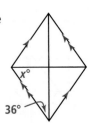

10. If $m\angle 1 = 36$ and $m\angle 2 = 54$, is *PQRS* a rhombus, a square, a rectangle, or none of these? Explain.

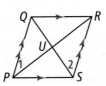

UNDERSTAND

11. Construct Arguments Write a proof for Theorem 8-19 using the following diagram.

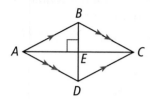

12. Error Analysis Becky is asked to classify *PQRS*. What is her error?

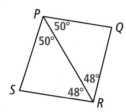

$\overline{PR}$ bisects opposite angles ∠SPQ and ∠QRS, so PQRS must be a rhombus. ✗

13. Construct Arguments Write a proof for Theorem 8-21 using the following diagram.

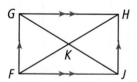

14. Construct Arguments Write a proof to show that if *ABCD* is a parallelogram and ∠*ABE* ≅ ∠*BAE*, then *ABCD* is a rectangle.

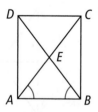

15. Mathematical Connections If *WXYZ* is a rhombus with *W*(−1, 3) and *Y*(9, 11), what must be an equation of $\overleftrightarrow{XZ}$ in order for *WXYZ* to be a rhombus? Explain how you found your answer.

16. Higher Order Thinking The longer diagonal of a rhombus is three times the length of the shorter diagonal. If the shorter diagonal is *x*, what expression gives the perimeter of the rhombus?

PRACTICE

For Exercises 17 and 18, determine whether each figure is a rhombus. Explain your answer.
SEE EXAMPLES 1 AND 2

17.

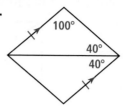

18.

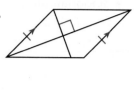

19. What is the perimeter of parallelogram *WXYZ*? SEE EXAMPLE 3

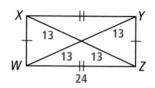

For Exercises 20 and 21, determine the name that best describes each figure: parallelogram, rectangle, square, or rhombus. SEE EXAMPLE 4

20.

21.

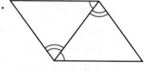

For Exercises 22–24, give the condition required for each figure to be the specified shape.
SEE EXAMPLES 5 AND 6

22. rectangle

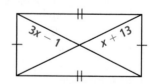

23. rhombus

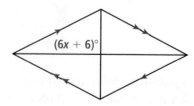

24. rhombus

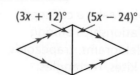

APPLY

25. Look for Relationships Melissa charges $1.50 per square meter for laying sod. She says she can compute the amount to charge for the pentagonal lawn by evaluating $1.50(12^2 + 0.25(12^2))$. Do you agree? Explain.

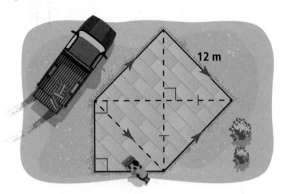

12 m

26. Make Sense and Persevere Jeffery is making a wall design with tape. How much tape does he need to put the design shown on his wall? Explain how you used the information in the diagram to find your answer.

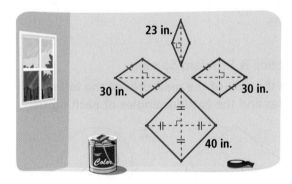

23 in.

30 in.　30 in.

40 in.

27. Use Structure After knitting a blanket, Monisha washes and stretches it out to the correct size and shape. Opposite sides line up with the edges of a rectangular table. She plans to sew a ribbon around the edge of the blanket. How much ribbon will she need?

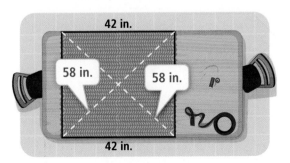

42 in.

58 in.　58 in.

42 in.

ASSESSMENT PRACTICE

28. Are the terms below valid classifications for the figure? Select *Yes* or *No*.

	Yes	No
Square	☐	☐
Rhombus	☐	☐
Parallelogram	☐	☐
Rectangle	☐	☐
Trapezoid	☐	☐

29. SAT/ACT Parallelogram *ABCD* has diagonals with lengths $AC = 7x + 6$ and $BD = 9x - 2$. For which value of *x* is *ABCD* a rectangle?

Ⓐ 2　　Ⓑ 4　　Ⓒ 7　　Ⓓ 9　　Ⓔ 34

30. Performance Task Zachary is using the two segments shown as diagonals of quadrilaterals he is making for a decal design for the cover of his smart phone.

5 cm　　5 cm

Part A Make a table showing at least four types of different quadrilaterals that Zachary can make using the segments as diagonals. For each type of quadrilateral, draw a diagram showing an example. Label angle measures where the diagonals intersect, and label segment lengths of the diagonals.

Part B Are some types of quadrilaterals not possible using these diagonals? Explain.

Part C Which has the greater area, a square or a rectangle? Explain.

Topic Review

1. How are properties of parallelograms used to solve problems and to classify quadrilaterals?

Vocabulary Review

Choose the correct term to complete each sentence.

2. A parallelogram is a(n) _____ if its diagonals are perpendicular and congruent.

3. A(n) _____ is a quadrilateral with two pairs of adjacent sides congruent and no pairs of opposite sides congruent.

4. The sum of the measures of the _____ angles of a convex polygon is 180° • (n − 2), where n is the number of sides of the polygon.

5. The length of the _____ is the average of its two bases.

- exterior
- interior
- kite
- midsegment of a trapezoid
- rectangle
- rhombus
- square

Concepts & Skills Review

LESSON 8-1 | **The Polygon Angle-Sum Theorems**

Quick Review

The sum of the measures of the exterior angles of a convex polygon, one at each vertex, is 360°.

The sum of the measures of the interior angles of a convex polygon is 180° • (n − 2), where n is the number of sides of the polygon.

Example

What is the sum of the measures of the interior angles of the regular hexagon?

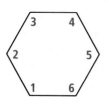

$180° • (6 − 2) = 720°$

Practice & Problem Solving

Find the sum of the measures of the interior angles and the exterior angles of each figure.

6. 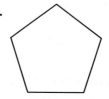　　7.

8. **Make Sense and Persevere** Is there enough information to determine the measures of the interior angles of the polygon shown? If so, find the measures. If not, explain.

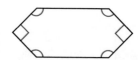

Quick Review

A kite is a quadrilateral with two pairs of adjacent sides congruent and no pairs of opposite sides congruent.

A trapezoid is a quadrilateral with exactly one pair of parallel sides. The length of the midsegment of a trapezoid is the average of the two bases.

Example

Given trapezoid ABCD, what is EF?

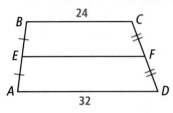

The midsegment of trapezoid ABCD is $\overline{EF}$, so $EF = \frac{1}{2}(24 + 32) = 28$.

Practice & Problem Solving

Find each measure.

9. $m\angle 1$

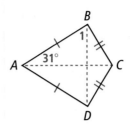

10. BC

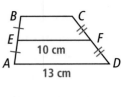

11. Use Structure Shannon wants to hang curtains using a tension rod across the top of the trapezoid-shaped window that is shown. Is a 36-inch tension rod long enough to go across the top of the window? Explain.

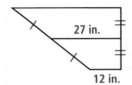

Quick Review

The sides, diagonals, and angles of parallelograms have special relationships.

• Opposite sides are congruent.
• Diagonals bisect each other.
• Consecutive angles are supplementary.
• Opposite angles are congruent.

Example

Given parallelogram ABCD, if ED = 3 and $BD = \frac{3}{4}(AC)$, what is AC?

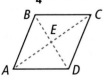

Since $ED = BE$, $BD = 6$. Substitute into $BD = \frac{3}{4}(AC)$ to get $6 = \frac{3}{4}(AC)$, and then solve to get $AC = 8$.

Practice & Problem Solving

Use the diagram to find each angle measure.

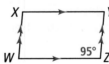

12. $m\angle W$

13. $m\angle X$

14. Construct Arguments The outline of a planned parking lot in the shape of a parallelogram is shown. Elijah says the north side of the lot is 130 ft and the west side of the lot is 240 ft. What is Elijah's mistake?

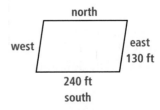

LESSON 8-4 Proving a Quadrilateral Is a Parallelogram

Quick Review

A quadrilateral is a parallelogram if any of the following conditions is true.

- Both pairs of opposite sides are congruent.
- One pair of opposite sides is congruent and parallel.
- An angle is supplementary to both of its consecutive angles.
- Both pairs of opposite angles are congruent.
- The diagonals bisect each other.

Example

Explain why the quadrilateral is a parallelogram.

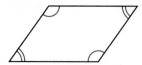

Two pairs of opposite angles are congruent, so the quadrilateral is a parallelogram.

Practice & Problem Solving

For what value of *x* is each quadrilateral a parallelogram?

15.

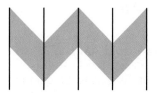

16.

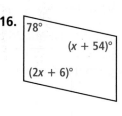

17. Communicate Precisely All the black lines in the pattern shown are vertical. What measurements can be used to show that each gray quadrilateral is a parallelogram? Explain.

LESSON 8-5 Properties of Special Parallelograms

Quick Review

The diagonals of a rhombus are perpendicular bisectors of each other. The diagonals of a rectangle are congruent. The diagonals of a square are perpendicular bisectors of each other and congruent.

Example

Given that *WXYZ* is a rhombus, show that $\overline{PW} \cong \overline{PY}$.

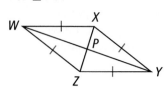

Quadrilateral *WXYZ* is a rhombus, so it is a parallelogram. Diagonals of parallelograms bisect each other, so $\overline{PW} \cong \overline{PY}$ by definition of bisect.

Practice & Problem Solving

18. Given that *ABCD* is a rhombus, what is *BD*?

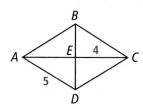

19. Given that *PQRS* is a rectangle, what is *QS*?

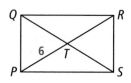

20. Construct Arguments Is any quadrilateral with four congruent sides a square? Explain.

Quick Review

Suppose a figure is a parallelogram.

- If the diagonals are perpendicular, then the parallelogram is a rhombus.
- If the diagonals are congruent, then the parallelogram is a rectangle.
- If the diagonals are perpendicular and congruent, then the parallelogram is a square.

Example

Show that the parallelogram is a square.

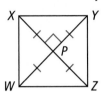

Since $XP = ZP = WP = YP$, $XZ = WY$, the diagonals are congruent. Since the diagonals are congruent, the parallelogram is a rectangle. The diagonals are also given to be perpendicular to each other, so the rectangle is a square.

Practice & Problem Solving

Is the parallelogram a rhombus, a rectangle, or a square?

21.

22.

23. **Make Sense and Persevere** For what value of x is *GHJK* a rhombus? Explain.

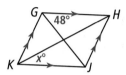

24. **Construct Arguments** Can Nora construct a kite with diagonals that bisect each other? Explain.

TOPIC 9

Similarity and Right Triangles

? TOPIC ESSENTIAL QUESTION

How are properties of similar figures used to solve problems?

Topic Overview

enVision® STEM Project:
Design With a 3D Printer

9-1 Dilations

9-2 Similarity Transformations

9-3 Proving Triangles Similar

9-4 Similarity in Right Triangles

Mathematical Modeling in 3 Acts:
Make It Right

9-5 Proportions in Triangles

9-6 Right Triangles and the Pythagorean Theorem

9-7 Trigonometric Ratios

Extension 9-7a: The Pythagorean Identity

Topic Vocabulary

- center of dilation
- cosine
- geometric mean
- Pythagorean triple
- similarity transformation
- sine
- tangent
- trigonometric ratios

Digital Experience

 INTERACTIVE STUDENT EDITION Access online or offline.

 ACTIVITIES Complete *Explore & Reason, Model & Discuss*, and *Critique & Explain* activities. Interact with Examples and Try Its.

 ANIMATION View and interact with real-world applications.

 PRACTICE Practice what you've learned.

 Go online | PearsonRealize.com

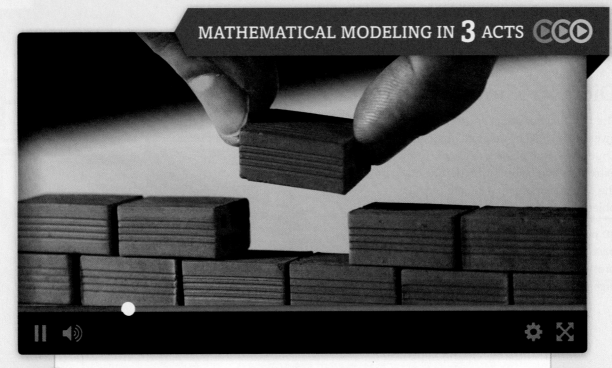

▶ Make It Right

Architects often make a scale physical model of a new building project. The scale model is usually a miniature version of the project it is representing.

When making a model, architects need to make sure that all of the parts of the model are the right size. Think about this during the Mathematical Modeling in 3 Acts lesson.

TOPIC 9

▶ **VIDEOS** Watch clips to support *Mathematical Modeling in 3 Acts Lessons* and **enVision® *STEM Projects.***

⚷ **CONCEPT SUMMARY** Review key lesson content through multiple representations.

☑ **ASSESSMENT** Show what you've learned.

A-Z **GLOSSARY** Read and listen to English and Spanish definitions.

⏻ **TUTORIALS** Get help from *Virtual Nerd*, right when you need it.

🔧 **MATH TOOLS** Explore math with digital tools and manipulatives.

Video

Did You Know?

The **first 3-dimensional printer** was invented in **1983** by Colorado engineer Chuck Hull. Hull's idea was to "print" extremely thin layers of plastic, one atop the other, building up a 3-dimensional object.

3D printers make **toys, replacement parts for machines, and medical prosthetics**. They also make architectural and scale models.

Grecia, a toucan, eats and sings using a **3D-printed prosthetic** upper beak.

The **first printing press** was invented by Johannes Gutenberg around the year **1450**. To print a page, Gutenberg made individual letters from metal and arranged the letters **on a block**. Then he inked the letters and **stamped them** on paper.

▶ Your Task: Design With a 3D Printer

An engineer has built a scale model of a part for a rocket engine. Full-size, the part will be mass-produced using 3D printing. You and your classmates will use similarity to scale up the dimensions of the part. Then you'll describe and draw steps for the production of the part.

9-1
Dilations

🔘 PearsonRealize.com

I CAN... dilate figures and identify characteristics of dilations.

VOCABULARY
• center of dilation

🖐 EXPLORE & REASON

Roosevelt High School sells a sticker and a larger car decal with the school logo.

A. Look for Relationships How are the sticker and the car decal alike? How are they different?

B. Suppose the sticker and decal are shown next to each other on a computer screen. If you zoom in to 125%, what would stay the same on the figures? What would be different?

❓ ESSENTIAL QUESTION   How does a dilation affect the side lengths and angle measures of a figure?

CONCEPTUAL UNDERSTANDING

🖐 EXAMPLE 1   Dilate a Figure

How can you draw a dilated image?

A dilation produces an image that is a different size than the preimage.

Method 1 The Ratio Method

Dilate $\triangle ABC$ by a scale factor of $\frac{1}{2}$ with fixed center P. This fixed center is called the **center of dilation**.

STUDY TIP
Recall that in a dilation, the preimage is enlarged or reduced in size by a given scale factor.

Step 2 Mark point A' at a point that is half the distance from P to A. Repeat for B' and C'.

Step 1 Draw rays from P through each vertex of $\triangle ABC$.

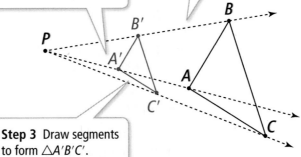

Step 3 Draw segments to form $\triangle A'B'C'$.

Triangle $A'B'C'$ is a copy of $\triangle ABC$ with side lengths that are $\frac{1}{2}$ the lengths of the corresponding sides of $\triangle ABC$.

CONTINUED ON THE NEXT PAGE

EXAMPLE 1 CONTINUED

Method 2 The Parallel Method

Dilate *WXYZ* by 2 with center of dilation *Q*.

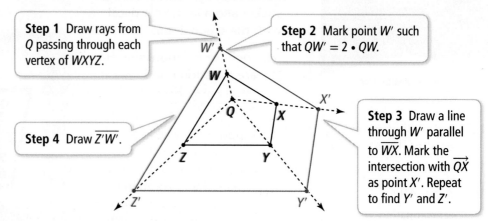

Step 1 Draw rays from *Q* passing through each vertex of *WXYZ*.

Step 2 Mark point *W'* such that $QW' = 2 \cdot QW$.

Step 3 Draw a line through *W'* parallel to $\overline{WX}$. Mark the intersection with $\overrightarrow{QX}$ as point *X'*. Repeat to find *Y'* and *Z'*.

Step 4 Draw $\overline{Z'W'}$.

MAKE SENSE AND PERSEVERE

Consider the two methods for dilating figures. How are they alike? How are they different?

Segment *W'Z'* is parallel to $\overline{WZ}$.

Quadrilateral *W'X'Y'Z'* is a copy of *WXYZ* with side lengths that are twice the lengths of the corresponding sides of *WXYZ*.

Try It!

1. a. Trace △*JKL* and point *R*. Use Method 1 to dilate △*JKL* by a scale factor of 3 with center of dilation *R*.

b. Trace △*PQR* and point *M*. Use Method 2 to dilate △*PQR* by a scale factor of $\frac{1}{3}$ with center of dilation *M*.

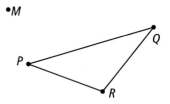

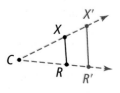

CONCEPT Dilations

A dilation $D_{(n, C)}$ is a transformation that has center of dilation *C* and scale factor *n*, where $n > 0$, with the following properties:

- Point *R* maps to *R'* in such a way that *R'* is on $\overrightarrow{CR}$ and $CR' = n \cdot CR$.

- Each length in the image is *n* times the corresponding length in the preimage (i.e., $X'R' = n \cdot XR$).

- The image of the center of dilation is the center itself (i.e., $C' = C$).

- If $n > 1$, the dilation is an *enlargement*.

- If $0 < n < 1$, the dilation is a *reduction*.

- Every angle is congruent to its image under the dilation.

On a coordinate plane, the notation D_n describes the dilation with the origin as center of dilation.

EXAMPLE 2 Analyze Dilations

Rectangle *A'B'C'D'* is a dilation with center *P* of *ABCD*. How are the side lengths and angle measures of *ABCD* related to those of *A'B'C'D'*?

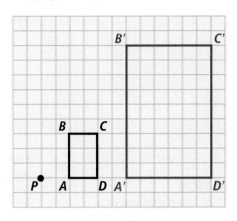

Step 1 Compare the angles.

All angles of rectangles are right angles, so each angle in image *A'B'C'D'* is congruent to the corresponding angle in *ABCD*.

Step 2 Compare the side lengths.

Find the side lengths in the preimage and image.

$AB = 3$	$BC = 2$	$CD = 3$	$DA = 2$
$A'B' = 9$	$B'C' = 6$	$C'D' = 9$	$D'A' = 6$

Find the ratios of the corresponding side lengths.

$$\frac{A'B'}{AB} = \frac{9}{3} = 3 \qquad \frac{B'C'}{BC} = \frac{6}{2} = 3 \qquad \frac{C'D'}{CD} = \frac{9}{3} = 3 \qquad \frac{D'A'}{DA} = \frac{6}{2} = 3$$

The ratios are equal, so the lengths of corresponding sides of the two figures are proportional.

 Try It! 2. Rectangle *W'X'Y'Z'* is a dilation with center *P* of *WXYZ*. How are the side lengths and angle measures of the two figures related?

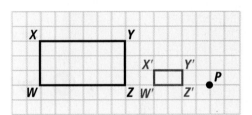

EXAMPLE 3 Find a Scale Factor

Quadrilateral *J'K'L'M'* is a dilation of *JKLM*. What is the scale factor?

The scale factor is the ratio of side lengths in the image to the corresponding side lengths in the preimage.

$$\frac{K'L'}{KL} = \frac{18}{12} = \frac{3}{2}$$

The scale factor is $\frac{3}{2}$.

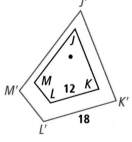

COMMON ERROR
Be careful to find the scale factor and not its reciprocal. Think about whether the dilation is an enlargement or reduction to see whether the scale factor makes sense.

 Try It! 3. Consider the dilation shown.

a. Is the dilation an enlargement or a reduction?

b. What is the scale factor?

EXAMPLE 4 **Dilate a Figure With Center at the Origin**

What are the vertices of $D_3(\triangle ABC)$?

The notation $D_3(\triangle ABC)$ means the image of $\triangle ABC$ after a dilation centered at the origin, with scale factor 3.

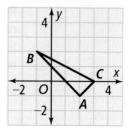

For a dilation with scale factor 3 centered at the origin, each image point is 3 times farther away from the origin than the corresponding preimage point.

Multiply each coordinate of each preimage point by 3 to find the coordinates of the image points.

$$A(2, -1) \rightarrow A'(3 \cdot 2, 3 \cdot -1) = A'(6, -3)$$
$$B(-1, 2) \rightarrow B'(3 \cdot -1, 3 \cdot 2) = B'(-3, 6)$$
$$C(3, 0) \rightarrow C'(3 \cdot 3, 3 \cdot 0) = C'(9, 0)$$

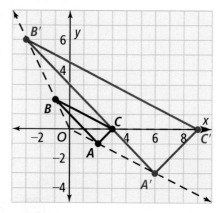

REASON

Think about distances on a coordinate plane. How could you show algebraically that multiplying each coordinate by the scale factor n produces a point that is n times the distance from the origin?

The vertices of $D_3(\triangle ABC)$ are $A'(6, -3)$, $B'(-3, 6)$, and $C'(9, 0)$.

☑ **Try It!** **4.** Use $\triangle PQR$.

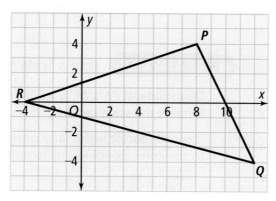

a. What are the vertices of $D_{\frac{1}{4}}(\triangle PQR)$?

b. How are the distances to the origin from each image point related to the distance to the origin from each corresponding preimage point?

EXAMPLE 5 · Dilate a Figure With Center Not at the Origin

What are the vertices of $D_{(\frac{1}{2}, R)}(QRST)$?

The dilation is centered at $R(-2, 7)$ with a scale factor of $\frac{1}{2}$. So each image point is half the distance from R as the corresponding preimage point is. For each preimage point, multiply the horizontal and vertical changes from R by $\frac{1}{2}$. Then add the horizontal and vertical half-changes to the coordinates of the center of dilation.

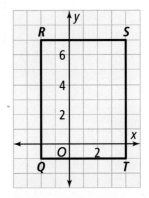

Preimage Point	Change From $R(-2, 7)$		Half of the Change From $R(-2, 7)$		Add to $R(-2, 7)$	Image Point
	horiz.	vert.	horiz.	vert.		
$Q(-2, -1)$	0	−8	0	−4	$(-2 + 0, 7 - 4)$	$Q'(-2, 3)$
$S(4, 7)$	6	0	3	0	$(-2 + 3, 7 + 0)$	$S'(1, 7)$
$T(4, -1)$	6	−8	3	−4	$(-2 + 3, 7 - 4)$	$T'(1, 3)$

Graph the preimage and image on the same coordinate plane.

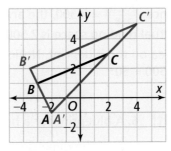

Since the center is R, points R and R' have the same coordinates.

The vertices of $D_{(\frac{1}{2}, R)}(QRST)$ are $Q'(-2, 3)$, $R'(-2, 7)$, $S'(1, 7)$, and $T'(1, 3)$.

STUDY TIP
Remember to check your answers by measuring the distances between the center of dilation and the image and preimage vertices.

☑ Try It! 5. A dilation of △ABC is shown.

a. What is the center of dilation?

b. What is the scale factor?

APPLICATION   **EXAMPLE 6**   **Use a Scale Factor to Find Length and Area**

A blueprint for a new library uses a scale factor of $\frac{1}{50}$. Mr. Ayer measures the reading space on the blueprint to find the actual dimensions and area so he can order furniture.

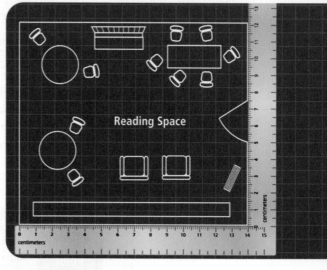

Reading Space

A. What are the actual dimensions of the reading space?

Let x represent the length and y represent the width.

$$\frac{14}{x} = \frac{1}{50}$$

$$x = 14 \cdot 50$$

$$x = 700$$

> The ratio of image side length to actual side length is $\frac{1}{50}$.

$$\frac{12}{y} = \frac{1}{50}$$

$$y = 12 \cdot 50$$

$$y = 600$$

The reading space is 700 cm, or 7 m, long and 600 cm, or 6 m, wide.

B. What is the actual area of the reading space? How does the actual area relate to the area on the blueprint?

Find the area of the reading space.

$$7 \cdot 6 = 42, \text{ or } 700 \cdot 600 = 420{,}000$$

The area is 420,000 cm^2, or 42 m^2.

> The actual area is more useful in square meters, but the actual area in square centimeters is needed to compare to the area on the blueprint.

Then find the area of the reading space on the blueprint.

$$14 \cdot 12 = 168$$

The area on the blueprint is 168 cm^2.

Since $\frac{420{,}000}{168} = 2{,}500$, the area of the actual reading space is 2,500 times the area on the blueprint. Notice that $2{,}500 = 50^2$.

> In general, the ratio of the area of the image to the area of the preimage is the square of the scale factor.

LOOK FOR RELATIONSHIPS
Think about equivalent expressions to understand how quantities are related. How does writing 700 × 600 as (50 × 14) × (50 × 12) help you to understand the relationship between the areas?

 Try It!   **6.** A blueprint for a house uses a scale factor of $\frac{1}{20}$.

   a. If the dimensions of the actual kitchen are 3.1 m by 3.4 m, what are the dimensions of the kitchen on the blueprint?

   b. What is the relationship between the area of the actual kitchen and the area of the kitchen on the blueprint?

CONCEPT SUMMARY Dilations

WORDS A dilation is a transformation that maps point X to point X' such that X' lies on $\overrightarrow{CX}$ and $CX' = k \cdot CX$ for a center of dilation C and a scale factor k. Dilations preserve angle measures.

DIAGRAM

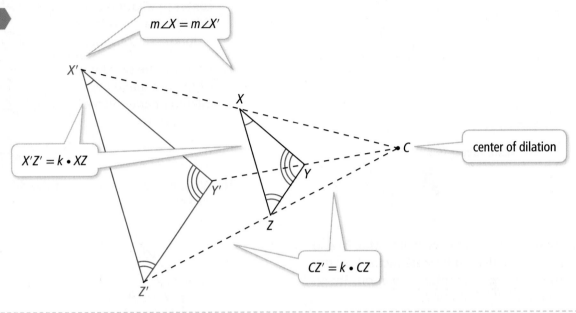

$m\angle X = m\angle X'$

$X'Z' = k \cdot XZ$

center of dilation

$CZ' = k \cdot CZ$

NOTATION Dilation centered at the origin: $D_k(X)$

Dilation centered at point C: $D_{(k,\ C)}(X)$

✓ Do You UNDERSTAND?

1. **ESSENTIAL QUESTION** How does a dilation affect the side lengths and angle measures of a figure?

2. **Error Analysis** Emilia was asked to find the coordinates of $D_2(\triangle ABC)$ for $A(2, 4)$, $B(0, 5)$, and $C(-2, 1)$. What is Emilia's error?

$$A(2, 4) \rightarrow A'(4, 6)$$
$$B(0, 5) \rightarrow B'(2, 7)$$
$$C(-2, 1) \rightarrow C'(0, 3)$$ ✗

3. **Vocabulary** In the definition of a dilation D_n, why can't n be equal to 0? What would a transformation like D_0 look like?

4. **Construct Arguments** Compare the vertices of $D_1(\triangle ABC)$ for any points A, B, and C. Justify your answer.

Do You KNOW HOW?

5. Trace $\triangle JKL$ and point P. Draw the dilation of $\triangle JKL$ using scale factor 3 and P as the center of dilation.

6. What is the scale factor for the dilation?

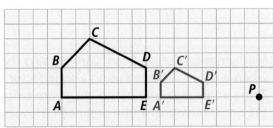

Give the coordinates of the dilation.

7. $D_5(\triangle PQR)$ for $P(1, -3)$, $Q(-5, -4)$, $R(6, 2)$

8. $D_{(3,\ B)}(\triangle ABC)$ for $A(0, 4)$, $B(0, 2)$, $C(-3, 2)$

9. $D_{(4,\ F)}(FGHJ)$ for $F(0, -1)$, $G(4, -1)$, $H(4, -3)$, $J(0, -3)$

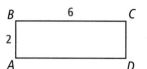
UNDERSTAND

10. Error Analysis Kendall was asked to find the scale factor for the dilation. What is Kendall's error?

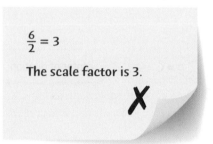

$\frac{6}{2} = 3$

The scale factor is 3.

✗

11. Higher Order Thinking Points $M(a, b)$ and $N(c, d)$ are dilated by scale factor k, with the origin as the center of dilation. Show algebraically that $\overleftrightarrow{MN} \parallel \overleftrightarrow{M'N'}$.

12. Communicate Precisely Suppose you want to dilate a figure on the coordinate plane with a center of dilation at point (a, b) that is not the origin and with a scale factor k. Describe how you can use a composition of translations and a dilation centered at the origin to dilate the figure. Then write the transformation rule.

13. Reason Rectangle $J'K'L'M'$ is a dilation of $JKLM$ with scale factor k. What are the perimeter and area of $JKLM$?

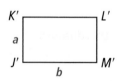

14. Mathematical Connections Carolina says that when a figure is dilated using a scale factor of 2, the angle measures in the image are twice the angle measures in the preimage. How could you use the Triangle Angle Sum Theorem to explain why this cannot be true?

15. Generalize Is it always true that $(D_m \circ D_n)(X) = D_{mn}(X)$? Explain.

PRACTICE

16. Trace $ABCD$ and point P. Draw the dilation of $ABCD$ using P as the center of dilation and sides that are two times as long. SEE EXAMPLE 1

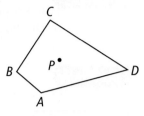

17. How are the side lengths of the preimage and dilated image related? SEE EXAMPLE 2

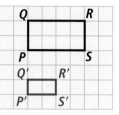

18. What is the scale factor of the dilation shown? SEE EXAMPLE 3

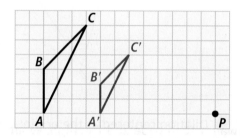

19. What are the coordinates of $D_{1.5}(ABCD)$ for $A(2, 0)$, $B(8, -4)$, $C(4, -6)$, and $D(-5, -10)$? SEE EXAMPLE 4

20. What are the coordinates of $D_{(2, X)}(\triangle XYZ)$ for $X(1, 1)$, $Y(2, 2)$, and $Z(3, 0)$? SEE EXAMPLE 5

21. A figure is dilated using a scale factor of 8. If the area of the image is 832 square units, what is the area of the preimage? SEE EXAMPLE 6

22. If $\triangle F'G'H'$ is a dilation of $\triangle FGH$ with a scale factor of 3, what are the values of x and y?

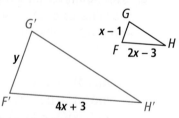

23. What are the coordinates of the center of dilation for the dilation shown?

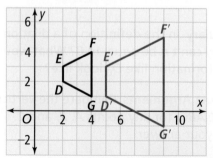

PRACTICE & PROBLEM SOLVING

APPLY

24. Reason The images on Henry's digital camera have a width-to-length ratio of 2 : 3. He wants to make an 8 in.-by-10 in. print of one of his photographs.

   a. Is this possible? Explain.

   b. How can Henry crop an image so that an 8 in.-by-10 in. print can be made?

25. Model With Mathematics Alex draws the scale model shown as a plan for a large wall mosaic.

10 cm

12 cm

   a. The wall is 10 m wide and 7 m high. What are the dimensions of the largest mosaic he can make on that wall? Explain.

   b. He will use 2-cm square tiles to make his mosaic. How many tiles will he need? Explain how you found your answer.

26. Look for Relationships How far from the screen should the light be placed in order for the shadow of the puppet to be 30 in. tall? Explain how you found your answer.

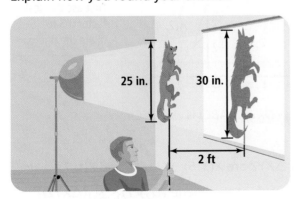

25 in.   30 in.

2 ft

ASSESSMENT PRACTICE

27. Copy and complete the table to show information about dilations centered at the origin.

Preimage Coordinates	Scale Factor	Image Coordinates
(5, –2)	4	■
(9, 3)	■	(3, 1)
■	1.5	(–6, 0)
(–1, 2)	■	(–5, 10)

28. SAT/ACT A dilation maps $\triangle ABC$ to $\triangle A'B'C'$. The area of $\triangle ABC$ is 13 square units, and the area of $\triangle A'B'C'$ is 52 square units. What is the scale factor?

   Ⓐ 2   Ⓒ 4

   Ⓑ 13   Ⓓ 26

29. Performance Task Alberto wants to make a scale model of the Wright brothers' glider.

Wingspan: 9.8 m

Wing Area: 28.3 m²

Height: 2.4 m

Length: 4.9 m

Part A The wingspan of the scale model must be between 15 cm and 18 cm. What scale factor should he use? Explain.

Part B Use your scale factor from Part A. What will be the length, wingspan, and height of the model glider?

Part C What will be the wing area of the model glider? If both wing sections are the same size, what will be the dimensions of each wing section?

9-2

Similarity Transformations

I CAN... determine whether figures are similar.

VOCABULARY
• similarity transformation

CRITIQUE & EXPLAIN

Helena and Edwin were asked to apply a composition of transformations to *ABCD*.

Helena

Edwin

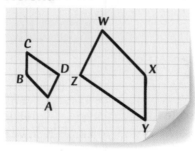
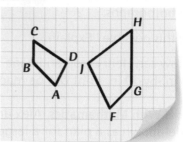

A. Use Appropriate Tools Is there a composition of transformations that maps *ABCD* to the second figure in each student's work? If so, what is it?

B. For each student whose work shows a composition of transformations, describe the relationship between the figures.

ESSENTIAL QUESTION

What makes a transformation a similarity transformation? What is the relationship between a preimage and the image resulting from a similarity transformation?

EXAMPLE 1   Graph a Composition of a Rigid Motion and a Dilation

COMMON ERROR
Be careful to use the correct center of dilation. When the notation does not specify the center of dilation, the center of dilation is at the origin.

If line *m* is represented by the equation $x = -3$, what is a graph of the image $(R_m \circ D_{0.5})(\triangle ABC)$?

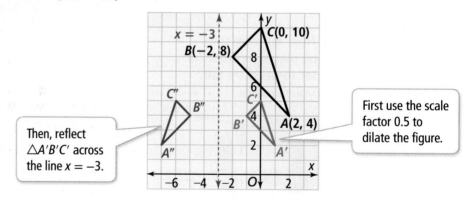

Then, reflect $\triangle A'B'C'$ across the line $x = -3$.

First use the scale factor 0.5 to dilate the figure.

The graph of the image $(R_m \circ D_{0.5})(\triangle ABC)$ is $\triangle A''B''C''$.

 Try It!   **1.** The vertices of $\triangle XYZ$ are $X(3, 5)$, $Y(-1, 4)$, and $Z(1, 7)$.

   a. What is the graph of the image $(D_2 \circ T_{\langle 1, -2\rangle})(\triangle XYZ)$?

   b. What is the graph of the image $(D_3 \circ r_{(90°, O)})(\triangle XYZ)$?

EXAMPLE 2 **Describe a Composition of a Rigid Motion and a Dilation**

Is there a composition of transformations that maps △XYZ to △JKL? Explain.

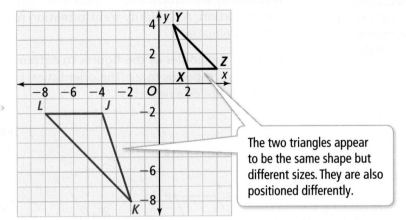

The two triangles appear to be the same shape but different sizes. They are also positioned differently.

> **MAKE SENSE AND PERSEVERE**
> Think about how you could use reflection, translation, or rotation to create an image of △XYZ with the orientation opposite of △JKL. Which rigid motion would you use?

Notice that Y in △XYZ is in the upper left of the first quadrant, but its corresponding vertex K in △JKL is in the lower right of the third quadrant, so it appears that △XYZ is rotated. Since △JKL is larger than △XYZ, it is also dilated.

Rotate △XYZ 180° about the origin to produce the image X'Y'Z'.

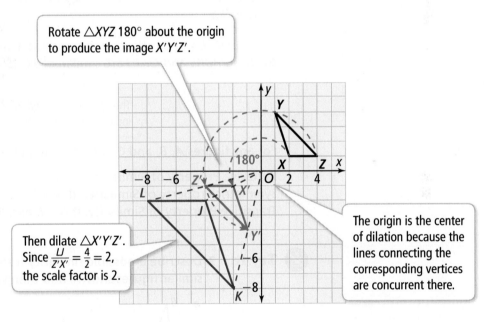

Then dilate △X'Y'Z'. Since $\frac{LJ}{Z'X'} = \frac{4}{2} = 2$, the scale factor is 2.

The origin is the center of dilation because the lines connecting the corresponding vertices are concurrent there.

So, the composition of transformations $D_2 \circ r_{(180°, O)}$ maps △XYZ to △JKL.

Try It! **2.** If the transformations in Example 2 are performed in the reverse order, are the results the same? Do you think your answer holds for all compositions of transformations? Explain.

CONCEPTUAL
UNDERSTANDING

👆 **EXAMPLE 3** **Find Similarity Transformations**

Why is *PQRS* similar to *GKJH*?

A **similarity transformation** is a composition of one or more rigid motions and a dilation. A similarity transformation results in an image that is similar to the preimage.

Measure the angles of the figures to determine that ∠S corresponds to ∠H and ∠R corresponds to ∠J. The orientation is reversed in *GHJK*, so the rigid motion includes a reflection.

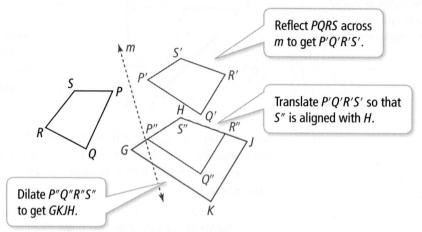

Reflect *PQRS* across *m* to get *P'Q'R'S'*.

Translate *P'Q'R'S'* so that *S"* is aligned with *H*.

Dilate *P"Q"R"S"* to get *GKJH*.

A composition of a reflection, a translation, and a dilation maps *PQRS* to *GKJH*, so *PQRS* and *GKJH* are similar, or *PQRS* ∼ *GKJH*.

The symbol ∼ is used to indicate similarity.

For any figures *A*, *B*, and *C*, the following properties hold.

Reflexive Property of Similarity: *A* ∼ *A*
Symmetric Property of Similarity: If *A* ∼ *B*, then *B* ∼ *A*.
Transitive Property of Similarity: If *A* ∼ *B* and *B* ∼ *C*, then *A* ∼ *C*.

 Try It!   3. Describe a possible similarity transformation for each pair of similar figures shown, and then write a similarity statement.

a.
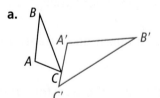

b.
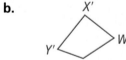

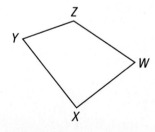

APPLICATION

EXAMPLE 4 Determine Similarity

Can the artist copy her sketch to cover an entire wall measuring 15 ft high by 20 ft wide so her wall mural is similar to her sketch? Explain.

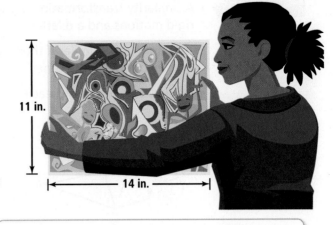

11 in.

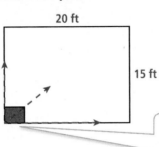

20 ft

15 ft

If the artist can map her sketch onto the wall, then she can place her sketch at the bottom left corner and dilate it.

14 in.

MAKE SENSE AND PERSEVERE
Suppose you found the scale factor needed to map the width of the sketch to the width of the wall. Would the results be the same?

To determine the scale factor, convert the dimensions of the wall into inches.

$15 \cdot 12 = 180$ $20 \cdot 12 = 240$

The dimensions of the wall are 180 in. high by 240 in. wide.

Divide the height of the wall by the height of the sketch to determine the scale factor needed to map the sketch to the height of the wall.

$180 \div 11 \approx 16.36$

Calculate to see whether the width of the sketch maps to the width of the wall.

$16.36 \cdot 14 \approx 229$

Since $229 < 240$, the sketch cannot be copied to cover the entire wall.

 Try It! 4. Suppose the artist cuts 2 inches from the width of her sketch in Example 4. How much should she cut from the height so she can copy a similar image to cover the wall?

PROOF

EXAMPLE 5 Identify Similar Circles

Write a proof that any two circles are similar.

Given: ⊙P with radius r, ⊙Q with radius s

Prove: ⊙P ~ ⊙Q

Proof: Translate P to Q, so P' coincides with Q. Then find a scale factor that dilates ⊙P' to the circle with radius s.

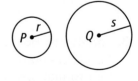

Let $k = \frac{s}{r}$. Then the translation followed by a dilation centered at Q with scale factor k maps ⊙P onto ⊙Q. Since a similarity transformation exists, ⊙P ~ ⊙Q.

 Try It! 5. Write a proof that any two squares are similar.

CONCEPT SUMMARY Similarity

WORDS • A similarity transformation is a composition of one or more rigid motions and a dilation.

• Two figures are similar if there is a similarity transformation that maps one to the other.

• All circles are similar to each other.

DIAGRAMS

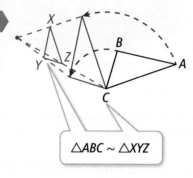

$\triangle ABC \sim \triangle XYZ$

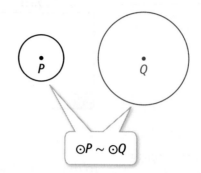

$\odot P \sim \odot Q$

Do You UNDERSTAND?

1. **ESSENTIAL QUESTION** What makes a transformation a similarity transformation? What is the relationship between a preimage and the image resulting from a similarity transformation?

2. **Error Analysis** Reese described the similarity transformation that maps $\triangle ABC$ to $\triangle XZY$. What is Reese's error?

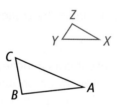

   △ABC is dilated and then rotated to produce the image △XZY. **X**

3. **Vocabulary** How are similarity transformations and congruence transformations alike? How are they different?

4. **Construct Arguments** A similarity transformation consisting of a reflection and a dilation is performed on a figure, and one point maps to itself. Describe one way this could happen.

Do You KNOW HOW?

For Exercises 5 and 6, what are the vertices of each image?

5. $r_{(90°, O)} \circ D_{0.5}(ABCD)$ for $A(5, 1)$, $B(-3, 4)$, $C(0, 2)$, $D(4, 6)$

6. $(D_3 \circ R_{x\text{-axis}})(\triangle GHJ)$ for $G(3, 5)$, $H(1, -2)$, $J(-1, 6)$

7. Describe a similarity transformation that maps $\triangle SQR$ to $\triangle DEF$.

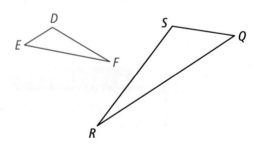

8. Do the two figures appear to be similar? Use transformations to explain.

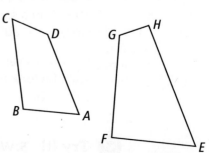

PRACTICE & PROBLEM SOLVING

UNDERSTAND

9. **Construct Arguments** Is it possible to use only translations and dilations to map one circle to another? Explain.

10. **Error Analysis** Keegan was asked to graph $(r_{90°} \circ D_2)(\triangle ABC)$. Explain Keegan's error.

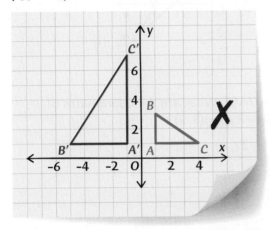

11. **Mathematical Connections** In the diagram, $ABCD \sim A'B'C'D'$. What are the angle measures of $A'B'C'D'$?

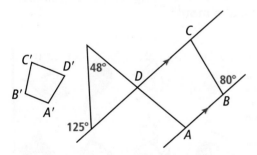

12. **Construct Arguments** Are all squares similar? Use transformations to explain.

13. **Generalize** Show whether a composition of a dilation and a translation can be performed in either order and result in the same image. (Hint: Test whether the equation $(D_k \circ T_{\langle a, b \rangle})(x, y) = (T_{\langle a, b \rangle} \circ D_k)(x, y)$ is true.)

14. **Higher Order Thinking** Given isosceles triangle ABC with $\overline{AB} \cong \overline{BC}$. Point D is the midpoint of $\overline{AB}$, E is the midpoint of $\overline{BC}$, and F is the midpoint of $\overline{CA}$. Use a similarity transformation and triangle congruence to show that $\triangle ABC \sim \triangle FEC$.

PRACTICE

What are the vertices of each image? SEE EXAMPLE 1

15. $(T_{\langle 5, -4 \rangle} \circ D_{1.5})(\triangle XYZ)$ for $X(6, -2)$, $Y(4, 1)$, $Z(-2, 3)$

16. $(R_{x\text{-axis}} \circ D_{0.5})(LMNP)$ for $L(2, 4)$, $M(4, 4)$, $N(4, -4)$, $P(2, -4)$

17. $(R_{y\text{-axis}} \circ D_2 \circ r_{270°})(\triangle PQR)$ for $P(1, 3)$, $Q(-4, 2)$, $R(0, 5)$

18. $(D_{0.25} \circ R_{x\text{-axis}})(ABCD)$ for $A(2, 6)$, $B(0, 0)$, $C(-5, 8)$, $D(-2, 10)$

For each black pre-image and red image describe the similarity transformation, and write a similarity statement. SEE EXAMPLES 2 AND 3

19.

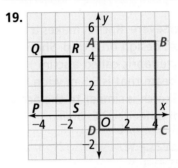

20.

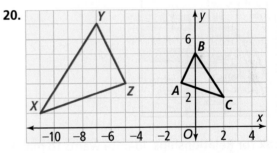

21.

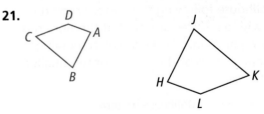

Do the figures appear to be similar? Explain.
SEE EXAMPLE 4

22.   23.

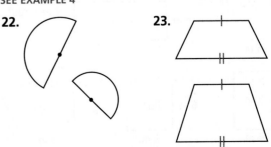

APPLY

24. Reason Can Ahmed use the larger sheets of paper shown to make paper cutouts similar to his original hummingbird cutout? If not, how can he trim the sheets of paper so he can use them? Justify your answer.

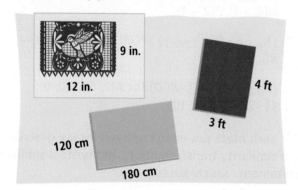

9 in.

12 in.

4 ft

3 ft

120 cm

180 cm

25. Make Sense and Persevere Rachel makes a sketch for a stage set design on a grid. She plans to have a gauze fabric called a scrim drop down from a beam that is 5.5 m wide. Assuming that her sketch is similar to the actual set, how much scrim is needed? Explain.

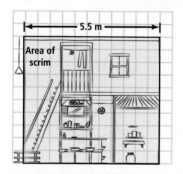

5.5 m

Area of scrim

26. Look for Relationships Juanita wants to make a dollhouse following the pattern shown but with a reduced size so that the floor has an area of 25 in.². Make a sketch showing the dimensions of the pieces for the smaller dollhouse.

Dollhouse Pattern

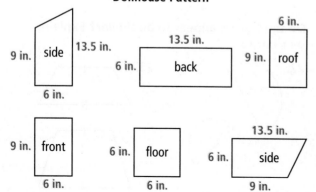

9 in. side 13.5 in.

13.5 in.

6 in. back

6 in.

6 in. roof

9 in.

6 in.

9 in. front

6 in.

6 in. floor

6 in.

6 in. side

13.5 in.

9 in.

ASSESSMENT PRACTICE

27. Graph the image of $(T_{\langle 1, -3 \rangle} \circ D_2)(\triangle ABC)$.

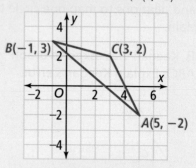

$B(-1, 3)$

$C(3, 2)$

$A(5, -2)$

28. SAT/ACT What are the coordinates of $(D_4 \circ R_{x\text{-axis}})(8, 2)$?

Ⓐ $(-32, 8)$

Ⓑ $(32, 8)$

Ⓒ $(-32, -8)$

Ⓓ $(32, -8)$

29. Performance Task Lourdes makes sketches for her graphic novel using a repeating similar shape as a motif.

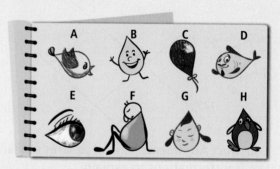

A   B   C   D

E   F   G   H

Part A On a separate sheet of paper, draw a small simple figure. Label it A.

Part B Use transformations, including similarity transformations, to create at least five images that are similar to figure A. Label the images B, C, D, E, and F.

Part C Is it possible to select any two of your figures and find a similarity transformation that maps one to the other? Explain.

9-3

Proving Triangles Similar

I CAN... use dilation and rigid motion to establish triangle similarity theorems.

🖐 EXPLORE & REASON

The measurements of two triangles are shown.

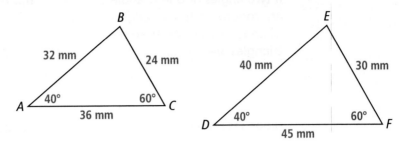

A. Are the triangles similar? Explain.

B. Construct Arguments Would any triangle with 40°- and 60°-angles be similar to △ABC? Explain.

❓ ESSENTIAL QUESTION

How can you use the angles and sides of two triangles to determine whether they are similar?

CONCEPTUAL UNDERSTANDING

🖐 EXAMPLE 1 Establish the Angle-Angle Similarity (AA ~) Theorem

If $\angle A \cong \angle R$ and $\angle B \cong \angle S$, is $\triangle ABC \sim \triangle RST$? Explain.

To show that the triangles are similar, determine whether there is a similarity transformation that maps △ABC to △RST.

Determine the center of dilation and the scale factor that map △ABC to image △A'B'C' such that A'B' = RS.

Let the scale factor k be $\frac{RS}{AB}$.

Then, $A'B' = k \cdot AB = RS$.

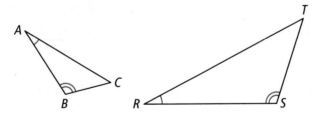

> Use vertex A as the center of dilation, so A = A' and $\angle A \cong \angle A' \cong \angle R$.

> Dilations preserve angle measure, so $\angle B \cong \angle B' \cong \angle S$.

REASON
Think about what it means for figures to be similar. Are congruent triangles similar to the same triangle?

The dilation $D_{(k, A)}$ maps △ABC to △A'B'C', and △A'B'C' ≅ △RST by ASA, so there is a rigid motion that maps △A'B'C' to △RST. Thus, the composition is a similarity transformation that maps △ABC to △RST. So, △ABC ~ △RST.

 Try It! 1. If $\angle A$ is congruent to $\angle R$, and $\angle C$ is congruent to $\angle T$, how would you prove the triangles are similar?

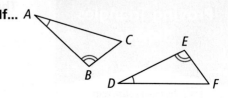

THEOREM 9-1 Angle-Angle Similarity (AA ~) Theorem

If two angles of one triangle
are congruent to two angles
of another triangle, then the
triangles are similar.

If...

$\angle A \cong \angle D$ and $\angle B \cong \angle E$

PROOF: SEE EXERCISE 10.

Then... $\triangle ABC \sim \triangle DEF$

EXAMPLE 2 **Establish the Side-Side-Side Similarity (SSS ~) Theorem**

If $\frac{LM}{PQ} = \frac{MN}{QR} = \frac{LN}{PR}$, is there a similarity transformation that maps $\triangle PQR$ to $\triangle LMN$? Explain.

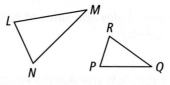

Dilate $\triangle PQR$ by scale factor $k = \frac{LM}{PQ} = \frac{MN}{QR} = \frac{LN}{PR}$ to map $\triangle PQR$ to $\triangle P'Q'R'$.

$$P'R' = k \cdot PR = \frac{LN}{PR} \cdot PR = LN$$

$$Q'R' = k \cdot QR = \frac{MN}{QR} \cdot QR = MN$$

$$P'Q' = k \cdot PQ = \frac{LM}{PQ} \cdot PQ = LM$$

Because $P'R' = LN$, $P'Q' = LM$, and $Q'R' = MN$, $\triangle P'Q'R' \cong \triangle LMN$ by SSS. By the definition of congruence, there is a rigid motion that maps $\triangle P'Q'R'$ to $\triangle LMN$.

So, $\triangle PQR$ was mapped to $\triangle LMN$ by a similarity transformation and $\triangle PQR$ is similar to $\triangle LMN$.

STUDY TIP
Remember, two figures are
similar if there is a similarity
transformation between them.

Try It! **2.** If $\frac{DF}{GJ} = \frac{EF}{HJ}$ and $\angle F \cong \angle J$, is there a similarity transformation
that maps $\triangle DEF$ to $\triangle GHJ$? Explain.

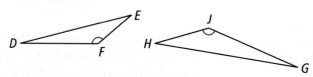

THEOREM 9-2 Side-Side-Side Similarity (SSS ~) Theorem

If the corresponding sides of two triangles are proportional, then the triangles are similar.

If...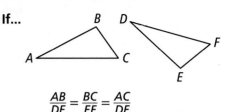

$$\frac{AB}{DE} = \frac{BC}{EF} = \frac{AC}{DF}$$

PROOF: SEE EXERCISE 20.

Then... △ABC ~ △DEF

THEOREM 9-3 Side-Angle-Side Similarity (SAS ~) Theorem

If an angle of one triangle is congruent to an angle of a second triangle, and the sides that include the two angles are proportional, then the triangles are similar.

If...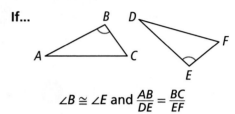

$$\angle B \cong \angle E \text{ and } \frac{AB}{DE} = \frac{BC}{EF}$$

PROOF: SEE EXERCISE 13.

Then... △ABC ~ △DEF

EXAMPLE 3 Verify Triangle Similarity

A. Are △ABC and △DEF similar?

Determine whether the ratios of the corresponding side lengths are equal.

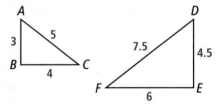

COMMON ERROR
When setting up ratios to check if triangles are similar, be sure you place sides from the same triangle in the same position in each ratio.

$$\frac{AB}{DE} = \frac{3}{4.5} = \frac{2}{3} \qquad \frac{BC}{EF} = \frac{4}{6} = \frac{2}{3} \qquad \frac{AC}{DF} = \frac{5}{7.5} = \frac{2}{3}$$

The ratios are equal, so the corresponding side lengths are proportional. △ABC ~ △DEF by SSS ~.

B. Are △PQS and △RQP similar?

The two triangles share an included angle, ∠Q. Separate the triangles and see whether the lengths of the corresponding sides are in proportion.

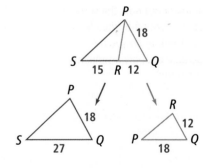

Since $\frac{SQ}{PQ} = \frac{27}{18} = \frac{3}{2}$ and $\frac{PQ}{RQ} = \frac{18}{12} = \frac{3}{2}$, the lengths of the sides that include ∠Q are proportional. By SAS ~, △PQS ~ △RQP.

 Try It! **3. a.** Is △ADE ~ △ABD? Explain.

b. Is △ADE ~ △BDC? Explain.

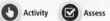
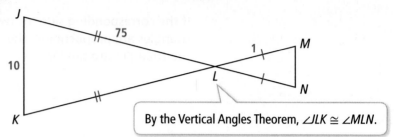

⏺ EXAMPLE 4 Find Lengths in Similar Triangles

What is MN?

By the Vertical Angles Theorem, $\angle JLK \cong \angle MLN$.

STUDY TIP
The measures of the two pairs of corresponding legs of any two isosceles triangles will always be proportional, even if the triangles are not similar.

The sides that include $\angle JLK$ and $\angle MLN$ are proportional.

By SAS ~, $\triangle JLK \sim \triangle MLN$.

Write a proportion using corresponding sides, and solve for MN.

$$\frac{MN}{10} = \frac{1}{75}$$

$$MN = \frac{2}{15}$$

 Try It! **4. a.** In Example 4, if the measure of $\overline{JL}$ were 150 instead of 75, how would the value of MN be different?

b. In Example 4, if the measure of $\overline{JK}$ were 20 instead of 10, how would the value of MN be different?

APPLICATION

⏺ EXAMPLE 5 Solve Problems Involving Similar Triangles

Avery puts up a radio antenna tower in his yard. Ella tells him that their city has a law limiting towers to 50 ft in height. How can Avery use the lengths of his shadow and the shadow of the tower to show that his tower is within the limit without directly measuring it?

You can consider the angles at which the sun hits Avery and the tower to be equal.

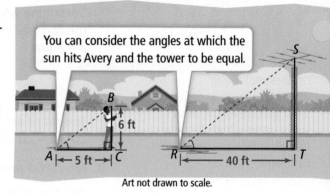

Art not drawn to scale.

MODEL WITH MATHEMATICS
Think about how the situation is modeled with triangles. What information do you need to be able to apply a similarity theorem?

Since $\angle BAC \cong \angle SRT$ and $\angle ACB \cong \angle RTS$, you can apply the AA ~ Theorem.

$$\frac{ST}{BC} = \frac{RT}{AC}$$

Corresponding sides of $\triangle ABC$ and $\triangle RST$ are proportional.

$$\frac{ST}{6} = \frac{40}{5}$$

$$ST = 48$$

The antenna tower is 48 ft high. Avery's tower is within the 50-ft limit.

 Try It! **5.** If the tower were 50 ft tall, how long would the shadow of the tower be?

CONCEPT SUMMARY Triangle Similarity Theorems

THEOREM 9-1

Angle-Angle Similarity

If...

$\angle A \cong \angle D$ and $\angle B \cong \angle E$

Then... $\triangle ABC \sim \triangle DEF$

THEOREM 9-2

Side-Side-Side Similarity

If...

$\dfrac{AB}{DE} = \dfrac{BC}{EF} = \dfrac{AC}{DF}$

Then... $\triangle ABC \sim \triangle DEF$

THEOREM 9-3

Side-Angle-Side Similarity

If...

$\angle B \cong \angle E$ and $\dfrac{AB}{DE} = \dfrac{BC}{EF}$

Then... $\triangle ABC \sim \triangle DEF$

Do You UNDERSTAND?

1. **ESSENTIAL QUESTION** How can you use the angles and sides of two triangles to determine whether they are similar?

2. **Error Analysis** Allie says $\triangle JKL \sim \triangle XYZ$. What is Allie's error?

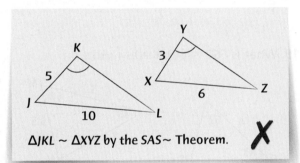

$\triangle JKL \sim \triangle XYZ$ by the SAS~ Theorem. ✗

3. **Make Sense and Persevere** Is any additional information needed to show $\triangle DEF \sim \triangle RST$? Explain.

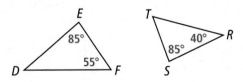

4. **Construct Arguments** Explain how you can use triangle similarity to show that $ABCD \sim WXYZ$.

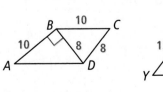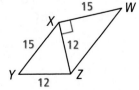

Do You KNOW HOW?

For Exercises 5 and 6, explain whether the two triangles are similar.

5.
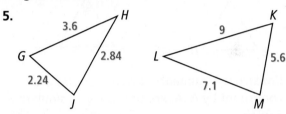

6.
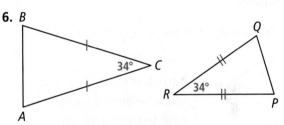

For Exercises 7 and 8, find the value of each variable such that the triangles are similar.

7. *a*
8. *b*

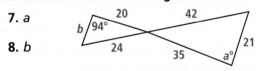

9. When Esteban looks at the puddle, he sees a reflection of the top of the cactus. How tall is the cactus?

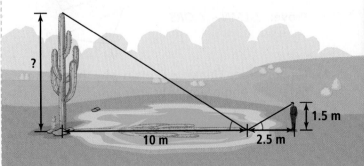

UNDERSTAND

10. Construct Arguments Write a proof of the Angle-Angle Similarity Theorem.

Given: $\angle T \cong \angle X$
$\angle U \cong \angle Y$

Prove: $\triangle TUV \sim \triangle XYZ$

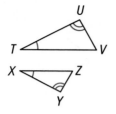

11. Use Structure For each triangle, name the triangle similar to $\triangle ABC$ and explain why it is similar.

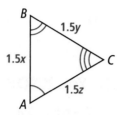

a.

b.

12. Construct Arguments If two triangles are congruent by ASA, are the triangles similar? Explain.

13. Error Analysis What is Russel's error?

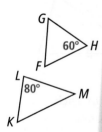

180 – 80 – 60 = 40, so the unlabeled angle in each triangle is 40°. So, $m\angle M = 60$, and thus $\triangle FGH \sim \triangle KLM$ by AA ~. ✗

14. Construct Arguments Write a proof of the Side-Angle-Side Similarity Theorem.

Given: $\dfrac{LM}{QR} = \dfrac{LN}{QS}$
$\angle L \cong \angle Q$

Prove: $\triangle LMN \sim \triangle QRS$

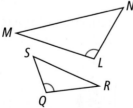

15. Higher Order Thinking Explain why there is no Side-Side-Angle Similarity Theorem.

PRACTICE

For Exercise 16–18, explain whether each pair of triangles is similar. SEE EXAMPLES 1–3

16.

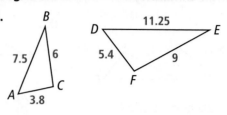

17.

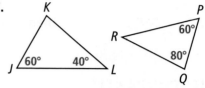

18.

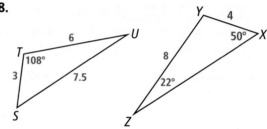

19. What is FG? SEE EXAMPLES 4 AND 5

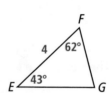 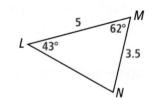

20. What is the value of x? SEE EXAMPLES 4 AND 5

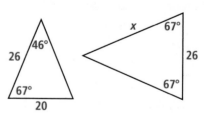

21. Write a proof of the Side-Side-Side Similarity Theorem.

Given: $\dfrac{AB}{EF} = \dfrac{BC}{FG} = \dfrac{AC}{AG}$

Prove: $\triangle ABC \sim \triangle EFG$

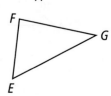

22. Communicate Precisely A building manager needs to order 9 replacement panes that are all the same size, each similar to the window itself. At what angles should each pane be cut in order to fit in the window? What are the dimensions of each pane? Explain.

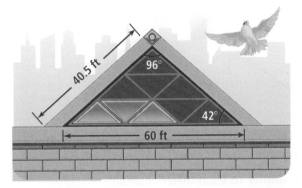

23. Use Structure The screen of a surveying device is 0.0026 m wide and is 0.1 m away from the lens. If the surveyor wants the image of the 2-m target to fit on the screen, what distance d should the lens be from the target? Explain.

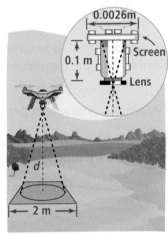

24. Mathematical Connections If a light beam strikes the inside of a fiber optic cable, it bounces off at the same angle. In a cable 1,200 micrometers (μm) long, if the beam strikes the wall after 720 μm what distance $x + y$ does the beam travel? Explain.

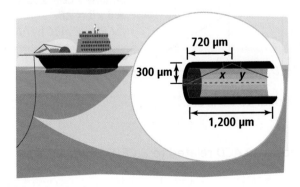

25. Which condition is sufficient to show that $\triangle ABC \sim \triangle QPR$? Select all that apply.

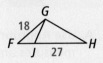

Ⓐ $RP = 4.5$

Ⓑ $m\angle Q = 63$

Ⓒ $m\angle P = 81$

Ⓓ $m\angle R = 81$

26. SAT/ACT For which value of FJ must $\triangle FGJ$ be similar to $\triangle FHG$?

Ⓐ 6   Ⓑ 8   Ⓒ 9   Ⓓ 12

27. Performance Task A rescue helicopter hovering at an altitude of 3.5 km sights a campsite just over the peak of a mountain.

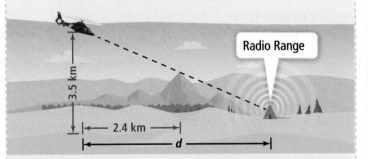

Part A The horizontal distance of the helicopter from the mountain is 2.4 km. If the height of the mountain is 2.8 km, what is the horizontal distance d of the helicopter from the campsite? Explain.

Part B The groundspeed (horizontal speed) of the helicopter is 1.6 km/min. When will the helicopter reach the campsite? Explain.

Part C The radio at the campsite can only transmit to a distance of 5 km. If the helicopter begins immediately to descend toward the campsite (along the diagonal line), how far will the pilot be, horizontally, when he contacts the campsite?

9-4
Similarity in Right Triangles

🔊 PearsonRealize.com

I CAN... use similarity and the geometric mean to solve problems involving right triangles.

VOCABULARY
• geometric mean

EXPLORE & REASON

Suppose you cut a rectangular sheet of paper to create three right triangles.

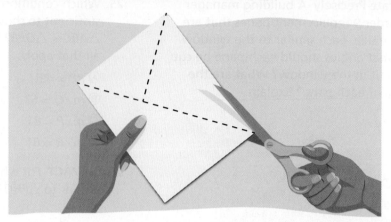

A. Use Appropriate Tools How can you compare leg lengths and angle measures among the triangles?

B. Are any of the triangles similar to each other? Explain.

❓ ESSENTIAL QUESTION In a right triangle, what is the relationship between the altitude to the hypotenuse, triangle similarity, and the geometric mean?

CONCEPTUAL UNDERSTANDING

🖐 EXAMPLE 1 **Identify Similar Triangles Formed by an Altitude**

When you draw an altitude to the hypotenuse of a right triangle, you create three right triangles. How are the triangles related?

USE STRUCTURE
Think about an altitude of a triangle. What type of angle does it form with the base?

The altitude $\overline{CD}$ divides $\triangle ABC$ into two right triangles, $\triangle ACD$ and $\triangle CBD$. Compare each triangle to $\triangle ABC$.

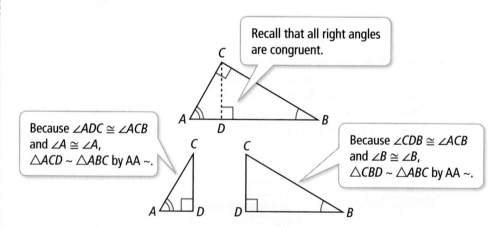

Recall that all right angles are congruent.

Because $\angle ADC \cong \angle ACB$ and $\angle A \cong \angle A$, $\triangle ACD \sim \triangle ABC$ by AA ~.

Because $\angle CDB \cong \angle ACB$ and $\angle B \cong \angle B$, $\triangle CBD \sim \triangle ABC$ by AA ~.

$\triangle ACD$ and $\triangle CBD$ are each similar to $\triangle ABC$.

☑ Try It! **1.** In Example 1, how is $\triangle ACD$ related to $\triangle CBD$? Explain.

THEOREM 9-4

The altitude to the hypotenuse of a right triangle divides the triangle into two triangles that are similar to the original triangle and to each other.

If...

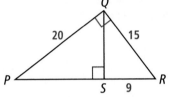

PROOF: SEE EXAMPLE 1.

Then... $\triangle CAB \sim \triangle DAC \sim \triangle DCB$

EXAMPLE 2   **Find Missing Lengths Within Right Triangles**

Given that $\triangle PQR \sim \triangle QSR$, what is QS?

Draw $\triangle PQR$ and $\triangle QSR$.

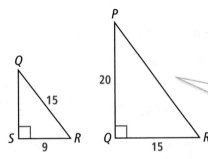

Because $\triangle QSR \sim \triangle PQR$, $\overline{QS}$ corresponds to $\overline{PQ}$, $\overline{SR}$ corresponds to $\overline{QR}$, and $\overline{QR}$ corresponds to $\overline{PR}$.

To find QS, write a proportion using corresponding legs of $\triangle QSR$ and $\triangle PQR$.

$$\frac{QS}{PQ} = \frac{SR}{QR}$$

$$\frac{QS}{20} = \frac{9}{15}$$

$$QS = \frac{9}{15} \cdot 20$$

$$QS = 12$$

STUDY TIP
With right triangles, you can apply the Pythagorean Theorem to verify your results.

The length of altitude $\overline{QS}$ is 12.

 Try It!   **2.** Refer to $\triangle PQR$ in Example 2.

         a. Write a proportion that you can use to solve for PS.

         b. What is PS?

DEFINITION

The **geometric mean** is the number x such that $\frac{a}{x} = \frac{x}{b}$, where a, b, and x are positive numbers.

EXAMPLE 3   Relate Altitude and Geometric Mean

Given △ACB, what is CD?

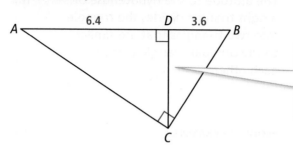

Notice that *CD* is the length of the longer leg of △*CDB* and is also the length of the shorter leg of △*ADC*.

By Theorem 9-4, △*ADC* ~ △*CDB*. Use the properties of similar triangles to write a proportion.

STUDY TIP
You can think about the geometric mean in another way. If $x^2 = ab$, then *x* is the geometric mean of *a* and *b*.

$$\frac{AD}{CD} = \frac{CD}{BD}$$

$$\frac{6.4}{CD} = \frac{CD}{3.6}$$

CD is the geometric mean of *AD* and *BD*.

$$(CD)^2 = 23.04$$

$$CD = 4.8$$

The length of altitude $\overline{CD}$ is 4.8.

 Try It!   **3.** Use △*ABC*.

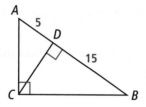

a. What is *CD*?

b. Describe how you can use the value you found for *CD* to find *AC* and *CB*.

COROLLARY 1 TO THEOREM 9-4

The length of the altitude to the hypotenuse of a right triangle is the geometric mean of the lengths of the segments of the hypotenuse.

If...

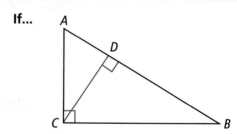

PROOF: SEE EXERCISE 14.

Then... $\frac{AD}{CD} = \frac{CD}{DB}$

EXAMPLE 4 **Relate Side Lengths and Geometric Mean**

Given △RST, what is RT?

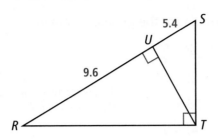

By Theorem 9-4, △RST ~ △RTU. Use the properties of similar triangles to write a proportion.

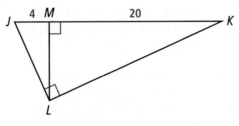

$$\frac{RS}{RT} = \frac{RT}{RU}$$

RT is the geometric mean of RS and RU.

$$\frac{15}{RT} = \frac{RT}{9.6}$$

$$(RT)^2 = 144$$

$$RT = 12$$

The length of $\overline{RT}$ is 12.

✅ **Try It!** **4.** Use △JKL.

a. What is JL?

b. What is KL?

COROLLARY 2 TO THEOREM 9-4

The altitude to the hypotenuse of a right triangle divides the hypotenuse so that the length of a given leg is the geometric mean of the length of the hypotenuse and the length of the segment of the hypotenuse that is adjacent to the leg.

PROOF: SEE EXERCISE 14.

If...

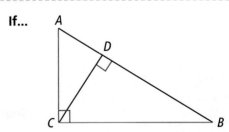

Then... $\frac{AB}{AC} = \frac{AC}{AD}$ and $\frac{AB}{CB} = \frac{CB}{DB}$

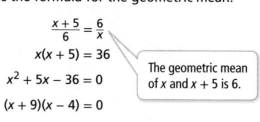

EXAMPLE 5 · Use the Geometric Mean to Solve Problems

What is the value of x?

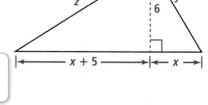

STUDY TIP
The length of the shared leg of the two smaller triangles (the altitude of the larger triangle) is the geometric mean of the lengths of the two triangles' non-shared legs.

Use the formula for the geometric mean.

$$\frac{x+5}{6} = \frac{6}{x}$$

$$x(x+5) = 36$$

The geometric mean of x and $x+5$ is 6.

$$x^2 + 5x - 36 = 0$$

$$(x+9)(x-4) = 0$$

$$x = -9 \text{ or } x = 4$$

The value of x is 4.

Length is always positive.

Try It! **5.** Use the geometric mean and Example 5 to find each unknown.

    a. Find the value of y.

    b. Find the value of z.

APPLICATION

EXAMPLE 6 · Apply Geometric Mean to Find a Distance

Zhang is constructing a 4-ft high loading ramp. The length of the back of the base must be 12.8 ft. How long must the entire base be?

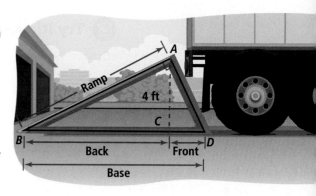

Formulate ◄ The ramp and the base form the long leg and the hypotenuse of a right triangle. The height of the ramp is the altitude of the triangle. The base of the ramp is composed of the front base x and the back base 12.8.

Compute ◄ **Step 1** Find the length of the front base x. Use the fact that the height is the geometric mean of the lengths of the front base and the back base.

$$\frac{x}{4} = \frac{4}{12.8}$$

$$12.8x = 16$$

The geometric mean of x and 12.8 is 4.

$$x = 1.25$$

Step 2 Find the length of the base.

$$12.8 + 1.25 = 14.05$$

Interpret ◄ The base of the ramp should be 14.05 feet long.

Try It! **6.** In Example 6, how long should Zhang make the ramp?

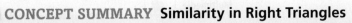

CONCEPT SUMMARY Similarity in Right Triangles

WORDS
- The altitude to the hypotenuse of a right triangle divides the triangle into two triangles that are similar to the original triangle and to each other.
- The length of the altitude is the geometric mean of the lengths of the segments of the hypotenuse.
- The length of each leg is the geometric mean of the length of the hypotenuse and the length of the segment adjacent to the leg.

DIAGRAMS

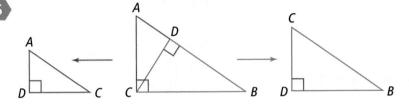

SYMBOLS $\triangle ACD$ ~ $\triangle ABC$ ~ $\triangle CBD$

$$\frac{AB}{AC} = \frac{AC}{AD}, \frac{AD}{CD} = \frac{CD}{DB}, \text{ and } \frac{AB}{CB} = \frac{CB}{DB}$$

✓ Do You UNDERSTAND?

1. **ESSENTIAL QUESTION** In a right triangle, what is the relationship between the altitude to the hypotenuse, triangle similarity, and the geometric mean?

2. **Error Analysis** Chris is asked to find a geometric mean in $\triangle JKL$. What is his error?

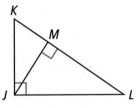

$\Delta JKL \sim \Delta MKJ$

$\frac{KL}{JK} = \frac{JK}{JM}$ ✗

3. **Vocabulary** Do the altitudes to the legs of a right triangle also create similar triangles? Explain.

Do You KNOW HOW?

For Exercises 4–6, use $\triangle DEF$ to find the lengths.

4. ER

5. DF

6. DE

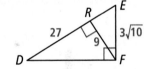

For Exercises 7–9, use $\triangle PQR$ to find the lengths.

7. QA

8. PQ

9. QR

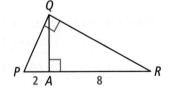

10. Deshawn installs a shelf bracket. What is the widest shelf that will fit without overhang? Explain.

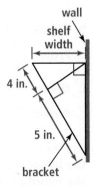

✏ PRACTICE & PROBLEM SOLVING

UNDERSTAND

11. Mathematical Connections Consider $\triangle XYZ$ with altitude to the hypotenuse $\overline{ZW}$.

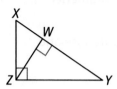

  a. Describe a sequence of transformations that maps $\triangle XYZ$ to $\triangle XZW$.

  b. Describe a sequence of transformations that maps $\triangle XYZ$ to $\triangle ZYW$.

12. Error Analysis Amaya was asked to find DC. What is Amaya's error?

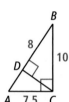

$\triangle ABC \sim \triangle ACD$ by Theorem 9-4.

$$\frac{AC}{BC} = \frac{AC}{DC} \rightarrow \frac{7.5}{10} = \frac{7.5}{DC}$$

$7.5 \times DC = 7.5 \times 10,$
so $DC = 10.$

13. Make Sense and Persevere Is CD the geometric mean of AD and BD? Explain.

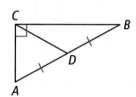

14. Construct Arguments Write proofs of Theorem 9-4 and its corollaries.

  a. Given: $m\angle JLK = 90$ and $\overline{LM} \perp \overline{JK}$

  Prove: $\triangle JKL \sim \triangle JLM \sim \triangle LKM$

  b. Given: $\triangle JLM \sim \triangle LKM$

  Prove: $\dfrac{JM}{LM} = \dfrac{LM}{KM}$

  c. Given: $\triangle JKL \sim \triangle JLM \sim \triangle LKM$

  Prove: $\dfrac{JK}{JL} = \dfrac{JL}{JM}$ and $\dfrac{JK}{LK} = \dfrac{LK}{MK}$

15. Higher Order Thinking Suppose the altitude to the hypotenuse of a right triangle also bisects the hypotenuse. What type of right triangle is it? Use the similarity of right triangles to explain your answer.

PRACTICE

16. In the figure, what two smaller triangles are similar to $\triangle ABC$? Explain. SEE EXAMPLE 1

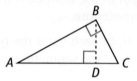

17. What are the values of h and x in the right triangle? Explain. SEE EXAMPLE 2

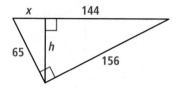

18. What is the value of y in the right triangle? Explain. SEE EXAMPLE 3

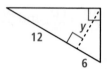

19. What are the values of a and b in each right triangle? Explain. SEE EXAMPLES 4 AND 6

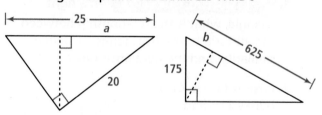

20. What are the values of m and n in each right triangle? Explain. SEE EXAMPLE 5

  a.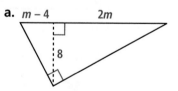

  b.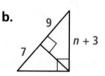

21. What is the value of w in the right triangle? Explain.

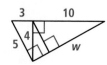

PRACTICE & PROBLEM SOLVING

APPLY

22. Reason Jake wants the profile of a hotel he is planning to be a right triangle with the dimensions shown. The city prohibits structures over 100 ft at the location where he would like to build. Can the hotel be located there? Explain.

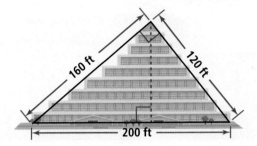

23. Look for Relationships Kiyo is repairing a wooden climbing tower.

a. He needs to cut two crossbars. What should the lengths of the two crossbars be? Explain.

b. Kiyo will make a notch in each crossbar in order to fit them together. Where should he make the notch on each crossbar? Explain.

24. Higher Order Thinking Write a proof.

Given: Right $\triangle WXY$ with altitude $\overline{XZ}$ to hypotenuse $\overline{WY}$

Prove: The product of the slopes of perpendicular lines is -1.

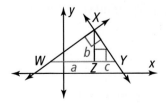

ASSESSMENT PRACTICE

25. For each figure, write an equation that you could use to find the value of x.

a.

b.

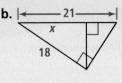

26. SAT/ACT Which triangle is similar to $\triangle ABC$?

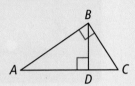

Ⓐ $\triangle CBA$ Ⓒ $\triangle CDB$

Ⓑ $\triangle ABD$ Ⓓ $\triangle BDC$

27. Performance Task To estimate the height of a tree, Tia and Felix walk away from the tree until the angle of sight with the top and bottom of the tree is a right angle. Let h represent the height of a person's eyes and d represent the distance away from the tree.

Part A If the height of Tia's eyes is 1.6 m and her distance away from the tree is 2.5 m, what is the height of the tree? Round to the nearest hundredth of a meter.

Part B If the height of Felix's eyes is 1.7 m, about how far from the tree is Felix if his angle of sight is a right angle? Round to the nearest hundredth of a meter.

Part C Suppose Tia and Felix stand the same distance away from another tree and their angles of sight are right angles, what is the height of the tree? Explain.

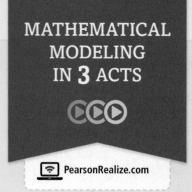

▶ **Make It Right**

Architects often make a scale physical model of a new building project. The scale model is usually a miniature version of the project it is representing.

When making a model, architects need to make sure that all of the parts of the model are the right size. Think about this during the Mathematical Modeling in 3 Acts lesson.

Scan for
Multimedia

ACT 1 ▸ **Identify the Problem**

1. What is the first question that comes to mind after watching the video?

2. Write down the main question you will answer about what you saw in the video.

3. Make an initial conjecture that answers this main question.

4. Explain how you arrived at your conjecture.

5. What information will be useful to know to answer the main question? How can you get it? How will you use that information?

ACT 2 ▸ **Develop a Model**

6. Use the math that you have learned in this Topic to refine your conjecture.

ACT 3 ▸ **Interpret the Results**

7. Did your refined conjecture match the actual answer exactly? If not, what might explain the difference?

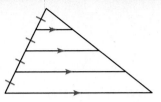
9-5

Proportions in Triangles

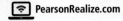
I CAN... find the lengths of segments using proportional relationships in triangles resulting from parallel lines.

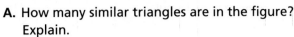

EXPLORE & REASON

Draw a triangle, like the one shown, by dividing one side into four congruent segments and drawing lines parallel to one of the other sides.

A. How many similar triangles are in the figure? Explain.

B. Look for Relationships How are the lengths of the parallel segments related to each other?

? ESSENTIAL QUESTION

When parallel lines intersect two transversals, what are the relationships among the lengths of the segments formed?

CONCEPTUAL UNDERSTANDING

EXAMPLE 1   Explore Proportions from Parallel Lines

In △*JLN*, if *LN* = 9.6, what are *LM* and *MN*? Are the sides divided proportionally? Explain.

Step 1 Determine how △*JLN* and △*KLM* are related.

The triangles share ∠*L*, and ∠*LJN* ≅ ∠*LKM* by the Corresponding Angles Theorem. Therefore, △*JLN* ~ △*KLM* by AA ~.

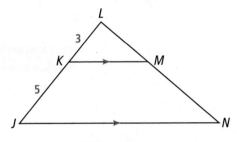

Step 2 Write a proportion to relate the corresponding sides.

$$\frac{LK}{LJ} = \frac{LM}{LN}$$

Step 3 Use the proportion to find *LM* and *MN*.

$$\frac{3}{8} = \frac{LM}{9.6}$$

$$LM = 3.6$$

> $LK = 3$, $LJ = LK + KJ = 3 + 5 = 8$, and $LN = 9.6$

Then $MN = LN - LM = 9.6 - 3.6 = 6$.

LOOK FOR RELATIONSHIPS
The length of the shorter segments, $\overline{LK}$ and $\overline{LM}$, are each the same fraction of the lengths of the corresponding longer segments, $\overline{KJ}$ and $\overline{MN}$.

Step 4 Find the ratios between the segments of each side divided by $\overline{KM}$.

$$\frac{LK}{KJ} = \frac{3}{5} = 0.6 \text{ and } \frac{LM}{MN} = \frac{3.6}{6} = 0.6$$

Since $\frac{LK}{KJ} = \frac{LM}{MN}$, $\overline{KM}$ divides $\overline{LJ}$ and $\overline{LN}$ proportionally.

☑ **Try It!**   **1.** $\overline{BD}$ bisects sides $\overline{AC}$ and $\overline{CE}$. Is $\overline{AE} \parallel \overline{BD}$? Explain.

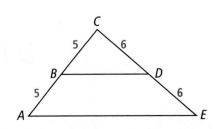

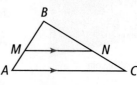
THEOREM 9-5 Side-Splitter Theorem

If a line is parallel to one side of a triangle and intersects the other two sides, then it divides those sides proportionally.

If... $\overline{MN} \parallel \overline{AC}$

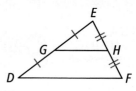

PROOF: SEE EXERCISE 14.

Then... $\dfrac{AM}{MB} = \dfrac{CN}{NB}$

THEOREM 9-6 Triangle Midsegment Theorem

If a segment joins the midpoints of two sides of a triangle, then the segment is parallel to the third side and is half as long.

If... $\overline{DG} \cong \overline{GE}$ and $\overline{FH} \cong \overline{HE}$

PROOF: SEE EXERCISE 24.

Then... $\overline{GH} \parallel \overline{DF}$ and $GH = \frac{1}{2}DF$

👆 EXAMPLE 2   Use the Side-Splitter Theorem

What is the value of *x* in △*PQR*?

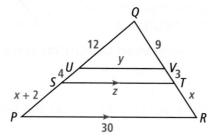

MAKE SENSE AND PERSEVERE
Consider other strategies you can use. Can you use proportions of similar triangles?

Since $\overline{ST} \parallel \overline{PR}$, $\dfrac{PS}{SQ} = \dfrac{RT}{TQ}$ by the Side-Splitter Theorem. Write a proportion in terms of *x* and solve.

$$\dfrac{PS}{SQ} = \dfrac{RT}{TQ}$$

    $SQ = 4 + 12 = 16$ and
    $TQ = 3 + 9 = 12$

$$\dfrac{x+2}{16} = \dfrac{x}{12}$$

$$48\left(\dfrac{x+2}{16}\right) = 48\left(\dfrac{x}{12}\right)$$

$$3x + 6 = 4x$$

$$x = 6$$

✅ Try It!   2. Refer to △*PQR* in Example 2.

    a. What is the value of *y*? Explain.

    b. What is the value of *z*? Explain.

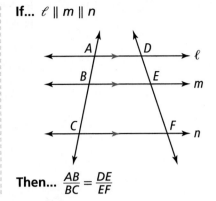

COROLLARY TO THE SIDE-SPLITTER THEOREM

If three parallel lines intersect two transversals, then the segments intercepted on the transversals are proportional.

If... $\ell \parallel m \parallel n$

PROOF: SEE EXERCISE 25.

Then... $\dfrac{AB}{BC} = \dfrac{DE}{EF}$

APPLICATION

EXAMPLE 3 **Find a Length**

A reflecting pool is separated by walkways parallel to Lincoln St. and Jefferson St., which are parallel to each other. The city wants to add additional tiling around the pool. How much tiling does *x* ft represent?

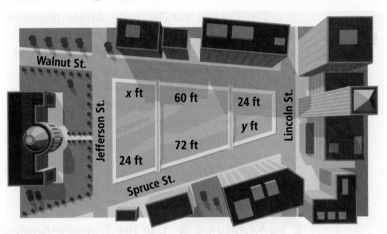

Formulate ◄ Walnut St. and Spruce St. are transversals of Jefferson St., Lincoln St., and the walkways that separate the pool.

Compute ◄ Write an equation with *x*.

$$\frac{x}{60} = \frac{24}{72}$$

Apply the Corollary to the Side-Splitter Theorem.

$$x = 60\left(\frac{24}{72}\right)$$

$$x = 20$$

Interpret ◄ The amount of tiling represented by *x* ft is 20 ft.

☑ **Try It!** 3. In Example 3, how much tiling does *y* ft represent?

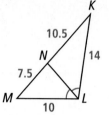
EXAMPLE 4   Investigate Proportionality with an Angle Bisector

In △KLM, $\overline{NL}$ bisects ∠KLM. Compare the ratios $\frac{KN}{MN}$ and $\frac{KL}{ML}$.
Is △LKN ~ △LMN? Explain.

Compute the ratios of the corresponding sides
for the given measures.

$$\frac{KN}{MN} = \frac{10.5}{7.5} = 1.4 \qquad \frac{KL}{ML} = \frac{14}{10} = 1.4$$

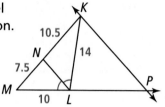

The ratios $\frac{KN}{MN}$ and $\frac{KL}{ML}$ are equal. However, the third pair is $\overline{NL}$ and $\overline{NL}$, and
that ratio is 1. So, the two triangles are not similar.

Try It!   4. Draw $\overrightarrow{ML}$ and a line through K parallel
to $\overline{NL}$. Let P be the point of intersection.

   a. Is △MNL ~ △MKP? Explain.

   b. Is ∠LKP ≅ ∠LPK? Explain.

THEOREM 9-7 Triangle-Angle-Bisector Theorem

If a ray bisects an angle of a triangle,
then it divides the opposite side into
two segments such that the ratio
between the segments is the same as
the ratio between the sides adjacent
to each segment.

If... ∠UVX ≅ ∠WVX

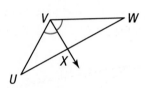

PROOF: SEE EXERCISE 16.

Then... $\frac{UX}{WX} = \frac{UV}{WV}$

EXAMPLE 5   Use the Triangle-Angle-Bisector Theorem

What are the values of AD and DC?

Since $\overline{BD}$ bisects ∠ABC, use the Triangle-Angle-
Bisector Theorem to write a proportion.

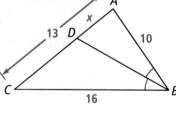

$$\frac{AD}{CD} = \frac{AB}{CB}$$

$$\frac{x}{13 - x} = \frac{10}{16}$$

$CD = AC - AD$ or
$CD = 13 - x$

$$16x = 130 - 10x$$
$$26x = 130$$
$$x = 5$$

In the figure, AD = 5 and CD = 13 − 5 = 8.

COMMON ERROR
You may incorrectly use 13 as
the length of one of the shorter
segments. Remember to
correctly identify the lengths of all
of the segments.

Try It!   5. a. What is the value of x?

   b. What are the values of GH
   and GK?

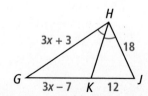

 CONCEPT SUMMARY Proportions in Triangles

THEOREM 9-5

Side-Splitter Theorem

If... $\overline{MN} \parallel \overline{AC}$

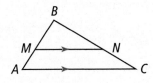

Then... $\dfrac{AM}{MB} = \dfrac{CN}{NB}$

THEOREM 9-6

Triangle Midsegment Theorem

If... $\overline{DG} \cong \overline{GE}$ and $\overline{FH} \cong \overline{HE}$

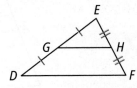

Then... $\overline{GH} \parallel \overline{DF}$ and $GH = \dfrac{1}{2}DF$

THEOREM 9-7

Triangle-Angle-Bisector Theorem

If... $\angle UVX \cong \angle WVX$

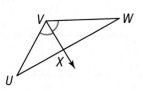

Then... $\dfrac{UX}{WX} = \dfrac{UV}{WV}$

☑ Do You UNDERSTAND?

1. **ESSENTIAL QUESTION** When parallel lines intersect two transversals, what are the relationships among the lengths of the segments formed?

2. **Error Analysis** Carmen thinks that $AD = BD$. What is Carmen's error?

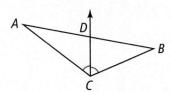

3. **Make Sense and Persevere** What information is needed to determine if x is half of y?

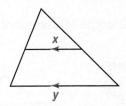

4. **Look for Relationships** If $\overline{RS} \cong \overline{QS}$, what type of triangle is $\triangle PQR$? Use the Triangle-Angle-Bisector Theorem to explain your reasoning.

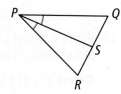

5. **Construct Arguments** Explain why LP must be less than LM.

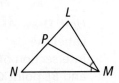

Do You KNOW HOW?

For Exercises 6–11, find each value of x.

6.

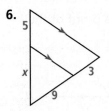

7.

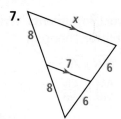

8.

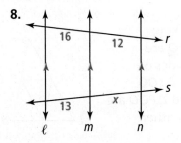

9.

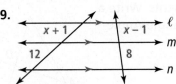

10.

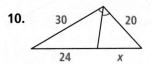

11.

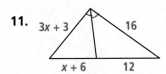

UNDERSTAND

12. Error Analysis What is Benson's error?

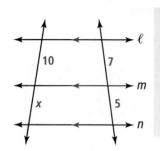

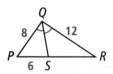

$$\frac{5}{10} = \frac{x}{7}$$

$$10x = 35$$

$$x = 3.5 \quad \text{✗}$$

13. Mathematical Connections What percent of the area of $\triangle PQR$ is the area of $\triangle QRS$? Explain.

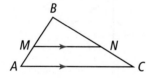

14. Construct Arguments Write a proof of the Side-Splitter Theorem.

Given: $\overline{MN} \parallel \overline{AC}$

Prove: $\frac{AM}{MB} = \frac{CN}{NB}$

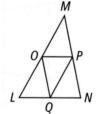

15. Higher Order Thinking Suppose O, P, and Q are midpoints of the sides of $\triangle LMN$. Show that $\triangle LOQ$, $\triangle OMP$, $\triangle QPN$, and $\triangle PQO$ are congruent to each other.

16. Construct Arguments Write a proof for the Triangle-Angle-Bisector Theorem.

Given: $\overrightarrow{AD}$ bisects $\angle A$.

Prove: $\frac{CA}{AB} = \frac{CD}{DB}$

Use the following outline.

- Extend $\overrightarrow{CA}$ and draw a line through point B parallel to $\overrightarrow{AD}$ that intersects $\overrightarrow{CA}$ at point E.
- Show that $\frac{CA}{AE} = \frac{CD}{DB}$.
- Then show that $\triangle AEB$ is isosceles.

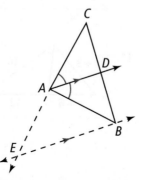

PRACTICE

For Exercises 17–19, find each value.
SEE EXAMPLES 1 AND 2

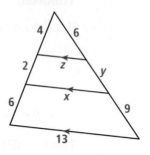

17. x **18.** y **19.** z

20. What is the value of x? SEE EXAMPLE 3

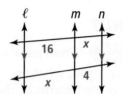

For Exercises 21–23, find each value of x for the given value of y. Round to the nearest tenth.
SEE EXAMPLES 4 AND 5

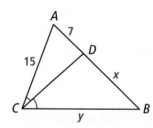

21. $y = 16$ **22.** $y = 20$ **23.** $y = 18$

24. Write a proof of the Triangle Midsegment Theorem.

Given: $\overline{DG} \cong \overline{GE}$, $\overline{FH} \cong \overline{HE}$

Prove: $\overline{GH} \parallel \overline{DF}$, $GH = \frac{1}{2}DF$

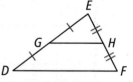

25. Write a proof of the Corollary to the Side-Splitter Theorem.

Given: $\ell \parallel m \parallel n$

Prove: $\frac{AB}{BC} = \frac{DE}{EF}$

Hint: Draw $\overline{AF}$. Label the intersection of $\overline{AF}$ and $\overleftrightarrow{BE}$ point G.

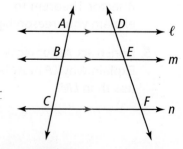

APPLY

26. **Use Structure** A building in the shape of a pyramid needs to have supports repaired, and two parallel sections need to be reinforced. The face of the building is an equilateral triangle. What are the lengths of $\overline{KO}$ and $\overline{LN}$?

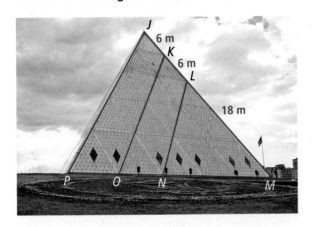

27. **Higher Order Thinking** Use the figure to prove: Two non-vertical lines are parallel if and only if they have the same slope.

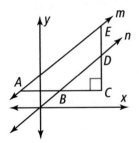

a. Assume the slopes of lines m and n are equal. Use proportions in $\triangle ACE$ and $\triangle BCD$ to show that $m \parallel n$.

b. Now assume that $m \parallel n$. Show that the slopes of m and n are equal.

28. **Use Structure** Aisha is building a roof and needs to determine the lengths of $\overline{CG}$ and $\overline{CF}$ from the design shown. How can she determine CG and CF? What are CG and CF?

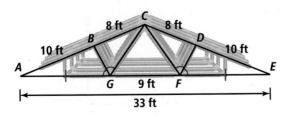

29. What is the value of x?

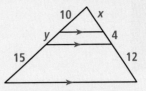

30. **SAT/ACT** What is the measure of side CB?

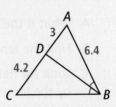

Ⓐ 4.57   Ⓑ 6.4   Ⓒ 8.96   Ⓓ 9.4

31. **Performance Task** Emma is determining measurements needed to simulate the distances in a shuffleboard computer game that she is programming.

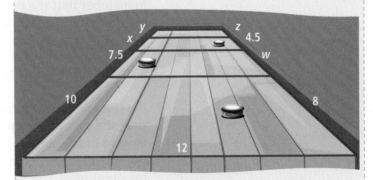

Part A The horizontal lines must be parallel and in proportion so that each zone of the shuffleboard appears to be the same length. What are the lengths w, x, and y?

Part B What is the length of each horizontal segment?

Part C Which horizontal segment is closest to the midsegment of the triangle that extends off of the screen? How do you know?

9-6

Right Triangles and the Pythagorean Theorem

I CAN... prove the Pythagorean Theorem using similarity and establish the relationships in special right triangles.

VOCABULARY

• Pythagorean triple

🖐 EXPLORE & REASON

Consider △ABC with altitude $\overline{CD}$ as shown.

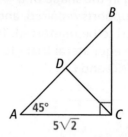

A. What is the area of △ABC? Of △ACD? Explain your answers.

B. Find the lengths of $\overline{AD}$ and $\overline{AB}$.

C. Look for Relationships Divide the length of the hypotenuse of △ABC by the length of one of its sides. Divide the length of the hypotenuse of △ACD by the length of one of its sides. Make a conjecture that explains the results.

❓ ESSENTIAL QUESTION

How are similarity in right triangles and the Pythagorean Theorem related?

Remember that the Pythagorean Theorem and its converse describe how the side lengths of right triangles are related.

THEOREM 9-8 Pythagorean Theorem

If a triangle is a right triangle, then the sum of the squares of the lengths of the legs is equal to the square of the length of the hypotenuse.

If... △ABC is a right triangle.

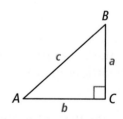

PROOF: SEE EXAMPLE 1.

Then... $a^2 + b^2 = c^2$

THEOREM 9-9 Converse of the Pythagorean Theorem

If the sum of the squares of the lengths of two sides of a triangle is equal to the square of the length of the third side, then the triangle is a right triangle.

If... $a^2 + b^2 = c^2$

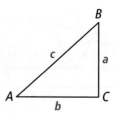

PROOF: SEE EXERCISE 17.

Then... △ABC is a right triangle.

PROOF 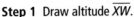 **EXAMPLE 1** Use Similarity to Prove the Pythagorean Theorem

Use right triangle similarity to write a proof of the Pythagorean Theorem.

Given: $\triangle XYZ$ is a right triangle.

Prove: $a^2 + b^2 = c^2$

Plan: To prove the Pythagorean Theorem, draw the altitude to the hypotenuse. Then use the relationships in the resulting similar right triangles.

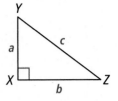

Proof:

Step 1 Draw altitude $\overline{XW}$.

Step 2 $\triangle XYZ \sim \triangle WXZ \sim \triangle WYX$

Step 3 Because $\triangle XYZ \sim \triangle WYX$, $\frac{c}{a} = \frac{a}{e}$. So $a^2 = ce$.

Step 4 Because $\triangle XYZ \sim \triangle WXZ$, $\frac{c}{b} = \frac{b}{f}$. So $b^2 = cf$.

LOOK FOR RELATIONSHIPS
Think about how you can apply properties of similar triangles. What is the relationship between corresponding sides of similar triangles?

Step 5 Write an equation that relates a^2 and b^2 to ce and cf.

$$a^2 + b^2 = ce + cf$$
$$a^2 + b^2 = c(e + f)$$
$$a^2 + b^2 = c(c)$$
$$a^2 + b^2 = c^2$$

 Try It! 1. Find the unknown side length of each right triangle.

a. AB

b. EF

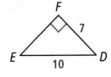

APPLICATION **EXAMPLE 2** Use the Pythagorean Theorem and Its Converse

9 ft

|←2.5 ft→|

A. To satisfy safety regulations, the distance from the wall to the base of a ladder should be at least one-fourth the length of the ladder. Did Drew set up the ladder correctly?

The floor, the wall, and the ladder form a right triangle.

Step 1 Find the length of the ladder.

$$a^2 + b^2 = c^2$$
$$2.5^2 + 9^2 = c^2$$
$$87.25 = c^2$$
$$9.34 \approx c$$

Use the Pythagorean Theorem with $a = 2.5$ and $b = 9$.

Step 2 Find $\frac{1}{4}$ the length of the ladder.

$$\frac{1}{4}c \approx \frac{1}{4}(9.34)$$
$$\approx 2.335$$

The length of the ladder is 9.34 ft.

Since $2.5 > 2.335$, Drew set up the ladder correctly.

B. The length of each crosspiece of the fence is 10 ft. Why would a rancher build this fence with the measurements shown?

The numbers 6, 8, and 10 form a *Pythagorean triple*. A **Pythagorean triple** is a set of three nonzero whole numbers that satisfy the equation $a^2 + b^2 = c^2$.

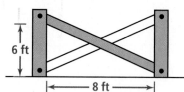

6 ft

|← 8 ft →|

Since $6^2 + 8^2 = 10^2$, the posts, the ground, and the crosspieces form right triangles.

By using those measurements, the rancher knows that the fence posts are perpendicular to the ground, which stabilizes the fence.

✓ **Try It!** **2. a.** What is *KL*?

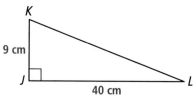

K
9 cm
J
40 cm
L

b. Is △*MNO* a right triangle? Explain.

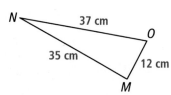

N
37 cm
O
35 cm
12 cm
M

CONCEPTUAL
UNDERSTANDING   👆 **EXAMPLE 3**   Investigate Side Lengths in 45°-45°-90° Triangles

Is there a relationship between the lengths of $\overline{AB}$ and $\overline{AC}$ in $\triangle ABC$? Explain.

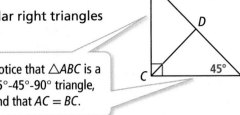

Draw altitude $\overline{CD}$ to form similar right triangles $\triangle ABC$, $\triangle ACD$, and $\triangle CBD$.

> Notice that $\triangle ABC$ is a 45°-45°-90° triangle, and that $AC = BC$.

REASON
Think about the properties of a triangle with two congruent angles. How do the properties of the triangle help you relate the side lengths?

Use right-triangle similarity to write an equation.

$$\frac{AB}{AC} = \frac{AC}{AD}$$

> Since $\triangle ABC \sim \triangle ACD$, AC is the geometric mean of AB and AD.

$$\frac{AB}{AC} = \frac{AC}{\frac{1}{2}AB}$$

$$\frac{1}{2}AB^2 = AC^2$$

> Because $\triangle ABC$ is isosceles, $\overline{CD}$ bisects $\overline{AB}$.

$$AB^2 = 2AC^2$$

$$AB = \sqrt{2} \cdot AC$$

The length of $\overline{AB}$ is $\sqrt{2}$ times the length of $\overline{AC}$.

✅ **Try It!**   **3.** Find the side lengths of each 45°-45°-90° triangle.

a. What are XZ and YZ?

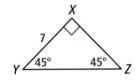

b. What are JK and LK?

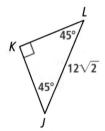

THEOREM 9-10   45°-45°-90° Triangle Theorem

In a 45°-45°-90° triangle, the legs are congruent and the length of the hypotenuse is $\sqrt{2}$ times the length of a leg.

If...

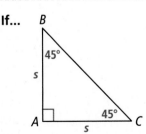

PROOF: SEE EXERCISE 18.

Then... $BC = s\sqrt{2}$

EXAMPLE 4   **Explore the Side Lengths of a 30°-60°-90° Triangle**

Using an equilateral triangle, show how the lengths of the short leg, the long leg, and the hypotenuse of a 30°-60°-90° triangle are related.

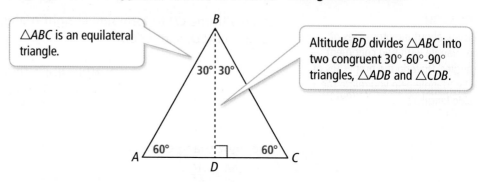

△ABC is an equilateral triangle.

Altitude $\overline{BD}$ divides △ABC into two congruent 30°-60°-90° triangles, △ADB and △CDB.

STUDY TIP
Recall that an altitude of a triangle is perpendicular to a side. Think about what properties of the triangle result in the altitude also being a segment bisector.

Look at △ADB. Let the length of the short leg $\overline{AD}$ be s.

Find the relationship between AD and AB.

$AD = CD = s$

$\overline{BD}$ bisects $\overline{AC}$.

$AC = AD + CD$

$AC = 2s$

$AB = 2s$

△ABC is equilateral, so AB = AC = 2s.

Find the relationship between AD and BD.

$AD^2 + BD^2 = AB^2$

$s^2 + BD^2 = (2s)^2$

Use the Pythagorean Theorem.

$BD^2 = 3s^2$

$BD = s\sqrt{3}$

In △ADB, the length of hypotenuse $\overline{AB}$ is twice the length of the short leg $\overline{AD}$. The length of the long leg $\overline{BD}$ is $\sqrt{3}$ times the length of the short leg.

Try It!   **4. a.** What are PQ and PR?   **b.** What are UV and TV?

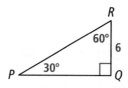

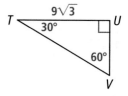

THEOREM 9-11 30°-60°-90° Triangle Theorem

In a 30°-60°-90° triangle, the length of the hypotenuse is twice the length of the short leg. The length of the long leg is $\sqrt{3}$ times the length of the short leg.

If... A

$30°$

C $60°$ B
      s

PROOF: SEE EXERCISE 19.

Then... $AC = s\sqrt{3}$, $AB = 2s$

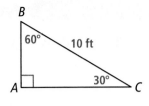
EXAMPLE 5 Apply Special Right Triangle Relationships

A. Alejandro needs to make both the horizontal and vertical supports, $\overline{AC}$ and $\overline{AB}$, for the ramp. Is one 12-foot board long enough for both supports? Explain.

The ramp and supports form a 30°-60°-90° triangle.

$BC = 2AB$ $\qquad\qquad$ $AC = AB\sqrt{3}$

$10 = 2AB$ $\qquad\qquad$ $AC = 5\sqrt{3}$ ft

$AB = 5$ ft

Find the total length of the supports.

$AB + AC = 5 + 5\sqrt{3}$

$\qquad\quad \approx 13.66$ ft

Since $13.66 > 12$, the 12-foot board will not be long enough for Alejandro to make both supports.

B. Olivia starts an origami paper crane by making the 200-mm diagonal fold. What are the side length and area of the paper square?

Step 1 Find the length of one side of the paper.

$s\sqrt{2} = 200$

$s = \dfrac{200}{\sqrt{2}}$

$s \approx 141.4$ mm

Step 2 Find the area of the paper square.

$A = s^2$

$A = \left(100\sqrt{2}\right)^2$

$A = 20{,}000$ mm^2

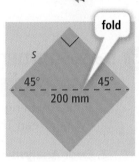

The paper square has side length 141.4 mm and area 20,000 mm^2.

☑ **Try It!** **5. a.** What are AB and BC? **b.** What are AC and BC?

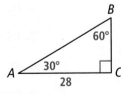

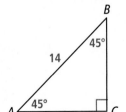

CONCEPT SUMMARY The Pythagorean Theorem and Special Right Triangles

THEOREM 9-8 Pythagorean Theorem

If... $\triangle ABC$ is a right triangle

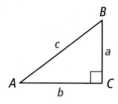

Then... $a^2 + b^2 = c^2$

THEOREM 9-9 Converse of the Pythagorean Theorem

If... $a^2 + b^2 = c^2$

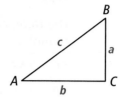

Then... $\triangle ABC$ is a right triangle.

THEOREM 9-10 45°-45°-90° Triangle Theorem

If...

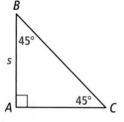

Then... $BC = s\sqrt{2}$

THEOREM 9-11 30°-60°-90° Triangle Theorem

If...

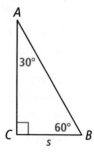

Then... $AC = s\sqrt{3}$, $AB = 2s$

Do You UNDERSTAND?

1. **ESSENTIAL QUESTION** How are similarity in right triangles and the Pythagorean Theorem related?

2. **Error Analysis** Casey was asked to find XY. What is Casey's error?

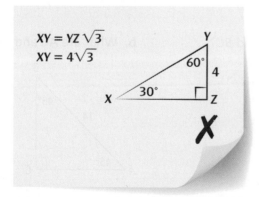

$XY = YZ \sqrt{3}$
$XY = 4\sqrt{3}$

3. **Reason** A right triangle has leg lengths 4.5 and $4.5\sqrt{3}$. What are the measures of the angles? Explain.

Do You KNOW HOW?

For Exercises 4 and 5, find the value of *x*.

4.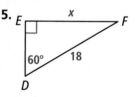

5.

For Exercises 6–8, is $\triangle RST$ a right triangle? Explain.

6. $RS = 20$, $ST = 21$, $RT = 29$

7. $RS = 35$, $ST = 36$, $RT = 71$

8. $RS = 40$, $ST = 41$, $RT = 11$

9. Charles wants to hang the pennant shown vertically between two windows that are 19 inches apart. Will the pennant fit? Explain.

41 in. 30°

PRACTICE & PROBLEM SOLVING

UNDERSTAND

10. Mathematical Connections Which rectangular prism has the longer diagonal? Explain.

Prism *P*   Prism *Q*

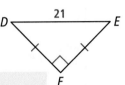

15
4
3
9
12
4

11. Error Analysis Dakota is asked to find *EF*. What is her error?

21
D   E
F

There is not enough information to find *EF* because you need to know either the length of $\overline{DF}$ or one of the other angle measures.

✗

12. Make Sense and Persevere What are expressions for *MN* and *LN*? *Hint*: Construct the altitude from *M* to $\overline{LN}$.

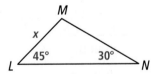

M
x
45°   30°
L   N

13. Higher Order Thinking Triangle *XYZ* is a right triangle. For what kind of triangle would $XZ^2 + XY^2 > YZ^2$? For what kind of triangle would $XZ^2 + XY^2 < YZ^2$? Explain.

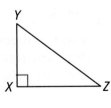

Y
X   Z

14. Look for Relationships Write an equation that represents the relationship between *JK* and *KL*.

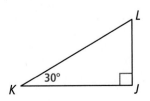

L
30°
K   J

PRACTICE

For Exercises 15 and 16, find the unknown side length of each triangle. SEE EXAMPLE 1

15. *RS*

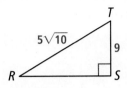

T
$5\sqrt{10}$
9
R   S

16. *XY*

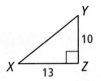

Y
10
X   Z
13

17. Given △*ABC* with $a^2 + b^2 = c^2$, write a paragraph proof of the Converse of the Pythagorean Theorem. SEE EXAMPLE 2

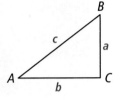

B
c   *a*
A   C
b

18. Write a two-column proof of the 45°-45°-90° Triangle Theorem. SEE EXAMPLE 3

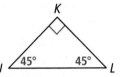

K
J 45°   45° L

19. Write a paragraph proof of the 30°-60°-90° Triangle Theorem. SEE EXAMPLE 4

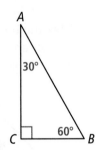

A
30°
C 60° B

For Exercise 20 and 21, find the side lengths of each triangle. SEE EXAMPLES 3 AND 4

20. What are *GJ* and *HJ*? **21.** What are *XY* and *YZ*?

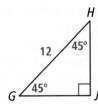

H
12 45°
45°
G   J

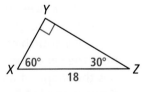

Y
X 60°   30° Z
18

22. What is *QS*? SEE EXAMPLE 5

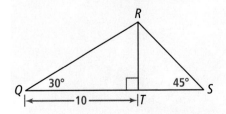

R
Q 30°   45° S
10   T

APPLY

23. Reason Esteban wants marble bookends cut at a 60° angle, as shown. If Esteban wants his bookends to be between 7.5 in. and 8 in. tall, what length d should the marble cutter make the base of the bookends? Explain.

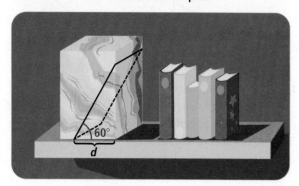

24. Communicate Precisely Sarah finds an antique dinner bell that appears to be in the shape of an isosceles right triangle, but the only measurement given is the longest side. Sarah wants to display the bell and wand in a 5.5-in. by 7.5-in. picture frame. Assuming that the bell is an isosceles right triangle, can Sarah display the bell and wand within the frame? Explain.

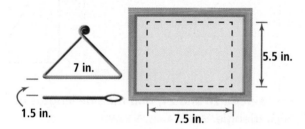

25. Construct Arguments When Carmen parks on a hill, she places chocks behind the wheels of her car. The height of the chocks must be at least one-fourth of the height of the wheels to hold the car securely in place. The chock shown has the shape of a right triangle. Is it safe for Carmen to use? Explain.

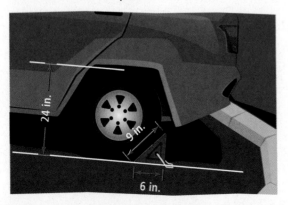

ASSESSMENT PRACTICE

26. Match each set of triangle side lengths with the best description of the triangle.

  I. $\sqrt{2}, \sqrt{2}, \sqrt{3}$ **A.** right triangle

  II. $5, 3\sqrt{2}, \sqrt{43}$ **B.** 30°-60°-90° triangle

  III. $8, 8, 8\sqrt{2}$ **C.** 45°-45°-90° triangle

  IV. $11, 11\sqrt{3}, 22$ **D.** not a right triangle

27. SAT/ACT What is GJ?

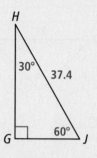

Ⓐ 18.7   Ⓒ $18.7\sqrt{3}$

Ⓑ $18.7\sqrt{2}$ Ⓓ 74.8

28. Performance Task Emma designed two triangular sails for a boat.

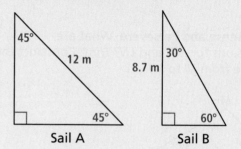

Sail A   Sail B

Part A What is the area of Sail A?

Part B What is the area of Sail B?

Part C Is it possible for Emma to cut both sails from one square of sailcloth with sides that are 9 meters in length? Draw a diagram to explain.

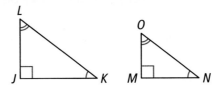
9-7
Trigonometric Ratios

PearsonRealize.com

I CAN...
use trigonometric ratios to find lengths and angle measures of right triangles.

VOCABULARY
- cosine
- sine
- tangent
- trigonometric ratios

🖐 **CRITIQUE & EXPLAIN**

A teacher asked students to write a proportion using the lengths of the legs of the two right triangles.

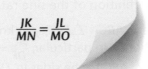
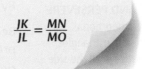

Two students' responses are shown.

Diego

$$\frac{JK}{MN} = \frac{JL}{MO}$$

Rebecca

$$\frac{JK}{JL} = \frac{MN}{MO}$$

A. Do you think that the proportion that Diego wrote is correct? Explain.

B. Do you think that the proportion that Rebecca wrote is correct? Explain.

C. Use Structure If $\frac{a}{b} = \frac{c}{d}$, how can you get an equivalent equation such that the left side of the equation is $\frac{a}{c}$?

❓ **ESSENTIAL QUESTION**

How do trigonometric ratios relate angle measures to side lengths of right triangles?

CONCEPT Trigonometric Ratios

The **trigonometric ratios**, or functions, relate the side lengths of a right triangle to its acute angles.

sine of $\angle A$

$$\sin A = \frac{\text{length of leg opposite } \angle A}{\text{length of hypotenuse}}$$

$$= \frac{BC}{AB}$$

cosine of $\angle A$

$$\cos A = \frac{\text{length of leg adjacent to } \angle A}{\text{length of hypotenuse}}$$

$$= \frac{AC}{AB}$$

tangent of $\angle A$

$$\tan A = \frac{\text{length of leg opposite } \angle A}{\text{length of leg adjacent to } \angle A}$$

$$= \frac{BC}{AC}$$

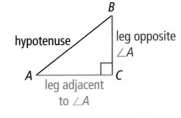

CONCEPTUAL
UNDERSTANDING

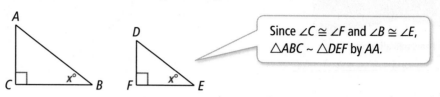

EXAMPLE 1 Understand Trigonometric Ratios Using Similarity

How are the sines of two different angles with the same measure related?

Let $\triangle ABC$ and $\triangle DEF$ be right triangles with $m\angle B = m\angle E$.

> Since $\angle C \cong \angle F$ and $\angle B \cong \angle E$, $\triangle ABC \sim \triangle DEF$ by AA.

You can use properties of similarity to determine the relationship between sin B and sin E.

MAKE SENSE AND PERSEVERE
There are many proportional relationships in similar triangles. Look for one that uses all the side lengths in the expressions for sin B and sin E.

By the definition of the sine ratio, $\sin B = \frac{AC}{AB}$ and $\sin E = \frac{DF}{DE}$.

Because $\triangle ABC \sim \triangle DEF$, you know that corresponding side lengths are proportional. In particular, $\frac{AC}{DF} = \frac{AB}{DE}$. Rewrite this equation to compare the sides in $\triangle ABC$ to the sides in $\triangle DEF$.

$$\frac{AC}{DF} \cdot \frac{DF}{AB} = \frac{AB}{DE} \cdot \frac{DF}{AB}$$

$$\frac{AC}{AB} = \frac{DF}{DE}$$

$$\sin B = \sin E$$

> Substitute sin B for $\frac{AC}{AB}$ and sin E for $\frac{DF}{DE}$.

Any two acute angles with the same measure have the same sine.

 Try It! 1. Show that any two acute angles with the same measure have the same cosine.

EXAMPLE 2 Write Trigonometric Ratios

What are the sine, cosine, and tangent ratios for $\angle H$?

Use the definitions of the trigonometric ratios.

COMMON ERROR
You may incorrectly assume the horizontal leg and vertical leg to be the adjacent and opposite legs. Remember that adjacent and opposite are relative to the angle.

$$\sin H = \frac{\text{length of leg opposite } \angle H}{\text{length of hypotenuse}} = \frac{12}{15}$$

$$\cos H = \frac{\text{length of leg adjacent } \angle H}{\text{length of hypotenuse}} = \frac{9}{15}$$

$$\tan H = \frac{\text{length of leg opposite } \angle H}{\text{length of leg adjacent } \angle H} = \frac{12}{9}$$

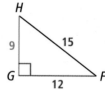

 Try It! 2. In Example 2, what are the sine, cosine, and tangent ratios of $\angle F$?

EXAMPLE 3 **Trigonometric Ratios of Special Angles**

A. **What are the sine, cosine, and tangent ratios for 30°, 45°, and 60° angles?**

You can use what you know about 45°-45°-90° and 30°-60°-90° right triangles to find the ratios.

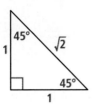 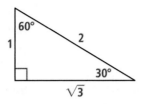

$\sin 45° = \frac{1}{\sqrt{2}} = \frac{\sqrt{2}}{2}$ $\sin 30° = \frac{1}{2}$ $\sin 60° = \frac{\sqrt{3}}{2}$

$\cos 45° = \frac{1}{\sqrt{2}} = \frac{\sqrt{2}}{2}$ $\cos 30° = \frac{\sqrt{3}}{2}$ $\cos 60° = \frac{1}{2}$

$\tan 45° = \frac{1}{1} = 1$ $\tan 30° = \frac{1}{\sqrt{3}} = \frac{\sqrt{3}}{3}$ $\tan 60° = \frac{\sqrt{3}}{1} = \sqrt{3}$

> **VOCABULARY**
> Recall that two angles are *complementary* if the sum of their measures is 90. If an angle has measure x, its complement has measure $90 - x$.

B. **How are the sine and cosine of complementary angles related?**

By the Triangle Angle-Sum Theorem, the two acute angles in any right triangle are complementary.

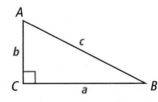

$m\angle A + m\angle B + m\angle C = 180$

$m\angle A + m\angle B + 90 = 180$

$m\angle A + m\angle B = 90$

Find the sine and cosine of the complementary angles $\angle A$ and $\angle B$.

$\sin A = \frac{a}{c}$ $\sin B = \frac{b}{c}$

$\cos A = \frac{b}{c}$ $\cos B = \frac{a}{c}$

So $\sin A = \cos B$ and $\sin B = \cos A$. The sine of an angle is equal to the cosine of its complement, and vice versa.

 Try It!   **3. a.** In $\triangle FGH$, what is the value of y?

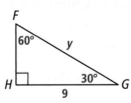

     b. How can you write an equivalent expression for cos 70° using sine? An equivalent expression for sin 34° using cosine?

APPLICATION → **EXAMPLE 4** **Use Trigonometric Ratios to Find Distances**

A plane takes off and climbs at a 12° angle. Is that angle sufficient enough to fly over an 11,088-foot mountain that is 12.5 miles from the runway or does the plane need to increase its angle of ascent?

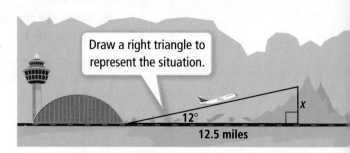

Draw a right triangle to represent the situation.

12°
12.5 miles
x

Step 1 You know the length of the side adjacent to the 12° angle, so use the tangent ratio to find the altitude of the plane as it passes the mountain.

$$\tan 12° = \frac{x}{12.5}$$

$$x = 12.5 \cdot \tan 12° \text{ — Use a calculator.}$$

$$\approx 2.66$$

12.5 TAN 12 ENTER

The altitude of the plane is about 2.66 miles.

Step 2 Compare the altitude of the plane to the height of the mountain.

$$11{,}088 \text{ ft} \cdot \frac{1 \text{ mi}}{5{,}280 \text{ ft}} = 2.1 \text{ mi} \text{ — Write the height of the mountain in miles.}$$

A 12° angle is sufficient because 2.1 mi < 2.66 mi.

 Try It! **4.** If a plane climbs at 5° and flies 20 miles through the air as it climbs, what is the altitude of the airplane, to the nearest foot?

 EXAMPLE 5 **Use Trigonometric Inverses to Find Angle Measures**

What are m∠A and m∠B?

If you know the sine, cosine, or tangent of an angle, you can use a *trigonometric inverse* ($\sin^{-1}$, $\cos^{-1}$, or $\tan^{-1}$) to find the angle measure.

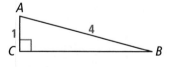

A
1
C
4
B

Since you know that $\cos A = \frac{1}{4}$, use $\cos^{-1}$ to find $m\angle A$.

$$m\angle A = \cos^{-1}\left(\frac{1}{4}\right)$$

$$\approx 75.5$$

Since you know that $\sin B = \frac{1}{4}$, use $\sin^{-1}$ to find $m\angle B$.

$$m\angle B = \sin^{-1}\left(\frac{1}{4}\right)$$

$$\approx 14.5$$

 Try It! **5. a.** What is $m\angle P$?

b. What is $m\angle Q$?

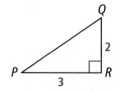

Q
2
P
3
R

Go Online | PearsonRealize.com

⊕ CONCEPT SUMMARY Trigonometric Ratios

WORDS For a right triangle, **the trigonometric ratios sine, cosine,** and **tangent** relate the measure of an acute angle of the triangle to the lengths of the sides.

DIAGRAM Triangle *ABC* is a right triangle.

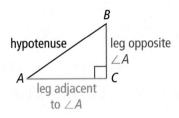

SYMBOLS

$$\sin A = \frac{\text{length of leg opposite } \angle A}{\text{length of hypotenuse}}$$

$$\cos A = \frac{\text{length of leg adjacent to } \angle A}{\text{length of hypotenuse}}$$

$$\tan A = \frac{\text{length of leg opposite } \angle A}{\text{length of leg adjacent to } \angle A}$$

☑ Do You UNDERSTAND?

1. **ESSENTIAL QUESTION** How do trigonometric ratios relate angle measures to side lengths of right triangles?

2. **Error Analysis** What is the error in this equation for a trigonometric ratio?

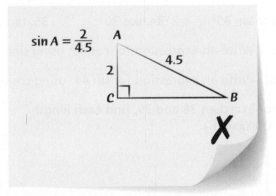

3. **Vocabulary** How are finding the inverses of trigonometric ratios similar to using inverse operations?

4. **Communicate Precisely** How is the sine ratio similar to the cosine ratio? How is it different?

5. **Look for Relationships** If $\sin A = \frac{a}{c}$, how could you use *a* and *c* to find cos *A*?

6. **Reason** What is an expression for *d* using $x°$, $y°$, and *h*?

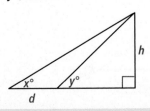

Do You KNOW HOW?

For Exercises 7–12, use △*ABC* to find each trigonometric ratio or angle measure.

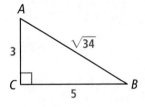

7. tan *B*

8. cos *B*

9. sin *A*

10. tan *A*

11. *m∠B*

12. *m∠A*

13. What are the sine and cosine of the smallest angle in the right triangle shown?

14. What is the measure of the largest acute angle in the right triangle shown?

15. In the figure shown, what are *m∠S* and *m∠T*?

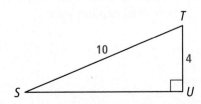

UNDERSTAND

16. Error Analysis Jacinta's teacher asks her to find the tangent of $\angle Y$. What is her error?

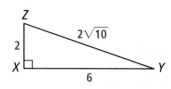

$\tan Y = \dfrac{XY}{XZ}$

$\tan Y = \dfrac{6}{2}$

$\tan Y = 3$

17. Make Sense and Persevere If $\sin B = 0.5$ in the triangle shown, what is an expression for AB?

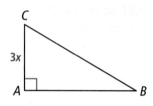

18. Reason Every tread of a staircase is 8 in. deep, and every riser is 6 in. high. How would you find the angle the staircase makes with the floor? Explain.

19. Mathematical Connections Find the values.

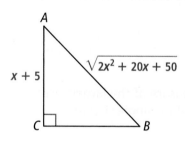

    a. $\sin B$ **b.** $m\angle B$

20. Higher Order Thinking Why are the sine and cosine ratios of $x°$ never greater than one? Use the triangle below to explain your reasoning.

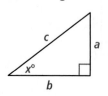

PRACTICE

For Exercises 21–23, write each ratio. SEE EXAMPLE 1

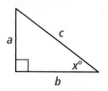

21. $\sin x°$ **22.** $\cos x°$ **23.** $\tan x°$

For Exercises 24–29, find each value. SEE EXAMPLE 2

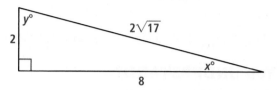

24. $\sin x°$ **25.** $\cos x°$ **26.** $\tan x°$

27. $\sin y°$ **28.** $\cos y°$ **29.** $\tan y°$

For Exercises 30–35, find each value. SEE EXAMPLE 3

30. $\sin 30°$ **31.** $\cos 60°$ **32.** $\sin 45°$

33. $\tan 45°$ **34.** $\cos 30°$ **35.** $\tan 60°$

36. Write an expression for $\cos 68°$ using sine.

37. Write an expression for $\sin 44°$ using cosine.

For Exercises 38 and 39, find each length.
SEE EXAMPLE 4

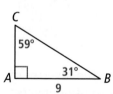

38. AC **39.** BC

For Exercises 40–43, find the angle measures in each triangle. SEE EXAMPLE 5

40. $m\angle B$

41. $m\angle C$

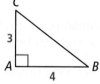

42. $m\angle K$

43. $m\angle L$

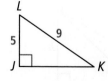

APPLY

44. Make Sense and Persevere Workers need to make repairs on a building. A boom lift has maximum height of 60 ft at an angle of 48°. If the bottom of the boom is 60 ft from the building, can the boom reach the top of the building? Explain.

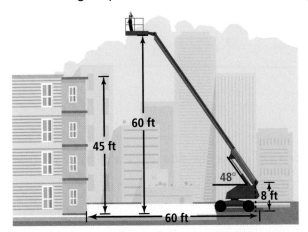

45. Model With Mathematics A coach draws up a play so a quarterback throws the football at the same time a receiver runs straight down the field. Suppose the quarterback throws the football at a speed of 20 ft/s and the receiver runs at a speed of 12 ft/s. At what angle $x°$ to the horizontal line must the quarterback throw the football in order for the receiver to catch it? Explain.

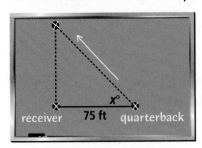

46. Use Structure Kelsey puts up an inflatable gorilla to advertise a sale. She realizes that she needs to secure the figure with rope. She estimates she needs to attach three pieces at the angles shown. How much rope does Kelsey need? Round to the nearest foot.

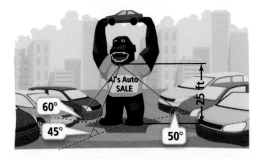

ASSESSMENT PRACTICE

47. Match each expression to a trigonometric ratio.

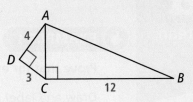

I. cos ∠ACD   A. $\frac{12}{13}$

II. tan ∠ABC   B. $\frac{4}{5}$

III. sin ∠BAC   C. $\frac{3}{5}$

IV. cos ∠CAD   D. $\frac{5}{12}$

48. SAT/ACT What is the value of cos $x°$?

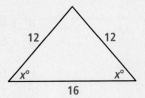

Ⓐ $\frac{\sqrt{5}}{2}$ Ⓑ $\frac{3}{2}$ Ⓒ $\frac{\sqrt{5}}{3}$ Ⓓ $\frac{2}{3}$

49. Performance Task Jacy anchors a retractable leash to a tree and attaches the leash to her dog's collar. When the dog fully extends the leash, the angle between the leash and the tree is 84°.

Part A If her neighbor's yard is 18 feet away from the tree, can Jacy's dog get into her neighbor's yard? If so, how far into the yard can the dog go? Round to nearest tenth of a foot.

Part B If Jacy wants to make sure her dog cannot get within 1 foot of her neighbor's yard, how high up the tree must she anchor the leash? Round to the nearest tenth of a foot.

9-7a

The Pythagorean Identity

 PearsonRealize.com

I CAN... prove the Pythagorean Identity and use it to find trigonometric ratios in right triangles.

VOCABULARY
• Pythagorean Identity

COMMON ERROR
Be careful not to interpret the notation $\sin^2 \theta$ as $\sin(\theta^2)$ or $\sin(\theta \cdot \theta)$. The notation $\sin^2 \theta$ means $(\sin \theta)(\sin \theta)$.

? ESSENTIAL QUESTION   How can you prove the Pythagorean Identity and use it to find trigonometric ratios in right triangles?

👆 EXAMPLE 1   Prove the Pythagorean Identity

Prove that for every right triangle, $\sin^2 \theta + \cos^2 \theta = 1$.

Draw and label a right triangle with angle θ.

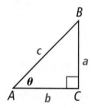

Use the Pythagorean Theorem to relate the side lengths of the right triangle.

$$a^2 + b^2 = c^2$$
$$\frac{a^2 + b^2}{c^2} = \frac{c^2}{c^2}$$
$$\frac{a^2}{c^2} + \frac{b^2}{c^2} = 1$$
$$\left(\frac{a}{c}\right)^2 + \left(\frac{b}{c}\right)^2 = 1$$
$$\sin^2 \theta + \cos^2 \theta = 1$$

Relate the side lengths to trigonometric ratios: $\sin \theta = \frac{a}{c}$; $\cos \theta = \frac{b}{c}$

This relationship is called the **Pythagorean Identity.**

☑ Try It!   **1.** Prove the Pythagorean Identity if $\angle B$ was labeled θ instead of $\angle A$.

👆 EXAMPLE 2   Use the Pythagorean Identity

A. What is $\tan \theta$ if $\cos \theta = \frac{3}{5}$?

Step 1 Use the Pythagorean Identity to find $\sin \theta$.

$$\sin^2 \theta + \cos^2 \theta = 1$$
$$\sin^2 \theta + \left(\frac{3}{5}\right)^2 = 1$$
$$\sin^2 \theta + \frac{9}{25} = 1$$
$$\sin^2 \theta = \frac{16}{25}$$
$$\sin \theta = \frac{4}{5}$$

Substitute $\frac{3}{5}$ for $\cos \theta$.

Step 2 Evaluate $\tan \theta$.

$$\tan \theta = \frac{\sin \theta}{\cos \theta}$$
$$= \frac{\frac{4}{5}}{\frac{3}{5}} = \frac{4}{3}$$

CONTINUED ON THE NEXT PAGE

 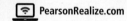

EXAMPLE 2 CONTINUED

B. If $\tan \theta = \frac{5}{12}$, what is $\sin \theta$?

Step 1 Use the Pythagorean Identity to find $\cos \theta$.

$$\sin^2 \theta + \cos^2 \theta = 1$$

$$\frac{\sin^2 \theta}{\cos^2 \theta} + \frac{\cos^2 \theta}{\cos^2 \theta} = \frac{1}{\cos^2 \theta}$$

You know **tan θ**, so write an equivalent form of the Pythagorean Identity that uses tangent.

$$\tan^2 \theta + 1 = \frac{1}{\cos^2 \theta}$$

$$\left(\frac{5}{12}\right)^2 + 1 = \frac{1}{\cos^2 \theta}$$

$$\frac{169}{144} = \frac{1}{\cos^2 \theta}$$

$$\frac{13}{12} = \frac{1}{\cos \theta}$$

$$\frac{12}{13} = \cos \theta$$

Step 2 Find $\sin \theta$.

$$\tan \theta = \frac{\sin \theta}{\cos \theta}$$

Use the definition of tangent.

$$\tan \theta \cdot \cos \theta = \sin \theta$$

$$\frac{5}{12} \cdot \frac{12}{13} = \sin \theta$$

$$\frac{5}{13} = \sin \theta$$

 Try It!   2a. If $\sin \theta = \frac{40}{41}$, what is $\tan \theta$?

b. If $\tan \theta = \frac{7}{24}$, what is $\sin \theta$?

 CONCEPT SUMMARY

The equation below is called the Pythagorean Identity.

$$\sin^2 \theta + \cos^2 \theta = 1$$

Do You UNDERSTAND?

1. **ESSENTIAL QUESTION** How can you use the Pythagorean Identity to find trigonometric ratios in right triangles?

2. **Reason** When you know the cosine ratio, how is finding the tangent ratio different than finding the sine ratio?

Do You KNOW HOW?

3. What is $\sin \theta$ if $\cos \theta = \frac{4}{5}$?

4. What is $\cos \theta$ if $\sin \theta = \frac{\sqrt{3}}{3}$?

5. What is $\tan \theta$ if $\cos \theta = \frac{15}{17}$?

6. What is $\tan \theta$ if $\sin \theta = \frac{\sqrt{2}}{2}$?

UNDERSTAND

7. Critique Others Nadeem said that to find the $\cos \theta$ when he knows $\sin \theta$, he can use the equation $\cos \theta = \sqrt{1 - \sin^2 \theta}$. Do you agree with Nadeem? Justify your response.

8. Prove the equation $\tan \theta = \sqrt{\dfrac{1}{\cos^2 \theta} - 1}$ can be used to find $\tan \theta$ when given $\cos \theta$.

9. Generalize Write an equation to find $\sin \theta$ when given $\tan \theta$. Prove your equation is true.

10. In Quadrant I, a triangle has a vertex at the origin. Side length a is on the x-axis and a side parallel to the y-axis has a length of 6 units. The acute angle between side a and the hypotenuse is θ.

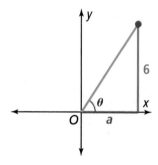

Express $\sin \theta$, $\cos \theta$ and $\tan \theta$ in terms of a.

11. Error Analysis A student was given the value for $\tan \theta$ and found $\sin \theta = \dfrac{5}{4}$. How do you know that the student made an error?

PRACTICE

12. If $\tan \theta = \dfrac{5}{12}$, what is $\sin \theta$?

13. If $\tan \theta = \dfrac{10}{15}$, what is $\cos \theta$?

14. If $\cos \theta = \dfrac{\sqrt{3}}{2}$, what is $\tan \theta$?

15. If $\sin \theta = \dfrac{\sqrt{15}}{\sqrt{31}}$, what is $\tan \theta$?

For each given trigonometric ratio in a right triangle, use the Pythagorean Identity to find two other trigonometric ratios.

16. $\sin \theta = \dfrac{45}{51}$

17. $\cos \theta = \dfrac{\sqrt{2}}{\sqrt{5}}$

18. $\tan \theta = \dfrac{1}{2}$,

19. $\tan \theta = \dfrac{\sqrt{46}}{\sqrt{3}}$

APPLY

20. Stacey is on a bench 20 feet away from a 100-foot tall building. The tangent of the angle θ when she looks up at the top of the building is $\dfrac{100}{20}$.

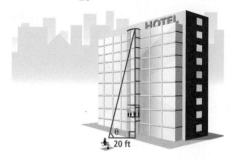

What are $\sin \theta$ and $\cos \theta$?

21. Make Sense and Persevere An architect is designing a sloped rooftop that is triangular from the side view.

If x represents the height of the triangle, then $\tan \theta = \dfrac{x}{12}$.

a. Write a formula to find $\sin \theta$, in terms of x.

b. Write a formula to find $\cos \theta$, in terms of x.

22. A carpenter is constructing a hexagonal floor for a treehouse. The floor will be made of six equilateral triangles. In an equilateral triangle, the cosine of each angle is $\dfrac{1}{2}$.

Use the Pythagorean Identity to find the sine and tangent of each angle of an equilateral triangle.

Topic Review

? TOPIC ESSENTIAL QUESTION

1. How are properties of similar figures used to solve problems?

Vocabulary Review

Choose the correct term to complete each sentence.

2. Two triangles that are _____ have two pairs of corresponding congruent angles.

3. A _____ is a composition of a dilation and one or more rigid motions.

4. A point that is its own image in a dilation is the _____.

5. As a result of a dilation, if $A'B' = n \cdot AB$, then n is the _____.

- center of dilation
- dilation
- geometric mean
- scale factor
- similar
- similarity transformation

Concepts & Skills Review

LESSONS 9-1 & 9-2 ▶ Dilations and Similarity Transformations

Quick Review

A **dilation** is a transformation that maps a point X to X' such that X' lies on $\overrightarrow{CX}$ and $CX' = k \cdot CX$, with **center of dilation** C and **scale factor** k.

Two figures are **similar** if there is a **similarity transformation** that maps one figure onto the other.

Example

Are △ABC and △DEF similar? Explain.

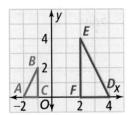

The reflection $R_{y\text{-axis}}$ maps △ABC to a triangle with vertices $A'(2, 0)$, $B'(1, 2)$ and $C'(1, 0)$. The dilation D_2 maps the image to △DEF. Since the composition $D_2 \circ R_{y\text{-axis}}$ maps △ABC to △DEF, the triangles are similar.

Practice & Problem Solving

Give the coordinates of each image.

6. $D_{\frac{1}{2}}(\triangle FGH)$ for $F(5, -2)$, $G(-2, -4)$, $H(0, 6)$

7. $D_{(3, K)}(\triangle KLM)$ for $K(0, 4)$, $L(3, 0)$, $M(-2, 4)$

8. What is a similarity transformation from $PQRS$ to $WXYZ$?

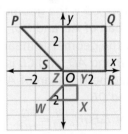

9. **Construct Arguments** Isabel says that the scale factor in the similarity transformation that maps △ABC to △PQR is 2. Is she correct? Explain.

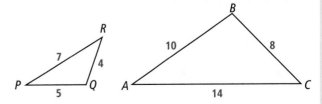

Proving Triangles Similar

Quick Review

A pair of triangles can be shown to be similar by using the following criteria.

- Two pairs of corresponding angles are congruent.
- All corresponding sides are proportional.
- Two pairs of corresponding sides are proportional and the included angles are congruent.

Example

Explain whether △ABE and △DBC are similar.

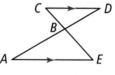

By the Alternate Interior Angles Theorem, $\angle A \cong \angle D$ and $\angle E \cong \angle C$. Since two pairs of corresponding angles are congruent, $\triangle ABE \sim \triangle DBC$.

Practice & Problem Solving

For Exercises 10 and 11, explain whether each triangle similarity is true.

10. △FGJ ~ △JGH

11. △KLN ~ △NLM

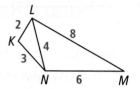

12. Communicate Precisely Explain what additional information is needed to use AA ~ to show that △TUV ~ △XZY.

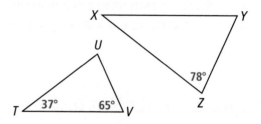

Similarity in Right Triangles and Proportions in Triangles

Quick Review

For right triangle △ABC, △ABC ~ △ACD ~ △CBD.

Also, CD is the **geometric mean** of AD and BD, AC is the geometric mean of AB and AD, and CB is the geometric mean of AB and DB.

For △FGH, $\frac{FJ}{HJ} = \frac{FG}{HG}$.

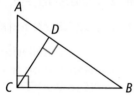

Example

For △LMN, what is x?

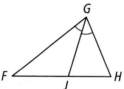

By the Side-Splitter Theorem, $\frac{LP}{PM} = \frac{NQ}{QM}$, so $\frac{6}{9} = \frac{4}{x}$. Solve for x to get $x = \frac{9}{6}(4) = 6$.

Practice & Problem Solving

For Exercises 13–15, use △RST to find each length.

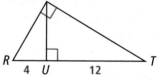

13. RS

14. ST

15. SU

For Exercises 16–19, find the value of x.

16.

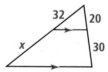

17.

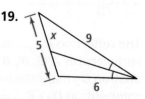

18.

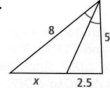

19.

20. Use Structure Given right triangle △GHJ with $\overline{JK}$ the altitude to hypotenuse $\overline{GH}$, what is GJ the geometric mean of? Explain.

Quick Review

Given $\triangle ABC$, the Pythagorean Theorem states $a^2 + b^2 = c^2$.

The **trigonometric ratios** are

$\sin A = \frac{a}{c}$ $\cos A = \frac{b}{c}$ $\tan A = \frac{a}{b}$.

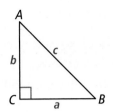

Example

Given $\triangle DEF$, what is $\sin D$?

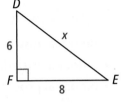

Step 1 Use the Pythagorean Theorem to find x.

$8^2 + 6^2 = x^2$

$10 = x$

Step 2 Use a trigonometric ratio to find $\sin D$.

$\sin D = \frac{8}{10} = \frac{4}{5}$

Practice & Problem Solving

For Exercises 21–23, use $\triangle ABC$ to find each value.

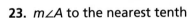
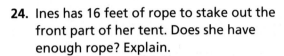

21. BC

22. $\cos B$

23. $m\angle A$ to the nearest tenth

24. Ines has 16 feet of rope to stake out the front part of her tent. Does she have enough rope? Explain.

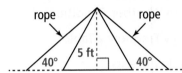

rope   rope

40°   5 ft   40°

25. **Make Sense and Persevere**
Given $\triangle XYZ$, what additional information do you need to find YZ? Explain.

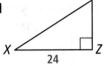

TOPIC 10

Probability

? TOPIC ESSENTIAL QUESTION

How can you find the probability of events and combinations of events?

Topic Overview

Topic Vocabulary

- binomial distribution
- binomial experiment
- binomial probability
- combination
- complement
- conditional probability
- conditional relative frequency
- dependent events
- expected value
- factorial
- Fundamental Counting Principle
- independent events
- joint frequency
- marginal frequency
- mutually exclusive
- permutation
- probability distribution
- uniform probability distribution

Digital Experience

 INTERACTIVE STUDENT EDITION
Access online or offline.

 ACTIVITIES Complete *Explore & Reason, Model & Discuss*, and *Critique & Explain* activities. Interact with Examples and Try Its.

 ANIMATION View and interact with real-world applications.

 PRACTICE Practice what you've learned.

 Go online | PearsonRealize.com

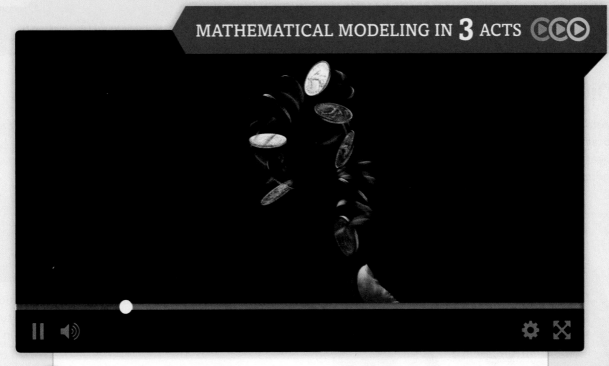

▶ Place Your Guess

A coin toss is a popular way to decide between two options or settle a dispute. The coin toss is popular because it is a simple and unbiased way of deciding. Assuming the coin being tossed is a fair coin, both parties have an equally likely chance of winning.

What other methods could you use to decide between two choices fairly? Think about this during the Mathematical Modeling in 3 Acts lesson.

VIDEOS Watch clips to support *Mathematical Modeling in 3 Acts Lessons* and **enVision® STEM Projects.**

CONCEPT SUMMARY Review key lesson content through multiple representations.

ASSESSMENT Show what you've learned.

GLOSSARY Read and listen to English and Spanish definitions.

TUTORIALS Get help from *Virtual Nerd*, right when you need it.

MATH TOOLS Explore math with digital tools and manipulatives.

Did You Know?

Meteorologists use past climate data for a particular location and date as well as weather models to make weather predictions. Some regions in the U.S. are more predictable than others.

The greatest temperature change in a one-day period occurred in Loma, Montana, in 1972. The temperature rose an incredible 103 degrees, from −54 to 49 °F, in 24 hours.

Weather events can surprise experts, and can vary greatly even within a few miles.

Climate is the long-term average of weather conditions. So the difference between weather and climate is a measure of time.

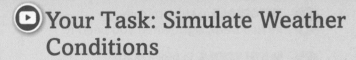

▶ Your Task: Simulate Weather Conditions

You and your classmates will research climate data for a specific location for one month. You'll use probability to simulate a plausible set of weather conditions for each day of February, including temperature and precipitation, and whether the precipitation will be rain or snow.

10-1

Two-Way Frequency Tables

PearsonRealize.com

I CAN... organize data in two-way frequency tables and use them to make inferences.

VOCABULARY
- conditional relative frequency
- joint frequency
- joint relative frequency
- marginal frequency
- marginal relative frequency

✋ **EXPLORE & REASON**

📶 🕐 Activity   ☑ Assess

Baseball teams at a high school and a college play at the same stadium. Results for every game last season are given for both teams. There were no ties.

Baseball Season Results at Mountain View Stadium

✦ ☆ *Wins!* ☆ ✦	HOME	AWAY
WEST MOUNTAIN HIGH SCHOOL	11 OUT OF 16	08 OUT OF 14
BIG MOUNTAIN COLLEGE	18 OUT OF 26	18 OUT OF 30

A. How could you organize the data in table form?

B. Look for Relationships How would you analyze the data to determine whether the data support the claim that the team that plays at home is more likely to win?

❓ **ESSENTIAL QUESTION** ▸ How can you use two-way frequency tables to analyze data?

APPLICATION ➜

✋ **EXAMPLE 1** Interpret a Two-Way Frequency Table

Owners of a major food chain are planning to add a vegetarian item to its menu. Customers were asked to choose one of two vegetarian items. The results are shown in the table. What trends do the results suggest?

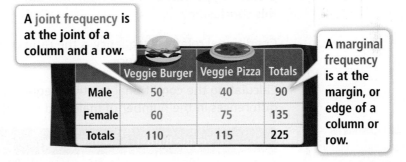

A **joint frequency** is at the joint of a column and a row.

A **marginal frequency** is at the margin, or edge of a column or row.

	Veggie Burger	Veggie Pizza	Totals
Male	50	40	90
Female	60	75	135
Totals	110	115	225

STUDY TIP
A two-way frequency table can show possible relationships between two sets of categorical data.

Joint frequencies indicate the frequency of a single option for one category; for example, the frequency of males choosing a veggie burger.

Marginal frequencies indicate the total frequency for each option or category, such as the total frequency of female respondents.

The joint frequencies suggest that male customers prefer veggie burgers over veggie pizzas, and female customers prefer veggie pizzas over veggie burgers.

The marginal frequencies suggest that all of the respondents showed only a slight preference for veggie pizza over a veggie burger. They also indicate that more females than males were surveyed.

Try It! 1. What do the marginal frequencies tell you about the number of male and female respondents?

APPLICATION

 EXAMPLE 2 Interpret a Two-Way Relative Frequency Table

What do the survey results reveal about male and female customer preferences for veggie burgers?

Joint relative frequency is the ratio, or percent, of the joint frequency to the total.

Marginal relative frequency is the ratio, or percent, of the marginal frequency to the total.

	Veggie Burger	Veggie Pizza	Totals
Male	$\frac{50}{225} \approx 22\%$	$\frac{40}{225} \approx 18\%$	$\frac{90}{225} = 40\%$
Female	$\frac{60}{225} \approx 27\%$	$\frac{75}{225} \approx 33\%$	$\frac{135}{225} = 60\%$
Totals	$\frac{110}{225} \approx 49\%$	$\frac{115}{225} \approx 51\%$	$\frac{225}{225} = 100\%$

Of the customers surveyed, about 22% were males who selected veggie burgers and about 27% were females who selected veggie burgers. So, a greater percent of females than males selected veggie burgers.

✓ **Try It!** **2.** How can you tell whether a greater percent of customers surveyed selected veggie burger or veggie pizza?

CONCEPTUAL
UNDERSTANDING

 EXAMPLE 3 Calculate Conditional Relative Frequency

Using data from Examples 1 and 2, a marketing team concludes that females prefer veggie burgers more than men do. Do the survey results support this conclusion?

Conditional relative frequency is the ratio of the joint frequency and the related marginal frequency.

Calculating the conditional relative frequency for each row will adjust for differences in the number of male and female customers surveyed.

	Veggie Burger	Veggie Pizza	Totals
Male	$\frac{50}{90} \approx 56\%$	$\frac{40}{90} \approx 44\%$	$\frac{90}{90} = 100\%$
Female	$\frac{60}{135} \approx 44\%$	$\frac{75}{135} \approx 56\%$	$\frac{135}{135} = 100\%$

$$\text{Conditional relative frequency} = \frac{\text{joint frequency}}{\text{marginal frequency}}$$

The results do not support this conclusion. The conditional relative frequencies show that while about 56% of the males surveyed prefer veggie burgers, only about 44% of the females prefer veggie burgers.

✓ **Try It!** **3.** What conclusion could the marketing team make about male and female preferences for veggie pizza? Justify your answer.

 EXAMPLE 4   Interpret Conditional Relative Frequency

The marketing team also concludes that there is a greater variation between the percent of men and women who like veggie pizza than there is for those who prefer veggie burgers. Do the survey results support this conclusion?

Calculating the conditional relative frequency for each column allows you to analyze male and female preferences within each food choice category.

<table>
<tr><td></td><th>Veggie Burger</th><th>Veggie Pizza</th></tr>
<tr><th>Male</th><td>$\frac{50}{110} \approx 45\%$</td><td>$\frac{40}{115} \approx 35\%$</td></tr>
<tr><th>Female</th><td>$\frac{60}{110} \approx 55\%$</td><td>$\frac{75}{115} \approx 65\%$</td></tr>
<tr><th>Totals</th><td>$\frac{110}{110} = 100\%$</td><td>$\frac{115}{115} = 100\%$</td></tr>
</table>

The conclusion is supported by the survey results. Conditional relative frequencies show that of the customers who prefer veggie pizza, 65% are female and only 35% are male. Of those who prefer veggie burgers, 55% are female and 45% are male.

USE STRUCTURE
The conditional relative frequencies calculated for rows are not the same as those calculated for columns. How are the questions you can answer looking at the table in Example 3 different from the questions you can answer looking at the table in Example 4?

✅ **Try It!**   **4.** What conclusion could you draw if the percentages for male and female customers were the same across the rows in this table?

 EXAMPLE 5   Interpret Data Frequencies

A random sample of spectators entering a stadium were asked whether they were cheering for the Bears or the Tigers in a championship game. The sample was categorized according to gender and team.

<table>
<tr><td></td><th>Cheering for Bears</th><th>Cheering for Tigers</th><th>Total</th></tr>
<tr><th>Male</th><td>72</td><td>65</td><td>137</td></tr>
<tr><th>Female</th><td>49</td><td>44</td><td>93</td></tr>
<tr><th>Totals</th><td>121</td><td>109</td><td>230</td></tr>
</table>

A. What does the joint relative frequency $\frac{65}{230}$ represent in this context?

Joint relative frequency is the ratio of the joint frequency to the total.

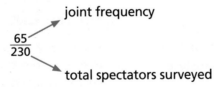

Find the joint frequency 65 in the table. You can see that 65 males cheered for the Tigers, so $\frac{65}{230}$ represents the ratio of male Tigers fans to the total number of people surveyed.

B. What does the conditional relative frequency $\frac{49}{93}$ represent in this context?

Conditional relative frequency is the ratio of the joint frequency to the related marginal frequency.

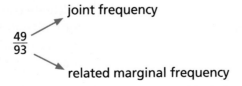

The number $\frac{49}{93}$ represents the ratio of female Bears fans to the number of females surveyed.

✅ **Try It!**   **5.** What does the conditional relative frequency $\frac{72}{137}$ represent in this context?

WORDS Two-way frequency tables show relationships between two sets of categorical data. Entries can be frequency counts or relative frequencies. Entries in the body of the table are **joint frequencies** (counts) or **joint relative frequencies** (ratios). Entries in the totals column or row are **marginal frequencies** or **marginal relative frequencies**.

Conditional relative frequencies show the frequency of responses for a given condition, or the ratio of the joint frequencies to the corresponding marginal frequency.

TABLES

Movie Time Preferences

	Afternoon	Evening	Totals
Student	$\frac{90}{200} = 45\%$	$\frac{50}{200} = 25\%$	$\frac{140}{200} = 70\%$
Adult	$\frac{20}{200} = 10\%$	$\frac{40}{200} = 20\%$	$\frac{60}{200} = 30\%$
Totals	$\frac{110}{200} = 55\%$	$\frac{90}{200} = 45\%$	$\frac{200}{200} = 100\%$

20 of the 200 respondents, or 10%, were adults who prefer the afternoon show.

70% of the respondents were students.

Conditional Relative Frequency

	Afternoon	Evening	Totals
Student	$\frac{90}{140} \approx 64\%$	$\frac{50}{140} \approx 36\%$	$\frac{140}{140} = 100\%$
Adult	$\frac{20}{60} \approx 33\%$	$\frac{40}{60} \approx 67\%$	$\frac{60}{60} = 100\%$

Of all of the adult respondents, 33% prefer afternoon shows.

Conditional Relative Frequency

	Afternoon	Evening
Student	$\frac{90}{110} \approx 82\%$	$\frac{50}{90} \approx 56\%$
Adult	$\frac{20}{110} \approx 18\%$	$\frac{40}{90} \approx 44\%$
Totals	$\frac{110}{110} = 100\%$	$\frac{90}{90} = 100\%$

Of all of the respondents that prefer evening shows, 44% were adults.

Do You UNDERSTAND?

1. **ESSENTIAL QUESTION** How can you use two-way frequency tables to analyze data?

2. **Communicate Precisely** How are joint frequencies and marginal frequencies similar? How are they different?

3. **Look for Relationships** How are conditional relative frequencies related to joint frequencies and marginal frequencies?

4. **Error Analysis** Zhang says that the marginal relative frequency for a given variable is 10. Could Zhang be correct? Explain your reasoning.

Do You KNOW HOW?

In a survey, customers select Item A or Item B. Item A is selected by 20 males and 10 females. Of 20 customers who select Item B, five are males.

5. Make a two-way frequency table to organize the data.

6. Make a two-way relative frequency table to organize the data.

7. Calculate conditional relative frequencies for males and females. Is it reasonable to conclude that males prefer Item A more than females do?

8. Calculate conditional relative frequencies for Item A and Item B. Is it reasonable to conclude that a customer who prefers Item B is more likely to be a female than a male?

UNDERSTAND

9. Reason An equal number of juniors and seniors were surveyed about whether they prefer lunch item A or B. Is it reasonable to infer from the table that more juniors prefer lunch item B while more seniors prefer lunch item A? Explain.

	Item A	Item B	Totals
Junior	0.1	0.4	0.5
Senior	0.3	0.2	0.5
Totals	0.6	0.4	1.0

10. Error Analysis Describe and correct the errors a student made when making a generalization based on a two-way frequency table.

Which subject do you prefer?			
	Math	Language Arts	Totals
Male	45	45	90
Female	30	30	60
Totals	75	75	150

Male students prefer math more than female students do.

11. Look for Relationships In a two-way relative frequency table, how are joint relative frequencies and marginal relative frequencies related?

12. Higher Order Thinking Students are surveyed to see how long they studied for a test.

- 10% of the students who studied 3 hours or more failed the test.
- 40% of the students who studied less than 3 hours passed the test.
- 2 students who studied 3 hours or more failed the test.
- 4 students who studied less than 3 hours passed the test.

a. Make a two-way frequency table that shows the association between hours spent studying and passing the test.

b. Does the association appear to be significant? Explain.

PRACTICE

In a survey, music club members select their preference between Song A or Song B. Song A is selected by 30 teens and 10 adults. Of 20 members who select Song B, five are teens. SEE EXAMPLES 1–4

Make a two-way frequency table to organize the data.

13. Is it reasonable to say that more people surveyed prefer Song A? Explain.

14. Is it reasonable to say that more adults than teens participated in the survey? Explain.

Calculate conditional relative frequencies.

15. Is it reasonable to say that teens prefer Song A more than adults do? Explain.

16. Is a member who prefers Song B significantly more likely to be an adult than a teen? Explain.

In the two-way frequency table, frequencies are shown on the top of each cell in blue, and relative frequencies are shown at the bottom in red. Most of the frequencies are missing. SEE EXAMPLES 1–5

High School Graduate?	Choice A	Choice B	Totals
Yes	16 / 0.08	——	—— / 0.56
No	——	24 / ——	——
Totals	——	——	——

17. Complete the table.

18. Calculate conditional relative frequencies for yes and no.

19. Calculate conditional relative frequencies for Choices A and B.

20. Is a high school graduate more likely to prefer Choice A or B? Explain.

21. Is someone who prefers Choice A more likely to be a high school graduate than not? Explain.

22. What does the joint relative frequency $\frac{64}{200}$ represent in this context?

23. What does the conditional relative frequency $\frac{96}{120}$ represent in this context?

APPLY

24. Construct Arguments Is there a significant association between income and whether or not a voter supports the referendum? Justify your answer.

Do you support the referendum?			
Income	Yes	No	Totals
≤ $100,000	80	20	100
> $100,000	40	10	50
Totals	120	30	150

25. Make Sense and Persevere A gardener is only satisfied when a hydrangea bush has at least 14 blooms. How can you organize the data shown in the dot plots into two-way frequency tables to make inferences about the new plant food and the number of blooms?

Hydrangeas Without New Plant Food

10 11 12 13 14 15 16 17 18
Number of Blooms

Hydrangeas with New Plant Food

8 9 10 11 12 13 14 15 16 17 18 19 20 21 22 23
Number of Blooms

26. Construct Arguments Based on the survey data below, a marketing team for an airline concludes that someone between 18 and 24 years of age is more likely never to have flown on a commercial airliner than someone 25 years or older. Do you agree with this conclusion? Justify your answer.

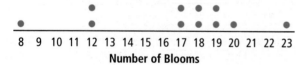

Terminal			
Have you ever flown on a commercial airline?			
	Yes	No	Totals
18-24 yrs	198	81	279
25 - yrs	2,539	448	2,987
Totals	2,737	529	3,266

ASSESSMENT PRACTICE

27. Consider a two-way frequency table. Select all that apply.

Ⓐ The sum of all joint frequencies equals the total frequency.

Ⓑ The sum of all marginal frequencies equals the total frequency.

Ⓒ The sum of all marginal frequencies in a row equals the total frequency.

Ⓓ The sum of all joint frequencies in a column equals the marginal frequency at the bottom of the column.

Ⓔ A relative frequency is the ratio of a joint frequency and a marginal frequency.

28. SAT/ACT In a two-way frequency table, the joint frequency in a cell is 8 and the marginal frequency in the same row is 32. What is the conditional relative frequency for the cell?

Ⓐ 0.12

Ⓑ 0.20

Ⓒ 0.25

Ⓓ 0.40

Ⓔ 0.50

29. Performance Task A high school offers a prep course for students who are taking a retest for a college entrance exam.

• Of 25 students who took the prep course, 20 scored at least 50 points higher on the retest than on the original exam.

• Overall, 100 students took the retest and 50 students scored at least 50 points higher on the retest than on the original exam.

Part A Create a two-way frequency table to organize the data.

Part B Funding for the prep course may be cut because more students scored at least 50 points higher on the retest without taking the prep course. Do you agree with this decision? If not, how could you use a two-way frequency table to construct an argument to keep the funding?

10-2
Probability Events

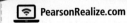

PearsonRealize.com

I CAN... use relationships among events to find probabilities.

VOCABULARY
- complement
- independent events
- mutually exclusive

👆 **EXPLORE & REASON**

Allie spins the spinner and draws one card without looking. She gets a 3 on the spinner and the 3 card. Then she sets the card aside, spins again, and draws another card.

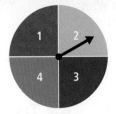

A. Is it possible for Allie to get a 3 on her second spin? On her second card? Explain.

B. Construct Arguments How does getting the 3 card on her first draw affect the probability of getting the 2 card on her second draw? Explain.

❓ **ESSENTIAL QUESTION** How does describing events as mutually exclusive or independent affect how you find probabilities?

👆 **EXAMPLE 1** Find Probabilities of Mutually Exclusive Events

You roll a standard number cube once. Let *E* represent the event "roll an even number." Let *T* represent the event "roll a 3 or 5."

A. What is the probability that you roll an even number or roll a 3 or 5?

Show the outcomes of events *E* and *T* as a subset of the sample space *S*.

Events *E* and *T* are **mutually exclusive** because there is no outcome in both sets.

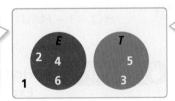

There are 5 outcomes that are even numbers or a 3 or 5. {2, 3, 4, 5, 6}
There are a total of 6 possible outcomes in the sample space.

$$P(E \text{ or } T) = \frac{\text{number of favorable outcomes}}{\text{number of total possible outcomes}}$$

$$= \frac{3 + 2}{6}$$ There are 3 outcomes in event *E* and 2 outcomes in event *T*.

$$= \frac{3}{6} + \frac{2}{6}$$ This is equivalent to $P(E) + P(T)$.

$$= \frac{5}{6}$$

The probability of rolling an even number or rolling a 3 or a 5 is $\frac{5}{6}$.

VOCABULARY

A *favorable* outcome is an outcome that is being tested or observed and not necessarily a desirable result. A "favorable" outcome may be a loss for the home team or testing positive for a disease.

B. You roll a standard number cube once. What is the probability that you roll an even number and a 3 or 5?

$$P(E \text{ and } T) = \frac{\text{number of favorable outcomes}}{\text{number of total possible outcomes}}$$

$$= \frac{0}{6}$$ Because events *E* and *T* are mutually exclusive, there are no outcomes that are in both sets.

$$= 0$$

The probability of rolling an even number and rolling a 3 or a 5 is 0.

CONTINUED ON THE NEXT PAGE

EXAMPLE 1 CONTINUED

C. You roll a standard number cube once. What is the probability that you do *not* roll an even number?

$$P(\text{not } E) = \frac{3}{6} \text{ or } \frac{1}{2}$$

There are 3 outcomes that are not even numbers.

The probability of not rolling an even number is $\frac{1}{2}$.

GENERALIZE
Notice that E and *not E* are mutually exclusive events. What would the sum of $P(E)$ and $P(\text{not } E)$ be equal to?

 Try It! **1.** A box contains 100 balls. Thirty of the balls are purple and 10 are orange. If you select one of the balls at random, what is the probability of each of the following events?

a. The ball is purple or orange.

b. The ball is not purple and not orange.

CONCEPT Probabilities of Mutually Exclusive Events

If A and B are mutually exclusive events, then

- $P(A \text{ or } B) = P(A) + P(B)$
- $P(A \text{ and } B) = 0$

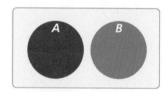

The **complement** of an event is the set of all outcomes in a sample space that are not included in the event.

If C is the event that A does not occur, then

$$P(C) = 1 - P(A).$$

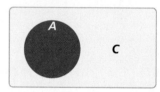

APPLICATION  **EXAMPLE 2** Find the Probabilities of Non-Mutually Exclusive Events

A student-made target includes two overlapping squares. Assume that a sticky ball thrown at the target is equally likely to land anywhere on the target. What is the probability that the ball lands inside one or both of the squares?

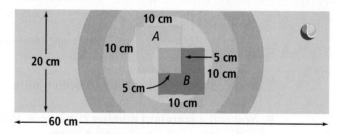

Step 1 Find the area of the squares, and their overlapping area.

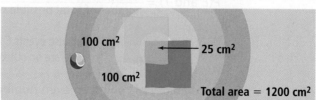

CONTINUED ON THE NEXT PAGE

Go Online | PearsonRealize.com

EXAMPLE 2 CONTINUED

Step 2 Find the probabilities.

One method: $75 \text{ cm}^2 + 25 \text{ cm}^2 + 75 \text{ cm}^2 = 175 \text{ cm}^2$

$$P(A \text{ or } B) = \frac{175}{1,200} = \frac{7}{12}$$

Another method: $P(A \text{ or } B) = \frac{100}{1,200} + \frac{100}{1,200} - \frac{25}{1,200}$

$$= \frac{175}{1,200} = \frac{7}{48}$$

> Subtract the probability of the overlapping area because it was included twice, once for each large square.

The probability that the ball will land inside one or both squares is $\frac{7}{48}$, or about 15%.

> **USE STRUCTURE**
> To avoid counting the overlapping region twice, you need to subtract $P(A \text{ and } B)$ from the sum of $P(A)$ and $P(B)$.

 Try It! **2.** A video game screen is a rectangle with dimensions 34 cm and 20 cm. A starship on the screen is made of two circles with radius 6 cm, and overlapping area of 20 cm². A black hole appears randomly on the screen. What is the probability that it appears within the starship?

CONCEPT Probabilities of Non-Mutually Exclusive Events

If A and B are not mutually exclusive events, then
$P(A \text{ or } B) = P(A) + P(B) - P(A \text{ and } B)$.

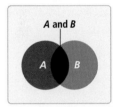

CONCEPTUAL UNDERSTANDING

EXAMPLE 3 **Identify Independent Events**

A jar contains 12 green marbles and 8 violet marbles.

A. A marble is chosen at random from the jar and replaced. Another marble is chosen at random from the jar. Does the color of the first marble chosen affect the possible outcomes for the second marble chosen?

Determine the probabilities for each choice to decide whether the first marble chosen affects the possibilities for the second marble.

First Choice-Sample Space
12 Green
8 Violet

Second Choice-Sample Space
12 Green
8 Violet

$$P(G) = \frac{12}{20} = \frac{3}{5}$$
$$P(V) = \frac{8}{20} = \frac{2}{5}$$

$$P(G) = \frac{12}{20} = \frac{3}{5}$$
$$P(V) = \frac{8}{20} = \frac{2}{5}$$

 The probabilities are the same.

The color of the first marble chosen does not affect the possible outcomes for the second marble chosen.

Two events are **independent events** if and only if the occurrence of one event does not affect the probability of a second event.

CONTINUED ON THE NEXT PAGE

EXAMPLE 3 CONTINUED

B. A marble is chosen at random from the jar and not replaced. Another marble is chosen at random from the jar. Does the color of the first marble chosen affect the possible outcomes for the second marble chosen?

Determine whether the events are independent.

First Choice-Sample Space
12 Green
8 Violet

$P(G) = \frac{12}{20} = \frac{3}{5}$ $P(V) = \frac{8}{20} = \frac{2}{5}$

Assume a green marble was chosen first.

Assume a violet marble is chosen first.

Second Choice-Sample Space
11 Green
8 Violet

Second Choice-Sample Space
12 Green
7 Violet

$P(G) = \frac{11}{19}$ $P(V) = \frac{8}{19}$

$P(G) = \frac{12}{19}$ $P(V) = \frac{7}{19}$

When the first marble is not replaced in the jar, the color of the first marble chosen does affect the possible outcomes for the second marble chosen. These events are not independent.

COMMON ERROR
When two or more items are selected from the same set, you must determine whether the first item(s) is replaced before the next item is selected. Then find the probabilities.

 Try It!   **3.** There are 10 cards in a box, 5 black and 5 red. Two cards are selected from the box, one at a time.

  a. A card is chosen at random and then replaced. Another card is chosen. Does the color of the first card chosen affect the possibilities of the second card chosen? Explain.

  b. A card is chosen at random and *not* replaced. Another card is chosen. Does the color of the first card chosen affect the possibilities of the second card chosen? Explain.

CONCEPT Probability of Independent Events

If A and B are independent events, then $P(A \text{ and } B) = P(A) \cdot P(B)$.

If $P(A \text{ and } B) = P(A) \cdot P(B)$, then A and B are independent events.

Example: When rolling a die and tossing a coin, the result of the die roll and the result of the coin toss are independent events.

$P(4) = \frac{1}{6}$ $P(H) = \frac{1}{2}$

$P(4 \text{ and } H) = \frac{1}{6} \cdot \frac{1}{2} = \frac{1}{12}$

APPLICATION EXAMPLE 4 **Find Probabilities of Independent Events**

Alex cannot decide which shirt to wear today, so she chooses one at random.

The probability of rain today is 40%, or $\frac{2}{5}$.

A. What is the probability that Alex chooses a yellow shirt and it does not rain today?

Let Y represent the event "yellow shirt." Let N represent "no rain."

Y and N are independent because Alex's choice of shirt does not affect the weather, and the weather does not affect Alex's choice of shirt. Use the formula to find $P(Y \text{ and } N)$.

Step 1 Find $P(N)$ and $P(Y)$.

> Subtract the probability that it will rain, $\frac{2}{5}$, from 1 to find the probability that it will *not* rain.

$$P(N) = 1 - \frac{2}{5} = \frac{3}{5}.$$

$$P(Y) = \frac{\text{number of favorable outcomes}}{\text{total number of outcomes}} = \frac{2}{4} \text{ or } \frac{1}{2}$$

Step 2 Apply the formula and multiply the probabilities of Y and N.

$$P(Y \text{ and } N) = P(Y) \cdot P(N) = \frac{1}{2} \cdot \frac{3}{5} = \frac{3}{10} = 30\%$$

> Use the rule for the probability of independent events.

The probability that Alex chooses a yellow shirt and it does not rain is 30%.

B. What is the probability that Alex chooses a yellow shirt and it does not rain today or that Alex chooses a green shirt and it rains today?

Let G represent "green shirt."   Let R represent "rain."

The events "Y and N" and "G and R" are mutually exclusive because no outcomes are in both events.

Step 1 Find $P(G \text{ and } R)$

> Add to find the probability that either event will occur.

$$P(G \text{ and } R) = P(G) \cdot P(R) = \frac{1}{4} \cdot \frac{2}{5} = \frac{2}{20} = \frac{1}{10} = 10\%$$

Step 2 Find $P((Y \text{ and } N) \text{ or } (G \text{ and } R))$

$$P((Y \text{ and } N) \text{ or } (G \text{ and } R)) = P(Y \text{ and } N) + P(G \text{ and } R)$$

$$= 30\% + 10\% = 40\%$$

The probability that Alex chooses a yellow shirt and it does not rain or that Alex chooses a green shirt and it rains is 40%.

 Try It! **4.** You spin the spinner two times. Assume that the probability of Blue each spin is $\frac{1}{3}$ and the probability of Orange each spin is $\frac{2}{3}$. What is the probability of getting the same color both times? Explain.

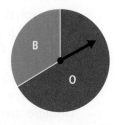

CONCEPT SUMMARY Probability Events

	Mutually Exclusive Events	Independent Events
WORDS	A and B are mutually exclusive because no outcome is in both A and B.	D and M are independent because the occurrence of one does not affect the probability of the other.
ALGEBRA	If A and B are mutually exclusive events, then $P(A \text{ or } B) = P(A) + P(B)$. If C is the event that A does not occur, then $P(C) = 1 - P(A)$.	If D and M are independent events, then $P(D \text{ and } M) = P(D) \cdot P(M)$. If $P(D \text{ and } M) = P(D) \cdot P(M)$, then D and M are independent events.
EXAMPLES	Experiment: spin the spinner.  Event A: number less than 3 Event B: number greater than 5 $P(A \text{ or } B) = P(A) + P(B) = \frac{2}{6} + \frac{1}{6} = \frac{1}{2}$	Experiment: spin the spinner and roll a number cube Event D: odd number on spinner Event M: number greater than 4 on number cube $P(D \text{ and } M) = P(D) \cdot P(M) = \frac{1}{2} \cdot \frac{1}{3} = \frac{1}{6}$

☑ Do You UNDERSTAND?

1. **ESSENTIAL QUESTION** How does describing events as independent or mutually exclusive affect how you find probabilities?

2. **Reason** Two marbles are chosen, one at a time, from a bag containing 6 marbles, 4 red marbles and 2 green marbles. Suppose the first marble chosen is green. Is the probability that the second marble will be red greater if the first marble is returned to the bag or if it is not returned to the bag? Explain.

3. **Error Analysis** The probability that Deshawn plays basketball (event B) after school is 20%. The probability that he talks to friends (event T) after school is 45%. He says that P(B or T) is 65%. Explain Deshawn's error.

4. **Vocabulary** What is the difference between mutually exclusive events and independent events?

Do You KNOW HOW?

5. A bag contains 40 marbles. Eight are green and 2 are blue. You select one marble at random. What is the probability of each event?

   a. The marble is green or blue.

   b. The marble is not green and not blue.

6. A robot at a carnival booth randomly tosses a dart at a square target with 8 inch sides and a circle with a 3 inch radius in the middle. To the nearest whole percent, what is the probability that the dart will land in the circle?

For Exercises 7 and 8, assume that you roll a standard number cube two times.

7. What is the probability of rolling an even number on the first roll and a number less than 3 on the second roll?

8. What is the probability of rolling an odd number on the first roll and a number greater than 3 on the second roll?

UNDERSTAND

9. Construct Arguments Let S be a sample space for an experiment in which every outcome is both equally likely and mutually exclusive. What can you conclude about the sum of the probabilities for all of the outcomes? Give an example.

10. Error Analysis At Lincoln High School, 6 students are members of both the Chess Club and the Math Club. There are 20 students in the Math Club, 12 students in the Chess Club, and 400 students in the entire school.

Danielle calculated the probability that a student chosen at random belongs to the Chess Club or the Math Club. Explain her error.

Event C: Student is in Chess Club
Event M: Student is in Math Club

$$P(C \text{ or } M) = P(C) + P(M)$$
$$= \frac{12}{400} + \frac{20}{400}$$
$$= \frac{32}{400} = 0.08 \quad ✗$$

11. Higher Order Thinking Murphy's math teacher sometimes wears scarves to class. Murphy has been documenting the relationship between his teacher wearing a scarf and when the class has a math quiz. The probabilities are as follows:

- $P(\text{wearing a scarf}) = 10\%$
- $P(\text{math quiz}) = 15\%$
- $P(\text{wearing a scarf and math quiz}) = 5\%$

Are the events "the teacher is wearing a scarf" and "there will be a quiz" independent events? Explain.

Reason A card is drawn from a box containing 5 cards, each showing a different number from 1 to 5. Consider the events "even number," "odd number," "less than 3," and "greater than 3." Determine whether each pair of events mutually exclusive.

12. $< 3, > 3$

13. even, > 3

14. odd, > 3

15. odd, even

PRACTICE

16. Hana is playing a virtual reality game in which she must toss a disc to land on the largest triangular section of the board. If the disc is equally likely to land anywhere on the board, what is the probability that she will succeed? Explain. SEE EXAMPLE 1

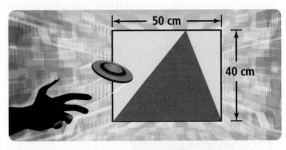

In a class of 25 students, 8 students have heights less than 65 inches and 10 students have heights of 69 inches or more. For Exercises 17–19, find the probabilities described. SEE EXAMPLE 1

17. $P(\text{less than 65 inches or greater than 69 inches})$

18. $P(\text{greater than or equal to 65 inches})$

19. $P(\text{greater than or equal to 65 inches and less than or equal to 69 inches})$

20. A skydiver is equally likely to land at any point on a rectangular field. Two overlapping circular targets of radius 5 meters are marked on the field. To the nearest percent, what is the probability that the sky diver will land in one or both of the circles? SEE EXAMPLE 2

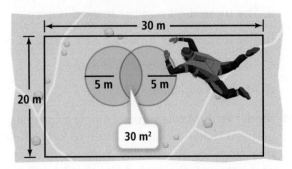

21. Two marbles are chosen at random, one at a time from a box that contains 7 marbles, 5 red and 2 green. SEE EXAMPLES 3 AND 4

a. Find the probability of drawing 2 red marbles when the first marble is replaced before the second marble is chosen.

b. Determine whether the situation described is independent.

APPLY

22. Mathematical Connections For a science fair project, Paige wants to test whether ants prefer certain colors. She releases ants on the colored surface shown. If the ants are randomly distributed across the entire surface, what is the probability that any given ant will be within the blue circle, but not within the yellow circle? Round to the nearest whole percent.

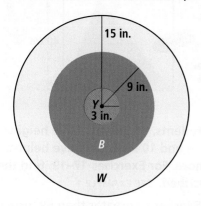

23. Use Structure A city issues 3-digit license plates for motorized scooters. The digits 0–9 are chosen at random by a computer program. What is the probability that a license plate issued meets each set of criteria?

a. The three-digit number formed is even.

b. The first number is not 7.

c. The first two digits are the same.

d. All three digits are the same.

24. Model With Mathematics During a football game, a kicker is called in twice to kick a field goal from the 30 yard line. Suppose that for each attempt, the probability that he will make the field goal is 0.8.

a. What is the probability that he will make both field goals?

b. What is the probability that he will make neither field goal?

ASSESSMENT PRACTICE

25. The probability of events A and B both occurring is 15%. The probability of event A or B occurring is 60%. The probability of B occurring is 50%. What is the probability of A occurring?

26. SAT/ACT A robot spins the spinner shown twice. Assume that the outcomes 1, 2, 3, and 4 are equally likely for each spin. What is the probability that the sum of the two outcomes will be 6?

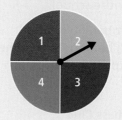

Ⓐ $\frac{1}{16}$ Ⓓ $\frac{1}{4}$

Ⓑ $\frac{1}{8}$ Ⓔ $\frac{3}{4}$

Ⓒ $\frac{3}{16}$

27. Performance Task Paula is packing to visit a friend in another city for a long weekend. She looks at the weather forecast shown below to find the chance of rain. Assume that whether it rains on each day is independent of whether it rains on any other day.

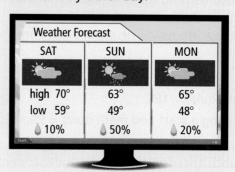

Weather Forecast		
SAT	SUN	MON
high 70°	63°	65°
low 59°	49°	48°
10%	50%	20%

Part A What is the probability that it will not rain on any of the three days to the nearest percent?

Part B What is the probability that it will rain at least one of the three days to the nearest percent?

Part C Do you think Paula should pack an umbrella? Explain.

10-3

Conditional Probability

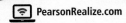
PearsonRealize.com

I CAN... find the probability of an event given that another event has occurred.

VOCABULARY
- conditional probability
- dependent events

EXPLORE & REASON

At Central High School, 85% of all senior girls attended and 65% of all senior boys attended the Spring Dance. Of all attendees, 20% won a prize.

A. Assuming that the number of senior girls at Central High School is about equal to the number of senior boys, estimate the probability that a randomly selected senior won a prize at the dance. Explain.

B. Construct Arguments If you knew whether the selected student was a boy or a girl, would your estimate change? Explain.

? ESSENTIAL QUESTION

How are conditional probability and independence related in real-world experiments?

EXAMPLE 1   Understand Conditional Probability

A student committee is being formed to decide how after-school activities will be funded. The committee members are selected at random from current club members. The frequency table shows the current club membership data.

Monday Club Memberships by Grade

	Drama	Science	Art	Total
Sophomore	3	9	24	36
Junior	6	18	16	40
Senior	8	13	18	39
Total	17	40	58	115

What is the probability that a member of the art club selected at random is a junior?

One Method Use the frequency table to find the probability that the student chosen is a junior given that the student is a member of the art club.

> The probability that an event B will occur given that another event A has already occurred is called a **conditional probability** and is written as $P(B \mid A)$.

COMMON ERROR
Avoid confusing $P(A \mid B)$ with $P(B \mid A)$. In the first case the prior event is B, but in the second case the prior event is A.

$$P(\text{junior} \mid \text{member of the art club}) = \frac{\text{number of juniors in art club}}{\text{total number of art club members}}$$

$$= \frac{16}{58} = \frac{8}{29}$$

Another Method Use the formula for conditional probability.

For any two events A and B, with $P(A) \neq 0$, $P(B \mid A) = \frac{P(B \text{ and } A)}{P(A)}$.

$$P(\text{junior} \mid \text{art}) = \frac{P(\text{junior and art})}{P(\text{art})} = \frac{\frac{16}{115}}{\frac{58}{115}} = \frac{8}{29}$$

> Of the 115 Monday club members and 58 art club members, 16 are juniors and in the art club.

The probability that the student chosen is a junior member from the art club is $\frac{8}{29}$.

CONTINUED ON THE NEXT PAGE

EXAMPLE 1 CONTINUED

 Try It! **1. a.** What is the probability that a member of the drama club is a sophomore, P(sophomore | drama)?

b. What is the probability that a sophomore is a member of the drama club, P(drama | sophomore)? Is P(sophomore | drama) the same as P(drama | sophomore)? Explain.

CONCEPT Conditional Probability and Independent Events

Let A and B be events with P(A) ≠ 0 and P(B) ≠ 0.

If events A and B are independent, then the conditional probability of B given A equals the probability of B and the conditional probability of A given B equals the probability of A.	If events A and B are independent, then P(B | A) = P(B) and P(A | B) = P(A).
If the conditional probability of B given A equals the probability of B and the conditional probability of A given B equals the probability of A, then events A and B are independent.	If P(B | A) = P(B) and P(A | B) = P(A), then events A and B are independent.

CONCEPTUAL
UNDERSTANDING

 **EXAMPLE 2** **Use the Test for Independence**

The table below shows the vehicles in a parking garage one afternoon. A vehicle in the garage will be selected at random. Let B represent "the vehicle is black" and V represent "the vehicle is a van." Are the events B and V independent or dependent?

STUDY TIP
When looking at a table of probabilities, consider events that are impossible or guaranteed to occur. For example, it is impossible to select a red van.

	Car	Van	Pickup	Totals
Red	5	0	2	7
White	0	0	2	2
Black	6	3	4	13
Totals	11	3	8	22

One Method

Since $P(B) = \frac{13}{22} \neq 0$ and $P(V \text{ and } B) = \frac{3}{22}$,

$$P(V \mid B) = \frac{P(V \text{ and } B)}{P(B)} = \frac{\frac{3}{22}}{\frac{13}{22}} = \frac{3}{13}$$

Since $P(V \mid B) \neq P(V)$, B and V are not independent events, they are **dependent events**.

CONTINUED ON THE NEXT PAGE

EXAMPLE 2 CONTINUED

Another Method

Since $P(V) = \frac{3}{22} \neq 0$ and $P(B \text{ and } V) = P(V \text{ and } B)$,

$$P(B \mid V) = \frac{P(B \text{ and } V)}{P(V)}$$

$$= \frac{\frac{3}{22}}{\frac{3}{22}} = 1$$

> A probability of 1, or 100%, indicates that the event is certain. Given that a van is selected, it must be black.

Again, Since $P(B \mid V) \neq P(B)$, the events B and V are dependent events.

 Try It! **2.** Let R represent "the vehicle is red" and C represent "the vehicle is a car." Are the events R and C independent or dependent? Explain.

EXAMPLE 3   **Apply the Conditional Probability Formula**

A band's marketing agent conducted a survey to determine how many high school fans the band has. What is the probability that a surveyed student plans to attend the band's concert and is a fan of the group?

Concert Survey Results

Students who plan to attend concert

- 70% of students plan to attend,
- 80% of students who plan to attend are fans of the band.

Students who do not plan to attend

- 30% of students do not plan to attend,
- 25% are fans of the band.

Use the conditional probability formula to find the combined probability.

Rewrite $P(B \mid A) = \frac{P(A \text{ and } B)}{P(A)}$ as $P(A \text{ and } B) = P(A) \cdot P(B \mid A)$.

$$P(A \text{ and } B) = P(A) \cdot P(B \mid A)$$

$$P(\text{attend and fan}) = P(\text{attend}) \cdot P(\text{fan} \mid \text{attend})$$

> Event A is "attend."
> Event B is "fan."

$$= 0.7 \cdot 0.8$$

> Substitute 0.7 for $P(\text{attend})$ and 0.8 for $P(\text{fan} \mid \text{attend})$.

$$= 0.56, \text{ or } 56\%$$

LOOK FOR RELATIONSHIPS
Why might $P(\text{fan} \mid \text{attend})$ not equal $P(\text{attend} \mid \text{fan})$ in this situation?

The probability that a surveyed student plans to attend the concert and is a fan of the group is 0.56, or 56%.

 Try It! **3.** What is the probability that a surveyed student plans to attend but is not a fan of the group?

👆 **EXAMPLE 4** Use Conditional Probability to Make a Decision

A marketer is looking at mobile phone statistics to help plan an online advertising campaign. She wants to find out which of her company's products is most likely to be purchased after a related search after a search for that product on a mobile phone.

Mobile Phone Search and Buying Behavior		
Product	Search(S)	Search & Buy (S and B)
W	46%	16%
X	32%	14%
Y	35%	12%
Z	40%	15%

MAKE SENSE AND PERSEVERE
Product W has the highest $P(S \text{ and } B)$ of 16% but not the highest $P(B \mid S)$. Can you explain why?

Find the probability a mobile phone customer buys, given that they performed a related search. Use the formula $P(B \mid S) = \dfrac{P(S \text{ and } B)}{P(S)}$.

Product	$P(B \mid S)$
W	$\dfrac{0.16}{0.46} \approx 0.348$ or about 34.8%
X	$\dfrac{0.14}{0.32} = 0.4375$ or 43.75%
Y	$\dfrac{0.12}{0.35} \approx 0.343$ or 34.3%
Z	$\dfrac{0.15}{0.40} = 0.375$ or 37.5%

Product X has the highest probability of being purchased given that a related search was performed.

 Try It! 4. The marketer also has data from desktop computers. Which product is most likely to be purchased after a related search?

Computer Search and Buying Behavior
(% of computer-based site visitors)

Product	Search	Search & Buy
J	35%	10%
K	28%	9%
L	26%	8%
M	24%	5%

CONCEPT SUMMARY Conditional Probability

Conditional Probability Formula	Conditional Probability and Independent Events
WORDS The probability that an event B will occur given that another event A has already occurred is called a **conditional probability**.	Events A and B are independent events if and only if the conditional probability of A given B is the same as the probability of A, and the conditional probability of B given A is the same as the probability of B.
ALGEBRA For any two events A and B, with $P(A) \neq 0$, $$P(B \mid A) = \frac{P(A \text{ and } B)}{P(A)}$$	For any events A and B with $P(A) \neq 0$ and $P(B) \neq 0$, A and B are independent if and only if $P(B \mid A) = P(B)$ and $P(A \mid B) = P(A)$.

☑ Do You UNDERSTAND?

1. **ESSENTIAL QUESTION** How are conditional probability and independence related in experiments?

2. **Vocabulary** How is the sample space for $P(B \mid A)$ different from the sample space for $P(B)$?

3. **Vocabulary** Why does the definition of $P(B \mid A)$ have the condition that $P(A) \neq 0$?

4. **Use Structure** Why is $P(A) \cdot P(B \mid A) = P(B) \cdot P(A \mid B)$?

5. **Error Analysis** Taylor knows that $P(R) = 0.8$, $P(B) = 0.2$, and $P(R \text{ and } B) = 0.05$. Explain Taylor's error.

$$P(B \mid R) = \frac{0.05}{0.2}$$
$$= 0.25 \quad ✗$$

6. **Reason** At a sports camp, a coach wants to find the probability that a soccer player is a local camper. Because 40% of the students in the camp are local, the coach reasons that the probability is 0.4. Is his conclusion justified? Explain.

Do You KNOW HOW?

7. Let $P(A) = \frac{3}{4}$, $P(B) = \frac{2}{3}$, and $P(A \text{ and } B) = \frac{1}{2}$. Find each probability.

   a. What is $P(B \mid A)$?

   b. What is $P(A \mid B)$?

8. Students randomly generate two digits from 0 to 9 to create a number between 0 and 99. Are the events "first digit 5" and "second digit 6" independent or dependent in each case? What is $P(56)$ in each experiment?

   a. The digits may not be repeated.

   b. The digits may be repeated.

9. Suppose that you select one card at random from the set of 6 cards below.

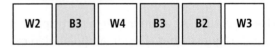

Let B represent the event "select a blue card" and T represent the event "select a card with a 3." Are B and T independent events? Explain your reasoning.

PRACTICE & PROBLEM SOLVING

UNDERSTAND

10. Mathematical Connections How can the formula $P(A \text{ and } B) = P(A) \cdot P(B \mid A)$ be simplified to find the probability of A and B when the events are independent? Explain.

11. Error Analysis From a bag containing 3 red marbles and 7 blue marbles, 2 marbles are selected without replacement. Esteban calculated the probability that two red marbles are selected. Explain Esteban's error.

$$P(red) = 0.3$$
$$P(red \text{ and } red) = P(red) \cdot P(red)$$
$$= 0.3 \cdot 0.3$$
$$= 0.09 \quad \text{✗}$$

12. Generalize Kiyo is creating a table using mosaic tiles chosen and placed randomly. She is picking tiles without looking. How does $P(\text{yellow second} \mid \text{blue first})$ compare to $P(\text{yellow second} \mid \text{yellow first})$ if the tiles are selected without replacement? If the tiles are selected and returned to the pile because Kiyo wants a different color?

13. Use Structure At a fundraiser, a participant is asked to guess what is inside an unlabeled can for a possible prize. If there are two crates of cans to choose from, each having a mixture of vegetables and soup, what is the probability that the first participant will select a vegetable can from the left crate given each situation?

a. The left crate has 2 cans of vegetables and 8 cans of soup, and the right crate has 7 cans of vegetables and 3 cans of soup.

b. The left crate has 8 cans of vegetables and 2 cans of soup, and the right crate has 5 cans of vegetables and 5 cans of soup.

PRACTICE

For Exercises 14–18, use the data in the table to find the probability of each event. SEE EXAMPLE 1

Technology Class Enrollment by Year

	Sophomore	Junior
Robotics	16	24
Game Design	18	22

14. $P(\text{Junior} \mid \text{Robotics})$

15. $P(\text{Robotics} \mid \text{Junior})$

16. $P(\text{Game Design} \mid \text{Sophomore})$

17. $P(\text{Sophomore} \mid \text{Game Design})$

18. Are year and technology class enrollment dependent or independent events? Explain. SEE EXAMPLE 2

19. At a high school, 40% of the students play an instrument. Of those students, 20% are freshmen. Of the students who do not play an instrument, 30% are freshmen. What is the probability that a student selected at random is a freshman who plays an instrument? SEE EXAMPLE 3

In a study of an experimental medication, patients were randomly assigned to take either the medication or a placebo.

Effectiveness of New Medication As Compared to a Placebo

	Medication	Placebo
Health Improved	53	47
Health Did Not Improve	65	35

20. What is the probability that a patient taking the medication showed improvement? Round to the nearest whole percent. SEE EXAMPLE 1

21. Are taking the medication and having improved health independent or dependent events? SEE EXAMPLE 2

22. Based on the data in the table, would you recommend that the medication be made available to doctors? Explain. SEE EXAMPLE 4

APPLY

23. Reason In a recreation center with 1,500 members, 200 are high school students. Of the members, 300 regularly swim. The 45 students of the high school swim team are all members and practice at the pool every week. What is the probability that a high school member selected at random is on the swim team?

24. Use Structure At the school fair, 5% of students will win a prize. A winner has an equally likely chance to win each prize type shown. What is the probability that a student at the fair will win a comic book? Explain.

PRIZES

25. Make Sense and Persevere A box contains 50 batteries, of which 10 are dead and 5 are weak. Suppose you select batteries at random from the box and set them aside for recycling if they are dead or weak. If the first battery you select is dead and the second one is weak, what is the probability that the next battery you select will be weak?

26. Higher Order Thinking An inspector at a factory has determined that 1% of the flash drives produced by the plant are defective. If assembly line A produces 20% of all the flash drives, what is the probability that a defective flash drive chosen at random is from the corresponding conveyor belt A? Explain.

Conveyor Belt A
Defective Rate: 1.5%

ASSESSMENT PRACTICE

27. Which of the following pairs of events are independent? Select all that apply.

Ⓐ A student selected at random has a backpack. A student selected at random has brown hair.

Ⓑ Events A and B, where $P(B \mid A) = \frac{1}{3}$, $P(A) = \frac{3}{5}$ and $P(B) = \frac{5}{9}$

Ⓒ A student selected at random is a junior. A student selected at random is a freshman.

Ⓓ Events A and B, where $P(A) = 0.30$, $P(B) = 0.25$ and $P(A \text{ and } B) = 0.075$

Ⓔ Events A and B, where $P(A) = 0.40$, $P(B) = 0.3$ and $P(A \text{ and } B) = 0.012$

28. SAT/ACT The table shows student participation in the newspaper and yearbook by year. A student on the newspaper staff is selected at random to attend a symposium. What is the probability that the selected student is a senior?

Journalism Club Members

	Junior	Senior
Newspaper	16	9
Yearbook	8	17

Ⓐ $\frac{9}{50}$ Ⓓ $\frac{9}{17}$

Ⓑ $\frac{9}{26}$ Ⓔ $\frac{9}{16}$

Ⓒ $\frac{9}{25}$

29. Performance Task In a survey of 50 male and 50 female high school students, 60 students said they exercise daily. Of those students, 32 were female.

Part A Use the data to make a two-way frequency table.

Part B What is the probability that a surveyed student who exercises daily is female? What is the probability that a surveyed student who exercises regularly is male?

Part C Based on the survey, what can you conclude about the relationship between exercise and gender? Explain.

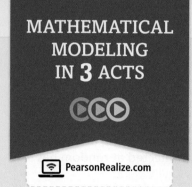

Video

▶ Place Your Guess

A coin toss is a popular way to decide between two options or settle a dispute. The coin toss is popular because it is a simple and unbiased way of deciding. Assuming the coin being tossed is a fair coin, both parties have an equally likely chance of winning.

What other methods could you use to decide between two choices fairly? Think about this during the Mathematical Modeling in 3 Acts lesson.

Scan for Multimedia

ACT 1 Identify the Problem

1. What is the first question that comes to mind after watching the video?

2. Write down the main question you will answer about what you saw in the video.

3. Make an initial conjecture that answers this main question.

4. Explain how you arrived at your conjecture.

5. What information will be useful to know to answer the main question? How can you get it? How will you use that information?

ACT 2 Develop a Model

6. Use the math that you have learned in this Topic to refine your conjecture.

ACT 3 Interpret the Results

7. Did your refined conjecture match the actual answer exactly? If not, what might explain the difference?

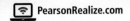
10-4
Permutations and Combinations

🖥 **PearsonRealize.com**

I CAN... use permutations and combinations to find the number of outcomes in a probability experiment.

VOCABULARY
• combination
• factorial
• Fundamental Counting Principle
• permutation

👆 **EXPLORE & REASON**

Holly, Tia, Kenji, and Nate are eligible to be officers of the Honor Society. Two of the four students will be chosen at random as president and vice-president. The table summarizes the possible outcomes.

Honor Society Officers

		Vice-President			
		Holly	Tia	Kenji	Nate
President	**Holly**	–	HT	HK	HN
	Tia	TH	–	TK	TN
	Kenji	KH	KT	–	KN
	Nate	NH	NT	NK	–

A. Holly wants to be an officer with her best friend Tia. How many outcomes make up this event?

B. How many outcomes show Holly as president and Tia as vice-president?

C. Generalize How many outcomes have only one of them as an officer? Explain.

❓ **ESSENTIAL QUESTION** How are permutations and combinations useful when finding probabilities?

👆 **EXAMPLE 1** Use the Fundamental Counting Principle

Manuel wants to advertise the number of one-topping pizzas he offers to his customers. How many different one-topping pizzas are available at Manuel's Pizzeria?

MANUEL'S PIZZERIA
Choose a Size:
large, medium
Choose a Crust:
deep dish or thin
Choose One Topping:
sausage, pepperoni, cheese

Make a tree diagram to find the number of pizzas.

COMMON ERROR
When you compare a tree diagram to the Fundamental Counting Principle, remember to count the total number of paths from the beginning to the end of the tree diagram, not the number of branches in each section.

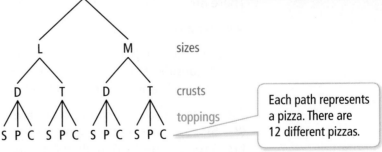

Each path represents a pizza. There are 12 different pizzas.

sizes × crusts × toppings = number of pizzas
  2   ×   2   ×   3   =   12

This example illustrates the **Fundamental Counting Principle**. If there are m ways to make the first selection and n ways to make the second selection, then there are $m \times n$ ways to make the two selections. If a third selection with p choices is added, then there are $m \times n \times p$ ways to make all three selections, and so on.

CONTINUED ON THE NEXT PAGE

EXAMPLE 1 CONTINUED

  Activity Assess

 Try It! **1.** The car that Ms. Garcia is buying comes with a choice of 3 trim lines (standard, sport, or luxury), 2 types of transmission (automatic or manual), and 8 colors. How many different option packages does Ms. Garcia have to choose from? Explain.

CONCEPTUAL UNDERSTANDING

👆 **EXAMPLE 2** **Find the Number of Permutations**

A. Gabriela is making a playlist with her 3 favorite songs. How many possible orders are there for the songs?

Method 1 Use an organized list.

Let A, B, and C represent the 3 songs.
There are 6 different possible orders for the songs.

ABC	ACB
BAC	BCA
CAB	CBA

Method 2 Use the Fundamental Counting Principle.

$3 \cdot 2 \cdot 1$ — There are 3 choices for the first song, 2 choices for the second song, and 1 choice for the third song.

REASON
How many ways are there to create a playlist with 0 songs?

The **factorial** of a positive integer n is the product of all positive integers less than or equal to n. It is written $n!$ and is read as n *factorial*. By definition, 0! equals 1.

$$n! = n \cdot (n-1) \cdot (n-2) \cdot \ldots \cdot 2 \cdot 1$$

The number of different possible orders for the songs is 3!.

$$3! = 3 \cdot 2 \cdot 1 = 6$$

There are 6 different possible orders for the 3 songs.

B. Gabriela wants to make another playlist using 5 of the 8 songs from her favorite artist's latest album. How many playlists are possible?

Method 1 Use the Fundamental Counting Principle.

There are 8 choices for the first song, 7 choices for the second song, and so on.

$$8 \cdot 7 \cdot 6 \cdot 5 \cdot 4 = 6{,}720$$

There are 6,720 possible playlists with 5 of the 8 songs.

Method 2 Use factorials.

To count the number of ways to order 5 songs from A, B, C, D, E, F, G, and H, consider the list ABCDE. The diagram shows all the possible ways that sequence appears among the 8! ways to list all songs.

For any sequence of 5 songs, there are $(8-5)! = 3!$ ways that sequence appears as the first 5 songs when listing all 8! lists. So divide 8! by 3! to find the number of 5-song playlists.

ABCDEFGH	ABCDEFHG
ABCDEGFH	ABCDEGHF
ABCDEHFG	ABCDEHGF

$$\frac{8!}{3!} = \frac{8 \cdot 7 \cdot 6 \cdot 5 \cdot 4 \cdot 3 \cdot 2 \cdot 1}{3 \cdot 2 \cdot 1} = 6{,}720$$

There are 6,720 possible playlists with 5 of the 8 songs.

CONTINUED ON THE NEXT PAGE

Try It!   **2.** How many possibilities are there for each playlist?

a. Gabriela's 4 favorite songs   **b.** 5 of the 10 most popular songs

---

CONCEPT Permutations

A **permutation** is an arrangement of objects in a specific order.

The number of permutations of r objects taken from a set of n objects is

$$_nP_r = \frac{n!}{(n-r)!} \text{ for } 0 \leq r \leq n.$$

CONCEPTUAL UNDERSTANDING

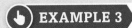 **EXAMPLE 3**   **Find the Number of Combinations**

Marisol is planning to be a counselor at summer camp. She can choose 3 activities for her session. How many different combinations of 3 activities are possible?

Use the formula to write an expression for the number of permutations of 3 objects chosen from a group of 10.

$$_{10}P_3 = \frac{10!}{(10-3)!} = 720$$

However, in this situation, the order of the 3 chosen activities does not matter, so you must adjust the formula.

A **combination** is a set of objects with no specific order.

3! Permutations   1 Combination

ABC	ACB
BAC	BCA
CAB	CBA

→   {A, B, C}

A group of 3 items can be arranged in 3! ways, so you must divide the the the number of permutations, $_{10}P_3$, by the number of arrangements of each group of 3 items, 3!.

USE APPROPRIATE TOOLS
Most scientific and graphing calculators can calculate permutations ($_nP_r$) and combinations ($_nC_r$). They often use the notation $P(n,r)$ and $C(n,r)$.

The notation $_nC_r$ indicates the number of combinations of r items from a set of n items.

$$_{10}C_3 = \frac{_{10}P_3}{3!} = \frac{10!}{3!(10-3)!}$$

$$= \frac{720}{6}$$

$$= 120$$

$_{10}C_3$ denotes the number of combinations of 3 items from a set of 10 items.

There are 120 different combinations of activities that Marisol can choose.

 Try It!   **3.** How many ways can a camper choose 5 activities from the 10 available activities at the summer camp?

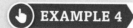 Combinations

A **combination** is a set of objects with no specific order.

The number of combinations of r objects taken from a set of n objects is

$$_nC_r = \frac{n!}{r!(n-r)!} \text{ for } 0 \le r \le n.$$

APPLICATION   **EXAMPLE 4**   **Use Permutations and Combinations to Find Probabilities**

A teacher chooses 5 students at random from the names shown to work together on a group project. What is the probability that the 5 students' names begin with a consonant?

Formulate ◀   Determine if the problem is about permutations or combinations.

Since the order in which the students are chosen does not matter, use combinations to find the numbers of possible outcomes and desirable outcomes to calculate the probability.

Compute ◀   **Step 1** Find the total number of possible outcomes.

$$_{18}C_5 = \frac{18!}{5!(18-5)!} = 8{,}568$$

There are 8,568 ways the teacher could choose 5 students.

Step 2 Find the number of possible outcomes in which all the names begin with a consonant and none of the names begin with a vowel.

$$_{13}C_5 = \frac{13!}{5!(13-5)!} = 1{,}287 \qquad\qquad _5C_0 = \frac{5!}{0!(5-0)!} = 1$$

> Choose 5 out of 13 names.   Choose 0 out of 5 names.

Use the Fundamental Counting Principle. Multiply the number of possible outcomes for the two subsets to find the total number of outcomes.

$$_{13}C_5 \cdot {_5C_0} = 1{,}287 \cdot 1 = 1{,}287$$

There are 1,287 outcomes with all the names beginning with consonants.

Step 3 Find the probability.

$$P(\text{all consonants}) = \frac{\text{number of outcomes with all consonants}}{\text{total number of possible outcomes}}$$

$$= \frac{1{,}287}{8{,}568} \approx 0.15$$

Interpret ◀   The probability that all 5 names begin with a consonant is about 0.15, or 15%.

✓ **Try It!**   **4.** Using the data from Example 4, what is the probability that the 5 students' names end with a vowel?

CONCEPT SUMMARY Permutations and Combinations

	Permutation	Combination
WORDS	A selection of items in which the order of the items is important	A selection of items in which the order of the items is not important
	$_nP_r$ represents the number of permutations of r objects taken from a set of n objects.	$_nC_r$ represents the number of combinations of r objects taken from a set of n objects.
ALGEBRA	$_nP_r = \dfrac{n!}{(n-r)!}$ for $0 \le r \le n$	$_nC_r = \dfrac{n!}{r!(n-r)!}$ for $0 \le r \le n$
NUMBERS	The number of permutations of 3 objects taken from a set of 6 objects is $$_6P_3 = \frac{6!}{3!} = \frac{6 \cdot 5 \cdot 4 \cdot 3 \cdot 2 \cdot 1}{3 \cdot 2 \cdot 1} = 120$$	The number of combinations of 3 objects taken from a set of 6 objects is $$_6C_3 = \frac{6!}{3!3!} = \frac{6 \cdot 5 \cdot 4 \cdot 3 \cdot 2 \cdot 1}{(3 \cdot 2 \cdot 1)(3 \cdot 2 \cdot 1)} = 20$$

✓ Do You UNDERSTAND?

1. **? ESSENTIAL QUESTION** How are permutations and combinations useful when finding probabilities?

2. **Use Structure** How is the formula for combinations related to the formula for permutations?

3. **Vocabulary** Why is it important to distinguish between a *permutation* and a *combination* when counting possible outcomes?

4. **Look for Relationships** How is $_9C_2$ related to $_9C_7$? Explain. How can you generalize this observation for any values of n and r?

5. **Error Analysis** Explain Beth's error.

$$\frac{_3P_3}{_5P_3} = \frac{3!}{\dfrac{5!}{(5-3)!}} = \frac{3!}{5!2!} = \frac{1}{40} \quad ✗$$

6. **Construct Arguments** A company wants to form a committee of 4 people from its 12 employees. How can you use combinations to find the probability that the 4 people newest to the company will be selected?

Do You KNOW HOW?

Do the possible outcomes represent permutations or combinations?

7. Jennifer will invite 3 of her 10 friends to a concert.

8. Jennifer must decide how she and her 3 friends will sit at the concert.

Find the number of permutations.

9. How many ways can 12 runners in a race finish first, second, and third?

Find the number of combinations.

10. In how many ways can 11 contestants for an award be narrowed down to 3 finalists?

11. How many different ways can a 4-person team be chosen from a group of 8 people?

Students will be chosen at random for school spirit awards. There are 6 athletes and 8 non-athletes who are eligible for 2 possible prizes. What is each probability?

12. P(both prizes are awarded to athletes)

13. P(both prizes are awarded to non-athletes)

14. P(no prize is awarded to an athlete)

15. P(no prize is awarded to a non-athlete)

16. Explain how Exercises 12 and 13 are similar to Exercises 14 and 15.

PRACTICE & PROBLEM SOLVING

UNDERSTAND

17. Use Structure Dwayne bought a new bike lock, and the lock came with instructions to choose 3 out of 30 numbers on a circular dial to keep his bike secure. The numbers cannot be repeated. How many possible arrangements can Dwayne choose for his lock? Do the arrangements represent permutations or combinations? Explain.

18. Construct Arguments Sage volunteers to read and play with sick children in a hospital. She selects some erasers at random from a bag to use as prizes. There are 8 alien erasers and 10 flying saucer erasers.

   a. How many groups of 6 erasers can be formed from the 18 erasers? Explain.

   b. In how many ways can 3 aliens be selected? Explain.

   c. In how many ways can 3 aliens and 3 flying saucers be selected? Explain.

   d. What is the probability that 3 aliens and 3 flying saucers will be selected? Explain.

19. Error Analysis There are 6 tiles numbered 1 to 6 in a box. Two tiles are selected at random without replacement to form a 2-digit number. Jeffrey found the probability that the number selected is 16. Explain his error.

> The number of ways to select 1 and 6 is given by $_6C_2 = 15$
>
> $P(16) = \frac{1}{_6C_2} = \frac{1}{15}$ ✗

20. Mathematical Connections How many lines are determined by the points, *P, Q, R,* and *S*? Explain.

S•

Q•

P•   R•

21. Higher Order Thinking There are 11! different ways for a group of people to sit around a circular table. How many people are in the group? Explain.

PRACTICE

For Exercises 22–27, state if the possible arrangements represent permutations or combinations, then state the number of possible arrangements. SEE EXAMPLES 1, 2, AND 3

22. A student chooses at random 4 books from a reading list of 11 books.

23. At the end of a season, 10 soccer teams are ranked by the state.

24. A committee of 5 people is being selected from a group of 9 to choose the food for a sport's banquet.

25. Hugo displays his 8 model planes in a single row.

26. A class president, secretary, and treasurer are chosen from 12 students running for office.

27. A food truck has a lunch special on tacos. Customers choose a shell, three toppings, and two sides for one price.

Menu	
Shell:	Hard, Soft, Wheat
Toppings:	Ground Beef, Chicken, Steak, Cheese, Lettuce, Tomato, Sour Cream
Sides:	Fountain Drink, Rice, Beans, Fruit

28. There are 4 comedians and 5 musicians performing in a variety show. The order in which the performers are chosen is random. SEE EXAMPLE 4

   a. What is the probability that the first 3 performers are comedians?

   b. What is the probability that the first two performers are a comedian followed by a musician?

29. A jewelry maker chooses three beads at random from a bag with 10 beads labeled A, B, C, D, E, F, G, H, I, and J. SEE EXAMPLES 2, 3, AND 4

   a. How can you use permutations or combinations to find *P*(selected beads spell the initials DEB)? What is the probability?

   b. How can you use permutations or combinations to find *P*(selected beads are all vowels)? What is the probability?

APPLY

30. Make Sense and Persevere Amaya's wallet contains three $1 bills, two $5 bills, and three $10 bills. If she pulls 2 bills without looking, what is the probability that she draws a $1-bill and a $10-bill? Explain.

31. Model with Mathematics Raul's favorite restaurant is running a prize game. Five of each of the winning tickets shown are available, and a customer must collect three winning tickets to receive the prize. What is the probability Raul will receive the prize for the baseball cap with his first 3 tickets?

WIN A... WIN A...

WIN A... WIN A...

32. Look for Relationships Smart Phones, Inc. chooses a 5-digit security code at random from the digits 0–9.

   a. Suppose the digits cannot be repeated. What is the probability that the security code is 30429? Explain.

   b. Suppose the digits can be repeated. What is the probability that the security code is 30429? Explain.

33. Make Sense and Persevere Edwin randomly plays 6 different songs from his playlist.

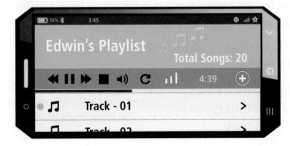

🔋72% ⚡   3:45

Edwin's Playlist 🎵🎵
Total Songs: 20

⏪ ⏸ ⏩ ⏹ 🔊 C 📶 4:39 ➕

🎵 Track - 01 ＞

🎵 Track - 02 ＞

   a. What is the probability that Edwin hears his 6 favorite songs?

   b. What is the probability that he hears the songs in order from his most favorite to his sixth most favorite?

ASSESSMENT PRACTICE

34. Consider an arrangement of 8 items taken 3 at a time in which order is not important. Does each expression give the correct number of arrangements? Select *Yes* or *No*.

	Yes	No
$_8P_3$	☐	☐
$_8C_3$	☐	☐
$\dfrac{_8P_3}{3!}$	☐	☐
$8! \cdot 3!$	☐	☐
$\dfrac{8!}{3!}$	☐	☐
$\dfrac{8!}{5!}$	☐	☐
$\dfrac{8!}{3!5!}$	☐	☐
$8 \cdot 7$	☐	☐

35. SAT/ACT Fifteen students enter a Safety Week poster contest in which prizes will be awarded for first through fourth place. In how many ways could the prizes be given out?

Ⓐ 4

Ⓑ 60

Ⓒ 1,365

Ⓓ 32,760

Ⓔ 50,625

36. Performance Task Use the word shown on the tiles below to find each probability.

| S | U | R | F | B | O | A | R | D |

Part A Two tiles are chosen at random without replacement. Use conditional probability to find the probability that both letters are vowels. Then find the probability using permutations or combinations. Explain.

Part B Four of the tiles are chosen at random and placed in the order in which they are drawn. Use conditional probability to find the probability the tiles spell the word SURF. Then find the probability using permutations or combinations. Explain.

10-5
Probability Distributions

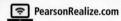

I CAN... define probability distributions to represent experiments and solve problems.

VOCABULARY
- binomial experiment
- probability distribution
- uniform probability distribution

🖐 MODEL & DISCUSS

Mr. and Mrs. Mason have three children. Assume that the probability of having a baby girl is 0.5 and the probability of having a baby boy is also 0.5.

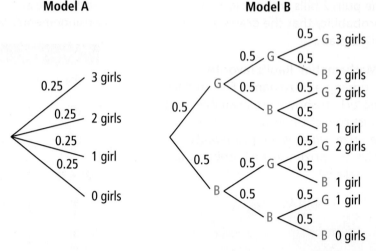

Model A

Model B

A. Reason Which model represents the situation correctly, Model A or Model B? Explain.

B. What is the probability that Mr. and Mrs. Mason have 3 girls?

C. Compare the probability that the Masons' first child was a boy and they then had two girls to the probability that their first two children were girls and they then had a boy. Does the order affect the probabilities? Explain.

❓ ESSENTIAL QUESTION

What does a probability distribution tell you about an experiment?

CONCEPTUAL UNDERSTANDING

🖐 EXAMPLE 1 Develop a Theoretical Probability Distribution

A. Teo and Henry are running for President of the Student Council. You will select a campaign button at random from the box containing 3 Teo buttons and 3 Henry buttons. You will record the number of Teo buttons that you get. What is the theoretical probability distribution for the sample space {0, 1}?

COMMUNICATE PRECISELY
The sample space {0, 1} represents how many Teo buttons you can select in one trial.

A **probability distribution** for an experiment is a function that assigns a probability to each outcome of a sample space for the experiment.

Since you are selecting a button at random, you are equally likely to get 0 buttons or 1 button for Teo.

The theoretical probability distribution for this experiment is the function P, defined on the set {0, 1}, such that $P(0) = \frac{1}{2}$ and $P(1) = \frac{1}{2}$.

> A theoretical probability is based upon assumptions rather than on experimentation.

CONTINUED ON THE NEXT PAGE

EXAMPLE 1 CONTINUED

B. Now you plan to select a button at random, put it back in the box, and then select another button at random. You will record the total number of times that you get a Teo button in the experiment. Define the theoretical probability distribution for the sample space {0, 1, 2}. How does this probability distribution differ from the distribution in Part A?

Make a tree diagram for the experiment.

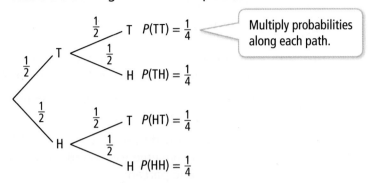

Multiply probabilities along each path.

Add the probabilities of TH and HT to find the probability of getting one Teo button.

$$P(1) = \frac{1}{4} + \frac{1}{4} = \frac{1}{2}$$

The theoretical probability distribution is the function P, defined on the set {0, 1, 2}, such that $P(0) = \frac{1}{4}$, $P(1) = \frac{1}{2}$, and $P(2) = \frac{1}{4}$.

Compare this probability distribution to the one in Part A.

A **uniform probability distribution** assigns the same probability to each outcome.

Comparing Probability Distributions		
Select one button	$P(0) = \frac{1}{2}$, $P(1) = \frac{1}{2}$.	uniform
Select two buttons	$P(0) = \frac{1}{4}$, $P(1) = \frac{1}{2}$, $P(2) = \frac{1}{4}$	not uniform

The probability distribution in Part A is a uniform probability distribution. The probability distribution in this part is not.

STUDY TIP
One way to check your work is to check that the sum of the probabilities of all the outcomes is 1.

 Try It!   **1.** You select two marbles at random from the bowl. For each situation, define the theoretical probability distribution for selecting a number of red marbles on the sample space {0, 1, 2}. Is it a uniform probability distribution?

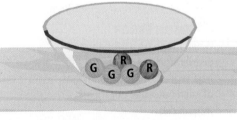

a. You select one marble and put it back in the bowl. Then you select a second marble.

b. You select one marble and do not put it back in the bowl. Then you select a second marble.

APPLICATION

EXAMPLE 2 ▶ Develop an Experimental Probability Distribution

A cell phone company surveyed 500 households about the number of smartphones they have that are in use.

Number of Smartphones per Household							
Number	0	1	2	3	4	5	6 or more
Frequency	10	66	120	144	79	37	44

Would you recommend that the company concentrate on selling data plans for individuals or plans for families with three or more smartphones? Explain.

Step 1 Define an experimental probability distribution on the sample space {0, 1, 2, 3, 4, 5, 6 or more}.

First divide each frequency by 500 to find each relative frequency. For convenience, round each relative frequency to the nearest whole percent.

Number of Smartphones per Household							
Number	0	1	2	3	4	5	6 or more
Frequency	10	66	120	144	79	37	44
Relative Frequency	2%	13%	24%	29%	16%	7%	9%

Each relative frequency represents the experimental probability that a household selected at random from the 500 households has a given number of smartphones.

> An experimental probability is based upon collecting real-world data and finding relative frequencies.

An experimental probability distribution for the experiment is the function P such that if n is an outcome of the sample space, then $P(n)$ is the probability of that outcome. For example, $P(0) = 2\%$.

Step 2 Graph the probability distribution.

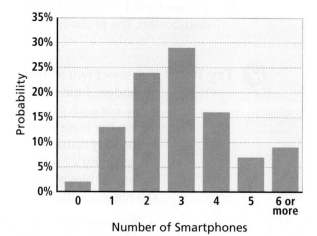

COMMON ERROR
When graphing a probability distribution, the heights of the bars represent the probabilities of each outcome, not their frequencies.

Step 3 Interpret the results.

The probability that a household has 3 or more cell phones is 61%.

Therefore, the company should probably focus on family plans rather than individual plans.

CONTINUED ON THE NEXT PAGE

EXAMPLE 2 CONTINUED

 Activity Assess

 Try It! **2.** Suppose that you selected a student at random from the Drama Club and recorded the student's age.

Ages of Students in Drama Club					
Age	14	15	16	17	18
Students	4	7	10	7	9

a. Define an experimental probability distribution on the sample space {14, 15, 16, 17, 18}.

b. Graph the probability distribution you defined.

CONCEPT Binomial Experiments

A **binomial experiment** is an experiment that consists of a fixed number of trials, with the following features.

- Each trial has two possible outcomes, one of which is denoted as "success."
- The results of the trials are independent events.
- The probability of "success" is the same for every trial.

EXAMPLE 3 **Binomial Experiments**

Is the experiment a binomial experiment?

A. This spinner is spun 3 times. Assume that the spinner is equally likely to stop in any of the sections. Success is landing on a section marked "Go Forward 2 Spaces."

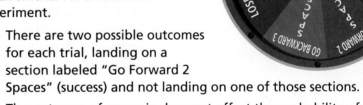

Compare the experiment to the requirements for a binomial experiment.

- There are two possible outcomes for each trial, landing on a section labeled "Go Forward 2 Spaces" (success) and not landing on one of those sections.
- The outcome of one spin does not affect the probability of success on any other spin.
- The probability of success is 0.25 for every trial.

The experiment is a binomial experiment.

B. In a class of 23 students, 7 students completed the term project. Two students selected at random have to give presentations. Success is that the student has completed the project.

The probability that the first student has completed the project is $\frac{7}{23}$.

If the first student completed the project, the probability that the second student did is $\frac{6}{22}$. If the first student is not, the probability is $\frac{7}{22}$.

Because the probabilities for each trial are different, the experiment is not a binomial experiment.

GENERALIZE
Would the experiment be a binomial experiment if there were 25 students in the class? Some other number?

CONTINUED ON THE NEXT PAGE

EXAMPLE 3 CONTINUED

 Activity  Assess

 Try It! 3. Is the experiment a binomial experiment? If so, find the probability of success. Explain.

  a. You select one card at random from a set of 7 cards, 4 labeled A and 3 labeled B. Then you select another card at random from the cards that remain. For each selection, success is that the card is labeled A.

  b. You roll a standard number cube 4 times. Assume that each time you roll the number cube, each number is equally likely to come up. For each roll, success is getting an even number.

CONCEPT Binomial Probability Formula

For a binomial experiment consisting of n trials with the probability of success p for each trial, the probability of exactly r successes out of the n trials is given by the following formula:

$P(r) =$ (ways to get r successes in n trials) • $P(r$ successes) • $P(n-r$ failures)

$P(r) = {}_nC_r \cdot p^r(1-p)^{n-r}$

 EXAMPLE 4 **Probabilities in a Binomial Experiment**

A grocery store gives away scratch-off cards with a purchase of more than $100.

Terrell has 5 scratch-off cards. What is the probability that he has exactly 3 winning cards if each card has a 30% chance of being a winner?

Step 1 Determine whether the situation is a binomial experiment.

  • Terrell's 5 cards represent 5 trials.

  • Each card is either a winning card (success) or not.

  • Whether one card is a winning card does not affect the probability that another card is a winning card.

  • The probability of success, 0.3, is the same for every trial.

So this is a binomial experiment.

REASON
In the formula for binomial probability, what probability does the term $1 - p$ represent?

Step 2 Find the probability of 3 successes.

The formula $P(r) = {}_nC_r \cdot p^r(1-p)^{n-r}$ gives the probability of r successes out of n trials. Use $n = 5$, $r = 3$, and $p = 0.3$.

$${}_5C_3 = \frac{5!}{3!(5-3)!}$$

$$= \frac{5 \cdot 4}{2 \cdot 1}$$

$$= 10$$

$$P(3) = {}_5C_3 \cdot (0.3)^3(1-0.3)^{5-3}$$

$$= 10(0.3)^3(0.7)^2$$

$$= 10(0.027)(0.49)$$

$$= 0.1323$$

The probability of having exactly 3 winning cards is about 13%.

 Try It! 4. To the nearest tenth of a percent, what is the probability that Terrell has more than 3 winning cards? Explain.

🔑 **CONCEPT SUMMARY** Probability Distributions

TYPES OF DISTRIBUTIONS ▶

A probability distribution for an experiment is a function that assigns a probability to each outcome of a sample space for the experiment.

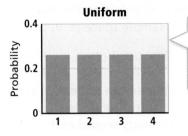

A uniform probability distribution assigns the same probability to each outcome.

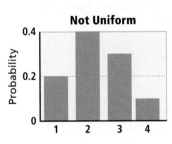

BINOMIAL EXPERIMENT ▶

A binomial experiment is an experiment that consists of a fixed number of trials, in which:

- each trial has two possible outcomes, one of which is denoted as "success";
- the results of the trials are independent events; and
- the probability of "success" is the same for every trial.

If the probability of success is p for each trial, then the probability of exactly r successes out of n trials is $P(r) = {}_nC_r \cdot p^r(1 - p)^{n-r}$.

☑️ **Do You UNDERSTAND?**

1. ❓ **ESSENTIAL QUESTION** What does a probability distribution tell you about an experiment?

2. **Vocabulary** What are the characteristics of a *binomial experiment*?

3. **Error Analysis** A regular tetrahedron has four triangular sides, with one of the letters A, B, C, and D on each side. Assume that if you roll the tetrahedron, each of the letters is equally likely to end up on the bottom. {A, B, C, D} is a sample space for the experiment. Rochelle was asked to find the theoretical probability distribution for the experiment. Explain and correct the error.

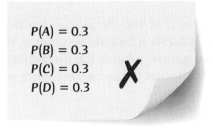

$P(A) = 0.3$
$P(B) = 0.3$
$P(C) = 0.3$
$P(D) = 0.3$ ✗

Do You KNOW HOW?

Graph the probability distribution P.

4. Theoretical probabilities from selecting a student at random from a group of 3 students, Jack, Alani, and Seth

5. Probabilities from flipping a fair coin 3 times and counting the number of heads. The sample space is the set of numbers 0, 1, 2, 3. $P(0) = 0.125$, $P(1) = 0.375$, $P(2) = 0.375$, $P(3) = 0.125$

A bag contains 5 balls: 3 green, 1 red, and 1 yellow. You select a ball at random 4 times, replacing the ball after each selection. Calculate the theoretical probability of each event to the nearest whole percent.

6. getting a green ball exactly 3 times

7. getting a green ball exactly 4 times

8. getting a green ball at least 3 times

9. getting a yellow ball twice

10. getting only red and green balls

UNDERSTAND

11. Communicate Precisely Explain what it means for a coin to be a fair coin.

12. Reason You spin the spinner shown.

Describe a theoretical probability distribution for the experiment.

13. Communicate Precisely Five students in a class of 27 students ate hamburgers for lunch. Suppose the teacher selects a student in the class at random and then selects another student at random. Success for each selection is selecting a student who ate a hamburger. Is this a binomial experiment? Explain.

14. Error Analysis A standard number cube is rolled 7 times. Success for each roll is defined as getting a number less than 3. Abby tried to calculate the probability of 5 successes. Describe and correct her error.

$$P(5) = \left(\frac{1}{3}\right)^5 \left(\frac{2}{3}\right)^2 \approx 0.002 \quad ✗$$

15. Mathematical Connections A marble is selected from the bowl shown 4 times. The marble is returned to the bowl after each selection.

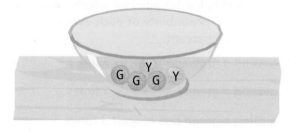

a. Show that there are exactly $_4C_2$ ways to get exactly 2 green marbles.

b. How are $_5C_3$ and $_5C_2$ related? Explain.

PRACTICE

A card is chosen at random from the box containing 10 cards: 3 yellow, 4 red, 2 green, and 1 blue. SEE EXAMPLES 1 AND 2

16. Define a probability distribution for this experiment on the sample space {Y, R, G, B}.

17. Graph the probability distribution.

In a certain game, the player can score 0, 1, 2, 3, or 4 points during their turn. The table shows the number of times Kennedy scored each number of points the last time she played the game. SEE EXAMPLE 2

Score	0	1	2	3	4
Frequency	3	7	9	6	5

18. Define an experimental probability distribution based on Kennedy's scores.

19. Graph the probability distribution you defined in Exercise 18.

Is the experiment a binomial experiment? Explain. SEE EXAMPLE 3

20. A quality control specialist tests 50 LED light bulbs produced in a factory. Success is that a tested light bulb burns for at least 2,000 hours without dimming. For each light bulb, the probability of success is 0.9.

21. There are 10 black and 10 red cards face down on the table. One card is selected at random. Then another card is selected at random. Success is getting a red card.

22. A basketball player is shooting 2 free throws. The probability of her making the first free throw is 0.86. The probability of her making the second free throw is 0.92.

Each time Bailey is at bat, the probability that he gets a hit is 0.250. If he bats 10 times in the course of two games, what is the probability of each result? Round to the nearest tenth of a percent. SEE EXAMPLE 4

23. He gets no hits.

24. He gets exactly 1 hit.

25. He gets exactly 2 hits.

26. He gets fewer than 3 hits.

PRACTICE & PROBLEM SOLVING

APPLY

27. Model with Mathematics The circle graph shows the result of a survey of the most popular types of music in the U.S., based on sales, downloads, and streaming.

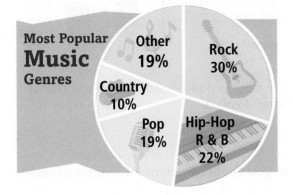

Most Popular **Music** Genres

- Other 19%
- Rock 30%
- Country 10%
- Pop 19%
- Hip-Hop R & B 22%

a. Define a probability distribution for the sample space.

b. Graph the probability distribution.

c. According to the survey, which is the most popular type of music in the United States?

28. Higher Order Thinking A pharmaceutical company is testing a new version of a medication. In a clinical trial of the old version of the medication, 18% of the subjects taking the old medication experienced headaches.

a. Suppose that 18% of the people taking the new medications will experience headaches. If 8 subjects are selected at random and given the new medication, what is the probability that less than two of them will experience headaches?

b. Suppose that two of the eight subjects experience headaches after taking the new medication. Is that cause for concern? Explain your reasoning.

29. Communicate Precisely In a quiz show, a contestant is asked 6 questions. Each question has 5 answer choices. Assume that the contestant picks an answer at random for each question and the probability of guessing the correct answer is 20%. What is the probability of guessing correctly on at least 4 of the questions? Round your answer to the nearest tenth of a percent.

ASSESSMENT PRACTICE

30. You are going to roll a game piece two times. The game piece has 10 sides of equal area, each with one of the numbers 0 through 9. Assume that it is equally likely to land with any of the sides on top. Success is defined as getting a 3 on top.

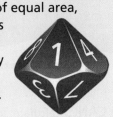

Let P be the function defined on {0, 1, 2} such that $P(n)$ is the probability of n successes. Select all that apply.

Ⓐ This is a binomial experiment.

Ⓑ P is a probability distribution for the sample space {0, 1, 2}.

Ⓒ $P(0) = 0.81$

Ⓓ $P(1) = 0.09$

Ⓔ $P(2) = 0.01$

31. SAT/ACT A standard number cube is rolled 6 times. Success is defined as getting a number greater than 4. Rounded to the nearest percent, what is the probability of exactly 2 successes?

Ⓐ 2%   Ⓑ 8%   Ⓒ 23%   Ⓓ 33%   Ⓔ 50%

32. Performance Task Get 5 index cards. Draw a picture on one side and no picture on the other side of each card.

Part A You are going to throw all 5 cards up in the air and count the number of cards that land face up. Assume that it is equally likely that each card will land face up and face down. Define a theoretical probability distribution for the sample space {0, 1, 2, 3, 4, 5}.

Part B Perform the experiment 20 times. Each time you perform the experiment, record the number of cards that land face up. Find the experimental probability for each outcome in the sample space {0, 1, 2, 3, 4, 5} and define an experimental probability distribution the sample space.

Part C Compare the results of Part A and B. If they are different, explain why you think they are different.

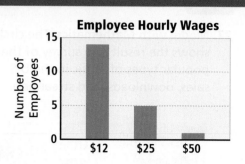
10-6

Expected Value

PearsonRealize.com

I CAN... calculate, interpret, and apply expected value.

VOCABULARY
- binomial distribution
- expected value

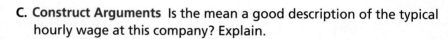
EXPLORE & REASON

A company has 20 employees whose hourly wages are shown in the bar graph.

Employee Hourly Wages

A. An employee is chosen at random. What is the probability that his or her hourly wage is $12? $25? $50?

B. What is the mean hourly wage? Explain your method.

C. **Construct Arguments** Is the mean a good description of the typical hourly wage at this company? Explain.

? **ESSENTIAL QUESTION**   What does expected value tell you about situations involving probability?

CONCEPTUAL UNDERSTANDING

EXAMPLE 1   **Evaluate and Apply Expected Value**

The table shows data on sales in one month for each item on a restaurant menu. To estimate future profits, the owner evaluates the average profit from each meal.

Meal	Profit per Serving	Percent Sold
Stew	$0.34	12%
Soup	$0.41	7%
Lasagna	$0.64	45%
Chili	$0.73	36%

A. Based on the data, what is the average profit that the owner can expect to make from each meal?

Expected value is the sum of the value of each outcome multiplied by the probability of the outcome.

$$E = x_1P(x_1) + x_2P(x_2) + x_3P(x_3) + \ldots + x_nP(x_n)$$

The outcomes are the profits for each meal. The probability for each meal is the percent sold. Multiply each outcome by its probability. Then add.

$$E = 0.34(0.12) + 0.41(0.07) + 0.64(0.45) + 0.73(0.36) = 0.6203$$

> Use the expected value formula when the probability of at least one outcome differs from any of the others.

COMMON ERROR
Note that average profit from each meal is not simply the average of the cost of 1 serving of each of the 4 meals because the number of each kind of meal varies.

If this expected value continues, the owner can expect to earn about $0.62 per meal.

B. What is the expected profit for the next 200 meals ordered?

$$\$0.6203 \times 200 = \$124.06$$

The owner can expect to net about $124.06 for the next 200 meals.

CONTINUED ON THE NEXT PAGE

Try It! 1. a. What would happen to the expected value if fewer people ordered chili and more people ordered stew? Explain.

b. Suppose the restaurant's profit on an order of stew increased by $0.05 and the profit on an order of chili decreased by $0.05. How would these changes affect the expected profit per meal?

 EXAMPLE 2 **Find Expected Payoffs**

A charity is considering a fundraising event in which donors will pay $1 to spin the wheel 3 times. What is the expected payoff for the charity for each game?

EVEN THREES

Spin 3 times
Get 3 even numbers
Win an item worth $4

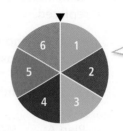

There are 6 possible outcomes. 3 of the possible outcomes are even numbers.

MAKE SENSE AND PERSEVERE
Think about methods used to find probabilities. What do you need to identify to find the probabilities for each situation?

Step 1 Find the probabilities for the donor.

There are 6^3, or 216 outcomes for spinning the wheel 3 times.

There are 3^3, or 27, ways to spin 3 even numbers in a row, so the probability of a donor winning a $4 prize is $\frac{27}{216}$, or $\frac{1}{8}$.

So, the probability of a donor not winning is $1 - \frac{1}{8}$, or $\frac{7}{8}$.

Step 2 Find probabilities for the charity.

The probability that the charity gains $1 is $P(1) = \frac{7}{8}$.

The probability that the charity loses $3 is $P(-3) = \frac{1}{8}$.

Step 3 Find the expected value of each game for the charity.
$$E(x) = 1\left(\frac{7}{8}\right) + (-3)\left(\frac{1}{8}\right)$$
$$= \frac{4}{8}$$
$$= \frac{1}{2}$$

The charity can expect to earn $0.50 each game.

 Try It! 2. What is the expected payoff for the person making the donation?

👆 **EXAMPLE 3**   **Use Expected Values to Evaluate Strategies**

You are considering options for an auto insurance policy. The insurance company offers new car replacement insurance, in the case your car is totaled. There is a 1% annual chance of the car being totaled.

Plan	Premium ($)	Deductible ($)
A	50	500
B	60	0

> The deductible is the portion of the cost that the car owner pays.

A. Which of the two plans has the lower expected cost?

The total expected cost is the sum of the known costs and the expected value of the unknown cost. The cost of a new car is higher than the deductible, so you would pay the full deductible if the car needs to be replaced.

Known cost   **Expected value of unknown cost**

Premium + Deductible • Probability of replacement = Expected cost of insurance

Plan A: $50 + $500 • 0.01 = $55

Plan B: $60 + $0 • 0.01 = $60

Plan A has the lower expected cost.

> **CONSTRUCT ARGUMENTS**
> If the expected costs were the same, what other criteria could the car owner use to decide? Why might the insurance company offer two different plans with the same expected cost?

B. How can you decide whether or not to purchase replacement insurance?

The cost of a new car is very high, so purchasing replacement insurance can be a good idea. Solve an inequality to determine when having no insurance is more costly than having insurance.

Known cost   **Expected value of unknown cost**

Premium + Cost of a new car • Probability of replacement > Expected cost of insurance

$0 + x • 0.01 > $55

$0.01x$ > $55

x > $5,500

> With or without insurance, you have the same chance of needing a new car.

You should buy replacement insurance if the cost of a new car is greater than $5,500.

✅ **Try It!**   **3.** The insurance company also offers safety glass coverage. There is a 50% chance of no repairs ($0), a 30% chance of minor repairs ($50), and 20% chance of full replacement ($300). Which plan for optional safety glass coverage has the lower expected cost?

Plan	Premium ($)	Deductible ($)
C	50	200
D	100	0

EXAMPLE 4 ▸ Use Binomial Probability to Find Expected Value

According to the weather app on Talisha's smartphone, there is a 40% chance of rain for each of the 5 days of her vacation. How many rainy days should Talisha expect during her vacation?

STUDY TIP
Organize your work in a table that clearly shows each outcome and its probability.

Days of Rain	Probability
0	$_5C_0(0.4)^0(0.6)^5 \approx 0.0778$
1	$_5C_1(0.4)^1(0.6)^4 = 0.2592$
2	$_5C_2(0.4)^2(0.6)^3 = 0.3456$
3	$_5C_3(0.4)^3(0.6)^2 = 0.2304$
4	$_5C_4(0.4)^4(0.6)^1 = 0.0768$
5	$_5C_5(0.4)^5(0.6)^0 \approx 0.0102$

Apply the binomial probability formula with $n = 5$, $p = 0.4$, and $1 - p = 0.6$ to find the probability of rain for each number of days of Talisha's vacation.

To find the expected number of rainy days, multiply each probability by the number of rainy days it corresponds to, and add those values together.

Expected number of rainy days

$$= 0 \cdot P(0) + 1 \cdot P(1) + 2 \cdot P(2) + 3 \cdot P(3) + 4 \cdot P(4) + 5 \cdot P(5)$$

$$= 0(0.0778) + 1(0.2592) + 2(0.3456) + 3(0.2304) + 4(0.0768) + 5(0.0102) \approx 2$$

Talisha should expect 2 rainy days during her vacation.

The table shows the probability of every outcome of a binomial experiment. This probability distribution is called a **binomial distribution**. A special relationship exists for the expected value for any binomial distribution.

$$E = np$$

$$2 = 5(0.4)$$

E expected value n trials p probability

Try It!

4. A carnival game has 4 orange lights and 1 green light that flash rapidly one at a time in a random order. When a player pushes a button, the game stops, leaving one light on. If the light is green, the player wins a prize. Copy and complete the table, then determine the number of prizes that a player can expect to win if the game is played 4 times.

Number of Green Lights	Probability
0	$_4C_0(0.2)^0(0.8)^4 = \blacksquare$
1	$_4C_\blacksquare(0.2)^\blacksquare(0.8)^\blacksquare = \blacksquare$
2	$_\blacksquare C_\blacksquare(0.2)^\blacksquare(0.8)^\blacksquare = \blacksquare$
3	$_\blacksquare C_\blacksquare(0.2)^\blacksquare(0.8)^\blacksquare = \blacksquare$
4	$_\blacksquare C_\blacksquare(0.2)^\blacksquare(0.8)^\blacksquare = \blacksquare$

CONCEPT SUMMARY Expected Value

WORDS	ALGEBRA
Expected value is the average outcome that will occur with many trials of an experiment. It is the sum of the value of each outcome times the probability of the outcome.	Let x_1, x_2, x_3, … x_n represent the values of the outcomes of a set of trials. You can find the expected value, E, with this formula. $$E = x_1P(x_1) + x_2P(x_2) + … + x_nP(x_n)$$

Do You UNDERSTAND?

1. **ESSENTIAL QUESTION** What does expected value tell you about situations involving probability?

2. **Error Analysis** Benjamin is finding the expected value of the number of heads when tossing a fair coin 10 times. What is Benjamin's error?

   > Toss a coin 10 times
   > $E = 50\%$
   > **X**

3. **Construct Arguments** A carnival game costs $1 to play. The expected payout for each play of this game is $1.12. Should the carnival operators modify the game in any way? Explain.

4. **Reason** The students in Ms. Kahn's class are raising money to help earthquake victims. They expect to raise $0.52 for each raffle ticket they sell. If each raffle ticket is sold for $2, what can you conclude?

5. **Reason** A spinner is divided into 6 equal-sized sectors, numbered 1, 1, 1, 4, 7, and 10. Is the expected value of a spin the same as the mean of the numbers? Explain.

Do You KNOW HOW?

6. What is the expected value when rolling a standard number cube?

7. What is the expected value of the sum when rolling two standard number cubes?

8. A travel website reports that in a particular European city, the probability of rain on any day in April is 40%. What is the expected number of rainy days in this city during the month of April?

9. You buy an airplane ticket for $900. You discover that if you cancel or rebook your vacation flight to Europe, you will be charged an extra $300. There is a 20% chance that you will have to rebook your flight.

   a. What is the expected value of the cost of the ticket?

   b. Is the expected value the amount you will pay to book the ticket whether or not you have to rebook? Explain.

10. A child-care service charges families an hourly rate based upon the age of the child. Their hourly rate per child is $20 per hour for infants less than 1 year old, $18 for toddlers 1 to 3 years old, $15 per hour children 3 or more years old. The ratios of infants : toddlers : 3+ years is 2 : 3 : 5. What is the expected charge per child per hour?

UNDERSTAND

11. Error Analysis For the dartboard shown, Deshawn calculated the expected number of points per dart. Explain Deshawn's error. What is the correct expected value?

$$\text{Expected value} = \frac{2}{7}(4) + \frac{5}{7}(1)$$
$$= \frac{8}{7} + \frac{5}{7}$$
$$= \frac{13}{7} \approx 1.86 \quad ✗$$

12. Reason A nonrefundable plane ticket costs $600, while a refundable ticket costs $900. A traveler estimates there is a 20% chance he will have to cancel his upcoming trip. Should the traveler purchase a refundable or nonrefundable ticket? Explain.

13. Construct Arguments A consumer determines that her expected cost for Option B is $528 per year.

Option	Annual Premium	Deductible
A	$600	$0
B	$500	$1,000

a. Why might this consumer select the policy with the $1000 deductible?

b. Why might this consumer select the policy with no deductible?

14. Mathematical Connections How is expected value related to the mean?

PRACTICE

A farmer estimates her hens will produce 3,000 dozen more eggs this year than last year. She estimates the probability of her net profit or loss on each dozen eggs based on her costs.
SEE EXAMPLE 1

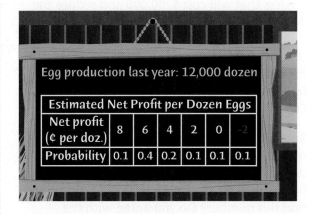

Egg production last year: 12,000 dozen

Estimated Net Profit per Dozen Eggs

Net profit (¢ per doz.)	8	6	4	2	0	-2
Probability	0.1	0.4	0.2	0.1	0.1	0.1

15. What is her expected profit per dozen eggs?

16. What is her expected profit on the total egg production?

17. An electronics store offers students a discount of 10% on purchases of computers. They estimate that $\frac{1}{16}$ of computer sales are to students. The average sale per customer is $498 and the store's profit is $80 before the discount. What is the expected profit on the sale of a computer? SEE EXAMPLE 2

18. An insurance company offers three policy options. The probability a car will be damaged in a given year is 5%, and if a car is damaged, the cost of the repairs will be $1000. Which option has the least expected annual cost for the car owner? Explain. SEE EXAMPLE 3

Insurance Policy Options

Option	Annual Premium ($)	Deductible ($)
A	900	0
B	800	400
C	700	1000

On a tropical island, the probability of sunny weather is 90% each day. SEE EXAMPLE 4

19. What is the expected number of sunny days in a non-leap year?

20. What is the expected number of sunny days during the month of June?

APPLY

21. Model With Mathematics A solar panel company has found that about 1% of its panels are defective. The company's cost to replace each defective panel is $600. A consultant recommends changes to the manufacturing process that will cost $200,000 and reduce the defective rate to 0.2%. The company estimates that it will sell 30,000 panels next year and that sales will increase by 5,000 panels per year for the next 10 years. Should the company follow the consultant's recommendation? Explain.

22. Reason A student tosses a coin 4 times and the results are heads, tails, heads, and heads. The student concludes that the expected number of heads for 100 tosses is 75. How did the student find this number? Do you agree with the student's reasoning? Explain.

23. Higher Order Thinking Your family is going to buy a new TV set for $599. You find out that the probability that the TV set will need to be serviced in the second year is 0.05 and the probability that the TV set will need to be serviced in the third year is 0.08. A 2-year warranty costs $55, and a 3-year warranty costs $80. The average cost of repairing the TV set is $278. What would you advise your family to do, get a 2-year extended warranty, a 3-year extended warranty or not to get any extended warranty? Explain your reasoning.

24. Make Sense and Persevere A company makes tablets that are guaranteed for one year. On average, one out of every 200 tablets needs to be repaired or replaced within the first year. If a tablet needs to be repaired, the company loses an average of $140. If the company sells 2,600,000 of the tablets in a year, what is their net profit on the sale of the tablets in that year?

If no repairs or replacement is needed for a tablet, the company makes a $24 profit on that tablet.

✓ ASSESSMENT PRACTICE

25. A commuter recorded data on the arrival time of his morning train each weekday for 5 weeks. According to the data, he should expect the train to be 1.16 minutes late on any given day. What are the missing values in the commuter's table?

Arrival Time for Train

Minutes late	0	1	2	3	4	5
Number of days	■	5	1	■	1	3

26. SAT/ACT What is the expected total for 20 spins?

Ⓐ 100
Ⓑ 105
Ⓒ 110
Ⓓ 115
Ⓔ 120

27. Performance Task A toy company is designing a children's game in which players toss chips onto a board. The square board will contain a smaller square at its center.

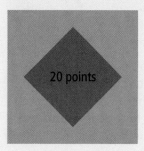

20 points

Part A Write design instructions for the board so that a chip tossed randomly onto the board is 8 times more likely to land in the outer region than in the inner square. Explain your reasoning.

Part B Assign a whole number of points to the outer region so that the expected score on a single toss is as close as possible to 5. Explain your reasoning.

Part C If the area of the inner square is doubled and the overall size of the board remains the same, how does the expected score change? Is it also doubled? Explain.

10-7

Probability and Decision Making

 PearsonRealize.com

I CAN... use probability to make decisions.

CRITIQUE & EXPLAIN

Your friend offers to play the following game with you "If the product of the roll of two number cubes is 10 or less, I win. If not, you win!"

A. If you were to play the game many times, what percent of the games would you expect to win?

B. Is the game fair? Should you take the offer? Explain.

C. Make Sense and Persevere Suggest a way to change the game from fair to unfair, or vice versa, while still using the product of the two number cubes. Explain.

? ESSENTIAL QUESTION

How can you use probability to make decisions?

APPLICATION

EXAMPLE 1   Use Probability to Make Fair Decisions

Sadie, Tamira, River, Victor, and Jae are candidates to represent their school at an event. How can you use random integers to select 2 students from the 5 candidates, so that each one is equally likely to be selected?

There are 5 students. Assign a number to each student.

1	2	3	4	5
Sadie	Tamira	River	Victor	Jae

To select a student, use a calculator or other random number generator to generate a random integer from 1 to 5. Repeat to select the second student.

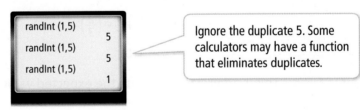

Ignore the duplicate 5. Some calculators may have a function that eliminates duplicates.

Jae (5) and Sadie (1) are selected.

MAKE SENSE AND PERSEVERE
Consider how you would assign integers from 1 to 10 among the 5 students. How do you adjust this for a random number generator that gives a number r from the interval $0 \leq r < 1$?

Try It!

1. Your trainer creates training programs for you. How can you use index cards to randomly choose the following: Strength training 1 day per week; Cardio training 2 days per week, with no consecutive days; Swimming 1 day per week.

CONCEPTUAL
UNDERSTANDING

EXAMPLE 2 **Determine Whether a Decision Is Fair or Unfair**

Thato places three cards in a hat
and challenges Helena to a game.

A. Thato says, "If you draw a
number greater than 2,
you earn 2 points. Otherwise,
I earn 2 points." Is the game
fair, or unfair? If it is unfair,
which player has the advantage? Explain.

In each round, Thato either wins
2 points or loses 2 points.

> If Helena draws a "3" and gets
> 2 points, Thato considers this a
> loss of 2 points for himself.

COMMON ERROR
Recall that the expected value
is the sum of the products of
the outcomes' values by their
respective probabilities. Be
careful not to use the sum of the
probabilities.

Find the probability of each outcome.
Then find the expected value.

$$P(-2) = \frac{1}{3} \text{ and } P(+2) = \frac{2}{3}.$$
$$E = -2 \cdot \left(\frac{1}{3}\right) + 2 \cdot \left(\frac{2}{3}\right)$$
$$= \frac{2}{3}$$

> A game is considered "fair" if and
> only if the expected value is 0.

The game is unfair and is skewed to Thato's advantage. The probability
of his scoring 2 points is twice the probability of Helena scoring 2 points.

B. Helena proposes a change to the scoring of the game. She says,
"If I draw a number greater than 2, I get 2 points. Otherwise, you get
1 point." Is the game fair, or unfair? If it is unfair, which player has
the advantage? Explain.

In each round, Thato either scores 1 point or he loses 2 points.

Find the probability of each outcome. Then find the expected value.

$$P(-2) = \frac{1}{3} \text{ and } P(+1) = \frac{2}{3}.$$
$$E = -2 \cdot \left(\frac{1}{3}\right) + 1 \cdot \left(\frac{2}{3}\right)$$
$$= -\frac{2}{3} + \frac{2}{3} = 0$$

This is a fair game because the expected value is 0. Neither player has an
advantage over the other.

 Try It! 2. Justice and Tamika use the same 3 cards but change the game.
In each round, a player draws a card and replaces it, and then
the other player draws. The differences between the two cards
are used to score each round. Order matters, so the difference
can be negative. Is each game fair? Explain.

  a. If the difference between the first and second cards is 2,
  Justice gets a point. Otherwise Tamika gets a point.

  b. They take turns drawing first. Each round, the first player to
  draw subtracts the second player's number from her own and
  the result is added to her total score.

APPLICATION

EXAMPLE 3 Make a Decision Based on Expected Value

The Silicon Valley Company manufactures tablets and computers. Their tablets are covered by a warranty for one year, so that if the tablet fails, the company replaces it. Since the failure rate of their model TAB5000 tablet is high, the head of production has a plan for replacing certain components inside the TAB5000 and calling the new model TAB5001.

Model TAB5000
- Cost to produce: $100
- Price: $150
- 5% fail within first year
- Replacement cost to company: $130

Model TAB5001
- Cost to produce: $105
- Price: $150
- 1% fail within first year (estimate)
- Replacement cost to company: $135

If you were the head of production, would you recommend switching to selling the TAB5001?

Formulate ◀ Find the expected profit for each model.

Expected profit = price − cost − (cost to replace)(failure rate)

Compute ◀ Expected profit of TAB5000 = $150 − $100 − ($130)(0.05)

$$= \$50 - \$6.50$$

$$= \$43.50$$

Expected profit of TAB5001 = $150 − $105 − ($135)(0.01)

$$= \$45 - \$1.35$$

$$= \$43.65$$

Interpret ◀ The expected profit of the TAB5001 is more than the expected profit of the TAB5000. It makes sense to sell the TAB5001 instead of the TAB5000. Also, customers who bought a tablet would be more likely to be pleased with their purchase and buy from the same company in the future.

Try It! **3.** Additional data is collected for the TAB5000 and TAB5001. The production and replacement costs for the TAB5001 remain unchanged.

    a. The production and replacement costs for the TAB5000 increased by $10. What would the expected profit be for the TAB5000?

    b. The failure rate for the TAB5001 increased by 1%. What would the expected profit be for the TAB5001?

    c. As a consultant for the company, what would you recommend they do to maximize their profit?

EXAMPLE 4 Use a Binomial Distribution to Make Decisions

An airport shuttle company takes 8 reservations for each trip because 25% of their reservations do not show up. Is this a reasonable policy?

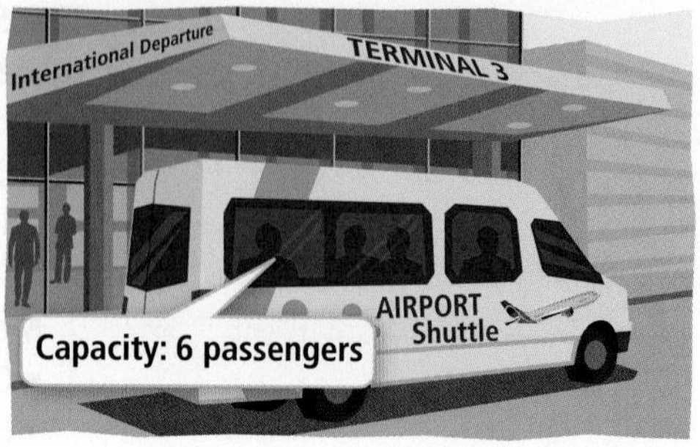
International Departure
TERMINAL 3
AIRPORT Shuttle
Capacity: 6 passengers

Find the probability that more passengers show up than the van can carry.

For 8 reservations, the graph shows the number of possible combinations of passengers showing up.

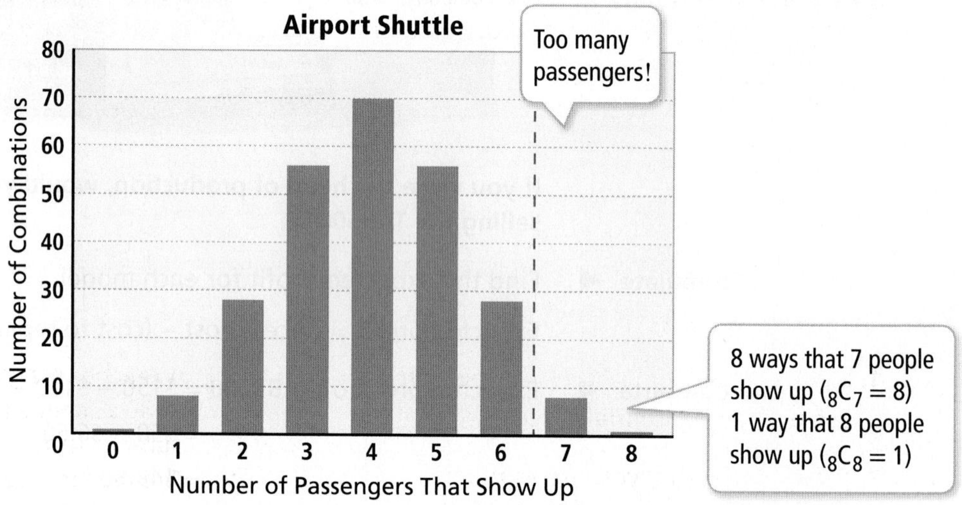
Airport Shuttle
Too many passengers!
Number of Combinations
0
10
20
30
40
50
60
70
80
Number of Passengers That Show Up
0
1
2
3
4
5
6
7
8
8 ways that 7 people show up (${}_8C_7 = 8$)
1 way that 8 people show up (${}_8C_8 = 1$)

USE APPROPRIATE TOOLS
How does the graph of the number of combinations help you think about the situation?

To find the probability that too many reservations show up, compute the probability that either 7 or 8 passengers show up. Each reservation has a 75% chance of showing up and a 25% chance of not showing up. Use $P(r) = {}_nC_r\, p^r(1-p)^{n-r}$.

Find the probability that 7 reservations show up.

$$P(7) = {}_8C_7(0.75)^7(0.25)^1 \approx 8(0.1335)(0.25) \approx 0.267$$

Find the probability that 8 reservations show up.

$$P(8) = {}_8C_8(0.75)^8(0.25)^0 \approx 1(0.1001)(1) \approx 0.100$$

The probability that more reservations will show up than the van can carry is $P(7) + P(8)$, or about $0.267 + 0.100 = 0.367$.

Over one third of the trips will have passengers who can not get a seat in the van. This will result in dissatisfied customers, so this is not a reasonable policy.

Try It! 4. A play calls for a crowd of 12 extras with non-speaking parts. Because 10% of the extras have not shown up in the past, the director selects 15 students as extras. Find the probabilities that 12 extras show up to the performance, 15 extras show up to the performance, and more than 12 extras show up to the performance.

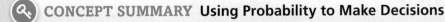

CONCEPT SUMMARY Using Probability to Make Decisions

METHOD	DESCRIPTION	APPLICATIONS
Simple Probability	Find the probability of random events.	• Select the most favorable among random events.
Expected Value	Multiply the probability of each outcome by its value. Add to find the expected value.	• Compare expected values to choose the best of several options. • Compare expected values to decide if a game is fair.
Probability Distribution	Find the probability distribution of all possible outcomes.	• Compare probabilities of outcomes in a binomial experiment. • Create a graph of a probability distribution to present the distribution visually.

 Do You UNDERSTAND?

1. **ESSENTIAL QUESTION** How can you use probability to make decisions?

2. **Reason** How can you use random numbers to simulate rolling a standard number cube?

3. **Error Analysis** Explain the error in Diego's reasoning.

> If a game uses random numbers, it is always fair. ✗

4. **Use Structure** Describe what conditions are needed for a fair game.

5. **Use Appropriate Tools** Explain how you can visualize probability distributions to help you make decisions.

6. **Reason** Why must the expected value of a fair game of chance equal zero?

Do You KNOW HOW?

7. A teacher assigns each of 30 students a unique number from 1 to 30. The teacher uses the random numbers shown to select students for presentations. Which student was selected first? second?

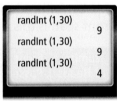

randInt (1,30)   9
randInt (1,30)   9
randInt (1,30)   4

8. Three friends are at a restaurant and they all want the last slice of pizza. Identify three methods involving probability that they can use to determine who gets the last slice. Explain mathematically why each method will guarantee a fair decision.

9. Edgar rolls one number cube and Micah rolls two. If Edgar rolls a 6, he wins a prize. If Micah rolls a sum of 7, she gets a prize. Is this game fair? Explain.

10. The 10 parking spaces in the first row of the parking lot are reserved for the 12 members of the Student Council. Usually an average of ten percent of the Student Council does not drive to school dances. What is the probability that more members of the Student Council will drive to a dance than there are reserved parking spaces?

UNDERSTAND

PRACTICE

11. Reason Suppose Chris has pair of 4-sided dice, each numbered from 1 to 4, and Carolina has a pair of 10-sided dice, each numbered from 1 to 10. They decide to play a series of games against each other, using their own dice.

a. Describe a game that would be fair. Explain.

b. Describe an unfair game. Explain.

12. Construct Arguments Mr. and Ms. Mitchell have 3 children, Luke, Charlie, and Aubrey. All 3 children want to sit in the front seat. Charlie suggests that they flip a coin two times to decide who will sit in the front seat. The number of heads determines who sits in the front seat. Is this a fair method? Explain.

Number of Heads	Front Seat Passenger
0	Luke
1	Charlie
2	Aubrey

13. Error Analysis Mercedes is planning a party for 10 people. She knows from experience that about 20% of those invited will not show up. If she invites 12 people, how can she calculate the probability that more than 10 people will show up. What error did she make? What is the correct probability?

> Use the binomial distribution for 12 trials, with a 20% probability, and more than 10 show up.
> $(12)(0.80)^1(0.20)^{11} +$
> $(1)(0.80)^0(0.20)^{12}$ ✗

14. How can you use random integers to select 3 students from a group of 8 to serve as student body representatives, so that each student is equally likely to be selected? SEE EXAMPLE 1

Explain whether each game is fair or unfair.
SEE EXAMPLE 2

15. When it is your turn, roll a standard number cube. If the number is even, you get a point. If it is odd, you lose a point.

16. When it is your turn, roll two standard number cubes. If the product of the numbers is even, you get a point. If the product is odd, you lose a point.

Fatima is a contestant on a game show. So far, she has won $34,000. She can keep the $34,000 or spin the spinner shown below and add or subtract the amount shown from $34,000. SEE EXAMPLE 3

17. If Fatima spins the spinner, what are her expected total winnings?

18. Would you advise Fatima to keep the $34,000 or to spin the spinner? Explain your reasoning.

19. Suppose 0.5% of people who file federal tax returns with an adjusted gross income (AGI) between $50,000 and $75,000 are audited. Of 5 people in that tax bracket for whom ABC Tax Guys prepared their taxes, 2 were audited. SEE EXAMPLE 4

a. If 5 people with an AGI between $50,000 and $75,000 are selected at random from all the people who filed federal tax returns, what is the probability that at least 2 people are audited?

b. Would you recommend that a friend with an AGI between $50,000 and $75,000 use ABC Tax Guys to prepare her tax returns? Explain.

APPLY

20. Model With Mathematics For $5.49 per month, Ms. Corchado can buy insurance to cover the cost of repairing a leak in the natural gas lines within her house. She estimates that there is a 3% chance that she will need to have such repairs made next year.

a. What is the expected cost of a gas leak, if Ms. Corchado does not buy insurance? Use the cost shown in the middle of the graph.

b. With more recent information, Ms. Corchado learns that repair costs could be as much as $1,200 dollars with an 8% probability of a leak. What is the expected cost of a gas leak with these assumptions?

c. Would you advise Ms. Corchado to buy the insurance? Explain.

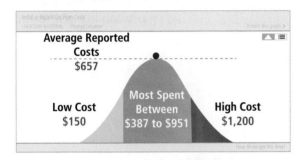

Average Reported Costs
$657
Low Cost $150
Most Spent Between $387 to $951
High Cost $1,200

21. Higher Order Thinking You are a consultant to a company that manufactures components for cell phones. One of the components the company manufactures has a 4% failure rate. Design changes have improved the quality of the component. A test of 50 of the new components found that only one of the new components is defective.

a. Before the design improvements what was the probability that among 50 of the items, at most one of the items was defective?

b. Is it reasonable to conclude that the new components have a lower failure rate than 4%?

c. Would you recommend further testing to determine whether the new parts have a lower failure rate than 4%? Explain.

ASSESSMENT PRACTICE

22. Paula, Sasha, and Yumiko live together. They want a system to determine who will wash the dinner dishes on any given night. Select all of the methods that are fair.

Ⓐ Roll a standard number cube. If the result is 1 or 2, Paula does the dishes; if 3 or 4, Sasha; if 5 or 6, Yumiko.

Ⓑ Roll a standard number cube. If the result is 1, Paula does the dishes; if 2, Sasha; if 4, Yumiko. If the result is 3, 5, or 6, roll again.

Ⓒ Roll two standard number cubes. If the sum of the numbers that come up is less than 6, Paula washes the dishes; if the sum is 8, 9, or 12, Sasha; if the sum is 6 or 7, Yumiko. If the sum is 10 or 11, roll again.

Ⓓ Write the name of each girl on a slip of paper, place the slips in a box, mix them up, and select one at random. The person whose name is selected does the dishes.

23. SAT/ACT A fair choice among a group of students may be made by flipping three coins in sequence, and noting the sequences of heads and tails. If each student is assigned one of these sequences, how many students can be selected fairly by this method?

Ⓐ 4   Ⓑ 5   Ⓒ 6   Ⓓ 7   Ⓔ 8

24. Performance Task Acme Tire Company makes two models of steel belted radial tires, Model 1001 and Model 1002.

Model	1001
Blowouts per 200,000 tires	2
Profits before any lawsuits	$60

Model	1002
Blowouts per 200,000 tires	1
Profits before any lawsuits	$56

If one of these tires fails and the company is sued, the average settlement is $1,200,000.

Part A Find the expected profit for both models of tires after any potential lawsuits. Explain.

Part B Would you recommend that the company continue selling both models? Explain.

Topic Review

1. How can you find the probability of events and combinations of events?

Vocabulary Review

Choose the correct term to complete each sentence.

2. An arrangement of items in a specific order is called a(n) _____.

3. Two events are _____ if there is no outcome that is in both events.

4. Two events are _____ if the occurrence of one event affects the probability of the other event.

5. An arrangement of items in which order is not important is called a(n) _____.

6. The predicted average outcome of many trials in an experiment is called the _____.

- combination
- complement
- conditional probability
- dependent events
- expected value
- independent events
- mutually exclusive
- permutation
- probability distribution

Concepts & Skills Review

LESSON 10-1 **Two-Way Frequency Tables**

Quick Review

Two-way frequency tables show relationships between two sets of categorical data. **Joint frequencies** indicate the frequency of one category. **Marginal frequencies** indicate the total frequency for each category.

Example

A teacher asked her students to choose between the museum or the zoo for a class trip. The results are shown in the table. What trends do the results suggest?

	Museum	Zoo	Totals
Male	5	7	12
Female	12	6	18
Totals	17	13	30

The joint frequencies suggest that males prefer the zoo and females prefer the museum. The marginal frequencies suggest that all respondents showed a slight preference for going to the museum.

Practice & Problem Solving

In a survey, TV viewers can choose between two movies. 40 men and 10 women choose the action movie that is featured. Of the 30 people who chose the comedy, 20 are women and 10 are men.

7. Make a two-way frequency table to organize the data. Is it reasonable to say that more people surveyed prefer action movies? Explain.

8. **Construct Arguments** According to the data below, is there a significant association between age and a person's news source? Justify your answer.

Where do you get most of your news?			
Age	TV	Internet	Totals
≤ 30	50	80	130
> 30	30	40	70
Totals	80	120	200

LESSON 10-2 — Probability Events

Quick Review

Two events are **mutually exclusive** if and only if there is no outcome that lies in the sample space of both events. Two events are **independent events** if and only if the occurrence of one event does not affect the probability of a second event.

Example

Let *A* represent the event "even number," or
A = {2, 4, 6, 8}.

Let *B* represent the event "odd number," or
B = {1, 3, 5, 7}.

Let *C* represent the event "divisible by 3," or *C* = {3, 6}.

Are *A* and *B* mutually exclusive? Explain.
    Yes; all of their elements are different.

Are *A* and *C* mutually exclusive? Explain.
    No; they both have a 3 in their sample space.

Practice & Problem Solving

Ten craft sticks lettered A through J are in a coffee cup. Consider the events "consonant," "vowel," "letter before D in the alphabet," "letter after A in the alphabet," and "letter after E in the alphabet." State whether each pair of events is mutually exclusive.

9. vowel, letter before D

10. letter before D, letter after E

11. **Communicate Precisely** Edward is rolling a number cube to decide on the new combination for his bicycle lock. If he only has one number to go, find the probability of each event. Use what you know about mutually exclusive events to explain your reasoning.

   a. Edward rolls a number that is both even and less than 2. Explain.

   b. Edward rolls a number that is even or less than 2. Explain.

LESSON 10-3 — Conditional Probability

Quick Review

For any two events *A* and *B*, with $P(A) \neq 0$, $P(A \text{ and } B) = P(A) \cdot P(B \mid A)$. Events *A* and *B* are independent if and only if $P(B \mid A) = P(B)$.

Example

One of these students is selected at random for an interview. Are selecting a sophomore and selecting a member of the track team independent events?

Team Enrollment by Year

	Sophomore	Junior
Cross Country	9	6
Track	12	23

$P(\text{Soph}) = 0.42$, $P(\text{Track}) = 0.70$, and $P(\text{Track and Soph}) = 0.24$

$P(\text{Soph}|\text{Track}) = \dfrac{P(\text{Track and Soph})}{P(\text{Track})} \approx 0.34$

$P(\text{Soph}|\text{Track}) \neq P(\text{Soph})$

No, these are dependent events.

Practice & Problem Solving

Use the table in the Example for Exercises 12–14. Find each probability for a randomly-selected student.

12. *P*(Junior)

13. *P*(Cross Country)

14. *P*(Junior | Cross Country)

15. *P*(Cross Country | Junior)

16. **Error Analysis** One card is selected at random from five cards numbered 1–5. A student says that drawing an even number and drawing a prime number are dependent events because $P(\text{prime} \mid \text{even}) = 0.5$ and $P(\text{even}) = 0.4$. Describe and correct the error the student made.

17. **Use Structure** A person entered in a raffle has a 3% chance of winning a prize. A prize winner has a 25% chance of winning two theater tickets. What is the probability that a person entered in the raffle will win the theater tickets?

Permutations and Combinations

Quick Review

The number of permutations of r items from a set of n items is $_nP_r = \frac{n!}{(n-r)!}$ for $0 \le r \le n$.

The number of combinations of r items from a set of n items is $_nC_r = \frac{n!}{r!(n-r)!}$ for $0 \le r \le n$.

Example

A bag contains 4 blue tiles and 4 yellow tiles. Three tiles are drawn from the bag at random without replacement. What is the probability all three tiles are blue?

Use combinations since order does not matter. Select 3 blue from 4 blue tiles $_4C_3$, or 4, ways.

Select 0 yellow from 4 yellow tiles $_4C_0$, or 1, way. Select 3 tiles from 8 total tiles $_8C_3$, or 56, ways.

$P(3 \text{ blue}) = \frac{4 \cdot 1}{56} = \frac{1}{14} = 0.07 \approx 7\%$

Practice & Problem Solving

In Exercises 18 and 19, determine whether the situation involves finding permutations or combinations. Then find the number.

18. How many ways can a team choose a captain and a substitute captain from 8 players?

19. How many ways can 3 numbers be selected from the digits 0–9 to set a lock code if the digits cannot be repeated?

20. **Error Analysis** A student computed $_5C_2$, and said that it is equal to 20. Describe and correct the error the student made.

21. **Look for Relationships** The formulas for permutations and combinations must always evaluate to a natural number. Explain why.

Probability Distributions

Quick Review

For a binomial experiment consisting of n trials, the probability of r successes out of n trials is given by the **binomial probability** formula:

$$P(r) = {_nC_r} \cdot p^r(1-p)^{n-r}$$

Example

Curtis scores a touchdown 24% of the time he receives the ball. If Curtis receives the ball 7 times, what is the probability he scores a touchdown 4 of those times?

$$P(4 \text{ touchdowns}) = {_7C_4} \cdot 0.24^4(1-0.24)^{7-4}$$
$$= 35 \cdot 0.24^4(0.76)^3$$
$$\approx 0.051 = 5.1\%$$

Practice & Problem Solving

Rhoda finds that every seed she plants has a 56% chance to grow to full height. If she plants 10 seeds, what is the probability each number of plants grows to full height? Round to the nearest hundredth of a percent.

22. 1 plant

23. 3 plants

24. 5 plants

25. 10 plants

26. **Error Analysis** Using the Example, Akasi tried to calculate Curtis' probable success rate of 3 touchdowns if he received the ball 5 times, but could not get an answer. Find and correct her mistake.

$$P(3) = {_3C_5} \cdot 0.24^5 (1-0.24)^{3-5}$$
$$= ?$$ ✗

LESSON 10-6   Expected Value

Quick Review

The **expected value** E of a trial of an experiment is the sum of the value of each possible outcome times its probability or

$E = x_1 P(x_1) + x_2 P(x_2) + \ldots + x_n P(x_n).$

Example

The outer ring on a dartboard is worth 10 points, the middle ring is worth 25 points, and the bullseye is worth 100 points. When throwing darts, Ravi has a 45% chance of hitting the outer ring, a 40% chance of hitting the inner ring, a 5% chance of hitting the bullseye, and a 10% chance of missing the board. What is the expected value of a single dart throw?

$E = 10(0.45) + 25(0.4) + 100(0.05) + 0(0.1)$

$\quad = 4.5 + 10 + 5 + 0$

$\quad = 19.5$

Practice & Problem Solving

Use the information in the Example to find the expected value of 15 throws from each of the following people.

27. Rosa: 20% outer ring; 65% inner ring, 10% bullseye, 5% miss

28. Vicki: 60% outer ring; 20% inner ring, 12% bullseye, 8% miss

29. Higher Order Thinking A basketball player takes 2 shots from the 3-point line and misses them both. She calculates the expected value of taking a shot from the 3-point line is 0 points. Do you agree with the player's calculation? Her reasoning? How could the player improve the accuracy of her estimate?

LESSON 10-7   Probability and Decision Making

Quick Review

Combined with probability, expected value can be used to help make decisions.

Example

Frederica is playing a game tossing 20 beanbags from a choice of three lines. Frederica has a 90% chance of success from the 5-point line, a 65% chance of success from the 10-point line, and a 20% chance from the 20-point line. Frederica wants to toss every beanbag from the same line. From which line should Frederica expect to score the most points?

Find the expected points per toss, or expected value.

5-point line:
5 points • 0.90 = 4.5 points per toss

10-point line:
10 points • 0.65 = 6.5 points per toss

20-point line:
20 points • 0.20 = 4 points per toss

Frederica should toss from the 10-point line.

Practice & Problem Solving

Both situations have the same expected value. Find the missing information.

30. Situation 1: Paul hits a dart target worth 15 points 45% of the time.

    Situation 2: He hits a dart target worth 10 points x% of the time.

31. Situation 1: Lenora has a success rate of 25% when selling bracelets at $15 each.

    Situation 2: She has a success rate of 20% when selling bracelets at $$x$ each.

32. Make Sense of Problems Use the information from the Example. Frederica practices her shots and increases her chances from the 20-point line to 30%. Should she now toss the beanbag from the 20-point line? Explain your reasoning.

TOPIC 11

Coordinate Geometry

? TOPIC ESSENTIAL QUESTION

How can geometric relationships be proven by applying algebraic properties to geometric figures represented in the coordinate plane?

Topic Overview

enVision® STEM Project:
   Design a Solar Collector

11-1   Polygons in the Coordinate Plane

Mathematical Modeling in 3 Acts:
   You Be the Judge

11-2   Proofs Using Coordinate Geometry

11-3   Circles in the Coordinate Plane

11-4   Parabolas in the Coordinate Plane

Topic Vocabulary

• directrix

• focus

• parabola

Digital Experience

📖 **INTERACTIVE STUDENT EDITION**
Access online or offline.

👆 **ACTIVITIES** Complete *Explore & Reason, Model & Discuss*, and *Critique & Explain* activities. Interact with Examples and Try Its.

👁 **ANIMATION** View and interact with real-world applications.

✏️ **PRACTICE** Practice what you've learned.

 Go online | **PearsonRealize.com**

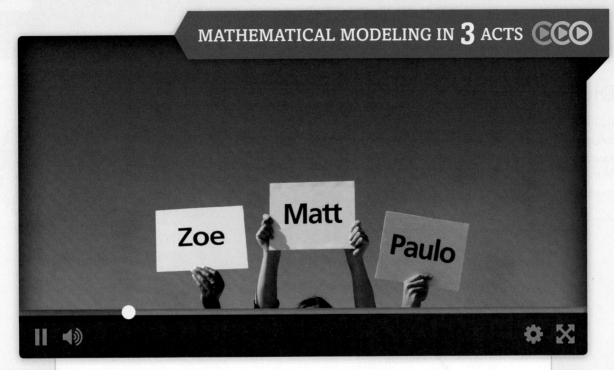

▶ You Be the Judge

Have you ever been a judge in a contest or competition? What criteria did you use to decide the winner? If you were one of many judges, did you all agree on who should win?

Often there is a set of criteria that judges use to help them score the performances of the contestants. Having criteria helps all of the judges be consistent regardless of the person they are rating. Think of this during the Mathematical Modeling in 3 Acts lesson.

TOPIC 11

VIDEOS Watch clips to support *Mathematical Modeling in 3 Acts Lessons* and **enVision®** *STEM Projects.*

CONCEPT SUMMARY Review key lesson content through multiple representations.

ASSESSMENT Show what you've learned.

GLOSSARY Read and listen to English and Spanish definitions.

TUTORIALS Get help from *Virtual Nerd*, right when you need it.

MATH TOOLS Explore math with digital tools and manipulatives.

Did You Know?

Solar reflectors are made of mirrors or pieces of glass in many shapes and sizes. **Parabolic reflectors** collect the sun's rays from a wide area and **focus them on a small area**, concentrating the energy.

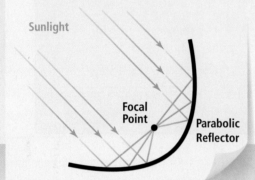

Sunlight

Focal Point

Parabolic Reflector

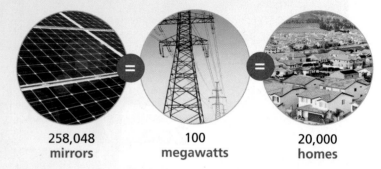

258,048 **mirrors** = 100 **megawatts** = 20,000 **homes**

The world's largest power station, the SHAMS 1 in the United Arab Emirates, uses **258,048 mirrors**. That's enough to generate **100 megawatts** of electricity per day and power **20,000 homes.**

In 2016, the United States produced more than 40 billion kilowatt-hours of **solar energy,** 40 times more than it did a decade earlier.

▶ Your Task: Design a Solar Collector

Giant solar power plants are not the only place to see parabolic trough collectors—you might find a water purifier made from a single 6 ft-x-4 ft mirror in a neighbor's back yard! You and your classmates will analyze parabolas and design a solar collector for use in your school or community.

11-1

Polygons in the Coordinate Plane

I CAN... use the coordinate plane to analyze geometric figures.

EXPLORE & REASON

Players place game pieces on the board shown and earn points from the attributes of the piece placed on the board.

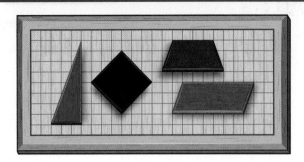

- 1 point for a right angle

- 2 points for a pair of parallel sides

- 3 points for the shortest perimeter

A. Which game piece is worth the greatest total points? Explain.

B. Make Sense and Persevere Describe a way to determine the perimeters that is different from the way you chose. Which method do you consider better? Explain.

? ESSENTIAL QUESTION   How are properties of geometric figures represented in the coordinate plane?

CONCEPTUAL UNDERSTANDING

EXAMPLE 1   Connect Algebra and Geometry Through Coordinates

What formulas can you use to identify properties of figures on the coordinate plane?

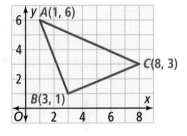

A. Which formula can you use to find AB?

Use the Distance Formula to find segment length.

$$AB = \sqrt{(3-1)^2 + (1-6)^2} = \sqrt{29}$$

B. What point bisects $\overline{AB}$?

Use the Midpoint Formula to find a segment bisector.

$$\text{midpoint of } \overline{AB} = \left(\frac{1+3}{2}, \frac{6+1}{2}\right) = \left(2, \frac{7}{2}\right)$$

> **COMMON ERROR**
> Recall that the slope of a line is the ratio of the difference in the y-coordinates to the difference in the x-coordinates. Be careful not to reverse the ratio.

C. Why do slopes of $\overline{AB}$ and $\overline{BC}$ show that $m\angle ABC = 90°$?

Use the slopes of the two segments to show that they are perpendicular.

$$\text{slope of } \overline{AB} = \frac{1-6}{3-1} = -\frac{5}{2}$$

$$\text{slope of } \overline{BC} = \frac{3-1}{8-3} = \frac{2}{5}$$

The product of the slopes is −1. So $\overline{AB} \perp \overline{BC}$, and $m\angle ABC = 90°$.

 Try It!   **1.** Given $\triangle ABC$ in Example 1, what is the length of the line segment connecting the midpoints of $\overline{AC}$ and $\overline{BC}$?

👆 **EXAMPLE 2** **Classify a Triangle on the Coordinate Plane**

A. Is △XYZ equilateral, isosceles, or scalene?

Find the length of each side.

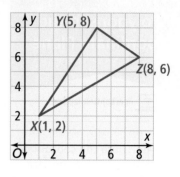

$$XY = \sqrt{(5-1)^2 + (8-2)^2} = \sqrt{52}$$

$$YZ = \sqrt{(8-5)^2 + (6-8)^2} = \sqrt{13}$$

$$XZ = \sqrt{(8-1)^2 + (6-2)^2} = \sqrt{65}$$

No two sides are congruent. The triangle is scalene.

B. Is △XYZ a right triangle?

If △XYZ is a right triangle, then $\overline{XZ}$ is the hypotenuse because it is the longest side, and XY, YZ, and XZ satisfy the Pythagorean Theorem.

$$\left(\sqrt{52}\right)^2 + \left(\sqrt{13}\right)^2 \overset{?}{=} \left(\sqrt{65}\right)^2$$

$$65 = 65 \checkmark$$

Triangle XYZ is a right triangle.

☑ **Try It!** **2.** The vertices of △PQR are P(4, 1), Q(2, 7), and R(8, 5).

a. Is △PQR equilateral, isosceles, or scalene? Explain.

b. Is △PQR a right triangle? Explain.

👆 **EXAMPLE 3** **Classify a Parallelogram on the Coordinate Plane**

What type of parallelogram is RSTU?

Determine whether RSTU is a rhombus, a rectangle, or a square. First calculate ST and SR:

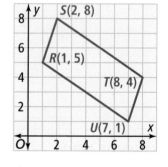

$$ST = \sqrt{(2-8)^2 + (8-4)^2} = \sqrt{52}$$

$$RS = \sqrt{(2-1)^2 + (8-5)^2} = \sqrt{10}$$

Since not all side lengths are equal, RSTU is not a rhombus or a square.

Check for right angles by finding the slopes.

$$\text{slope of } \overline{ST} = \frac{4-8}{8-2} = -\frac{2}{3}$$

$$\text{slope of } \overline{RS} = \frac{8-5}{2-1} = 3$$

The product of the slopes is not −1, so $\overline{ST}$ and $\overline{RS}$ are not perpendicular. At least one angle is not a right angle, and RSTU is not a rectangle. Therefore, quadrilateral RSTU is a parallelogram that is neither a square, nor a rhombus, nor a rectangle.

MAKE SENSE AND PERSEVERE
Consider other formulas you use on the coordinate plane. What are some ways to show that a quadrilateral is not a rectangle or a rhombus?

☑ **Try It!** **3.** The vertices of a parallelogram are A(−2, 2), B(4, 6), C(6, 3), and D(0, −1).

a. Is ABCD a rhombus? Explain.

b. Is ABCD a rectangle? Explain.

Classify Quadrilaterals as Trapezoids and Kites on the Coordinate Plane

A. Is *ABCD* a trapezoid?

A trapezoid has exactly one pair of parallel sides. Use the slope formula to determine if only one pair of opposite sides is parallel.

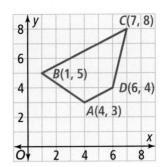

slope of $\overline{AB} = \frac{5-3}{1-4} = -\frac{2}{3}$

slope of $\overline{BC} = \frac{8-5}{7-1} = \frac{1}{2}$

slope of $\overline{CD} = \frac{4-8}{6-7} = \frac{4}{1}$

slope of $\overline{AD} = \frac{4-3}{6-4} = \frac{1}{2}$

Since only the slopes of $\overline{BC}$ and $\overline{AD}$ are equal, $\overline{BC} \parallel \overline{AD}$, and only one pair of opposite sides is parallel. Therefore, quadrilateral *ABCD* is a trapezoid.

COMMUNICATE PRECISELY
Think about the properties of a trapezoid. Why do you need to find the slopes for all four sides?

B. Is *JKLM* a kite?

A kite has two pairs of consecutive congruent sides and no opposite sides congruent. Use the Distance Formula to find the lengths of the sides.

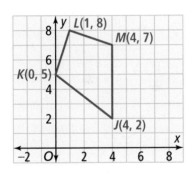

$JK = \sqrt{(0-4)^2 + (5-2)^2} = 5$

$KL = \sqrt{(1-0)^2 + (8-5)^2} = \sqrt{10}$

$LM = \sqrt{(4-1)^2 + (7-8)^2} = \sqrt{10}$

$MJ = \sqrt{(4-4)^2 + (2-7)^2} = 5$

Consecutive pair $\overline{KL}$ and $\overline{LM}$ and consecutive pair $\overline{JK}$ and $\overline{MJ}$ are congruent. No opposite pair is congruent, so *JKLM* is a kite.

✓ **Try It!** 4. Is each quadrilateral a kite, trapezoid, or neither?

a.
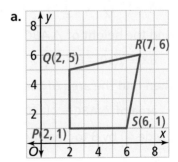

b.
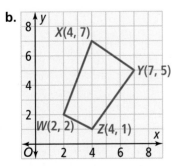

APPLICATION ☞ **EXAMPLE 5** Find Perimeter and Area

Dylan draws up a plan to fence in a yard for his chickens. The distance between grid lines is 1 foot.

A. Is 30 feet of fencing enough to enclose the yard?

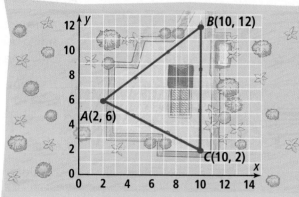

Find the lengths of the sides.

$$AB = \sqrt{(2 - 10)^2 + (6 - 12)^2} = 10 \text{ ft}$$

$$BC = \sqrt{(10 - 10)^2 + (12 - 2)^2} = 10 \text{ ft}$$

$$AC = \sqrt{(2 - 10)^2 + (6 - 2)^2} = \sqrt{80} \text{ ft}$$

Find the perimeter of the yard.

$$P = 10 + 10 + \sqrt{80}$$

$$\approx 28.9 \text{ ft}$$

The perimeter is about 28.9 feet, which is less than 30 feet. Dylan has enough fencing material.

B. **For a healthy flock, each chicken needs at least 8 square feet of space. What is the maximum number of chickens Dylan can put in the yard?**

CONSTRUCT ARGUMENTS
Consider the properties of an isosceles triangle. What property of an isosceles triangle justifies that $\overline{BX}$ is a height of the triangle?

The yard is an isosceles triangle. To find the area, you need the height of the triangle. The height of $\triangle ABC$ is BX, where X is the midpoint of $\overline{AC}$.

Find the midpoint of $\overline{AC}$.

$$X = \left(\frac{2 + 10}{2}, \frac{6 + 2}{2}\right) = (6, 4)$$

Find the height of $\triangle ABC$.

$$BX = \sqrt{(10 - 6)^2 + (12 - 4)^2} = \sqrt{80} \text{ ft}$$

Then find the area of the yard.

$$\text{area of } \triangle ABC = \frac{1}{2}(\sqrt{80})(\sqrt{80}) = 40 \text{ ft}^2$$

Divide 40 by 8 to find the number of chickens.

$$40 \div 8 = 5$$

Dylan can keep as many as 5 chickens in the yard.

 Try It! 5. The vertices of WXYZ are W(5, 4), X(2, 9), Y(9, 9), and Z(8, 4).

a. What is the perimeter of WXYZ?

b. What is the area of WXYZ?

CONCEPT SUMMARY Connecting Algebra and Geometry

You can use algebra to determine properties of and to classify geometric figures on the coordinate plane.

WORDS

Use the Distance Formula to find the lengths of segments to classify figures.

Use the Slope Formula to determine whether two lines or segments are parallel or perpendicular.

Use the Midpoint Formula to determine if a point bisects a segment.

GRAPH

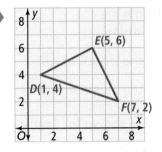

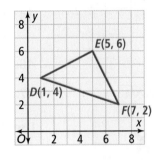

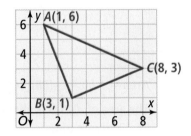

NUMBERS

$DE = \sqrt{(5-1)^2 + (6-4)^2}$

$= \sqrt{20}$

slope of $\overline{DE} = \dfrac{6-4}{5-1}$

$= \dfrac{1}{2}$

midpoint of $\overline{DF}$

$= \left(\dfrac{1+7}{2}, \dfrac{4+2}{2}\right) = (4, 3)$

✓ Do You UNDERSTAND?

1. **ESSENTIAL QUESTION** How are properties of geometric figures represented in the coordinate plane?

2. **Error Analysis** Chen is asked to describe two methods to find BC. Why is Chen incorrect?

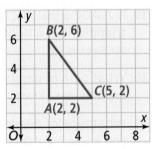

The only possible method is to use the Distance Formula because you only know the endpoints of $\overline{BC}$.

3. **Communicate Precisely** Describe three ways you can determine whether a quadrilateral is a parallelogram given the coordinates of the vertices.

Do You KNOW HOW?

Use *JKLM* for Exercises 4–6.

4. What is the perimeter of *JKLM*?

5. What is the relationship between $\overline{JL}$ and $\overline{KM}$? Explain.

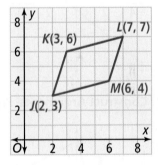

6. What type of quadrilateral is *JKLM*? Explain.

Use △*PQR* for Exercises 7 and 8.

7. What kind of triangle is *PQR*? Explain.

8. What is the area of *PQR*?

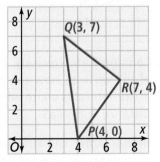

PRACTICE & PROBLEM SOLVING

UNDERSTAND

9. Error Analysis What error did Kelley make in finding the area of △PQR?

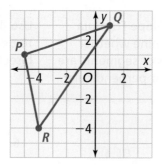

Area $= \frac{1}{2}bh = \frac{1}{2}(PR)(PQ) = \frac{1}{2}\sqrt{26}\sqrt{40}$

The area of △PQR is about 16.12 square units. ✗

10. Mathematical Connections Find the equation of the line that passes through point R and is perpendicular to line m.

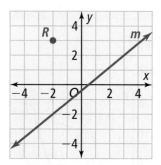

11. Construct Arguments Prove △ABC ≅ △DEF.

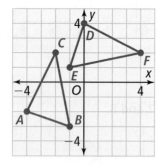

12. Communicate Precisely Given the coordinates of the vertices, how can you show that a quadrilateral is a kite without using the Distance Formula?

13. Higher Order Thinking Let line p be the perpendicular bisector of $\overline{AB}$ that has endpoints and $A(x_1, y_1)$ and $B(x_2, y_2)$. Describe the process for writing a general equation in slope-intercept form for line p.

PRACTICE

Use the figure shown for Exercises 14–17.
SEE EXAMPLE 1

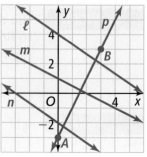

14. Which lines are parallel?

15. Which lines are perpendicular?

16. What is the length of $\overline{AB}$?

17. What is the midpoint of $\overline{AB}$?

Use the figure shown for Exercises 18–23.

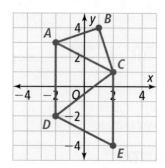

18. Is △ABC a scalene, isosceles, or equilateral triangle? Is it a right triangle? Explain.
SEE EXAMPLE 2

19. Is △ADC a scalene, isosceles, or equilateral triangle? Is it a right triangle? Explain.
SEE EXAMPLE 2

20. What type of parallelogram is ACED? Explain. SEE EXAMPLE 3

21. What type of quadrilateral is ABCD? How do you know? SEE EXAMPLE 4

22. Find the area and perimeter of △ABC.
SEE EXAMPLE 5

23. Find the area and perimeter of ABCD.
SEE EXAMPLE 6

Three vertices of a quadrilateral are P(−2, 3), Q(2, 4), and R(1, 0). SEE EXAMPLE 3

24. Suppose PQRS is a parallelogram. What are the coordinates of vertex S? What type of parallelogram is PQRS?

25. Suppose PQSR is a parallelogram. What are the coordinates of vertex S? What type of parallelogram is PQSR?

APPLY

26. Use Appropriate Tools An architect overlays a coordinate grid on her plans for attaching a greenhouse to the side of a house. She wants to locate point D so that $ABCD$ is a trapezoid and $\overline{CD}$ is perpendicular to the house. What are the coordinates for point D?

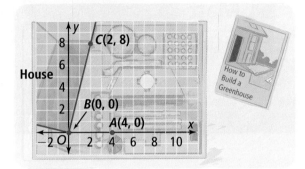

27. Model With Mathematics Yuson thinks the design she made is symmetric across the dashed line she drew. How can she use coordinates to show that her design is symmetric?

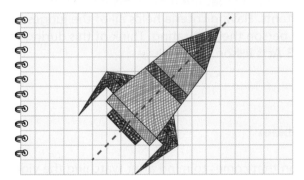

28. Construct Arguments The map shows the regions that Anna and Richard have explored. Each claims to have explored the greater area. Who is correct? Explain.

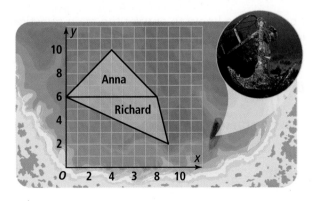

ASSESSMENT PRACTICE

29. Triangle ABC has vertices $A(2, 5)$, $B(6, 8)$, and $C(5, 1)$. Determine whether each statement about $\triangle ABC$ is true. Select *Yes* or *No*.

	Yes	No
$\overline{AB} \cong \overline{AC}$	❑	❑
$BC = AB\sqrt{2}$	❑	❑
The midpoint of BC is $(5.5, 4)$.	❑	❑
The perimeter is 12.5 units.	❑	❑

30. SAT/ACT Quadrilateral $JKLM$ has vertices $J(1, -2)$, $K(7, 1)$, $L(8, -1)$, and $M(2, -4)$. Which is the most precise classification of $JKLM$?

Ⓐ rectangle

Ⓑ rhombus

Ⓒ trapezoid

Ⓓ kite

31. Performance Task Dana draws the side view of a TV stand that has slanted legs. Each unit in his plan equals half of a foot.

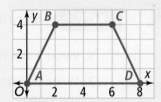

Part A Dana thinks his TV stand is in the shape of isosceles trapezoid. Is he correct? Explain.

Part B Dana adds an additional support by connecting the midpoints of the legs. How long is the support?

Part C Dana decides he wants to make the TV stand a half foot higher by placing B at $(2, 5)$ and C at $(6, 5)$. How much longer will the legs and support connecting the midpoints be?

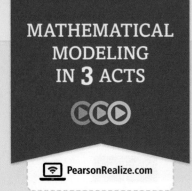

MATHEMATICAL MODELING IN **3** ACTS

💻 ⊡ ▶ Video

▶ You Be the Judge

Have you ever been a judge in a contest or competition? What criteria did you use to decide the winner? If you were one of many judges, did you all agree on who should win?

Often there is a set of criteria that judges use to help them score the performances of the contestants. Having criteria helps all of the judges be consistent regardless of the person they are rating. Think of this during the Mathematical Modeling in 3 Acts lesson.

Scan for Multimedia

ACT 1 ▸ Identify the Problem

1. What is the first question that comes to mind after watching the video?

2. Write down the main question you will answer about what you saw in the video.

3. Make an initial conjecture that answers this main question.

4. Explain how you arrived at your conjecture.

5. What information will be useful to know to answer the main question? How can you get it? How will you use that information?

ACT 2 ▸ Develop a Model

6. Use the math that you have learned in this Topic to refine your conjecture.

ACT 3 ▸ Interpret the Results

7. Did your refined conjecture match the actual answer exactly? If not, what might explain the difference?

11-2

Proofs Using Coordinate Geometry

I CAN... prove geometric theorems using algebra and the coordinate plane.

CRITIQUE & EXPLAIN

Dakota and Jung are trying to show that $\triangle ABC$ is a right triangle. Each student uses a different method.

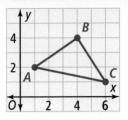

Dakota

slope of $\overline{AB} = \frac{2}{3}$, slope of $\overline{BC} = -\frac{3}{2}$

slope of $\overline{AB}$ • slope of $\overline{BC} = -1$

Triangle ABC is a right triangle.

Jung

$AB = BC = \sqrt{13}, AC = \sqrt{26}$

$(\sqrt{13})^2 + (\sqrt{13})^2 = (\sqrt{26})^2$

Triangle ABC is a right triangle.

A. Did Dakota and Jung both show $\triangle ABC$ is a right triangle? Explain.

B. Reason If the coordinates of $\triangle ABC$ were changed to (2, 3), (5, 5), and (7, 2), how would each student's method change? Explain.

 ESSENTIAL QUESTION How can geometric relationships be proven algebraically in the coordinate plane?

CONCEPTUAL UNDERSTANDING

EXAMPLE 1 Plan a Coordinate Proof

How can you use coordinates to prove geometric relationships algebraically? Plan a proof for the Trapezoid Midsegment Theorem.

Draw and label a diagram that names all points to be used in the proof.

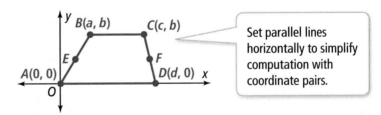

Set parallel lines horizontally to simplify computation with coordinate pairs.

Restate the Trapezoid Midsegment Theorem so the statement can be proved using algebra on the coordinate plane.

Theorem: The midsegment of a trapezoid is parallel to each base and its length is one half the sum of the lengths of the bases.

USE STRUCTURE
Variables are used according to the properties of trapezoids. Why is the proof valid for all trapezoids?

Restatement: If $\overline{EF}$ is the midsegment of trapezoid $ABCD$, then slope $\overline{EF}$ = slope $\overline{AD}$ = slope $\overline{BC}$ and $EF = \frac{AD + BC}{2}$.

Plan: To show that the midsegment is parallel to the bases, show that their slopes are equal. Then show that the mean of the base lengths is the length of the midsegment.

✓ **Try It!** **1.** Plan a proof to show that the diagonals of a square are congruent and perpendicular.

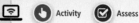

PROOF → **EXAMPLE 2** **Write a Coordinate Proof**

Write a coordinate proof of the Trapezoid Midsegment Theorem. Use the conditional statement from Example 1 to decide what is given and what is to be proved.

Given: Trapezoid $ABCD$, with midpoints E and F

Prove: $\overline{EF} \parallel \overline{AD} \parallel \overline{BC}$ and $EF = \dfrac{AD + BC}{2}$

Plan: Apply the plan and diagram from Example 1. Use the coordinates in the diagram to show that slope $\overline{EF}$ = slope $\overline{AD}$ = slope $\overline{BC}$, and $EF = \dfrac{AD + BC}{2}$.

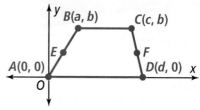

Proof:

Step 1 Use the Midpoint Formula to find the coordinates of points E and F.

$$E = \left(\frac{0 + a}{2}, \frac{0 + b}{2}\right) \qquad F = \left(\frac{c + d}{2}, \frac{b + 0}{2}\right)$$
$$= \left(\frac{a}{2}, \frac{b}{2}\right) \qquad\qquad = \left(\frac{c + d}{2}, \frac{b}{2}\right)$$

Step 2 The slopes of $\overline{AD}$, $\overline{BC}$, and $\overline{EF}$ all equal zero, because the segments are horizontal.

Therefore, $\overline{EF} \parallel \overline{AD} \parallel \overline{BC}$.

Step 3 Determine AD, BC, and EF.

Since the segments are horizontal lines, the lengths are differences of the x-coordinates.

$$AD = d - 0 \qquad BC = c - a \qquad EF = \frac{c + d}{2} - \frac{a}{2}$$
$$= d \qquad\qquad\qquad\qquad\qquad = \frac{c + d - a}{2}$$

Step 4 Use algebra to show that $\dfrac{AD + BC}{2} = EF$.

$$\frac{AD + BC}{2} = \frac{d + (c - a)}{2} = \frac{c + d - a}{2} = EF$$

The bases and the midsegment are parallel, and the length of the midsegment is equal to the mean of the base lengths.

Therefore, $\overline{EF} \parallel \overline{AD} \parallel \overline{BC}$ and $EF = \dfrac{AD + BC}{2}$.

☑ **Try It!** 2. Use coordinate geometry to prove that the diagonals of a rectangle are congruent.

PROOF   **EXAMPLE 3** Plan and Write a Coordinate Proof

Write a coordinate proof of the Concurrency of Medians Theorem.

Given: $\triangle ABC$ with medians $\overline{AD}$, $\overline{BE}$, and $\overline{CF}$

Prove: The medians are concurrent at point P such that

$$AP = \tfrac{2}{3}AD, \ BP = \tfrac{2}{3}BE, \text{ and } CP = \tfrac{2}{3}CF.$$

Plan: Draw and label a triangle in the coordinate plane. Then use the Midpoint Formula to locate the midpoints. Draw two medians and locate the point of intersection P. Use algebra to determine that the medians are concurrent at P. Finally, find the distance from P to each vertex.

Proof: Draw the triangle with the coordinates shown.

Find the coordinates of D, E, and F using the Midpoint Formula.

$$D = (a + c, b) \qquad E = (c, 0) \qquad F = (a, b)$$

Then find the slopes of the lines containing the medians $\overline{AD}$ and $\overline{CF}$.

slope of $\overline{AD} = \dfrac{b - 0}{a + c - 0} = \dfrac{b}{a + c}$ slope of $\overline{CF} = \dfrac{b - 0}{a - 2c} = \dfrac{b}{a - 2c}$

Write equations for $\overleftrightarrow{AD}$ and $\overleftrightarrow{CF}$ using point-slope form.

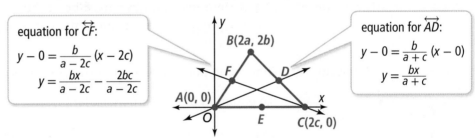

equation for $\overleftrightarrow{CF}$:

$$y - 0 = \dfrac{b}{a - 2c}(x - 2c)$$

$$y = \dfrac{bx}{a - 2c} - \dfrac{2bc}{a - 2c}$$

equation for $\overleftrightarrow{AD}$:

$$y - 0 = \dfrac{b}{a + c}(x - 0)$$

$$y = \dfrac{bx}{a + c}$$

Set the expressions for y equal to each other. Solve for x to get $x = \dfrac{2(a + c)}{3}$.

Then substitute the expression for x into $y = \dfrac{bx}{a + c}$ to get $y = \dfrac{2b}{3}$.

Let point P be $\left(\dfrac{2(a + c)}{3}, \dfrac{2b}{3}\right)$.

To show that point P is on $\overline{BE}$, find an equation for the line containing $\overline{BE}$. Start by finding the slope of $\overline{BE}$.

$$\text{slope of } \overline{BE} = \dfrac{0 - 2b}{c - 2a} = -\dfrac{2b}{c - 2a}$$

Then, using point-slope form, an equation for $\overleftrightarrow{BE}$ is $y = -\dfrac{2bx}{c - 2a} + \dfrac{2bc}{c - 2a}$.

Substituting $\dfrac{2(a + c)}{3}$ for x into the equation results in $y = \dfrac{2b}{3}$, so point P is on $\overline{BE}$. The three medians are concurrent at P.

To complete the proof in the Try It, use the Distance Formula to show that $AP = \tfrac{2}{3}AD$, $BP = \tfrac{2}{3}BE$, and $CP = \tfrac{2}{3}CF$.

CONTINUED ON THE NEXT PAGE

EXAMPLE 3 CONTINUED

 Try It! **3.** To complete the proof in Example 3, use the coordinates to show that $AP = \frac{2}{3}AD$, $BP = \frac{2}{3}BE$, and $CP = \frac{2}{3}CF$.

APPLICATION **EXAMPLE 4** **Use Coordinate Proofs to Solve Problems**

An interior designer wants the center of a circular fountain to be equidistant from the corners of a triangular lobby. Where should he place the center of the fountain?

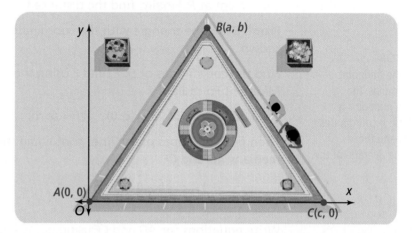

Formulate ◄ The center of the fountain must be at the circumcenter of the triangle. Find the point of intersection of the perpendicular bisectors of two sides of the triangle.

Compute ◄ Determine the intersection of the perpendicular bisectors of $\overline{AC}$ and $\overline{AB}$.

An equation of the perpendicular bisector of $\overline{AC}$ is $x = \frac{c}{2}$.

The perpendicular bisector of $\overline{AB}$ contains the point $\left(\frac{a}{2}, \frac{b}{2}\right)$ and has slope $-\frac{a}{b}$. Its point-slope equation is $y - \frac{b}{2} = -\frac{a}{b}\left(x - \frac{a}{2}\right)$, which simplifies to $y = -\frac{a}{b}x + \frac{a^2 + b^2}{2b}$.

Calculate the intersection of the two lines.

$$y = -\frac{a}{b}x + \frac{a^2 + b^2}{2b}$$

$$y = -\frac{a}{b} \cdot \frac{c}{2} + \frac{a^2 + b^2}{2b}$$

$$y = \frac{a^2 - ac + b^2}{2b}$$

> Substitute $\frac{c}{2}$ for x, and then solve for y.

Interpret ◄ The center of the fountain should be at the point $\left(\frac{c}{2}, \frac{a^2 - ac + b^2}{2b}\right)$.

 Try It! **4.** A table has a top that is a right triangle and a single support leg. Where should the center of the leg be placed so it corresponds with the center of gravity of the table top? Plan a coordinate geometry proof to find its location.

CONCEPT SUMMARY Writing a Coordinate Proof

WORDS
- Determine which numerical relationships you must calculate to show the statement is true.
- Draw and label a figure on a coordinate plane. Choose coordinates that simplify computations.
- Calculate the numerical values needed to prove a statement or solve a problem.

DIAGRAMS

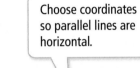
Choose coordinates so parallel lines are horizontal.

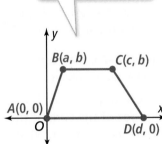

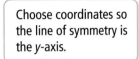
Choose coordinates so the line of symmetry is the y-axis.

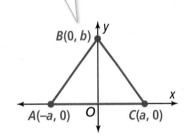

Choose coordinates so the coordinates of midpoints are convenient.

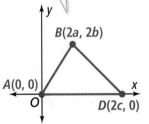

 Do You UNDERSTAND?

1. **ESSENTIAL QUESTION** How can geometric relationships be proven algebraically in the coordinate plane?

2. **Error Analysis** Venetta tried to find the slope of $\overline{AB}$. What is her error?

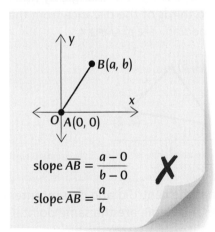

slope $\overline{AB} = \dfrac{a-0}{b-0}$ ✗

slope $\overline{AB} = \dfrac{a}{b}$

3. **Communicate Precisely** What is a coordinate geometry proof?

4. **Reason** Describe why it is important to plan a coordinate proof.

5. **Use Structure** What coordinates would you use to describe an isosceles triangle on a coordinate plane? Explain.

Do You KNOW HOW?

For Exercises 6–8, write a plan for a coordinate proof.

6. The diagonals of a rhombus are perpendicular.

7. The area of a triangle with vertices $A(0, 0)$, $B(0, a)$ and $C(b, c)$ is $\frac{ab}{2}$.

8. The lines that contain the altitudes of a triangle are concurrent.

For Exercises 9–12, plan and write a coordinate proof.

9. A point on the perpendicular bisector of a segment is equidistant from the endpoints.

10. The diagonals of a kite are perpendicular.

11. All squares are similar.

12. The area of a rhombus is half the product of the lengths of its diagonals.

Scan for Multimedia

Practice   Tutorial

Additional Exercises Available Online

UNDERSTAND

13. **Communicate Precisely** What coordinates would you use to describe an equilateral triangle in the coordinate plane? Explain.

14. **Error Analysis** Tonya drew a diagram to prove the Perpendicular Bisector Theorem using coordinate geometry. What coordinates should she use for point C?

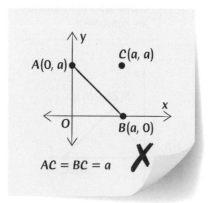

$AC = BC = a$ ✗

For Exercises 15 and 16, use the graph.

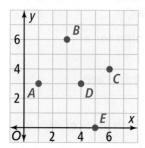

15. **Make Sense and Persevere** How would you plan a proof to show that $\triangle ABC$ is a right triangle?

16. **Make Sense and Persevere** Describe how you would prove points B, D, and E are collinear.

17. **Mathematical Connections** What is the equation of the line containing the perpendicular bisector of $\overline{AB}$?

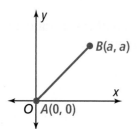

PRACTICE

For Exercises 18–21, write a plan for a coordinate proof. SEE EXAMPLE 1

18. The diagonals of a parallelogram that is not a rectangle are not congruent.

19. The length of a diameter of a circle is twice that of its radius.

20. The diagonals of a parallelogram bisect each other.

21. The area of $\triangle XYZ$ is twice the area of $\triangle XWZ$, where W is the midpoint of $\overline{YZ}$.

For Exercises 22–25, plan and write a coordinate proof. SEE EXAMPLES 2 AND 3

22. The length of a diagonal of a rectangle is the square root of the sum of the squares of the lengths of two adjacent sides.

23. All right triangles with one acute angle measuring $30°$ are similar.

24. One and only one diagonal of a kite bisects the other.

25. The length of the median to the hypotenuse of a right triangle is half the length of the hypotenuse.

26. Find the centroid of the triangle by finding the point two thirds of the distance from the vertex on one median. SEE EXAMPLE 4

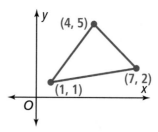

27. Show that the centroid and circumcenter of an equilateral triangle are the same point.

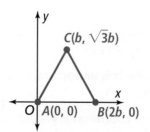

Go Online | PearsonRealize.com

APPLY

28. Model With Mathematics Each student in a woodworking class inlays brass wire along the lines connecting the midpoints of adjacent sides of a trivet. A trivet is six square inches. If the wire costs $0.54 per inch, what is the cost of the wire for making 12 trivets?

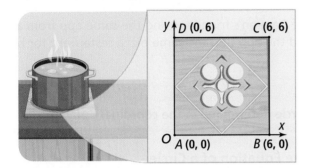

29. Make Sense and Persevere The owner of an animal park wants a quadrilateral trail that connects the four sides of the iscosceles-trapezoid-shaped park, with all sides of the trail the same length. Deon says that if the trail connects the midpoint of each side to the midpoints of the adjacent sides, the trail will be a rhombus. Write a coordinate proof to show that Deon is correct.

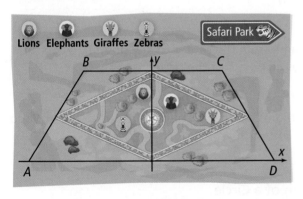

30. Higher Order Thinking The front of a sculpture is symmetric about the y-axis. Point A is located at $(-3, 0)$, and $\overline{AC}$ is the longest side of $\triangle ABC$. The perimeter of $\triangle ABC$ is 16. What is the value of a?

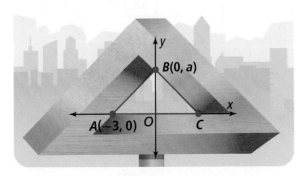

ASSESSMENT PRACTICE

31. A coordinate proof requires a ___?___ and then uses ___?___ on the ___?___ of the points in the diagram to complete the proof.

32. SAT/ACT Which statements are true?

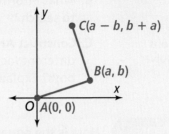

I. $AB = BC$

II. $\overline{AB} \perp \overline{BC}$

III. $AC = 2a^2 + 2b^2$

Ⓐ I only

Ⓒ I and II only

Ⓑ II only

Ⓓ I, II, and III

33. Performance Task Consider $\triangle ABC$ on the coordinate plane. Points D, E, and F are the midpoints of the sides.

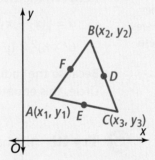

Part A What are the coordinates of D, E, and F?

Part B Prove that the coordinates of the point of concurrency of the medians is the average of the x and y coordinates of the vertices.

$$\left(\frac{x_1 + x_2 + x_3}{3}, \frac{y_1 + y_2 + y_3}{3} \right)$$

Hint: Apply the Concurrency of Medians Theorem and find the point $\frac{2}{3}$ of the way from A to D.

Part C Explain why it does not make sense to place one of the coordinates at the origin for this proof.

11-3

Circles in the Coordinate Plane

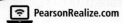 **PearsonRealize.com**

I CAN... use the equations and graphs of circles to solve problems.

MODEL & DISCUSS

Damian uses an app to find all pizza restaurants within a certain distance of his current location.

A. What is the shape of the region that the app uses to search for pizza restaurants? Explain how you know.

B. What information do you think the app needs to determine the area to search?

C. Construct Arguments If Damian's friend is using the same app from a different location, could the app find the same pizza restaurant for both boys? Explain.

? ESSENTIAL QUESTION

How is the equation of a circle determined in the coordinate plane?

CONCEPTUAL UNDERSTANDING

EXAMPLE 1   Derive the Equation of a Circle

What equation defines a circle in the coordinate plane?

Draw a circle with point (h, k) as the center of the circle. Then select any point (x, y) on the circle.

> Use variables that can apply to any circle on the coordinate plane.

Use the Distance Formula to find the distance r between the two points.

$$d = \sqrt{(x_2 - x_1)^2 + (y_2 - y_1)^2}$$

$$(x - h)^2 + (y - k)^2 = r^2$$

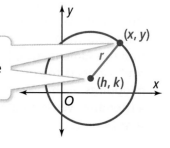

GENERALIZE
What other formula or formulas compares the sum of two squares to a third square? How do these formulas relate?

Because the radius is the same from the center to any point (x, y) on the circle, this equation satisfies all points of the circle.

✓ Try It!

1. What are the radius and center of the circle with the equation $(x - 2)^2 + (y - 3)^2 = 25$?

THEOREM 11-1 Equation of a Circle

An equation of a circle with center (h, k) and radius r is
$(x - h)^2 + (y - k)^2 = r^2$.

If...

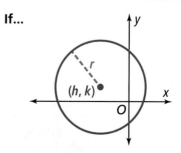

Then... $(x - h)^2 + (y - k)^2 = r^2$

PROOF: SEE EXERCISE 13.

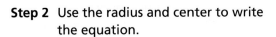
EXAMPLE 2 **Write the Equation of a Circle**

What is the equation for ⊙A?

The notation ⊙A means a circle with center at point A.

Step 1 Find the radius r.

The radius is the distance from P to A.

$$r = \sqrt{(-1 - 1)^2 + (2 - 5)^2} = \sqrt{13}$$

The radius of the circle is $\sqrt{13}$.

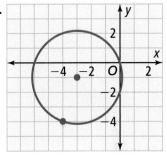

Step 2 Use the radius and center to write the equation.

$$(x - h)^2 + (y - k)^2 = r^2$$ ⟵ Use the equation of a circle.

$$(x - (-1))^2 + (y - 2)^2 = (\sqrt{13})^2$$

$$(x + 1)^2 + (y - 2)^2 = 13$$ ⟵ Substitute values for h, k, and r.

The equation for ⊙A is $(x + 1)^2 + (y - 2)^2 = 13$.

COMMON ERROR
Be careful with the signs of coordinates. Coordinates of the center are subtracted, so if a coordinate is negative, the expression will convert to addition.

✓ **Try It!** **2.** What is the equation for each circle?

a.

b.

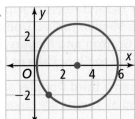

EXAMPLE 3 **Determine Whether a Point Lies on a Circle**

Circle Q has radius 7 and is centered at the origin. Does the point $(-3\sqrt{2}, 5)$ lie on ⊙Q?

Step 1 Write the equation for ⊙Q.

$$(x - h)^2 + (y - k)^2 = r^2$$

$$(x - 0)^2 + (y - 0)^2 = 7^2$$

$$x^2 + y^2 = 49$$

Step 2 Test the point $(-3\sqrt{2}, 5)$ in the equation.

$$(-3\sqrt{2})^2 + 5^2 \stackrel{?}{=} 49$$

$$18 + 25 \stackrel{?}{=} 49$$

$$43 \neq 49$$

STUDY TIP
Remember that to square an expression $a\sqrt{b}$, you square both factors: $(a\sqrt{b})^2 = a^2(\sqrt{b})^2$.

The point $(-3\sqrt{2}, 5)$ does not lie on ⊙Q.

 Try It! **3.** Determine whether each point lies on the given circle.

a. $(-3, \sqrt{11})$; circle with center at the origin and radius $2\sqrt{5}$

b. $(6, 3)$; circle with center at $(2, 4)$ and radius $3\sqrt{3}$

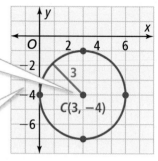
EXAMPLE 4   **Graph a Circle from Its Equation**

What is the graph of $(x - 3)^2 + (y + 4)^2 = 9$?

Write the equation in the form $(x - h)^2 + (y - k)^2 = r^2$ to identify the center and radius.

$(x - 3)^2 + (y - (-4))^2 = 3^2$

center $(h, k) = (3, -4)$

radius $r = 3$

> Plot the point $(3, -4)$.

> Plot points 3 units above, below, left, and right of the center. Use the points as a guide to draw the circle.

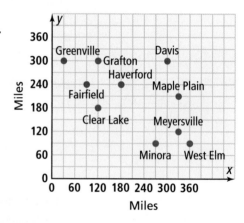

Try It!   **4.** What is the graph of each circle?

   a. $(x + 2)^2 + y^2 = 25$ **b.** $(x + 1)^2 + (y - 2)^2 = 1$

APPLICATION

EXAMPLE 5   **Use the Graph and Equation of a Circle to Solve Problems**

Doppler radar detects precipitation within a 90-mile radius. Doppler radar gear in Grafton and Meyersville does not extend to Clear Lake or Davis.

Where can a third Doppler station be placed so all towns are covered?

Draw circles with a 90-mile radius with centers at Grafton and Meyersville.

REASON
Think about the parts of the equation for a circle. How could you write an inequality to determine whether a point is within a circle?

A circle with a 90-mile radius has a diameter of 180 miles, so 180 miles is the farthest distance between two locations covered by the same radar.

Use the Distance Formula to find the distance between Clear Lake and Davis.

$$\sqrt{(300 - 180)^2 + (300 - 120)^2} \approx 216$$

The towns are more than 180 miles apart. Adding one more Doppler radar will not cover all the towns.

Try It!   **5.** If one or both of the existing radar stations could be moved to another town, would three radar stations be sufficient to cover all the towns? Explain.

CONCEPT SUMMARY Equations and Graphs of Circles

WORDS A circle is the set of points equidistant from a fixed point. The fixed point is the center.

ALGEBRA $(x - h)^2 + (y - k)^2 = r^2$ where (h, k) is the center and r is the radius.

GRAPH

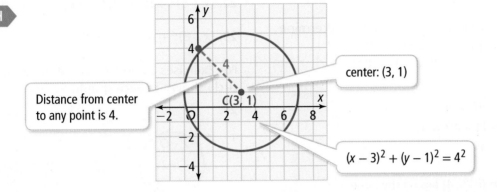

Distance from center to any point is 4.

center: (3, 1)

$(x - 3)^2 + (y - 1)^2 = 4^2$

✓ Do You UNDERSTAND?

1. **ESSENTIAL QUESTION** How is the equation of a circle determined in the coordinate plane?

2. **Error Analysis** Leo says that the equation for the circle is $(x - 1)^2 + (y - 2)^2 = 3$. What is his error?

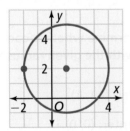

3. **Construct Arguments** If you are given the coordinates of the center and one point on a circle, can you determine the equation of the circle? Explain.

4. **Make Sense and Persevere** How could you write the equation of a circle given only the coordinates of the endpoints of its diameter?

Do You KNOW HOW?

5. What are the center and radius of the circle with equation $(x - 4)^2 + (y - 9)^2 = 1$?

6. What is the equation for the circle with center (6, 2) and radius 8?

7. What are the center and radius of the circle with equation $(x + 7)^2 + (y - 1)^2 = 9$?

8. What is the equation for the circle with center (−9, 5) and radius 4?

For Exercises 9 and 10, write an equation for each circle shown.

9.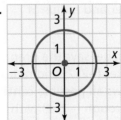

10.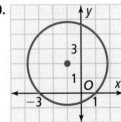

11. Is point (5, −2) on the circle with radius 5 and center (8, 2)?

12. What is the equation for the circle with center (5, 11) that passes through (9, −2)?

Scan for
Multimedia

Practice | Tutorial

Additional Exercises Available Online

UNDERSTAND

13. **Construct Arguments** Write a proof of Theorem 11-1.

14. **Mathematical Connections** What are the point(s) of intersection of $x^2 + y^2 = 25$ and $y = 2x - 5$? Graph both equations to check your answer.

15. **Error Analysis** LaTanya was asked to determine if $(3\sqrt{5}, 4)$ lies on the circle with radius 7 centered at $(0, -2)$. What is her error?

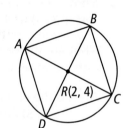

$x^2 + (y - 2)^2 = 49$
$(3\sqrt{5})^2 + (4 - 2)^2 \overset{?}{=} 49$
$45 + 4 = 49$

The point $(3\sqrt{5}, 4)$ lies on the circle with radius 7 and center $(0, -2)$. ✗

16. **Communicate Precisely** Describe the graph of $(x - a)^2 + (y - b)^2 = 0$.

17. **Reason** If the area of square $ABCD$ is 50, what is the equation for $\odot R$?

18. **Construct Arguments** The points (a, b) and (c, d) are the endpoints of a diameter of a circle. What are the center and radius of the circle?

19. **Higher Order Thinking** Isabel says the graph shows the circle with center $(-2, 2)$ and radius 3. Nicky says the graph shows all possible centers for a circle that passes through $(-2, 2)$ with radius 3. Which student is correct? Explain.

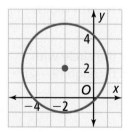

PRACTICE

For Exercises 20–23, find the center and radius for each equation of a circle. SEE EXAMPLE 1

20. $(x - 4)^2 + (y + 3)^2 = 64$

21. $(x + 2)^2 + y^2 = 13$

22. $(x + 5)^2 + (y + 11)^2 = 32$

23. $(x - 8)^2 + (y - 12)^2 = 96$

For Exercises 24 and 25, write the equation for the circle shown in each graph. SEE EXAMPLE 2

24.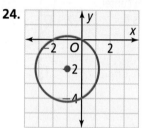

25.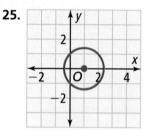

For Exercises 26–29, write the equation for each circle with the given radius and center. SEE EXAMPLE 2

26. radius: 4, center: $(5, 1)$

27. radius: 9, center: $(-3, 8)$

28. radius: $5\sqrt{5}$, center: $(2, -4)$

29. radius: $\sqrt{13}$, center: $(-5, -9)$

For Exercises 30–32, determine whether each given point lies on the circle with the given radius and center. SEE EXAMPLE 3

30. $(2, 4)$; radius: 4, center: $(-1, 1)$

31. $(\sqrt{17}, 8)$; radius: 9, center: $(0, 0)$

32. $(2, 0)$; radius: $\sqrt{10}$, center: $(3, -9)$

For Exercises 33–35, graph each equation.
SEE EXAMPLES 4 AND 5

33. $(x - 5)^2 + (y + 1)^2 = 4$

34. $x^2 + (y - 1)^2 = 16$

35. $(x + 3)^2 + (y + 4)^2 = 9$

36. The point $(2, b)$ lies on the circle with radius 5 and center $(-1, -1)$. What are the possible values of b?

37. Is $(7, 2)$ inside, outside, or on the circle $(x - 4)^2 + y^2 = 25$? Explain.

Go Online | PearsonRealize.com

APPLY

38. Model With Mathematics After an earthquake, a circle-shaped tsunami travels outward from the epicenter at an average speed of 420 miles per hour. If the earthquake with the epicenter shown occurred at 5:48 A.M., at what time will the tsunami reach Port Charles? Justify your answer.

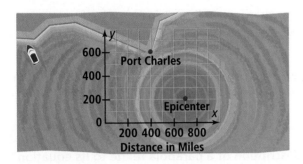

39. Make Sense and Persevere A cell phone tower is attached to the ground as shown. A circular security fence must be placed around the tower 10 feet from where the guy wires are attached to the ground. Can a cell phone tower be placed in the region enclosed by the red border? If so, what are possible coordinates of the tower?

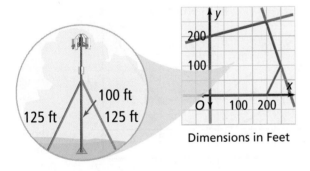

Dimensions in Feet

40. Reason Semitrailer trucks can be up to 14 feet tall. Should they be allowed in the outer lanes of the semicircular tunnel? Explain.

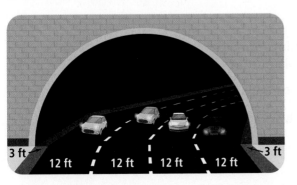

41. A circle has center (0, 0) and passes through the point (−5, 2). Which other points lie on the circle? Select all that apply.

Ⓐ (0, 6)   Ⓓ (−5, −2)

Ⓑ ($\sqrt{11}$, $3\sqrt{2}$)   Ⓔ (4, −$\sqrt{13}$)

Ⓒ (2, 5)   Ⓕ (−$\sqrt{29}$, 0)

42. SAT/ACT Which equation represents the circle with center (−3, 7) and radius 9?

Ⓐ $(x + 3)^2 + (y - 7)^2 = 3^2$

Ⓑ $(x - 3)^2 + (y + 7)^2 = 9^2$

Ⓒ $(x - 7)^2 + (y + 3)^2 = 9^2$

Ⓓ $(x + 3)^2 + (y - 7)^2 = 9^2$

Ⓔ $(x + 7)^2 + (y - 3)^2 = 3^2$

43. Performance Task A farmer can use up to four rotating sprinklers for the field shown. He has ten 50-meter sections that can be combined to form rotating arms with lengths from 50 m to 500 m. The irrigation circles cannot overlap and must not extend beyond the edges of the field. The distance between grid lines is 50 m.

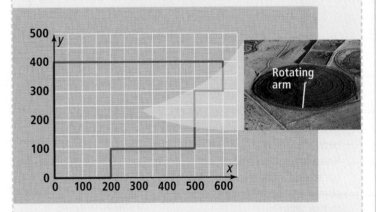

Rotating arm

Part A Design an irrigation system for the field that irrigates as much of the field as possible. Draw a sketch of your system. For each sprinkler, give the coordinates of the center of the sprinkler, the radius, and the equation.

Part B What is the total area of the field? What is the total area irrigated by your system? What percent of the field does your system irrigate?

11-4

Parabolas in the Coordinate Plane

I CAN... use the equations and graphs of parabolas to solve problems.

VOCABULARY
- directrix
- focus
- parabola

EXPLORE & REASON

Consider two points and two intersecting lines.

A. Describe the set of points that is equidistant from two points. Draw a diagram to support your answer.

B. Describe the set of points that is equidistant from each of two intersecting lines. Draw a diagram to support your answer.

C. **Look for Relationships** What do you think a set of points that is equidistant from a line and a point would look like? Draw a diagram to support your answer.

? ESSENTIAL QUESTION

How does the geometric description of a parabola relate to its equation?

CONCEPTUAL UNDERSTANDING

✋ EXAMPLE 1   Explore the Graph of a Parabola

What is the set of points that are equidistant from the graph of the equation $y = -2$ and the point $(0, 2)$?

Graph the line and the point.

Step 2 Find a point on the perpendicular that is equidistant from $(0, 2)$ and $y = -2$.

Step 1 Draw a line perpendicular to $y = -2$.

Step 3 Repeat to find other equidistant points.

Step 4 Connect the points.

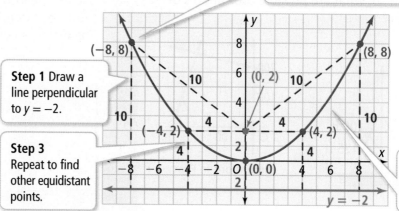

MAKE SENSE AND PERSEVERE
Think about the relationship between the point and line. How would the shape of the parabola change if the line and point were closer together or farther apart?

The set of points equidistant from $(0, 2)$ and $y = -2$ is a curve called a *parabola*.

 Try It!   **1.** The set of points equidistant from $(3, 5)$ and the line $y = 9$ is also a parabola.

    a. What is the vertex of the parabola?

    b. Describe the graph of the parabola.

     📶 Go Online | PearsonRealize.com

EXAMPLE 2 Derive the Equation of a Parabola

What is the equation of a parabola?

A **parabola** is the set of all points in a plane that are the same distance from a fixed point F, the **focus**, as they are from a line d, the **directrix**.

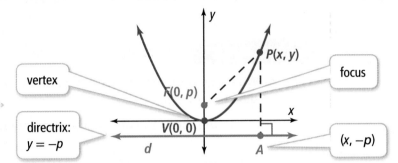

vertex

$F(0, p)$

$P(x, y)$

focus

directrix: $y = -p$

$V(0, 0)$

d

A

$(x, -p)$

Every point on the parabola is equidistant from F and line d.

$$PF = PA$$

$$\sqrt{(x - 0)^2 + (y - p)^2} = \sqrt{(x - x)^2 + (y - (-p))^2} \quad \text{Distance Formula}$$

$$\sqrt{x^2 + (y - p)^2} = \sqrt{(y + p)^2} \quad \text{Simplify.}$$

$$x^2 + (y - p)^2 = (y + p)^2 \quad \text{Square each side.}$$

$$x^2 + y^2 - 2py + p^2 = y^2 + 2py + p^2 \quad \text{Simplify.}$$

$$x^2 - 2py = 2py$$

$$x^2 = 4py$$

$$y = \frac{1}{4p} x^2 \quad \text{Solve for } y.$$

The equation for a parabola with vertex at the origin is $y = \frac{1}{4p} x^2$.

If the vertex is at (h, k), then the parabola is translated h units horizontally and k units vertically, and the equation is $y - k = \frac{1}{4p}(x - h)^2$.

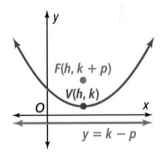

$F(h, k + p)$

$V(h, k)$

O

$y = k - p$

 Try It! 2. What expression represents the distance between the focus and the directrix?

CONCEPT Equation of a Parabola

Vertex at origin:

$$y = \frac{1}{4p} x^2$$

Vertex at (h, k):

$$y - k = \frac{1}{4p}(x - h)^2$$

The variable p represents the distance between the focus and the vertex.

EXAMPLE 3 Write the Equation of a Parabola

A. What equation represents the parabola with focus (5, 5) and directrix $y = 1$?

Graph the focus and directrix to determine the vertex and p.

The vertex is the midpoint of the segment connecting the focus and the directrix.

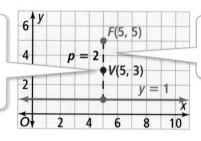

The value of p is the distance between the focus and the vertex.

Write the equation for the parabola with vertex (5, 3) and $p = 2$.

$$y - k = \frac{1}{4p}(x - h)^2$$

Write the formula for a parabola with vertex (h, k).

$$y - 3 = \frac{1}{4(2)}(x - 5)^2$$

$$y = \frac{1}{8}(x - 5)^2 + 3$$

COMMON ERROR
When substituting values into the equation of a parabola, be sure to use the coordinates of the vertex, not the coordinates of the focus.

B. Graph the parabola from part A.

Use the equation to make a table of values to help you sketch the graph.

x	y	(x, y)
1	$\frac{1}{8}(1 - 5)^2 + 3$	$(1, 5)$
3	$\frac{1}{8}(3 - 5)^2 + 3$	$\left(3, 3\frac{1}{2}\right)$
8	$\frac{1}{8}(8 - 5)^2 + 3$	$\left(8, 4\frac{1}{8}\right)$

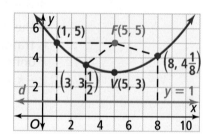

Try It! **3. a.** What equation represents the parabola with focus (−1, 4) and directrix $y = -2$?

b. What equation represents the parabola with focus (3, 5) and vertex (3, −1)?

APPLICATION

EXAMPLE 4 **Apply the Equation of a Parabola**

The cross section of a satellite dish is a parabola, with the feed horn at the focus. How long do the braces holding the feed horn need to be?

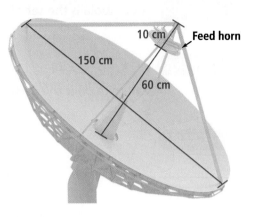

Formulate ◀ Place the parabola on a coordinate plane. Parabolas are symmetric, so computations are easier for a parabola with its vertex at the origin.

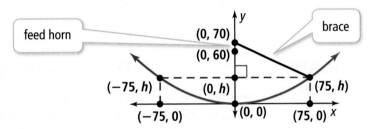

Write an equation for the parabola, and then use the equation to find the height h of the dish. Finally, use the Pythagorean Theorem to find the length of the brace.

Compute ◀ **Step 1** Write the equation.

$$y = \frac{1}{4p} x^2$$

Write the equation for a parabola with vertex at the origin, where p is the distance between the focus and the vertex.

$$y = \frac{1}{4(60)} x^2$$

Substitute 60 for p.

$$y = \frac{1}{240} x^2$$

Step 2 Evaluate for $x = 75$ to find the height h of the dish.

$$h = \frac{1}{240}(75)^2 \approx 23.4 \text{ cm}$$

Step 3 Use the Pythagorean Theorem to find the length of the brace.

$$(70 - 23.4)^2 + 75^2 = b^2$$

$$7{,}796.56 = b^2$$

$$b \approx 88.3$$

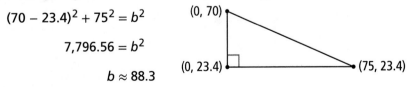

Interpret ◀ The braces need to be 88.3 cm long.

 Try It! 4. On a different satellite dish, the feed horn is 38 inches above the vertex. If the height of the dish is 22 inches, what is its width?

CONCEPT SUMMARY **Parabolas**

WORDS A parabola is the set of points equidistant from a focus and a directrix.

ALGEBRA $y - k = \frac{1}{4p}(x - h)^2$

where (h, k) is the vertex and p is the distance from the vertex to the focus

GRAPH

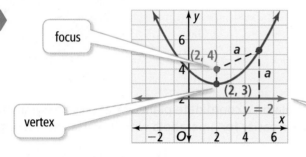

focus

(2, 4) a

a

(2, 3)

$y = 2$

vertex

directrix

Do You UNDERSTAND?

1. **ESSENTIAL QUESTION** How does the geometric description of a parabola relate to its equation?

2. **Error Analysis** Arthur says that an equation of the parabola with directrix $y = 0$ and focus $= (0, 6)$ is $y - 3 = \frac{1}{24}x^2$. What is his error?

3. **Vocabulary** How could the word *direction* help you remember that the directrix is a line?

4. **Reason** What are the coordinates of point P? Show your work.

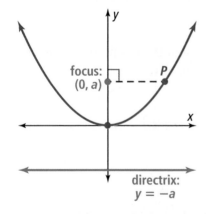

focus: (0, a)

P

x

y

directrix: $y = -a$

5. **Communicate Precisely** Given vertex (a, b) and focus (a, c), describe how you would write an equation for the parabola.

Do You KNOW HOW?

For Exercises 6–9, write an equation of each parabola with the given focus and directrix.

6. focus: $(0, 4)$; directrix: $y = -4$

7. focus: $(5, 1)$; directrix: $y = -5$

8. focus: $(4, 0)$; directrix: $y = -4$

9. focus: $(2, -1)$; directrix: $y = -4$

For Exercises 10–13, give the vertex, focus, and directrix of each parabola.

10. $y = \frac{1}{8}x^2$

11. $y - 2 = \frac{1}{6}x^2$

12. $y - 6 = \frac{1}{4}(x - 1)^2$

13. $y + 3 = \frac{1}{20}(x - 9)^2$

For Exercises 14–17, write an equation of each parabola with the given focus and vertex.

14. focus: $(6, 2)$; vertex: $(6, -4)$

15. focus: $(-1, 8)$; vertex: $(-1, 7)$

16. focus: $(4, 0)$; vertex: $(4, -2)$

17. focus: $(-3, -1)$; vertex: $(-3, -4)$

18. Consider the parabola $y = \frac{1}{36}x^2$.

a. What are the focus and directrix?

b. The parabola passes through $(12, 4)$. Show that this point is equidistant from the focus and the directrix.

UNDERSTAND

19. **Communicate Precisely** Use the graph to answer the questions. Line *m* is the directrix of the parabola.

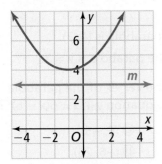

   a. How would you find the vertex of the parabola? Explain.

   b. How would you find the focus of the parabola? Explain.

   c. How would you find an equation of the parabola? Explain.

20. **Communicate Precisely** Define a parabola as a set of points. What is the relationship of the points to the lines and points associated with the parabola?

21. **Mathematical Connections** The general form of the equation of a parabola is $y = x^2 - 6x + 9$. What are the focus, vertex, and directrix of the parabola?

22. **Reason** How does changing the distance from the focus to the directrix change the shape of a parabola in the coordinate plane? Explain.

23. **Construct Arguments** The parabola has its focus at $\left(0, \frac{1}{4}\right)$ and vertex at (0, 0). How would you find the equation of the parabola?

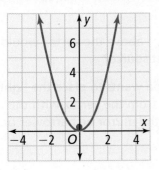

PRACTICE

For Exercises 24–27, find the vertex of each parabola. SEE EXAMPLE 1

24. focus: (3, 7); directrix: $y = -1$

25. focus: (6, 2); directrix: $y = -4$

26. focus: (−4, 3); directrix: $y = 0$

27. focus: (−2, −1); directrix: $y = -6$

For Exercises 28–31, find the vertex, focus and directrix of each parabola. SEE EXAMPLE 2

28. $y - 7 = \frac{1}{8}(x - 3)$ 29. $y + 4 = \frac{1}{36}(x - 1)$

30. $y - 3 = \frac{1}{16}(x + 6)$ 31. $y + 5 = \frac{1}{2}(x - 10)$

For Exercises 32–34, write an equation of each parabola with the given focus and directrix. SEE EXAMPLE 3

32. focus: (0, 4); directrix: $y = 0$

33. focus: (5, 1); directrix: $y = -9$

34. focus: (−4, 5); directrix: $y = 2$

For Exercises 35–37, write an equation of each parabola with the given focus and vertex. SEE EXAMPLE 3

35. focus: (4, 5); vertex: (4, −1)

36. focus: (−4, 9); vertex: (−4, 5)

37. focus: (2, 4); vertex: (2, 0)

For Exercises 38–40, use the graph of the parabola shown to answer each question. SEE EXAMPLE 4

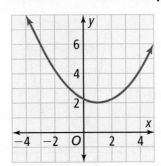

38. What is the vertex of the parabola?

39. Using a point on the parabola and the equation $y - k = \frac{1}{4p}(x - h)^2$, what is p?

40. What is the focus of the parabola?

APPLY

41. Reason Henry is building a model of the Clifton Suspension Bridge using a scale factor of 100 ft : 1 in. The cables between the towers are in the shape of a parabola. He writes an equation of the parabola to describe the model he is building and uses the equation to determine the distances from the cable to the deck of the bridge. Suppose the deck is the x-axis and the vertex lies on the y-axis. What is the equation that Henry writes?

702 ft
86 ft

42. Model With Mathematics Devin builds a solar hot dog cooker for the science fair. Suppose the base of the cooker is the x-axis and the hot dog is on the y-axis at the focus. What is the equation of the parabola that models the cooker?

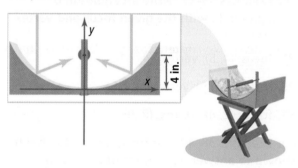

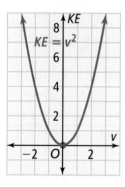

43. Higher Order Thinking
An engineer is making an impact analysis on a car bumper. He graphs the kinetic energy of a 2-kg steel ball as a function of the velocity of the ball. Kinetic energy is measured in joules (J) and velocity is measured in meters per second.

$KE = v^2$

a. What are the vertex, focus, and directrix of the parabola?

b. The car bumper has to withstand an impact of 25 J from the 2-kg steel ball without any damage. How fast is the ball moving when it strikes the bumper with that amount of energy?

ASSESSMENT PRACTICE

44. An equation of a parabola is $y - 5 = \frac{1}{8}(x - 4)$. Select all that apply.

Ⓐ The vertex of the parabola is (5, 4).

Ⓑ $p = 2$

Ⓒ The focus of the parabola is (4, 7).

Ⓓ The directrix of the parabola is $y = 3$.

45. SAT/ACT Which is the vertex of the parabola represented by the equation $y + 5 = 6(x - 6)^2$?

Ⓐ (6, 5)   Ⓒ (6, −5)

Ⓑ (−6, −5)   Ⓓ (−6, 25)

46. Performance Task Some flashlights are designed so that a parabolic mirror reflects light forward from a light source.

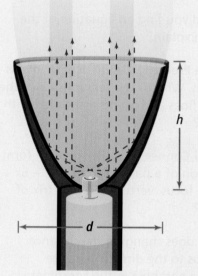
h
d

For the flashlight to work best, the light source is placed at the focus of the parabola. Deon designs a flashlight so $d = 4$ in. and $h = 3$ in.

Part A How could Deon model the mirror on the coordinate plane? What is an equation for the mirror?

Part B At what point above the vertex would Deon place the light source?

Part C Suppose Deon wants to place the light source $\frac{1}{2}$ in. farther from the vertex with the same $h = 3$ in. Will the mirror be narrower or wider? Explain.

Topic Review

? TOPIC ESSENTIAL QUESTION

1. How can geometric relationships be proven by applying algebraic properties to geometric figures represented in the coordinate plane?

Vocabulary Review

Choose the correct term to complete each sentence.

2. All the points on a parabola are the same distance from a fixed point, the _____ as they are from a line, the _____.

3. A _____ is a set of points equidistant from a point.

4. A _____ is the highest or lowest point on the graph of a function.

- circle
- directrix
- focus
- parabola
- radius
- vertex

Concepts & Skills Review

LESSON 11-1   Polygons in the Coordinate Plane

Quick Review

When a geometric figure is represented in a coordinate plane, you can use slope, distance, and midpoints to analyze properties of the figure.

Example

Is △ABC an isosceles triangle? Explain.

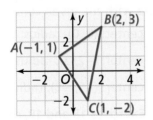

A triangle is isosceles if two sides are congruent. Use the Distance Formula to find the side lengths.

$$AB = \sqrt{(2-(-1))^2 + (3-1)^2} = \sqrt{13}$$
$$BC = \sqrt{(1-2)^2 + (-2-3)^2} = \sqrt{26}$$
$$CA = \sqrt{(1-(-1))^2 + (-2-1)^2} = \sqrt{13}$$

Since $AB = CA$, △ABC is isosceles.

Practice & Problem Solving

For Exercises 5–8, determine whether each figure is the given type of figure.

5. $F(-2, 4)$, $G(0, 0)$, $H(3, 1)$; right triangle

6. $A(7, 2)$, $B(3, -1)$, $C(3, 4)$; equilateral triangle

7. $J(-4, -4)$, $K(-7, 0)$, $L(-4, 4)$, $M(-1, 0)$; rhombus

8. What are the area and perimeter of PQRS?

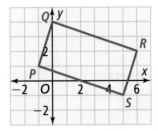

9. **Make Sense and Persevere** Parallelogram WXYZ has coordinates $W(a, b)$, $X(c, d)$, $Y(f, g)$, and $Z(h, j)$. What equation can you use to determine whether WXYZ is a rhombus? Explain.

Proofs Using Coordinate Geometry

Quick Review

To prove theorems using coordinate geometry, place the figure on the coordinate plane. Use slope, midpoint, and distance to write an algebraic proof.

Example

Prove that the diagonals of a rectangle are congruent.

Place a rectangle on a coordinate plane with one vertex at the origin and two sides along the axes.

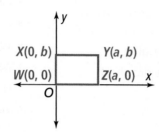

$$WY = \sqrt{(a-0)^2 + (b-0)^2} = \sqrt{a^2 + b^2}$$
$$XZ = \sqrt{(a-0)^2 + (0-b)^2} = \sqrt{a^2 + b^2}$$

Since $WY = XZ$, the diagonals of a rectangle are congruent.

Practice & Problem Solving

For Exercises 10–12, give the coordinates of each missing vertex.

10. *ABCD* is a parallelogram; *A*(0, 0), *B*(p, q), *D*(t, 0)

11. *JKLM* is a kite; *J*(0, 0), *K*(a, b), *L*(0, c)

12. *WXYZ* is a rhombus; *W*(0, 0), *Y*(0, h), *Z*(j, k)

13. **Communicate Precisely** If you are given the coordinates of a quadrilateral, how can you prove that the quadrilateral is an isosceles trapezoid?

14. The diagram shows a fenced garden area, where $PX = PY$. The gardener is dividing the garden with a fence from *P* to the midpoint of $\overline{XY}$. Will the new fence be perpendicular to $\overline{XY}$? Use coordinate geometry to explain.

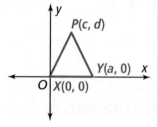

Circles in the Coordinate Plane

Quick Review

The equation of a circle in the coordinate plane is

$$(x - h)^2 + (y - k)^2 = r^2$$

where (h, k) is the center of the circle and r is the radius.

Example

What is the equation of $\odot Q$?

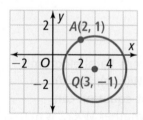

The center of the circle is $(3, -1)$, and the radius is *QA*.

$$QA = \sqrt{(2-3)^2 + (1-(-1))^2} = \sqrt{5}$$

So, the equation of $\odot Q$ is $(x - 3)^2 + (y + 1)^2 = 5$.

Practice & Problem Solving

For Exercises 15–17, write the equation for the circle with the given center and radius.

15. center: (0, 0), radius: 9

16. center: (−2, 3), radius: 5

17. center: (−5, −8), radius: $\sqrt{13}$

For Exercises 18 and 19, determine whether the given point lies on the circle with the given center and radius.

18. (−3, 0); center: (−5, 2), radius: $2\sqrt{2}$

19. (11, −1); center: (4, 4), radius: $6\sqrt{2}$

20. Suppose that $\overline{AB}$, with *A*(1, 15) and *B*(13, −1), and $\overline{CD}$, with *C*(15, 13) and *D*(−1, 1), are diameters of $\odot T$. What is the equation of $\odot T$?

21. **Construct Arguments** Is it possible to write the equation of a circle given only two points on the circle? Explain.

Quick Review

A **parabola** is the set of points that are equidistant from a fixed point, the **focus**, and a line, the **directrix**. The equation for a parabola in the coordinate plane is

$$y - k = \frac{1}{4p}(x - h)^2$$

where (h, k) is the vertex and p is the distance between the vertex and focus.

Example

What is the equation of the parabola with focus (4, 2) and directrix $y = 0$?

The vertex is the midpoint of the segment connecting the focus and the directrix, so the vertex is (4, 1). Since p is the distance between the focus and the vertex, $p = 1$. So, the equation of the parabola is

$$y - 1 = \frac{1}{4}(x - 4)^2.$$

Practice & Problem Solving

For Exercises 22 and 23, write the equation for the parabola with the given focus and directrix.

22. focus: (0, 0), directrix: $y = -6$

23. focus: (−1, −3), directrix: $y = -4$

24. **Reason** Point F is the focus and $y = -p$ is the directrix of the parabola shown. What is AB? Explain how you found your answer.

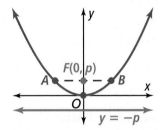

25. The cables for a suspension bridge are parabolic. The support towers are 40 m tall and 100 m apart. At its lowest point, the cable is 15 m above the bridge deck. If the bridge deck represents the x-axis and the vertex is on the y-axis, what equation represents the bridge cables?

TOPIC 12

Circles

? TOPIC ESSENTIAL QUESTION

When a line or lines intersect a circle how are the figures formed related to the radius, circumference, and area of the circle?

Topic Overview

enVision® STEM Project:
Design Space Cities

12-1 Arcs and Sectors

12-2 Lines Tangent to a Circle

Mathematical Modeling in 3 Acts:
Earth Watch

12-3 Chords

12-4 Inscribed Angles

12-5 Secant Lines and Segments

Topic Vocabulary

- arc length
- central angle
- chord
- inscribed angle
- intercepted arc
- major arc
- minor arc
- point of tangency
- radian
- secant
- sector of a circle
- segment of a circle
- tangent to a circle

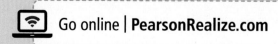

Go online | **PearsonRealize.com**

Digital Experience

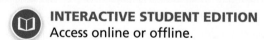

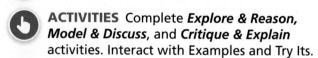

INTERACTIVE STUDENT EDITION
Access online or offline.

ACTIVITIES Complete *Explore & Reason,*
Model & Discuss, and *Critique & Explain*
activities. Interact with Examples and Try Its.

ANIMATION View and interact with
real-world applications.

PRACTICE Practice what
you've learned.

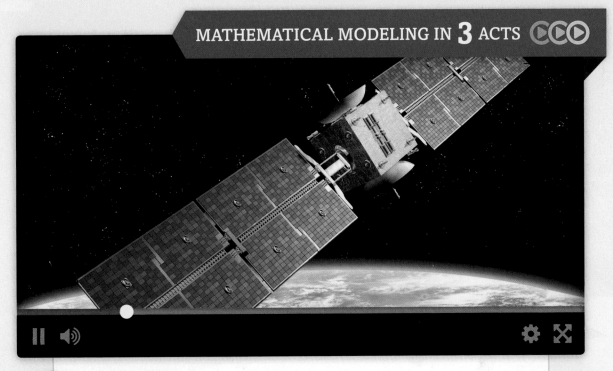

▶ **Earth Watch**

Scientists estimate that there are currently about 3,000 operational man-made satellites orbiting Earth. These satellites serve different purposes, from communication to navigation and global positioning. Some are weather satellites that collect environmental information.

The International Space Station is the largest man-made satellite that orbits Earth. It serves as a space environment research facility, and it also offers amazing views of Earth. Think about this during the Mathematical Modeling in 3 Acts lesson.

TOPIC 12

VIDEOS Watch clips to support *Mathematical Modeling in 3 Acts Lessons* and **enVision®** *STEM Projects.*

CONCEPT SUMMARY Review key lesson content through multiple representations.

ASSESSMENT Show what you've learned.

GLOSSARY Read and listen to English and Spanish definitions.

TUTORIALS Get help from *Virtual Nerd*, right when you need it.

MATH TOOLS Explore math with digital tools and manipulatives.

Did You Know?

Astronauts, six at a time, have lived and worked in the International Space Station (ISS) since 2000. Residents of 17 countries have visited the ISS.

The size of a football field, ISS circles the Earth every 90 minutes at an altitude of 248 miles and a speed of about 17,500 miles per hour.

At its closest, the planet Mars is 150 times as far from Earth as the Moon is. Despite the distance, the United States and Russia have been landing spacecraft and scientific instruments on Mars for several decades.

▶ Your Task: Design Space Cities

Suppose it's 500 years in the future. Space stations the size of small cities are journeying through space. Use trigonometry and the geometry of circles to calculate the measurements of two of these stations, then design, measure, and describe a group of three "space cities."

12-1

Arcs and Sectors

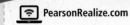
PearsonRealize.com

I CAN... find arc length and sector area of a circle and use them to solve problems.

VOCABULARY

- arc length
- central angle
- intercepted arc
- major arc
- minor arc
- radian
- sector of a circle
- segment of a circle

Activity   Assess

👆 EXPLORE & REASON

Darren bends a piece of wire using a circular disc to make the shape as shown.

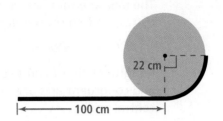

22 cm

|← 100 cm →|

A. How long does the piece of wire need to be to make the shape? Explain.

B. Construct Arguments What information do you think is needed to find part of the circumference of a circle? Justify your answer.

❓ ESSENTIAL QUESTION

How are arc length and sector area related to circumference and area of a circle?

👆 EXAMPLE 1   Relate Central Angles and Arc Measures

What are $m\overset{\frown}{AB}$ and $m\overset{\frown}{ACB}$?

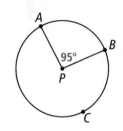

A **central angle** of a circle is an angle formed by two radii with the vertex at the center of the circle. Angle APB is a central angle.

A central angle creates two intercepted arcs. An **intercepted arc** is the part of a circle that lies between two segments, rays, or lines that intersect the circle.

A central angle and its intercepted minor arc have equal measure.

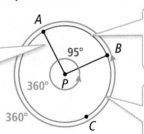

$\angle APB$ is a central angle, and $\overset{\frown}{AB}$ is its corresponding intercepted arc.

A **minor arc** of a circle is an arc that is smaller than a semicircle. $\overset{\frown}{AB}$ is a minor arc.

A **major arc** of a circle is an arc that is larger than a semicircle. $\overset{\frown}{ACB}$ is a major arc.

Find $m\overset{\frown}{AB}$.

$m\overset{\frown}{AB} = m\angle APB = 95$

The degree measure of $\overset{\frown}{AB}$ is equal to the measure of its corresponding central angle $\angle APB$.

Find $m\overset{\frown}{ACB}$.

$m\overset{\frown}{ACB} = 360 - 95 = 265$

✅ Try It!   1. Use ⊙W.

a. What is $m\overset{\frown}{XZ}$?

b. What is $m\overset{\frown}{XYZ}$?

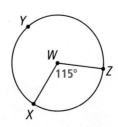

CONCEPT Arc Measure

The measure of an arc is equal to the measure of its corresponding central angle.

$m\widehat{JM} = m\angle JPM$

Congruent central angles intercept congruent arcs, and congruent arcs are intercepted by congruent central angles.

$\angle JPK \cong \angle KPL$ $\widehat{JK} \cong \widehat{KL}$

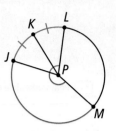

CONCEPTUAL UNDERSTANDING

EXAMPLE 2   **Relate Arc Length to Circumference**

A. How do you find the length s of an arc measured in degrees?

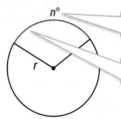

The *measure* of an arc is a fraction of 360°

The **arc length** is a fraction of the circumference.

$$\frac{\text{arc length}}{\text{circumference}} = \frac{\text{arc measure}}{360}$$

$$\frac{s}{2\pi r} = \frac{n}{360}$$

$$s = \frac{n}{360} \cdot 2\pi r$$

Use a proportion to represent the relationship between arc length s, radius r, and arc measure n.

The formula to find the length of an arc is $s = \frac{n}{360} \cdot 2\pi r$.

B. How do you find the length s of an arc measured in radians?

Besides degrees, angle measures can be expressed in *radians*.

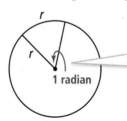

A **radian** is equal to the measure of a central angle that intercepts an arc with length equal to the radius of the circle.

Circumference is $2\pi r$, which is 2π arcs of length r. Since each arc of length r corresponds to 1 radian, there are 2π radians in a circle. So, 2π radians is equivalent to 360°.

To find the arc length, use the following proportion.

$$\frac{\text{arc length}}{\text{circumference}} = \frac{\text{arc measure (radians)}}{2\pi}$$

$$\frac{s}{2\pi r} = \frac{\theta}{2\pi}$$

$$s = \frac{\theta}{2\pi} \cdot 2\pi r = \theta r$$

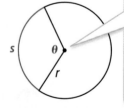

The variable theta (θ) is often used for angles measured in radians.

Arc length is proportional to radius, with θ as the constant of proportionality.

To find the length of an arc measured in radians, use the formula $s = \theta r$.

STUDY TIP
Remember that the circumference measures the distance around all of the circle and the arc length is the distance around part of the circle.

CONTINUED ON THE NEXT PAGE

EXAMPLE 2 CONTINUED

 Try It! **2. a.** In a circle with radius 4, what is the length of an arc that has a measure of 80? Round to the nearest tenth.

b. In a circle with radius 6, what is the length of an arc that has a measure of π radians? Round to the nearest tenth.

CONCEPT Arc Length

The length *s* of an arc of a circle is the product of the ratio relating the measure of the central angle in degrees to 360 and the circumference of the circle. The length of the arc is also the product of the radius and the central angle measure in radians.

Central angle in degrees:

$$s = \frac{n}{360} \cdot 2\pi r$$

Central angle in radians:

$$s = \theta r$$

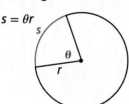

 EXAMPLE 3 **Apply Arc Length**

What is the length of $\overset{\frown}{AD}$? Express the answer in terms of π.

Step 1 Find the arc measure.

$$m\overset{\frown}{AD} = 360 - m\overset{\frown}{AB} - m\overset{\frown}{BC} - m\overset{\frown}{CD}$$

$$= 360 - 73 - 43 - 104$$

$$= 140$$

> Each arc measure is equal to the measure of the corresponding central angle.

MAKE SENSE AND PERSEVERE
Think about when you should express arc lengths in terms of π and when you should give approximate answers. How would you decide?

Step 2 Find the arc length.

$$s = \frac{n}{360} \cdot 2\pi r$$

$$= \frac{140}{360} \cdot 2\pi(4) = \frac{28}{9}\pi$$

> Use the formula for arc length for angles given in degrees.

The length of $\overset{\frown}{AD}$ is $\frac{28}{9}\pi$.

 Try It! **3.** Use $\odot Q$. Express answers in terms of π.

a. What is the length of $\overset{\frown}{JK}$?

b. What is the length of $\overset{\frown}{HK}$?

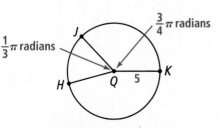

EXAMPLE 4   Relate the Area of a Circle to the Area of a Sector

A sector of a circle is the region bounded by two radii and the intercepted arc. What is the area of sector *MQN*?

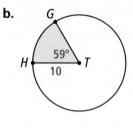

To find the area of the sector, find $\frac{78}{360}$ of the area of the circle.

$$A = \frac{78}{360} \cdot \pi r^2$$

$$= \frac{78}{360} \cdot \pi (10)^2 = \frac{65}{3}\pi$$

The area of sector *MQN* is $\frac{65}{3}\pi$ cm².

In general, the area of a sector is $A = \frac{n}{360} \cdot \pi r^2$, where $n°$ is the measure of the intercepted arc and *r* is the radius of the circle.

GENERALIZE
Compare the formulas for arc length and sector area. What relationships do you see between the arc length and sector area for any given arc?

Try It!   **4.** What is the area of each sector?

a.

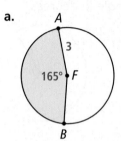

b.

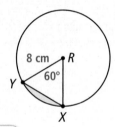

EXAMPLE 5   Find the Area of a Segment of a Circle

A segment of a circle is the part of a circle bounded by an arc and the segment joining its endpoints. What is the area of the shaded region?

To find the area of the segment, subtract the area of the triangle from the area of the sector.

Step 1 Find the area of the sector.

$$A = \frac{n}{360} \cdot \pi r^2 = \frac{32}{3}\pi$$

Use the formula for area of a sector.

Step 2 Find the area of the triangle.

Since $\overline{RX}$ and $\overline{RY}$ are both radii and the angle between them is 60°, $\triangle RYX$ is equilateral.

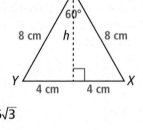

Use the Pythagorean Theorem to find *h*.

$$4^2 + h^2 = 8^2$$

$$h^2 = 8^2 - 4^2$$

$$h = \sqrt{48} = 4\sqrt{3}$$

Find the area of the triangle.

$$A = \frac{1}{2}bh$$

$$= \frac{1}{2}(8)(4\sqrt{3}) = 16\sqrt{3}$$

Step 3 Find the area of the segment.

area of segment = area of sector − area of triangle

$$= \frac{32}{3}\pi - 16\sqrt{3} \approx 5.8$$

The area of the shaded region is about 5.8 cm².

STUDY TIP
To find areas of triangles in circles, you may need to apply trigonometric ratios to find the base and height.

CONTINUED ON THE NEXT PAGE

EXAMPLE 5 CONTINUED

 Try It! **5.** What is the area of each segment?

a.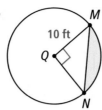

b.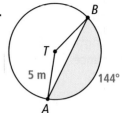

 APPLICATION

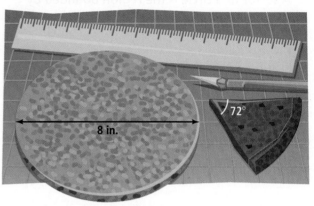

EXAMPLE 6 **Solve Problems Involving Circles**

Chen uses circular corkboards to make 18 watermelon coasters to sell at a craft fair.

A. He paints one side of each coaster with special paint. Each jar of paint covers 200 in.². Will one jar of paint be enough to paint all the coasters?

COMMON ERROR
Be careful not to confuse the formula for the area of a sector with the formula for arc length. Remember that the area of a sector is proportional to the area of the circle, and the arc length is proportional to the circumference.

Find the area of one watermelon coaster. Use 3.14 for π.

$$A = \frac{n}{360} \cdot \pi r^2$$ ← Use the formula for area of a sector.

$$= \frac{72}{360} \cdot \pi(4)^2$$

$$\approx 10.0$$

The area of one watermelon coaster is about 10 in.².

Chen can paint $200 \div 10 = 20$ coasters with one jar of paint, so he has enough paint for 18 coasters.

B. He puts decorative tape around the edge of each coaster. How much tape does he need for each coaster?

The perimeter of the coaster consists of two radii and an arc.

$$P = r + r + \frac{n}{360} \cdot 2\pi r$$

$$= 4 + 4 + \frac{72}{360} \cdot 2\pi(4)$$

$$\approx 13.0$$

Chen needs about 13 inches of tape for each coaster.

 Try It! **6.** What is the area and perimeter of sector QNR? Round to the nearest tenth.

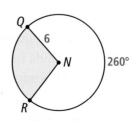

CONCEPT SUMMARY Arc Length and Sector Area

WORDS

Arc Length

The arc length is a fraction of the circumference.

Sector

A sector of a circle is the region bounded by two radii and the intercepted arc.

Segment

A segment of a circle is the part of a circle bounded by an arc and the segment joining its endpoints.

DIAGRAMS

Degrees

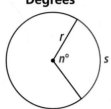

$$s = \frac{n}{360} \cdot 2\pi r$$

Radians

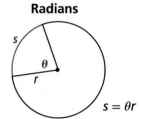

$$s = \theta r$$

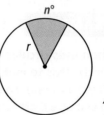

$$A = \frac{n}{360} \cdot \pi r^2$$

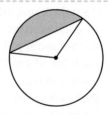

segment area =
sector area − triangle area

☑ Do You UNDERSTAND?

1. **ESSENTIAL QUESTION** How are arc length and sector area related to circumference and area of a circle?

2. **Error Analysis** Luke was asked to compute the length of $\widehat{AB}$. What is Luke's error?

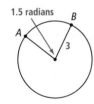

1.5 radians

$$S = \frac{n}{360} \cdot 2\pi r$$
$$= \frac{1.5}{360} \cdot 2\pi(3)$$
$$= 0.0785 \quad ✗$$

3. **Vocabulary** How can the word *segment* help you remember what a *segment of a circle* is?

4. **Reason** Mercedes says that she can find the area of a quarter of a circle using the formula $A = \frac{1}{4}\pi r^2$. Using the formula for the area of a sector, explain why Mercedes is correct.

Do You KNOW HOW?

For Exercises 5 and 6, find the measures and lengths of each arc. Express the answers in terms of π.

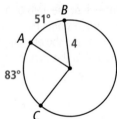

5. $\widehat{BC}$

6. $\widehat{ABC}$

7. Circle P has radius 8. Points Q and R lie on circle P, and the length of $\widehat{QR}$ is 4π. What is $m\angle QPR$ in radians?

8. What is the area of sector EFG? Express the answer in terms of π.

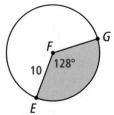

9. What is the area of the segment? Express the answer in terms of π.

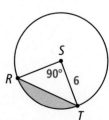

✎ PRACTICE & PROBLEM SOLVING

Scan for Multimedia

Practice   Tutorial

Additional Exercises Available Online

UNDERSTAND

10. Generalize Is it always true that two arcs with the same length have the same measure? Explain.

11. Error Analysis Steve is asked to compute the area of the shaded region. What is his error?

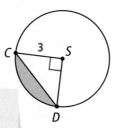

Segment area = sector area − triangle area

$= \frac{90}{360} \cdot 2\pi(3) - \frac{1}{2}(3)(3)$

≈ 0.21

12. Mathematical Connections The equation $(x - 2)^2 + (y - 3)^2 = 25$ represents $\odot T$. Points $X(-2, 6)$ and $Y(-1, -1)$ lie on $\odot T$. What is $m\widehat{XY}$? Explain how you know.

13. Reason Figure *GHJKL* is a regular pentagon. Rounded to the nearest tenth, what percent of the area of $\odot T$ is not part of the area of *GHJKL*? Explain.

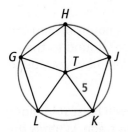

14. Use Structure Explain why the length of an arc with arc measure $a°$ is proportional to the radius of the circle.

15. Higher Order Thinking The areas of sectors *ACB* and *DEF* are equal. What expression gives the value of *x*? Show your work.

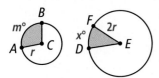

PRACTICE

For Exercises 16–19, find each arc measure.
SEE EXAMPLE 1

16. $m\widehat{FE}$

17. $m\widehat{BC}$

18. $m\widehat{CE}$

19. $m\widehat{CFE}$

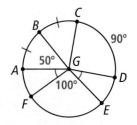

For Exercises 20 and 21, find each arc length in terms of π. SEE EXAMPLES 2 AND 3

20. length of $\widehat{JK}$

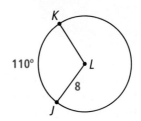

21. length of $\widehat{XYZ}$

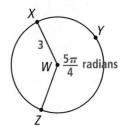

For Exercises 22 and 23, find the area of each sector. Round to the nearest tenth. SEE EXAMPLES 4 AND 6

22. sector *DEF*

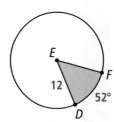

23. sector *GHJ*

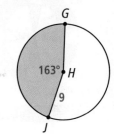

For Exercises 24 and 25, find the area of each segment. Round to the nearest tenth. SEE EXAMPLE 5

24.

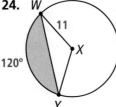

25.

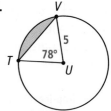

26. The length of $\widehat{ABC}$ is 110 ft. What is the radius of $\odot D$? Round to the nearest tenth.

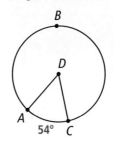

APPLY

27. Make Sense and Persevere Aubrey and Fatima will each run 150 m on the two inside lanes of the track, so the end markers need to be placed correctly. To the nearest hundredth, what are x and y?

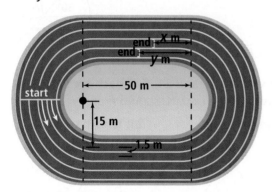

28. Reason Charlie is designing a dart board and wants the red sections to be 25% of the total area. What should be the radius of the inner circle? Round to the nearest tenth.

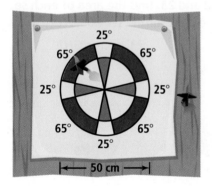

29. Look for Relationships Enrique is selling the drop-leaf table and wants to include the area of the table when the leaves are down in his ad. What is the area of the center section when the leaves are down? Round to the nearest square inch. Explain how you found your answer.

ASSESSMENT PRACTICE

30. What is the diameter of $\odot T$?

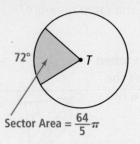

Sector Area $= \frac{64}{5}\pi$

31. SAT/ACT An arc has a central angle of $\frac{2}{5}\pi$ radians and a length of 6π. What is the circumference of the circle?

Ⓐ 12π Ⓑ 15π Ⓒ 30π Ⓓ 36π

32. Performance Task A carpenter is constructing the stage for a concert.

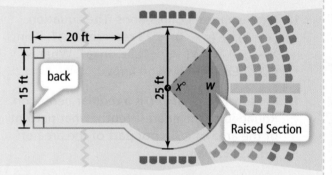

Part A What is the total amount of flooring needed to cover the stage? Round to the nearest square foot. Explain how you found your answer.

Part B A string of lights will be strung along the sides and front of the stage. What is the total length of light string needed? Show your work.

Part C One portion of the stage can be raised during the concert. The lift mechanism can lift a maximum area of 180 ft², but the band needs the width w of the raised area to be at least 20 ft. What could be the value of x? Justify your answer.

12-2

Lines Tangent to a Circle

🛜 PearsonRealize.com

I CAN... use properties of tangent lines to solve problems.

VOCABULARY
• point of tangency
• tangent to a circle

Alicia and Renaldo made conjectures about the lines that intersect a circle only once.

Alicia

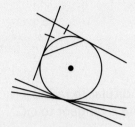

• Many lines intersect the circle once at the same point.
• Two lines that intersect the circle once and the segment connecting the points form an isosceles triangle.

Renaldo

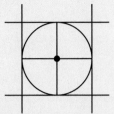

• Parallel lines intersect the circle at opposite ends of the same diameter.
• The lines intersecting the circle at one point are perpendicular to a diameter of the circle.

A. Use Appropriate Tools Which of the four conjectures do you agree with? Which do you disagree with? Draw sketches to support your answers.

B. What other conjectures can you make about lines that intersect a circle at one point?

❓ **ESSENTIAL QUESTION**   How is a tangent line related to the radius of a circle at the point of tangency?

CONCEPTUAL UNDERSTANDING

👆 **EXAMPLE 1**   Understand Tangents to a Circle

What is the relationship between a circle and a tangent to the circle?

A **tangent to a circle** is a line in the plane of the circle that intersects the circle in exactly one point. That point is the **point of tangency**.

Circle C has tangent line m with point of tangency X. Point Y is any other point on m.

GENERALIZE
Point Y represents any point other than the point of tangency. Would the result be true no matter where point Y is located on m?

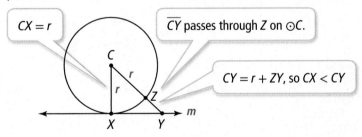

$CX = r$

$\overline{CY}$ passes through Z on $\odot C$.

$CY = r + ZY$, so $CX < CY$

So, $\overline{CX}$ is the shortest segment from C to line m. Since the shortest segment from a point to a line is perpendicular to the line, $\overline{CX} \perp m$.

✓ **Try It!**   **1.** Does Example 1 support Renaldo's conjecture that parallel lines intersect the circle at opposite ends of the same diameter? Explain.

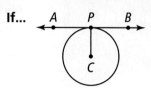

THEOREM 12-1 AND THE CONVERSE

Theorem

If $\overleftrightarrow{AB}$ is tangent to $\odot C$ at P, then $\overleftrightarrow{AB}$ is perpendicular to $\overline{CP}$.

If...

Then... $\overleftrightarrow{AB} \perp \overline{CP}$

Converse

If $\overleftrightarrow{AB}$ is perpendicular to radius $\overline{CP}$ at P, then $\overleftrightarrow{AB}$ is tangent to $\odot C$.

If...

PROOF: SEE EXERCISES 12 AND 13.

Then... $\overleftrightarrow{AB}$ is tangent to $\odot C$.

EXAMPLE 2 ▶ **Use Tangents to Solve Problems**

A. Is $\overline{KJ}$ tangent to $\odot P$ at J?

A segment or ray that intersects a circle in one point is tangent to the circle if it is part of a tangent line.

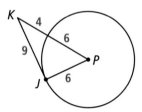

If $\overline{KJ}$ is part of a line that is tangent to $\odot P$ at J, then $\overline{PJ} \perp \overline{JK}$ and $\triangle PJK$ is a right triangle.

$$9^2 + 6^2 \overset{?}{=} (4 + 6)^2$$

$$117 \neq 100$$

> Use the Converse of the Pythagorean Theorem to determine whether $\triangle PJK$ is a right triangle.

So, $\overline{PJ}$ is not perpendicular to $\overline{KJ}$.

Therefore, $\overline{KJ}$ is not tangent to $\odot P$ at J.

B. Segment ST is tangent to $\odot R$. What is the radius of $\odot R$?

Since $\overline{ST}$ is tangent to $\odot R$, $\triangle RST$ is a right triangle.

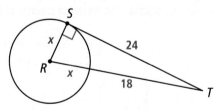

COMMON ERROR
You may incorrectly square just the terms x and 18. Recall how to square a binomial. It may be helpful to first write $(x + 18)^2$ as $(x + 18)(x + 18)$ and multiply.

$$x^2 + 24^2 = (x + 18)^2$$

$$x^2 + 576 = x^2 + 36x + 324$$

$$252 = 36x$$

$$7 = x$$

> Use the Pythagorean Theorem with length of the hypotenuse $x + 18$.

The radius of $\odot R$ is 7.

CONTINUED ON THE NEXT PAGE

EXAMPLE 2 CONTINUED

C. Line *m* is tangent to ⊙*T* at *B*, and line *n* is tangent to ⊙*T* at *C*. What is the value of *x*?

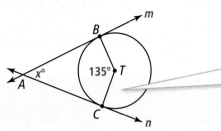

Points *B* and *C* are points of tangency, so $m\angle ABT = 90$ and $m\angle ACT = 90$.

Use the Polygon Angle-Sum Theorem to find *x*.

$$m\angle BAC + m\angle ACT + m\angle CTB + m\angle TBA = 360$$
$$x + 90 + 135 + 90 = 360$$
$$x = 45$$

☑ **Try It!** **2.** Use ⊙*N*.

    a. Is $\overleftrightarrow{MP}$ tangent to ⊙*N*? Explain.

    b. If $\overline{LK}$ is tangent to ⊙*N* at *L*, what is *KN*?

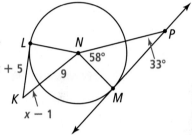

✋ **EXAMPLE 3**   **Find Lengths of Segments Tangent to a Circle**

What is the relationship between $\overline{YZ}$ and $\overline{XZ}$?

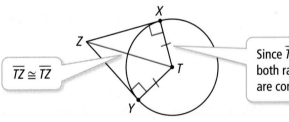

$\overline{TZ} \cong \overline{TZ}$

Since $\overline{TX}$ and $\overline{TY}$ are both radii of ⊙*T*, they are congruent.

By HL, $\triangle TXZ \cong \triangle TYZ$, so $\overline{YZ} \cong \overline{XZ}$ by CPCTC.

☑ **Try It!** **3.** If $TX = 12$ and $TZ = 20$, what are *XZ* and *YZ*?

THEOREM 12-2 Segments Tangent to a Circle Theorem

If two segments with a common endpoint exterior to a circle are tangent to the circle, then the segments are congruent.	**If...**

Then... $\overline{AB} \cong \overline{AC}$

PROOF: SEE EXERCISE 14.

EXAMPLE 4 **Find Measures Involving Tangent Lines**

A satellite requires a line of sight for communication. Between the ground stations farthest from the satellite, what is the amount of time needed for a signal to go from one station up to the satellite, and then down to the other station?

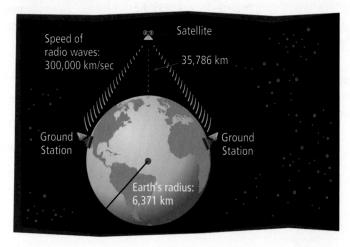

Formulate ◄ The lines from the satellite to the farthest ground stations are tangent to Earth's surface.

Use the Pythagorean Theorem to compute the distance to the ground stations. Then compute the time for radio waves to travel twice this distance.

Compute ◄ **Step 1** Find the distance from the farthest ground stations to the satellite.

$$x^2 + 6,371^2 = (6,371 + 35,786)^2$$

$$x^2 + 40,589,641 = 1,777,212,649$$

$$x^2 = 1,736,623,008$$

$$x \approx 41,673$$

Step 2 Find the time for radio waves to travel this distance twice.

$$(41,673 \times 2) \text{ km} \div 300,000 \text{ km/sec} \approx 0.28 \text{ sec}$$

Interpret ◄ The amount of time for a signal to travel from one of the farthest ground stations to the satellite and back to the other ground station is about 0.28 second.

 Try It! **4.** What is the perimeter of *ABCD*?

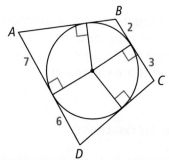

Go Online | PearsonRealize.com

EXAMPLE 5 **Construct Tangent Lines**

How do you construct a tangent to ⊙P passing through point T?

Step 1 Use a straightedge to draw $\overline{PT}$. Label point A where $\overline{PT}$ intersects the circle.

Step 2 Use a compass to construct a circle with center P and passing through T. Construct a perpendicular to $\overline{PT}$ at A. Label point B where the perpendicular intersects the outer circle.

> **COMMON ERROR**
> You may think that A is the midpoint of $\overline{PT}$. However, the construction of a perpendicular line here is different from constructing the perpendicular bisector of $\overline{PT}$.

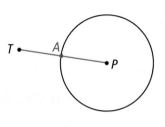

Step 3 Use a straightedge to construct $\overline{BP}$. Label point C where $\overline{BP}$ intersects the inner circle.

Step 4 Use a straightedge to construct $\overline{TC}$.

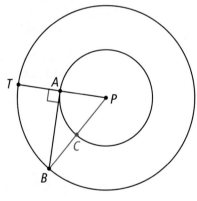
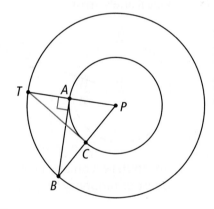

The tangent to ⊙P passing through T is $\overline{TC}$.

 Try It! **5.** Prove that $\overline{TC}$ is tangent to ⊙P.

Given: Two circles share center P, points A and C on the smaller circle, points T and B on the larger circle, $\overline{AB} \perp \overline{PT}$

Prove: $\overline{TC}$ is tangent to ⊙P at C.

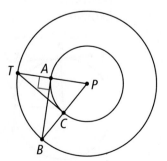

WORDS A tangent to a circle intersects the circle at exactly one point. The radius that contains the point of tangency is perpendicular to the tangent.

DIAGRAM

$\overline{CP} \perp m$

tangent line

point of tangency

Do You UNDERSTAND?

1. **ESSENTIAL QUESTION** How is a tangent line related to the radius of a circle at the point of tangency?

2. **Error Analysis** Kona looked at the figure shown and said that $\overline{AB}$ is tangent to ⊙G at A because it intersects ⊙G only at A. What was Kona's error?

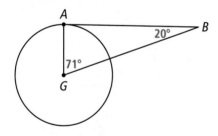

3. **Vocabulary** Can any point on a circle be a *point of tangency*? Explain.

4. **Reason** Lines *m* and *n* are tangent to circles *A* and *B*. What are the relationships between ∠PAS, ∠PQS, ∠RQS, and ∠RBS? Explain.

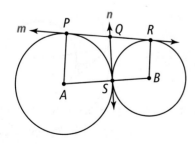

Do You KNOW HOW?

Tell whether each line or segment is a tangent to ⊙B.

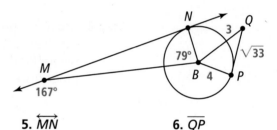

5. $\overleftrightarrow{MN}$

6. $\overline{QP}$

Segment *AC* is tangent to ⊙D at *B*. Find each value.

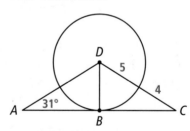

7. $m\angle ADB$

8. BC

Segment *FG* is tangent to ⊙K at *F* and $\overline{HG}$ is tangent to ⊙K at *H*. Find each value.

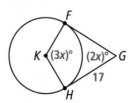

9. FG

10. $m\angle FGH$

UNDERSTAND

11. Error Analysis Segments $\overline{DF}$, $\overline{DH}$, and $\overline{GF}$ are tangent to the circle. Andrew was asked to find DF. Explain Andrew's error.

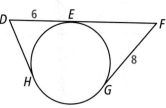

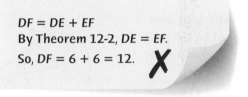

$DF = DE + EF$
By Theorem 12-2, $DE = EF$.
So, $DF = 6 + 6 = 12$. ✗

12. Construct Arguments Use the following outline to write an indirect proof of Theorem 12-1.

Given: Line m is tangent to $\odot T$ at G.

Prove: $\overline{GT} \perp m$

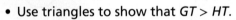

- Assume that $\overline{GT}$ is not perpendicular to m.
- Draw $\overline{HT}$ such that $\overline{HT} \perp m$.
- Use triangles to show that $GT > HT$.
- Show that this is a contradiction, since H is in the exterior of $\odot T$.

13. Construct Arguments Prove the Converse of Theorem 12-1.

Given: $\overline{QR} \perp n$

Prove: n is tangent to $\odot Q$ at R

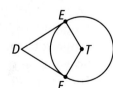

Hint: Select any other point S on line n. Show that $\overline{QS}$ is the hypotenuse of $\triangle QRS$, so $QS > QR$ and therefore S lies outside $\odot Q$.

14. Construct Arguments Prove Theorem 12-2.

Given: $\overline{DE}$ and $\overline{DF}$ are tangent to $\odot T$.

Prove: $\overline{DE} \cong \overline{DF}$

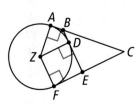

15. Higher Order Thinking If $AC = x$, what is the perimeter of $\triangle BCE$? Explain.

PRACTICE

The segments $\overline{AB}$ and $\overline{CD}$ are tangent to $\odot T$. Find each value. SEE EXAMPLES 1 AND 2

16. AB

17. $m\angle TDC$

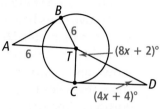

For Exercises 18–20, the segments are tangent to the circle. Find each value. SEE EXAMPLES 3 AND 4

18. DG

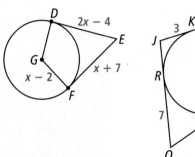

19. Perimeter of $JLNQ$

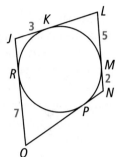

20. AC

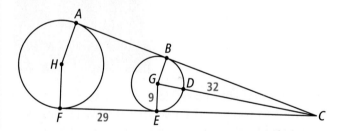

21. Trace $\odot P$ and point A. Construct a tangent to $\odot P$ that passes through A. SEE EXAMPLE 5

22. The diameter of $\odot F$ is 8; $AB = 10$; and $\overline{AB}$, $\overline{BC}$, and $\overline{AC}$ are tangent to $\odot F$. What is the perimeter of $\triangle ABC$?

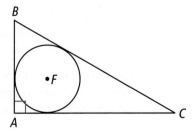

APPLY

23. Make Sense and Persevere Yumiko is shopping for a stand for a decorative glass ball with an 8-inch diameter. She is considering the stand shown and wants to know the height h of the portion of the ball that will be visible if the sides of the stand are tangent to the sphere. What is the value of h?

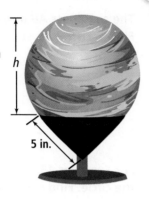

h

5 in.

24. Use Structure Samantha is looking out from the 103rd floor of the Willis Tower on a clear day. How far away is the horizon? Earth's radius is about 6,400 km.

412 m

25. Mathematical Connections Rail planners want to connect the two straight tracks with a curved track as shown. Any curves must have a radius of at least 450 m.

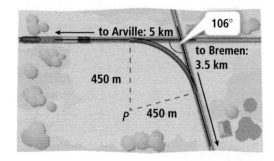

to Arville: 5 km

106°

to Bremen: 3.5 km

450 m

P 450 m

a. Explain how engineers can locate point P, the center of the curved section of track.

b. Once the curved track is constructed, what distance will trains travel between Arvillle and Bremen? Justify your answer.

ASSESSMENT PRACTICE

26. Circle P is described by the equation $(x + 3)^2 + (y - 2)^2 = 25$. Which of the following lines are tangent to $\odot P$? Select all that apply.

Ⓐ $y = x + 3$ Ⓓ $x = 2$

Ⓑ $y = 5$ Ⓔ $y = -3$

Ⓒ $y = x$ Ⓕ $y = x - 3$

27. SAT/ACT Line m is tangent to $\odot A$ at B. What is the area of $\triangle ABC$?

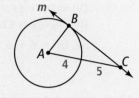

m

B

A

4

5

C

Ⓐ 10   Ⓒ $2\sqrt{65}$

Ⓑ 18   Ⓓ $\dfrac{5\sqrt{65}}{2}$

28. Performance Task The African art design below is based on circles that are tangent to each other.

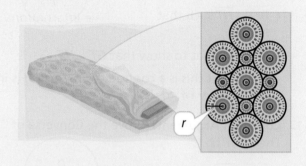

r

Part A If the radius of the larger circles is r, what is the radius of the smaller circles?

Part B Choose a value for the larger radius and draw the pattern. Measure the radii of the small and large circles. Are the values related in the way you described in Part A?

Part C In your diagram for Part B, mark the points where the small and large circles are tangent to each other. Add lines that are tangent to the circles at these points. Describe how the tangent lines you drew illustrate Theorems 10-1 and 10-2.

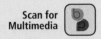

Video

▶ Earth Watch

Scientists estimate that there are currently about 3,000 operational man-made satellites orbiting Earth. These satellites serve different purposes, from communication to navigation and global positioning. Some are weather satellites that collect environmental information.

The International Space Station is the largest man-made satellite that orbits Earth. It serves as a space environment research facility, and it also offers amazing views of Earth. Think about this during the Mathematical Modeling in 3 Acts lesson.

Scan for Multimedia

ACT 1 ▶ Identify the Problem

1. What is the first question that comes to mind after watching the video?

2. Write down the main question you will answer about what you saw in the video.

3. Make an initial conjecture that answers this main question.

4. Explain how you arrived at your conjecture.

5. What information will be useful to know to answer the main question? How can you get it? How will you use that information?

ACT 2 ▶ Develop a Model

6. Use the math that you have learned in this Topic to refine your conjecture.

ACT 3 ▶ Interpret the Results

7. Did your refined conjecture match the actual answer exactly? If not, what might explain the difference?

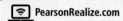
12-3

Chords

Activity   Assess

I CAN... relate the length of a chord to its central angle and the arc it intercepts.

VOCABULARY
• chord

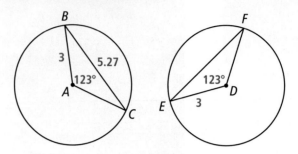

👆 **EXPLORE & REASON**

Use the diagram to answer the questions.

A. What figures in the diagram are congruent? Explain.

B. Look for Relationships How can you find *EF*?

❓ **ESSENTIAL QUESTION**   How are chords related to their central angles and intercepted arcs?

CONCEPTUAL
UNDERSTANDING ➡️

👆 **EXAMPLE 1**   Relate Central Angles and Chords

A chord is a segment whose endpoints are on a circle.
Why is $\overline{RS} \cong \overline{UT}$?

∠*RQS* ≅ ∠*UQT*
because they are
vertical angles.

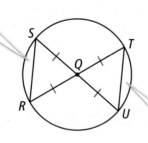

STUDY TIP
Refer to the diagram as you read
the proof. Note which parts of the
triangles are congruent.

$\overline{SQ} \cong \overline{TQ} \cong \overline{UQ} \cong \overline{RQ}$
because all radii of a
circle are ≅.

By the SAS Congruence Theorem, △*QRS* ≅ △*QUT*. Therefore $\overline{RS} \cong \overline{UT}$ because
they are corresponding parts of congruent triangles.

✅ **Try It!**   **1.** Why is ∠*BAC* ≅ ∠*DAE*?

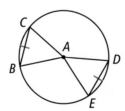

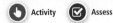

THEOREM 12-3 AND THE CONVERSE

Theorem

If two chords in a circle or in congruent circles are congruent, then their central angles are congruent.

Converse

If two central angles in a circle or in congruent circles are congruent, then their chords are congruent.

PROOF: SEE EXERCISES 12 AND 13.

If... $\overline{MN} \cong \overline{PQ}$
Then... $\angle MTN \cong \angle PTQ$

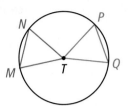

If... $\angle MTN \cong \angle PTQ$
Then... $\overline{MN} \cong \overline{PQ}$

THEOREM 12-4 AND THE CONVERSE

Theorem

If two arcs in a circle or in congruent circles are congruent, then their chords are congruent.

Converse

If two chords in a circle or in congruent circles are congruent, then their arcs are congruent.

PROOF: SEE EXAMPLE 2 AND EXAMPLE 2 TRY IT.

If... $\overparen{MN} \cong \overparen{PQ}$
Then... $\overline{MN} \cong \overline{PQ}$

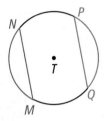

If... $\overline{MN} \cong \overline{PQ}$
Then... $\overparen{MN} \cong \overparen{PQ}$

PROOF ⟶   🖱 **EXAMPLE 2**   **Relate Arcs and Chords**

Write a proof of Theorem 12-4.

Given: $\overparen{AB} \cong \overparen{CD}$

Prove: $\overline{AB} \cong \overline{CD}$

Plan: Use the relationship between central angles and arcs by drawing the radii $\overline{PA}$, $\overline{PB}$, $\overline{PC}$, and $\overline{PD}$.

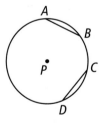

MAKE SENSE AND PERSEVERE
Think about other strategies you can use. How could you use congruent triangles to prove the relationship?

Proof: Since $\overparen{AB} \cong \overparen{CD}$, you know that $m\overparen{AB} = m\overparen{CD}$. And since the measure of a central angle is equal to the measure of its arc, $m\angle APB = m\overparen{AB}$ and $m\angle CPD = m\overparen{CD}$. By substitution, $m\angle APB = m\angle CPD$ and $\angle APB \cong \angle CPD$. So, by the Converse of Theorem 12-3, $\overline{AB} \cong \overline{CD}$.

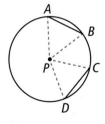

✅ **Try It!**   **2.** Write a flow proof of the Converse of Theorem 12-4.

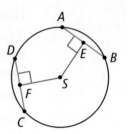
THEOREM 12-5 AND THE CONVERSE

Theorem

If chords are equidistant from the center of a circle or the centers of congruent circles, then they are congruent.

Converse

If chords in a circle or in congruent circles are congruent, then they are equidistant from the center or centers.

PROOF: SEE EXAMPLE 3 AND EXAMPLE 3 TRY IT.

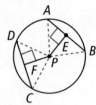

If... $\overline{SE} \cong \overline{SF}$, Then... $\overline{AB} \cong \overline{CD}$
If... $\overline{AB} \cong \overline{CD}$, Then... $\overline{SE} \cong \overline{SF}$

PROOF ⟶ 👆 **EXAMPLE 3**   **Relate Chords Equidistant from the Center**

Write a proof of Theorem 12-5.

Given: $\odot P$ with $\overline{AB} \perp \overline{PE}$,
$\overline{CD} \perp \overline{PF}$,
$\overline{PE} \cong \overline{PF}$

COMMON ERROR
Be sure to construct the triangles with corresponding parts that yield the desired conclusion.

Prove: $\overline{AB} \cong \overline{CD}$

Plan: Construct triangles by drawing the radii $\overline{PA}$, $\overline{PB}$, $\overline{PC}$, and $\overline{PD}$. Then show that the triangles are congruent in order to apply CPCTC.

Proof:

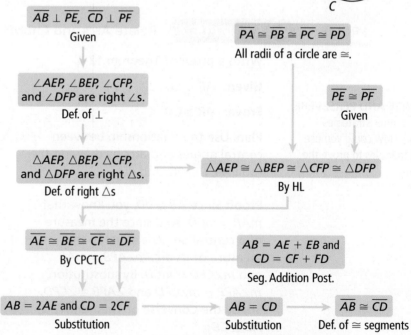

 Try It!   **3.** Write a flow proof of the Converse of Theorem 12-5.

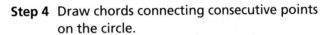
EXAMPLE 4 **Construct a Regular Hexagon Inscribed in a Circle**

STUDY TIP
Remember, a regular polygon is both equilateral and equiangular.

How do you draw a regular hexagon inscribed in ⊙P?

Step 1 Mark point Q on the circle.

Step 2 Set the compass the radius of the circle. Place the compass point at Q and draw an arc through the circle.

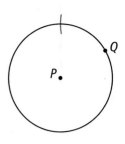

Step 3 Keep the compass setting. Move the compass point to the intersection of the arc and the circle. Draw another arc through the circle. Each point of intersection is a vertex of the hexagon. Continue this way until you have five arcs.

Step 4 Draw chords connecting consecutive points on the circle.

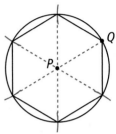

The side lengths of the resulting figure are all congruent because they have the same length as the radius of the circle.

Connecting the center of the circle with the six vertices of the inscribed polygon forms six equilateral triangles, so each angle measures 120. The figure is a regular hexagon.

 Try It! 4. Construct an equilateral triangle inscribed in a circle.

THEOREM 12-6 AND THE CONVERSE

Theorem

If a diameter is perpendicular to a chord, then it bisects the chord.

Converse

If a diameter bisects a chord (that is not a diameter), then it is perpendicular to the chord.

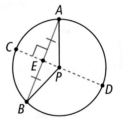

If... $\overline{CD}$ is a diameter, $\overline{AB} \perp \overline{CD}$
Then... $\overline{AE} \cong \overline{BE}$

If... $\overline{CD}$ is a diameter, $\overline{AE} \cong \overline{BE}$
Then... $\overline{AB} \perp \overline{CD}$

PROOF: SEE EXERCISES 15 AND 16.

THEOREM 12-7

The perpendicular bisector of a chord contains the center of the circle.

If...

Then... S is on $\overline{CD}$

PROOF: SEE EXERCISE 28.

APPLICATION 👆 **EXAMPLE 5**   Solve Problems Involving Chords of Circles

An engineer is designing a service tunnel to accommodate two trucks simultaneously. If the tunnel can accommodate a width of 18 ft, what is the greatest truck height that the tunnel can accommodate? Subtract 0.5 ft to account for fluctuations in pavement.

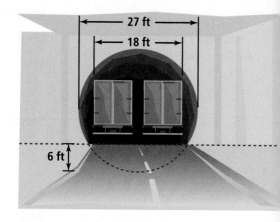

27 ft
18 ft
6 ft

Formulate ◀   Draw and label a sketch to help solve the problem.

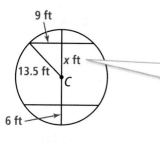

9 ft
13.5 ft
x ft
C
6 ft

Let x be the distance from the center to the greatest height. The radius is 13.5 ft.

Compute ◀   Write and solve an equation for x.

$$9^2 + x^2 = 13.5^2$$

Use the Pythagorean Theorem.

$$x^2 = 13.5^2 - 9^2$$

$$x = \sqrt{13.5^2 - 9^2}$$

$$x \approx 10.06$$

Add the distance from the ground to the center $13.5 - 6 = 7.5$ to x and subtract 0.5 ft to account for fluctuations in pavement.

$$7.5 + 10.06 - 0.5 = 17.06$$

Interpret ◀   The greatest height that the tunnel can accommodate is about 17.06 ft.

☑ **Try It!**   **5.** Fresh cut flowers need to be in at least 4 inches of water. A spherical vase is filled until the surface of the water is a circle 5 inches in diameter. Is the water deep enough for the flowers? Explain.

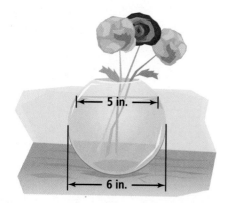

5 in.
6 in.

🛜 **Go Online** | PearsonRealize.com

🔍 CONCEPT SUMMARY Chords

Chords and Central Angles	Chords and Arcs
WORDS Two chords in a circle or in congruent circles are congruent if and only if the central angles of the chords are congruent.	Two chords in a circle or in congruent circles are congruent if and only if the chords intercept congruent arcs.

DIAGRAMS

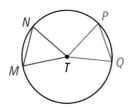

$\angle MTN \cong \angle PTQ$ if and only if $\overline{MN} \cong \overline{PQ}$.

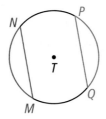

$\overarc{MN} \cong \overarc{PQ}$ if and only if $\overline{MN} \cong \overline{PQ}$.

☑ Do You UNDERSTAND?

1. **? ESSENTIAL QUESTION** How are chords related to their central angles and intercepted arcs?

2. **Error Analysis** Sasha writes a proof to show that two chords are congruent. What is her error?

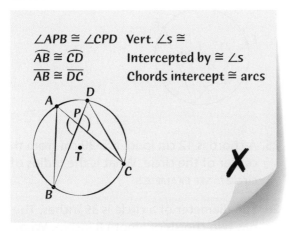

$\angle APB \cong \angle CPD$ Vert. $\angle$s $\cong$
$\overarc{AB} \cong \overarc{CD}$ Intercepted by $\cong$ $\angle$s
$\overline{AB} \cong \overline{DC}$ Chords intercept $\cong$ arcs

✗

3. **Vocabulary** Explain why all diameters of circles are also chords of the circles.

4. **Reason** Given $\overarc{RS} \cong \overarc{UT}$, how can you find UT?

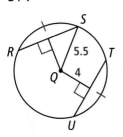

Do You KNOW HOW?

For Exercises 5–10, in ⊙P, $m\overarc{AB} = 43°$, and $AC = DF$. Find each measure.

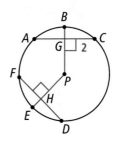

5. DF

6. $m\overarc{ABC}$

7. FH

8. $m\overarc{DE}$

9. AC

10. $m\overarc{DF}$

11. For the corporate headquarters, an executive wants to place a company logo that is six feet in diameter with the sides of the H five feet tall on the front wall. What is the width x of the crossbar for the H?

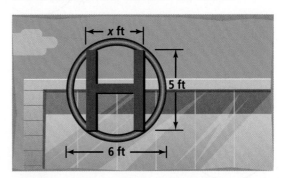

UNDERSTAND

12. Construct Arguments Write a paragraph proof of Theorem 12-3.

Given: $\overline{AB} \cong \overline{CD}$

Prove: $\angle AEB \cong \angle CED$

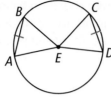

13. Construct Arguments Write a two-column proof of the Converse of Theorem 12-3.

Given: $\angle AEB \cong \angle CED$

Prove: $\overline{AB} \cong \overline{CD}$

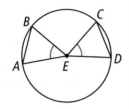

14. Error Analysis What is Ashton's error?

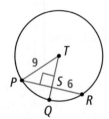

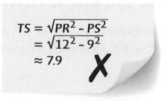

$$TS = \sqrt{PR^2 - PS^2}$$
$$= \sqrt{12^2 - 9^2}$$
$$\approx 7.9 \quad \times$$

15. Construct Arguments Write a proof of Theorem 12-6.

Given: $\overline{LN}$ is a diameter of $\odot Q$; $\overline{LN} \perp \overline{KM}$

Prove: $\overline{KP} \cong \overline{MP}$

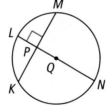

16. Construct Arguments Write a proof of the Converse of Theorem 12-6.

Given: $\overline{LN}$ is a diameter of $\odot Q$; $\overline{KP} \cong \overline{MP}$

Prove: $\overline{LN} \perp \overline{KM}$

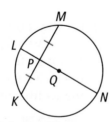

17. Higher Order Thinking $\triangle ABP \sim \triangle CDE$. How do you show that $\overset{\frown}{AB} \cong \overset{\frown}{CD}$?

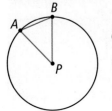

PRACTICE

For Exercises 18–21, in $\odot B$, $m\angle VBT = m\overset{\frown}{PR} = 90$, and $QR = TU$. SEE EXAMPLES 1 AND 2

18. Find $m\angle PBR$.

19. Find $m\overset{\frown}{TV}$.

20. Which angle is congruent to $\angle QBR$?

21. Which segment is congruent to $\overline{TV}$?

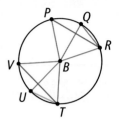

22. Construct a square inscribed in a circle. How is drawing an inscribed square different from drawing an inscribed hexagon or triangle? SEE EXAMPLE 4

23. Find CD. SEE EXAMPLE 3

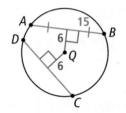

24. Find FG. SEE EXAMPLE 3

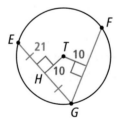

25. A chord is 12 cm long. It is 30 cm from the center of the circle. What is the radius of the circle? SEE EXAMPLE 5

26. The diameter of a circle is 39 inches. The circle has two chords of length 8 inches. What is the distance from each chord to the center of the circle?

27. A chord is 4 units from the center of a circle. The radius of the circle is 5 units. What is the length of the chord?

28. Write a proof of Theorem 12-7.

Given: $\overline{QR}$ is a chord in $\odot P$; $\overline{AB}$ is the perpendicular bisector of $\overline{QR}$.

Prove: $\overline{AB}$ contains P.

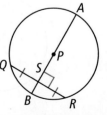

APPLY

29. Mathematical Connections Nadia designs a water ride and wants to use a half-cylindrical pipe in the construction. If she wants the waterway to be 8 ft wide when the water is 2 ft deep, what is the diameter of the pipe?

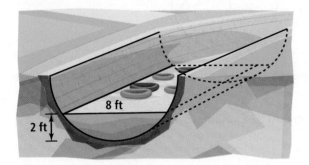

30. Model With Mathematics A bike trail has holes up to 20 in. wide and 5 in. deep. If the diameter of the wheels of Anna's bike is 26 in., can she ride her bike without the wheels hitting the bottom of the holes? Explain.

31. Make Sense and Persevere The bottom of a hemispherical cake has diameter 8 in.

a. If the cake is sliced horizontally in half so each piece has the same height, would the top half fit on a plate with diameter 6 in.? Explain.

b. If the cake is sliced horizontally in thirds so each piece has the same height, would the top third fit on a plate with diameter 5 in.? Explain.

ASSESSMENT PRACTICE

32. Which must be true? Select all that apply.

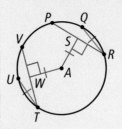

Ⓐ $\overset{\frown}{QR} \cong \overset{\frown}{TU}$ Ⓒ $VW = AS$

Ⓑ $PR = TV$ Ⓓ $PS = SR$

33. SAT/ACT The radius of the semicircle is r, and $CD = \frac{3}{4} \cdot AB$. What is the distance from the chord to the diameter?

Ⓐ $\frac{5}{4}r$ Ⓑ $\frac{\sqrt{7}}{4}r$ Ⓒ $\frac{\sqrt{7}}{4}\pi r$ Ⓓ $\frac{5}{4}\pi r$

34. Performance Task The radius of the range of a radar is 50 miles. At 1:00 P.M., a plane enters the radar screen flying due north. At 1:04 P.M. the aircraft is due east of the radar. At 1:08 P.M., the aircraft leaves the screen. The plane is moving at 8 miles per minute.

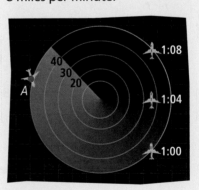

Part A What distance does the plane fly on the controller's screen?

Part B What is the distance of the plane from the radar at 1:04 P.M.?

Part C Another plane enters the screen at point A at 1:12 P.M. and flies in a straight line at 9 miles per minute. If it gets no closer than 40 miles from the radar, at what time does it leave the screen? Explain.

12-4

Inscribed Angles

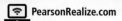
I CAN... use the relationships between angles and arcs in circles to find their measures.

VOCABULARY
• inscribed angle

Activity Assess

Consider ⊙T.

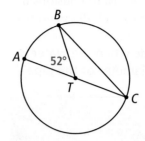

A. Make Sense and Persevere List at least seven things you can conclude about the figure.

B. How is ∠ACB related to ∠ATB? Explain.

ESSENTIAL QUESTION How is the measure of an inscribed angle related to its intercepted arc?

CONCEPTUAL UNDERSTANDING

👆 **EXAMPLE 1** Relate Inscribed Angles to Intercepted Arcs

What is the relationship between $\overset{\frown}{AB}$ and ∠ACB?

An **inscribed angle** has its vertex on a circle and its sides contain chords of the circle.

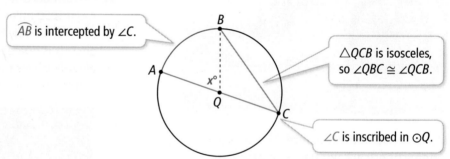

$\overset{\frown}{AB}$ is intercepted by ∠C.

△QCB is isosceles, so ∠QBC ≅ ∠QCB.

∠C is inscribed in ⊙Q.

Draw radius $\overline{QB}$ to form △QCB and central angle ∠AQB.

$m\angle QBC + m\angle QCB = x$ ⟵ Apply the Triangle Exterior Angle Theorem.

$2(m\angle QCB) = x$

$m\angle QCB = \frac{1}{2}x$ ⟵ $m\angle QBC = m\angle QCB$ since ∠QBC ≅ ∠QCB.

$m\angle ACB = \frac{1}{2}m\overset{\frown}{AB}$ ⟵ $m\angle QCB = m\angle ACB$ and $x = m\overset{\frown}{AB}$.

STUDY TIP
There are an infinite number of inscribed angles that intercept the arc. These inscribed angles all have the same angle measure.

The measure of an inscribed angle ∠ACB is half the measure of the intercepted arc $\overset{\frown}{AB}$.

✅ **Try It!** **1.** Given ⊙P with inscribed angle ∠S, if $m\overset{\frown}{RT} = 47$, what is $m\angle S$?

THEOREM 12-8 Inscribed Angles Theorem

The measure of an inscribed angle is half the measure of its intercepted arc.

Case 1

The center is on one side of the angle.

If...

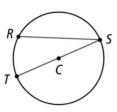

Then... $m\angle S = \frac{1}{2}m\widehat{RT}$

Case 2

The center is inside the angle.

If...

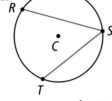

Then... $m\angle S = \frac{1}{2}m\widehat{RT}$

Case 3

The center is outside the angle.

If...

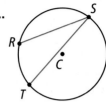

Then... $m\angle S = \frac{1}{2}m\widehat{RT}$

PROOF: SEE EXERCISES 19, 32, AND 33.

EXAMPLE 2   Use the Inscribed Angles Theorem

A. If $m\widehat{DG} = 45.6$, what are $m\angle E$ and $m\angle F$?

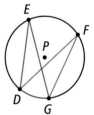

$$m\angle E = \frac{1}{2}m\widehat{DG} \qquad\qquad m\angle F = \frac{1}{2}m\widehat{DG}$$

$$= \frac{1}{2}(45.6) = 22.8 \qquad\qquad = \frac{1}{2}(45.6) = 22.8$$

LOOK FOR RELATIONSHIPS
The diameter of a circle is a straight angle. What is the measure of the arc intercepted by a diameter?

B. If $\widehat{RT}$ is a semicircle, what is $m\angle RST$?

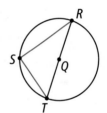

$$m\angle S = \frac{1}{2}m\widehat{RT}$$

$$= \frac{1}{2}(180) = 90$$

C. If $m\widehat{ABC} = 184$ and $m\widehat{BCD} = 242$, what are the measures of the angles of quadrilateral $ABCD$?

$$m\angle A = \frac{1}{2}m\widehat{BCD} \qquad\qquad m\angle B = \frac{1}{2}m\widehat{ADC}$$

$$= \frac{1}{2}(242) = 121 \qquad\qquad = \frac{1}{2}(360 - 184) = 88$$

$$m\angle D = \frac{1}{2}m\widehat{ABC} \qquad\qquad m\angle C = 360 - (121 + 88 + 92)$$

$$= \frac{1}{2}(184) = 92 \qquad\qquad = 59$$

 Try It!   **2. a.** If $m\widehat{RST} = 164$, what is $m\angle RVT$?

      b. If $m\angle SPU = 79$, what is $m\widehat{STU}$?

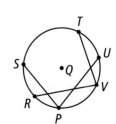

COROLLARIES TO THE INSCRIBED ANGLES THEOREM

Corollary 1	Corollary 2	Corollary 3
Two inscribed angles that intercept the same arc are congruent.	An angle inscribed in a semicircle is a right angle.	The opposite angles of an inscribed quadrilateral are supplementary.

If...

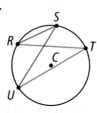

If... $m\widehat{RS} = 180$

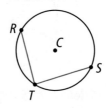

If...

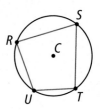

Then... $\angle S \cong \angle T$

Then... $m\angle T = 90$

Then...

$$m\angle R + m\angle T = 180$$
$$m\angle S + m\angle U = 180$$

👆 **EXAMPLE 3**   Explore Angles Formed by a Tangent and a Chord

Given chord $\overline{FH}$ and $\overleftrightarrow{HJ}$ tangent to $\odot E$ at point H, what is the relationship between $\angle FHJ$ and $\widehat{FGH}$?

Consider the angles and arcs formed by the chord, tangent line, and diameter.

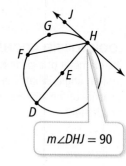

$m\angle DHJ = 90$

Let $m\angle FHJ = x$, so $m\angle FHD = 90 - x$.

$m\angle FHD = \frac{1}{2}m\widehat{DF}$ ⟵ Use the Inscribed Angles Theorem.

$90 - x = \frac{1}{2}m\widehat{DF}$

$m\widehat{DF} = 180 - 2x$

COMMON ERROR
Be careful not to assume arc measure relationships such as assuming $m\widehat{DF} = m\widehat{FH}$. Think about concepts and theorems you can apply when writing mathematical statements.

Since $\overline{DH}$ is a diameter, $m\widehat{DFH} = 180$.

$m\widehat{DF} + m\widehat{FGH} = m\widehat{DFH}$

$180 - 2x + m\widehat{FGH} = 180$

$m\widehat{FGH} = 2x$

$m\widehat{FGH} = 2m\angle FHJ$

$m\angle FHJ = \frac{1}{2}m\widehat{FGH}$

☑ **Try It!**   **3. a.** Given $\overleftrightarrow{BD}$ tangent to $\odot P$ at point C, if $m\widehat{AC} = 88$, what is $m\angle ACB$?

b. Given $\overleftrightarrow{EG}$ tangent to $\odot P$ at point F, if $m\angle GFC = 115$, what is $m\widehat{FAC}$?

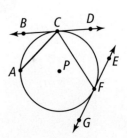

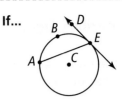
THEOREM 12-9

The measure of an angle formed by a tangent and a chord is half the measure of its intercepted arc.

If...

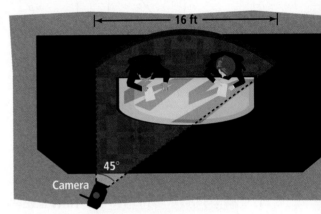

PROOF: SEE EXERCISE 34.

Then... $m\angle AED = \frac{1}{2}m\widehat{ABE}$

APPLICATION

✋ **EXAMPLE 4**   Use Arc Measure to Solve a Problem

A director wants to position two cameras to capture an entire circular backdrop behind two newscasters. Where should he position the cameras?

Formulate ◄ Represent the set as a chord $\overline{AB}$ of a circle that intercepts an arc measuring 90°.

16 ft

45°

Camera

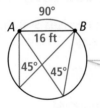

> Any point on the major arc $\widehat{AB}$ is the vertex of a 45° angle that intercepts arc $\widehat{AB}$.

To find the size of the circle, find the radius of the circle.

Compute ◄ Let P be the center of the circle.

$$m\angle APB = m\widehat{AB} = 90$$

Find r.

$$\sqrt{2} \cdot r = 16$$

> $\triangle APB$ is a 45°-45°-90° triangle, and the length of the hypotenuse is 16.

$$r = \frac{16}{\sqrt{2}}$$

$$r = 8\sqrt{2}$$

Center P is on the perpendicular bisector of $\overline{AB}$, so P is 8 ft from the midpoint of $\overline{AB}$.

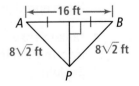

Interpret ◄ Position a camera on any point of circle with radius $8\sqrt{2}$ ft and center 8 ft from the midpoint of the set.

☑ **Try It!**   **4. a.** Given $\overleftrightarrow{WY}$ tangent to ⊙C at point X, what is $m\widehat{XZ}$?

b. What is $m\angle VXW$?

50°   Z

196°

•C

Y

X

W   V

CONCEPT SUMMARY Inscribed Angles and Intercepted Arcs

Inscribed Angles	**Angles Formed by a Tangent and a Chord**
WORDS The measure of an inscribed angle is one-half the measure of its intercepted arc.	The measure of an angle formed by a tangent and a chord is one-half the measure of its intercepted arc.

DIAGRAMS

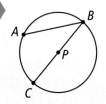 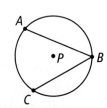 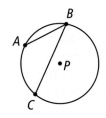

SYMBOLS $m\angle ABC = \frac{1}{2}m\widehat{AC}$ | $m\angle ABD = \frac{1}{2}m\widehat{BCD}$

✓ Do You UNDERSTAND?

1. **ESSENTIAL QUESTION** How is the measure of an inscribed angle related to its intercepted arc?

2. **Error Analysis** Darren is asked to find $m\widehat{XZ}$. What is his error?

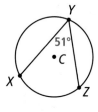

$$m\widehat{XZ} = \frac{1}{2}\,m\angle XYZ$$
$$= \frac{1}{2}(51)$$ ✗
$$= 25.5$$

3. **Reason** Can the measure of an inscribed angle be greater than the measure of the intercepted arc? Explain.

4. **Make Sense and Persevere** Is there enough information in the diagram to find $m\widehat{RST}$? Explain.

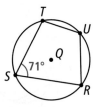

Do You KNOW HOW?

For Exercises 5–8, find each measure in $\odot Q$.

5. $m\widehat{JKL}$

6. $m\widehat{MJ}$

7. $m\angle KJM$

8. $m\angle KLM$

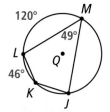

For Exercises 9–12, $\overleftrightarrow{DF}$ is tangent to $\odot Q$ at point E. Find each measure.

9. $m\widehat{EGH}$

10. $m\widehat{EKJ}$

11. $m\angle HEJ$

12. $m\angle DEJ$

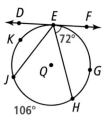

For Exercises 13–16, find each measure in $\odot M$.

13. $m\angle PRQ$

14. $m\angle PTR$

15. $m\angle RST$

16. $m\angle SRT$

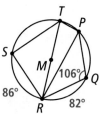

Scan for Multimedia

Practice Tutorial

Additional Exercises Available Online

17. **Mathematical Connections** Given $m\widehat{ABC} = x$, what is an expression for $m\widehat{DAB}$ in terms of x? Explain.

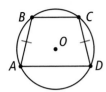

18. **Error Analysis** Casey is asked to find $m\widehat{WVZ}$. What is Casey's error?

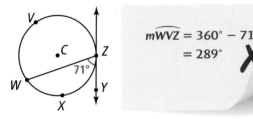

$$m\widehat{WVZ} = 360° - 71°$$
$$= 289° ✗$$

19. **Higher Order Thinking** Write a proof of the Inscribed Angles Theorem, Case 2.

Given: Center C is inside $\angle RST$.

Prove: $m\angle RST = \frac{1}{2}m\widehat{RT}$

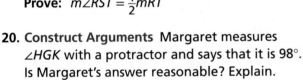

20. **Construct Arguments** Margaret measures $\angle HGK$ with a protractor and says that it is 98°. Is Margaret's answer reasonable? Explain.

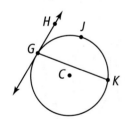

21. **Use Structure** Given $\odot Q$ with diameter $\overline{AC}$, if point B is located on $\odot Q$, can $\angle ABC$ ever be less than 90°? Can it ever be greater than 90°? Explain.

For Exercises 22–25, find each measure in $\odot P$.
SEE EXAMPLES 1 AND 2

22. $m\widehat{AD}$

23. $m\widehat{BDC}$

24. $m\angle ADC$

25. $m\angle BAD$

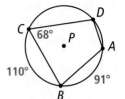

For Exercises 26–28, $\overleftrightarrow{SU}$ is tangent to $\odot P$ at point T. Find each measure. SEE EXAMPLES 2 AND 3

26. $m\widehat{TVW}$

27. $m\angle TWX$

28. $m\angle TWV$

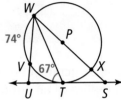

For Exercises 29–31, $\overleftrightarrow{HK}$ is tangent to $\odot C$ at point J. Find each measure. SEE EXAMPLES 3 AND 4

29. $m\angle KJM$

30. $m\angle MJN$

31. $m\angle HJN$

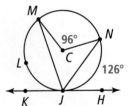

32. Write a proof of the Inscribed Angles Theorem, Case 1.

Given: Center C is on $\overline{ST}$.

Prove: $m\angle RST = \frac{1}{2}m\widehat{RT}$

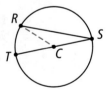

33. Write a proof of the Inscribed Angles Theorem, Case 3.

Given: Center C is outside $\angle RST$.

Prove: $m\angle RST = \frac{1}{2}m\widehat{RT}$

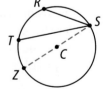

34. Write a two-column proof of Theorem 12-9.

Given: $\overleftrightarrow{AB}$ tangent to $\odot P$ at point B.

Prove: $m\angle ABD = \frac{1}{2}m\widehat{BCD}$

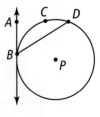

APPLY

35. Construct Arguments Deondra needs to know the angle measure for each notch in the 16-notch socket wrench she is designing. The notches will be the same size. What is the angle measure?

36. Use Structure Cheyenne wants to make a replica of an antique sundial using the fragment of the sundial she acquired. Is there enough information for her to determine the diameter of the sundial? Explain.

37. Use Appropriate Tools Malcom sets up chairs for a home theater showing on his television. His optimal viewing angle is 50°. Besides at chair A, where else could he sit with the same viewing angle? Draw a diagram and explain.

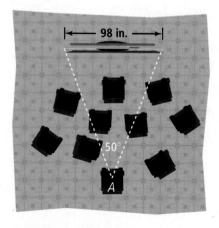

ASSESSMENT PRACTICE

38. Write an expression that represents $m\angle DGF$.

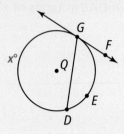

39. SAT/ACT Segment AB is tangent to $\odot M$ at Point A. What is $m\angle DAC$?

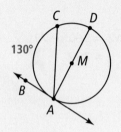

Ⓐ 25

Ⓑ 65

Ⓒ 50

Ⓓ 90

Ⓔ 100

40. Performance Task Triangle DEF is inscribed in $\odot G$, and $\overline{AB}$, $\overline{BC}$, and $\overline{AC}$ are tangent to $\odot G$.

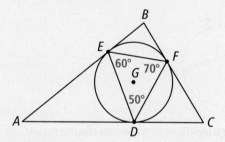

Part A Are there any isosceles triangles in the diagram? If so, explain why the triangles are isosceles. If not, explain why not.

Part B Are $\triangle ABC$ and $\triangle DEF$ similar? Explain.

12-5

Secant Lines and Segments

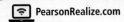 PearsonRealize.com

I CAN... use angle measures and segment lengths formed by intersecting lines and circles to solve problems.

VOCABULARY
• secant

CONCEPTUAL UNDERSTANDING

EXPLORE & REASON

Skyler made the design shown. Points *A*, *B*, *C*, and *D* are spaced evenly around the circle.

A. Using points *A*, *B*, *C*, and *D* as vertices, what congruent angles can you find? How can you justify that they are congruent?

B. Make Sense and Persevere What strategy did you use to make sure you found all congruent angles?

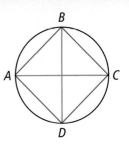

ESSENTIAL QUESTION How are the measures of angles, arcs, and segments formed by intersecting secant lines related?

EXAMPLE 1 Relate Secants and Angle Measures

A secant is a line, ray, or segment that intersects a circle at two points. Secants $\overleftrightarrow{AC}$ and $\overleftrightarrow{BD}$ intersect to form ∠1. How can you use arc measures to find $m\angle 1$?

Draw $\overline{AB}$ to form △*AEB*.

Since ∠*BAC* is an inscribed angle, $m\angle BAC = \frac{1}{2}m\widehat{BC}$.

Since ∠*ABD* is an inscribed angle, $m\angle ABD = \frac{1}{2}m\widehat{AD}$.

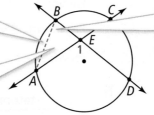

MAKE SENSE AND PERSEVERE
Consider other relationships in the diagram. What is an alternate plan you could use to solve the problem?

Apply the Triangle Exterior Angle Theorem.

$$m\angle 1 = m\angle ABD + m\angle BAC$$
$$= \frac{1}{2}m\widehat{AD} + \frac{1}{2}m\widehat{BC}$$

So the measure of the angle is half the sum of the measures of the two intercepted arcs.

 Try It! **1.** If $m\widehat{AD} = 155$ and $m\widehat{BC} = 61$, what is $m\angle 1$?

THEOREM 12-10

The measure of an angle formed by two secant lines that intersect inside a circle is half the sum of the measures of the intercepted arcs.

If...

Then... $m\angle 1 = \frac{1}{2}(x + y)$

PROOF: SEE EXERCISE 18.

THEOREM 12-11

The measure of an angle formed by two lines that intersect outside a circle is half the difference of the measures of the intercepted arcs.

Case 1	Case 2	Case 3
If...	If...	If...
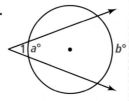	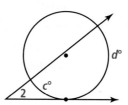	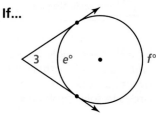
Then...	Then...	Then...
$m\angle 1 = \frac{1}{2}(b - a)$	$m\angle 2 = \frac{1}{2}(d - c)$	$m\angle 3 = \frac{1}{2}(f - e)$

PROOF: SEE EXAMPLE 2, TRY IT 2, AND EXERCISE 19.

EXAMPLE 2   Prove Theorem 12-11, Case 1

Write a proof for Theorem 12-11, Case 1.

Given: Secants $\overrightarrow{PS}$ and $\overrightarrow{PT}$

Prove: $m\angle P = \frac{1}{2}(m\widehat{ST} - m\widehat{QR})$

Proof:

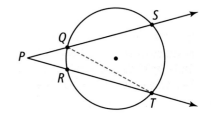

STUDY TIP
Remember to look for helpful relationships that you can draw on the given figure when completing a proof. Drawing $\overline{QT}$ forms inscribed angles, which are needed for this proof.

Statement	Reason
1) $\overrightarrow{PS}$ and $\overrightarrow{PT}$ are secants.	1) Given
2) Draw $\overline{QT}$.	2) Two points determine a segment.
3) $m\angle QTP = \frac{1}{2}m\widehat{QR}$	3) Inscribed Angles Theorem
4) $m\angle SQT = \frac{1}{2}m\widehat{ST}$	4) Inscribed Angles Theorem
5) $m\angle SQT = m\angle P + m\angle QTP$	5) Triangle Exterior Angle Theorem
6) $m\angle P = m\angle SQT - m\angle QTP$	6) Subtraction Property of Equality
7) $m\angle P = \frac{1}{2}m\widehat{ST} - \frac{1}{2}m\widehat{QR}$	7) Substitution
8) $m\angle P = \frac{1}{2}(m\widehat{ST} - m\widehat{QR})$	8) Distributive Property

---

Try It!   **2.** Prove Theorem 12-11, Case 2.

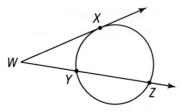

EXAMPLE 3   Use Secants and Tangents to Solve Problems

A. What is $m\angle ABD$?

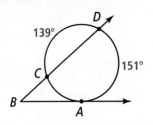

Step 1 Find $m\widehat{AC}$.

$$m\widehat{AC} = 360 - m\widehat{AD} - m\widehat{CD}$$

$$= 360 - 151 - 139$$

$$= 70$$

Step 2 Find $m\angle ABD$.

$$m\angle ABD = \tfrac{1}{2}(m\widehat{AD} - m\widehat{AC})$$

$$= \tfrac{1}{2}(151 - 70)$$

$$= 40.5$$

> Since the angle is formed outside the circle by a secant and a tangent, apply Theorem 12-11, Case 2.

B. What is $m\widehat{LM}$?

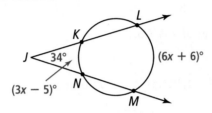

COMMON ERROR
Remember to add the arc measures when the vertex is inside the circle and to subtract them when it is outside the circle.

Step 1 Find x.

$$m\angle LJM = \tfrac{1}{2}(m\widehat{LM} - m\widehat{KN})$$

$$34 = \tfrac{1}{2}((6x + 6) - (3x - 5))$$

$$34 = \tfrac{1}{2}(3x + 11)$$

$$68 = 3x + 11$$

$$19 = x$$

> Since the angle is formed outside the circle by two secants, apply Theorem 12-11, Case 1.

Step 2 Find $m\widehat{LM}$.

$$m\widehat{LM} = 6x + 6$$

$$= 6(19) + 6$$

$$= 120$$

> Substitute the value of x found in Step 1.

 Try It!   3. a. What is $m\widehat{WX}$?

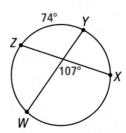

b. What is $m\angle PSQ$?

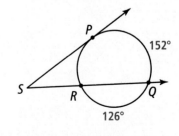

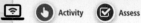
👆 **EXAMPLE 4** Develop Chord Length Relationships

What is the value of *x*?

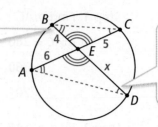

∠A and ∠B are inscribed angles that intercept the same arc.

∠C and ∠D are inscribed angles that intercept the same arc.

By the Angle-Angle Similarity Theorem, △AED ∼ △BEC.

$$\frac{ED}{EC} = \frac{EA}{EB}$$

$$\frac{x}{5} = \frac{6}{4}$$

The ratios of corresponding sides of similar triangles are equal.

$4 \cdot x = 6 \cdot 5$

$x = 7.5$

The value of *x* is 7.5.

COMMON ERROR
Be careful to correctly identify corresponding sides in similar triangles. The sides opposite congruent angles are the corresponding sides.

 Try It! **4.** What is the value of *y*?

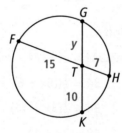

THEOREM 12-12

For a given point and circle, the product of the lengths of the two segments from the point to the circle is constant along any line through the point and circle.

Case 1	Case 2	Case 3
If...	If...	If...
	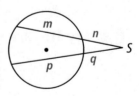	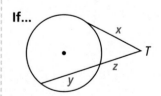
Then...	Then...	Then...
$ab = cd$	$(n + m)n = (q + p)q$	$x^2 = (z + y)z$

PROOF: SEE EXERCISES 11, 23, and 24.

APPLICATION

EXAMPLE 5 **Use Segment Relationships to Find Lengths**

Archaeologists found part of the circular wall that surrounds an ancient city. They measure the distances shown. The 272-m segment lies on a line through the center of the circular wall. What was the diameter of the circular wall?

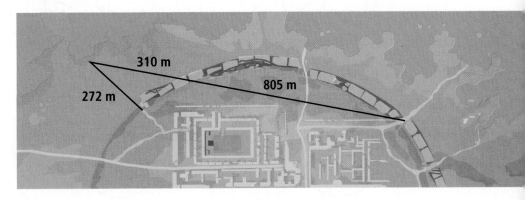

Draw a diagram to represent the situation.

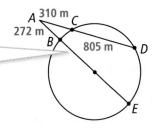

The line through $\overline{AB}$ continues to the center of the circle, so $\overline{BE}$ is a diameter.

MAKE SENSE AND PERSEVERE
Are there other measurements that archaeologists could have taken to help find the diameter using another method?

Write an equation to relate the segment lengths.

$$(AB + BE)AB = (AC + CD)AC$$

$$(272 + BE)(272) = (310 + 805)(310)$$

Apply Theorem 12-12 and substitute known segment lengths.

$$73{,}984 + 272 \cdot BE = 345{,}650$$

$$272 \cdot BE = 271{,}666$$

$$BE \approx 998.8$$

The diameter of the circular wall was about 998.8 meters.

 Try It! **5. a.** What is the value of a?   **b.** What is EC?

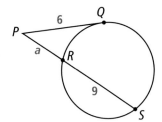

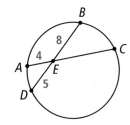

CONCEPT SUMMARY Angle and Segment Relationships in a Circle

Vertex Inside the Circle	Vertex Outside the Circle
ANGLES 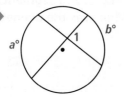	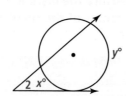 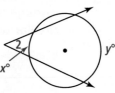 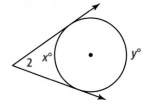
$m\angle 1 = \frac{1}{2}(a + b)$	$m\angle 2 = \frac{1}{2}(y - x)$
SEGMENTS	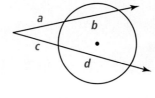 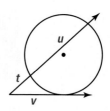
$wx = yz$	$(a + b)a = (c + d)c$ $(t + u)t = v^2$

☑ Do You UNDERSTAND?

1. ❓ **ESSENTIAL QUESTION** How are the measures of angles, arcs, and segments formed by intersecting secant lines related?

2. Error Analysis Derek is asked to find the value of *x*. What is his error?

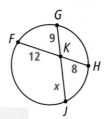

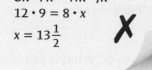

$GK \cdot FK = HK \cdot JK$
$12 \cdot 9 = 8 \cdot x$
$x = 13\frac{1}{2}$ ✗

3. Vocabulary How are *secants* and *tangents* to a circle alike and different?

4. Construct Arguments The rays shown are tangent to the circle. Show that $m\angle 1 = (x - 180)$.

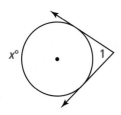

Do You KNOW HOW?

For Exercises 5 and 6, find each angle measure. Rays *QP* and *QR* are tangent to the circle in Exercise 6.

5. $m\angle BEC$

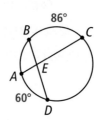

6. $m\angle PQR$

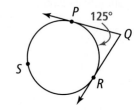

For Exercises 7 and 8, find each length. Ray *HJ* is tangent to the circle in Exercise 7.

7. *GF*

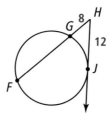

8. *LM*

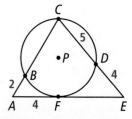

For Exercises 9 and 10, $\overline{AE}$ is tangent to ⊙*P*. Find each length.

9. *BC*

10. *EF*

PRACTICE & PROBLEM SOLVING

UNDERSTAND

11. Construct Arguments Given ⊙X, write a two-column proof of Theorem 12-12, Case 2.

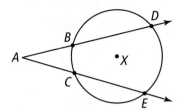

12. Error Analysis Cindy is asked to find m∠VXZ. What is her error?

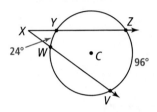

$$m\angle VXZ = \frac{1}{2}\left(m\widehat{WY} + m\widehat{VZ}\right)$$
$$= \frac{1}{2}(24 + 96)$$
$$= 60 \quad \textbf{✗}$$

13. Mathematical Connections Given ⊙P, secant $\overrightarrow{CA}$, and tangent $\overrightarrow{CD}$, what is the area of ⊙P?

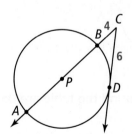

14. Higher Order Thinking Given ⊙T, and tangents $\overline{AD}$ and $\overline{CD}$, what is the measure of ∠ADC?

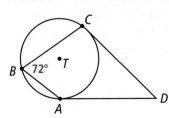

15. Communicate Precisely How would you describe each case of Theorem 12-11?

PRACTICE

For Exercises 16 and 17, find each measure.
SEE EXERCISE 1

16. m∠1

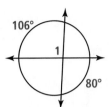

17. x

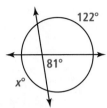

18. Given ⊙A and secants $\overline{PR}$ and $\overline{QS}$, write a paragraph proof of Theorem 12-10. SEE EXAMPLE 1

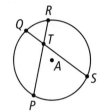

19. Given ⊙Q and tangents $\overrightarrow{AB}$ and $\overrightarrow{AC}$, write a two-column proof of Theorem 12-11, Case 3.
SEE EXAMPLE 2

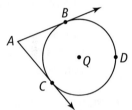

20. Given ⊙C, inscribed angle ∠RWV, and secants $\overrightarrow{TR}$ and $\overrightarrow{TV}$, what is the measure of ∠RTV?
SEE EXAMPLE 3

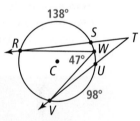

For Exercises 21 and 22, find each length.
SEE EXERCISE 4

21. a

22. b

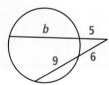

23. Given ⊙T and secants $\overline{JK}$ and $\overline{LM}$ intersecting at point N, write a paragraph proof of Theorem 12-12, Case 1.
SEE EXAMPLE 4

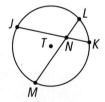

24. Given ⊙C, secant $\overrightarrow{QS}$ and tangent $\overline{PQ}$, write a two-column proof of Theorem 12–12, Case 3.
SEE EXAMPLE 5

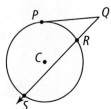

APPLY

25. Use Structure Chris stands in the position shown to take a picture of a sculpture with a circular base.

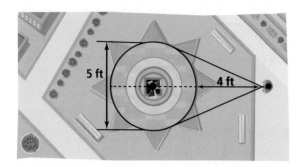

a. Chris is deciding on which lens to use. What is the minimum view angle from where he stands so he can get as much of the base as possible in his picture?

b. If Chris uses a lens with a view angle of 40°, what is the shortest distance he could stand from the sculpture?

26. Reason A satellite orbits above the equator of Mars as shown and transmits images back to a scientist in the control room. What percent of the equator is the scientist able to see? Explain.

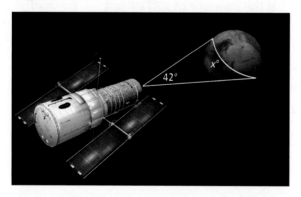

27. Use Structure Carolina wants to etch the design shown onto a circular piece of glass. At what measure should she cut ∠1? Explain.

ASSESSMENT PRACTICE

28. For what measure of $\widehat{UW}$ does $m\angle TVX = 34$?

$m\widehat{UW} = $ _____

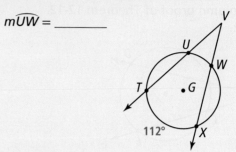

29. SAT/ACT Given $\odot P$ and secants $\overline{FH}$ and $\overline{FK}$, what is FG?

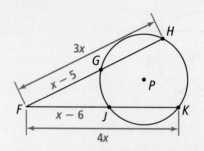

Ⓐ 3　　Ⓑ 4　　Ⓒ 9　　Ⓓ 27　　Ⓔ 36

30. Performance Task Alberto, Benson, Charles, and Deon sit at a round lunch table with diameter 54 inches. The salt shaker is 27 inches from Charles, 18 inches from Benson, 20 inches from Deon, and 30 inches from Alberto.

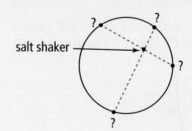

Part A In what order around the table are they seated? Explain.

Part B Alberto, Benson, Charles, and Deon change the positions of their seats and sit evenly spaced around the table. If the location of the salt shaker does not change, what is the closest that one of them could be from the salt shaker? What is the farthest?

Topic Review

? TOPIC ESSENTIAL QUESTION

1. When a line or lines intersect a circle how are the figures formed related to the radius, circumference, and area of the circle?

Vocabulary Review

Choose the correct term to complete each sentence.

2. A(n) _____ is a region of a circle with two radii and an arc of the circle as borders.

3. A(n) _____ is an angle with its vertex on the circle.

4. A(n) _____ and the corresponding circle have exactly one point in common.

5. When both rays of an angle intersect a circle, the _____ is the portion of the circle between the rays.

- central angle
- chord
- inscribed angle
- intercepted arc
- secant
- sector of a circle
- segment of a circle
- tangent to a circle

Concepts & Skills Review

LESSON 12-1 **Arcs and Sectors**

Quick Review

Arc length and the area of a **sector of a circle** are proportional to the corresponding central angle.

The length of an arc is $\frac{n}{360}$ of the circumference, where n is the measure of the central angle in degrees, and the area of a sector is $\frac{n}{360}$ of the area of the circle.

Example

Circle *J* has a radius of 6 cm. What is the area of a sector with a central angle of 80°?

Write the formula for the area of a sector:

$$A = \frac{n}{360} \cdot \pi r^2$$

$$= \frac{80}{360} \cdot \pi(6)^2$$

$$\approx 25.1$$

The area of the sector is about 25.1 cm².

Practice & Problem Solving

Find each arc length in terms of π.

6. $\widehat{JK}$

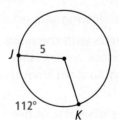

7. $\widehat{ABC}$

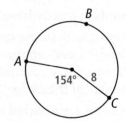

Find the area of each sector in terms of π.

8. sector *NRM*

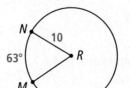

9. sector *DSE*

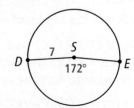

10. **Reason** If you know the circumference of a circle and the area of a sector of the circle, how could you determine the central angle of the sector? Explain.

Lines Tangent to a Circle

Quick Review

A **tangent to a circle** is perpendicular to the radius of the circle at the **point of tangency**. You can use properties of right triangles to solve problems involving tangents.

Example

Lines *m* and *n* are tangent to ⊙*T*. What is *m∠ATB*?

Since lines *m* and *n* are tangent lines, *m∠SAT* = *m∠SBT* = 90. Points *A*, *T*, *B*, and *S* form a quadrilateral, so use the angle sum of a quadrilateral to solve the problem.

$$m∠SAT + m∠ASB + m∠SBT + m∠ATB = 360$$
$$90 + 61 + 90 + m∠ATB = 360$$
$$m∠ATB = 119$$

So, *m∠ATB* = 119.

Practice & Problem Solving

For Exercises 11–12, $\overline{QR}$ and $\overline{AB}$ are tangent to the circle. Find each value.

11. *QR*

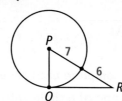

12. *m∠CAB*

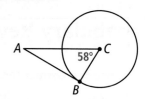

13. Construct Arguments If $\overline{GH}$ is a diameter of ⊙*T*, is it possible to draw tangents to *G* and *H* from the same point external to ⊙*T*? Explain.

14. Segment MN is tangent to ⊙ *L*. What is the radius of the circle? Explain.

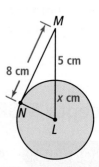

Chords

Quick Review

Chords in a circle have the following properties:

- Two chords in the same circle with the same length have congruent central angles, have congruent arcs, and are equidistant from the center of the circle.

- Chords are bisected by the diameter of the circle that is perpendicular to the chord.

Example

What is the radius of ⊙*T*?

Since $\overline{CT} \perp \overline{AB}$, $\overline{CT}$ bisects $\overline{AB}$. So, *CB* = 7. Use the Pythagorean Theorem to find the radius.

$$(CT)^2 + (CB)^2 = (BT)^2$$
$$3^2 + 7^2 = (BT)^2$$
$$BT \approx 7.6$$

The radius of ⊙*T* is about 7.6.

Practice & Problem Solving

For Exercises 15–17, the radius of ⊙*T* is 7. Find each value. Round to the nearest tenth.

15. *FH*

16. *CD*

17. *m∠BTA*

18. Look for Relationships Circles *T* and *S* intersect at points *A* and *B*. What is the relationship between $\overline{AB}$ and $\overleftrightarrow{TS}$? Explain.

19. A contractor cuts off part of a circular countertop so that it fits against a wall. What should be the length *x* of the cut? Round to the nearest tenth.

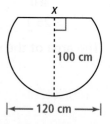

 Go Online | PearsonRealize.com

Inscribed Angles

Quick Review

The measure of an **inscribed angle** is half the measure of its intercepted arc. As a result:

- Opposite angles of an inscribed quadrilateral are supplementary.
- The measure of an angle formed by a tangent and chord is half the measure of the intercepted arc.

Example

What are the angle measures of △ABC?

Use inscribed angles:

$m\angle BAC = \frac{1}{2}(84) = 42$

$m\angle BCA = \frac{1}{2}(116) = 58$

$m\angle ABC = 180 - 42 - 58 = 80$

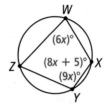

Practice & Problem Solving

Find each value.

20. $m\widehat{EF}$

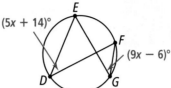

21. $m\angle MNP$

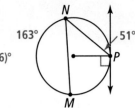

22. $m\angle WZY$

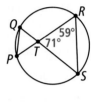

23. $m\angle QPR$

24. Generalize If a rectangle is inscribed in a circle, what must be true about the diagonals of the rectangle? Explain.

Secant Lines and Segments

Quick Review

Secant lines form angles with special relationships:

- The measure of an angle formed by secants intersecting inside a circle is half the sum of the measures of the intercepted arcs.
- The measure of an angle formed by secants intersecting outside a circle is half the difference of the measures of the intercepted arcs.

Example

What is the value of x?

Use secant segment relationships.

$(AE)(AE + ED) = (AB)(AB + BC)$

$6(6 + 12) = 4(4 + x)$

$108 = 16 + 4x$

$92 = 4x$

$23 = x$

The value of x is 23.

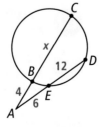

Practice & Problem Solving

For Exercises 25 and 26, find each value in the figure shown.

25. QR

26. $m\angle NRP$

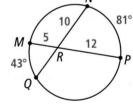

For Exercises 27 and 28, find each value in the figure shown. The segment $\overline{WZ}$ is tangent to the circle.

27. WZ

28. $m\widehat{XZ}$

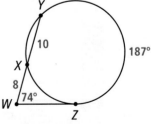

29. Construct Arguments A student said that if $\angle A$ is formed by two secants intersecting outside of a circle, then $m\angle A < 90$. Do you agree? Explain.

TOPIC 13

Two- and Three-Dimensional Models

? TOPIC ESSENTIAL QUESTION

How is Cavalieri's Principle helpful in understanding the volume formulas for solids?

Topic Overview

enVision® STEM Project:
Design a Rigid Package

13-1 Three-Dimensional Figures and Cross Sections

13-2 Volumes of Prisms and Cylinders

Mathematical Modeling in 3 Acts:
Box 'Em Up

13-3 Pyramids and Cones

13-4 Spheres

Topic Vocabulary

- Cavalieri's Principle
- hemisphere
- oblique cylinder
- oblique prism

Digital Experience

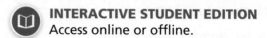

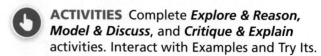

INTERACTIVE STUDENT EDITION
Access online or offline.

ACTIVITIES Complete *Explore & Reason, Model & Discuss*, and *Critique & Explain* activities. Interact with Examples and Try Its.

ANIMATION View and interact with real-world applications.

PRACTICE Practice what you've learned.

 Go online | **PearsonRealize.com**

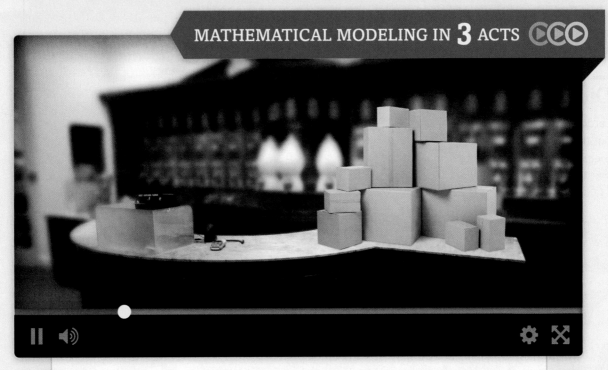

MATHEMATICAL MODELING IN **3** ACTS

▶ Box 'Em Up

With so many people and businesses shopping online, retailers, and especially e-retailers, ship more and more packages every day. Some of the products people order have unusual sizes and shapes and need custom packaging. Imagine how you might package a surfboard, or a snow blower, or even live crawfish to ship to someone's house!

Think about this during the Mathematical Modeling in 3 Acts lesson.

TOPIC 13

VIDEOS Watch clips to support *Mathematical Modeling in 3 Acts Lessons* and **enVision® STEM Projects.**

CONCEPT SUMMARY Review key lesson content through multiple representations.

ASSESSMENT Show what you've learned.

GLOSSARY Read and listen to English and Spanish definitions.

TUTORIALS Get help from *Virtual Nerd*, right when you need it.

MATH TOOLS Explore math with digital tools and manipulatives.

Did You Know?

Cardboard boxes look simple, but the machines that make them are not. This **cartoning machine** is capable of making **15,000 boxes per day**.

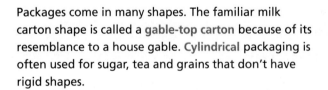

Packages come in many shapes. The familiar milk carton shape is called a **gable-top carton** because of its resemblance to a house gable. **Cylindrical** packaging is often used for sugar, tea and grains that don't have rigid shapes.

Manufacturers consider many factors when designing a package.

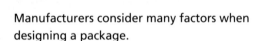

- ☑ Marketing appeal
- ☑ Cost of materials
- ☑ Simplicity
- ☑ Safety
- ☑ Recyclability

▶ Your Task: Design a Rigid Package

You will design a rigid package for a product of your choice. Your design will address factors such as attractiveness, protection for the product, and cost. You will then draw two- and three-dimensional representations of your package and build a prototype.

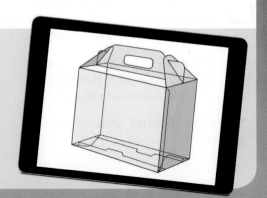

13-1

Three-Dimensional Figures and Cross Sections

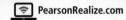
PearsonRealize.com

I CAN... identify three-dimensional figures and their relationships with polygons to solve problems.

EXPLORE & REASON

Consider a cube of cheese. If you slice straight down through the midpoints of four parallel edges of the cube, the outline of the newly exposed surface is a square.

A. How would you slice the cube to expose a triangular surface?

B. Communicate Precisely How would you slice the cube to expose a triangular surface with the greatest possible area?

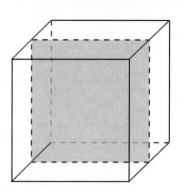

? ESSENTIAL QUESTION

How are three-dimensional figures and polygons related?

CONCEPTUAL UNDERSTANDING

EXAMPLE 1 Develop Euler's Formula

How many faces, vertices, and edges does each prism contain? Do you notice any patterns in these quantities?

    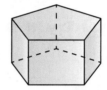

Make a table of the number of vertices, edges, and faces for each prism. Look for patterns and relationships.

Type of Prism	Faces (F)	Vertices (V)	Edges (E)
triangular	5	6	9
rectangular	6	8	12
pentagonal	7	10	15
hexagonal	8	12	18

> For each additional face on the prism, the prism gains 2 vertices and 3 edges.

MODEL WITH MATHEMATICS
Look at the relationships between the number of vertices, faces, and edges. How might you represent these relationships in an equation?

Look at the sums of the faces and vertices. Compare it to the number of edges.

$$5 + 6 = 9 + 2$$
$$6 + 8 = 12 + 2$$
$$7 + 10 = 15 + 2$$
$$8 + 12 = 18 + 2$$

> The sum of the faces and vertices is always 2 more than the number of edges.

 Try It! **1.** How many faces, vertices, and edges do the pyramids have? Name at least three patterns you notice.

  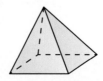   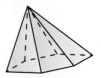

CONCEPT Euler's Formula

The sum of the number of faces (*F*) and vertices (*V*) of a polyhedron is 2 more than the number of its edges (*E*).

$$F + V = E + 2$$

$$F + V = E + 2$$
$$4 + 4 = E + 2$$
$$E = 6$$

APPLICATION

 EXAMPLE 2 Apply Euler's Formula

To make polyhedron-shaped game pieces using a 3D printer, Juanita enters the number of faces, edges, and vertices into a program. If she wants a game piece with 20 faces and 30 edges, how many vertices does the piece have?

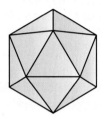

COMMON ERROR
Remember to add the number of faces and vertices on one side of the equation and to add the number of edges plus 2 on the other side of the equation.

$$F + V = E + 2$$
$$20 + V = 30 + 2$$ ⟵ Apply Euler's Formula.
$$V = 12$$

The game piece has 12 vertices.

✓ **Try It!** **2. a.** A polyhedron has 12 faces and 30 edges. How many vertices does it have?

b. Can a polyhedron have 4 faces, 5 vertices, and 8 edges? Explain.

 EXAMPLE 3 Describe a Cross Section

Plane *M* and plane *N* intersect the regular octahedron as shown. What is the shape of each cross section?

STUDY TIP
Recall that a *cross section* is the intersection of a solid and a plane.

Plane *M* slices the octahedron in half through the top and bottom vertices. The cross section is a rhombus.

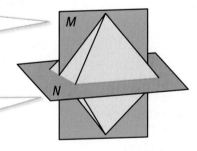

Plane *N* slices horizontally between the bases of two square pyramids. The cross section is a square.

✓ **Try It!** **3. a.** What shape is the cross section shown?

b. What shape is the cross section if the plane is perpendicular to the base and passes through the vertex of the pyramid?

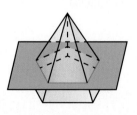

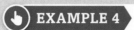 **EXAMPLE 4** **Draw a Cross Section**

A plane intersects a tetrahedron parallel to the base. How do you draw the cross section?

Step 1 Visualize the plane intersecting the tetrahedron.

Step 2 Draw lines where the plane cuts the surface of the polyhedron.

Step 3 Shade the cross section.

☑ **Try It!** **4. a.** Draw the cross section of a plane intersecting the tetrahedron through the top vertex and perpendicular to the base.

b. Draw the cross section of a plane intersecting a hexagonal prism perpendicular to the base.

🖐 **EXAMPLE 5** **Rotate a Polygon to Form a Three-Dimensional Figure**

If you rotate an isosceles triangle about the altitude, what three-dimensional figure does the triangle form?

As the triangle rotates, each point on the sides traces out a circle about the axis of rotation.

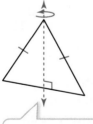  

The line containing the altitude is the axis of rotation.

The rotation forms a stack of circles.

The three-dimensional figure is a cone.

☑ **Try It!** **5. a.** What three-dimensional figure is formed by rotating equilateral triangle △*ABC* about $\overline{BD}$?

b. What three-dimensional figure is formed by rotating △*ABC* about $\overline{BC}$?

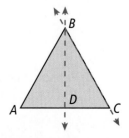

LESSON 13-1 Three-Dimensional Figures and Cross Sections **617**

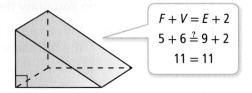

| WORDS | | DIAGRAMS | |

Euler's Formula The faces of a polyhedron are polygons. The sum of the number of faces F and vertices V of a polyhedron is 2 more than the number of its edges E.

$$F + V = E + 2$$

$$F + V = E + 2$$
$$5 + 6 \overset{?}{=} 9 + 2$$
$$11 = 11$$

Cross Sections A cross section is the intersection of a plane and a solid. The cross section of a plane and a convex polyhedron is a polygon.

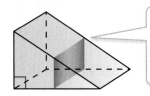

A cross section perpendicular to the base of the triangular prism is a rectangle.

Rotation of Polygons Rotating a polygon about an axis forms a three-dimensional figure with at least one circular cross section.

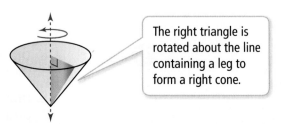

The right triangle is rotated about the line containing a leg to form a right cone.

☑ Do You UNDERSTAND?

1. **ESSENTIAL QUESTION** How are three-dimensional figures and polygons related?

2. **Error Analysis** Nicholas drew a figure to find a cross section of an icosahedron, a polyhedron with 20 faces. What is Nicholas's error?

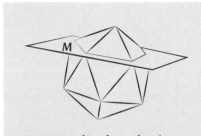

Because the plane that intersects the icosahedron is a rectangle, the cross section is a rectangle. ✗

3. **Reason** Can a polyhedron have 3 faces, 4 vertices, and 5 edges? Explain.

Do You KNOW HOW?

For Exercises 4–7, copy and complete the table.

	Faces	Vertices	Edges
4.	5	6	
5.	8		18
6.		12	20
7.	22	44	

8. What polygon is formed by the intersection of plane N and the octagonal prism shown?

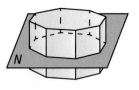

9. Describe the three-dimensional figure that is formed from rotating the isosceles right triangle about the hypotenuse.

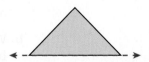

PRACTICE & PROBLEM SOLVING

Practice   Tutorial

UNDERSTAND

10. Mathematical Connections If you rotate rectangle *ABCD* about $\overleftrightarrow{CD}$, what is the volume of the resulting three-dimensional figure?

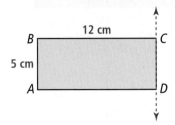

12 cm

5 cm

11. Error Analysis Philip was asked to find the number of vertices of a polyhedron with 32 faces and 60 edges. What is his error?

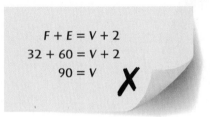

$$F + E = V + 2$$
$$32 + 60 = V + 2$$
$$90 = V \quad ✗$$

12. Make Sense and Persevere A tetrahedron is a polyhedron with four triangular faces. Can a plane intersect the tetrahedron shown to form a cross section with four sides? Explain.

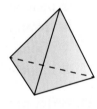

13. Use Appropriate Tools Can the intersection of a plane and a triangular prism produce a rectangular cross section? Draw a diagram to explain.

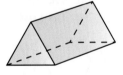

14. Higher Order Thinking Is it possible to rotate a polygon to form a cube? Explain.

15. Make Sense and Persevere Use the polyhedron shown.

a. Does the figure have a cross section with five sides? Copy the figure and draw the cross section or explain why not.

b. What is the maximum number of sides that a cross section of this figure can have?

PRACTICE

For Exercises 16–20, find the missing number for each polyhedron. SEE EXAMPLES 1 AND 2

16. A polyhedron has 24 edges and 12 vertices. How many faces does it have?

17. A polyhedron has 20 faces and 12 vertices. How many edges does it have?

18. A polyhedron has 8 faces and 15 edges. How many vertices does it have?

19. A polyhedron has 16 edges and 10 vertices. How many faces does it have?

20. Draw the cross section formed by the intersection of plane *A* and the polyhedron shown. What type of polygon is the cross section? SEE EXAMPLE 3

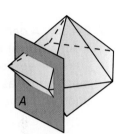

For Exercises 20 and 21, use the square pyramid shown. SEE EXAMPLE 4

21. Visualize a plane intersecting the square pyramid parallel to the base. Describe the cross section.

22. Visualize a plane intersecting the square pyramid through the vertex and perpendicular to opposite edges of the base. Describe the cross section.

23. Describe the three-dimensional figure that is formed from by rotating the rectangle about the side. SEE EXAMPLE 5

24. Describe the three-dimensional figure that is formed by rotating the pentagon about the line shown. SEE EXAMPLE 5

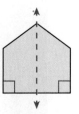

25. Describe the three-dimensional figure that is formed by rotating the circle about a diameter.

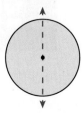

APPLY

26. Model With Mathematics Parker cuts 12 pentagons and 20 hexagons out of fabric to make the pillow shown. The pillow has 60 vertices. If it takes 20 inches of thread per seam to connect the edges of the polygons, how many inches of thread does Parker need to make the pillow?

27. Reason A gem cutter cuts a polyhedral crystal from a garnet gemstone. The crystal has 10 fewer vertices than edges and twice as many edges as faces. How many faces, vertices, and edges does the crystal have?

28. Communicate Precisely Rebecca wants to install a safety mat under the path of a revolving door. What shape should she make the mat? Explain.

ASSESSMENT PRACTICE

29. Complete the table for each polyhedron.

Polyhedron	Faces (F)	Vertices (V)	Edges (E)
regular dodecahedron	12		30
heptagonal pyramid	8	9	
octahedron	8		12
rhombohedron		8	12

30. SAT/ACT Which best describes the cross section of plane *X* and the polyhedron shown?

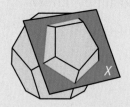

Ⓐ hexagon

Ⓑ pentagon

Ⓒ rectangle

Ⓓ trapezoid

Ⓔ triangle

31. Performance Task Draw a polyhedron with the fewest possible faces, vertices, and edges. Choose the faces from the polygons shown. You may use a polygon more than once.

Part A Explain why the polygon or polygons you chose minimize the number of vertices and edges.

Part B How do you know that there is no polyhedron with fewer faces, vertices, or edges than the one you drew?

13-2
Volumes of Prisms and Cylinders

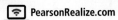
PearsonRealize.com

I CAN... use the properties of prisms and cylinders to calculate their volumes.

VOCABULARY
• Cavalieri's Principle
• oblique cylinder
• oblique prism

MODEL & DISCUSS

The Environmental Club has a piece of wire mesh that they want to form into an open-bottom and open-top compost bin.

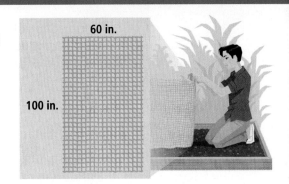

60 in.

100 in.

A. Using one side as the height, describe how you can form a compost bin in the shape of a rectangular prism using all of the mesh with no overlap.

B. Construct Arguments Which height would result in the largest volume? Explain.

C. Suppose you formed a cylinder using the same height as a rectangular prism. How would the volumes compare?

? ESSENTIAL QUESTION
How does the volume of a prism or cylinder relate to a cross section parallel to its base?

CONCEPTUAL UNDERSTANDING

EXAMPLE 1   Develop Cavalieri's Principle

How are the volumes of the two different stacks of index cards related?

The first stack forms a right prism. The second stack forms an *oblique prism*. An **oblique prism** is a prism such that some or all of the lateral faces are nonrectangular.

VOCABULARY
Remember that in a right prism, the sides are perpendicular to the bases. In an *oblique prism*, one or more sides are not perpendicular to the bases.

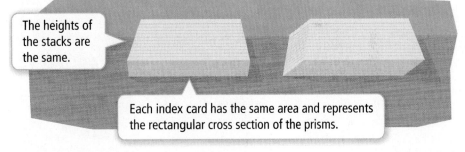

The heights of the stacks are the same.

Each index card has the same area and represents the rectangular cross section of the prisms.

The volumes of the two stacks are the same because the sums of the areas of the cards are the same.

 Try It!   **1.** Do you think that right and oblique cylinders that have the same height and cross-sectional area also have equal volume? Explain.

CONCEPT   Cavalieri's Principle

Cavalieri's Principle states that if two three-dimensional figures have the same height and the same cross-sectional area at every level, then they have the same volume.

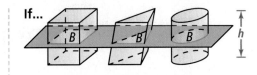

If...

h

Then... the volumes are equal.

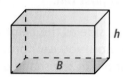

CONCEPT Volumes of Prisms and Cylinders

The volume of a prism is the product of the area of the base and the height of the prism.	The volume of a cylinder is the product of the area of the base and the height of the cylinder.
$V = Bh$	$V = Bh$
	$V = \pi r^2 h$

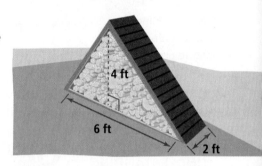

👆 **EXAMPLE 2** Find the Volumes of Prisms and Cylinders

A. Lonzell needs to store 20 ft³ of firewood. Could he use the storage rack shown?

The rack is a triangular prism.

$$V = Bh$$
$$= \left[\frac{1}{2}(4)(6)\right](2) = 24$$

The volume of the storage rack is 24 ft³, so Lonzell can store his firewood in the rack.

B. Keisha is deciding between the two canisters shown. Which canister holds more? What is the volume of the larger canister?

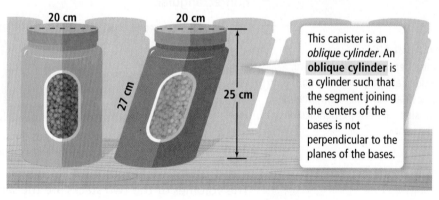

This canister is an *oblique cylinder*. An **oblique cylinder** is a cylinder such that the segment joining the centers of the bases is not perpendicular to the planes of the bases.

COMMON ERROR
The height of an oblique cylinder or prism is the length perpendicular to the bases, not the length of the sides of the figure.

The canisters have the same cross-sectional area at every height. So, by Cavalieri's Principle, the canisters have the same volume.

Use the volume formula to find the volume of the canister on the left.

$$V = \pi r^2 h$$
$$= \pi(10)^2(25) \approx 7,854$$

The diameter is 20 cm, so the radius is 10 cm.

The volume of both canisters is about 7,854 cm³.

 Try It! **2. a.** How would the volume of the storage shed change if the length of the triangular base is reduced by half?

b. How would the volume of the canisters change if the diameter is doubled?

APPLICATION   **EXAMPLE 3** **Apply the Volumes of Prisms to Solve Problems**

Marta is repurposing a sandbox as a garden and is buying the soil from her school's fundraiser. Estimate the number of bags she should buy.

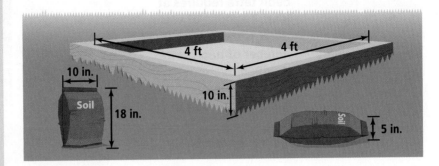

Step 1 Determine the volume of soil needed.

Compute the volume of the sandbox in cubic inches.

$V = Bh$

$= (48 \cdot 48)(10)$ ⟵ Use 4 ft = 48 in.

$= 23{,}040$

Marta needs 23,040 in.^{3} of soil.

Step 2 Estimate the volume of soil in each bag by modeling the bag of soil as a rectangular prism.

> The height of the bag is tapered on the ends, but thicker in the middle, so we still use 5 inches to estimate the height.

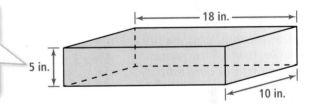

$V = Bh$

$= (10 \cdot 18)(5) = 900$

The volume of one bag of soil is about 900 in.^{3}.

MODEL WITH MATHEMATICS
Think about other ways to model the bag. Is a rectangular prism with the values used a reasonable model?

Step 3 Estimate the number of bags needed.

$23{,}040 \div 900 \approx 26$

Marta should buy 26 bags of soil to fill the sandbox.

✅ **Try It!** **3.** Kathryn is using cans of juice to fill a cylindrical pitcher that is 11 in. tall and has a radius of 4 in. Each can of juice is 6 in. tall with a radius of 2 in. How many cans of juice will Kathryn need?

EXAMPLE 4 **Apply Volume of Cylinders to Solve Problems**

Benito has 15 neon tetras in his aquarium. Each neon tetra requires at least 2 gallons of water. What is the maximum number of neon tetras that Benito should have in his aquarium?
(*Hint:* 1 gal = 231 in.³)

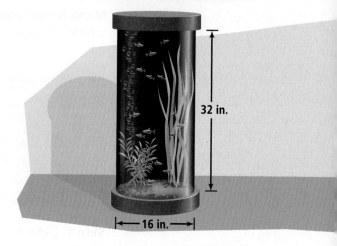

32 in.

16 in.

Step 1 Compute the volume of water in cubic inches.

$$V = \pi r^2 h$$
$$= \pi(8)^2(32)$$

The radius is half the diameter.

$$\approx 6{,}434$$

The volume of the water in the aquarium is about 6,434 in.³

Step 2 Find the volume of water in gallons.

$$6{,}434 \text{ in.}^3 \cdot \frac{1 \text{ gal}}{231 \text{ in.}^3} \approx 27.85 \text{ gal}$$

The volume of the water in the aquarium is about 27.85 gal.

STUDY TIP
You can also think about this step as finding the maximum number of fish for the tank using a density of 0.5 tetra per gallon.

Step 3 Compute the number of neon tetras that Benito's tank should hold.

Use a proportion to find the maximum number x of neon tetras that should be in 27.85 gal of water.

$$\frac{x \text{ fish}}{27.85 \text{ gal}} = \frac{1 \text{ fish}}{2 \text{ gal}}$$

$$\frac{x}{27.85} = \frac{1}{2}$$

$$2x = 27.85$$

$$x = 13.925$$

Benito should have no more than 13 neon tetras in his aquarium.

 Try It! 4. Benito is considering the aquarium shown. What is the maximum number of neon tetras that this aquarium can hold?

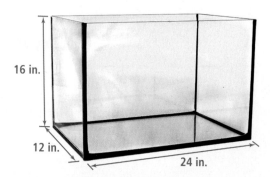

16 in.

12 in.

24 in.

APPLICATION  **EXAMPLE 5** **Determine Whether Volume or Surface Area Best Describes Size**

A forester surveys giant sequoias by gathering data about the heights and circumference of the trees.

	A	B	C
Height	270 ft	258 ft	248 ft
Circumference (measured at 4.5 ft)	101 ft	109 ft	106 ft

A. Should the forester use surface area or volume to describe the sizes of the sequoias? Explain.

The amount of wood in a tree is represented by its volume, so she should use volume to determine the size of a giant sequoia.

> **MODEL WITH MATHEMATICS**
> Think about other shapes you could use to represent the tree. What is another mathematical model you could use for this problem?

B. What are the sizes of the sequoias shown? Rank them in order by size from largest to smallest.

Although the sequoias have branches and the trunk tapers gradually toward the top of the tree, each tree can be modeled as a cylinder. Find the volume of each cylinder to estimate the volume of each tree.

	Radius (ft)	Volume of Trunk (ft³)
Tree A 270 ft	$r = \dfrac{101}{2\pi} \approx 16.1$	$\begin{aligned} V &= \pi r^2 h \\ &= \pi (16.1)^2 (270) \\ &\approx 219{,}870 \end{aligned}$
Tree B 258 ft	$r = \dfrac{109}{2\pi} \approx 17.3$	$\begin{aligned} V &= \pi r^2 h \\ &= \pi (17.3)^2 (258) \\ &\approx 242{,}584 \end{aligned}$
Tree C 248 ft	$r = \dfrac{106}{2\pi} \approx 16.9$	$\begin{aligned} V &= \pi r^2 h \\ &= \pi (16.9)^2 (248) \\ &\approx 222{,}523 \end{aligned}$

In order from largest to smallest, the three trees are: Tree B, Tree C, Tree A.

 Try It! **5.** Describe a situation when surface area might be a better measure of size than volume.

CONCEPT SUMMARY Volumes of Prisms and Cylinders

WORDS **Cavalieri's Principle** Figures with the same height and same cross-sectional area at every level have the same volume.

As a result, right and oblique prisms and cylinders with the same base area and height have the same volume.

DIAGRAMS

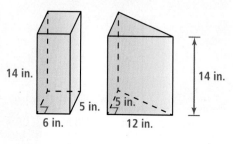

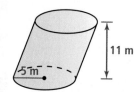

$V = Bh$

$V = 30 \cdot 14$

$V = 420$ cubic inches

$V = Bh$

$V = \pi r^2 h$

$= \pi \cdot 5^2 \cdot 11$

$= 863.9$ cubic meters

Do You UNDERSTAND?

1. **ESSENTIAL QUESTION** How does the volume of a prism or cylinder relate to a cross section parallel to its base?

2. **Error Analysis** Sawyer says that Cavalieri's Principle proves that the two prisms shown have the same volume. Explain Sawyer's error.

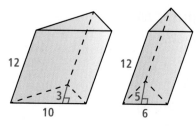

3. **Vocabulary** How are an oblique prism and an oblique cylinder alike and different?

4. **Reason** The circumference of the base of a cylinder is x, and the height of the cylinder is x. What expression gives the volume of the cylinder?

5. **Construct Arguments** Denzel kicks a large dent into a trash can and says that the volume does not change because of Cavalieri's Principle. Do you agree with Denzel? Explain.

Do You KNOW HOW?

For Exercises 6–11, find the volume of each figure. Round to the nearest tenth.

6.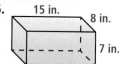

7.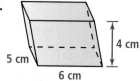

8.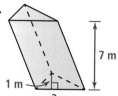

9.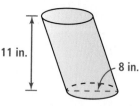

10.

11.

12. Which figures have the same volume? Explain.

 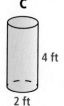

UNDERSTAND

13. Error Analysis Dylan compares the volumes of two bottles. What is Dylan's error?

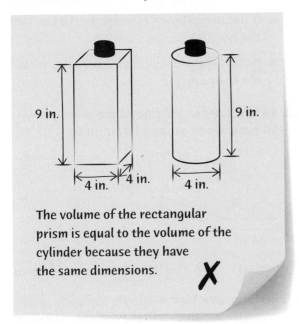

The volume of the rectangular prism is equal to the volume of the cylinder because they have the same dimensions. **X**

14. Higher Order Thinking Does Cavalieri's Principle apply to the volumes of the cones shown? Explain.

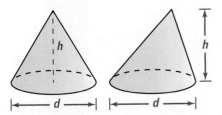

15. Mathematical Connections Does rotating the rectangle about line m result in a cylinder with the same volume as rotating the rectangle about line n? Explain.

16. Use Appropriate Tools Do the prisms shown have equivalent volumes? Explain.

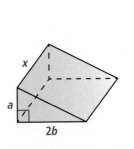 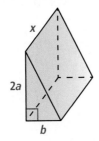

PRACTICE

17. Katrina buys the two vases shown. How do the volumes of the vases compare? Explain.
SEE EXAMPLE 1

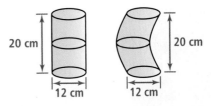

18. Talisa plans a 6-foot deep pond. While digging, she hits rock 5 feet down. How can Talisa modify the radius to maintain the original volume of the pond? SEE EXAMPLE 2

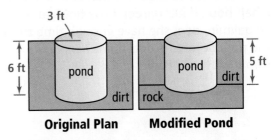

Original Plan   Modified Pond

19. The instructions for plant food say to use 0.25 gram per cubic inch of soil. How many grams of plant food should Jordan use if the planter box shown is full of soil? SEE EXAMPLE 3

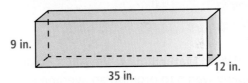

20. If a stack of 40 nickels fits snugly in the coin wrapper shown, how thick is 1 nickel? Round to the nearest hundredth. SEE EXAMPLE 4

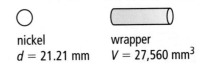

nickel   wrapper
$d = 21.21$ mm $V = 27{,}560$ mm^3

21. Sections of two flood-control ditches are shown. Which one holds the greater volume of water per foot? Explain. SEE EXAMPLE 5

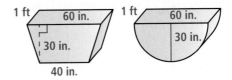

APPLY

22. Use Appropriate Tools How many 3-inch-thick bags of mulch should Noemi buy to cover 100 square feet at a depth of 4 inches?

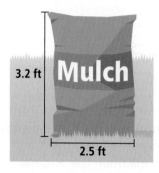

3.2 ft

Mulch

2.5 ft

23. Reason Ines's younger brother will be home in a half hour. If her garden hose flows at a rate 24 gal/min, does she have enough time to fill the pool before he gets home? Explain. (*Hint:* 1 ft^3 = 7.48 gal)

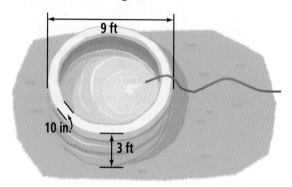

9 ft

10 in.

3 ft

24. Model With Mathematics The ABC Cookie Company wants to promise an average of "12 chocolate chips per cookie." Assuming that the cookies fill about 80% of the box by volume, will 600 chocolate chips for each box of cookies be sufficient to make the claim? Explain.

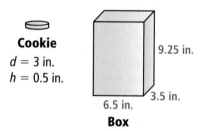

Cookie
d = 3 in.
h = 0.5 in.

9.25 in.

3.5 in.

6.5 in.

Box

ASSESSMENT PRACTICE

25. Cylinders A, B, and C have the same volume. Cylinder A has diameter 12 cm and height 8 cm.

a. If the diameter of cylinder B is 16 cm, what is the height?

b. If the height of cylinder C is 32 cm, what is the diameter?

26. SAT/ACT If the volume of the prism shown is 70 cubic yards, what is its length?

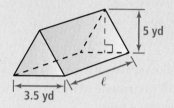

5 yd

3.5 yd

ℓ

Ⓐ 4 yd   Ⓑ 8 yd   Ⓒ 16 yd   Ⓓ 28 yd

27. Performance Task A candle company receives an order for an overnight delivery of 8 short candles and 6 tall candles. The overnight service has a weight limit of 23 kg.

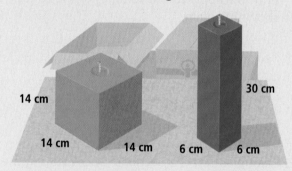

14 cm

14 cm   14 cm

30 cm

6 cm   6 cm

Part A The density of the wax used to make each candle is 0.0009 kg/cm^3. What is the weight of the order? Can the order be filled and shipped for delivery?

Part B If no tall candles are included in the order, what is the greatest number of short candles that can be delivered?

Part C What combination of tall and short candles can be delivered if the total number of candles delivered is 10?

PearsonRealize.com

▶ Box 'Em Up

With so many people and businesses shopping online, retailers, and especially e-retailers, ship more and more packages every day. Some of the products people order have unusual sizes and shapes and need custom packaging. Imagine how you might package a surfboard, or a snow blower, or even live crawfish to ship to someone's house!

Think about this during the Mathematical Modeling in 3 Acts lesson.

Scan for Multimedia

ACT 1 ▸ Identify the Problem

1. What is the first question that comes to mind after watching the video?

2. Write down the main question you will answer about what you saw in the video.

3. Make an initial conjecture that answers this main question.

4. Explain how you arrived at your conjecture.

5. What information will be useful to know to answer the main question? How can you get it? How will you use that information?

ACT 2 ▸ Develop a Model

6. Use the math that you have learned in this Topic to refine your conjecture.

ACT 3 ▸ Interpret the Results

7. Did your refined conjecture match the actual answer exactly? If not, what might explain the difference?

13-3
Pyramids and Cones

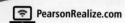
PearsonRealize.com

I CAN... use the volumes of right and oblique pyramids and cones to solve problems.

✋ EXPLORE & REASON

Consider the cube and pyramid.

A. How many pyramids could you fit inside the cube? Explain.

B. Write an equation that shows the relationship between *C* and *P*.

C. Look for Relationships Make a conjecture about the volume of any pyramid. Explain your reasoning.

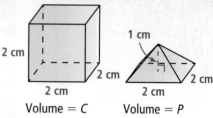

Volume = *C*   Volume = *P*

? ESSENTIAL QUESTION

How are the formulas for volume of a pyramid and volume of a cone alike?

CONCEPTUAL UNDERSTANDING

✋ EXAMPLE 1   Apply Cavalieri's Principle to Pyramids and Cones

How are the volumes of pyramids and cones with the same base area and height related?

Imagine a set of cardboard discs, each with a slightly smaller radius than the previous disc. You can stack the discs in different ways.

GENERALIZE
Think about the shape formed by the stacks. What would happen if the number of discs increases while the difference in the radii and the thickness of each disc decreases?

The heights of the stacks are the same, and the area at each level is the same. The total volume of cardboard in each stack is the same.

The stacks approximate cones. You can apply Cavalieri's Principle to cones and pyramids.

If two figures have the same height and equal area at every cross section, they have equal volumes.

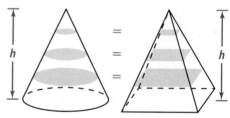

☑ Try It!   1. Is it possible to use only Cavalieri's Principle to show that a cone and a cylinder have equal volumes? Explain.

CONCEPT Volumes of Pyramids and Cones

The volume of a pyramid is one-third the product of the area of the base and the height of the pyramid.

$$V = \frac{1}{3} Bh$$

The volume of a cone is one-third the product of the area of the base and the height of the cone.

$$V = \frac{1}{3} Bh$$
$$V = \frac{1}{3} \pi r^2 h$$

 Go Online | PearsonRealize.com

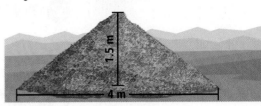

EXAMPLE 2 | Find the Volumes of Pyramids and Cones

A. Kyle's truck can haul 1.75 tons of corn per load. One cubic meter of corn weighs 0.8 ton. How many loads will Kyle haul to move this pile of corn?

$$V = \frac{1}{3}\pi r^2 h$$

> The pile is shaped like a cone, so use the volume formula for cones.

$$= \frac{1}{3}\pi(2)^2(1.5) \approx 6.3 \text{ m}^3$$

Since 6.3 m³ • 0.8 ton/m³ = 5.04 tons, Kyle will need to haul 5.04 ÷ 1.75 = 2.88 or 3 loads.

B. Jason is using the mold to make 12 candles. How many cubic inches of wax does he need?

$$V = \frac{1}{3}Bh$$

> Use the volume formula for a pyramid.

$$= \frac{1}{3}\left[\frac{1}{2}(4)(3)\right](6) = 12 \text{ in.}^3$$

> Use the area formula for a triangle to find the base.

STUDY TIP
The base of a pyramid can be any polygon, so the formula you use to determine the area of the base *B* depends on the shape of the base.

For 12 candles, Jason needs 12 in.³ • 12, or 144 in.³ of wax.

✓ Try It!

2. a. What is the volume of a cone with base diameter 14 and height 16?

b. What is the volume of a pyramid with base area 10 and height 7?

EXAMPLE 3 | Apply the Volumes of Pyramids to Solve Problems

Dyani is 1.8 m tall and wants to be able to stand inside her new tent. Should she buy this tent?

> Tent Features:
> - 3.4 cubic meters
> - Square floor with 8.4 m perimeter
> - Height:
> Clearance Price: $59.00

Step 1 Draw and label a square pyramid to represent the tent.

> Since the perimeter of the square floor is 8.4 m, s = 2.1 m.

Step 2 Find the height of the pyramid.

$$V = \frac{1}{3}Bh$$

$$3.4 = \frac{1}{3}(2.1)^2 h$$

$$h \approx 2.3$$

The height of the pyramid is approximately 2.3 m.

Dyani will be able to stand in the tent, so she should buy this tent.

CONTINUED ON THE NEXT PAGE

EXAMPLE 3 CONTINUED

  Activity Assess

Try It! 3. A rectangular pyramid has a base that is three times as long as it is wide. The volume of the pyramid is 75 ft^3 and the height is 3 ft. What is the perimeter of the base?

APPLICATION

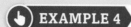 **EXAMPLE 4** Apply the Volumes of Cones to Solve Problems

A restaurant sells smoothies in two sizes. Which size is a better deal?

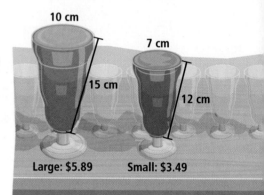

10 cm
7 cm
15 cm
12 cm
Large: $5.89   Small: $3.49

Formulate ◄ Compare the prices by determining the cost per cubic centimeter for each size.

The volume of fruit smoothie in each glass can be approximated as the volume of a cone.

Compute ◄ **Step 1** Calculate the height of each cone using the Pythagorean Theorem.

Large	Small

Large

$5^2 + h^2 = 15^2$

$h^2 = 200$

$h \approx 14.1$

The height of the large cone is approximately 14.1 cm.

Small

$3.5^2 + h^2 = 12^2$

$h^2 = 131.75$

$h \approx 11.5$

The height of the small cone is approximately 11.5 cm.

Step 2 Calculate the volume of each cone.

Large

$V = \frac{1}{3}\pi r^2 h$

$= \frac{1}{3}\pi(5)^2(14.1)$

≈ 369.1

The volume of the large cone is approximately 369.1 cm^3.

Small

$V = \frac{1}{3}\pi r^2 h$

$= \frac{1}{3}\pi(3.5)^2(11.5)$

≈ 147.5

The volume of the small cone is approximately 147.5 cm^3.

Step 3 Calculate the cost per cubic centimeter for each size.

Large

$\frac{\$5.89}{369.1 \text{ cm}^3} \approx \$0.016 \text{ per cm}^3$

Small

$\frac{\$3.49}{147.5 \text{ cm}^3} \approx \$0.024 \text{ per cm}^3$

Interpret ◄ The large size smoothie costs less per cubic centimeter, so the large size smoothie is a better deal.

CONTINUED ON THE NEXT PAGE

EXAMPLE 4 CONTINUED

 Try It! **4.** A cone has a volume of 144π and a height of 12.

    a. What is the radius of the base?

    b. If the radius of the cone is tripled, what is the new volume? What is the relationship between the volumes of the two cones?

APPLICATION

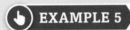 **EXAMPLE 5**   Measure a Composite Figure

Kaitlyn is making a concrete animal sculpture. Each bag of concrete mix makes 0.6 ft³ of concrete. How many bags of concrete mix does Kaitlyn need?

16 in.

20 in.   16 in.

18 in.

15 in.

22 in.

16 in. 4 in.

Calculate the volume of each part.

Step 1 Calculate the volume of one of the legs.

$$V = \pi r^2 h$$

$$= \pi(2)^2(16)$$

$$\approx 201 \text{ in.}^3$$

> The legs are oblique cylinders.

Step 2 Calculate the volume of the body.

$$V = Bh$$

$$= (22 \cdot 18)(15)$$

$$= 5{,}940 \text{ in.}^3$$

> The body is a rectangular prism.

Step 3 Calculate the volume of the head.

$$V = \frac{1}{3}Bh$$

$$= \frac{1}{3}(16 \cdot 16)(20)$$

$$\approx 1{,}707 \text{ in.}^3$$

> The head is a square pyramid.

COMMON ERROR
When multiple parts of a composite figure have the same volume, make sure you account for each part in your total.

Step 4 Calculate the total volume.

$$V = 4(201) + 5{,}940 + 1{,}707$$

$$= 8{,}451$$

> Add the volumes of the parts of the sculpture.

The total volume is 8,451 in.³. Convert to cubic feet to determine the amount of concrete needed.

$$8{,}451 \cdot \frac{1}{1{,}728} = 4.9$$

> $1 \text{ ft}^3 = (12 \text{ in.})^3 = 1{,}728 \text{ in.}^3$

To make the sculpture, 4.9 ft³ of concrete is needed. Kaitlyn needs $4.9 \div 0.6 \approx 8.2$ or 9 bags of concrete mix.

 Try It! **5.** A cone-shaped hole is drilled in a prism. The height of the triangular base is 12 cm. What is the volume of the remaining figure? Round to the nearest tenth.

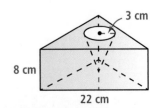

3 cm

8 cm

22 cm

CONCEPT SUMMARY Pyramids and Cones

| WORDS | The volume of a pyramid is one-third the volume of a prism with the same base area and height. | The volume of a cone is one-third the volume of a cylinder with the same base area and height. |

DIAGRAMS

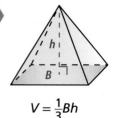

$$V = \frac{1}{3}Bh$$

$$V = \frac{1}{3}Bh \text{ or } V = \frac{1}{3}\pi r^2 h$$

Do You UNDERSTAND?

1. **ESSENTIAL QUESTION** How are the formulas for volume of a pyramid and volume of a cone alike?

2. **Error Analysis** Zhang is finding the height of a square pyramid with a base side length of 9 and a volume of 162. What is his error?

$$V = Bh$$
$$162 = 9^2(h)$$
$$h = 2 \quad \text{✗}$$

3. **Reason** A cone and cylinder have the same radius and volume. If the height of the cone is h, what is the height of the cylinder?

4. **Construct Arguments** Do you have enough information to compute the volume of the cone? Explain.

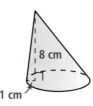

8 cm

1 cm

Do You KNOW HOW?

For Exercises 5–10, find the volume of each figure. Round to the nearest tenth. Assume that all angles in each polygonal base are congruent.

5.
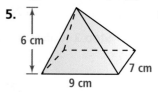
6 cm
7 cm
9 cm

6.
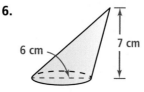
6 cm
7 cm

7.
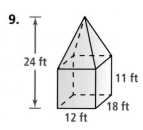
8 in.
3 in.

8.
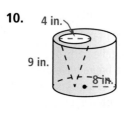
5 m
2 m

9.
24 ft
11 ft
18 ft
12 ft

10.
4 in.
9 in.
8 in.

11. A solid metal square pyramid with a base side length of 6 in. and height of 9 in. is melted down and recast as a square pyramid with a height of 4 in. What is the base side length of the new pyramid?

UNDERSTAND

12. Construct Arguments A stack of 39 pennies is exactly as tall as a stack of 31 nickels. Do the two stacks have the same volume? Explain.

13. Error Analysis Jacob is finding the volume of the cylinder. What is his error?

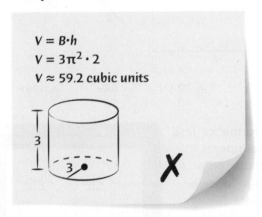

$V = B \cdot h$
$V = 3\pi^2 \cdot 2$
$V \approx 59.2$ cubic units

14. Communicate Precisely How would you find the volume of a right square pyramid with a base side length of 10 cm, and the altitude of a triangular side is 13 cm? Explain.

15. Mathematical Connections In terms of the radius r, what is the volume of a cone whose height is equal to its radius?

16. Higher Order Thinking A plane slices a cone parallel to the base at one-half of the height of the cone. What is the volume of the part of the cone lying below the plane?

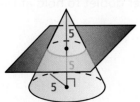

PRACTICE

17. The plane intersects sections of equal area in the two solids. Are the volumes equal? SEE EXAMPLE 1

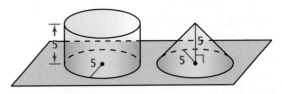

For Exercises 18–21, find the volume of each solid. Assume that all angles in each polygonal base are congruent. SEE EXAMPLE 2

18.

19.

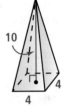

20.

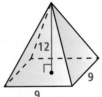

21.

22. A cone is inscribed in a right square pyramid. What is the remaining volume if the cone is removed? SEE EXAMPLES 3 AND 4

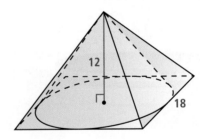

For Exercises 23 and 24, find the volume of each composite figure. SEE EXAMPLE 5

23.

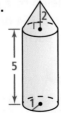

24.

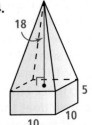

APPLY

25. Make Sense and Persevere Chiang makes gift boxes in the shape of a right square pyramid. She fills each box with chocolate cubes with $\frac{7}{8}$-in. sides. She can fill about 75% of a box. How many pieces can she fit in each box?

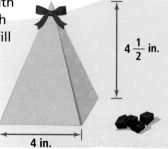

$4\frac{1}{2}$ in.

4 in.

26. Reason A pile of snow is plowed into the shape of a right cone. How many trucks with a capacity of 10 yd³ per truck will be needed to move the pile?

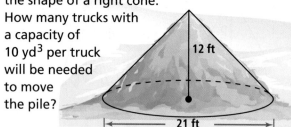

12 ft

21 ft

27. Use Structure The basin beneath a fountain is a right cone that is 7 m across and 1 m deep at the center. After the fountain is cleaned, the pool is refilled at a rate of 300 L/min. One cubic meter is 1,000 L. How long does it take to refill the pool?

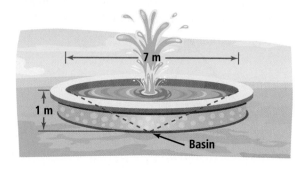

7 m

1 m

Basin

28. Model With Mathematics A physicist wants to know what percentage of gas is empty space. A molecule of methane can be modeled by a regular tetrahedron with side length 0.154 nm (1 nm = 1×10^{-9} m). The altitude of each triangular side is 0.133 nm. If 6.022×10^{23} molecules make up 0.0224 m³ of gas, how does the volume of the molecules compare to the volume of the gas?

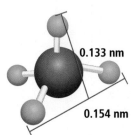

0.133 nm

0.154 nm

ASSESSMENT PRACTICE

29. Cavalieri's Principle states that if two solids have the same ____?____ and the same ____?____ at every cross section, then the two solids have the same ____?____ .

30. SAT/ACT Which is the volume of the largest cone that will fit entirely within the right square prism?

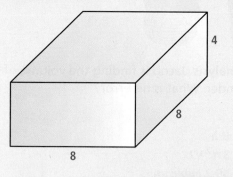

4

8

8

Ⓐ $\frac{16\pi}{3}$ Ⓑ $\frac{32\pi}{3}$ Ⓒ $\frac{64\pi}{3}$ Ⓓ $\frac{128\pi}{3}$

31. Performance Task A designer is working on a design for two goblets. Design A is based on a cylinder and design B is based on a cone. The client wants both goblets to be the same height and width.

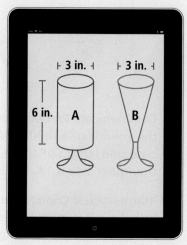

⊢ 3 in. ⊣   ⊢ 3 in. ⊣

6 in.   A   B

Part A The client wants the smaller goblet to hold at least 10 fl oz. One fluid ounce is 1.8 in.³. Will design B be large enough to meet the client's requirements? Explain.

Part B The client wants the larger goblet to hold 20 fl oz. Does design A meet the client's requirement? Explain.

Part C How could design B be changed if the client wants the smaller goblet to hold at least 12 fl oz?

13-4

Spheres

I CAN... calculate the volume of a sphere and solve problems involving the volumes of spheres.

VOCABULARY

• hemisphere

CRITIQUE & EXPLAIN

Ricardo estimates the volume of a sphere with radius 2 by placing the sphere inside a cylinder and placing two cones inside the sphere. He says that the volume of the sphere is less than 16π and greater than $\frac{16}{3}\pi$.

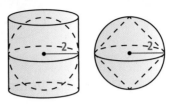

A. Do you agree with Ricardo? Explain.

B. Reason How might you estimate the volume of the sphere?

ESSENTIAL QUESTION

How does the volume of a sphere relate to the volumes of other solids?

CONCEPTUAL UNDERSTANDING

EXAMPLE 1   Explore the Volume of a Sphere

What is the volume of a sphere? Why does the volume formula for a sphere make sense?

A plane, parallel to the bases, intersects half of a sphere with radius r and a cylinder with radius r and height r. The cylinder has a cone with radius r and height r removed from its center.

USE APPROPRIATE TOOLS
Think about how you can draw the section of the cylinder with the cone removed. What does the cross section look like?

By the Pythagorean Theorem, the cross section is a circle with radius $\sqrt{r^2 - h^2}$.

The cross section of the cylinder has radius r. The cross section of the cone has radius h.

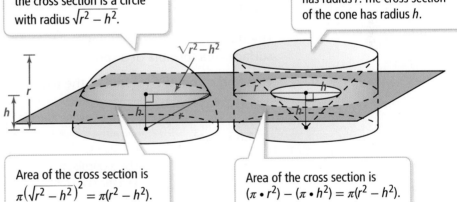

Area of the cross section is $\pi\left(\sqrt{r^2 - h^2}\right)^2 = \pi(r^2 - h^2)$.

Area of the cross section is $(\pi \cdot r^2) - (\pi \cdot h^2) = \pi(r^2 - h^2)$.

Once the cone is removed, the areas of the cross sections of the solids are equal at any height. Therefore, by Cavalieri's Principle, the two solids have the same volume.

$$\text{volume of half a sphere} = \text{volume of cylinder} - \text{volume of cone}$$

$$= \pi r^2 \cdot r - \frac{1}{3}\pi r^2 \cdot r$$

$$= \frac{2}{3}\pi r^3$$

The volume of a sphere is twice the volume of half of the sphere, so the volume of a sphere with radius r is $\frac{4}{3}\pi r^3$.

CONTINUED ON THE NEXT PAGE

EXAMPLE 1 CONTINUED

 Try It! 1. Find the volumes of the three solids. What do you notice?

10 m

10 m

10 m

10 m

10 m

CONCEPT Volume of a Sphere

The volume of a sphere is four-thirds of the product of π and the cube of the radius of the sphere.

$$V = \frac{4}{3}\pi r^3$$

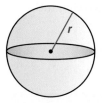

r

APPLICATION  **EXAMPLE 2** Use the Volumes of Spheres to Solve Problems

The drama club makes a big ball from foam to hang above the stage for a play. They plan to cover the surface of the ball with metallic fabric. What is the minimum number of square meters of fabric that the club needs?

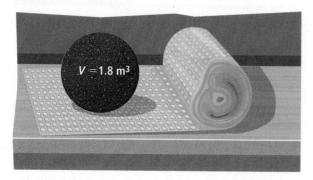

$V = 1.8 \text{ m}^3$

Use the volume formula to determine the radius of the ball. Then use the surface area formula of a sphere.

First find r from the volume of the ball.

$$V = \frac{4}{3}\pi r^3$$ ⟵ Use the volume formula.

$$1.8 = \frac{4}{3}\pi r^3$$

$$r^3 = \frac{1.35}{\pi}$$ ⟵ Use a calculator to find the cube root.

$$r \approx 0.75$$

STUDY TIP
Remember that the surface area of a sphere is four times the area of a circle with the same radius.

The radius of the ball is about 0.75 m. Next, calculate the surface area.

The surface area of a sphere with radius r is S.A. $= 4\pi r^2$.

$$\text{S.A.} = 4\pi r^2$$

$$\text{S.A.} = 4\pi(0.75)^2$$ ⟵ Substitute the radius into the surface area formula.

$$\text{S.A.} \approx 7.1$$

The club needs at least 7.1 m^2 of fabric.

 Try It! 2. What is the largest volume a sphere can have if it is covered by 6 m^2 of fabric?

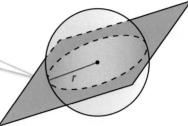

EXAMPLE 3 Find the Volumes of Hemispheres

What is the volume of the hemisphere?

A *great circle* is the intersection of a sphere and a plane containing the center of the sphere.

A great circle divides a sphere into two **hemispheres**.

The volume of a hemisphere is one-half the volume of a sphere with the same radius.

$$V = \frac{2}{3}\pi r^3$$

$$V = \frac{2}{3}\pi \cdot 4^3 \approx 134.04$$

☑ **Try It!** **3. a.** What is the volume of a hemisphere with radius 3 ft?

b. What is the volume of a hemisphere with diameter 13 cm?

EXAMPLE 4 Find the Volumes of Composite Figures

A solid is composed of a right cylinder and a hemisphere as shown. If the density of the solid is 100 kg/m³, what is the mass of the solid?

Find the volume of the solid.

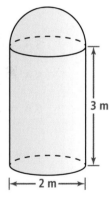

volume of solid = volume of cylinder
                + volume of hemisphere

$$= \pi r^2 h + \frac{2}{3}\pi r^3$$

$$= \pi (1)^2 (3) + \frac{2}{3}\pi (1)^3$$

$$\approx 11.5$$

The volume of the solid is about 11.5 m³. Next, find the mass of the solid.

$$11.5 \cdot 100 = 1,150$$

The mass of the solid is about 1,150 kg.

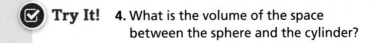

☑ **Try It!** **4.** What is the volume of the space between the sphere and the cylinder?

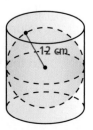

CONCEPT SUMMARY Volume of Spheres

WORDS Cavalieri's Principle can be used to show how the volume of the sphere is related to the volumes of a cylinder and cone. The area of a cross section of a hemisphere is the same as the area of a cross section of a cylinder with height equal to the radius minus the cross section of a cone with height equal to the radius.

DIAGRAMS

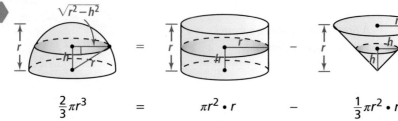

$$\frac{2}{3}\pi r^3 \qquad = \qquad \pi r^2 \cdot r \qquad - \qquad \frac{1}{3}\pi r^2 \cdot r$$

✓ Do You UNDERSTAND?

1. **ESSENTIAL QUESTION** How does the volume of a sphere relate to the volumes of other solids?

2. **Error Analysis** Reagan is finding the volume of the sphere. What is her error?

S.A. $= \frac{4}{3}\pi r^3$

S.A. $= \frac{4}{3} \cdot \pi \cdot 3^3$

S.A. ≈ 113.1 square units

✗

3. **Vocabulary** How does a great circle define a hemisphere?

4. **Reason** The radius of a sphere, the base radius of a cylinder, and the base radius of a cone are r. What is the height of the cylinder if the volume of the cylinder is equal to the volume of the sphere? What is the height of the cone if the volume of the cone is equal to the volume of the sphere?

Do You KNOW HOW?

For Exercises 5 and 6, find the surface area of each solid.

5.
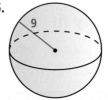

6.
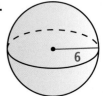

For Exercises 7 and 8, find the volume of each solid.

7.

8.

9. Find the volume of the largest sphere that can fit entirely in the rectangular prism.

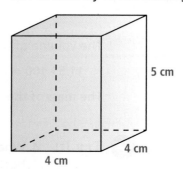

10. Find the volume and surface area of a sphere with radius 1.

PRACTICE & PROBLEM SOLVING

UNDERSTAND

11. Construct Arguments How does Cavalieri's Principle apply to finding the volume of a hemisphere? Explain.

12. Error Analysis Kayden is finding the surface area of the sphere. What is her error?

S.A. = $4\pi r^2$

S.A. = $4 \cdot \pi \cdot 14^2$

S.A. ≈ 2,463.0 square units ✗

13. Mathematical Connections Given the surface area of a sphere, write a formula for the volume of a sphere in terms of the surface area.

14. Construct Arguments Fifteen cylinders and 15 rectangular prisms are stacked. Each cylinder has the same top surface area and height as each rectangular prism. What can you determine about the volumes of the two stacks of 15 solids? Explain.

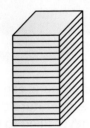

15. Reason A sphere is divided by two great circles that are perpendicular to each other. How would you find the surface area and volume of each part of the sphere between the two planes containing the great circles? Explain.

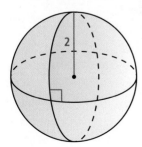

PRACTICE

For Exercises 16–18, find the area of each cross section. SEE EXAMPLE 1

16.

17.

18.

For Exercises 19–22, find the surface area of each solid to the nearest tenth. SEE EXAMPLE 2

19.

20.

21. sphere with volume 35 cm^3

22. sphere with volume 100 in.^{3}

For Exercises 23–26, find the volume of each solid to the nearest tenth. SEE EXAMPLES 2 AND 3

23.

24.

25. hemisphere with radius 12 ft

26. sphere with radius 25 m

For Exercises 27 and 28, find the volume of each composite figure to the nearest tenth.
SEE EXAMPLE 4

27.
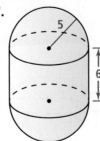

28.
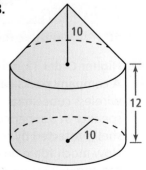

APPLY

29. Make Sense and Persevere To reach the regulation pressure for a game ball, the amount of air pumped into a ball is 1.54 times the volume of the ball. A referee adds 15 in.³ of air for each pump of air. How many pumps of air will it take the referee to fill an empty ball?

9.55 in.

30. Reason Jeffery uses a block of clay to make round beads. How many beads can he make from the block?

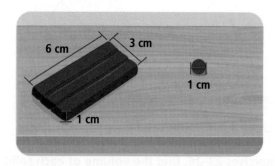

6 cm   3 cm

1 cm

1 cm

31. Felipe places a spherical round-bottom flask in a cylindrical beaker containing hot water. The flask must fit into the beaker with 2 cm of space around the flask. What is the minimum diameter d of the beaker?

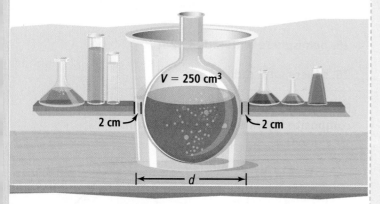

$V = 250$ cm³

2 cm   2 cm

d

32. Higher Order Thinking A company packs each wireless cube-shaped speaker in a spherical shell protected by foam. How much foam does the company use for each speaker?

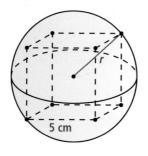

r

5 cm

ASSESSMENT PRACTICE

33. Match each description with its expression.

I. volume of a sphere with radius 1

A. $\frac{4}{3}\pi$

II. surface area of a sphere with radius 2

B. $\frac{16}{3}\pi$

III. circumference of a great circle for a sphere with radius 3

C. 6π

IV. volume of a hemisphere with radius 2

D. 16π

34. SAT/ACT The surface area of a sphere is 64π ft². What is the radius of the sphere?

Ⓐ 64 ft

Ⓑ 16 ft

Ⓒ 8 ft

Ⓓ 4 ft

35. Performance Task Jayesh is to fill the tank shown with liquid propane.

4 m   1.2 m

Part A The liquid propane expands and contracts as the temperature changes, so a propane tank is never filled to more than 80% capacity with liquid propane. How much liquid propane should Jayesh put in the tank?

Part B If Jayesh has 20 m³ of liquid propane to fill another tank, what are the dimensions of the tank if the length of the cylindrical part is three times the diameter?

Topic Review

1. How is Cavalieri's Principle helpful in understanding the volume formulas for solids?

Vocabulary Review

Choose the correct term to complete each sentence.

2. A prism is _____ if one or more faces are not perpendicular to the bases.

3. _____ describes the relationship between the volumes of three-dimensional figures that have the same height and the same cross sectional area at every level.

4. A great circle divides a sphere into two _____.

- Cavalieri's Principle
- cones
- cylinders
- hemispheres
- oblique
- right
- spheres

Concepts & Skills Review

| LESSON 13-1 | Three-Dimensional Figures and Cross Sections |

Quick Review

The faces of a polyhedron are polygons. Euler's Formula states that the relationship between the number of faces F, number of vertices V, and number of edges E is

$$F + V = E + 2$$

The cross section of a plane and a convex polyhedron is a polygon.

Rotating a polygon about an axis forms a three-dimensional figure.

Example

A triangular prism has 5 faces and 9 edges. How many vertices does it have?

$$F + V = E + 2$$

$$5 + V = 9 + 2$$

$$V = 6$$

The prism has 6 vertices.

Practice & Problem Solving

For Exercises 5 and 6, use the pyramid shown.

5. The pyramid has 6 vertices and 10 edges. How many faces does it have?

6. Visualize a plane intersecting the pyramid parallel to the base. Describe the cross section.

7. Describe the three-dimensional figure that is formed by rotating the rectangle about the line shown.

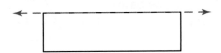

8. **Reason** Can a polyhedron have the same number of faces, edges, and vertices? Explain.

LESSON 13-2 ► Volumes of Prisms and Cylinders

Quick Review

Cavalieri's Principle states that figures with the same height and same area at every horizontal cross section have the same volume.

$V = Bh$
$V = (\ell \cdot w)h$
$V = (9\pi)(20)$
$V = 180\pi$

$V = Bh$
$V = (\pi r^2)h$
$V = (9\pi)(20)$
$V = 180\pi$

Example

Do the cylinders have the same volume? Explain.

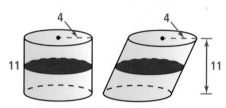

Yes, cylinders with the same base area and height have the same volume. The height of each cylinder is 11. The area of the base of each cylinder is $\pi(4)^2$, or 16π.

Practice & Problem Solving

For Exercises 9 and 10, find the volume of each figure. Round to the nearest tenth.

9.  30 mm

70 mm

10. 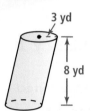 3 yd
8 yd

11. **Reason** What does the expression $\frac{3}{4}xyz$ represent for the prism shown?

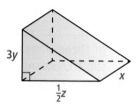
3y
x
$\frac{1}{2}z$

12. Malia pours wax in molds to make candles. Compare the amount of wax each mold holds.

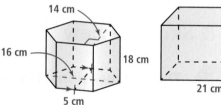
14 cm
16 cm
18 cm
5 cm

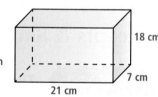
18 cm
7 cm
21 cm

LESSON 13-3 ► Pyramids and Cones

Quick Review

The volume of a pyramid is one-third the volume of a prism with the same base area and height.

$V = \frac{1}{3}Bh$

The volume of a cone is one-third the volume of a cylinder with the same base area and height.

$V = \frac{1}{3}Bh$

Example

What is the volume?

$V = \frac{1}{3}Bh = \frac{1}{3} \cdot \frac{1}{2}(6 \cdot 3)(9)$

$= 27$

9
3
6

The volume of the pyramid is 27 cubic units.

Practice & Problem Solving

For Exercises 13 and 14, find the volume of each figure. Round to the nearest tenth.

13.
7 in.
12 in.
4 in.

14.
24 m
15 m

15. A sculptor cuts a pyramid from a marble cube with volume t^3 ft³. The pyramid is t ft tall. The area of the base is t^2 ft². Write an expression for the volume of marble removed.

16. A company cuts 2 in. from the tops of the solid plastic cones. How much less plastic is used in the new design?

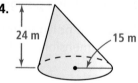
2 in.
3.5 in.
10 in.
21 in.

📶 **Go Online** | PearsonRealize.com

Quick Review

The volume of a sphere is
$V = \frac{4}{3}\pi r^3$.

The volume of a hemisphere is one-half the volume of a sphere with the same radius,
$V = \frac{2}{3}\pi r^3$.

Example

What is the volume of the sphere shown?

$$V = \frac{4}{3}\pi r^3$$
$$= \frac{4}{3}\pi(3)^3 = 36\pi$$

The volume of the sphere is 36π m³.

Practice & Problem Solving

For Exercises 17 and 18, find the volume of each figure. Round to the nearest tenth.

17.

2.4 in.

18.

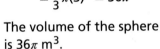
1.8 cm

19. **Use Structure** A golf ball has a radius of r centimeters. What is the least possible volume of a rectangular box that can hold 2 golf balls?

20. A capsule of liquid cold medicine is shown. If 1 dose is about 23 ml, how many capsules make up 1 dose? (*Hint:* 1 ml = 1 cm³)

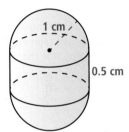
1 cm
0.5 cm

Visual Glossary

English

Absolute value function $f(x) = |x|$

Example

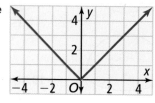

Altitude *See* **cone; cylinder; parallelogram; prism; pyramid; trapezoid; triangle.**

Altitude of a triangle An altitude of a triangle is the perpendicular segment from a vertex to the line containing the side opposite that vertex.

Example

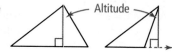

Arc *See* **major arc; minor arc.** *See also* **arc length; measure of an arc.**

Arc length The length of an arc of a circle is the product of the circumference of the circle and the ratio of the corresponding central angle measure in degrees and 360. The length of the arc is also the product of the radius and central angle measure in radians.

Example

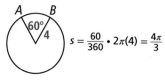

$$s = \frac{60}{360} \cdot 2\pi(4) = \frac{4\pi}{3}$$

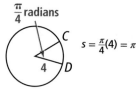

$$s = \frac{\pi}{4}(4) = \pi$$

Asymptote A line that the graph of a function gets closer to as x or y gets larger in absolute value.

Example

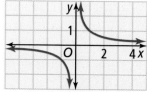

The y-axis is a vertical asymptote for $y = \frac{1}{x}$.
The x-axis is a horizontal asymptote for $y = \frac{1}{x}$.

Spanish

Función de valor absoluto $f(x) = |x|$

Altura *Ver* **cone; cylinder; parallelogram; prism; pyramid; trapezoid; triangle.**

Altura de un triángulo Una altura de un triángulo es el segmento perpendicular que va desde un vértice hasta la recta que contiene el lado opuesto a ese vértice.

Arco *Ver* **major arc; minor arc.** *Ver también* **arc length; measure of an arc.**

Longitud de un arco La longitud del arco de un círculo es el producto de la circunferencia del círculo y la razón de la medida del ángulo central correspondiente en grados y 360. La longitud del arco es también el producto del radio y de la medida del ángulo central en radianes.

Asíntota Línea recta a la que la gráfica de una función se acerca indefinidamente, mientras el valor absoluto de x o y aumenta.

English

Spanish

Axis of symmetry   The line that intersects the vertex, and divides the graph into two congruent halves that are reflections of each other.

Eje de simetría   El eje de simetría es la línea que corta el vértice y divide la gráfica en dos mitades congruentes que son reflexiones una de la otra.

Example

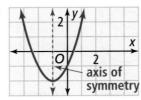

B

Base(s)   *See* **cone; cylinder; isosceles triangle; parallelogram; prism; pyramid; trapezoid; triangle.**

Base(s)   *Ver* **cone; cylinder; isosceles triangle; parallelogram; prism; pyramid; trapezoid; triangle.**

Binomial experiment   A binomial experiment is one in which the situation involves repeated trials. Each trial has two possible outcomes (success or failure), and the probability of success is constant throughout the trials.

Experimento binomial   Un experimento binomial es un experimento que requiere varios ensayos. Cada ensayo tiene dos resultados posibles (éxito o fracaso), y la probabilidad de éxito es constante durante todos los ensayos.

Binomial probability   For a binomial experiment consisting of n trials with probability of success p for each trial, the binomial probability is the probability of r successes out of n trials given by the function $P(r) = {_n}C_r \cdot p^r(1 - p)^{n-r}$.

Probabilidad binomial   En un experimento que incluye n ensayos con una probabilidad p de cada ensayo, la probabilidad binomial es la probabilidad de r éxitos de n ensayos dados por la función $P(r) = {_n}C_r \cdot p^r(1 - p)^{n-r}$.

Example   Suppose you roll a standard number cube and that you call rolling a 1 a success. Then $p = \frac{1}{6}$. The probability of rolling nine 1s in twenty rolls is
$${_{20}}C_9 \left(\frac{1}{6}\right)^9 \left(1 - \frac{1}{6}\right)^{20-9} \approx 0.022.$$

Binomial Theorem   For every positive integer n, $(a + b)^n = P_0a^n + P_1a^{n-1}b + P_2\,a^{n-2}b^2 + \ldots + P_{n-1}\,ab^{n-1} + P_n\,b^n$ where $P_0, P_1, \ldots, P_n$ are the numbers in the row of Pascal's Triangle that has n as its second number.

Teorema binomial   Para cada número entero positivo n, $(a + b)^n = P_0a^n + P_1a^{n-1}\,b + P_2a^{n-2}\,b^2 + \ldots + P_{n-1}ab^{n-1} + P_nb^n$, donde $P_0, P_1, \ldots, P_n$ son los números de la fila del Triángulo de Pascal cuyo segundo número es n.

Example $(x + 1)^3 = {_3}C_0(x)^3 + {_3}C_1(x)^2(1)^1$
$+ \; {_3}C_2(x)^1(1)^2 + {_3}C_3(1)^3$
$= x^3 + 3x^2 + 3x + 1$

C

Cavalieri's Principle   If two space figures have the same height and the same cross-sectional area at every level, then they have the same volume.

Principio de Cavalieri   Si dos figuras sólidas tienen la misma altura y la misma área transversal en todos los niveles, entonces también tienen el mismo volumen.

Example

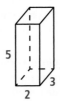

Both figures are prisms with height 5 units and horizontal cross-sectional area 6 square units.
$V = B \cdot h = (6)(5) = 30$ cubic units

Ceiling function   A function that rounds numbers up to the nearest integer.

Función techo   Función que redondea los números hacia arriba al entero más cercano.

English

Spanish

Central angle of a circle A central angle of a circle is an angle formed by two radii with the vertex at the center of the circle.

Ángulo central de un círculo Un ángulo central de un círculo es un ángulo formado por dos radios que tienen el vértice en el centro del círculo.

Example

$\angle ROK$ is a central angle of $\odot O$.

Centroid of a triangle The centroid of a triangle is the point of concurrency of the medians of the triangle.

Centroide de un triángulo El centroide de un triángulo es el punto de intersección de sus medianas.

Example P is the centroid of $\triangle ABC$.

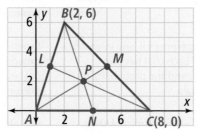

Chord A chord of a circle is a segment whose endpoints are on the circle.

Cuerda Una cuerda de un círculo es un segmento cuyos extremos son dos puntos del círculo.

Example

$\overline{HD}$ and $\overline{HR}$ are chords of $\odot C$.

Circle A circle is the set of all points in a plane that are a given distance, the radius, from a given point, the center. The standard form for an equation of a circle with center (h, k) and radius r is $(x - h)^2 + (y - k)^2 = r^2$.

Círculo Un círculo es el conjunto de todos los puntos de un plano situados a una distancia dada, el radio, de un punto dado, el centro. La fórmula normal de la ecuación de un círculo con centro (h, k) y radio r es $(x - h)^2 + (y - k)^2 = r^2$.

Example

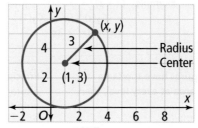

The equation of the circle whose center is $(1, 3)$ and whose radius is 3 is $(x - 1)^2 + (y - 3)^2 = 9$.

Circumcenter of a triangle The circumcenter of a triangle is the point of concurrency of the perpendicular bisectors of the sides of the triangle.

Circuncentro de un triángulo El circuncentro de un triángulo es el punto de intersección de las bisectrices perpendiculares de los lados del triángulo.

Example

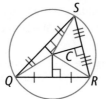

$QC = SC = RC$

C is the circumcenter.

English

Circumference   The circumference of a circle is the distance around the circle. Given the radius r of a circle, you can find its circumference C by using the formula $C = 2\pi r$.

Example
$$C = 2\pi r$$
$$= 2\pi(4)$$
$$= 8\pi$$

Circumference is the distance around the circle.

Circumscribed   A circumscribed circle of a triangle is the circle that contains the three vertices of the triangle.

Example

$\odot P$ is the circumscribed circle of $\triangle ABC$.

Closure property   A set of numbers is closed under an operation when the result of the operation is also part of the same set of numbers.

Example   The set of integers is closed under addition because the sum of two integers is always an integer.

Combination   Any unordered selection of r objects from a set of n objects is a combination. The number of combinations of n objects taken r at a time is $_nC_r = \frac{n!}{r!(n-r)!}$ for $0 \leq r \leq n$.

Example   The number of combinations of seven items taken four at a time is $_7C_4 = \frac{7!}{4!(7-4)!} = 35$. There are 35 ways to choose four items from seven items without regard to order.

Compass   A compass is a tool for drawing arcs and circles of different sizes and can be used to copy lengths.

Complement of an event   All possible outcomes that are not in the event.
$P(\text{complement of event}) = 1 - P(\text{event})$

Example   The complement of rolling a 1 or a 2 on a standard number cube is rolling a 3, 4, 5, or 6.

Completing the square   Completing the square is the process of adding $\left(\frac{b}{2}\right)^2$ to $x^2 + bx$ to form a perfect-square trinomial.

Example
$$x^2 - 12x + \blacksquare$$
$$x^2 - 12x + \left(\frac{-12}{2}\right)^2$$
$$x^2 - 12x + 36$$

Spanish

Circunferencia   La circunferencia de un círculo es la distancia alrededor del círculo. Dado el radio r de un círculo, se puede hallar la circunferencia C usando la fórmula $C = 2\pi r$.

Circunscrito   El círculo circunscrito de un triángulo es el círculo que contiene los tres vértices del triángulo.

Propiedad de cerradura   Un conjunto de números está cerrado bajo una operación cuando el resultado de la operación también forma parte del mismo conjunto de números.

Combinación   Cualquier selección no ordenada de r objetos tomados de un conjunto de n objetos es una combinación. El número de combinaciones de n objetos, cuando se toman r objetos cada vez, $_nC_r = \frac{n!}{r!(n-r)!}$ para $0 \leq r \leq n$.

Compás   El compás es un instrumento que se usa para dibujar arcos y círculos de diferentes tamaños, y que se puede usar para copiar longitudes.

Complemento de un suceso   Todos los resultados posibles que no se dan en el suceso.
$P(\text{complemento de un suceso}) = 1 - P(\text{suceso})$

Completar el cuadrado   Completar un cuadrado es el proceso mediante el cual se suma $\left(\frac{b}{2}\right)^2$ a $x^2 + bx$ para formar un trinomio cuadrado perfecto.

English	Spanish

Complex conjugates   Complex numbers with equivalent real parts and opposite imaginary parts are complex conjugates.

Conjugados complejos   Los números complejos con partes reales equivalentes y partes imaginarias opuestas son conjugados complejos.

Example   The complex numbers $2 - 3i$ and $2 + 3i$ are complex conjugates.

Complex number   Complex numbers are numbers that can be written in the form $a + bi$, where a and b are real numbers and i is the square root of -1.

Número complejo   Los números complejos son los números que se pueden escribir como $a + bi$, donde a y b son números reales y donde i es la raíz cuadrada de -1.

Example $6 + i$
7
$2i$

Composite space figures   A composite space figure is the combination of two or more figures into one object.

Figuras geométricas compuestas   Una figura geométrica compuesta es la combinación de dos o más figuras en un mismo objeto.

Example

Composition of rigid motions   A composition of rigid motions is a transformation with two or more rigid motions in which the second rigid motion is performed on the image of the first rigid motion.

Composición de movimientos rígidos   Una composición de movimientos rígidos es una transformación de dos o más movimientos rígidos en la que el segundo movimiento rígido se realiza sobre la imagen del primer movimiento rígido.

Example

If you reflect $\triangle ABC$ across line m to get $\triangle A'B'C'$ and then reflect $\triangle A'B'C'$ across line n to get $\triangle A''B''C''$, you perform a composition of rigid motions.

Compound event   A compound event is an event that consists of two or more events linked by the word *and* or the word *or*.

Suceso compuesto   Un suceso compuesto es un suceso que consiste en dos o más sucesos unidos por medio de la palabra *y* o la palabra *o*.

Example   Rolling a 5 on a standard number cube and then rolling a 4 is a compound event.

Compound interest   Interest that is paid on both the principal and the interest that has already been paid is compound interest.

Interés compuesto   El interés calculado tanto sobre el capital como sobre los intereses ya pagados es el interés compuesto.

Compound interest formula   This formula is an exponential model that is used to calculate the value of an investment when interest is compounded.

Fórmula de interés compuesto   Esta fórmula es un modelo exponencial que se usa para calcular el valor de una inversión cuando el interés es compuesto.

Concentric circles   Concentric circles lie in the same plane and have the same center.

Círculos concéntricos   Los círculos concéntricos están en el mismo plano y tienen el mismo centro.

Example

The two circles both have center D and are therefore concentric.

Conditional relative frequency   The ratio of the joint frequency and the related marginal frequency.

Frecuencia relativa condicional   La razón de la frecuencia conjunta y la frecuencia marginal relacionada.

Example

	Afternoon	Evening	Totals
Student	$\frac{90}{140} = 64\%$	$\frac{50}{140} = 36\%$	$\frac{140}{140} = 100\%$
Adult	$\frac{20}{60} = 33\%$	$\frac{40}{60} = 67\%$	$\frac{60}{60} = 100\%$

Concurrent   Three or more lines are concurrent if they intersect at one point. The point at which they intersect is the *point of concurrency*.

Concurrente   Tres o más rectas son concurrentes si se intersecan en un punto. El punto en el que se intersecan es el *punto de concurrencia*.

Example

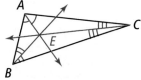

Point E is the point of concurrency of the bisectors of the angles of $\triangle ABC$. The bisectors are concurrent.

Conditional probability   A conditional probability is the probability that an event B will occur given that another event A has already occurred. The notation $P(B|A)$ is read "the probability of event B, given event A." For any two events A and B in the sample space, $P(B|A) = \frac{P(A \text{ and } B)}{P(A)}$.

Probabilidad condicional   Una probabilidad condicional es la probabilidad de que ocurra un suceso B cuando ya haya ocurrido otro suceso A. La notación $P(B|A)$ se lee "la probabilidad del suceso B, dado el suceso A". Para dos sucesos cualesquiera A y B en el espacio muestral $P(B|A) = \frac{P(A \text{ and } B)}{P(A)}$.

Example
$$= \frac{P(\text{departs and arrives on time})}{P(\text{departs on time})}$$
$$= \frac{0.75}{0.83}$$
$$\approx 0.9$$

Cone   A cone is a three-dimensional figure that has a circular *base*, a *vertex* not in the plane of the circle, and a curved lateral surface, as shown in the diagram. The *altitude* of a cone is the perpendicular segment from the vertex to the plane of the base. The *height* is the length of the altitude. In a *right* cone, the altitude contains the center of the base. The *slant height* of a right cone is the distance from the vertex to the edge of the base.

Cono   Un cono es una figura tridimensional que tiene una *base* circular, un *vértice* que no está en el plano del círculo y una superficie lateral curvada (indicada en el diagrama). La *altura* de un cono es el segmento perpendicular desde el vértice hasta el plano de la base. La *altura*, por extensión, es la longitud de la altura. Un *cono recto* es un cono cuya altura contiene el centro de la base. La *longitud de la generatriz* de un cono recto es la distancia desde el vértice hasta el borde de la base.

Example

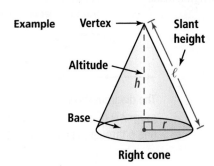

Right cone

English	Spanish
Congruent arcs Congruent arcs are arcs that have the same measure and are in the same circle or congruent circles.	**Arcos congruentes** Arcos congruentes son arcos que tienen la misma medida y están en el mismo círculo o en círculos congruentes.

Example

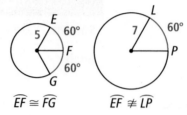

$$\overset{\frown}{EF} \cong \overset{\frown}{FG} \qquad \overset{\frown}{EF} \not\cong \overset{\frown}{LP}$$

English	Spanish
Congruent circles Congruent circles are circles whose radii are congruent.	**Círculos congruentes** Los círculos congruentes son círculos cuyos radios son congruentes.

Example

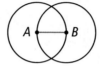

$\odot A$ and $\odot B$ have the same radius, so $\odot A \cong \odot B$.

English	Spanish
Continuously compounded interest formula This formula is a model for interest that has an infinitely small compounding period. The number e is the base in the formula $A = Pe^{rt}$.	**Fórmula de interés compuesto continuo** Esta fórmula es un modelo para calcular el interés que tiene un período de capitalización muy reducido. El número e es la base de la fórmula $A = Pe^{rt}$.

Example Suppose that $P = \$1200$, $r = 0.05$, and $t = 3$. Then
$$A = 1200e^{0.05 \cdot 3}$$
$$= 1200(2.718 \ldots)^{0.15}$$
$$\approx 1394.20$$

English	Spanish
Consecutive angles Consecutive angles of a polygon share a common side.	**Ángulos consecutivos** Los ángulos consecutivos de un polígono tienen un lado común.

Example

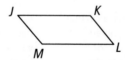

In $\square JKLM$, $\angle J$ and $\angle M$ are consecutive angles, as are $\angle J$ and $\angle K$. $\angle J$ and $\angle L$ are *not* consecutive.

English	Spanish
Construction A construction is a geometric figure made with only a straightedge and compass.	**Construcción** Una construcción es una figura geométrica trazada solamente con una regla sin graduación y un compás.

Example

The diagram shows the construction (in progress) of a line perpendicular to a line ℓ through a point P on ℓ.

Corollary A corollary is a theorem that can be proved easily using another theorem.

Corolario Un corolario es un teorema que se puede probar fácilmente usando otro teorema.

Example **Theorem:** If two sides of a triangle are congruent, then the angles opposite those sides are congruent.
Corollary: If a triangle is equilateral, then it is equiangular.

Cosine ratio See **trigonometric ratios.**

Razón coseno *Ver* **trigonometric ratios.**

Cross section A cross section is the intersection of a solid and a plane.

Sección de corte Una sección de corte es la intersección de un plano y un cuerpo geométrico.

Example
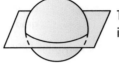
The cross section is a circle.

Cube A cube is a polyhedron with six faces, each of which is a square.

Cubo Un cubo es un poliedro de seis caras, cada una de las caras es un cuadrado.

Example

Cube root function $f(x) = \sqrt[3]{x}$

Función de raíz cúbica $f(x) = \sqrt[3]{x}$

Example
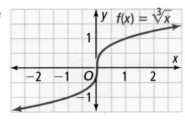

Cylinder A cylinder is a three-dimensional figure with two congruent circular bases that lie in parallel planes. An *altitude* of a cylinder is a perpendicular segment that joins the planes of the bases. Its length is the *height* of the cylinder. In a *right cylinder*, the segment joining the centers of the bases is an altitude. In an *oblique cylinder*, the segment joining the centers of the bases is not perpendicular to the planes containing the bases.

Cilindro Un cilindro es una figura tridimensional con dos bases congruentes circulares en planos paralelos. Una *altura* de un cilindro es un segmento perpendicular que une los planos de las bases. Su longitud es, por extensión, la *altura* del cilindro. En un *cilindro recto*, el segmento que une los centros de las bases es una altura. En un *cilindro oblicuo*, el segmento que une los centros de las bases no es perpendicular a los planos que contienen las bases.

Example
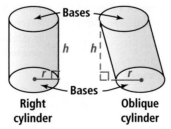
Right cylinder   Oblique cylinder

English

Dependent events   When the outcome of one event affects the probability of a second event, the events are dependent events.

Example   You have a bag with marbles of different colors. If you pick a marble from the bag and pick another without replacing the first, the events are dependent events.

Degree of a monomial   The sum of the exponents of the variables of a monomial.

Example $-4x^3y^2$ is a monomial of degree 5.

Degree of a polynomial   The highest degree of any term of the polynomial.

Example   The polynomial $P(x) = x^6 + 2x^3 - 3$ has degree 6.

Diameter of a circle   A diameter of a circle is a segment that contains the center of the circle and whose endpoints are on the circle. The term *diameter* can also mean the length of this segment.

Example

$\overline{DM}$ is a diameter of $\odot C$.

Diameter of a sphere   The diameter of a sphere is a segment passing through the center, with endpoints on the sphere.

Example

Difference of two squares   A difference of two squares is an expression of the form $a^2 - b^2$. It can be factored as $(a + b)(a - b)$.

Examples $25a^2 - 4 = (5a + 2)(5a - 2)$
$m^6 - 1 = (m^3 + 1)(m^3 - 1)$

Dilation   A dilation is a transformation that has *center C* and *scale factor n*, where $n > 0$, and maps a point R to R' in such a way that R' is on $\overrightarrow{CR}$ and $CR' = n \cdot CR$. The center of a dilation is its own image. If $n > 1$, the dilation is an *enlargement*, and if $0 < n < 1$, the dilation is a *reduction*.

Example

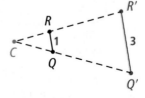

$\overline{R'Q'}$ is the image of $\overline{RQ}$ under a dilation with center C and scale factor 3.

Spanish

Sucesos dependientes   Dos sucesos son dependientes si el resultado de un suceso afecta la probabilidad del otro.

Grado de un monomio   La suma de los exponentes de las variables de un monomio.

Grado de un polinomio   El grado de un polinomio es el grado mayor de cualquier término del polinomio.

Diámetro de un círculo   Un diámetro de un círculo es un segmento que contiene el centro del círculo y cuyos extremos están en el círculo. El término *diámetro* también puede referirse a la longitud de este segmento.

Diámetro de una esfera   El diámetro de una esfera es un segmento que contiene el centro de la esfera y cuyos extremos están en la esfera.

Diferencia de dos cuadrados   La diferencia de dos cuadrados es una expresión de la forma $a^2 - b^2$. Se puede factorizar como $(a + b)(a - b)$.

Dilatación   Una dilatación, o *transformación de semejanza*, tiene *centro C* y *factor de escala n* para $n > 0$, y asocia un punto R a R' de tal modo que R' está en $\overrightarrow{CR}$ y $CR' = n \cdot CR$. El centro de una dilatación es su propia imagen. Si $n > 1$, la dilatación es un aumento, y si $0 < n < 1$, la dilatación es una reducción.

English	Spanish

Discriminant The discriminant of a quadratic equation in the form $ax^2 + bx + c = 0$ is the value of the expression $b^2 - 4ac$. The value of the discriminant determines the number of solutions of the equation.

Discriminante El discriminante de una ecuación cuadrática en la forma $ax^2 + bx + c = 0$ es el valor de la expresión $b^2 - 4ac$. El valor del discriminante determina el número de soluciones de la ecuación.

Example $3x^2 - 6x + 1$
discriminant $= (-6)^2 - 4(3)(1)$
$= 36 - 12 = 24$

Distance from a point to a line The distance from a point to a line is the length of the perpendicular segment from the point to the line.

Distancia desde un punto hasta una recta La distancia desde un punto hasta una recta es la longitud del segmento perpendicular que va desde el punto hasta la recta.

Example

The distance from point P to a line ℓ is PT.

E

Edge *See* **polyhedron**.

Arista *Ver* **polyhedron**.

Elements (of a set) Members of a set.

Elementos Partes integrantes de un conjunto.

Example Cats and dogs are elements of the set of mammals.

Enlargement *See* **dilation**.

Aumento *Ver* **dilation**.

Event Any group of outcomes in a situation involving probability.

Suceso En la probabilidad, cualquier grupo de resultados.

Example When rolling a number cube, there are six possible outcomes. Rolling an even number is an event with three possible outcomes, 2, 4, and 6.

Expected value The average value you can expect for a large number of trials of an experiment; the sum of each outcome's value multiplied by its probability.

Valor esperado El valor promedio que se puede esperar para una cantidad grande de pruebas en un experimento; la suma de los valores de los resultados multiplicados cada uno por su probabilidad.

Example In a game, a player has a 25% probability of earning 10 points by spinning an even number and a 75% probability of earning 5 points by spinning an odd number.

expected value $= 0.25(10) + 0.75(5) = 6.25$

Experimental probability The ratio of the number of times an event actually happens to the number of times the experiment is done.

$$P(\text{event}) = \frac{\text{number of times an event happens}}{\text{number of times the experiment is done}}$$

Probabilidad experimental La razón entre el número de veces que un suceso sucede en la realidad y el número de veces que se hace el experimento.

$$P(\text{suceso}) = \frac{\text{número de veces que sucede un suceso}}{\text{número de veces que se hace el experimento}}$$

Example A baseball player's batting average shows how likely it is that a player will get a hit, based on previous times at bat.

English	Spanish

Exterior angle of a polygon   An exterior angle of a polygon is an angle formed by a side and an extension of an adjacent side.

Ángulo exterior de un polígono   El ángulo exterior de un polígono es un ángulo formado por un lado y una extensión de un lado adyacente.

Example

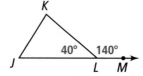

∠*KLM* is an exterior angle of △*JKL*.

Factorial   The factorial of a positive integer *n* is the product of all positive integers less than or equal to *n* and written *n*!

Factorial   El factorial de un número entero positivo *n* es el producto de todos los números positivos menores que o iguales a *n*, y se escribe *n*!

Example $4! = 4 \cdot 3 \cdot 2 \cdot 1 = 24$

Floor function   The floor function rounds numbers down to the nearest integer.

Función piso   La función piso redondea los números hacia abajo al entero más cercano.

Frequency table   A table that groups a set of data values into intervals and shows the frequency for each interval.

Tabla de frecuencias   Tabla que agrupa un conjunto de datos en intervalos y muestra la frecuencia de cada intervalo.

Example

Interval	Frequency
0−9	5
10−19	8
20−29	4

Fundamental Counting Principle   If there are *m* ways to make the first selection and *n* ways to make the second selection, then there are *m* • *n* ways to make the two selections.

Principio fundamental de Conteo   Si hay *m* maneras de hacer la primera selección y *n* maneras de hacer la segunda selección, quiere decir que hay *m* • *n* maneras de hacer las dos selecciones.

Example   For 5 shirts and 8 pairs of shorts, the number of possible outfits is $5 \cdot 8 = 40$.

G

Geometric mean   The geometric mean is the number *x* such that $\frac{a}{x} = \frac{x}{b}$, where *a*, *b*, and *x* are positive numbers.

Media geométrica   La media geométrica es el número *x* tanto que $\frac{a}{x} = \frac{x}{b}$, donde *a*, *b* y *x* son números positivos.

Example   The geometric mean of 6 and 24 is 12.

$$\frac{6}{x} = \frac{x}{24}$$
$$x^2 = 144$$
$$x = 12$$

Geometric probability   Geometric probability is a probability that uses a geometric model in which points represent outcomes.

Probabilidad geométrica   La probabilidad geométrica es una probabilidad que utiliza un modelo geométrico donde se usan puntos para representar resultados.

Example

$P(H \text{ on } \overline{BC}) = \frac{BC}{AD}$

English	Spanish

Great circle   A great circle is the intersection of a sphere and a plane containing the center of the sphere. A great circle divides a sphere into two *hemispheres*.

Círculo máximo   Un círculo máximo es la intersección de una esfera y un plano que contiene el centro de la esfera. Un círculo máximo divide una esfera en dos *hemisferios*.

Example   Hemispheres   Great circle

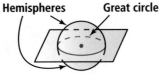

I

Identity   An identity is an equation between two polynomial expressions in which one side can be transformed into the other side using defined rules of calculation.

Identidad   Una ecuación entre dos expresiones polinomiales para la cual un lado se puede transformar en el otro lado usando reglas de cálculo definidas.

Imaginary number   An imaginary number is any number of the form bi, where b is a nonzero real number and i is the square root of −1.

Número imaginario   Un número imaginario es cualquier número de la forma bi, donde b es un número real distinto de cero y donde i es la raíz cuadrada de −1.

Example $7i$
i

Imaginary unit   The imaginary unit i is the complex number whose square is −1.

Unidad imaginaria   La unidad imaginaria i es el número complejo cuyo cuadrado es −1.

Incenter of a triangle   The incenter of a triangle is the point of concurrency of the angle bisectors of the triangle.

Incentro de un triángulo   El incentro de un triángulo es el punto donde concurren las tres bisectrices de los ángulos del triángulo.

Example

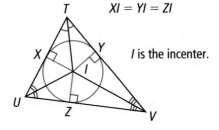

$XI = YI = ZI$

I is the incenter.

Independent events   When the outcome of one event does not affect the probability of a second event, the two events are independent.

Sucesos independientes   Cuando el resultado de un suceso no altera la probabilidad de otro, los dos sucesos son independientes.

Example   The results of two rolls of a number cube are independent. Getting a 5 on the first roll does not change the probability of getting a 5 on the second roll.

English

Spanish

Inscribed The inscribed circle of a triangle is the circle that intersects each side of the triangle at exactly one point.

Inscrito El círculo inscrito de un triángulo es el círculo que interseca cada lado del triángulo en exactamente un punto.

Example

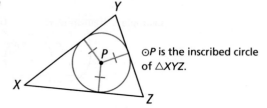

⊙*P* is the inscribed circle of △*XYZ*.

Inscribed angle An angle is inscribed in a circle if the vertex of the angle is on the circle and the sides of the angle are chords of the circle.

Ángulo inscrito Un ángulo está inscrito en un círculo si el vértice del ángulo está en el círculo y los lados del ángulo son cuerdas del círculo.

Example

∠*C* is inscribed in ⊙*M*.

Intercepted arc An intercepted arc is the part of a circle that lies between two segments that intersect the circle.

Arco interceptor Un arco interceptor es la parte de un círculo que yace entre dos segmentos de recta que intersecan al círculo.

Example

$\overarc{UV}$ is the intercepted arc of inscribed ∠*T*.

Inverse function If function *f* pairs a value *b* with *a*, then its inverse, denoted f^{-1}, pairs the value *a* with *b*. If f^{-1} is also a function, then *f* and f^{-1} are inverse functions.

Funcion inversa Si la función *f* empareja un valor *b* con *a*, entonces su inversa, cuya notación es f^{-1}, empareja el valor *a* con *b*. Si f^{-1} también es una función, entonces *f* y f^{-1} son funciones inversas.

Example If $f(x) = x + 3$, then
$f^{-1}(x) = x - 3$.

Joint frequency The frequency of a single option for one category.

Frecuencia conjunta La frecuencia de una única opción por categoría.

Example

	Afternoon	Evening	Totals
Student	90	50	140
Adult	20	40	60
Totals	110	90	200

90, 50, 20, and 40 are joint frequencies.

English	Spanish
Joint relative frequency The ratio, or percent, of the joint frequency to the total.	**Frecuencia relativa conjunta** La razón, o porcentaje, de la frecuencia conjunta al total.

Example

	Afternoon	Evening	Totals
Student	$\frac{90}{200} = 45\%$	$\frac{50}{200} = 25\%$	$\frac{140}{200} = 70\%$
Adult	$\frac{20}{200} = 10\%$	$\frac{40}{200} = 20\%$	$\frac{60}{200} = 30\%$
Totals	$\frac{110}{200} = 55\%$	$\frac{90}{200} = 45\%$	$\frac{200}{200} = 100\%$

45%, 25%, 10%, and 20% are joint relative frequencies.

K

English	Spanish
Kite A kite is a quadrilateral with two pairs of consecutive sides congruent and no opposite sides congruent.	**Cometa** Una cometa es un cuadrilátero con dos pares de lados congruentes consecutivos y sin lados opuestos congruentes.

Example

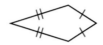

L

English	Spanish
Lateral area The lateral area of a prism or pyramid is the sum of the areas of the lateral faces. The lateral area of a cylinder or cone is the area of the curved surface.	**Área lateral** El área lateral de un prisma o pirámide es la suma de las áreas de sus caras laterals. El área lateral de un cilindro o de un cono es el área de la superficie curvada.

Example

6 cm

5 cm

5 cm

$$\text{L.A. of pyramid} = \tfrac{1}{2}p\ell$$
$$= \tfrac{1}{2}(20)(6)$$
$$= 60 \text{ cm}^2$$

English	Spanish
Lateral face *See* **prism; pyramid.**	**Cara lateral** *Ver* **prism; pyramid.**
Linear-quadratic system A system of equations that includes a linear equation and a quadratic equation and is represented on a graph by the corresponding line and parabola.	**Sistema cuadrático lineal** Un sistema de ecuaciones que incluye una ecuación lineal y una ecuación cuadrática y se representa en una gráfica con su línea y su parábola correspondientes.

Example

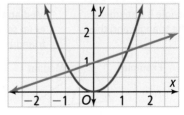

English   Spanish

Major arc   A major arc of a circle is an arc that is larger than a semicircle.

Arco mayor   Un arco mayor de un círculo es cualquier arco más grande que un semicírculo.

Example

$\widehat{DEF}$ is a major arc of $\odot C$.

Marginal frequency   The total frequency for each option or category.

Frecuencia marginal   La frecuencia total para cada opción o categoría.

Example

	Afternoon	Evening	Totals
Student	90	50	140
Adult	20	40	60
Totals	110	90	200

140, 60, 110, and 90 are marginal frequencies.

Marginal relative frequency   The ratio, or percent, of the marginal frequency to the total.

Frecuencia relativa marginal   La razón, o porcentaje, de la frecuencia marginal al total.

Example

	Afternoon	Evening	Totals
Student	$\frac{90}{200} = 45\%$	$\frac{50}{200} = 25\%$	$\frac{140}{200} = 70\%$
Adult	$\frac{20}{200} = 10\%$	$\frac{40}{200} = 20\%$	$\frac{60}{200} = 30\%$
Totals	$\frac{110}{200} = 55\%$	$\frac{90}{200} = 45\%$	$\frac{200}{200} = 100\%$

70%, 30%, 55%, and 45% are marginal relative frequencies.

Measure of an arc   The measure of a minor arc is the measure of its central angle. The measure of a major arc is 360° minus the measure of its related minor arc.

Medida de un arco   La medida de un arco menor es la medida de su ángulo central. La medida de un arco mayor es 360° menos la medida en grados de su arco menor correspondiente.

Example

$m\widehat{TY} = 70$
$m\widehat{TXY} = 290$

Median of a triangle   A median of a triangle is a segment that has as its endpoints at a vertex of the triangle and the midpoint of the opposite side.

Mediana de un triángulo   Una mediana de un triángulo es un segmento que tiene en sus extremos el vértice del triángulo y el punto medio del lado opuesto.

Example

Median

English	Spanish
Midsegment of a trapezoid The midsegment of a trapezoid is the segment that joins the midpoints of the nonparallel opposite sides of a trapezoid.	**Segmento medio de un trapecio** El segmento medio de trapecio es el segmento que une los puntos medios de los lados no paralelos de un trapecio.

Example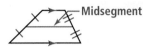 Midsegment

Midsegment of a triangle A midsegment of a triangle is a segment that joins the midpoints of two sides of the triangle.	**Segmento medio de un triángulo** Un segmento medio de un triángulo es un segmento que une los puntos medios de dos lados del triángulo.

Example Midsegment

Minor arc A minor arc is an arc that is smaller than a semicircle.	**Arco menor** Un arco menor de un círculo es un arco más corto que un semicírculo.

Example $\overset{\frown}{KC}$ is a minor arc of $\odot S$.

Monomial A real number, a variable, or a product of a real number and one or more variables with whole-number exponents.	**Monomio** Número real, variable o el producto de un número real y una o más variables con números enteros como exponentes.

Example   9, n, and $-5xy^2$ are examples of monomials.

Mutually exclusive events When two events cannot happen at the same time, the events are mutually exclusive. If A and B are mutually exclusive events, then $P(A \text{ or } B) = P(A) + P(B)$.	**Sucesos mutuamente excluyentes** Cuando dos sucesos no pueden ocurrir al mismo tiempo, son mutuamente excluyentes. Si A y B son sucesos mutuamente excluyentes, entonces $P(A \text{ o } B) = P(A) + P(B)$.

Example   Rolling an even number E and rolling a multiple of five M on a standard number cube are mutually exclusive events.

$$P(E \text{ or } M) = P(E) + P(M)$$
$$= \frac{3}{6} + \frac{1}{6}$$
$$= \frac{4}{6}$$
$$= \frac{2}{3}$$

N

Natural base e The value that the expression $(1 + \frac{1}{x})^x$ approaches as $x \to \infty$. The value is approximately 2.7818282 . . .	**Base natural** e El valor al que se acerca la expresión $(1 + \frac{1}{x})^x$ a medida que $x \to \infty$. El valor es aproximadamente igual a 2.7818282 . . .

n-gon An n-gon is a polygon with n sides.	**n-ágono** Un n-ágono es un polígono de n lados.

Example   A polygon with 25 sides is a 25-gon.

English

Spanish

Opposite sides   Opposite sides of a quadrilateral are two sides that do not share a vertex.

Lados opuestos   Los lados opuestos de un cuadrilátero son dos lados que no tienen un vértice en común.

Example

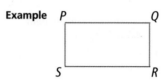

$\overline{PQ}$ and $\overline{SR}$ are opposite sides, as are $\overline{PS}$ and $\overline{QR}$.

Orthocenter of a triangle   The orthocenter of a triangle is the point of concurrency of the lines containing the altitudes of the triangle.

Ortocentro de un triángulo   El ortocentro de un triángulo es el punto donde se intersecan las alturas de un triángulo.

Example

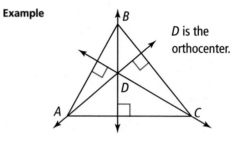

D is the orthocenter.

Outcome   An outcome is the result of a single trial in a probability experiment.

Resultado   Un resultado es que se obtiene al hacer una sola prueba en un experimento de probabilidad.

Example   The outcomes of rolling a number cube are 1, 2, 3, 4, 5, and 6.

Overlapping events   Overlapping events are events that have at least one common outcome. If A and B are overlapping events, then $P(A \text{ or } B) = P(A) + P(B) - P(A \text{ and } B)$.

Sucesos traslapados   Sucesos traslapados son sucesos que tienen por lo menos un resultado en común. Si A y B son sucesos traslapados, entonces $P(A \text{ ó } B) = P(A) + P(B) - P(A \text{ y } B)$.

Example   Rolling a multiple of 3 and rolling an odd number on a number cube are overlapping events.

$$P(\text{multiple of 3 or odd}) = P(\text{multiple of 3}) + P(\text{odd}) - P(\text{multiple of 3 and odd})$$
$$= \frac{1}{3} + \frac{1}{2} - \frac{1}{6}$$
$$= \frac{2}{3}$$

Parabola   The graph of a quadratic function.

Parábola   La gráfica de una función cuadrática.

Example

English	Spanish

Pascal's Triangle   Pascal's Triangle is a triangular array of numbers in which the first and last number in each row is 1. Each of the other numbers in the row is the sum of the two numbers above it.

Triángulo de Pascal   El Triángulo de Pascal es una distribución triangular de números en la cual el primer número y el último número son 1. Cada uno de los otros números en la fila es la suma de los dos números de encima.

Example   **Pascal's Triangle**

```
            1
          1   1
        1   2   1
      1   3   3   1
    1   4   6   4   1
  1   5   10  10  5   1
```

Perfect-square trinomial   Any trinomial of the form $a^2 + 2ab + b^2$ or $a^2 - 2ab + b^2$. It is the result when a binomial is squared.

Trinomio cuadrado perfecto   Todo trinomio de la forma $a^2 + 2ab + b^2$ ó $a^2 - 2ab + b^2$. Es el resultado cuando un binomio se eleva al cuadrado.

Example $(x + 3)^2 = x^2 + 6x + 9$

Permutation   A permutation is an arrangement of some or all of a set of objects in a specific order. You can use the notation $_nP_r$ to express the number of permutations, where n equals the number of objects available and r equals the number of selections to make.

Permutación   Una permutación es una disposición de algunos o de todos los objetos de un conjunto en un orden determinado. El número de permutaciones se puede expresar con la notación $_nP_r$, donde n es igual al número total de objetos y r es igual al número de selecciones que han de hacerse.

Example   How many ways can you arrange 5 objects 3 at a time?

$$_5P_3 = \frac{5!}{(5-3)!} = \frac{5!}{2!} = \frac{5 \cdot 4 \cdot 3 \cdot 2 \cdot 1}{2 \cdot 1} = 60$$

There are 60 ways to arrange 5 objects 3 at a time.

Piecewise-defined function   A piecewise-defined function has different rules for different parts of its domain.

Función definida por fragmentos   Una función definida por fragmentos tiene reglas diferentes para diferentes partes de su dominio.

Polygon   A polygon is a closed plane figure formed by three or more segments. Each segment intersects exactly two other segments, but only at their endpoints, and no two segments with a common endpoint are collinear. The *vertices* of the polygon are the endpoints of the sides. A *diagonal* is a segment that connects two nonconsecutive vertices. A polygon is *convex* if no diagonal contains points outside the polygon. A polygon is *concave* if a diagonal contains points outside the polygon.

Polígono   Un polígono es una figura plana compuesta por tres o más segmentos. Cada segmento interseca los otros dos segmentos exactamente, pero únicamente en sus puntos extremos y ningúno de los segmentos con extremos comunes son colineales. Los *vértices* del polígono son los extremos de los lados. Una *diagonal* es un segmento que conecta dos vértices no consecutivos. Un polígono es *convexo* si ninguna diagonal tiene puntos fuera del polígono. Un polígono es *cóncavo* si una diagonal tiene puntos fuera del polígono.

Example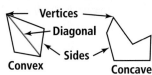
Vertices — Diagonal — Sides
Convex   Concave

English

Spanish

Polyhedron A polyhedron is a three-dimensional figure whose surfaces, or *faces*, are polygons. The vertices of the polygons are the *vertices* of the polyhedron. The intersections of the faces are the *edges* of the polyhedron.

Poliedro Un poliedro es una figura tridimensional cuyas superficies, o *caras*, son polígonos. Los vértices de los polígonos son los *vértices* del poliedro. Las intersecciones de las caras son las *aristas* del poliedro.

Example

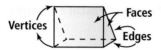

Polynomial A monomial or the sum or difference of two or more monomials.

Polinomio Un monomio o la suma o diferencia de dos o más monomios.

Example $2x^2$, $3x + 7$, 28, and $-7x^3 - 2x^2 + 9$ are all polynomials.

Postulate A postulate is an accepted statement of fact.

Postulado Un postulado es un enunciado que se acepta como un hecho.

Example **Postulate:** Through any two points there is exactly one line.

Prism A prism is a polyhedron with two congruent and parallel faces, which are called the *bases*. The other faces, which are parallelograms, are called the *lateral faces*. An *altitude* of a prism is a perpendicular segment that joins the planes of the bases. Its length is the *height* of the prism. A *right prism* is one whose lateral faces are rectangular regions and a lateral edge is an altitude. In an *oblique prism*, some or all of the lateral faces are nonrectangular.

Prisma Un prisma es un poliedro con dos caras congruentes paralelas llamadas *bases*. Las otras caras son paralelogramos llamados *caras laterales*. La *altura* de un prisma es un segmento perpendicular que une los planos de las bases. Su longitud es también la *altura* del prisma. En un *prisma rectangular*, las caras laterales son rectangulares y una de las aristas laterales es la altura. En un *prisma oblicuo*, algunas o todas las caras laterales no son rectangulares.

Example

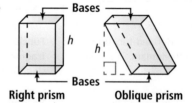

Right prism   Oblique prism

Probability Probability is the likelihood that an event will occur (written formally as $P(\text{event})$).

Probabilidad Probabilidad es la posibilidad de que un suceso ocurra, escrita formalmente $P(\text{suceso})$.

Example You have 4 red marbles and 3 white marbles. The probability that you select one red marble, and then, without replacing it, randomly select another red marble is $P(\text{red}) = \frac{4}{7} \cdot \frac{3}{6} = \frac{2}{7}$.

English

Spanish

Probability distribution A probability distribution for an experiment is a function that assigns a probability to each outcome of a sample space for the experiment.

Distribución de probabilidades La distribución de probabilidades de un experimento es una función que asigna una probabilidad a cada resultado de un espacio muestral del experimento.

Example

Roll	Fr.	Prob.
1	5	0.125
2	9	0.225
3	7	0.175
4	8	0.2
5	8	0.2
6	3	0.075

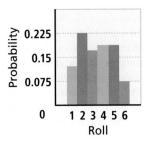

The table and graph both show the experimental probability distribution for the outcomes of 40 rolls of a standard number cube.

Product Property of Square Roots $\sqrt{ab} = \sqrt{a} \cdot \sqrt{b}$, when both a and b are greater than or equal to 0.

Propiedad del producto de las raíces cuadradas $\sqrt{ab} = \sqrt{a} \cdot \sqrt{b}$, cuando tanto a como b son mayores que o iguales a 0.

Example $\sqrt{16 \cdot 25} = \sqrt{16} \cdot \sqrt{25}$

Proof A proof is a convincing argument that uses deductive reasoning. A proof can be written in many forms. In a two-column proof, the statements and reasons are aligned in columns. In a paragraph proof, the statements and reasons are connected in sentences. In a flow proof, arrows show the logical connections between the statements. In a coordinate proof, a figure is drawn on a coordinate plane and the formulas for slope, midpoint, and distance are used to prove properties of the figure. An indirect proof involves the use of indirect reasoning.

Prueba Una prueba es un argumento convincente en el cual se usa el razonamiento deductivo. Una prueba se puede escribir de varias maneras. En una *prueba de dos columnas*, los enunciados y las razones se alinean en columnas. En una *prueba de párrafo*, los enunciados y razones están unidos en oraciones. En una *prueba de flujo*, hay flechas que indican las conexiones lógicas entre enunciados. En una *prueba de coordenadas*, se dibuja una figura en un plano de coordenadas y se usan las fórmulas de la pendiente, punto medio y distancia para probar las propiedades de la figura. Una *prueba indirecta* incluye el uso de razonamiento indirecto.

Example

Given: $\triangle EFG$, with right angle $\angle F$
Prove: $\angle E$ and $\angle G$ are complementary.

Paragraph Proof: Because $\angle F$ is a right angle, $m\angle F = 90$. By the Triangle Angle-Sum Theorem, $m\angle E + m\angle F + m\angle G = 180$. By substitution, $m\angle E + 90 + m\angle G = 180$. Subtracting 90 from each side yields $m\angle E + m\angle G = 90$. $\angle E$ and $\angle G$ are complementary by definition.

English	Spanish

Proportion A proportion is a statement that two ratios are equal. An *extended proportion* is a statement that three or more ratios are equal.

Proporción Una proporción es un enunciado en el cual dos razones son iguales. Una *proporción extendida* es un enunciado que dice que tres razones o más son iguales.

Example $\frac{x}{5} = \frac{3}{4}$ is a proportion.

$\frac{9}{27} = \frac{3}{9} = \frac{1}{3}$ is an extended proportion.

Pyramid A pyramid is a polyhedron in which one face, the *base*, is a polygon and the other faces, the *lateral faces*, are triangles with a common vertex, called the *vertex* of the pyramid. An *altitude* of a pyramid is the perpendicular segment from the vertex to the plane of the base. Its length is the *height* of the pyramid. The *slant height* of a regular pyramid is the length of an altitude of a lateral face.

Pirámide Una pirámide es un poliedro en donde una cara, la *base*, es un polígono y las otras caras, las *caras laterales*, son triángulos con un vértice común, llamado el *vértice* de la pirámide. Una *altura* de una pirámide es el segmento perpendicular que va del vértice hasta el plano de la base. Su longitud es, por extensión, la *altura* de la pirámide. La *apotema* de una pirámide regular es la longitud de la altura de la cara lateral.

Example

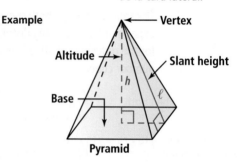

Pythagorean triple A Pythagorean triple is a set of three nonzero whole numbers a, b, and c, that satisfy the equation $a^2 + b^2 = c^2$.

Tripleta de Pitágoras Una tripleta de Pitágoras es un conjunto de tres números enteros positivos a, b, and c que satisfacen la ecuación $a^2 + b^2 = c^2$.

Example The numbers 5, 12, and 13 form a Pythagorean triple because $5^2 + 12^2 = 13^2 = 169$.

 Q

Quadratic equation An equation of the second degree.

Ecuación cuadrática Una ecuación de segundo grado.

Example $4x^2 + 9x - 5 = 0$

Quadratic formula If $ax^2 + bx + c = 0$ and $a \neq 0$, then $x = \frac{-b \pm \sqrt{b^2 - 4ac}}{2a}$.

Fórmula cuadrática Si $ax^2 + bx + c = 0$ y $a \neq 0$, entonces $x = \frac{-b \pm \sqrt{b^2 - 4ac}}{2a}$.

Example $2x^2 + 10x + 12 = 0$

$$x = \frac{-b \pm \sqrt{b^2 - 4ac}}{2a}$$

$$x = \frac{-10 \pm \sqrt{10^2 - 4(2)(12)}}{2(2)}$$

$$x = \frac{-10 \pm \sqrt{4}}{4}$$

$$x = \frac{-10 + 2}{4} \text{ or } \frac{-10 - 2}{4}$$

$$x = -2 \text{ or } -3$$

English

Quadratic function A function of the form $y = ax^2 + bx + c$, where $a \neq 0$. The graph of a quadratic function is a parabola, a U-shaped curve that opens up or down.

Example $y = 5x^2 - 2x + 1$ is a quadratic function.

Quadratic parent function The simplest quadratic function $f(x) = x^2$ or $y = x^2$.

Example $y = x^2$ is the parent function for the family of quadratic equations of the form $y = ax^2 + bx + c$.

R

Radian A radian is equal to the measure of a central angle that intercepts an arc with length equal to the radius of the circle.

Example

$$s = \theta r$$
$$\theta = \frac{s}{r}$$
$$\theta = \frac{3}{2} = 1.5 \text{ radians}$$

Radius of a sphere The radius of a sphere is a segment that has one endpoint at the center and the other endpoint on the sphere.

Example

Rational exponent Another way to express radicals.

Example $\sqrt[3]{x} = x^{\frac{1}{3}}$

$\frac{1}{3}$ is the rational exponent.

Reduction *See* **dilation**.

Relative frequency The relative frequency of an event is the ratio of the number of times the event occurs to the total number of trials.

Example

Archery Results					
Scoring Region	Yellow	Red	Blue	Black	White
Arrow Strikes	52	25	10	8	5

Relative frequency of striking red $= \dfrac{\text{frequency of striking red}}{\text{total frequencies}}$

$= \dfrac{25}{100} = \dfrac{1}{4}$

Spanish

Función cuadrática La función $y = ax^2 + bx + c$, en la que $a \neq 0$. La gráfica de una función cuadrática es una parábola, o curva en forma de U que se abre hacia arriba o hacia abajo.

Función cuadrática madre La función cuadrática más simple $f(x) = x^2$ ó $y = x^2$.

Radián Un radián es igual a la medida de un ángulo central que interseca a un ángulo de la misma longitud que el radio del círculo.

Radio de una esfera El radio de una esfera es un segmento con un extremo en el centro y otro en la esfera.

Exponente racional Otra forma de expresar los radicales.

Reducción *Ver* **dilation**.

Frecuencia relativa La frecuencia relativa de un suceso es la razón del número de veces que ocurre un evento al número de eventos en el espacio muestral.

English	Spanish

Right triangle A right triangle contains one right angle. The side opposite the right angle is the *hypotenuse* and the other two sides are the *legs*.

Triángulo rectángulo Un triángulo rectángulo contiene un ángulo recto. El lado opuesto del ángulo recto es la *hipotenusa* y los otros dos lados son los *catetos*.

Example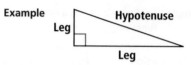

Root The input values for which the related function is zero.

Raíz Los valores de entrada para los cuales la función relacionada es cero.

Sample space A sample space is the set of all possible outcomes of a situation or experiment.

Espacio muestral Un espacio muestral es el conjunto de todos los resultados posibles de un suceso.

Example When you roll a standard number cube, the sample space is {1, 2, 3, 4, 5, 6}.

Scale A scale is the ratio of any length in a scale drawing to the corresponding actual length. The lengths may be in different units.

Escala Una escala es la razón de cualquier longitud en un dibujo a escala en relación a la longitud verdadera correspondiente. Las longitudes pueden expresarse en distintas unidades.

Example 1 cm to 1 ft
1 cm = 1 ft
1 cm : 1 ft

Scale drawing A scale drawing is a drawing in which all lengths are proportional to corresponding actual lengths.

Dibujo a escala Un dibujo a escala es un dibujo en el que todas las longitudes son proporcionales a las longitudes verdaderas correspondientes.

Example  Scale:
1 in. = 30 ft

Scale factor A scale factor is the ratio of corresponding linear measurements of two similar figures.

Factor de escala El factor de escala es la razón de las medidas lineales correspondientes de dos figuras semejantes.

Example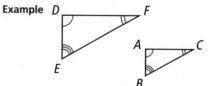

$$\triangle ABC \sim \triangle DEF$$

$$\frac{AB}{DE} = \frac{BC}{EF} = \frac{CA}{FD}$$

Scale factor of a dilation The scale factor of a dilation is the ratio of the distances from the center of dilation to an image point and to its preimage point.

Factor de escala de dilatación El factor de escala de dilatación es la razón de las distancias desde el centro de dilatación hasta un punto de la imagen y hasta un punto de la preimagen.

Example

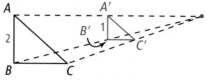

The scale factor of the dilation that maps $\triangle ABC$ to $\triangle A'B'C'$ is $\frac{1}{2}$.

English

Secant   A secant is a line, ray, or segment that intersects a circle at two points.

Example

$\overleftrightarrow{AB}$ is a secant of $\odot C$.

Sector of a circle   A sector of a circle is the region bounded by two radii and the intercepted arc.

Example

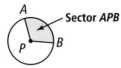

Sector *APB*

Segment of a circle   A segment of a circle is the part of a circle bounded by an arc and the segment joining its endpoints.

Example

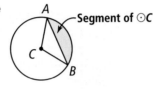

Segment of $\odot C$

Semicircle   A semicircle is half a circle.

Example

Semicircle

Set   A well-defined collection of elements.

Example   The set of integers:
$\{\ldots, -3, -2, -1, 0, 1, 2, 3, \ldots\}$

Similar figures   Similar figures are two figures that have the same shape, but not necessarily the same size. Two figures are similar if there is a similarity transformation that maps one figure to the other.

Example

Similarity transformation   A composition of one or more rigid motions and a dilation.

Spanish

Secante   Una secante es una recta, semirrecta o segmento que corta un círculo en dos puntos.

Sector de un círculo   Un sector de un círculo es la región limitada por dos radios y el arco abarcado por ellos.

Segmento de un círculo   Un segmento de un círculo es la parte de un círculo bordeada por un arco y el segmento que une sus extremos.

Semicírculo   Un semicírculo es la mitad de un círculo.

Conjunto   Un grupo bien definido de elementos.

Figuras semejantes   Los figuras semejantes son dos figuras que tienen la misma forma pero no necesariamente el mismo tamaño. Dos figuras son semejantes si hay una transformación de semajanza en la que una figura es la imagen de la otra.

Transformación de semejanza   Una composición de uno o más movimientos rígidos y una dilatación.

English	Spanish
Similar polygons Similar polygons are polygons having corresponding angles congruent and the lengths of corresponding sides proportional. Similarity is denoted by ~.	**Polígonos semejantes** Los polígonos semejantes son polígonos cuyos ángulos correspondientes son congruentes y las longitudes de los lados correspondientes son proporcionales. El símbolo ~ significa "es semejante a".

Example

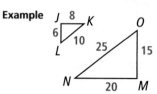

$\triangle JKL \sim \triangle MNO$

Scale factor $= \frac{2}{5}$

English	Spanish
Sine ratio *See* **trigonometric ratios**.	**Razón seno** *Ver* **trigonometric ratios**.

English	Spanish
Sphere A sphere is the set of all points in space that are a given distance *r*, the *radius*, from a given point *C*, the *center*. A *great circle* is the intersection of a sphere with a plane containing the center of the sphere. The *circumference* of a sphere is the circumference of any great circle of the sphere.	**Esfera** Una esfera es el conjunto de los puntos del espacio que están a una distancia dada *r*, el *radio*, de un punto dado *C*, el *centro*. Un *círculo máximo* es la intersección de una esfera y un plano que contiene el centro de la esfera. La *circunferencia* de una esfera es la circunferencia de cualquier círculo máximo de la esfera.

Example

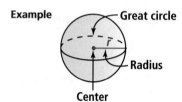

- Great circle
- Radius
- Center

English	Spanish
Square root function A function that contains the independent variable in the radicand.	**Función de raíz cuadrada** Una función que contiene la variable independiente en el radicando.

Example $y = \sqrt{2x}$ is a square root function.

English	Spanish
Standard form of a polynomial The form of a polynomial that places the terms in descending order by degree.	**Forma normal de un polinomio** Cuando el grado de los términos de un polinomio disminuye de izquierda a derecha, está en forma normal, o en orden descendente.

Example $15x^3 + x^2 + 3x + 9$

English	Spanish
Standard form of a quadratic equation The standard form of a quadratic equation is $ax^2 + bx + c = 0$, where $a \neq 0$.	**Forma normal de una ecuación cuadrática** Cuando una ecuación cuadrática se expresa de forma $ax^2 + bx + c = 0$.

Example $-x^2 + 2x - 9 = 0$

English	Spanish
Standard form of a quadratic function The standard form of a quadratic function is $f(x) = ax^2 + bx + C$, where $a \neq 0$.	**Forma normal de una función cuadrática** La forma normal de una función cuadrática es $f(x) = ax^2 + bx + C$, donde $a \neq 0$.

Example $f(x) = 2x^2 - 5x + 2$

English	Spanish
Step-function A step-function pairs every number in an interval with a single value. The graph of a step function can look like the steps of a staircase.	**Función escalón** Una función escalón empareja cada número de un intervalo con un solo valor. La gráfica de una función escalón se puede parecer a los peldaños de una escalera.

English	Spanish
Subset A subset of a set consists of elements from the given set.	**Subconjunto** Un subconjunto de un conjunto consiste en elementos del conjunto dado.

Example If $B = \{1, 2, 3, 4, 5, 6, 7\}$
and $A = \{1, 2, 5\}$, then A is a subset of B.

English

Straightedge   A straightedge is a tool for drawing straight lines.

Surface area   The surface area of a prism, cylinder, pyramid, or cone is the sum of the lateral area and the areas of the bases. The surface area of a sphere is four times the area of a great circle.

Example

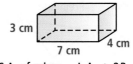

S.A. of prism = L.A. + 2B
= 66 + 2(28)
= 122 cm^2

T

Tangent ratio   *See* **trigonometric ratios**.

Tangent to a circle   A tangent to a circle is a line in the plane of the circle that intersects the circle in exactly one point. That point is the *point of tangency*.

Example

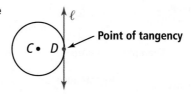

Line ℓ is tangent to ⊙C. Point D is the point of tangency.

Theorem   A theorem is a conjecture that is proven.

Example   The theorem "Vertical angles are congruent" can be proven by using postulates, definitions, properties, and previously stated theorems.

Theoretical probability   The theoretical probability is the ratio of the number of favorable outcomes to the number of possible outcomes if all outcomes have the same chance of happening.

$P(\text{event}) = \dfrac{\text{number of favorable outcomes}}{\text{number of possible outcomes}}$

Example   In tossing a coin, the events of getting heads or tails are equally likely. The likelihood of getting heads is $P(\text{heads}) = \frac{1}{2}$.

Spanish

Regla sin graduación   Una regla sin graduación es un instrumento para dibujar líneas rectas.

Área   El área de un prisma, pirámide, cilindro o cono es la suma del área lateral y las áreas de las bases. El área de una esfera es igual a cuatro veces el área de un círculo máximo.

Razón tangente   *Ver* **trigonometric ratios**.

Tangente de un círculo   Una tangente de un círculo es una recta en el plano del círculo que corta el círculo en exactamente un punto. Ese punto es el *punto de tangencia*.

Teorema   Un teorema es una conjetura que se demuestra.

Probabilidad teórica   Si cada resultado tiene la misma probabilidad de darse, la probabilidad teórica de un suceso se calcula como la razón del número de resultados favorables al número de resultados posibles.

$P(\text{suceso}) = \dfrac{\text{numero de resultados favorables}}{\text{numero de resultados posibles}}$

English

Transformation   A transformation is a change in the position, size, or shape of a geometric figure. The given figure is called the *preimage* and the resulting figure is called the *image*. A transformation *maps* a figure onto its image. *Prime notation* is sometimes used to identify image points. In the diagram, *X*′ (read "*X* prime") is the image of *X*.

Spanish

Transformación   Una transformación es un cambio en la posición, tamaño o forma de una figura. La figura dada se llama la *preimagen* y la figura resultante se llama la *imagen*. Una transformación *traza* la figura sobre su propia imagen. La *notación prima* a veces se utilize para identificar los puntos de la imagen. En el diagrama de la derecha, *X*′ (leído *X* prima) es la imagen de *X*.

Example

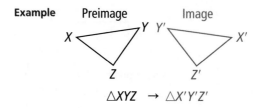

$$\triangle XYZ \;\rightarrow\; \triangle X'Y'Z'$$

Trigonometric ratios   The trigonometric ratios, or functions, relate the side lengths of a right triangle to its acute angles. In right $\triangle ABC$ with acute $\angle A$,

$$\text{sine } \angle A = \sin A = \frac{\text{length of leg opposite } \angle A}{\text{length of hypotenuse}}$$

$$\text{cosine } \angle A = \cos A = \frac{\text{length of leg adjacent to } \angle A}{\text{length of hypotenuse}}$$

$$\text{tangent } \angle A = \tan A = \frac{\text{length of leg opposite } \angle A}{\text{length of leg adjacent to } \angle A}$$

Razones trigonométricas   Las razones trigonométricas, o funciones, relacionan las longitudes de lado de un triángulo rectángulo con sus ángulos agudos. En un triángulo rectángulo $\triangle ABC$ con ángulo agudo $\angle A$,

$$\text{seno } \angle A = \text{sen } A = \frac{\text{cateto opuesto a } \angle A}{\text{hipotenusa}}$$

$$\text{coseno } \angle A = \cos A = \frac{\text{cateto adyecente a } \angle A}{\text{hipotenusa}}$$

$$\text{tangente } \angle A = \tan A = \frac{\text{cateto opuesto a } \angle A}{\text{cateto adyecente a } \angle A}$$

Example

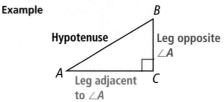

Two-way frequency table   A two-way frequency table is a table that displays frequencies in two different categories.

Tabla de frecuencias de doble entrada   Una tabla de frecuencias de doble entrada es una tabla de frecuencias que contiene dos categorías de datos.

Example

	Male	Female	Totals
Juniors	3	4	7
Seniors	3	2	5
Totals	6	6	12

The last column shows a total of 7 juniors and 5 seniors.
The last row shows a total of 6 males and 6 females.

U

Uniform probability distribution   A uniform probability distribution assigns the same probability to each outcome.

Distribución uniforme de probabilidad   Una distribución uniforme de probabilidad le asigna la misma probabilidad a cada resultado.

English

V

Vertex   The highest or lowest point on the graph of a function.

Example

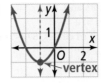

Vertex form of a quadratic function   The function $f(x) = a(x - h)^2 + k$, where $a \neq 0$. The vertex of the graph is at (h, k).

Example   If the vertex form of a function is $f(x) = 5(x + 3)^2 + 7$, the vertex of the graph is $(-3, 7)$.

Vertical motion model   The vertical motion model is the quadratic function $h(t) = -16t^2 + v_0t + h_0$. The variable h represents the height of an object, in feet, t seconds after it is launched into the air. The term v_0 is the object's initial velocity and h_0 is its initial height.

Example   If an object is launched from a height of 10 ft with an initial velocity of 8 ft/s, then the equation of the object's height over time is $h(t) = -16t^2 + 8t + 10$.

Volume   Volume is a measure of the space a figure occupies.

Z

Zero of a function   An x-intercept of the graph of a function.

Example   The zeros of $y = x^2 - 4$ are ± 2.

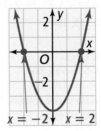

Spanish

Vértice   El punto más alto o más bajo de la gráfica de una función.

Forma canónica de una función cuadrática   La función $f(x) = a(x - h)^2 + k$, donde $a \neq 0$. El vértice de la gráfica está en (h, k).

Modelo de movimiento vertical   El modelo de movimiento vertical es la función cuadrática $h(t) = -16t^2 + v_0t + h_0$. La variable h representa la altura en pies de un objeto t segundos después de lanzarlo al aire. El término v_0 es la velocidad inicial del objeto y h_0 es su altura inicial.

Volumen   El volumen es una medida del espacio que ocupa una figura.

Cero de una función   Intercepto x de la gráfica de una función.

Index

A

AA ~ (Angle-Angle Similarity) Theorem, 430

absolute value functions
  defined, 229
  graphing, 229–235, 249–255
  vertex of, 229

addition
  of complex numbers, 184
  of functions, 275–280
  of monomials, 49
  of polynomials, 47–54
  of rational numbers, 6–7
  of real numbers, 6

algebra, 535–536

Alternate Exterior Angles Theorem, 306

Alternate Interior Angles Theorem, 305–306

altitude, 328–335, 436–437, 438

Angle-Angle Similarity (AA ~) Theorem, 430

angle bisectors
  equidistant points and, 314–316
  proportionality and, 448
  of triangles, 322, 448

Angle Bisector Theorem, 315

angles
  bisectors of. *see* angle bisectors
  parallel lines and, 304–310
  of parallelograms, 374–382, 384
  of polygons, 357–363
  of rhombuses, 391–392, 398–399
  of squares, 394
  trigonometric inverses and, 464
  vertex, 603

angles, types of
  central, 569, 586–587
  complementary, 299
  congruent, 299
  consecutive, 377
  corresponding, 306
  exterior. *see* exterior angles
  inscribed, 594–600
  interior. *see* interior angles
  opposite, 377
  vertical, 298

angle-sum theorems of polygons, 357–363

arc length, 570–571, 597

arcs, 569–576, 587, 594, 596–598

area

  coordinate plane and, 538
  scale factors and, 418
  of sectors, 572
  of segment of circles, 572–573
  surface, 625

asymptote, 259

axis of symmetry, 110–116, 229, 250, 258

B

binomial, expand a power of a, 215

binomial distribution, 524

binomial experiments, 509–510

binomial probability, 510, 517

Binomial Probability Formula, 510

binomials
  multiplying, 56–59, 64–65
  rewriting as a polynomial, 57
  squaring, 63–68

Binomial Theorem, 216

bisectors. *see* perpendicular bisectors

C

Cavalieri's Principle, 621, 630, 637

ceiling function, 243

center of dilation, 413, 422

center of gravity, 330

central angles, 569, 586–587

centroids, 329–330

change, rate of, 29, 37–38, 232

chords, 586–593, 604

circles
  arcs of, 569–576
  chords of, 586–593, 604
  circumscribed, 320–321
  in coordinate plane system, 550–555
  hexagon inscribed in, 589
  inscribed, 322
  inscribed angles of, 594–600
  notations for, 551
  secant lines and segments, 601–608
  sectors of, 572–576
  similar, 425
  tangent lines of, 577–584, 603

circumcenters, 321

circumference, 570

circumscribed circles, 320–321

classifying
  real numbers, 5–10

Closure Property, 50, 58

combinations, 499–505

common factors, 90

compasses, 311

complementary angles, 299

complement of an event, 484

completing the square, 191–197

complex conjugates, 185

complex numbers, 183–189

complex roots, 220

composite figures, 633, 639

compound interest, 19–21

compressions
  absolute value functions, 251
  of functions, 269–274

Concurrency of Altitudes, 331

Concurrency of Angle Bisectors, 322

Concurrency of Medians, 329, 545–546

Concurrency of Perpendicular Bisectors, 319–320

concurrent lines, 320

conditional probability
  decision-making using, 494
  defined, 491
  formula, 493
  independent events and, 492–493

conditional relative frequency, 478–479

cones, 630–636

45°-45°-90° Triangle Theorem, 455

frequency
  conditional relative, 478–479
  interpreting, 477–482
  joint, 477
  joint relative, 478
  marginal, 477
  marginal relative, 478

frequency table, 477–482

function(s)
  absolute value, 249–255
  adding, 275–280
  analyzing graphically, 256–262
  assess fit of, 126
  axis of symmetry, 258
  compressions of, 269–274
  domain, 256
  end behavior, 259
  inverse, 281–286
  maximum values, 257
  minimum values, 257
  multiplying, 276–280
  one-to-one, 281, 282
  piecewise-defined, 237–242, 249–255
  quadratic parent, 103
  range of, 256
  real-world application, 134–135
  reciprocal, 469
  step, 243–248
  stretches of, 269–274
  subtracting, 275–280
  translations of, 263–268

Fundamental Counting Principle, 499

Fundamental Theorem of Algebra, 220–221

G

GCF (greatest common factor), 69–74

geometric means, 437–438

graph(s)
  of absolute value functions, 229–235, 249–255
  analyzing functions using, 256–262
  of circles, 552
  circles on, 238
  composition of rigid motion and dilation, 422
  cube root function, 34–40
  end behavior, 259
  of equations, 153
  of horizontal translations, 250–251, 271
  of inverse functions, 282
  of parabola, 556
  of piece-wise defined functions, 237–242
  of quadratic equations, 153
  of quadratic formula, 200

  of quadratic functions, 103–104, 110–112, 117–123
  sketching, 256
  of solutions of equations, 145–150
  solving linear-quadratic equations using, 171
  solving quadratic equations using, 145–150
  of square root functions, 28–30
  of vertical translations, 250–251, 270

great circles, 639

Greatest Common Factor (GCF), 69–74, 84

grouping, factoring by, 84

growth rate, 18

H

hemispheres, 639

hexagon, inscribed in circles, 589

Hinge Theorem, 344

horizontal asymptote, 259

horizontal translations, 250–251, 264

I

identity(ies)
  polynomial, 212–219
  Pythagorean Identity, 468–470
  sum of cubes, 213

imaginary numbers, 184

imaginary unit i, 183

incenter, 322–323

independent events, 485–487, 492–493

inequalities in triangles, 336–342, 343–348

inscribed angles, 594–600

Inscribed Angles Theorem, 595–596

inscribed circles, 322

intercepted arcs, 569, 594, 596–598

interest, 19–21

interior angles
  of parallel lines, 305–306
  of polygons, 357–358

inverse functions, 281–286

irrational numbers, 7

isosceles trapezoids, 367–368

J

joint frequency, 477

joint relative frequency, 478

K

kites, 365–366, 537

L

length, finding, 447

like terms
  combining, 49
  defined, 49

linear functions
  identifying, 132–138
  modeling data sets, 132–138
  piecewise-defined functions, 237

linear models, 132–138

Linear Pairs Theorem, 300

linear-quadratic systems
  defined, 170
  determining number of solutions with, 205
  of equations, 170–175
  of inequalities, 207–208
  with no solution, 205
  solving using graphing technology, 208
  solving using substitution, 206

linear regressions, 127

lines
  intersecting a parabola, 170
  secant, 601–608
  tangent, of circles, 577–584

M

major arcs, 569

marginal frequency, 477

marginal relative frequency, 478

mathematical modeling, of quadratic functions, 124–130

maximum value, of functions, 257

means, geometric, 437–438

median, 328–335

midpoints, 535

midsegments
  of trapezoids, 369–370, 543–544
  of triangles, 446

minimum value, of functions, 257

minor arcs, 569

monomials
  adding, 49
  defined, 47
  multiplying, 55
  subtracting, 49

multiplication
  of binomials, 56–59, 64–65
  of closure, 58
  of complex numbers, 185
  of exponents, 11
  of expressions using polynomial
    identities, 213
  of functions, 276–280
  of monomials, 55
  of polynomials, 55–62, 65, 276
  of radical expressions, 160
  of rational numbers, 6–7
  of real numbers, 6
  of trinomial, 57–58
  of trinomials, 55

multiplicity of the root, 220

mutually exclusive events, 483–484

N

natural base e, 20

non-mutually exclusive events,
  484–485

notations
  for circles, 551
  for dilations, 414, 416

numbers
  complex, 183–189
  imaginary, 184
  integers, 5
  irrational, 7

O

oblique cylinders, 621

oblique prisms, 621

one-to-one, 281, 282

operations, 5–10

opposite angles, 377

orthocenters, 331–332

P

parabolas
  axis of symmetry of, 110–116
  defined, 103
  graphs of, 556–562
  lines intersecting, 170
  in quadratic graphs, 110–112
  symmetry of, 110–112, 153
  vertex of, 112–113, 153

paragraph proofs, 299, 301

parallel lines
  angle pair relationships with,
    304–310
  transversals and, 304–310
  triangle proportions and, 445–446

parallel method, 414

parallelograms
  classification of, 536
  conditions of, 398–405
  properties of, 374–382, 391–397
  quadrilaterals as, 383–390

parent functions, 103

**parentheses, for negative values when
  substituting**, 199

Pascal's Triangle, 215

patterns, in squares of binomials,
  63–68

payoffs, expected, 515

perfect-square trinomials, 89–90

perimeter, 538

permutations, 499–505

perpendicular bisectors
  of segments, 311–314
  of triangle, 319–326

Perpendicular Bisector Theorem, 312,
  314

piecewise-defined function
  defined, 237–242
  step functions as, 243–248
  transformations of, 249–255

planes
  coordinate. *see* coordinate plane
    systems
  cross-sections as, 616–618, 637, 639

points
  on circles, 551
  of concurrency, 320
  equidistant, 311, 314–316, 556
  midpoints, 535
  of tangency, 577

Polygon Exterior Angle-Sum Theorem,
  359

Polygon Interior Angle-Sum Theorem,
  358

polygons
  angle-sum theorems of, 357–363
  in coordinate geometry, 535–541
  rotations of, 617
  three-dimensional figures related
    to, 615–620

polyhedrons, 616–618

polynomial equations, 220–221

polynomial identities
  defined, 212
  to factor polynomials, 214
  to multiply expressions, 213
  proving, 213

polynomial(s)
  adding, 47–54
  binomials written as, 57
  defined, 48
  degrees, 48

  factoring, 69–74, 214
  multiplying, 55–62, 64, 276
  naming, 48
  standard form of, 48
  subtracting, 47–54

population growth rate, 19

Postulates
  Same-Side Interior Angles, 305

Power of a Power Property, 11–13

Power of a Product Property, 13

prime factorization, 69

prisms, 621–628

probability
  binomial, 517
  combinations to find, 499–505
  conditional, 491–497
  decision-making using, 494, 521–527
  Fundamental Counting Principle, 499
  permutations to find, 499–505

probability distributions, 506–511

probability events
  complements, 484
  dependent, 492
  independent, 485–487, 492–493
  mutually exclusive, 483–484
  non-mutually exclusive, 484–485

Product of Powers Property, 12

Product Property of Square Roots, 158

proofs
  for Alternate Interior Angles
    Theorem, 305
  Concurrency of Perpendicular
    Bisectors, 320
  for Converse of Hinge Theorem, 345
  of coordinate geometry, 543–549
  defined, 297, 301
  diagonals confirming parallelogram,
    386
  for Fundamental Theorem of
    Algebra, 221
  paragraph, 299, 301
  parallel lines to prove angle
    relationships, 307
  for Perpendicular Bisector Theorem,
    312
  Pythagorean Identity, 468
  for Pythagorean Theorem, 453
  of quadrilaterals as parallelograms,
    383–390
  of rectangle diagonal congruency,
    393
  relate arcs and chords, 587
  for similar circles, 425
  for similar triangles, 429–435
  two-column, 297–298, 300, 301
  writing, 297–303

property(ies)
Closure Property, 50
Distributive Property, 56–58, 64–65
Power of a Power Property, 11–13
Power of a Product Property, 13
Product of Powers Property, 12
Product Property of Square Roots, 158
Quotient of Powers Property, 14

proportions, 445–451, 461–467

pyramids, 630–636

Pythagorean Identity, 468–470

Pythagorean Theorem, 166, 452–460

Pythagorean triple, 454

Q

quadratic equations
with complex solutions, 186
defined, 145
Fundamental Theorem of Algebra for, 221
graphing, 153
solving by factoring, 151–157
solving by graphing, 145–150
solving by tables, 145–150
solving using completing the square, 191–197
solving using square roots, 164–169, 183
solving with factoring, 186
standard form of, 152
systems of, 145–150, 171–172
vertex form, 194

Quadratic Formula, 198–204

quadratic functions
compare properties of, 119–120
graphs of, 103–104, 106, 110–112, 117–123
identifying, 132–138
modeling data sets, 132–138
modeling with, 124–130
parent function, 103
real-world application, 105
standard form of, 117–123
vertex form, 110–116

quadratic graphs, 103–104, 110–112, 117–123

quadratic models, 124–130, 132–138

quadratic parent function, 103

quadratic regressions, 127, 134

quadrilaterals
classification of, on coordinate plane, 537
as parallelograms, 383–390

Quotient of Powers Property, 14

R

radians, 570

radical expressions, 158–163

radicand, 200

radius, 550–555

range
of absolute value functions, 230–231
of functions, 256

rate
of change, 29, 37–38, 106, 231
exponential function for, 18

ratio method, 413

rational exponents, 11–17

rational numbers, operations with, 6–7

ratios, trigonometric, 461–467

real numbers, operations on, 5–10

reciprocal functions, 469

rectangles, 393–394, 400

reduction dilation, 414

reflections
across *x*-axis, 269
of rigid motions and dilations, 424

regressions
of exponential model, 22
linear, 127
quadratic, 127, 134

residuals, 126

rhombuses, 391–392, 398–399

right cylinders, 621

right triangles
Pythagorean Theorem and, 452–460
ratios of, 461–467
similarity of, 436–443

rigid motions, composition of, 422–423

roots, 200

rotations, of polygons, 617

S

Same-Side Interior Angles Postulate, 305

SAS ~ (Side-Angle-Side Similarity) Theorem, 431

scale factors, 415, 418

secants, 601–608

sectors of circles, 572–576

segments
of circles, 572
perpendicular bisectors of, 311–314
secant, 601–608
tangent to circles, 579

Segments Tangent to a Circle Theorem, 579

set(s), 5

Side-Angle-Side Similarity (SAS ~) Theorem, 431

Side-Side-Side Similarity (SSS ~) Theorem, 430–431

Side-Splitter Theorem, 446–447

similarity
dilations, 413–421
proving, 429–435
Pythagorean Theorem proof and, 453
of right triangles, 436–443
transformations, 422–428
of triangle proportions, 445–451
trigonometric ratios and, 462

sine (sin), 461–463, 469

slopes, 535, 537

solving equations
approximately, 147
by factoring, 186
inequalities with linear-quadratic, 207–208
linear-quadratic, using elimination, 171–172
linear-quadratic, using substitution, 172
linear-quadratic systems, 206, 208
quadratic equations, 183, 186
with rational exponents, 11–17
using elimination, 171–172
using graphs, 208
using square roots, 183
using substitution, 172, 206

spheres, 637–642

square of a sum, 212

square root, 183

square root function(s), 27–30

square roots
defined, 158
solving quadratic equations using, 164–169, 183

square(s)
of a binomial, 63–68
completing, 191–197
diagonal and angle measurements of, 394
difference of two, 64–65
factoring a sum of, 186
perfect-square trinomials, 89–90

SSS ~ (Side-Side-Side Similarity) Theorem, 430–431

standard form
of polynomials, 48
of quadratic equations, 152
of quadratic functions, 117–123

step function, 243–248, 249

stretches
absolute value functions, 251
of functions, 269–274

subset, 5

Acknowledgments

Photographs

Cover:

Mikhail Leonov/Shutterstock

Topic 1:

3 Amaia Arozena & Gotzon Iraola/Moment Open/Getty Images; **4** (TL) Dikobraziy/Shutterstock, (TR) Greens87/Shutterstock, (CL) Greens87/Shutterstock, (CR) Greens87/Shutterstock, (BL) Razvan Sera/Shutterstock, (BR) Stockshoppe/Shutterstock; **17** (T) Cultura Creative/Alamy Stock Photo, (B) Dmussman/Shutterstock; **27** Marco Diaz Segura/Shutterstock; **29** Amaia Arozena & Gotzon Iraola/Moment Open/Getty Images; **30** Joern Sackermann/Alamy Stock Photo; **33** (L) Jason Edwards/National Geographic/Getty Images, (R) Efrain Padro/Alamy Stock Photo; **36** Double Photo Studio/Shutterstock

Topic 02:

45 Agencja Fotograficzna Caro/Alamy Stock Photo; **46** (TL) 1r1ska/Shutterstock, (TC) Hand Idea/Shutterstock, (TR) Robuart/Shutterstock, (C) Veronchick84/Shutterstock, (BL) Sean Pavone/Shutterstock, (BR) Stockbroker/Alamy Stock Photo; **51** Paul White/UK Industries/Alamy Stock Photo; **59** Gunter Marx/BI/Alamy Stock Photo; **68** (T) Asiapics/Alamy Stock Photo, (B) Vittorio Valletta/Agf Srl/Alamy Stock Photo; **70** (T) Monkey Business/Fotolia, (B) Redsnapper/Alamy Stock Photo; **71** (T) Monkey Business/Fotolia, (B) Redsnapper/Alamy Stock Photo; **74** Design56/123RF; **82** Agencja Fotograficzna Caro/Alamy Stock Photo; **83** Brian Kinney/Shutterstock; **88** Jose Luis Stephens/Alamy Stock Photo

Topic 03:

101 Larry w. Smith/epa/Newscom; **102** (T) Hero Images Inc./Alamy Stock Photo, (C) Jeff Gilbert/Alamy Stock Photo, (B) Marcin Balcerzak/Shutterstock; **109** Studio Source/Alamy Stock Photo; **119** Wdg Photo/Shutterstock; **131** Larry w. Smith/epa/Newscom

Topic 04:

143 R. Mackay Photography, LLC/Shutterstock; **144** (T) Eugene Onischenko/Shutterstock, (CL) Somchai Som/Shutterstock, (C) NASA Images/Shutterstock, (CR) Claudio Divizia/Shutterstock, (BL) Martin Rickett/PA Images/Alamy Stock Photo, (BR) Vadim Sadovski/Shutterstock; **169** Mario Hagen/Shutterstock; **170** Joel Sartore/National Geographic/Getty Images; **176** R. Mackay Photography, LLC/Shutterstock

Topic 05:

181 Aksonov/E+/Getty Images; **182** (TL) Chuck Franklin/Alamy Stock Photo, (TR) Tim Sharp/Reuters/Alamy Stock Photo, (CL) Dejan Popovic/Shutterstock, (CR) Chingachgook/Shutterstock, (B) learchitecto/Fotolia; **190** Aksonov/E+/Getty Images

Topic 06:

227 Maridav/Fotolia; **228** (TL) Roger Bacon/Reuters/Alamy Stock Photo, (TR) Maksimilian/Shutterstock, (CL) Robert/Fotolia, (CR) Clarence Holmes Wildlife/Alamy Stock Photo, (B) Fotoschab/Fotolia; **236** Maridav/Fotolia; **255** (T) Natallia Vintsik/Fotolia, (B) Hamdan/Shutterstock; **262** ariosStudio/Alamy Stock Photo; **280** Marc Xavier/Fotolia; **283** Erick Nguyen/Alamy Stock Photo; **286** World Foto/Alamy Stock Photo

Topic 07:

295 Rexi Video/Shutterstock; **296** **(T)** Neil Webb/Ikon Images/Alamy Stock Photo, **(CL)** Jacob Lund/Fotolia, **(CR)** Maksym Protsenko/Fotolia, **(B)** Aleksandr Simonov/Shutterstock; **327** Rexi Video/Shutterstock

Topic 08:

355 Africa Studio/Fotolia; **356** (BKGD) Dushlik/Fotolia, (T) Zastolskiy Victor/Shutterstock, (C) Julen Garces Carro/EyeEm/Alamy Stock Photo, (B) Taina Sohlman/Fotolia; **364** Africa Studio/Fotolia; **382** Rukawajung/Fotolia

Acknowledgments

Topic 09:
411 Maxisport/Fotolia; **412** (T) Pressmaster/Fotolia, (CL) Juan Carlos Ulate/Reuters/Alamy Stock Photo, (CR) Chris Hill/National Geographic Creative/Alamy Stock Photo, (B) Petrovich12/Fotolia; **444** Maxisport/Fotolia; **451** Oleksii Nykonchuk/Fotolia

Topic 10:
475 Jacques Beauchamp/Glow Images; **476** (TL) Harvepino/Shutterstock, (TC) Tainar/Shutterstock, (TR) Marina Zezelina/Shutterstock, (C) Vasin Lee/Shutterstock, (B) Zeljko Radojko/Fotolia; **498** Jacques Beauchamp/Glow Images; **513** Grum_l/Shutterstock; **526** Blackregis/123RF

Topic 11:
534 (TL) Hayate/Fotolia, (TC) Aleksandr Lesik/Fotolia, (TR) Andy Dean/Fotolia, (C) Jdoms/Fotolia, (B) Mike Flippo/Shutterstock; **541** Karen Doody/Stocktrek Images,Inc./Alamy Stock Photo; **555** Rgb Ventures/SuperStock/Ed Darack/Alamy Stock Photo; **559** Africa Rising/Shutterstock; **562** Stocker1970/Shutterstock

Topic 12:
567 Paul Fleet/Shutterstock; **568** (T) 3Dsculptor/Shutterstock, (CL) Tryfonov/Fotolia, (CR) Olekcii Mach/Alamy Stock Photo, (B) Algol/Shutterstock; **584** Songquan Deng/Shutterstock; **585** Paul Fleet/Shutterstock; **600** Vasilii Gubskii/Shutterstock; **608** Friedrich Saurer/Alamy Stock Photo

Topic 13:
613 Andersphoto/Shutterstock; **614** (T) Heiner Heine/ImageBroker/Alamy Stock Photo, (C) Katyr/Fotolia, (B) AD unter/Shutterstock; **620** (T) Perutskyi Petro/Shutterstock, (CL) Imfotograf/Fotolia, (CR) Yellow Cat/Shutterstock, (B) Monkey Business/Fotolia; **624** Cynoclub/Fotolia; **625** Joerg Hackemann/123RF; **629** Andersphoto/Shutterstock; **642** Sorapong Chaipanya/123RF